A-Z SHEFFIELD

C000182515

Key to Map Pages	2-3
Large Scale City Centre	4-5
Map Pages	6-177

REFERENCE

Motorway	**M1**
A Road	A629
B Road	B6150
Dual Carriageway	
One-way Street Traffic flow on A Roads is also indicated by a heavy line on the driver's left.	
Road Under Construction Opening dates are correct at time of publication.	
Proposed Road	
Restricted Access	
Pedestrianized Road	
Track / Footpath	
Residential Walkway	
Railway	Level Crossing / Station / Heritage Sta. / Tunnel
Supertram The boarding of Supertrams at stops may be limited to a single direction, indicated by the arrow.	Stop
Built-up Area	BURGESS ST
Local Authority Boundary	
National Park Boundary	
Posttown Boundary	
Postcode Boundary (within Posttown)	
Map Continuation	86 / Large Scale City Centre 4

Car Park (selected)	P
Church or Chapel	†
Cycleway (selected)	
Fire Station	■
Hospital	H
House Numbers (A & B Roads only)	13 8
Information Centre	i
National Grid Reference	445
Park & Ride (Bus or Tram)	Abbeydale P+R
Police Station	▲
Post Office	★
Safety Camera with Speed Limit Fixed cameras and long term road works cameras. Symbols do not indicate camera direction.	(30)
Toilet: without facilities for the Disabled	▽
with facilities for the Disabled	▽
Disabled use only	▽
Viewpoint	☀
Educational Establishment	▢
Hospital or Healthcare Building	▢
Industrial Building	▢
Leisure or Recreational Facility	▢
Place of Interest	▢
Public Building	▢
Shopping Centre or Market	▢
Other Selected Buildings	▢

SCALE

Map Pages 4-5 1:9,051

0 — ⅛ — ¼ Mile

0 — 100 — 200 — 300 Metres

7 inches (17.78 cm) to 1 mile   11.05 cm to 1 km

Map Pages 6-177 1:18,103

0 — ¼ — ½ Mile

0 — 250 — 500 — 750 Metres

3½ inches (8.89 cm) to 1 mile   5.52 cm to 1 km

A-Z AZ AtoZ
registered trade marks of
Geographers' A-Z Map Company Ltd

www./az.co.uk

EDITION 7 2016
Copyright ©Geographers' A-Z Map Co. Ltd.
Telephone: 01732 781000 (Enquiries & Trade Sales)
01732 783422 (Retail Sales)

KEY TO MAP PAGES

A-Z WEST YORKSHIRE COUNTY ATLAS

WOOLLEY EDGE

Hemsworth

ROYSTON Shafton
38
6 | 7 | 8 | 9 | 10 | 11 | 12 | 13
Darton | Athersley | Carlton | Grimethorpe

Denby Dale
Cawthorne | Barugh Green | Monk Bretton Cudworth
Holmfirth
14 | 15 | 16 | 17 | 18 | 19 | 20 | 21
Higham | **BARNSLEY** | Great Houghton

Thurlstone | **176-177** | 28 | 29 | 30 | 31 | 32 | 33 | 34 | 35
Penistone | Dodworth **WORSBROUGH** | Kendray | Ardsley | Darfield

WOMBWELL
44 | 45 | 46 | 47 | 48 | 49
Birdwell **HOYLAND** | **WATH UPON**

Winscar Resr.
174 175 | Tankersley 36 | Elsecar | **DEARNE**
STOCKSBRIDGE | 60 | 61 | 62 | 63 | 64 | 65
High Green 35a | Wentworth

PEAK DISTRICT | Langsett Resr. | A629 Chapeltown | Thorpe Hesley **RAWMARSH**
Wharncliffe | Inset Page 90 | 78 | 79 | 80 | 81 | 82 | 83
Side | Burncross | 35 | Greasbrough

NATIONAL PARK | Agden Res. | Grenoside Ecclesfield M1 | **ROTHERHAM**
Howden Resr. | 90 | 91 | 92 | 93 | 94 | 95 | 96 | 97
Derwent Resr. | Oughtibridge | Parson Shiregreen
Strines Resr. | Cross | Owlerton Meadowhall | **Moorgate**
Hillsborough | 104 105 106 107 108 109 110 111
Ladybower Resr. | **Stannington** | Walkley | Attercliffe **Brinsworth**

Darnall | **Treeton**
LARGE SCALE | 116 117 118 119 120 121 122 123
4 5 | Handsworth
CITY CENTRE | **SHEFFIELD**

Greystones | Brincliffe | Arbourthorne | Woodhouse
130 131 132 133 134 135 136 137
Hathersage | Whirlow Millhouses Norton Gleadless **Hackenthorpe**
Woodseats

Dore | Greenhill | Norton | **Mosborough**
144 145 146 147 148 149 150 151
Totley | Bradway Coal Aston | Marsh | Halfway
Dronfield | Lane | **Eckington**
Woodhouse | **DRONFIELD** | 158 159 Renishaw
154 155 156 157
Unstone

Unstone Green | Barrow Hill
160 161 162 163 164
Sheepbridge **Whittington** Staveley

Newbold **Brimington** | Inset Page 173
166 167 168 169
CHESTERFIELD | Calow

DERBYSHIRE | Boythorpe | Hasland Arkwright Town
170 171 172 173
Walton | **Wingerworth**

Bakewell

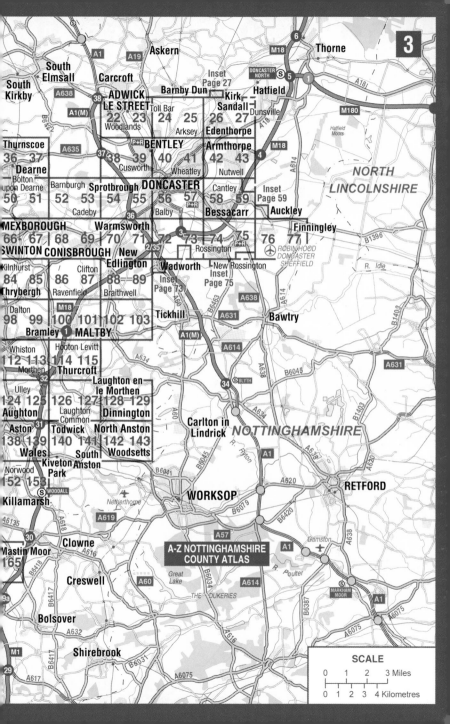

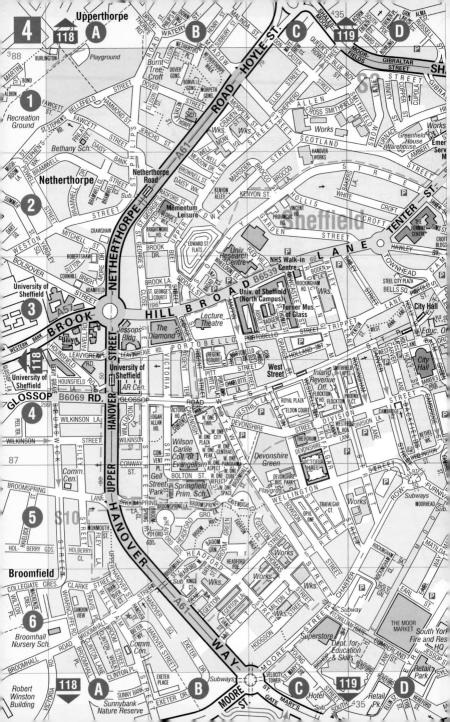

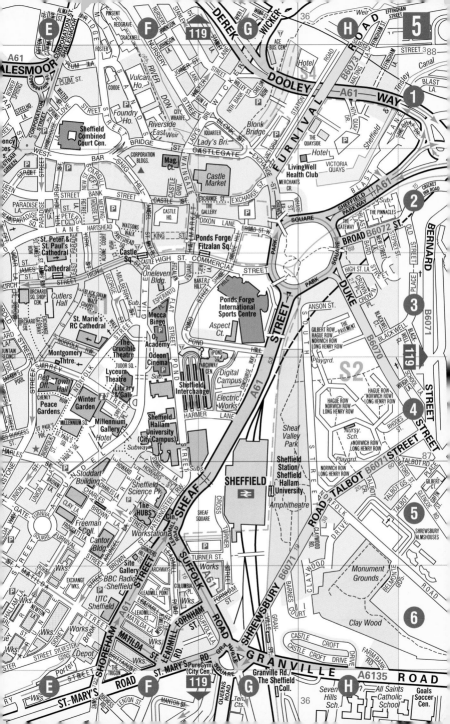

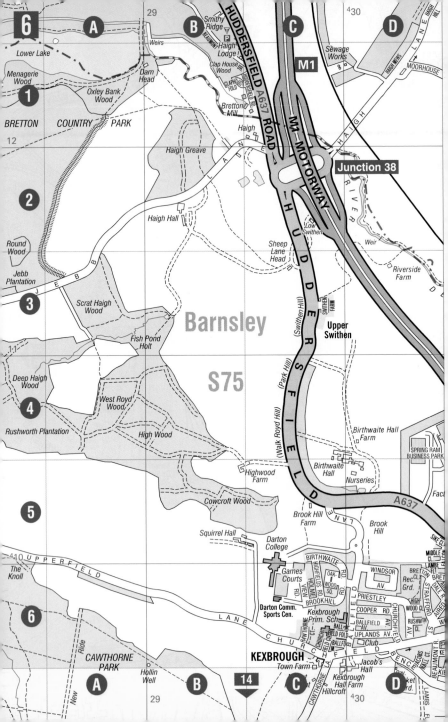

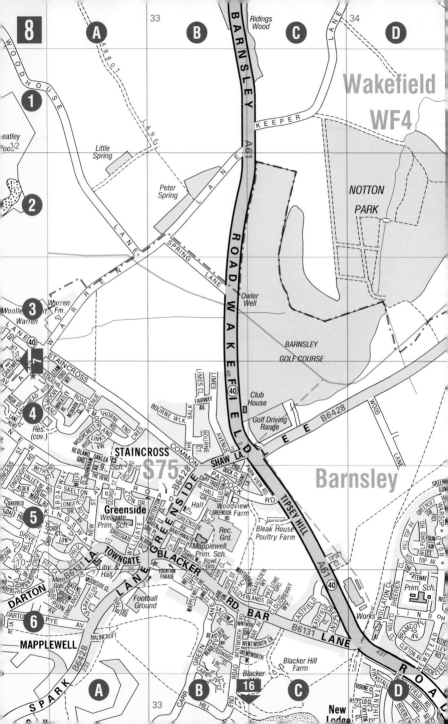

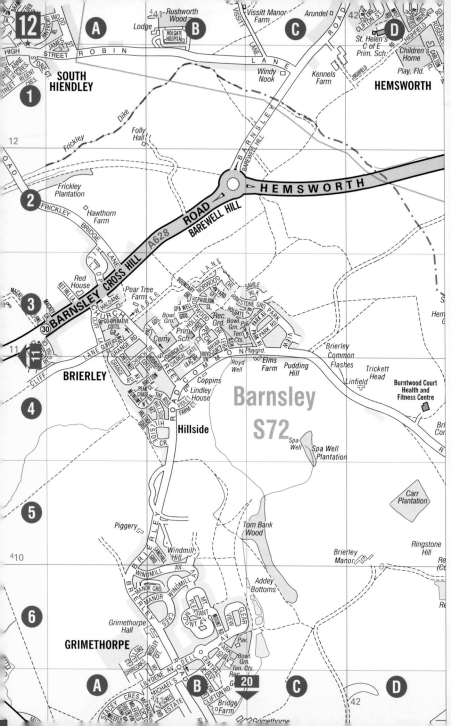

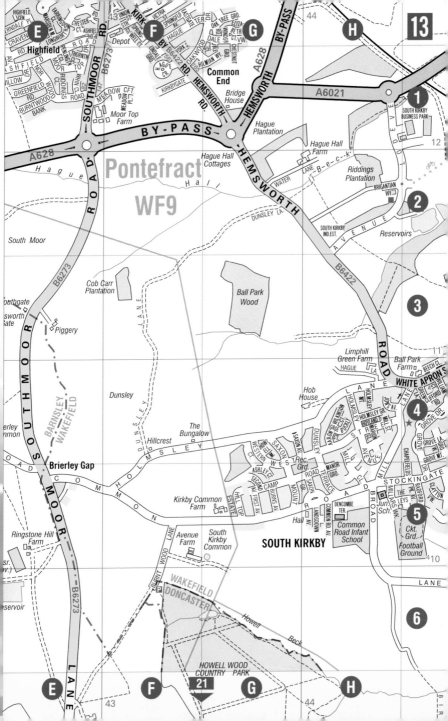

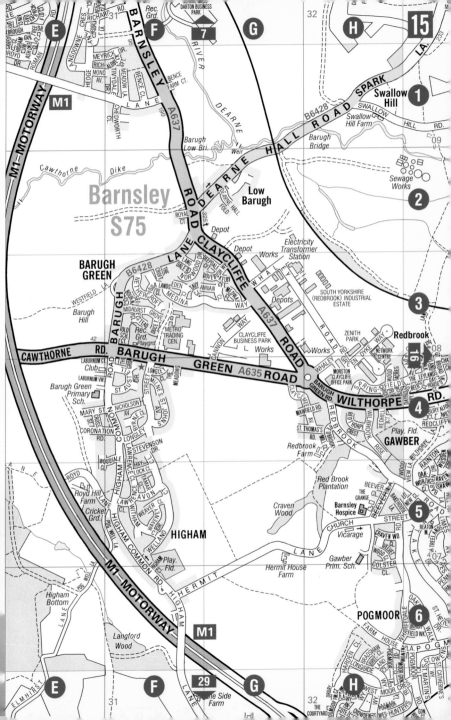

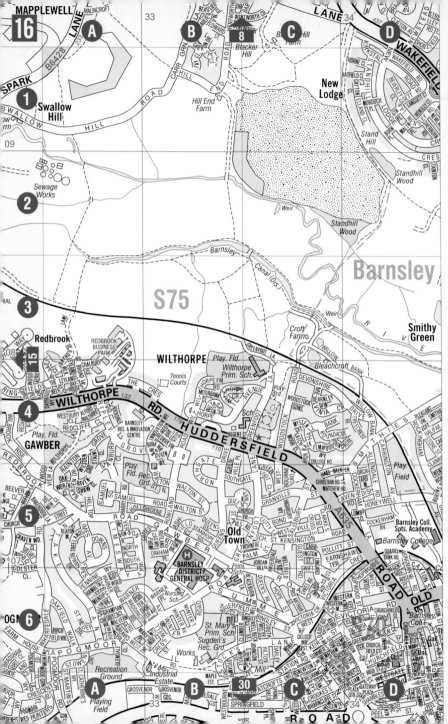

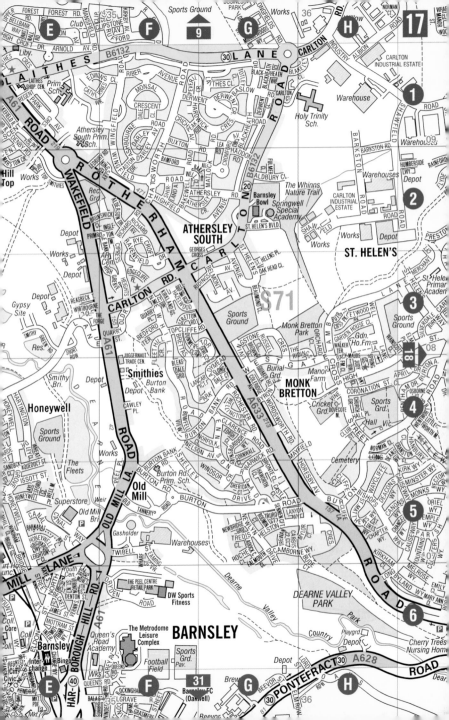

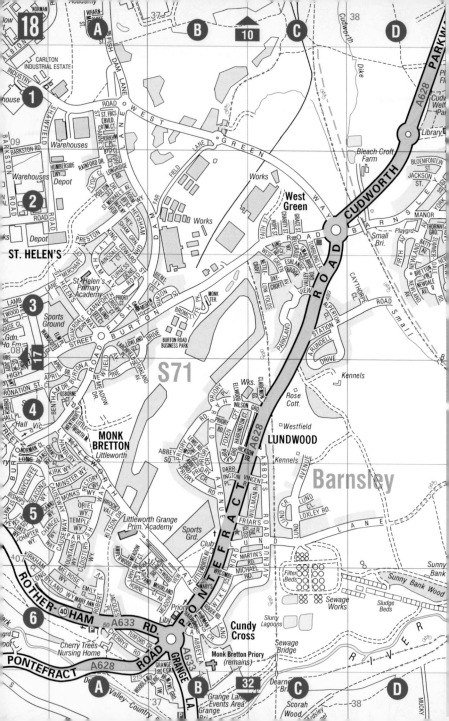

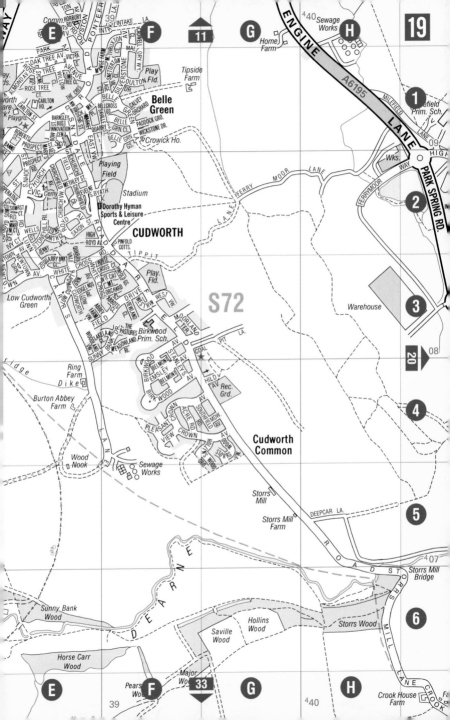

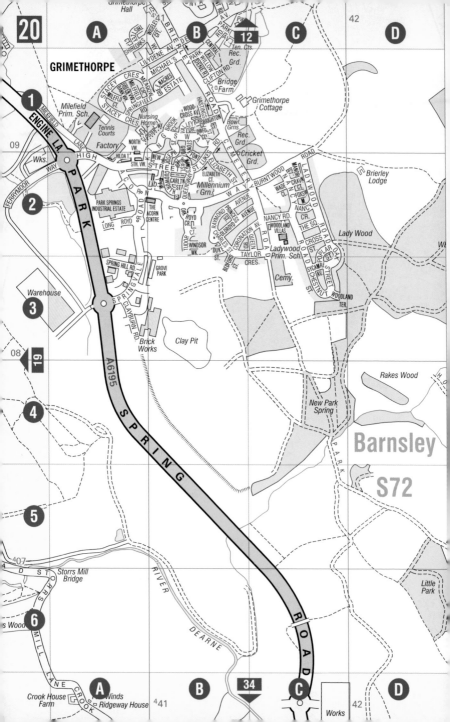

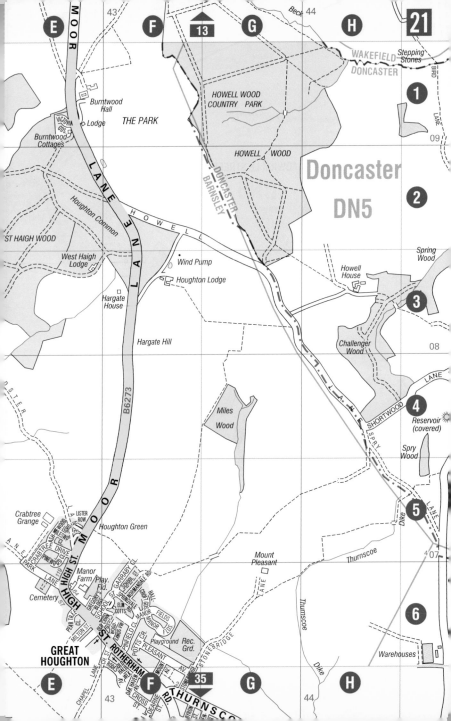

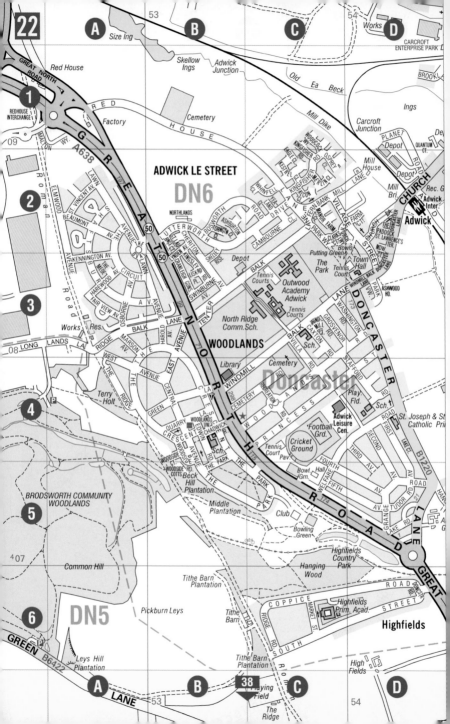

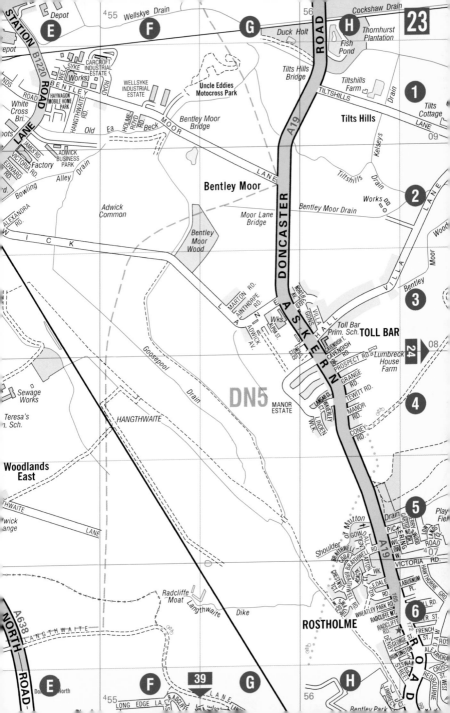

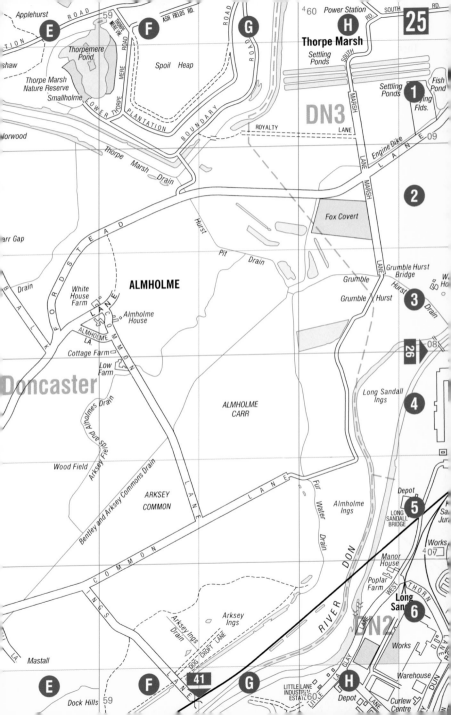

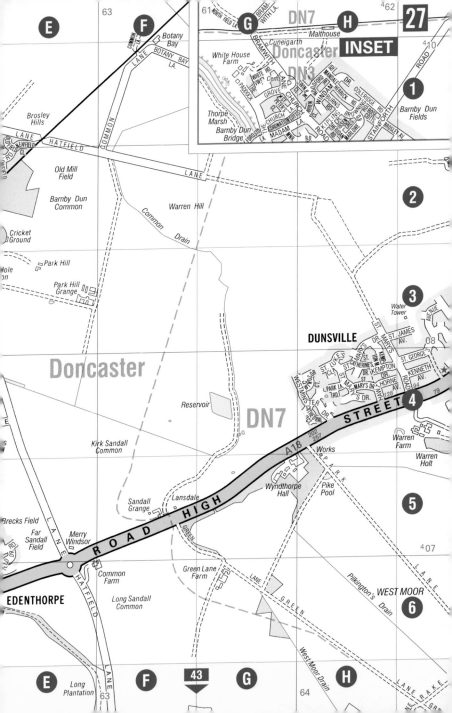

E 63 **F**

27

Botany Bay

Cuneigarth
Malthouse
Doncaster **INSET**

BOTANY BAY LA.
White House Farm
DN3

Brosley Hills

Thorpe Marsh

Barnby Dun Bridge

HATFIELD LANE

NEWFIELD CL.

Old Mill Field

LANE

COMMON LANE

Barnby Dun Common

1

Barnby Dun Fields

ROAD

410

2

Warren Hill

Common Drain

Cricket Ground

Park Hill

Park Hill Grange

3

Water Tower

DUNSVILLE

08

AVENUE

ST. GEORGE

KENNETH AV.

Doncaster

Reservoir

DN7

ST. JAMES AV.

ST. MARY'S

ST. LUKE'S CLN.
ST. CATHERINE'S
ST. KEMPTON
DR.
MARYS DR.
THORNE AV.
PARK LA.

★

79

Kirk Sandall Common

4

A18

Works

Warren Farm

Warren Holt

Lansdale

Wyndthorpe Hall

Pike Pool

PARK

5

Brecks Field

Far Sandall Field

Merry Windsor

Sandall Grange

ROAD HIGH

GREEN LANE

Common Farm

Green Lane Farm

LANE

GREEN

Pilkington's Drain

WEST MOOR

407

LANE

6

EDENTHORPE

HATFIELD LANE

Long Sandall Common

STREET

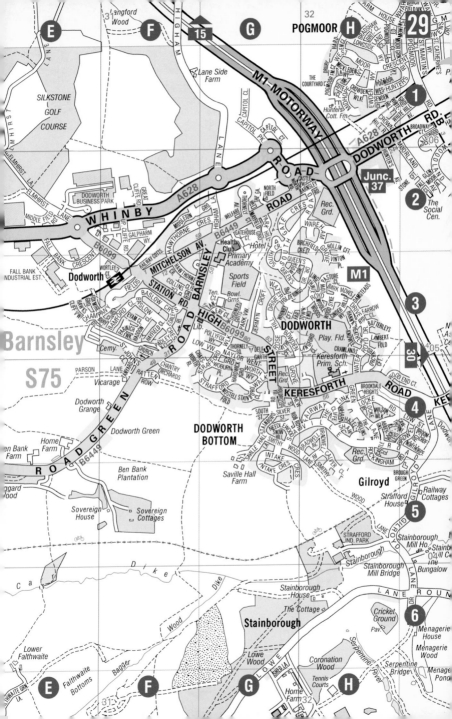

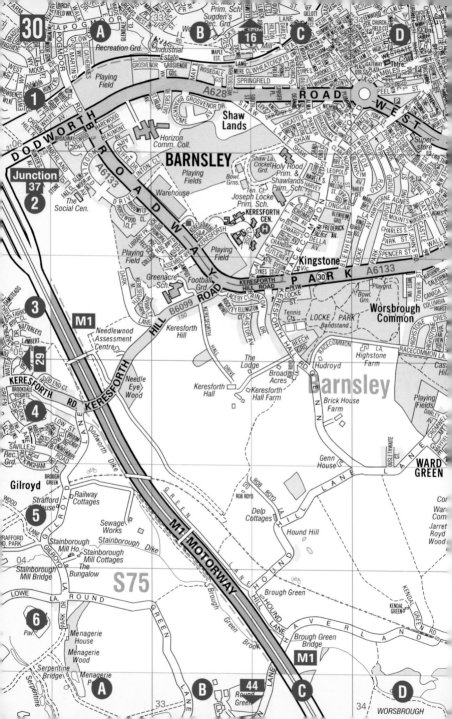

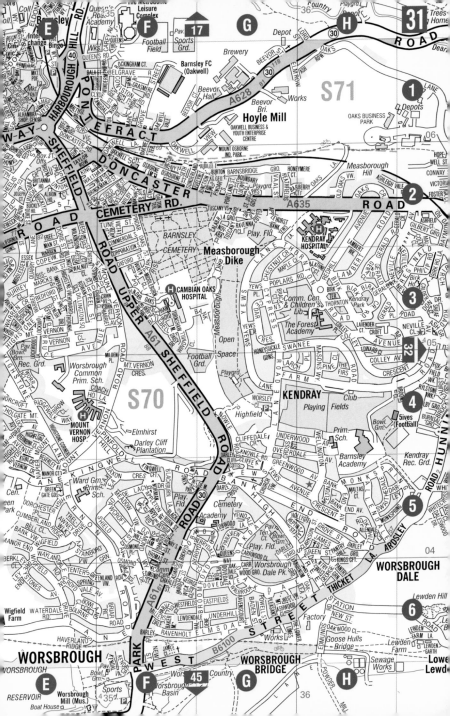

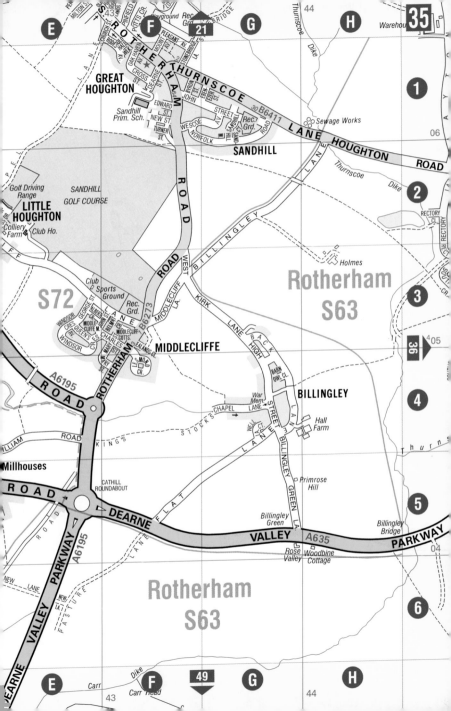

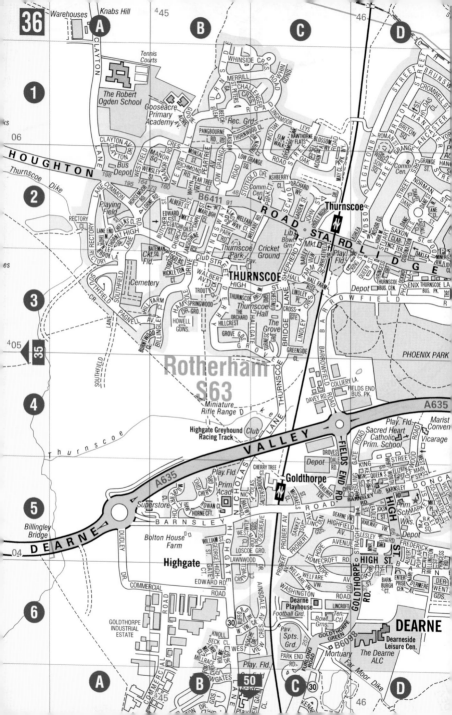

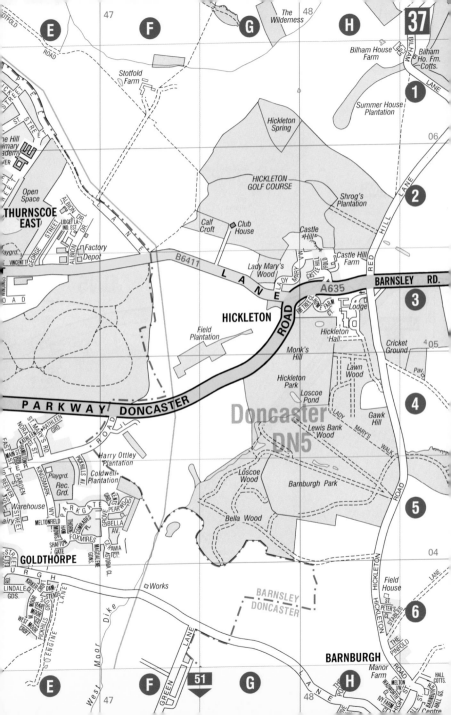

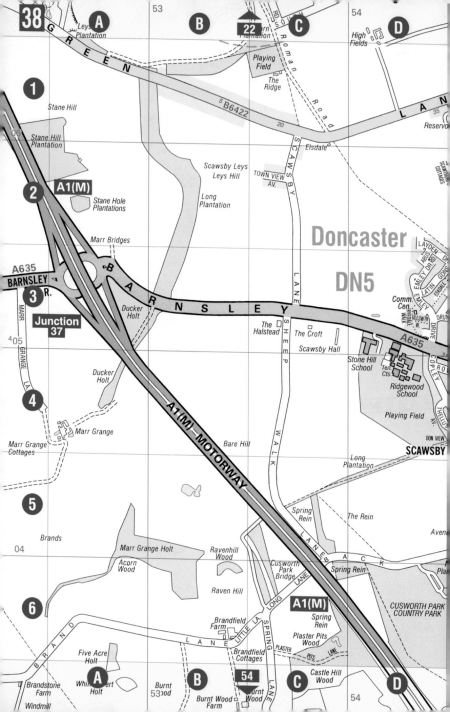

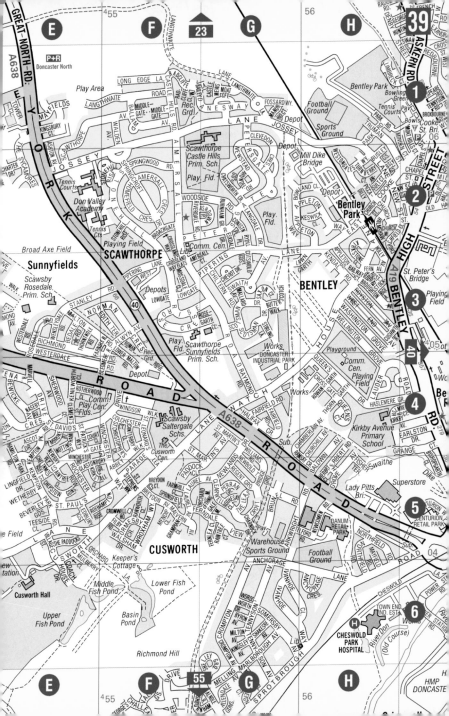

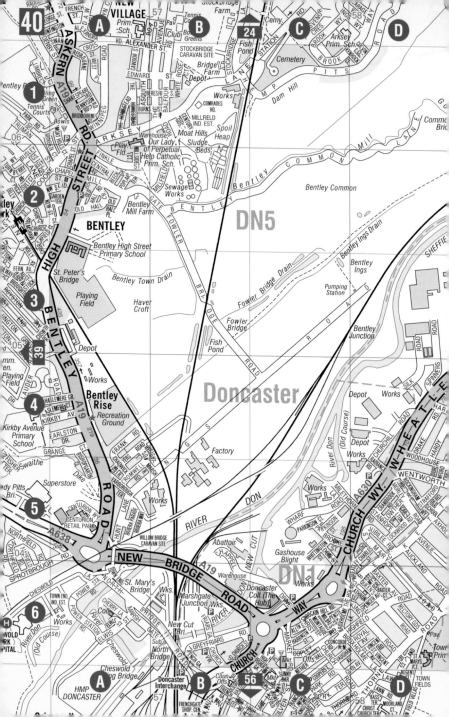

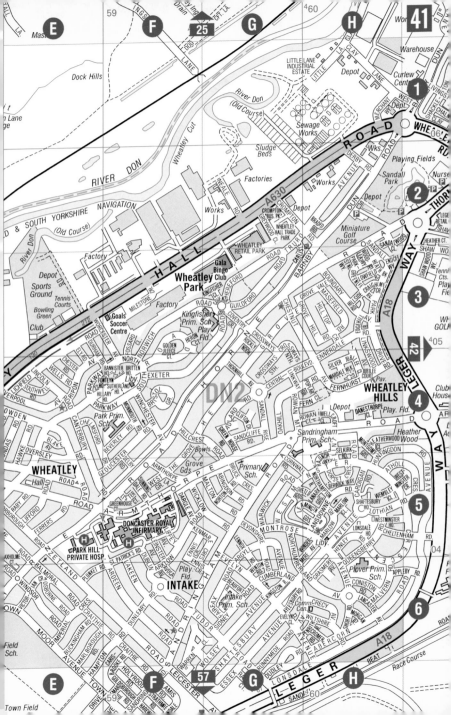

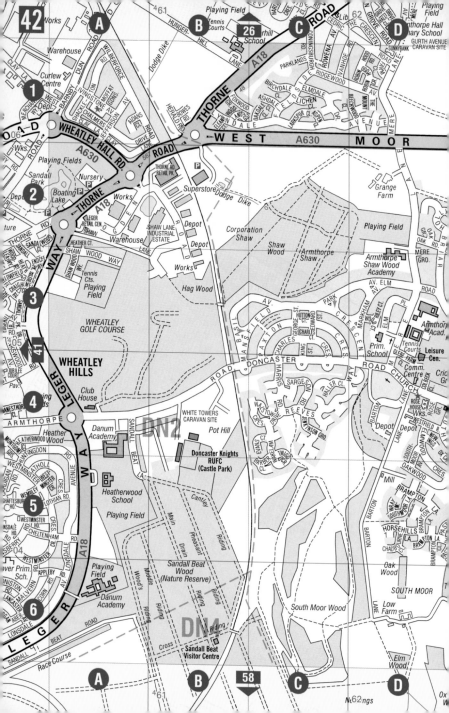

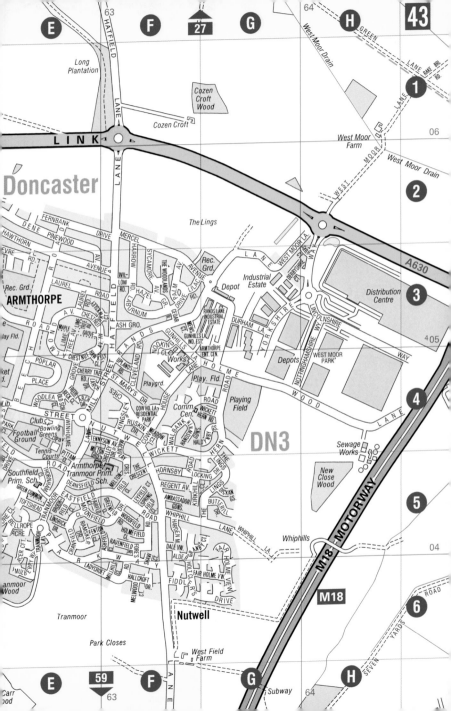

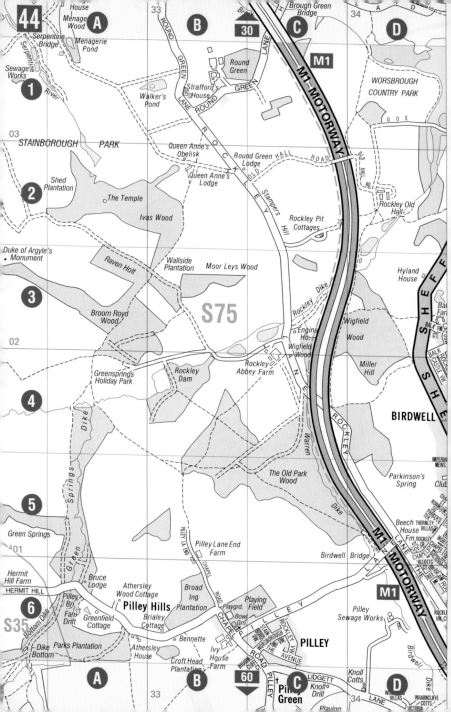

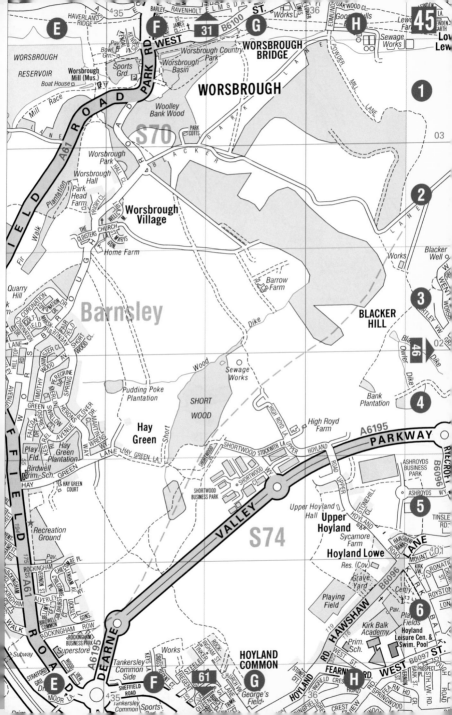

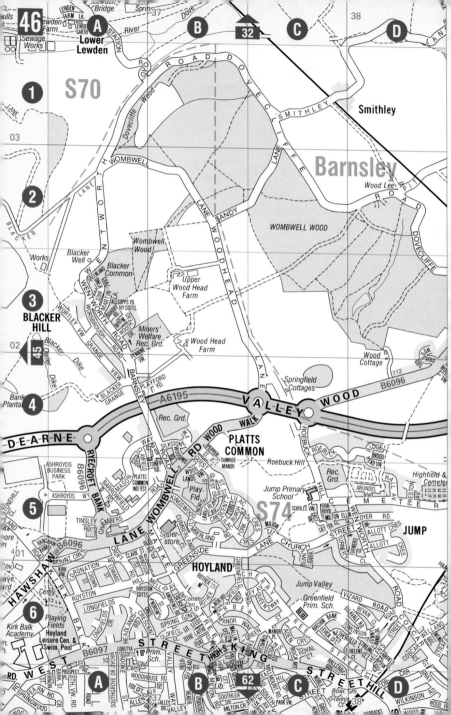

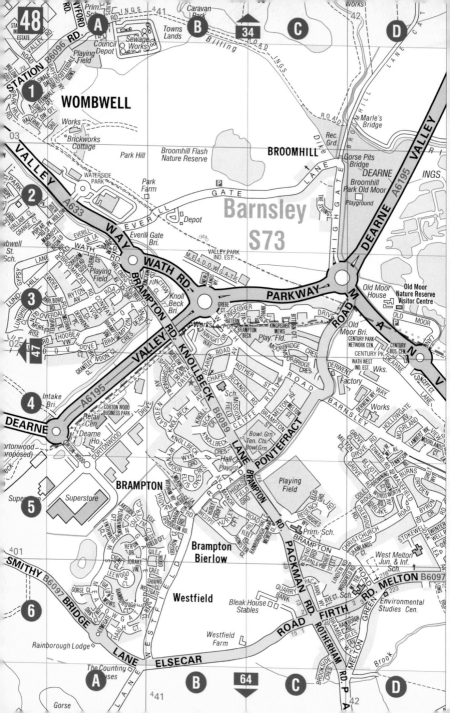

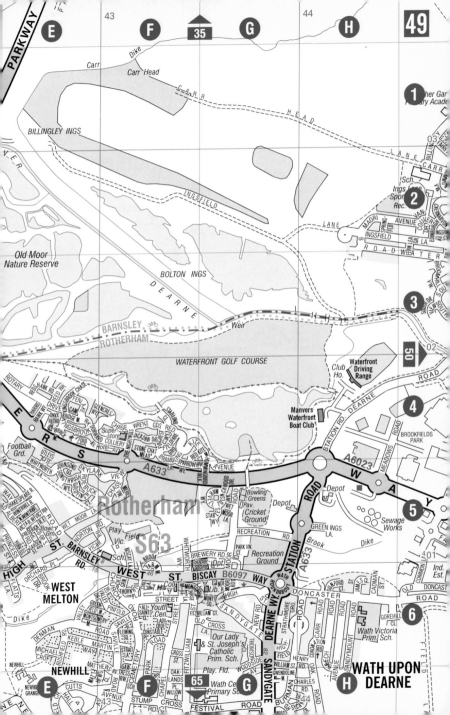

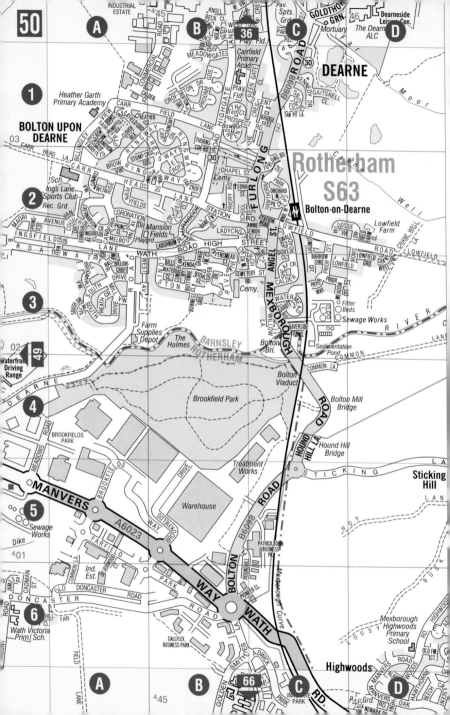

52

A **B** **C** **D**

BARNBURGH

Manor Farm

HALL COTTS.

Fish Pond

Centre Farm

Low Farm

St. Helen's Spring

HANGMAN LANE

STONE ROAD

CHURCH VW. THE GREEN

FOX LA.

Fox Lane Farm

DONCASTER VW.

Barnburgh Primary Sch. Play. Flds.

Church Lane Bridge

HARLINGTON

Road (HARLINGTON

DONCASTER

ROAD

Springfield Spring

Ludwell Cl.

LUDWELL

ST. HELEN'S

Melton Warren

Filter Beds

Sewage Works

Sludge Beds

BARNBURGH COMMON

Ludwell Spring

St. Helen's Lane

Ludwell Spring

Barnburgh Grange

The Temple

HANGMAN HILL

DONCASTER

51

OWLER CARR

MELTON LANE

The Ripple

Bath House Bath Farm Pond

Bath House Plantation

Sewage Works

River

Dearne (old course)

NORTH INGS

DEARNE

Mexborough

S64

WINDSOR DR.

Windhill Prim. Sch.

ULLSWATER

CONISTON RD.

CLAYFIELD

ROAD

DONNINGTON

POULTON RD.

MALLORY RD.

RIVER DEARNE

VALLEY

Dearne Bridge

Mexborough Low Pasture

ROAD PASTURE

Denaby Ings Nature Reserve

WINDHILL

WINDHILL CR.

WINDHILL

WINDHILL

HADDON RISE

CLAYFIELD VW.

CLAYFIELD

P

DN12

A **B** **C** **D**

DRIVE

CYGNET

BANK DR.

ANGEL CL.

CYGNET DR.

BUZZARD AVENUE

68

PASTURES

The Ings

Hotel

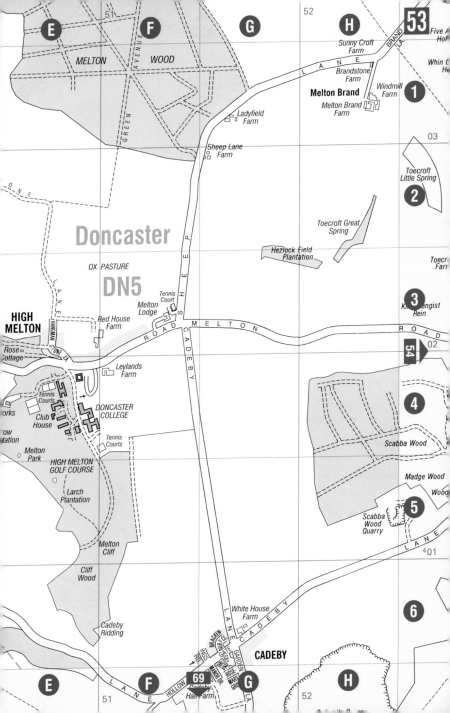

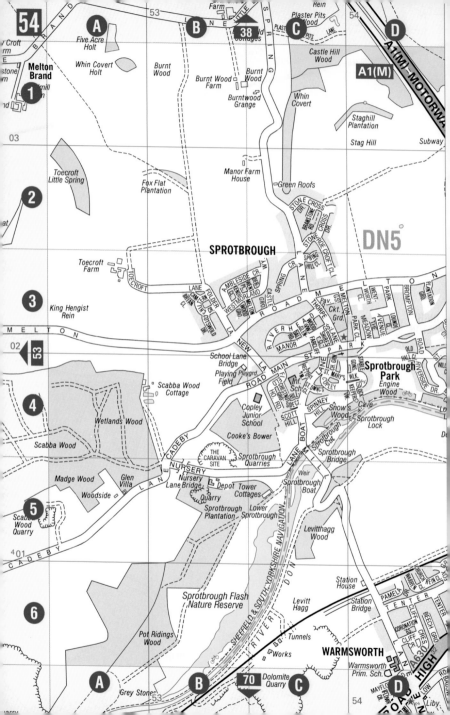

54

A B 38 C D

A1(M) — MOTORWAY

53 Farm LITTLE SPRING Plaster Pits Wood 54

Melton Brand

Five Acre Holt

Whin Covert Holt

Burnt Wood

Burnt Wood Farm

Burnt Wood

Burntwood Grange

Castle Hill Wood

Rein

Plaster Pits

Lane

A1(M)

1

Whin Covert

Staghill Plantation

Stag Hill

Subway

03

Toecroft Little Spring

Fox Flat Plantation

Manor Farm House

Green Roofs

STONE CROSS DR.

BRANSTONE RD.

CROSS DR.

STONE RIGE CROFT CLI.

SPRING HILL CL.

2

SPROTBROUGH

DN5

Toecroft Farm

TOECROFT LANE

King Hengist Rein

AMBLESIDE CR.

FOLDER LANE

GRASMERE CR.

WINDERMERE CR.

WESTMORLAND

CASTLE GRO.

SPRING LANE

COTSWOLD DR.

PLANTATION GRO.

BROMPTON

WENTWORTH CL.

PARK

LOUNDE AVENUE

MEADOW CL.

PARK CL.

Pav.

Ckt. Grd.

3

MELTON 53

02

RIVERHEAD

NEW LANE

MANOR ROAD

THORPE LANE

MELTON ROAD

SHURT GDNS.

FAIRCROFT

ST. CATHERINES AVE.

Cave

OLD ROAD

HALL CL.

RIVERSIDE DR.

WILL CL.

School Lane Bridge

Playing Field

Playgrd Field

MAIN ST.

FLORENCE RD.

SIDE CT.

Inf. Sch.

ST. MARY'S

CH. CT.

COLEY

SPINNEY

Sprotbrough Park

Engine Wood

KEEPERS GDNS.

WLK.

4

Wetlands Wood

Scabba Wood Cottage

CADEBY LANE

NURSERY LANE

Copley Junior School

Cooke's Bower

SCOTT HILL

SNOW HILL

Snow's Wood

Sprotbrough Lock

Scabba Wood

Madge Wood

Glen Villa

Woodside

THE CARAVAN SITE

Sprotbrough Quarries

Nursery Lane Bridge

Depot

Tower Cottages

Quarry

Sprotbrough Plantation

Lower Sprotbrough

Weir

Sprotbrough Boat

Sprotbrough Bridge

Levitthagg Wood

5

Scabba Wood Quarry

01

CADEBY

Sprotbrough Flash Nature Reserve

SHEFFIELD & SOUTH YORKSHIRE NAVIGATION

RIVER DON

Levitt Hagg

Station House

Station Bridge

CHURCH RD.

PAMELA

REIN CL.

CLIFF

TENTER LANE

CORONATION CRES.

BEECH GRO.

6

Pot Ridings Wood

Tunnels

Works

WARMSWORTH

Warmsworth Prim. Sch.

MAYFLOW CT.

CLIFF

HIGH ROAD A630

Liby.

A B 70 C D

Grey Stone 53 Dolomite Quarry 54

Warmsworth

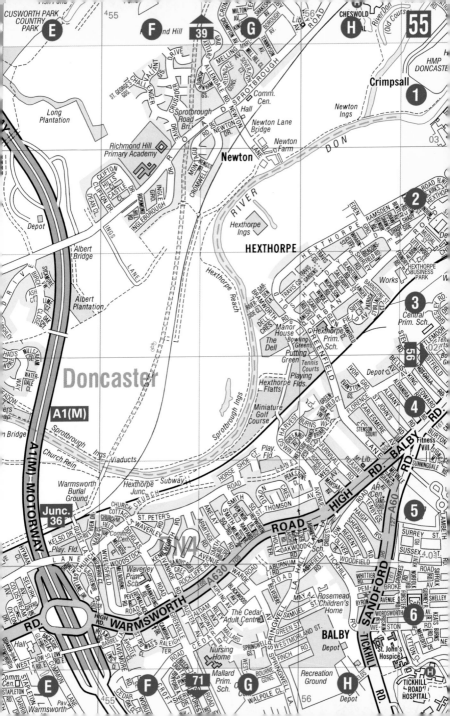

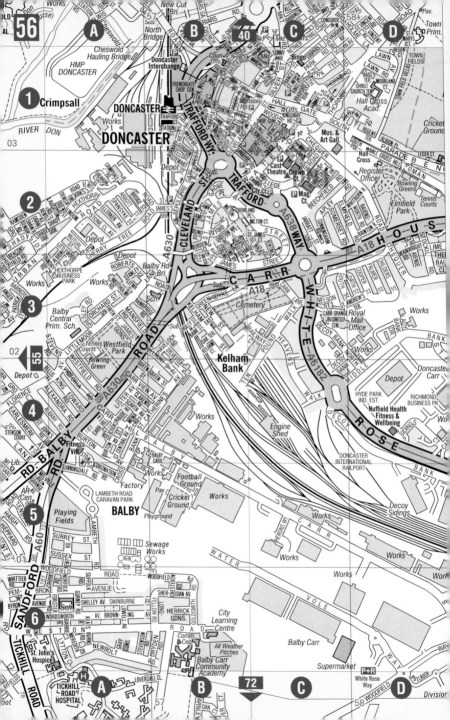

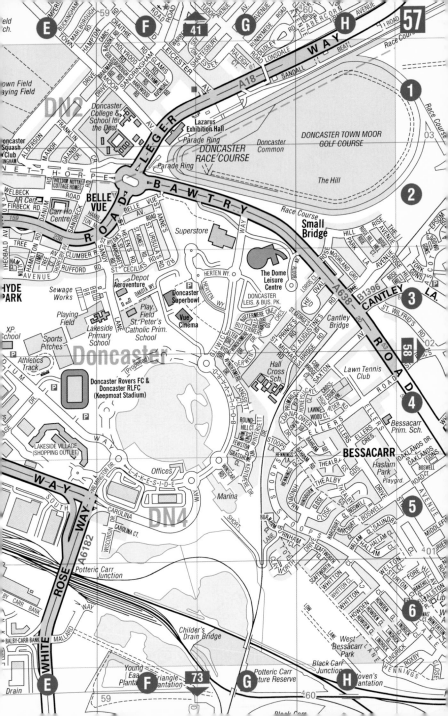

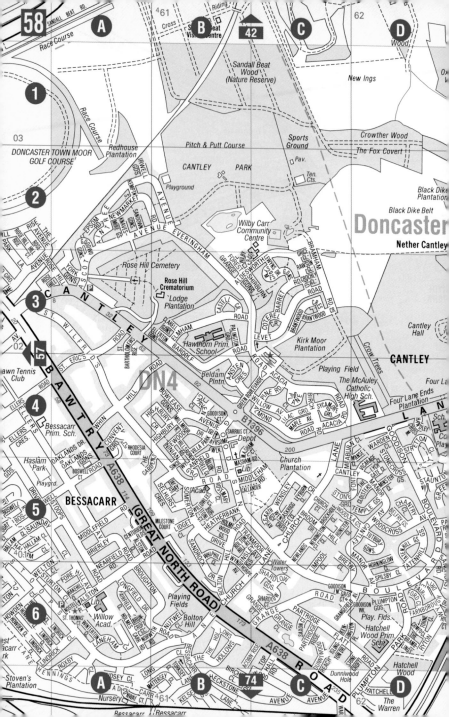

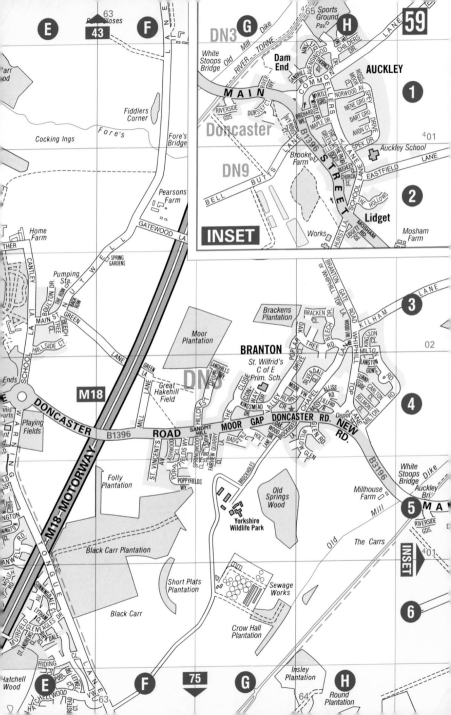

E 63 Pye Roses **F**

G DN3 **H** 59

43

White Stoops Bridge

Dam End

AUCKLEY

MAIN

Fiddlers Corner

Doncaster

Fore's

1

Cocking Ings

Fore's Bridge

Auckley School

DN9

Brooke Farm

Eastfield

2

Lidget

Pearsons Farm

BELL BUTTS

Mosham Farm

Works

INSET

Home Farm

GATEWOOD LA

SPRING GARDENS

Brackens Plantation

Bracken

KILHAM

3

Pumping Sta.

Moor Plantation

BRANTON

St. Wilfrid's C of E Prim. Sch.

4

M18

DN9

Great Hakehill Field

DONCASTER

Playing Fields

B1396

ROAD

MOOR GAP

DONCASTER RD.

NEW RD.

White Stoops Bridge

Auckley Bri

5

Sandpit Hill

Millhouse Farm

M18 MOTORWAY

Folly Plantation

POPPYFIELDS WY.

Old Springs Wood

The Carrs

RIVERSIDE GDS

INSET

401

Black Carr Plantation

Yorkshire Wildlife Park

Short Plats Plantation

Sewage Works

6

Black Carr

Crow Hall Plantation

Hatchell Wood

E 63 **F** **75** **G** 64 **H** Round Plantation

Insley Plantation

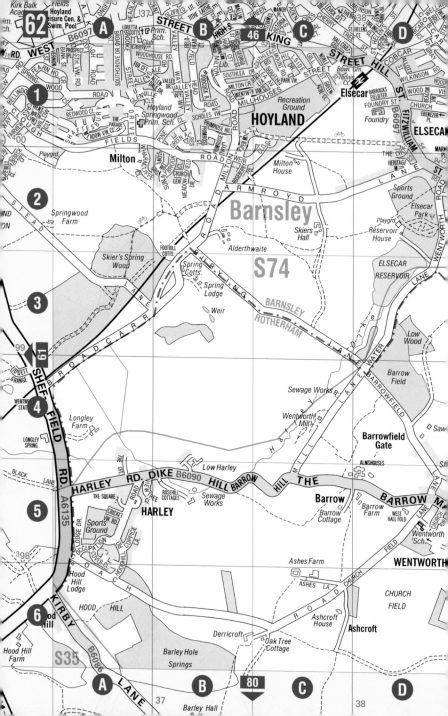

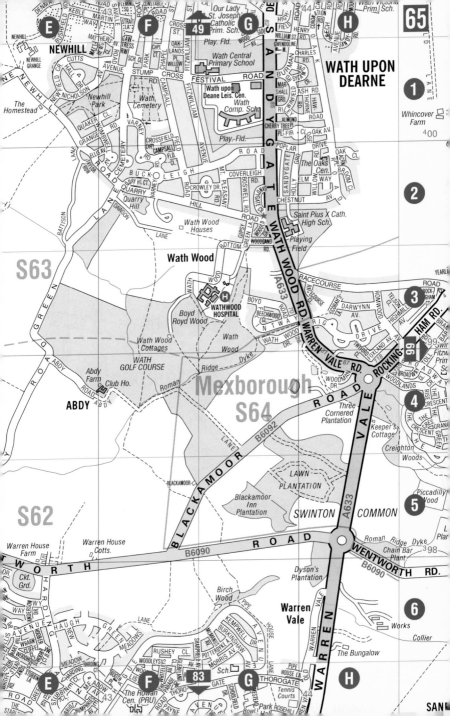

WATH UPON DEARNE

NEWHILL

Wath Central Primary School

Wath Comp. Sch

Wath Wood

WATHWOOD HOSPITAL

Boyd Royd Wood

Mexborough

S64

ABDY

WATH GOLF COURSE

S63

S62

SWINTON COMMON

Warren Vale

Three Cornered Plantation

LAWN PLANTATION

Blackamoor Inn Plantation

Dyson's Plantation

Birch Wood

The Bungalow

The Homestead

Newhill Grange

Newhill Park

Wath Cemetery

Wath Wood Houses

Wath Wood Cottages

Abdy Farm

Warren House Farm

Warren House Cotts.

Whincover Farm

The Oaks Cen.

Saint Pius X Cath. High Sch.

Playing Field

Keeper's Cottage

Creighton Woods

Piccadilly Wood

Wath Victoria Prim. Sch.

Our Lady St. Joseph Catholic Prim. Sch.

Three Cornered Plantation

Wath upon Deane Leis. Cen.

Chain Bar Plant.

Roman Ridge Dyke

65

① ② ③ ④ ⑤ ⑥

E **F** **G** **H**

49 83

99

ROCKINGHAM

WENTWORTH RD.

B6090

B6092

B6090

WARREN VALE

A633

WATH WOOD RD.

WARREN VALE RD.

SANDYGATE

GREEN ROAD

BLACKAMOOR LANE

WENTWORTH ROAD

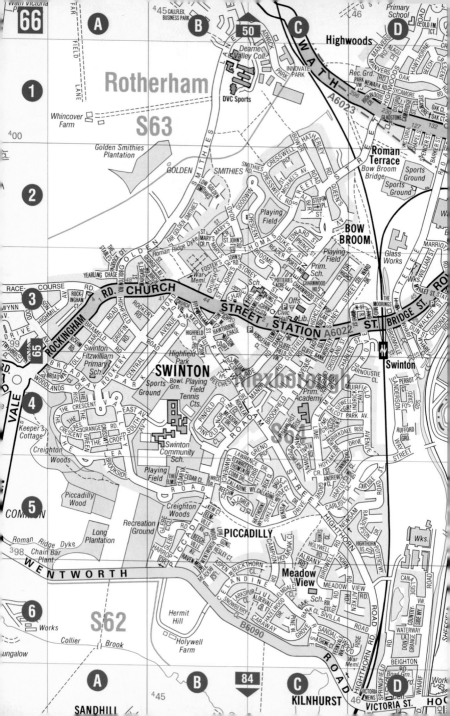

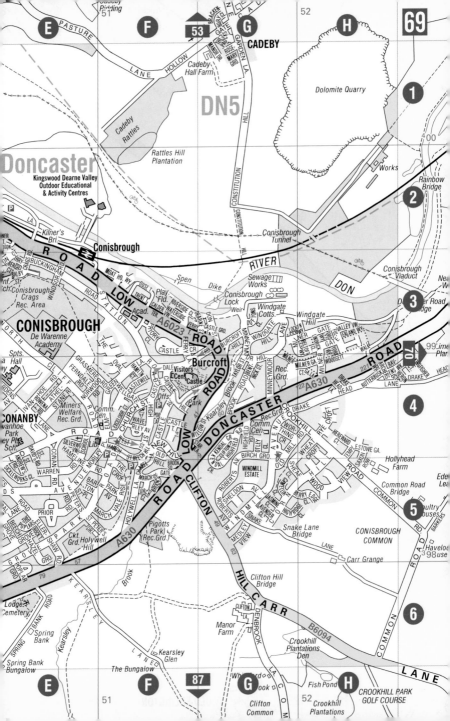

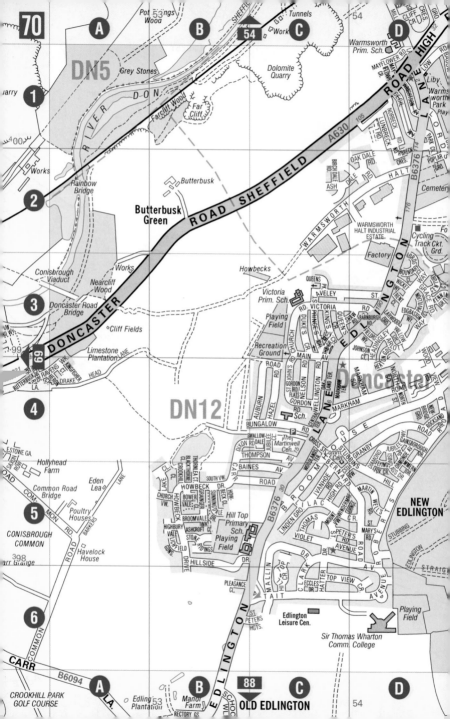

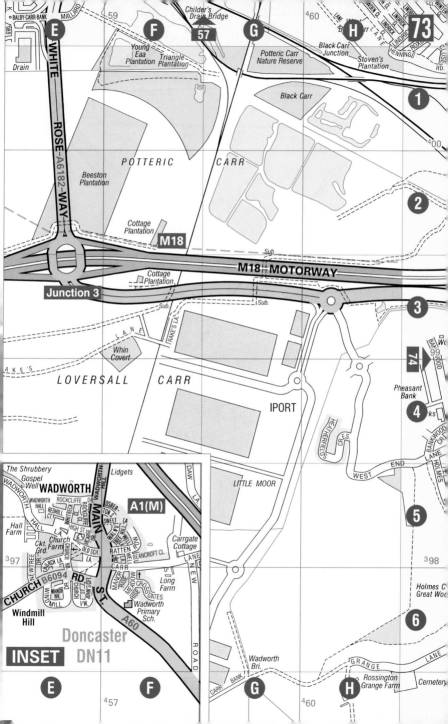

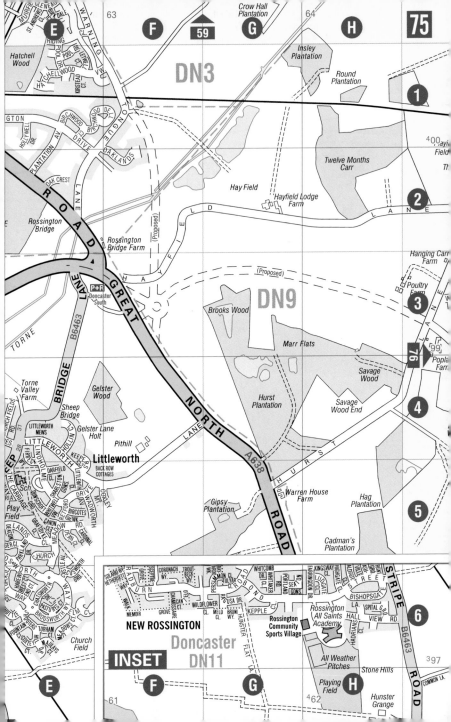

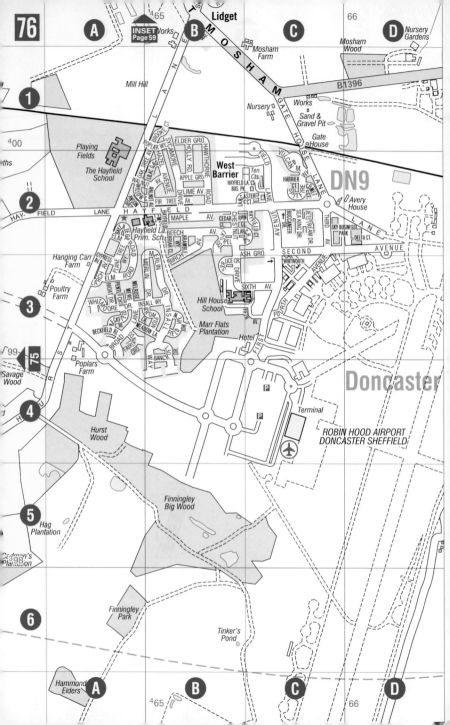

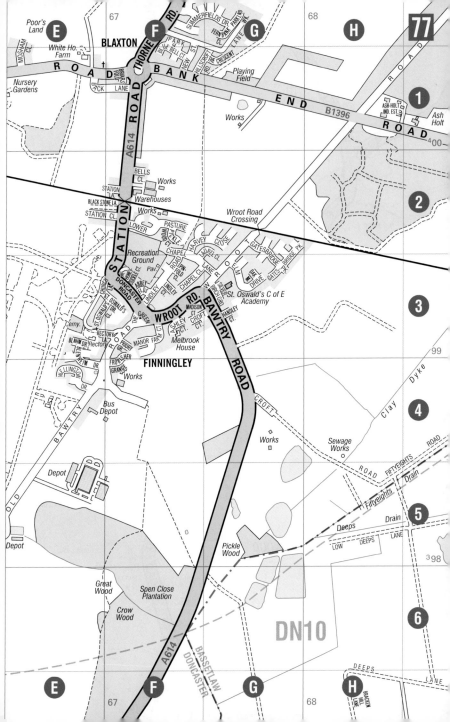

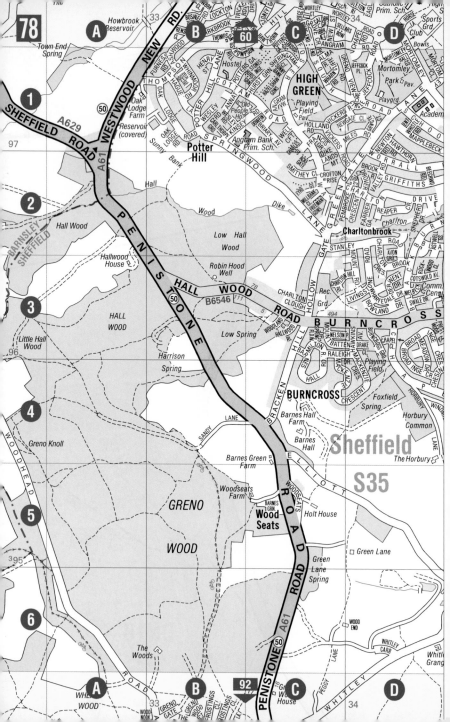

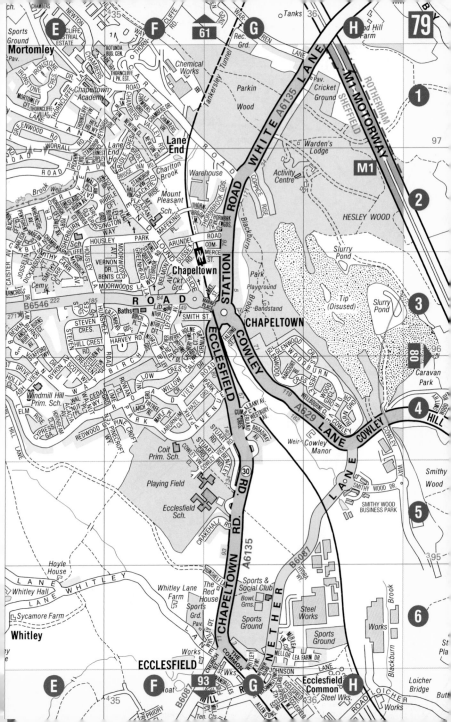

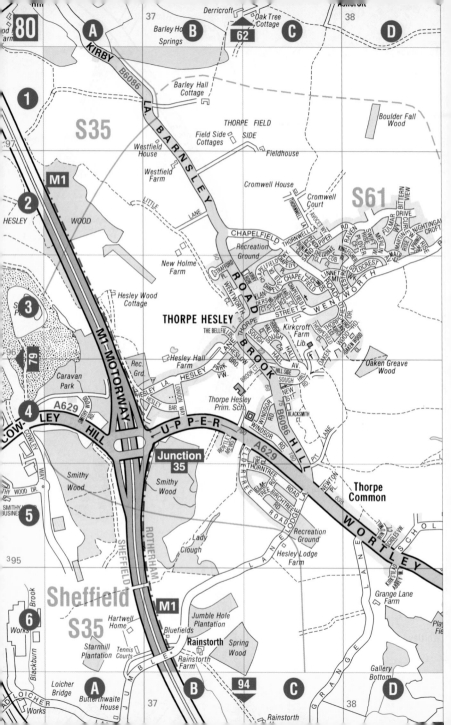

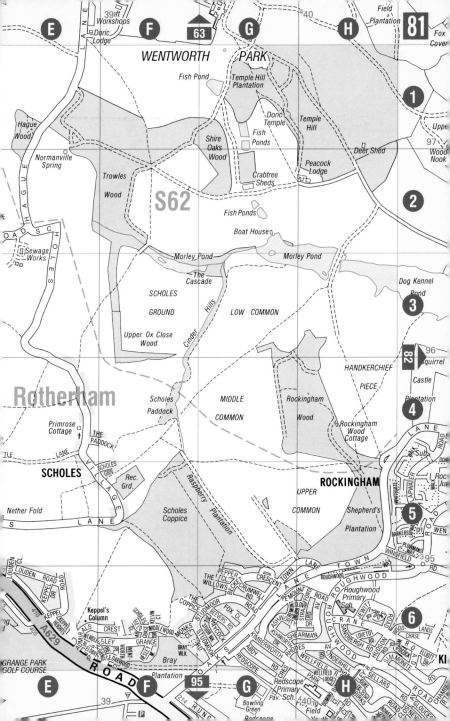

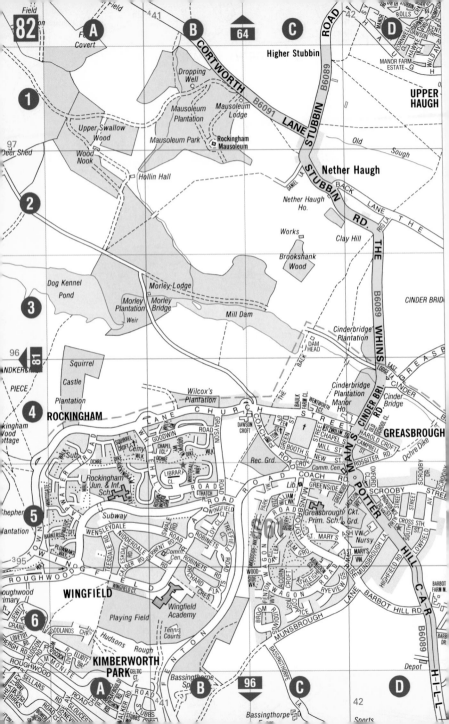

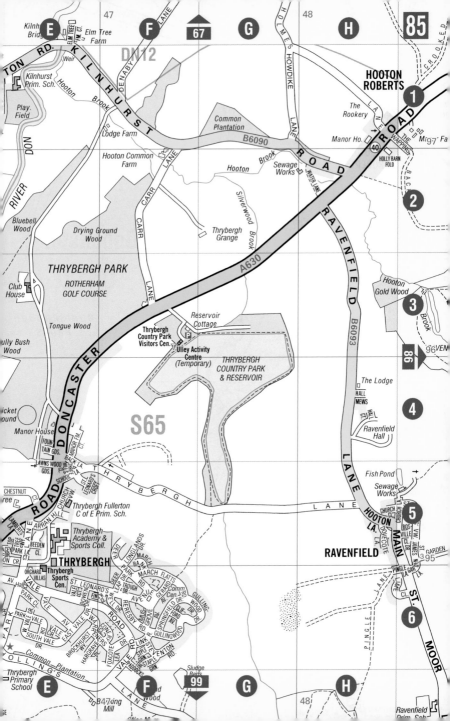

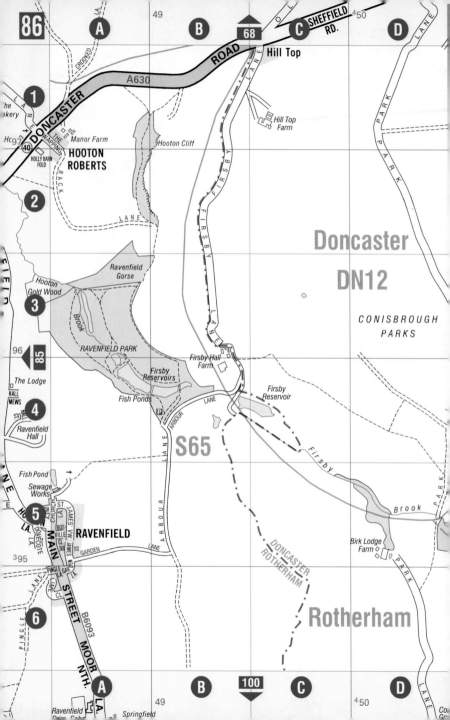

A   49   **B**   68   **C**   SHEFFIELD RD.   450   **D**

ROAD

Hill Top

1

A630

DONCASTER

The Rookery

Hc9?   40

The WAPPING

Manor Farm

Hooton Cliff

HILL TOP FARM

Hill Top Farm

HOOTON ROBERTS

HOLLY BARN FOLD

Holly Barn Fold

CROOKED LANE

LANE

BACK   LANE

2

FIRSBY   LANE

FIRSBY   LANE

Doncaster

DN12

Ravenfield Gorse

Hooton Gold Wood

CONISBROUGH PARKS

3

Brook

96   ◀ 85

RAVENFIELD PARK

Firsby Hall Farm

The Lodge

HALL MEWS

Firsby Reservoirs

Firsby Reservoir

Fish Ponds

LANE

4

Ravenfield Hall

ARBOUR   LANE

S65

Firsby   Brook

Fish Pond

Sewage Works

ST.   JAMES VW.

CHURCH LA.   JAMES WAY

DOVECOTE LA.   BOSVILLE CT.

JAMES ST.

GARDEN

DONCASTER

ROTHERHAM

Birk Lodge Farm

PARK   LANE

5

RAVENFIELD

MAIN   STREET

HOLL LA.

ARBOUR   LANE

Rotherham

395

PINGLE LA.   GAR. LA.

CL.

6

PINGLE   LANE

B6093

MOOR   NTH.

Ravenfield Prim. Sch.

Springfield

Co. Gr

A   49   **B**   100   **C**   450   **D**

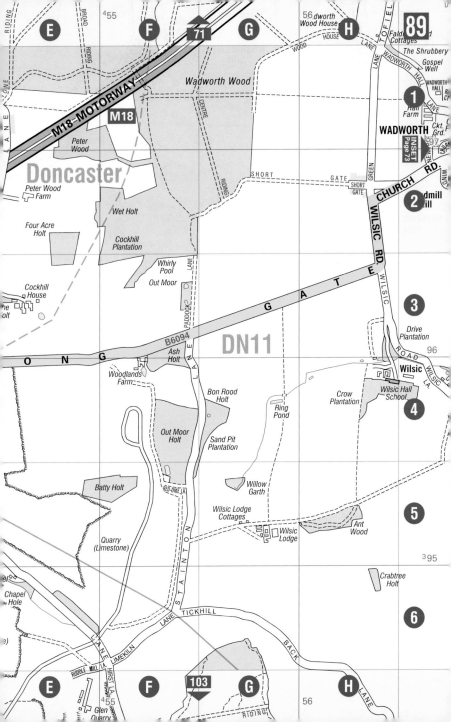

90

INSET

A

B
WHARNCLIFFE
SIDE
Wharncliffe Side
Packhorse Bridge

INSET

C

D

Water
Treatment
Works

Swinnock Hall

Long
Wood

Ewden Beck

MAIN

RIVER DON

Grove
Wood

Hagg
Wood

Bitholmes
House

Glen Howe

Glen Howe
Park

School
Fm.

Weir

Damsel

Weir

Sheffield

1

THE CARLTON

MORE HALL

WHARNCLIFFE RI

BROOMHEAD RD.

A6102

GROVE AVE

Glen Howe
Tower

THE GLEN

SPRING GROVE

P

A6102 RD. LANGSETT

Weir

Works

S35

BRIGHTHOLMLEE

Wharncliffe Side
Primary School

2
WHARNCLIFFE
SIDE

STORTH LANE

DIXON DRIVE

DYSON HOLMES LA.

DYSON
HOLMES
Long
Wood

DON LANE

DAMASK LANE

ROAD

395

40

Tennis
Courts

Slack
Fields

SLACKFIELDS LA.

Works

Delf Hill

GATE LANE

HILL TOP DR.

COCKSHUTTS LANE

Hill Top Usher
Wood

VIEW

Foldrings

Folderings
Fm.

RAYNOR SIKE LA.

OWLER LANE

ACRE LA.

Foldrings

Field Farm

Foldrings
Bush

HORSE CROFT

LUMB LANE

GREEN LANE

LONG LANE

Sheffield

Top Hill
Farm

Pav.

ONESACRE
UC

Onesacre Hall

Onesacre

Don Vie
House

Gilbert Wood

Brook

CHURCH

Com
Cer

3

ONESMOOR

Lumb
Bush

Coumes

FARMHOUSE

Greave
Bush

Coldwell

Cold Well
Farm

JACKEY LANE

COLDWELL HI.

WHEEL

Coumes

LANE

HAGG LANE

POPLAR
RD.

POPLAR
NAYLOR

MAYFLD
GRO.

93

Coumes Vale
Plantation

Brook

Old
School
House

Coumes Wood

HOLLIN
RD.

Hollin
Hill

HILLCREST

HAGGS

4

ONESMOOR

S6

LANE

Coumes
Vale

Coumes

Gate
Farm

BURTON LANE

Cemetery

BOGGARD

The Aspland

S35

**PEAK
DISTRICT
NATIONAL
PARK**

OLD BOTTOM LANE

WAL
LO

LONING

BRIARFIELDS LA.

5

Prospect
Farm

Convent of the
Holy Ghost

BURNT HILL LANE

Burnt Hill
Farm

**Bradfield
Sch.**

KIRK EDGE RD.

392

BROOMFIELD TER.

COAL PIT LA.

KIRK

EDGE

LANE

KIRK
EDG
DR

6

Holdworth
Hall

Holdworth

Trickett
Edge Farm

Far
House

HOLDWORTH LANE

STONY LANE

ROAD

White
Green End

Spitewinter
Farm

Haighen Field

Haighenfield

LOW ASH COMMON

DARWENT LANE

Low Ash
Farm

STUBBING LANE

Lang Hou
Farm

A

B

104

C

D

29

430

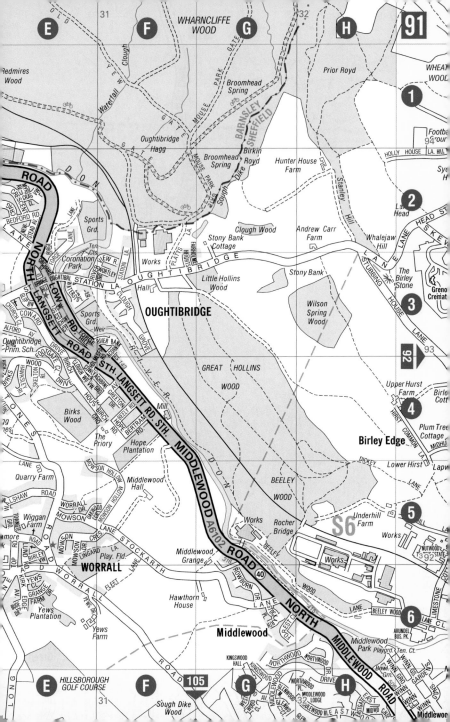

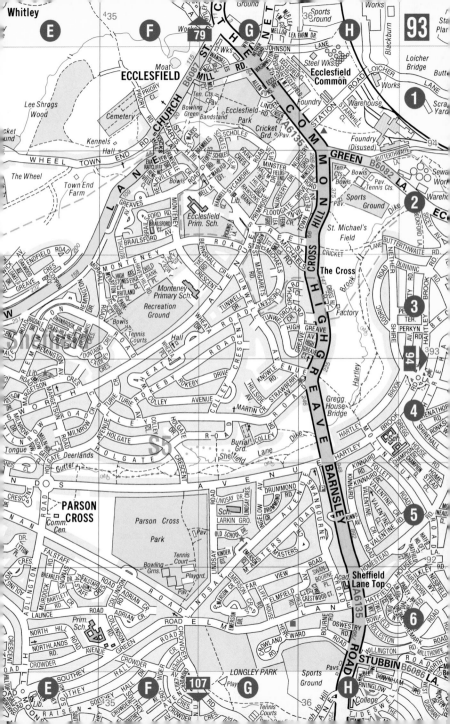

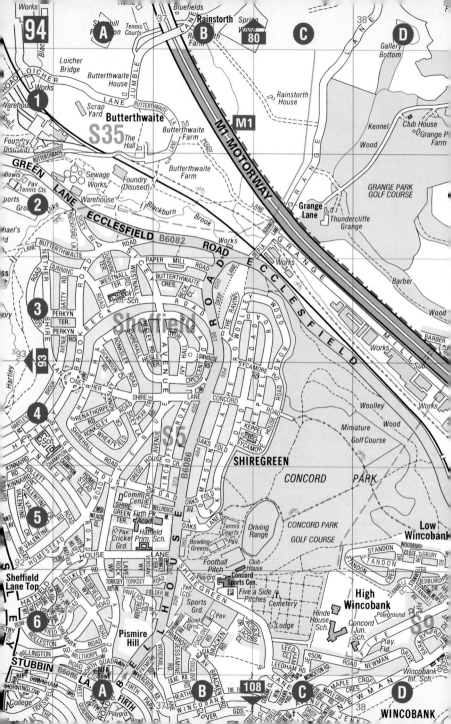

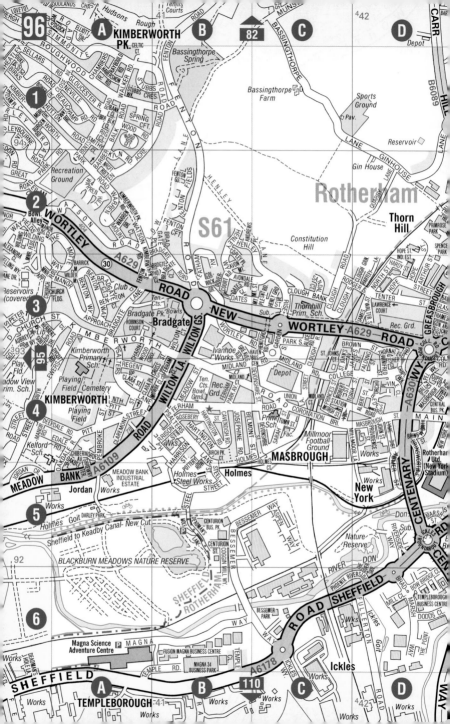

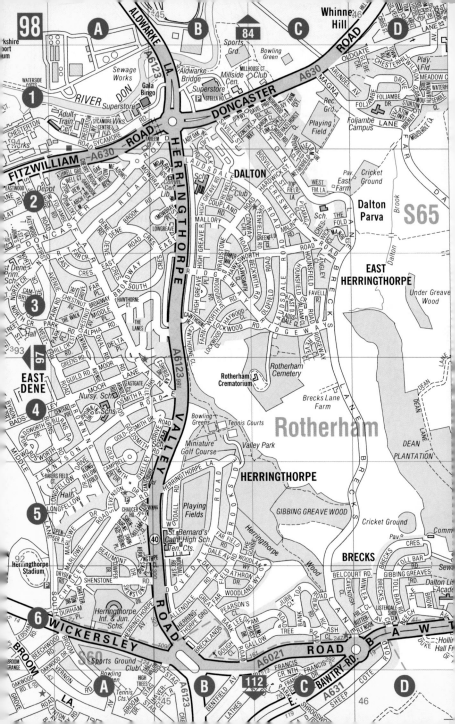

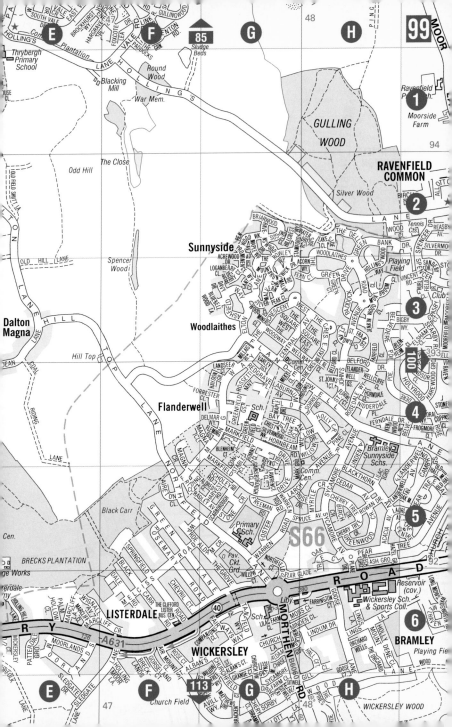

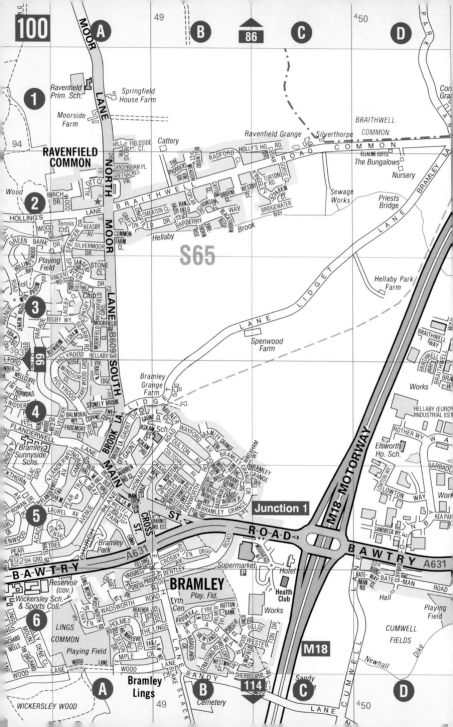

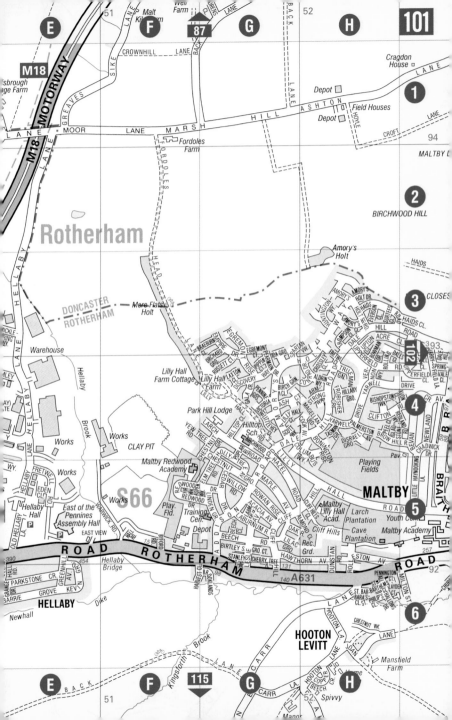

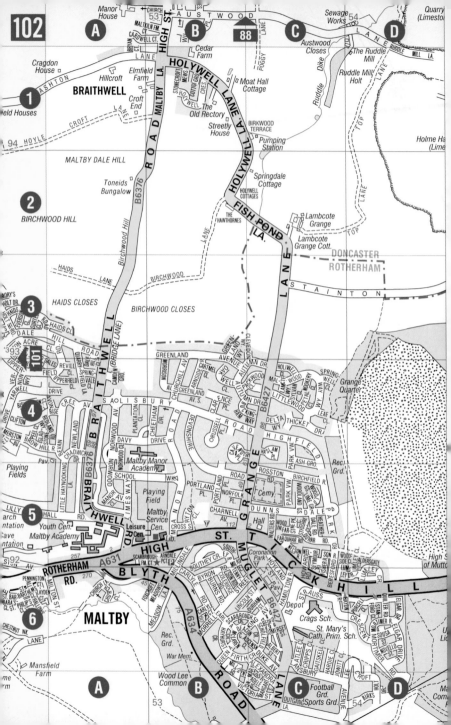

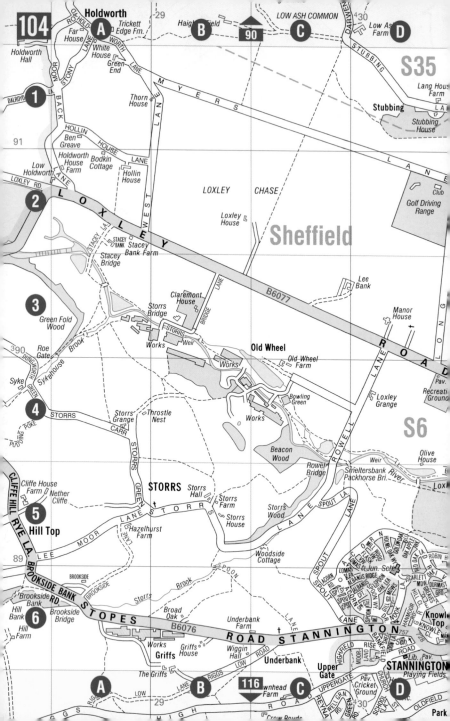

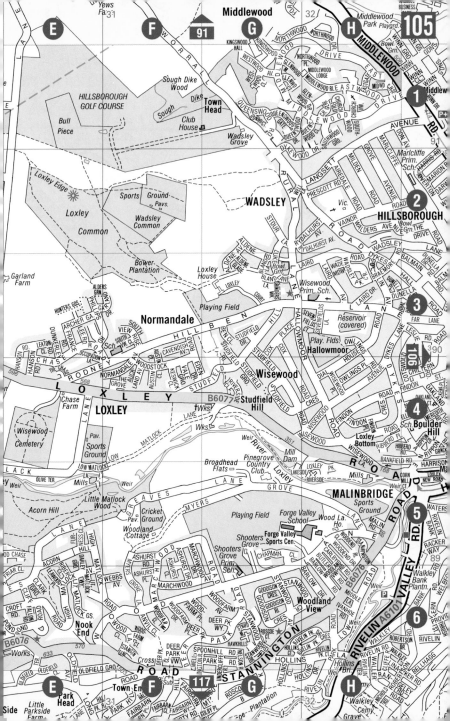

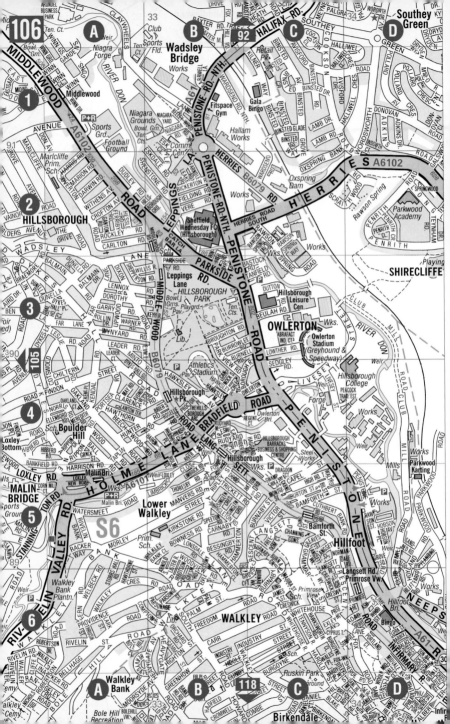

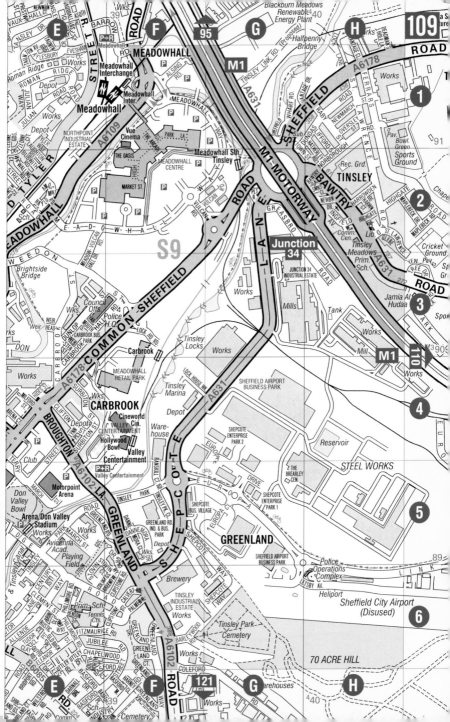

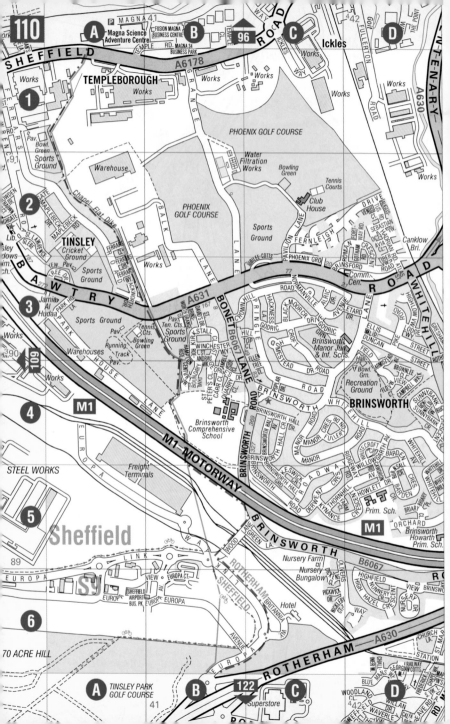

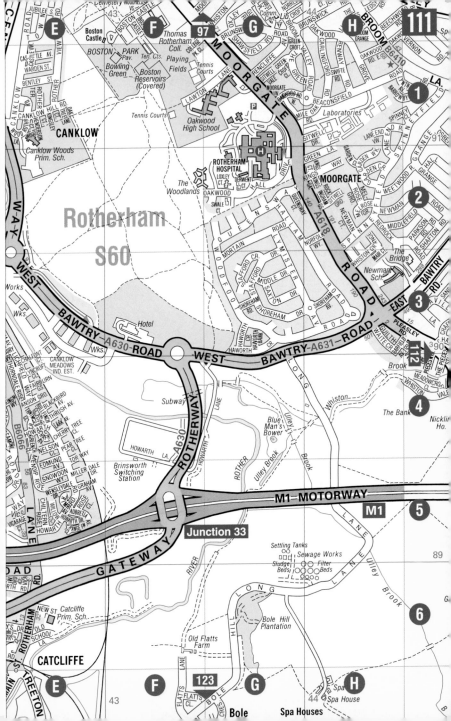

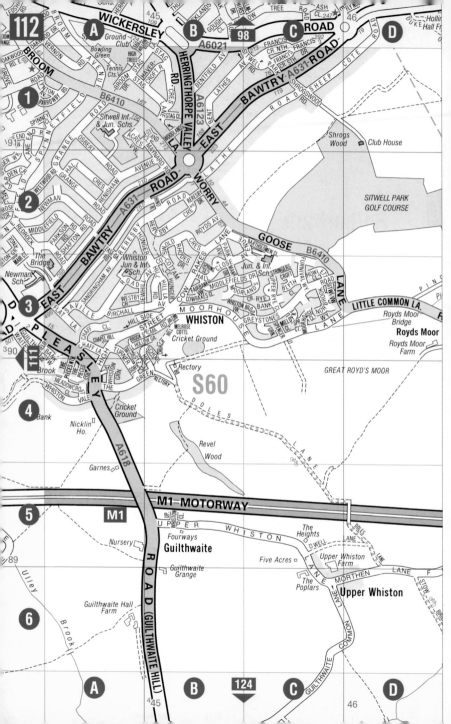

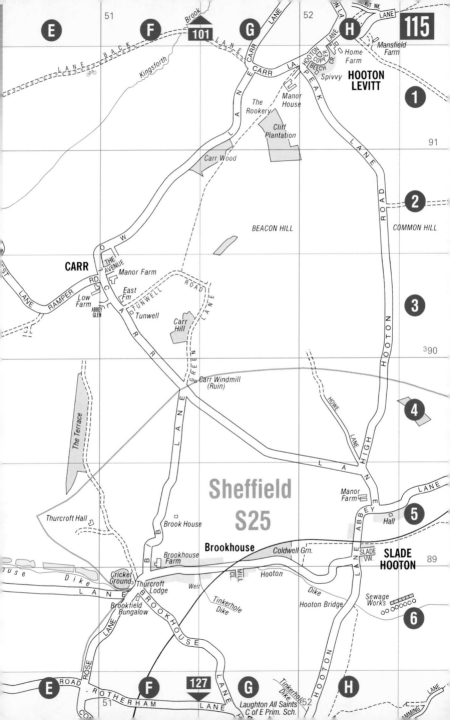

E 51 F Brook 101 G 52 H **115**

LANE NUT WK LANE
LANE BACK Kingsforth CARR LA HOOTON COPPER CR BEECH Mansfield Farm **1** 91
Kingsforth CARR LANE Spivvy Home Farm **HOOTON LEVITT**
The Rookery Manor House PEAK
Cliff Plantation LANE
Carr Wood

BEACON HILL ROAD COMMON HILL **2**

W THE AVENUE Manor Farm ROAD HOOTON **3** 390
CARR RAMPER RD C East Fm TUNWELL GREEN Road
LANE Low Farm ABBEY GLEN Tunwell Carr Hill LANE
C A R R Carr Windmill (Ruin) HOME LANE HIGH **4**

The Terrace LANE LANE ROAD

Sheffield Manor Farm LANE **5**
S25 Thurcroft Hall Brook House Hall ABBEY
B Brookhouse Farm **Brookhouse** Coldwell Grn. SLADE VW. **SLADE HOOTON** 89
use Dike LANE Cricket Ground Thurcroft Lodge Hooton Weir MILL Hooton Dike Hooton Bridge Sewage Works **6**
Brookfield Bungalow BROOKHOUSE Tinkerhole Dike Tinkerhole Dike

E ROAD F 127 G 52 H
ROSE ROTHERHAM LANE LANE Laughton All Saints HOOTON LANE
CO 51 LANE C of E Prim. Sch. AMMING

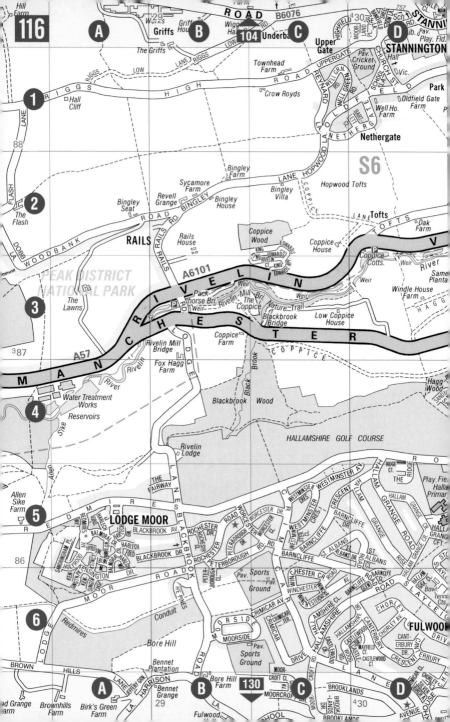

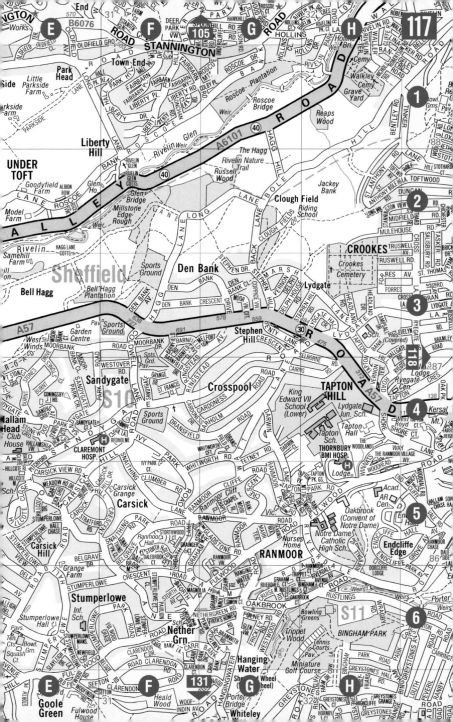

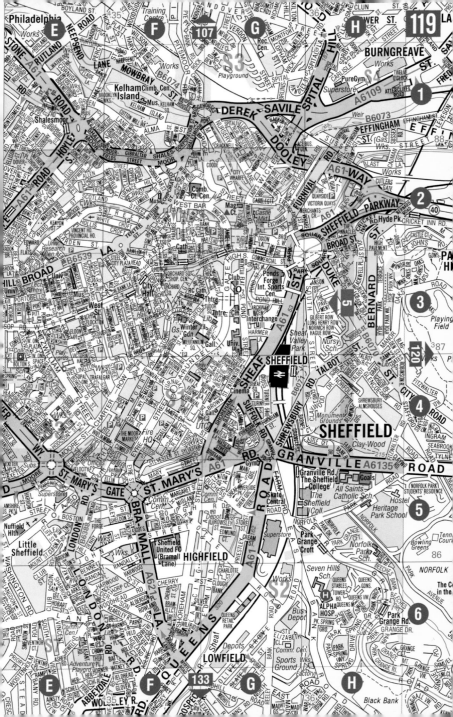

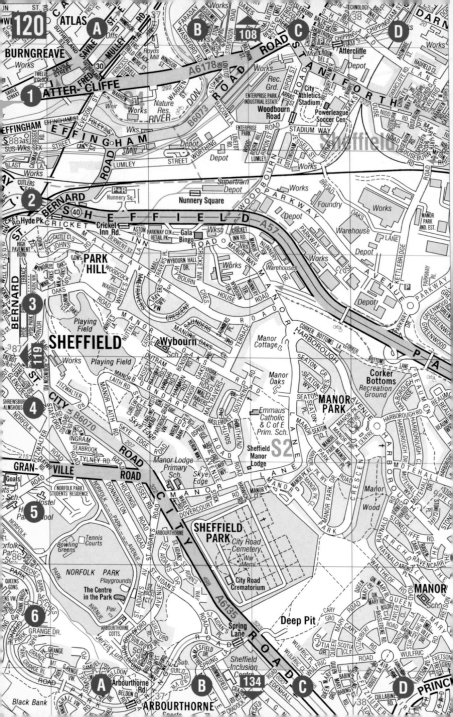

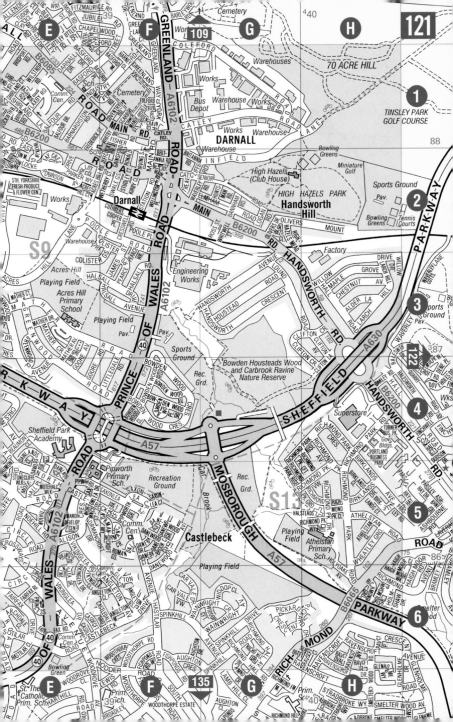

E **F** 111 **G** **H**

1

2

3

4

5

6

43 44 88 387 86 44

CATCLIFFE

TREETON

Bole Hill

Spa Well
Spa House

Spa Houses

Spa Hill

Rotherham
S60

Burnt Wood

Treeton Junction Sports Ground

Mill Ho.

Weir

OPENCAST WORKINGS

Treeton Grange

Sludge Tanks

B6067

LANE

124
TREETON WOOD

Hail Mary Hill Wood

Falconer Wood

Nurseries

Falconer Farm

Smallage Farm

Stevenage

LANE

WE

SMALLAGE

Woodhouse Mill

Sewage Works

Recreation Ground

RIVER

Pumping Station

Rec. Grd.

FALCONER LA.

FALCONER LA.

ROAD

Fence

Playing Field
Fence Farm

Sch.

SHEFFIELD

ASTON BY-PASS

ROAD PARK

Park Hill Farm

Woodhouse

SHEFFIELD ROAD

Forge

Works

Works

FURNACE LA.

B6064

137

Woodhouse Washlands

E **F** **G** **H**

43 44

124

A B **112** C D

1

Rotherham S60

Ulley Brook

PLEASLEY (GUILTHWAITE HILL)

GUILTHWAITE

Depot

88

Burnt Wood

2

Packman's Bridge

Gas Valve Compound

A618

Guilthwaite Common

Weir

Ulley Reservoir

RESERVOIR

Sluice

Sandstone Quarry

GREEN

West End Farm

P

Ulley Country Park Visitor Centre

ULLEY COUNTRY PARK

LANE

ROAD

MAIN

POYNTON WY
POYNTON AV.

3

WOOD B6067 LA. TREETON

387-

◄ **123**

TREETON WOOD

LA.

ROAD ST.

ULLEY

Ulley Holt

Weirs

LANE

Turnshaw Plantation

4

29

NASCOT GDNS.

DRIVE

HALL

HALL FARM

CORAL CORS.

CORAL DR.

WELL LA.

MARTIN

Play-Fld
Sch.

RISE

AUGHTON

ASTON

MANOR FM.

ULLEY VIEW

RICKNALD CL.

Sunnyside

B6067

Turnshaw Common

5

Nurseries

Reservoir (Covered)

Kenville

DANIELS DR.

RAMBLER

LANE

Aughton

AVENUE GRAY AV.

Sheffield S26

SMALLAGE LA.

Smallage

WEST

Stevenage

WESTFIELD

SPRINGWOOD AV.

GRANGE AV.

HALLAM AV.

AUGHTON AV.

MAIN

HALL

Aughton Prim. Sch.

30

WINDY RIDGE

Turnshaw Heights WY

WW1

MASON DR.

WESTCOTT

ALDERSON AV.

WALPOLE GR.

MASON

GREEN

WHARTON

SPROWD

AVENUE

AV.

AVENUE

VERBEST AV.

LOVETOT AV.

CONYRS

TOWN

119

6

86

Aston Academy

Aston-cum-Aughton Leis. Cen.

ROAD

SWALLOWNEST COURT

BEECH

Playgrd.

Cemetery

ALEXANDRA

Bowl. Green

ROSE

MEWS

AUGHTON A618

HIGH

SWALLOWNEST

Tennis Cts.

Park Farm

Comm. Cen.

NURSERY RD.

JASMINE GDNS.

ALPINE

CAMELI

MANVERS RD.

Jun. Acad.

CANTILUPE

ARCUBUS

AV.

PAGNALL

AV.

WESLEY

CERELENE

DRIVE

ROSEGARTH

AV.

ROSE

MELBOURNE AV.

AVENUE

EDEN GLADE

EDEN GROVE

AVENUE

HOLDERNE

MILLSTON

BRAMLEY

ROSSLYN

CHELMSFORD

ROAD

MALTON

Sch.

138

Comm. Cen.

Mill Stone Hill

ROAD PARK

MOOR

WAY

MAIN

ST.

ROTHERHAM

B6053

SCH. ST.

PARK

GATE

WORKSOP

THORNE PL.

PRIORY

A B C D

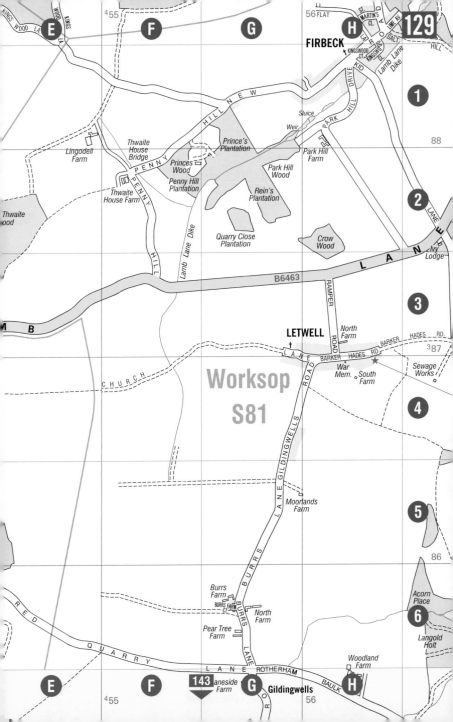

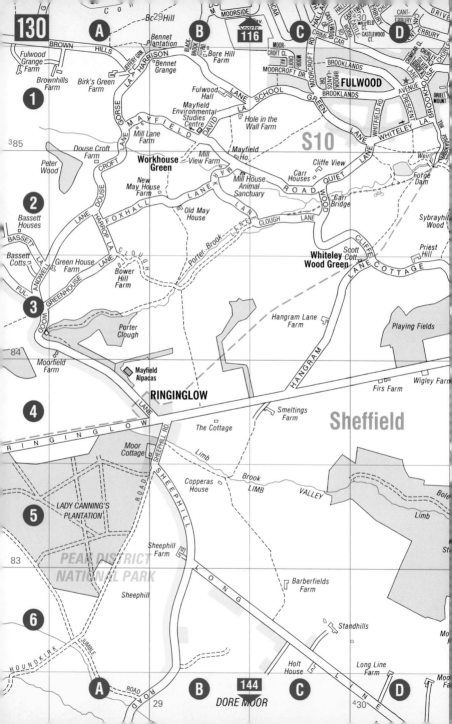

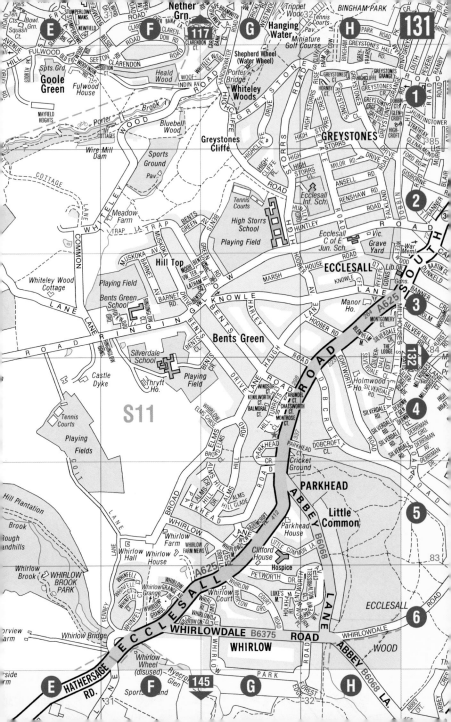

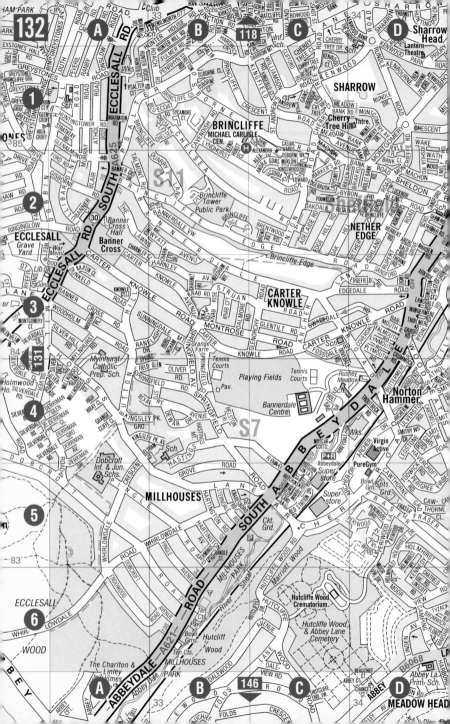

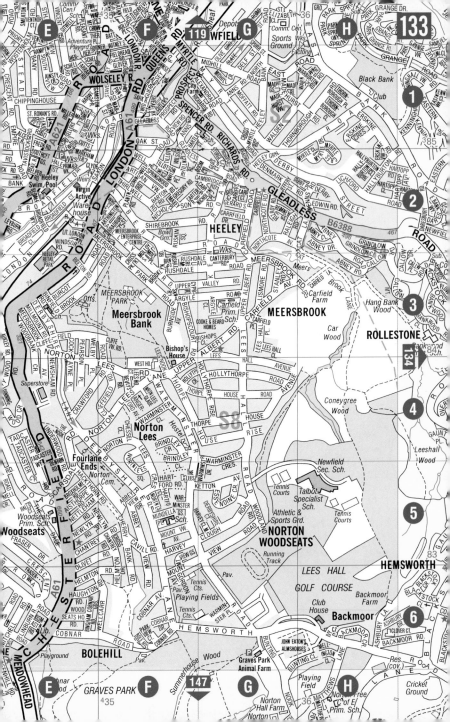

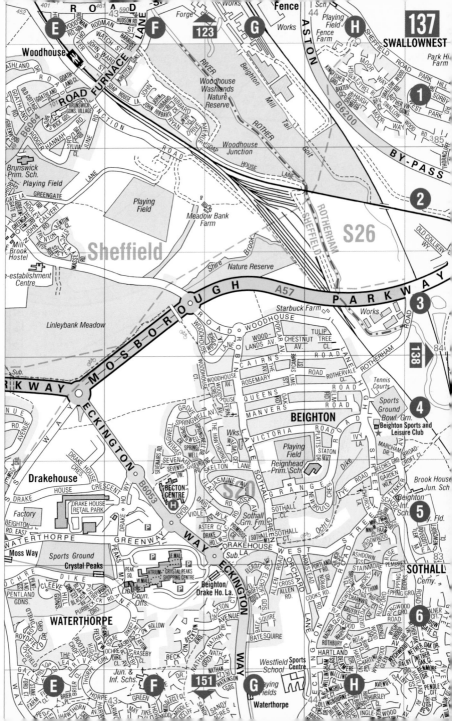

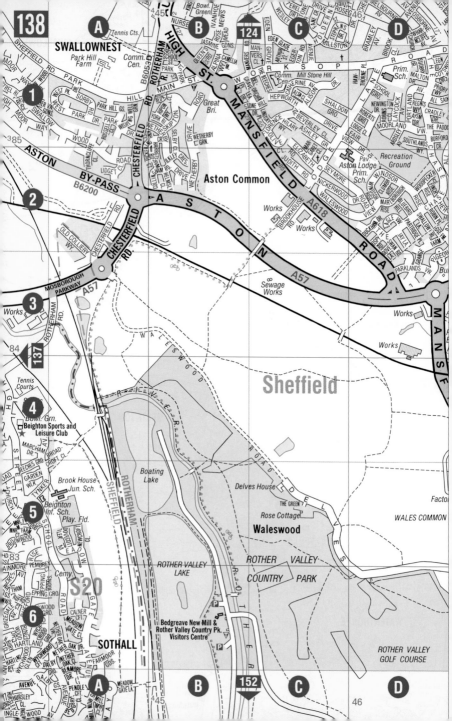

138

SWALLOWNEST

A **B** **124** **C** **D**

1

Aston Common

2

ASTON BY-PASS
B6200

3

137

Sheffield

4

Beighton Sports and
Leisure Club

5

Brook House
Jun. Sch.

Beighton
Inf. Sch.
Play. Fld.

Boating
Lake

Delves House

Rose Cottage

Waleswood

ROTHER VALLEY
COUNTRY PARK

WALES COMMON

Facto

S20

6

ROTHER VALLEY
LAKE

Bedgreave New Mill &
Rother Valley Country Pk.
Visitors Centre

SOTHALL

ROTHER VALLEY
GOLF COURSE

A **B** **152** **C** **D**

46

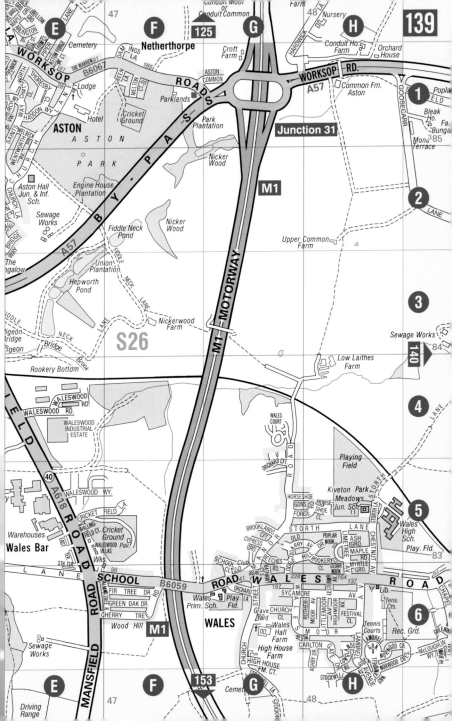

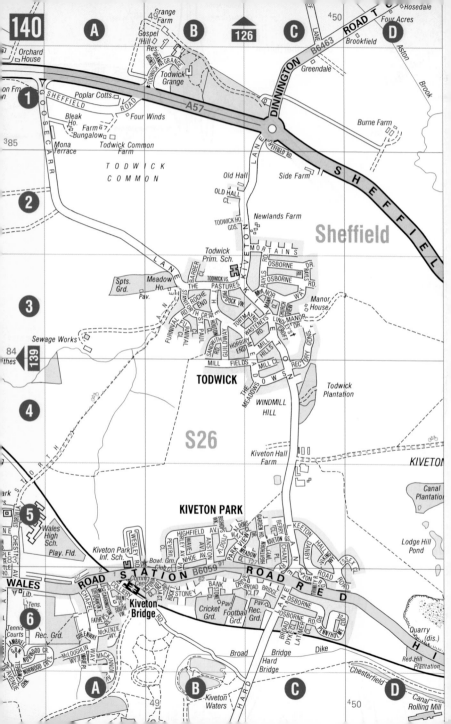

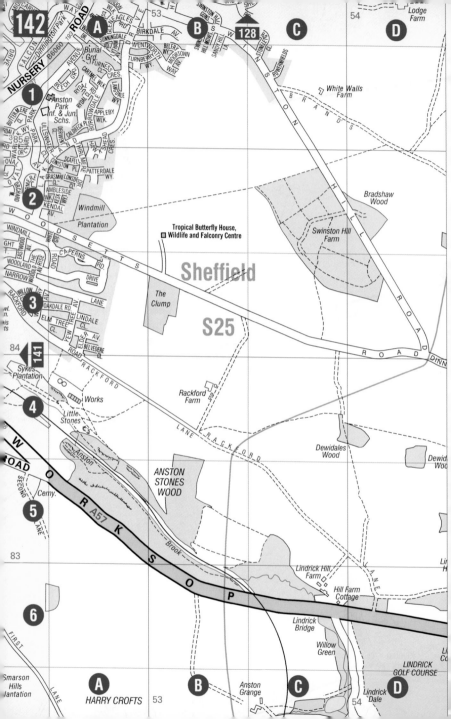

142

A B C D

NURSERY ROAD

B6060

FALCON

Dinnington Park

53

SWINSTON

SWINSTON HILL

SANDY HILL

54

Lodge Farm

128

ROAD

WAY

A

B

CLEVE EAGLES

BIRKDALE AV.

WENTWORTH

SUNNINGDALE

FURNESS CL.

CARTMEL WLK.

TURNBERRY WY.

RYDAL CT.

MORTOWN CL.

BELFRY WAY

BELTRY

WK.

C

STONEHILLS

POWERFIELDS

White Walls Farm

1

Anston Park Inf. & Jun. Schs.

Burial Grd.

BEECH GRO.

AVENUE

PARK

RYDAL

LO. RD.

BROWNHILL

APPLEBY WLK.

LANGDALE

BUTTERMERE

385

BROW

B6060

RD.

WARD

DENWICK CL.

CALDBECK RD.

THIRLMERE CRES.

PARK

WINDSETTS

HILL

Bradshaw Wood

S

T

O

N

S

BRANDS

WINDMERE

OVAL

AV.

PARK

ULLSWATER

CL.

HAWKS

SCAFELL PL.

PATTERDALE WY.

Swinston Hill Farm

2

ORCHARD

GRASMERE

CON/STON

AMBLESIDE

LONSDALE

CL.

KENDAL AV.

KESWICK

Windmill Plantation

WOODSETTS

WINDMILL

GHT

EASTWOOD

THE

CAPERNS

RD.

RISE

Tropical Butterfly House, Wildlife and Falconry Centre

Sheffield

ROAD

HILL

WOODLAND

WOOD

NARROW

DRIVE

LANE

The Clump

3

WILLOW

RACKFORD

OAKDALE RD.

TREE AV.

YEW

TREE CL.

LINDALE CL.

LINDALE AV.

S25

141

84

ELM TREE CL.

ELDER CL.

BELVEDERE CL.

ROAD

RACKFORD

Sykes Plantation

LANE

Rackford Farm

ROAD

DINN

4

Works

Little Stones

LANE

CRACKFORD

Dewidales Wood

Dewid Woo

ROAD

W

O

O

Anston

ANSTON STONES WOOD

5

Cerny.

SECOND

LANE

R

A57

K

S

O

P

Brook

Dewidales Wood

83

LANE

Lindrick Hill Farm

Li

H

Hill Farm Cottage

6

Lindrick Bridge

Willow Green

LINDRICK GOLF COURSE

Li

Co

FIRST

LANE

Smarson Hills Plantation

A

HARRY CROFTS

53

B

Anston Grange

C

54

Lindrick Dale

D

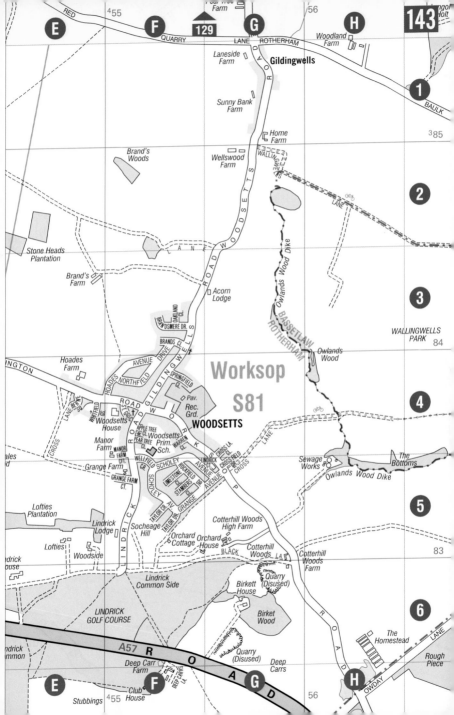

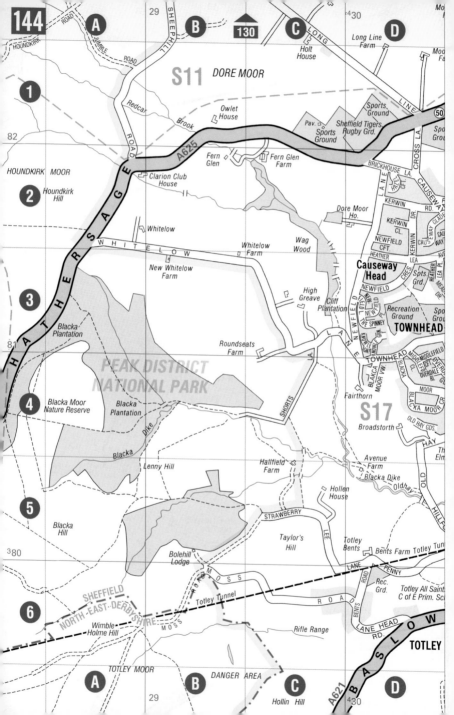

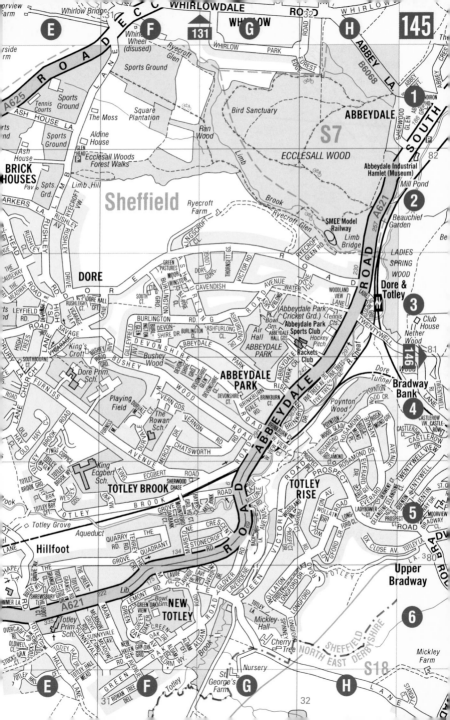

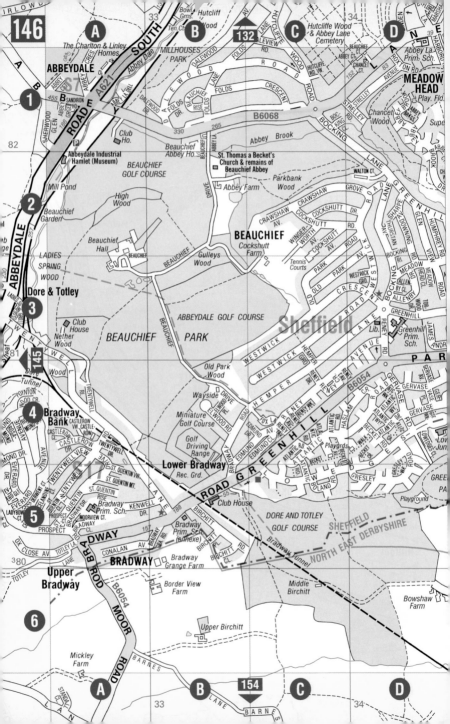

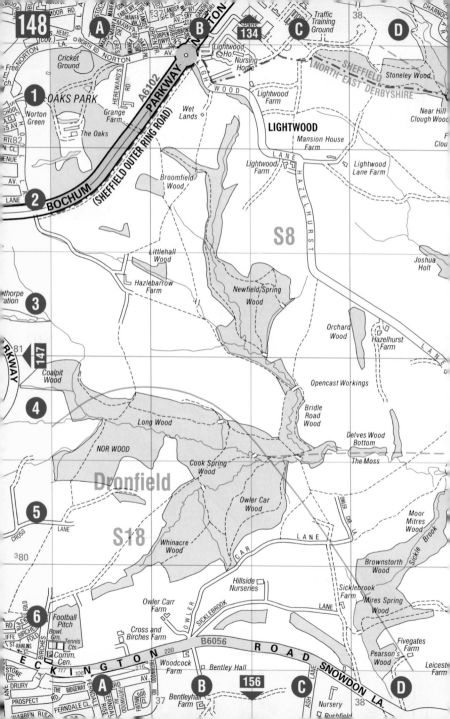

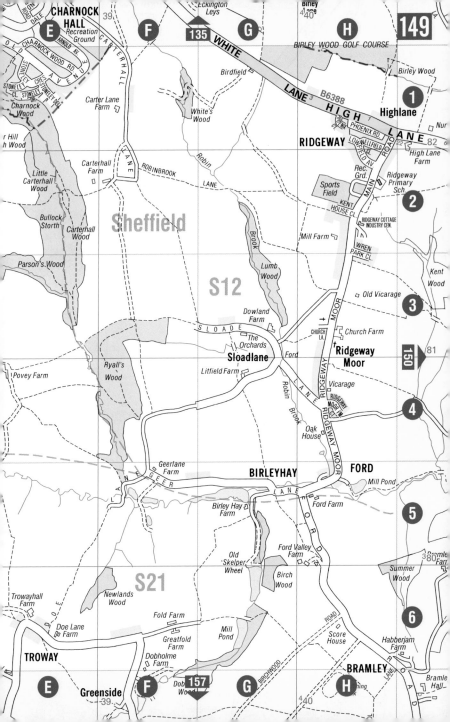

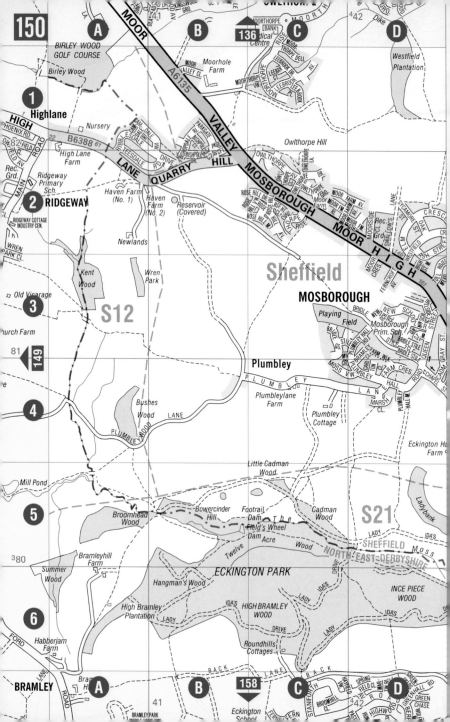

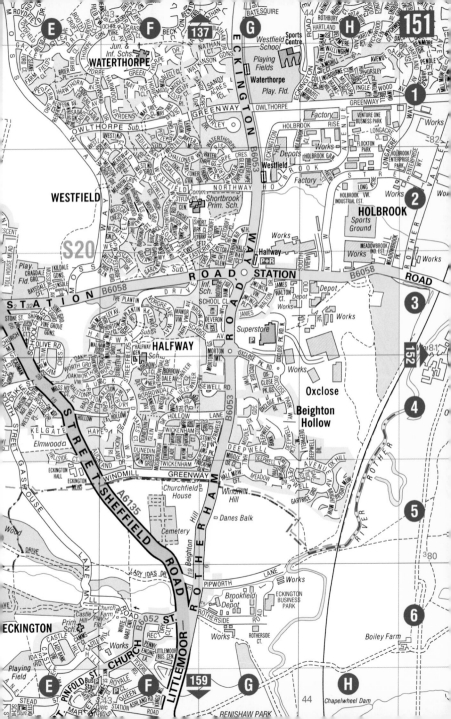

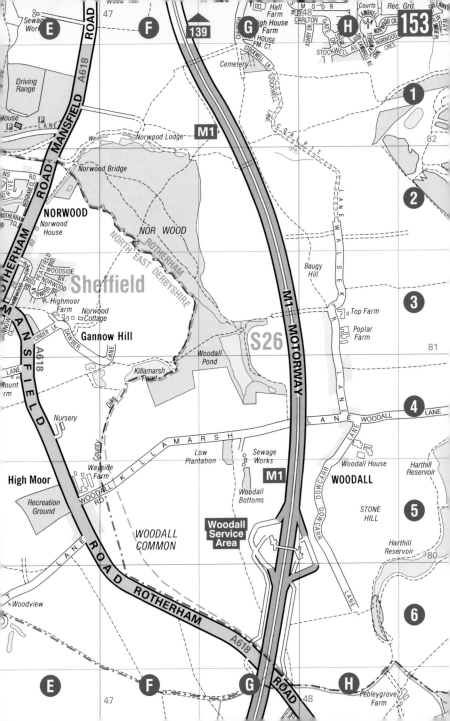

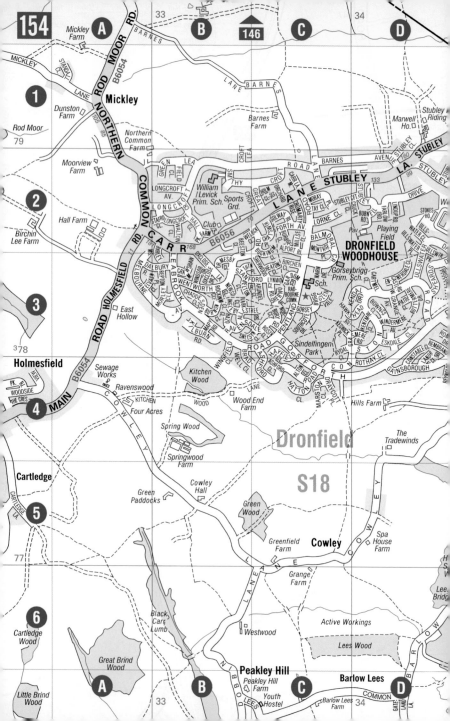

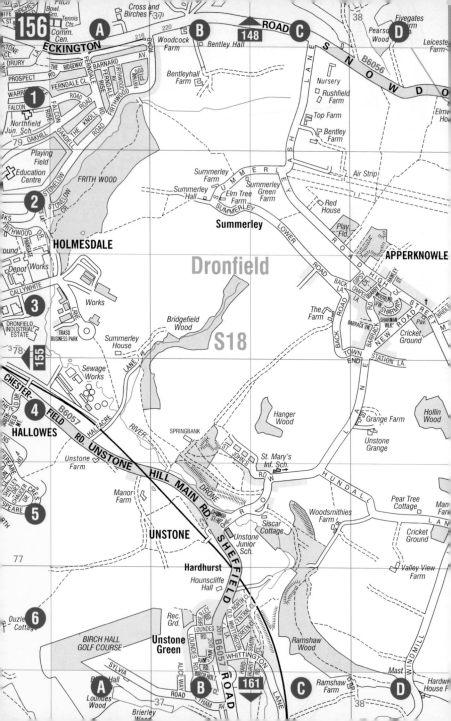

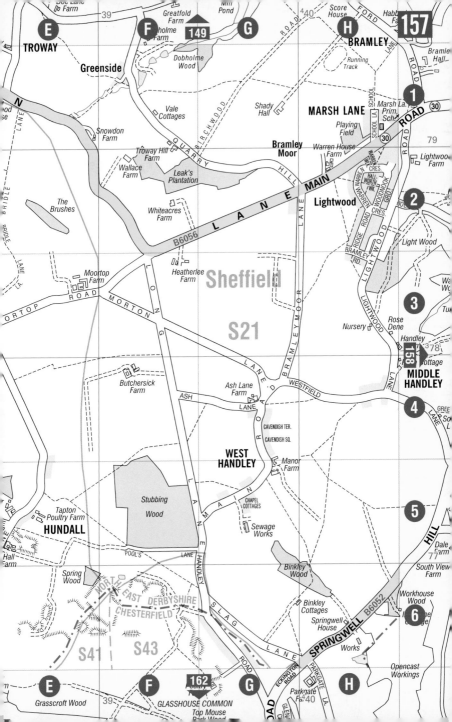

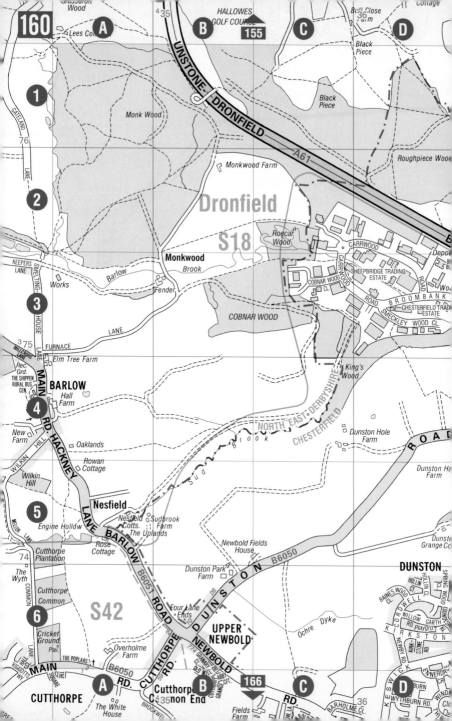

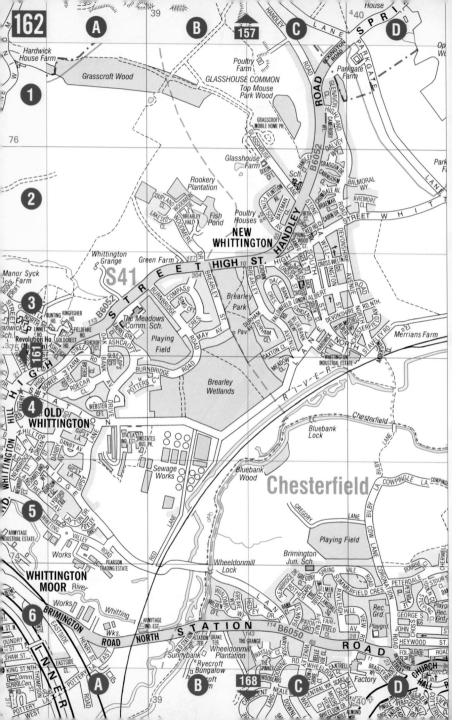

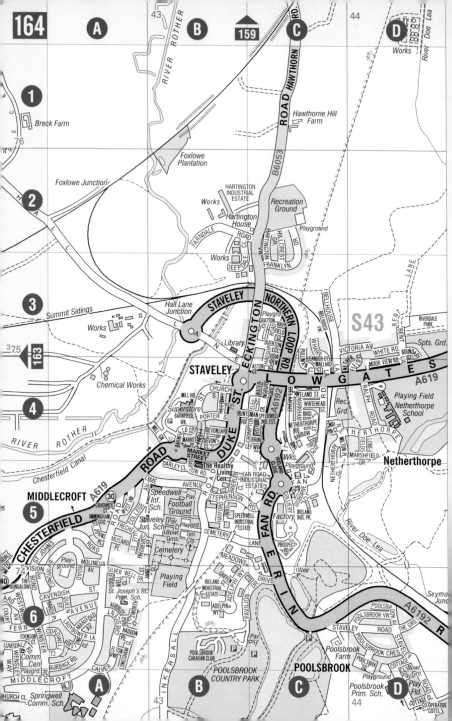

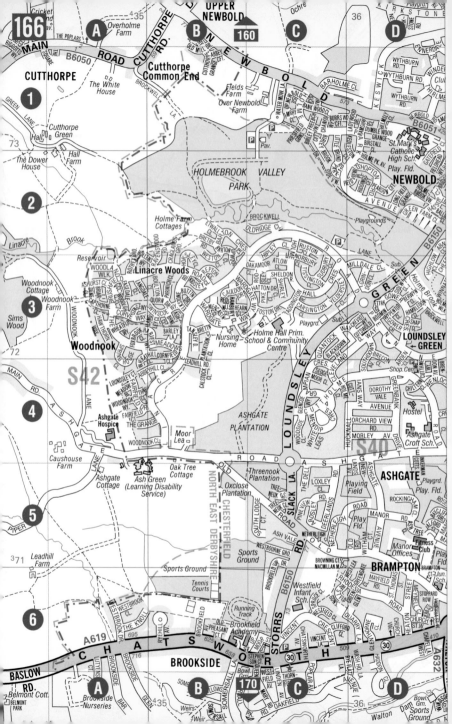

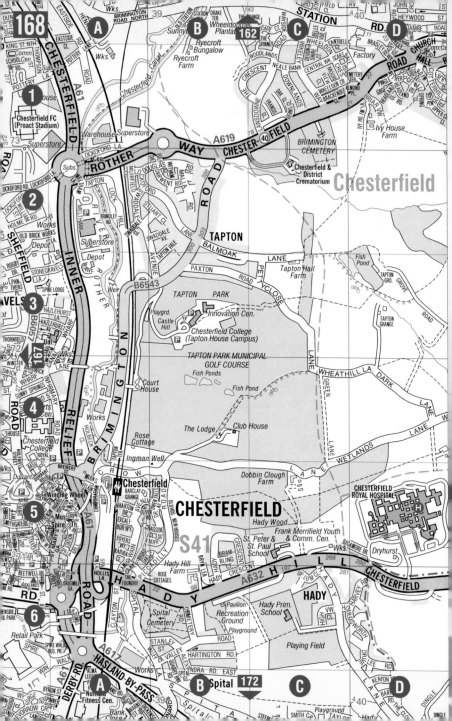

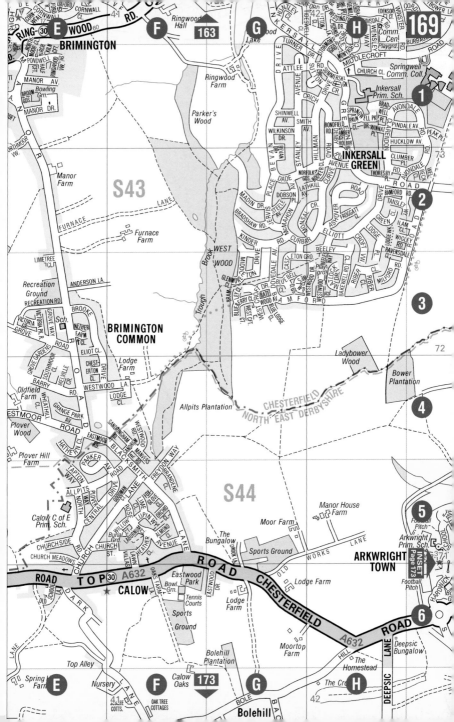

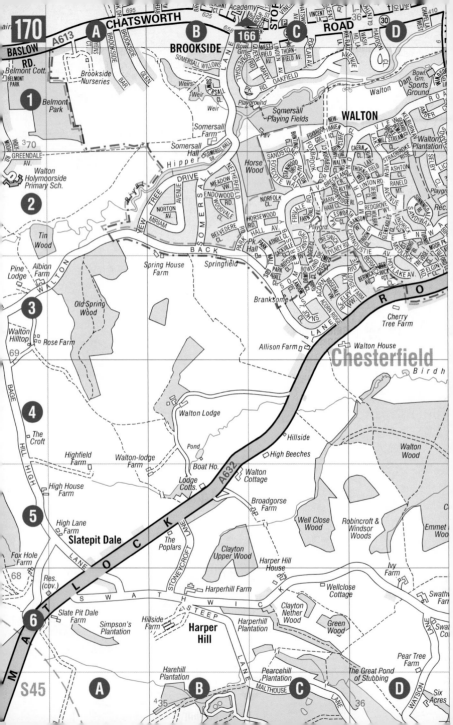

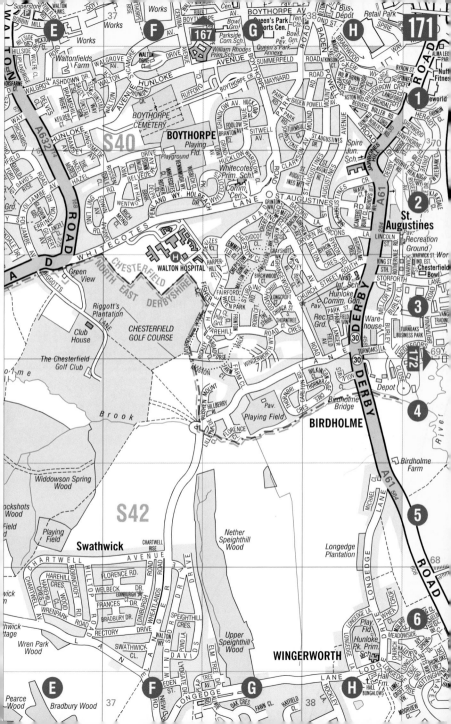

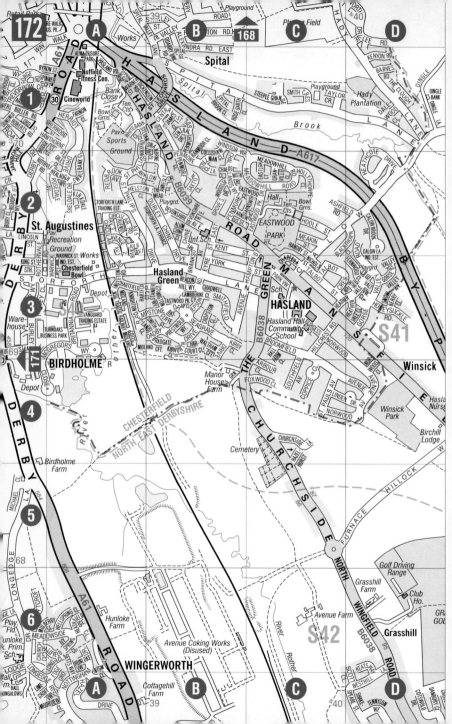

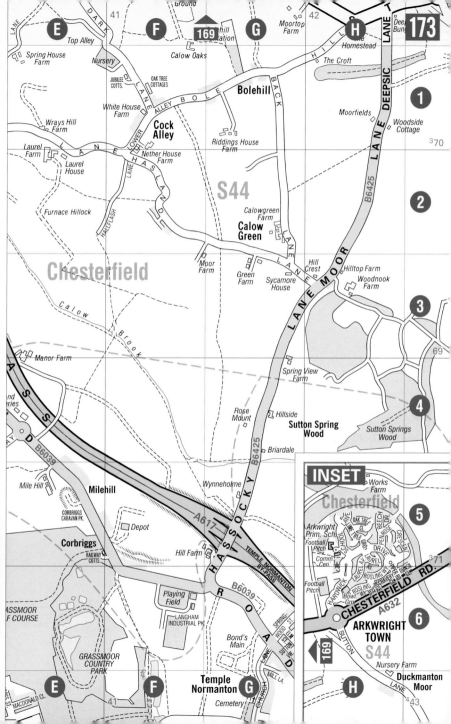

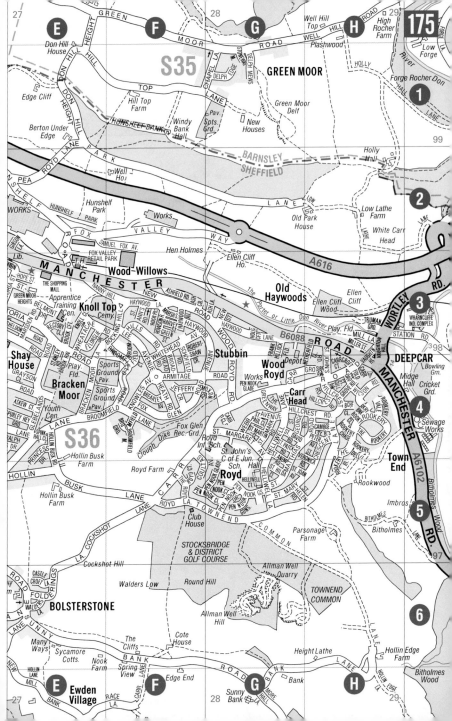

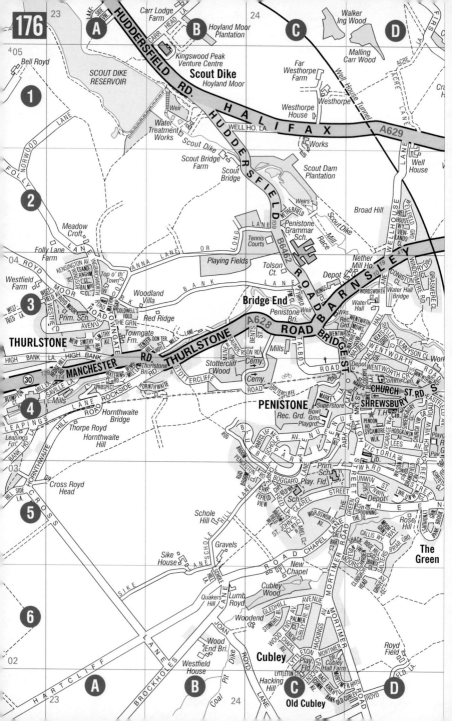

INDEX

Including Streets, Places & Areas, Industrial Estates, Selected Flats & Walkways,
Junction Names & Service Areas, Stations and Selected Places of Interest.

HOW TO USE THIS INDEX

1. Each street name is followed by its Postcode District, then by its Locality abbreviation(s) and then by its map reference;
e.g. **Abbey Brook Dr.** S8: Shef . . . .1D **146** is in the S8 Postcode District and the Sheffield Locality and is to be found in
square 1D on page **146**. The page number is shown in bold type.

2. A strict alphabetical order is followed in which Av., Rd., St., etc. (though abbreviated) are read in full and as part of the street name;
e.g. **Abbeyfield Rd.** appears after **Abbey Farm Vw.** but before **Abbey Flds.**

3. Streets and a selection of flats and walkways that cannot be shown on the mapping, appear in the index with the thoroughfare to which
they are connected shown in brackets; e.g. **Abbeydale Ct.** *S17: Dore* . . . .3H **145** *(off Ladies Spring Dr.)*

4. Addresses that are in more than one part are referred to as not continuous.

5. Places and areas are shown in the index in **BLUE TYPE** and the map reference is to the actual map square in which the town centre or
area is located and not to the place name shown on the map; e.g. **ARKSEY.** 6C **24**

6. An example of a selected place of interest is **Abbeydale Industrial Hamlet (Mus.)** 2A **146**

7. Examples of stations are:
Adwick Station (Rail) . . . .2D **22**; **Arbourthorne Road Stop (ST)** . . . .1A **134**; **Abbeydale (Park & Ride)** 4C **132**
Eckington Bus Station 1E **159**

8. Junction Names & Service Areas are shown in the index in **BOLD CAPITAL TYPE**; e.g. **BRIDGEHOUSES RDBT.** 1F **119**

9. Map references for entries that appear on large scale pages **4** & **5** are shown first, with small scale map references shown in brackets;
e.g. **Abney St.** S1: Shef 3C **4** (3E **119**)

GENERAL ABBREVIATIONS

All. : Alley	**Fld.** : Field	**Nth.** : North
App. : Approach	**Flds.** : Fields	**Pde.** : Parade
Arc. : Arcade	**Gdn.** : Garden	**Pk.** : Park
Av. : Avenue	**Gdns.** : Gardens	**Pl.** : Place
Bk. : Back	**Gth.** : Garth	**Pct.** : Precinct
Blvd. : Boulevard	**Ga.** : Gate	**Quad.** : Quadrant
Bri. : Bridge	**Gt.** : Great	**Ri.** : Rise
Bldgs. : Buildings	**Grn.** : Green	**Rd.** : Road
Bungs. : Bungalows	**Gro.** : Grove	**Rdbt.** : Roundabout
Bus. : Business	**Hgts.** : Heights	**Shop.** : Shopping
Cvn. : Caravan	**Ho.** : House	**Sth.** : South
Cen. : Centre	**Ho's.** : Houses	**Sq.** : Square
Chu. : Church	**Ind.** : Industrial	**Sta.** : Station
Circ. : Circle	**Info.** : Information	**St.** : Street
Cl. : Close	**Intl.** : International	**Ter.** : Terrace
Comn. : Common	**La.** : Lane	**Twr.** : Tower
Cnr. : Corner	**Lit.** : Little	**Trad.** : Trading
Cott. : Cottage	**Lwr.** : Lower	**Up.** : Upper
Cotts. : Cottages	**Mnr.** : Manor	**Va.** : Vale
Ct. : Court	**Mans.** : Mansions	**Vw.** : View
Cres. : Crescent	**Mkt.** : Market	**Vs.** : Villas
Cft. : Croft	**Mdw.** : Meadow	**Vis.** : Visitors
Dr. : Drive	**Mdws.** : Meadows	**Wlk.** : Walk
E. : East	**M.** : Mews	**W.** : West
Ent. : Enterprise	**Mt.** : Mount	**Yd.** : Yard
Est. : Estate	**Mus.** : Museum	

LOCALITY ABBREVIATIONS

Abdy: S62 .Abdy	**Beighton:** S20 . . . . .Beig	**Bromley:** S35 . . . . .Brom
Adwick le Street: DN6 . . . . .Adw S	**Bentley:** DN5 . . . . .Bntly	**Brookhouse:** S25 . . . . .Brookh
Aldwarke: S65 . . . . .Ald	**Bessacarr:** DN4 . . . . .Bess	**Burncross:** S35 . . . . .Burn
Almholme: DN5 . . . . .Alm	**Billingley:** S72 . . . . .Bill	**Cadeby:** DN5 . . . . .Cad
Alverley: DN4,DN11 . . . . .A'ley	**Birdholme:** S40 . . . . .Birdh	**Calow:** S44 .Cal
Apperknowle: S18 . . . . .App	**Birdwell:** S70,S75 . . . . .Birdw	**Cantley:** DN3-4 . . . . .Can
Ardsley: S71 . . . . .Ard	**Blacker Hill:** S74 . . . . .Black H	**Carcroft:** DN6 . . . . .Carc
Arksey: DN5 . . . . .Ark	**Blaxton:** DN9 . . . . .Blax	**Carlton:** S71 . . . . .Car
Arkwright Town: S44 . . . . .Ark T	**Bolsover:** S44 . . . . .Bols	**Carr:** S66 . . . . .Carr
Armthorpe: DN3 . . . . .Arm	**Bolsterstone:** S36 . . . . .Bolst	**Catcliffe:** S60 . . . . .Cat
Ashgate: S40,S42 . . . . .Ash	**Bolton upon Dearne:** S63 . . . . . . .Bolt D	**Cawthorne:** S75 . . . . .Cawt
Ashover: S45 . . . . .Asho	**Bradfield:** S6,S35 . . . . .Brad	**Chapeltown:** S35 . . . . .Chap
Aston: S26 . . . . .Aston	**Bradway:** S17 . . . . .Bradw	**Chesterfield:** S40-41 . . . . .C'fld
Athersley: S71 . . . . .Ath	**Braithwell:** S66 . . . . .B'well	**Clayton:** DN5 . . . . .Clay
Auckley: DN9 . . . . .Auck	**Bramley:** S65-66 . . . . .Bram	**Clifton:** S66 . . . . .Clftn
Aughton: S26 . . . . .Augh	**Brampton:** S40,S42,S73 . . . . .Bramp	**Clowne:** S43 . . . . .Clow
Balby: DN4 . . . . .Balb	**Brampton Bierlow:** S63 . . . . .Bramp B	**Coal Aston:** S18 . . . . .Coal A
Barlborough: S21,S43 . . . . .Barl	**Brampton en le Morthen:** S66 . . .Bramp M	**Conisbrough:** DN12 . . . . .Con
Barlow: S18 . . . . .Barl	**Branton:** DN3 . . . . .Brant	**Corbriggs:** S41 . . . . .Cor
Barnburgh: DN5 . . . . .Barnb	**Brierley:** S72 . . . . .Brier	**Cubley:** S36 . . . . .Cub
Barnby Dun: DN3 . . . . .Barn D	**Brighthlmlee:** S35 . . . . .Bright	**Cudworth:** S72 . . . . .Cud
Barnsley: S70-71,S75 . . . . .Barn	**Brimington:** S43 . . . . .Brim	**Cusworth:** DN5 . . . . .Cus
Barrow Hill: S43 . . . . .Bar H	**Brimington Common:** S43 . . . . . .Brim C	**Cutthorpe:** S42 . . . . .Cut
Barugh Green: S75 . . . . .Bar G	**Brinsworth:** S60 . . . . .Brins	**Dalton:** S65 . . . . .Dalt
Bawtry: DN11 . . . . .Baw	**Brodsworth:** DN5 . . . . .Brod	**Dalton Magna:** S65-66 . . . . .Dalt M

Locality Abbreviations

Darfield: S71,S73 ....D'fld
Darton: S75 ....Dart
Denaby Main: DN12 ....Den M
Dinnington: S25 ....Din
Dodworth: S75 ....Dod
Doncaster: DN1-2,DN4-5 .....Don
Dore: S11,S17 ....Dore
Dronfield: S18 ....Dron
Dronfield Woodhouse: S18 ...Dron W
Duckmanton: S44 ....Duck
Dungworth: S6 ....Dung
Dunsville: DN7 ....Dunsv
Ecclesfield: S35 ....Eccl
Eckington: S21 ....Ecki
Edenthorpe: DN3 ....Eden
Elsecar: S74 ....Els
Finningley: DN9 ....Finn
Firbeck: S81 ....Fir
Flanderwell: S66 ....Flan
Gildingwells: S81 ....Gild
Goldthorpe: S63 ....Gol
Grassmoor: S42 ....Gras
Greasbrough: S61 ....Grea
Great Houghton: S72 ....Gt H
Green Moor: S35 ....Green M
Grenoside: S6,S35 ....Gren
Grimethorpe: S72 ....Grim
Haigh: S75 ....Haigh
Halfway: S20 ....Half
Hampole: DN6 ....Ham
Harley: S62 ....H'ley
Harlington: DN5 ....Harl
Harthill: S26 ....Hart
Hasland: S40-41 ....Has
Hatfield: DN7 ....Hat
Hellaby: S66 ....Hel
Hemingfield: S73-74 ....Hem
Hemsworth: S72,WF9 ....Hems
Hexthorpe: DN4 ....Hex
Hickleton: DN5 ....Hick
Higham: S75 ....High'm
Highfields: DN6 ....Highf
High Green: S35 ....High G
High Hoyland: S75 ....High H
High Melton: DN5 ....High M
Holbrook: S20 ....Holb
Hollingwood: S43 ....Hol
Hollow Meadows: S6 ....Holl M
Holme: DN5 ....Holme
Holmesfield: S18 ....Holme
Holymoorside: S42 ....Holy
Hood Green: S75 ....Hood G
Hooton Levitt: S66 ....Hoot L
Hooton Pagnell: DN5 ......Hoot P
Hooton Roberts: S65 ......Hoot R
Howbrook: S35 ....Howb
Hoyland: S74 ....Hoyl
Hoylandswaine: S36 ....H'swne
Hundall: S18 ....Hun
Ingbirchworth: S36 ....Ingb
Inkersall: S43 ....Ink
Jump: S74 ....Jum
Kexborough: S75 ....Kexb
Killamarsh: S21 ....Killa
Kilnhurst: S64 ....Kiln
Kimberworth: S61 ....Kimb
Kimberworth Park: S61 ....Kimb P

Kirk Sandall: DN3 ....Kirk Sa
Kiveton Park: S26 ....Kiv P
Kiveton Park Station: S26 ...Kiv S
Laughton Common: S25 ....Laugh C
Laughton en le Morthen: S25 ..Laugh M
Letwell: S81 ....Letw
Little Houghton: S72 ....Lit H
Long Sandall: DN2 ....Long S
Loversall: DN11 ....Lov
Low Laithes: S71,S73 ......Low L
Loxley: S6 ....Lox
Lundwood: S71-72 ....Lund
Maltby: S66 ....Malt
Mapplewell: S75 ....Mapp
Marr: DN5 ....Marr
Marsh Lane: S21 ....Mar L
Mastin Moor: S43 ....Mas M
Mexborough: S64 ....Mexb
Micklebring: S66 ....Mick
Middlecliffe: S72 ....Midd
Middle Handley: S21 ......Midd H
Midhopestones: S36 ......Midh
Millhouse Green: S36 .....Mill G
Misson: DN10 ....Miss
Monk Bretton: S71 ....Monk B
Morthen: S66 ....Mort
Mosborough: S20 ....Mosb
Nether Handley: S21 ......Neth Han
Nether Haugh: S62 ....Neth Hau
New Edlington: DN12 ......New E
Newmillerdam: WF4 ....New
New Rossington: DN11 .....New R
New Whittington: S43 .....New W
North Anston: S25 ....Nth A
Notton: WF4 ....Nott
Old Brampton: S42 ....Old B
Old Denaby: DN12 ....Old D
Old Edlington: DN12 ....Old E
Old Tupton: S42 ....Old T
Old Whittington: S41 ......Old W
Oughtibridge: S6,S35 .....Ough
Oxspring: S36 ....Oxs
Parkgate: S62 ....P'gte
Penistone: S36 ....Pen
Pilley: S75 ....Pil
Poolsbrook: S43 ....Pool
Ravenfield: S65 ....Rav
Rawmarsh: S62 ....Rawm
Renishaw: S21 ....Reni
Ridgeway: S12 ....Ridg
Rossington: DN11 ....Ross
Rotherham: S60-61,S65 ...Roth
Roughbirchworth: S36 ....Rough
Royston: S71 ....R'ton
Scawsby: DN5 ....Scaws
Scawthorpe: DN5 ....Scawt
Scholes: S61 ....Scho
Shafton: S72 ....Shaft
Sheffield: S1-14,S60 .....Shef
Shuttlewood: S44 ....Shut
Silkstone: S75 ....Silk
Silkstone Common: S75 ...Silk C
Skelbrooke: DN6 ....Skelb
Skellow: DN6 ....Skell
Slade Hooton: S25 ....Slade H
Smithies: S71 ....Smi
Sothall: S20 ....Sot

South Anston: S25-26 .....Sth A
South Bramwith: DN7 .....Sth B
South Elmsall: WF9 ......Sth E
South Hiendley: S72 ......Sth H
South Kirkby: WF9 ....Sth K
Spinkhill: S21,S36 ....Spink
Sprotbrough: DN5 ....Sprot
Stainborough: S75 ....Stainb
Staincross: S71,S75 .....Stain
Stainton: S66 ....Stain
Stairfoot: S70-71 ....Stair
Stanfree: S44 ....Stan
Stannington: S6 ....Stan
Staveley: S43 ....Stav
Stocksbridge: S36 ....Stoc
Stone Edge: S45 ....Ston E
Sunnyside: S66 ....Sunn
Sutton Scarsdale: S44 ...Sut S
Swaithe: S70 ....Swai
Swallownest: S20,S26 ...Swal
Swinton: S64 ....Swin
Tankersley: S75 ....Tank
Temple Normanton: S42 ..Tem N
Thorpe Hesley: S61 .....Thorpe H
Thrybergh: S65 ....Thry
Thurcroft: S66 ....Thurc
Thurlstone: S36 ....Thurl
Thurnscoe: S63 ....Thurn
Tickhill: DN11 ....Tick
Tinsley: S9 ....Tins
Todwick: S26 ....Tod
Totley: S17 ....Tot
Treeton: S60 ....Tree
Troway: S21 ....Trow
Tupton: S42 ....Tup
Ulley: S26 ....Ull
Unstone: S18,S41 ......Uns
Upper Newbold: S40-42 ..Up N
Upper Whiston: S60 .....Up W
Wadworth: DN11 ....Wad
Wales: S26 ....Wales
Wales Bar: S26 ....Wales B
Walton: S40,S42 ....W'ton
Warmsworth: DN4 ......Warm
Waterthorpe: S20 ......Water
Wath upon Dearne: S63,S73 ..Wath D
Waverley: S13,S60 .....Wav
Wentworth: S62 ....Wentw
Westfield: S20 ....W'fld
West Handley: S21 .....West H
Wharncliffe Side: S35 ...Wharn S
Whiston: S60 ....Whis
Whittington Moor: S41 ..Whit M
Wickersley: S66 ....Wick
Wilsic: DN11 ....Wils
Wingerworth: S42 .....W'orth
Wingfield: S61 ....Wing
Wombwell: S73 ....Womb
Woodall: S26 ....Wooda
Woodlands: DN6 ......Woodl
Woodsetts: S81 ......Woods
Woodthorpe: S43 .....Woodt
Woolley: WF4 ....Wool
Woolley Grange: S75 ..Wool G
Worksop: S81 ....Work
Worsbrough: S70,S75 ..Wors
Wortley: S35 ....Wort

5ives
Barnsley 4A 32

A

Aaron Wilkinson Ct.
WF9: Sth K 4H 13
Abbey Brook Cl. S8: Shef 1D 146
Abbey Brook Ct. S8: Shef 1D 146
Abbey Brook Dr. S8: Shef 1D 146
Abbey Brook Gdns. S8: Shef ...1D 146
Abbey Cl. S25: Laugh M 1G 127
Abbey Ct. S8: Shef 1D 146
Abbey Cres. S7: Shef 1A 146
Abbey Cft. S7: Shef 1A 146
   S41: Up N 1B 166
ABBEYDALE 1A 146

Abbeydale Ct. S17: Dore 3H 145
   (off Ladies Spring Dr.)
Abbeydale Dr. S7: Shef 4C 132
Abbeydale Golf Course 3A 146
Abbeydale Hall Gdns. S17: Dore ..3G 145
Abbeydale Industrial Hamlet (Mus.)
   ....2A 146
ABBEYDALE PARK 4G 145
Abbeydale (Park & Ride) 4C 132
Abbeydale Pk. Cres. S17: Dore ..4G 145
Abbeydale Park Rackets & Fitness Club
   ....3H 145
Abbeydale Park Sports Club 3G 145
Abbeydale Pk. Ri. S17: Dore ...3F 145
Abbeydale Rd. S7: Shef 5C 132
Abbeydale Rd. Sth. S7: Shef ...4G 145
   S17: Dore, Tot 4G 145
Abbey Farm Vw. S72: Cud 3E 19
Abbeyfield Rd. S4: Shef 5G 107
Abbey Fids. DN9: Finn 3F 77
Abbey Glen S66: Carr 3E 115
Abbey Grange S7: Shef 1A 146

Abbey Grn. S75: Dod 4H 29
Abbey Gro. S71: Lund 5B 18
Abbeyhill Cl. S42: Ash 4A 166
Abbey La. S7: Shef 6H 131
   S8: Shef 6H 131
   S11: Shef 5G 131
   S25: Slade H 5H 115
   S71: Lund 6B 18
Abbey La. Dell S8: Shef 1A 146
Abbey Sq. S71: Lund 4B 18
Abbey Vw. Dr. S8: Shef 5F 133
Abbey Vw. Rd. S8: Shef 5F 133
Abbey Wlk. DN5: Scaws 5F 39
Abbey Way S25: Nth A 5E 127
Abbot La. WF4: Wool 1A 8
Abbots Cl. S72: Cud 3F 19
Abbots Ford Dr. S66: Thurc ...6B 114
Abbots Mdw. S20: Sot 1H 151
Abbots Rd. S71: Lund 5C 18
Abbott St. DN4: Hex 2A 56
ABDY 4E 65

Abdy La. S62: Abdy 4F 65
   S64: Swin 4F 65
Abdy Rd. S61: Kimb P 6G 81
   S62: Abdy 5D 64
Abell St. S65: Thry 6D 84
Aberconway Cres. DN11: New R 6B 74
Abercorn Rd. DN2: Don 6H 41
Abercrombie St. S41: C'fld 4H 167
Aberford Gro. S74: Els 6E 47
Abingdon Gdns. S61: Grea 5C 82
Abingdon Rd. DN2: Don 5G 41
Abney Cl. S14: Shef 2H 133
   S40: C'fld 2D 166
Abney Dr. S14: Shef 2H 133
Abney Rd. S14: Shef 2H 133
Abney St. S1: Shef 3C 4 (3E 119)
Abrafact Ind. Ct. S6: Shef 3C 106
Abus Rd. DN5: Scaws 3D 38
Acacia Av. S35: Chap 4E 79
   S43: Hol 6F 163
   S66: Bram 5H 99
   S66: Malt 5G 101
Acacia Ct. DN5: Bntly 6H 23
Acacia Cres. S21: Killa 5A 152
Acacia Gro. DN12: Con 6D 68
   S72: Shaft 4F 11
Acacia Rd. DN4: Can 4C 58
   S5: Shef 6B 94
Ace Bus. Cen. S3: Shef 1G 5 (1G 119)
Acer Cl. S21: Killa 5B 152
   S25: Sth A 5G 141
Acer Cft. DN3: Arm 5E 43
Ackworth Dr. S9: Tins 3A 110
Acorn Av. S63: Thurn 2C 36
Acorn Bus. Pk. S8: Shef 4D 132
   (off Woodseats Cl.)
Acorn Cen., The S72: Grim 2B 20
Acorn Ct. S35: Ough 3F 91
Acorn Cft. S61: Grea 6C 82
Acorn Dr. S6: Stan 6D 104
Acorn Hill S6: Stan 5E 105
Acorn Pl. S63: Wath D 2H 65
Acorn Ridge S42: W'ton 3C 170
Acorn Rd. DN4: Bess 6B 58
Acorn Rd. S6: Stan 6C 104
Acorn St. S3: Shef 1D 4 (1F 119)
Acorn Way S66: Sunn 3H 99
   S72: Grim 2A 20
Acre Cl. DN3: Eden 6C 26
   S66: Malt 3H 101
   S66: Thurc 5C 114
Acre Ga. S35: High G 2C 78
Acre La. S35: Ough 2B 90
   S36: H'swne 1D 176
Acre Rd. S72: Cud 4F 19
Acres Hill Ct. S9: Shef 2E 121
Acres Hill La. S9: Shef 3E 121
Acres Hill Rd. S9: Shef 2E 121
Acres Vw. S60: Roth 1A 112
Acrewood Dr. S66: Sunn 2G 99
Adamfield S3: Shef 3A 4
Adam La. S75: Cawt 6B 14
Adastral Av. S12: Shef 6D 134
Addison Rd. S5: Shef 2A 108
   S64: Mexb 1G 67
   S66: Malt 5G 101
Addison Sq. S25: Din 5A 128
Addy Cl. DN4: Balb 1B 72
   S6: Shef 1D 118
Addy Dr. S6: Shef 1D 118
Addy St. S6: Shef 1D 118
Adelaide La. S3: Shef 1E 119
Adelaide Rd. S7: Shef 2C 132
Adelaide St. S66: Malt 6C 102
Adelphi St. S6: Shef 1D 118
Adelphi Way S43: Stav 6B 164
Adkin Royd S75: Silk 2A 28
Adkins Dr. S5: Shef 1D 106
Adkins Rd. S5: Shef 1D 106
Adlard Rd. DN2: Don 4G 41
Adlington Cres. S5: Shef 6E 93
Adlington Rd. S5: Shef 6E 93
Admiral Biggs Dr. S60: Tree 2F 123
Admirals Crest S61: Scho 6E 81
Adrian Cres. S5: Shef 6F 93
Adsetts St. S4: Shef 3B 108
Advanced Manufacturing Pk.
   S60: Shef 2B 122
Adwick Av. DN5: Bntly 3G 23
Adwick Bus. Pk. DN6: Adw S 2E 23

Adwick Ct. S64: Mexb 2G 67
Adwick Interchange
   DN6: Adw S 2D 22
   (off Church La.)
Adwick La. DN5: Bntly 2D 22
   DN6: Adw S 2D 22
Adwick Leisure Cen. 4C 22
ADWICK LE STREET 2C 22
Adwick Pk. S63: Wath D 6C 50
Adwick Rd. S64: Mexb 5E 51
Adwick Station (Rail) 2D 22
ADWICK UPON DEARNE 4E 51
Aeroventure .3F 57
Agden Rd. S7: Shef 6D 118
Agnes Rd. S70: Barn 2D 30
   S75: Dart 6F 7
Agnes Ter. S70: Barn 2D 30
Ainsdale Av. S63: Gol 6C 36
Ainsdale Cl. S71: R'ton 1G 9
Ainsdale Cl. S71: Monk B 3A 18
Ainsdale Rd. S71: R'ton 1G 9
Ainsley Cl. DN9: Auck 1H 59
Ainsley Rd. S10: Shef 2B 118
Ainsty Rd. S7: Shef 1E 133
Ainthorpe Rd. DN5: Bntly 3G 23
Aintree Av. DN4: Can 2A 58
   S21: Ecki 1C 158
Aintree Cl. DN5: Scaws 5E 39
Aintree Dr. DN4: Balb 1B 72
   S64: Mexb 6G 51
Aire Cl. S35: Chap 2E 79
Airedale Cl. S66: Wick 5F 99
Airedale Rd. S6: Shef 2H 105
   S75: Kexb 6D 6
Aireton Cl. S66: Wick 5F 99
Aireton Rd. S70: Barn 6D 16
Air Mount Cl. S66: Wick 6F 99
Aisby Dr. DN11: Ross 4D 74
Aisthorpe Rd. S8: Shef 5E 133
Aitken Rd. S64: Kiln 6D 66
Aizlewood Rd. S8: Shef 1E 133
Akley Bank Cl. S17: Tot 5G 145
Alagu Cl. S64: Mexb 1D 66
Alan Rd. S75: Dart 6E 7
Alba Cl. S73: D'fld 4H 33
Albanus Cft. S6: Stan 6D 104
Albanus Ridge S6: Stan 6D 104
Albany Av. S35: Chap 4G 79
Albany Cl. S73: Womb 4D 32
Albany La. DN11: New R 5B 74
Albany Rd. DN4: Balb 4H 55
   S7: Shef 1E 133
   S36: Stoc 3D 174
   S64: Kiln 5C 66
Albany St. S65: Roth 4F 97
Albert Av. S43: New W 3C 162
Albert Cres. S72: Midd 3E 35
Albert Rd. S8: Shef 2F 133
   S12: Shef 5D 136
   S43: New W 3C 162
   S62: P'gte 4G 83
   S63: Gol 5D 36
   S63: Wath D 5E 49
   S64: Mexb 1F 67
Albert St. S21: Ecki 2E 159
   S60: Roth 4D 96
   S63: Thurn 2B 36
   S64: Swin 2C 66
   S66: Malt 6C 102
   S70: Barn 1E 31
   S72: Cud .5F 11
Albert St. E. S70: Barn 1E 31
Albert St. Nth. S41: Whit M 5G 161
Albert Ter. Rd. S6: Shef 1D 118
Albion S6: Shef 1A 4 (2D 118)
Albion Cl. S75: Mapp 5A 8
Albion Dr. S63: Thurn 2E 37
Albion Ho. S70: Barn 2E 31
Albion Pl. DN11: Don 1D 56
Albion Rd. S40: C'fld 5G 167
   S60: Roth 4F 97
   S71: Car 1H 17
Albion Row S6: Shef 2E 117
Albion St. S6: Shef 2D 118
Albion Ter. DN4: Hex 3A 56
   S70: Barn 2F 31
Alcester Rd. S7: Shef 1E 133
Aldam Chase S66: Wick 6G 99
Aldam Cl. S17: Tot 6F 145
   S65: Roth 3C 98
Aldam Cft. S17: Tot 6F 145

Aldam Rd. DN4: Balb 6G 55
   S17: Tot 6G 145
Aldam Way S17: Tot 6F 145
Aldbeck Cft. S75: Dart 1F 15
Aldbury Cl. S71: Ath 2G 17
Aldcliffe Cres. DN4: Balb 2G 71
Aldene Av. S6: Shef 3G 105
Aldene Glade S6: Shef 3G 105
Aldene Rd. S6: Shef 2G 105
Alder Chase S61: Scho 6F 81
Alder Cl. S75: Mapp 5H 7
Alderford Dr. DN4: Balb 1A 72
Alder Gdns. S43: Hol 5F 163
Alder Gro. DN4: Balb 5H 55
   S73: D'fld 6A 34
Alder Holt Cl. DN3: Arm 5F 43
Alder La. S9: Shef 3H 121
Alder M. S74: Hoyl 1B 62
Alderney Rd. S2: Shef 1F 133
Alder Rd. S18: Dron 1F 155
Aldersgate Cl.
   DN11: New R 6D 74, 6H 75
Aldersgate Cl. S66: Malt 5D 102
Alders Grn. S6: Lox 3E 105
Alderson Av. S62: Rawm 1G 83
Alderson Cl. S26: Swal 5C 124
Alderson Dr. DN2: Don 2E 57
   S71: Smi 2F 17
Alderson Pl. S2: Shef 6F 119
Alderson Rd. S2: Shef 6F 119
   (not continuous)
Alderson Rd. Nth. S2: Shef 6F 119
Aldervale Cl. S64: Swin 6C 66
Alderwood Cl. S66: Sunn 3G 99
Aldesworth Rd. DN4: Can 3B 58
Aldfield Way S5: Shef 3G 107
Aldham Cotts. S73: Shef 5F 33
Aldham Cres. S73: Womb 4D 32
Aldham Ho. La. S73: Womb 5E 33
Aldham Ind. Est. S73: Womb 5F 33
Aldham Vw. S73: Womb 6E 33
Aldine Cl. S1: Shef 3F 5
Aldous Cl. S26: Kiv P 5B 140
Aldous Way S26: Kiv P 5B 140
Aldred Cl. S21: Killa 2D 152
   S66: Wick 5G 99
Aldred Ct. S65: Roth 5F 97
Aldred Rd. S10: Shef 1B 118
Aldred St. S65: Roth 5F 97
Aldrens Cl. S66: Mick 6G 87
Aldrin Way S66: Malt 4H 101
ALDWARKE 6A 84
Aldwarke La. S65: Ald 5H 83
Aldwarke Rd. S62: P'gte 5G 83
Aldwarke Ter. S62: P'gte 5H 83
Aleem Cl. S66: Malt 5B 102
   (off High St.)
Alexander St. DN5: Bntly 1A 40
Alexandra S11: Shef 2C 132
Alexandra Cen. S62: P'gte 6G 83
Alexandra Cl. S61: Kimb 2H 95
Alexandra Gdns. S11: Shef 2C 132
Alexandra Rd. DN4: Balb 4A 56
   DN5: Bntly 6A 24
   DN6: Adw S 2E 23
   S2: Shef 1G 133
   S18: Dron 2G 155
   S26: Swal 6B 124
   S64: Mexb 1G 67
Alexandra Rd. E. S41: C'fld 6B 168
Alexandra Rd. W. S40: C'fld 5G 167
Alexandra St. S66: Malt 6C 102
Alexandra Ter. S71: Ard 2C 32
Alford Av. S35: Ough 3E 91
Alford Cl. S40: Ash 5D 166
   S75: Barn 4A 16
Alfred St. S9: Shef 5C 108
   (not continuous)
Alfred St. S71: R'ton 2B 10
Algar Cl. S2: Shef 1B 134
Algar Cres. S2: Shef 1C 134
Algar Dr. S2: Shef 1B 134
Algar Pl. S2: Shef 1B 134
Algar Rd. S2: Shef 1B 134
Alhambra Shop. Cen. S70: Barn 1E 31
Alice Rd. S61: Roth 3C 96
Alice Way S18: Uns 6B 156
Alison Cl. S26: Swal 1C 138
Alison Cres. S21: Shef 5E 121
Alison Dr. S26: Swal 1C 138
Allan St. S65: Roth 4F 97

Allatt Cl. S70: Barn 2E **31**
Alldred Cres. S64: Swin 5B **66**
Allenby Cl. S8: Shef 3D **146**
Allenby Cres. DN11: New R 6B **74**
Allenby Dr. S8: Shef 3D **146**
Allendale S70: Wors 5H **31**
Allendale Ct. S70: Wors 5H **31**
Allendale Dr. S74: Hoyl 1B **62**
Allendale Gdns. DN5: Don 1G **55**
Allendale Rd. DN5: Don 1G **55**
　　　　S42: W'orth 6G **171**
　　　　S65: Roth 6B **98**
　　　　S74: Hoyl 1A **62**
　　　　S75: Barn 4D **16**
　　　　S75: Kexb 6E **7**
Allende Way S9: Shef 6E **109**
Allen Gdns. S35: Eccl 1G **93**
Allen Rd. S20: Beig 6G **137**
Allen St. S3: Shef 1C **4** (2E **119**)
Allerton St. DN1: Don 6C **40**
Allestree Dr. S18: Dron W 3B **154**
All Hallows Dr. S66: Malt 6H **101**
Alliance St. S4: Shef 5A **108**
Alliss Rd. DN3: Brant 4H **59**
Allott Cl. S65: Rav 2A **100**
Allott Cres. S74: Jum 5D **46**
Allotts Ct. S70: Birdw 5D **44**
Allott St. S74: Els 1D **62**
　　　　S74: Hoyl 1G **61**
Allpits Rd. S44: Cal 5E **169**
Allport Ter. S43: Bar H 2G **163**
All Saints Cl. DN5: Ark 6C **24**
　　　　S63: Wath D 6F **49**
　　　　S75: Silk 1B **28**
All Saints Mdws. S25: Laugh C 3F **127**
All Saints Sq. DN12: Den M 2D **68**
　　　　S60: Roth 4E **97**
All Saints Way S26: Aston 1D **138**
Allsopps Yd. S74: Black H 3A **46**
Allsops Pl. S41: C'fld 6G **161**
Allt St. S62: P'gte 4G **83**
Alma Cres. S18: Dron 1F **155**
Alma Leisure Pk. S40: C'fld 1A **172**
Alma Rd. S35: High G 1C **78**
　　　　S60: Roth 5E **97**
Alma Row S60: Whis 3B **112**
Alma St. S3: Shef 1D **4**, 1E **5** (1F **119**)
　　　　S70: Barn 1C **30**
　　　　S73: Womb 2G **47**
Alma St. W. S40: C'fld 6F **167**
ALMHOLME 3E **25**
Almholme La. DN5: Alm, Ark 5D **24**
Almholme M. DN5: Ark 5D **24**
Almond Av. DN3: Arm 3E **43**
　　　　S72: Cud 1E **19**
Almond Cl. S44: Cal 5F **169**
　　　　S66: Malt 5H **101**
Almond Cres. S43: Mas M 2F **165**
Almond Cft. S73: Womb 3F **47**
Almond Dr. S21: Killa 5B **152**
Almond Glade S66: Wick 1H **113**
Almond Pl. S43: Brim 1D **168**
　　　　S63: Wath D 1G **65**
Almond Rd. DN4: Can 4C **58**
Almond Tree Rd. S26: Wales 6F **139**
Alms Hill Cres. S11: Shef 5G **131**
Alms Hill Dr. S11: Shef 5G **131**
Alms Hill Glade S11: Shef 5G **131**
Alms Hill Rd. S11: Shef 5G **131**
Alms Houses S60: Roth 5G **97**
Almshouses S42: Wentw 4D **62**
Alney Pl. S6: Shef 6C **92**
Alnwick Dr. S12: Shef 3E **135**
Alnwick Rd. S12: Shef 3D **134**
Alperton Cl. S71: Lund 3C **18**
Alpha Rd. S65: Roth 3A **98**
Alpha St. DN5: Bntly 3G **23**
Alpina Way S26: Swal 1B **138**
Alpine Cl. S36: Stoc 3C **174**
Alpine Cft. S36: Stoc 3C **174**
Alpine Gro. S43: Hol 6F **163**
Alpine Rd. S6: Shef 1C **118**
　　　　S36: Stoc 3C **174**
Alport Av. S12: Shef 3H **135**
Alport Dr. S12: Shef 3H **135**
Alport Gro. S12: Shef 3H **135**
Alport Pl. S12: Shef 4H **135**
Alport Ri. S18: Dron W 2C **154**
Alport Rd. S12: Shef 3H **135**
Alric Dr. S60: Brins 3C **110**
　　　　S71: Barn 1B **32**

Alrich M. S36: Stoc 2B **174**
Alsing Rd. S9: Shef 1F **109**
Alston Cl. DN4: Bess 5A **58**
　　　　S75: Silk 2A **28**
Alston Rd. DN4: Bess 6A **58**
Alton Cl. S11: Shef 6H **131**
　　　　S18: Dron W 4C **154**
　　　　S42: W'ton 2C **170**
Alton Way S75: Mapp 5H **7**
Alum Chine Cl. S41: Has 2B **172**
Alvaston Wlk. DN12: Den M 3D **68**
ALVERLEY 3G **71**
Alverley Gdns. S43: Stav 6A **164**
Alverley La. DN4: Balb 2H **71**
Alverley Vw. DN11: A'ley 3H **71**
Alverley Way S70: Birdw 6E **45**
Alwyn Av. DN5: Scaws 3F **39**
Amalfi Cl. S73: D'fld 5A **34**
Ambassador Gdns. DN3: Arm 5F **43**
Amber Cres. S40: W'ton 1D **170**
Amber Cft. S43: Ink 1H **169**
Amberley Ct. S9: Shef 5D **108**
Amberley St. S9: Shef 4D **108**
Amberwood Dr. S71: Lund 5A **18**
Ambler Ri. S26: Augh 5B **124**
Ambleside Cl. S20: Half 4F **151**
　　　　S41: C'fld 1D **166**
　　　　S60: Brins 4B **110**
Ambleside Cres. DN5: Sprot 3B **54**
Ambleside Gro. S71: Ard 2D **32**
Ambleside Wlk. S25: Nth A 2A **142**
Amen Corner S60: Roth 3D **96**
　　　　　　　　　　　(not continuous)
America La. S62: Wentw 5C **64**
　　　　S63: Wath D 3D **64**
Amersall Cl. DN5: Scawt 3F **39**
Amersall Cres. DN5: Scawt 2F **39**
Amersall Rd. DN5: Scawt 2F **39**
Amesbury Cl. S41: C'fld 1F **167**
Ami Ct. S62: P'gte 6F **83**
Amory's Holt Cl. S66: Malt 3H **101**
Amory's Holt Dr. S66: Malt 3H **101**
Amory's Holt Rd. S66: Malt 3H **101**
Amory's Holt Way S66: Malt 4G **101**
Amos Rd. S9: Shef 2E **109**
Amy Rd. DN5: Bntly 5B **24**
Anchorage Cres. DN5: Don 6H **39**
Anchorage La. DN5: Don 5G **39**
Ancona Ri. S73: D'fld 4A **34**
Ancote Cl. S75: Barn 1H **29**
Anderson Cl. S43: New W 3D **162**
Anderson Dr. S62: Rawm 6E **65**
Anderson La. S43: Brim C 3E **169**
Andover Dr. S3: Shef 6F **107**
Andover St. S3: Shef 6F **107**
Andrew La. S3: Shef 1G **5**
Andrews Pl. DN5: Roth 2B **96**
Andwell La. S10: Shef 3A **130**
Anelay Rd. DN4: Balb 5G **55**
Anfield Rd. DN4: Can 5B **58**
Angel La. S62: Wentw 6A **64**
Angel St. S3: Shef 2F **5** (2G **119**)
　　　　S63: Bolt D 3C **50**
Angel Yd. S40: C'fld 5H **167**
Angerford Av. S8: Shef 4F **133**
Anglesey Rd. S18: Dron 4F **155**
Angleton Av. S2: Shef 6F **121**
Angleton Cl. S2: Shef 6F **121**
Angleton Gdns. S2: Shef 6F **121**
Angleton Grn. S2: Shef 6F **121**
Angleton M. S2: Shef 6F **121**
Angram St. S35: High G 6C **60**
Angram Vw. S35: High G 1C **78**
Annan Cl. S75: Bar G 3G **15**
Annat Pl. S35: High G 1B **78**
Anne Cres. S72: Sth H 1H **11**
Annesley Cl. S8: Shef 3E **147**
　　　　S41: Has 2B **172**
Annesley Rd. S8: Shef 2E **147**
Anne St. S25: Din 3A **128**
Annie Senior Gdns. S63: Bolt D 2C **50**
Anns Rd. S2: Shef 1F **133**
Anns Rd. Nth. S2: Shef 1G **133**
Ann St. S62: P'gte 5G **83**
Ansdell Rd. DN5: Bntly 6A **24**
Ansell Rd. S11: Shef 2H **131**
Anson Gro. DN9: Auck 2A **76**
　　　　S60: Brins 4E **98**
Anson St. S2: Shef 3H **5** (3H **119**)
Ansten Cres. DN4: Can 4B **58**
Anston Av. S26: Kiv P 5B **140**

Anston Cl. S25: Nth A 2G **141**
Ansult Ct. DN5: Bntly 2H **39**
Antrim Av. S10: Shef 4C **118**
Anvil Cl. S6: Shef 6F **105**
Anvil Cres. S35: Eccl 2G **93**
Apley Rd. DN1: Don 2C **56**
Apollo Cl. S62: Rawm 1A **84**
Apostle Cl. DN4: Balb 6F **55**
APPERKNOWLE 3D **156**
Appleby Cl. S75: Dart 5G **7**
Appleby Rd. DN2: Don 6H **41**
Appleby Wlk. S25: Nth A 1A **142**
Applegarth Cl. S12: Shef 2D **134**
Applegarth Dr. S12: Shef 2D **134**
Apple Gro. DN9: Auck 2B **76**
Applehaigh Ct. WF4: Nott 1F **9**
Applehaigh Dr. DN3: Kirk Sa 3B **26**
Applehaigh La. WF4: Nott 1F **9**
Applehaigh Vw. S71: R'ton 3F **9**
Applehurst Bank S70: Barn 2G **31**
Application Cl. S65: Dalt 1C **98**
Appleton Gdns. DN5: Scawt 3H **39**
Appleton Way
　　　　DN5: Scawt 2G **39**
　　　　S70: Wors 5F **31**
Apple Tree Cl. DN4: Bess 1D **74**
　　　　S81: Woods 4F **143**
Appletree Dr. S18: Dron 3F **155**
Appletree Wlk. S18: Dron 3G **155**
　　　　　　　　　　(off Appletree Dr.)
April Cl. S71: Monk B 4A **18**
April Dr. S71: Monk B 4A **18**
Apy Hill La. DN11: Tick, Wils 2H **103**
Aqueduct St. S71: Barn 5E **17**
Arbour Cl. S41: Has 4C **172**
Arbour Cres. S66: Thurc 6C **114**
Arbour Dr. S66: Thurc 6C **114**
Arbour La. S65: Rav 5B **86**
ARBOURTHORNE 1A **134**
Arbourthorne Ct. S2: Shef 5B **120**
Arbourthorne Cotts. S2: Shef 6A **120**
Arbourthorne Est. S2: Shef 2B **134**
Arbourthorne Rd. S2: Shef 1A **134**
Arbourthorne Road Stop (ST) 1A **134**
Arcade, The S9: Shef 1F **109**
　　　　S70: Barn 1E **31**
Archdale Cl. S2: Shef 6E **121**
　　　　S40: C'fld 1H **171**
Archdale Pl. S2: Shef 6D **120**
Archdale Rd. S2: Shef 5D **120**
Archer Dr. S8: Shef 5C **132**
　　　　　　　　　　　(not continuous)
Archer Ga. S6: Lox 3E **105**
Archer Ho. S65: Roth 3F **97**
　　　　　　　　　　(off Wharncliffe Hill)
Archer La. S7: Shef 3C **132**
Archer M. S8: Shef 4D **132**
Archer Rd. S8: Shef 5C **132**
Archers Way DN12: Con 4H **69**
Archery Cl. S66: Wick 1G **113**
Archibald Rd. S7: Shef 2D **132**
Archway Cen. S1: Shef 4G **5** (3G **119**)
Archways S1: Shef 6F **5**
Arcon Pl. S62: Rawm 2H **83**
Arcubus Av. S26: Swal 6C **124**
Ardeen Rd. DN2: Don 6F **41**
Arden Cl. S40: C'fld 4D **166**
Arden Ga. DN4: Balb 2G **71**
Ardmore St. S9: Shef 1D **120**
Ardron Wlk. S62: Rawm 2A **84**
ARDSLEY 2D **32**
Ardsley Av. S26: Aston 1D **138**
Ardsley Cl. S20: Mosb 6A **136**
Ardsley Dr. S20: Mosb 6A **136**
Ardsley Gro. S20: Mosb 6A **136**
Ardsley M. S71: Ard 2D **32**
Ardsley Rd. S40: Ash 5C **166**
　　　　S70: Wors 5H **31**
Arena Ct. S9: Shef 4E **109**
Arena Stop (ST) 5E **109**
Argyle Cl. S8: Shef 3G **133**
Argyle La. DN11: New R 5B **74**
Argyle Rd. S8: Shef 3F **133**
Argyle St. S64: Mexb 1F **67**
Argyll Av. DN2: Don 5G **41**
Arklow Cl. S41: Has 2A **172**
Arklow Rd. DN2: Don 6F **41**
ARKSEY 6C **24**
Arksey Comn. La. DN5: Alm, Ark . . .6D **24**

Arksey La. DN5: Bntly 1A 40
Arkwright Rd. DN5: Don 5G 39
ARKWRIGHT TOWN 5H 173
Arley St. S2: Shef 5F 119
(not continuous)
Arlington Av. S26: Aston 6E 125
Arlott Way DN12: New E 3D 70
Armer St. S60: Roth 4D 96
Armistead Av. S60: Brins 4D 110
Armitage Bldgs. S36: Pen 4C 176
(off Stottercliffe Rd.)
Armitage Rd. DN4: Balb 5G 55
S36: Spink 4F 175
Armroyd La. S74: Els, Hoyl 2B 62
Arms Pk. Dr. S20: Half 4G 151
Armstead Rd. S20: Beig 5H 137
Armstrong Wlk. S66: Malt 4H 101
ARMTHORPE 4D 42
Armthorpe Ent. Cen. DN3: Arm 3G 43
Armthorpe La. DN2: Don 5F 41
DN3: Barn D, Kirk Sa 3D 26
Armthorpe Leisure Cen. 3D 42
Armthorpe Rd. DN2: Don 5F 41
S11: Shef 6G 117
Armyne Gro. S71: Barn 1B 32
Army Row S71: R'ton 2A 10
Armytage Ind. Est. S41: Whit M 5H 161
(not continuous)
Arncliffe Dr. S35: Chap 2E 79
S70: Barn 1A 30
Arndale Pct. S66: Malt 5B 102
Arnold Av. S12: Shef 6D 134
S71: Ath 1E 17
Arnold Cres. S64: Mexb 6F 51
Arnold Rd. S65: Roth 4A 98
Arnold St. S6: Shef 5B 106
Arnside Cl. S41: C'fld 5E 161
Arnside Rd. S8: Shef 3D 132
S66: Malt 4B 102
Arnside Ter. S8: Shef 3D 132
Arran Hill S65: Thry 5E 85
Arran Rd. S10: Shef 3A 118
Arras St. S9: Shef 1C 120
Arren Cl. DN3: Barn D 1H 27
Arrowsmith Ho. S65: Roth 3F 97
(off Wharncliffe Hill)
Arthington St. S8: Shef 2F 133
Arthur Av. DN5: Bntly 6A 24
Arthur Pl. DN5: Bntly 6A 24
Arthur Rd. S36: Stoc 3C 174
Arthur St. DN5: Bntly 6B 24
S26: Swal 1C 138
S60: Roth 3D 96
S62: Rawm 1H 83
S70: Wors 5F 31
Artisan Vw. S8: Shef 2F 133
Arundel Av. S60: Tree 2F 123
S65: Dalt 1C 98
Arundel Bus. Pk. S6: Shef 6A 92
Arundel Cl. S18: Dron W 3C 154
S41: C'fld 6G 161
Arundel Cotts. S60: Tree 2F 123
Arundel Ct. S11: Shef 4G 131
S43: Stav 4B 164
(off Porter St.)
Arundel Cres. S60: Tree 2F 123
Arundel Gdns. DN5: Scawt 2G 39
S71: R'ton 2H 9
Arundel Gate S1: Shef 5E 5 (4F 119)
Arundel La. S1: Shef 5F 5 (4G 119)
Arundell Dr. S71: Lund 3C 18
Arundel Rd. S35: Chap 2F 79
S60: Tree 2F 123
S65: Roth 5G 97
Arundel St. S1: Shef 6E 5 (4F 119)
S60: Tree 2F 123
Arundel Vw. S74: Jum 5D 46
Ascension Cl. S66: Malt 6C 102
Ascension M. S66: Malt 6B 102
(off Firth Cres.)
Ascot Av. DN4: Can 3A 58
Ascot Cl. S64: Mexb 6G 51
Ascot Dr. DN5: Scaws 4E 39
S25: Laugh C 4F 127
Ascot St. S2: Shef 5F 119
Ashberry Cl. S63: Thurn 2C 36
Ashberry Gdns. S6: Shef 1C 118
Ashberry Rd. S6: Shef 1C 118
Ashbourne Cl. S40: C'fld 3B 166
Ashbourne Gro. S13: Shef 5A 122
S35: Ough 4F 91

Ashbourne Rd. S13: Shef 5A 122
S71: Ath 1F 17
Ashbourne Way S60: Wav 3C 122
Ashburnham Gdns. DN5: Don 1F 55
Ashburton Cl. DN6: Adw S 2B 22
Ashbury Dr. S8: Shef 6H 133
Ashbury La. S8: Shef 6H 133
Ashby Ct. S70: Barn 2C 30
Ashby Dr. S26: Kiv P 6H 139
Ash Cl. S21: Killa 5B 152
S65: Roth 6C 98
Ash Cotts. S73: Womb 4E 33
Ash Ct. DN5: Sprot 3E 55
S66: Malt 4G 101
Ash Cres. S21: Ecki 2C 158
S36: Spink 3F 175
S64: Mexb 6E 51
ASHCROFT 6C 62
Ashcroft Cl. DN12: New E 5B 70
Ashcroft Ct. S41: Old W 3A 162
Ashcroft Dr. S41: Old W 3A 162
Ashdale Cl. S3: Eden 1C 42
Ash Dale Rd. DN4: Warm 2C 70
Ashdell S10: Shef 4B 118
Ashdell La. S10: Shef 4B 118
Ashdell Rd. S10: Shef 4B 118
Ashdene Ct. S64: Swin 6C 66
Ashdown Dr. S40: W'ton 1E 171
Ashdown Gdns. S20: Sot 5H 137
Ashdown Pl. DN5: Scawt 2G 39
Ash Dyke Cl. S75: Kexb 1E 15
Asher Rd. S7: Shef 6E 119
Ashes La. S62: Wentw 6C 62
Ashfield Cl. DN3: Arm 5F 43
S12: Shef 4C 134
S36: Pen 5D 176
S75: Barn 5B 16
Ashfield Ct. S70: Barn 2A 32
Ashfield Dr. S12: Shef 4C 134
Ashfield Ho. WF9: Hems 1E 13
Ashfield Rd. DN4: Balb 6H 55
S36: Spink 3F 175
S41: Has 2C 172
WF9: Hems 1E 13
Ash Flds. Rd. DN5: Bntly 1F 25
Ashfield Way S66: Sunn 3G 99
Ashford Cl. S18: Dron W 4C 154
Ashford Ct. S13: Wav 3C 122
S41: C'fld 3H 167
S71: R'ton 1H 9
Ashford Rd. S11: Shef 6C 118
S18: Dron W 4C 154
Ashfurlong Cl. S17: Dore 3G 145
Ashfurlong Dr. S17: Dore 3G 145
Ashfurlong Pk. S17: Dore 3G 145
Ashfurlong Rd. S17: Dore 3F 145
ASHGATE 4D 166
Ashgate Av. S40: Ash 5D 166
Ashgate Cl. S10: Shef 4B 118
Ashgate Ct. M. S10: C'fld 5G 167
Ashgate La. S10: Shef 4B 118
Ashgate Rd. S10: Shef 4B 118
S40: Ash, C'fld 4C 166
S42: Ash 4A 166
Ashgate Valley Rd. S40: C'fld 4E 167
Ash Gro. DN3: Arm 3F 43
DN9: Auck 2C 76
DN12: Con 5D 68
S10: Shef 4C 118
S26: Kiv P 5H 139
S43: Mas M 2E 165
S62: Rawm 3H 83
S66: Malt 4C 102
S66: Wick 5H 99
S70: Barn 3A 32
Ash-Holt Ind. Est. DN9: Finn 1H 77
Ash Ho. La. S17: Dore 1E 145
Ashland Ct. S7: Shef 2D 132
Ashland Rd. S7: Shef 2D 132
S21: Ecki 1F 159
Ash La. S18: App, Coal A 1C 156
S21: West H 4F 157
S36: Spink 3G 175
Ashlea S63: Thurn 2D 36
Ashleigh Av. S12: Shef 3C 134
Ashleigh Cl. S41: Old W 3A 162
Ashleigh Ct. S21: Ecki 3D 158
Ashleigh Cft. S12: Shef 3C 134
Ashleigh Dr. S12: Shef 3C 134

Ashleigh Gdns. S61: Grea 6C 82
Ashleigh Pl. S12: Shef 3C 134
Ashleigh Va. S70: Barn 2H 31
Ashley Cl. S21: Killa 4C 152
Ashley Ct. DN9: Finn 3F 77
WF9: Sth K 5G 13
Ashley Cft. S71: R'ton 2G 9
Ashley Gro. S26: Aston 1C 138
Ashley Ind. Est. S60: Roth 3E 97
Ashley La. S21: Killa 4C 152
Ashmore Av. S21: Ecki 2C 158
Ash Mt. S62: Rawm 3G 83
S65: Roth 4F 97
(off Doncaster Gate)
S72: Shaft 3F 11
Ashmount S6: Shef 5B 92
Ashopton Rd. S41: C'fld 2D 166
Ashover Cl. S70: Wors 6F 31
Ashover Cft. S60: Wav 2C 122
(off Stephenson Way)
Ashover Rd. S43: Ink 2H 169
Ashpool Cl. S13: Shef 2B 136
Ashpool Fold S13: Shef 2B 136
Ash Ridge S64: Swin 4C 66
Ash Rd. S63: Wath D 1H 65
S72: Shaft 4G 11
Ash Row S71: Barn 1H 31
Ashroyds Bus. Pk. S74: Hoyl 5A 46
Ashroyds Way S74: Hoyl 5A 46
Ash St. S6: Shef 6D 106
S20: Mosb 2D 150
S73: Womb 4D 32
Ashton Av. DN5: Scawt 1E 39
Ashton Cl. S21: Killa 4B 152
S40: W'ton 2D 170
Ashton Dr. DN3: Kirk Sa 4B 26
Ashton La. S66: B'well 1H 101
Ash Tree Cl. S40: Ash 5D 166
Ash Tree Ct. S9: Shef 6E 95
(off Eccles St.)
Ashurst Cl. S6: Shef 6F 105
S40: C'fld 3A 166
Ashurst Dr. S6: Shef 5F 105
Ashurst Pl. S6: Shef 6F 105
Ashurst Rd. S6: Shef 5F 105
Ash Va. S40: Bramp 5C 166
Ash Vw. S35: Chap 4E 79
S61: Grea 5D 82
Ashville DN11: New R 6D 74, 6H 75
Ashville Ct. S70: Stair 2A 32
Ashwell Cl. S72: Shaft 3F 11
Ashwell Gro. S65: Roth 2A 98
Ashwell Rd. S13: Shef 2B 136
Ashwood Cl. DN3: Brant 4F 59
S35: High G 6B 60
S70: Wors 6G 31
Ashwood Gro. S72: Gt H 5E 21
Ashwood Ho. DN6: Adw S 3D 22
Ashwood Rd. S35: High G 1B 78
S62: P'gte 4G 83
Ashworth Dr. S61: Kimb P 6G 81
Askam Cl. S66: Bram 4A 100
Askam Rd. S66: Bram 4A 100
Askern Ho. DN1: Don 2B 56
(off Oxford Pl.)
Askern Rd. DN5: Bntly 3G 23
Askew Cl. S36: Stoc 4E 175
Askew Way S40: C'fld 1H 171
Askrigg Cl. DN4: Can 5C 58
Asline Rd. S2: Shef 6F 119
Aspen Cl. DN3: Eden 1C 42
S21: Killa 4B 152
Aspen Gdns. S70: Wors 4G 31
(off Underwood Av.)
Aspen Gro. S73: D'fld 6B 34
Aspen Rd. S21: Ecki 3C 158
Aspen Wlk. S66: Malt 5F 101
Aspen Way S60: Roth 5C 96
S64: Swin 6B 66
Aspley Cl. S40: C'fld 3F 167
Asquith Rd. DN5: Bntly 1A 40
S9: Shef 6E 95
Assembly Way S70: Barn 3B 30
Astcote Ct. DN3: Kirk Sa 4B 26
Aster Cl. S20: Beig 5G 137
S25: Sth A 4G 141
ASTON 1E 139
Aston By-Pass S13: Shef 6H 123
S26: Aston, Swal 2B 138
Aston Cl. S18: Dron 1H 155
S26: Swal 5C 124

ASTON COMMON 2C 138
Aston Comn. S26: Aston 1G 139
Aston Ct. S43: Stav 4C 164
Aston-cum-Aughton Leisure Cen. . . .6A 124
Aston Dr. S71: Ath 2F 17
Aston Forge Ct. S26: Aston 1E 139
Aston Ho. S40: C'fld 1H 171
Aston La. S26: Augh 4C 124
Aston St. S2: Shef 2A 120
Aston Towers S18: Coal A 1H 155
Astoria Cl. S63: Gol 5F 37
Astrams Ct. S70: Barn 1C 30
Astwell Gdns. S35: Chap 2D 78
Atebanks Cl. DN4: Balb 2A 72
Athelstan Cl. S13: Shef 5H 121
Athelstane Cres. DN3: Eden 5C 26
Athelstane Dr. S66: Thurc 1B 126
Athelstane Rd. DN12: Con 4E 69
Athelstan Rd. S13: Shef 5H 121
Athersley Cres. S71: Ath 2F 17
Athersley Gdns. S20: Mosb 6B 136
ATHERSLEY NORTH 6E 9
Athersley Rd. S71: Ath 2F 17
ATHERSLEY SOUTH 2F 17
Atherton Cl. S2: Shef 2C 134
Atherton Rd. S2: Shef 2C 134
Atholl Cl. S42: W'ton 2C 170
Atholl Cres. DN2: Don 5H 41
Athol Rd. S8: Shef 4D 132
Athorpe Gro. S25: Din 5H 127
Athorpe Rd. S25: Din 5H 127
Athron Dr. S65: Roth 6B 98
Athron Ind. Est. DN1: Don 6D 40
(off Athron St.)
Athron St. DN1: Don 6D 40
Atkin Pl. S2: Shef 6F 119
Atkinson Ct. S40: C'fld 1H 171
Atlantic Cres. S8: Shef 4D 146
Atlantic Dr. S8: Shef 4D 146
Atlantic Rd. S8: Shef 4C 146
Atlantic Wlk. S8: Shef 4D 146
Atlantic Way S8: Shef 4D 146
ATLAS 6A 108
Atlas St. S4: Shef 6A 108
S60: Brins 3D 110
Atlas Way S4: Shef 5B 108
Atlee Cl. S66: Malt 6C 102
Atlow Cl. S40: C'fld 3C 166
Atrium S20: Water 6F 137
Atterby Dr. DN11: Ross 4D 74
ATTERCLIFFE 6C 108
Attercliffe Comn. S9: Shef 5D 108
Attercliffe Rd. S4: Shef 1H 119
S9: Shef 1H 119
Attercliffe Stop (ST) 6C 108
Attlee Av. DN11: New R 5A 74
Attlee Cres. S73: D'fld 5D 34
Attlee Rd. S43: Ink 1G 169
Aubretia Av. S60: Brins 5E 111
Aubrey Senior Way
S61: Kimb 3H 95
Auburn Rd. DN12: New E 4C 70
Auckland Av. S6: Lox 4F 105
Auckland Dr. S20: Half 4F 151
Auckland Ri. S20: Half 4F 151
Auckland Rd. DN2: Don 5D 40
S64: Mexb 1G 67
Auckland's Pl. S40: C'fld 6H 167
Auckland Way S20: Half 4F 151
AUCKLEY 1H 59
Audrey Rd. S13: Shef 1F 135
AUGHTON .5B 124
Aughton Av. S26: Augh 5B 124
Aughton Cl. S13: Shef 1G 135
Aughton Cres. S13: Shef 6F 121
Aughton Dr. S13: Shef 6F 121
Aughton La. S26: Aston 6D 124
Aughton Rd.
S26: Augh, Swal 6B 124
Augustus Rd. S60: Brins 2D 110
Aukley Rd. S8: Shef 3E 133
Aunby Dr. S26: Swal 6C 124
Austen Av. DN4: Balb 6F 55
Austen Dr. S66: Bram 5B 100
Austerfield Av. DN5: Don 3H 39
Austin Cl. S6: Lox 4F 105
Austin Ct. S6: Lox 3F 105
Austwick Cl. DN4: Balb 2G 71
S75: Mapp 4H 7
Austwick Wlk. S70: Barn 6C 16
Austwood La. S66: B'well 6B 88

Autumn Cl. S66: Thurc 6D 114
S71: R'ton 3G 9
Autumn Dr. S66: Malt 4B 102
Ava Ct. DN3: Brant 4G 59
Aven Ho. S64: Mexb 5G 103
Avenue, The DN4: Bess 2H 57
DN5: Bntly 5B 24
DN5: Harl 2G 51
S9: Shef 2F 121
S18: Dron 2G 155
S20: Beig 4G 137
S66: Carr 3F 115
S66: Stain 2F 103
S71: R'ton 2B 10
S75: Pil 6C 44
Avenue 1 S41: Has 2A 172
Avenue 2 S41: Has 2A 172
Avenue 3 S41: Has 2A 172
Avenue 4 S41: Has 2A 172
Avenue 5 S41: Has 2A 172
Avenue 6 S41: Has 2A 172
Avenue 7 S41: Has 2A 172
Avenue 8 S41: Has 2A 172
Avenue Ct. S10: Shef 6H 117
Avenue Lodge
WF9: Sth K 2H 13
Avenue Rd. DN2: Don 5D 40
S7: Shef 2E 133
S41: Whit M 6H 161
S63: Wath D 1H 65
Aviemore Cl. S43: New W 2D 162
Aviemore Rd.
DN4: Balb 6F 55
Avill Way S66: Wick 1G 113
Avisford Dr. S5: Shef 1C 106
Avisford Rd. S5: Shef 6C 92
Avoca Av. DN2: Don 6F 41
Avocet Cl. S64: Mexb 6B 52
Avocet Way S61: Thorpe H 2C 80
Avon Cl. S18: Dron 1G 155
S66: Malt 4A 102
S73: Womb 3A 48
S75: High'm 5F 15
Avon Ct. DN9: Auck 1H 59
Avondale Dr. S71: Car 5H 9
Avondale Rd. DN2: Don 1F 57
S6: Shef 4A 106
S40: C'fld 4G 167
S43: Ink 1H 169
S61: Roth 3B 96
Avon Gro. S35: Chap 2D 78
Avon Mt. S61: Roth 3B 96
Avonside Cl. S43: Bar H 3G 163
Avon St. S71: Barn 1F 31
Awesome Walls Climbing Cen.
. . . . .5A 108
Axe Edge Cl. S5: Shef 3F 93
Axholme Ct. DN2: Don 5E 41
Axholme Rd. DN2: Don 5D 40
Axle La. S25: Sth A 4E 141
Aylesbury Ct. S9: Shef 6E 95
Aylesbury Cres. S9: Shef 1E 109
Aylesbury Rd. DN2: Don 6G 41
Aylesford Cl. S71: Barn 5E 17
Aylsham Dr. S26: Aston 1D 138
Aylward Cl. S2: Shef 1C 134
Aylward Rd. S2: Shef 1C 134
Aymer Dr. S66: Thurc 6B 114
Ayrsome Wlk. DN4: Can 4B 58
Aysgarth Av. S71: Ard 2E 33
Aysgarth Cl. DN4: Can 5C 58
Aysgarth Ri. S26: Swal 6B 124
Aysgarth Rd. S6: Shef 6B 92
Ayton Wlk. DN5: Bntly 6H 23
Azalea Cl. S25: Sth A 5G 141

B

Babington Cl. S2: Shef 1C 134
Babington Ct. S2: Shef 1C 134
Babur Rd. S4: Shef 6A 108
Backfield Ri. S35: Chap 2F 79
Backfields S1: Shef 4D 4 (3F 119)
Back La. DN4: Warm 2F 71
DN5: Cus 5C 38
DN9: Blax 1E 77
DN12: Old E 1B 88
S6: Brad 1A 104
S10: Shef 2G 117
S13: Shef 2D 136

Back La. S17: Tot 5G 145
S18: App 3C 156
S21: Ecki 6B 150
S25: Nth A 2H 141
S36: Midh 2A 174
S36: Oxs, Rough 6G 177
S36: Pen 4D 176
S44: Cal 1G 173
S62: Neth Hau 2D 82
S65: Hoot R 2A 86
S65: Thry 4E 85
S66: Clftn 3H 87
S66: Hoot L 1D 114
S66: Mick 1F 101
S71: Monk B 4H 17
S72: Bill 3G 35
Back La. W. S71: R'ton 2F 9
BACKMOOR 6H 133
Backmoor Cres. S8: Shef 6H 133
Backmoor Rd. S8: Shef 6H 133
Bk. Poplar Ter. S71: R'ton 2B 10
Back Rd. S18: App 3C 156
Back Row DN3: Can 3E 59
Back Row Cotts. DN11: Ross 5E 75
Backside La. DN4: Warm 6E 55
Bk. South St. S43: New W 3C 162
(not continuous)
Bacon La. S9: Shef 1B 120
Bacons La. S40: Birdh 2G 171
Baden Powell Av. S40: C'fld 1G 171
Baden Powell Rd. S40: C'fld 6H 167
Baden St. S60: Roth 3D 96
S70: Wors 6G 31
Badger Cl. S13: Shef 1D 136
S42: W'ton 2C 170
Badger Dr. S13: Shef 1D 136
Badger La. S1: Shef 3C 4
Badger Pl. S13: Shef 1D 136
Badger Ri. S13: Shef 1D 136
Badger Rd. S13: Shef 1D 136
Badgers Holt DN3: Brant 4G 59
Badsley Cl. S65: Roth 4H 97
Badsley Moor La. S65: Roth 5G 97
Badsley St. S65: Roth 4G 97
Badsley St. Sth. S65: Roth 5G 97
Badsworth Cl. S66: Bram 5B 100
S73: Womb 2A 48
Badsworth Pl. S66: Bram 5B 100
Badsworth Rd. DN4: Warm 1D 70
Badsworth Way S66: Bram 5B 100
Bage Hill S42: W'ton 4A 170
Bagshaw's Rd. S12: Shef 2E 135
Bagshot St. S11: Shef 6C 118
Bahram Gro. DN11: New R 6B 74
Bahram Rd. DN4: Bess 4H 57
Bailey Cft. S70: Barn 2D 30
Bailey Dr. S21: Killa 2D 150
Bailey La. S1: Shef 3C 4 (3E 119)
Bailey M. DN5: Scawt 1F 39
Bailey St. S1: Shef 3D 4 (3F 119)
Bainbridge Rd. DN4: Balb 3A 56
Baines Av. DN12: New E 5B 70
Baines Wood Cl. S41: C'fld 6D 160
Bainton Dr. S70: Barn 3C 30
Bairstow Gdns. S62: Rawm 6D 64
Bakehouse La. S21: Ecki 1E 159
S75: Barn 5H 15
Baker Dr. S21: Killa 4B 152
Bakers Field Ct. S65: Roth 5A 98
Bakers Hill S1: Shef 3C 5 (3G 119)
Bakers La. S1: Shef 2C 4 (2F 119)
Baker St. S9: Shef 6C 108
S25: Laugh C 4F 127
Bakewell Cl. S71: Ath 2F 17
Bakewell Gdns. S60: Wav 2C 122
Bakewell Rd. S43: Ink 3H 169
S71: Ath 2F 17
Balaclava La. S6: Shef 6D 106
Balaclava Rd. S6: Shef 6D 106
Bala St. S71: Barn 1E 31
BALBY 6H 55
Balby Carr DN4: Balb 4B 56
Balby Carr Bank DN4: Balb 4B 56
Balby Rd. DN4: Balb 4A 56
Balby St. DN12: Den M 3E 69
Balcarres Rd. DN11: New R 5C 74
Baldwin Av. DN5: Don 5H 39
Baldwin St. S9: Shef 1B 120
Balfour Dr. S9: Shef 1E 121
Balfour Rd. DN5: Bntly 1B 40
S9: Shef 1E 121

Balk, The—Barrowfield Rd.

Balk, The DN5: Ark .3C 24
S61: Grea .4C 82
S75: Stain .4B 8
Balk Farm Ct. S70: Birdw .3D 44
Balk La. S60: Brins .2B 110
S66: Bram .5A 100
S70: Birdw .3D 44
Balkley La. S73: D'fld .5D 34
Ballam Av. DN5: Scawt .1F 39
Ballard Hall Chase S10: Shef .5H 117
Ballard Hall Ct. S10: Shef .5G 117
Ballard Hall M. S10: Shef .5G 117
Ballfield Av. S75: Kexb .6D 6
Ballfield Fold S75: Kexb .6C 6
Ballfield La. S75: Kexb .6D 6
Ballfield M. S75: Kexb .6C 6
Ballidon Cl. S40: C'fld .2D 166
Ballifield Av. S13: Shef .5B 122
Ballifield Cl. S13: Shef .5B 122
Ballifield Cres. S13: Shef .5C 122
Ballifield Dr. S13: Shef .5C 122
Ballifield Pl. S13: Shef .5B 122
Ballifield Ri. S13: Shef .5C 122
Ballifield Rd. S13: Shef .5B 122
Ballifield Way S13: Shef .5B 122
Ball Rd. S6: Shef .4A 106
Ball St. S3: Shef .1E 119
Balmain Dr. S6: Shef .3A 106
Balmain Rd. S6: Shef .3A 106
Balmer Ri. S66: Bram .6B 100
Balm Grn. S1: Shef .3D 4 (3F 119)
Balmoak La. S41: C'fld .2B 168
Balmoral Cl. DN5: Barnb .1H 51
S36: Thurl .3A 176
Balmoral Ct. S11: Shef .4G 131
Balmoral Cres. S10: Shef .5A 116
S18: Dron W .2C 154
Balmoral Glen S10: Shef .5A 116
Balmoral M. S10: Shef .5A 116
Balmoral Rd. DN2: Don .6E 41
S13: Shef .2D 136
Balmoral Way S43: New W .2D 162
S66: Bram .4A 100
Baltic La. *S9: Shef* .*6C 108*
(off Baltic Rd.)
Baltic Rd. S9: Shef .6C 108
Baltic Way S9: Shef .6C 108
Bamford Av. S71: Ath .2F 17
Bamford Cl. S75: Dod .3F 29
Bamford Rd. S43: Ink .3G 169
Bamford St. S43: New W .2C 162
Bamforth St. S6: Shef .5C 106
Bamforth Street Stop (ST) .5C 106
Banbury Cl. *DN12: Den M* .*3E 69*
(off Crags Rd.)
Bancroft Dr. DN9: Auck .3B 76
Bank Cl. S7: Shef .2D 132
S61: Kimb P .1A 96
Bank Ct. S43: Brim .6C 162
Bank End Av. S70: Wors .5H 31
Bank End Cl. S63: Bolt D .2B 50
Bank End Rd. DN9: Blax, Finn .1F 77
S70: Wors .5G 31
Bankfield La. S6: Stan .6D 104
Bankfield Rd. S6: Shef .4H 105
Bank Ho. La. S36: Thurl .4A 176
Bank Ho. Rd. S6: Shef .1B 118
Bank La. S36: Bolst .6G 175
Bank Rd. S41: C'fld .2H 167
Bank Sq. DN11: New R .6B 74
Bank St. DN1: Don .3B 56
S1: Shef .2E 5 (2G 119)
S25: Sth A .3G 141
S40: C'fld .5F 167
S43: Brim .6C 162
S64: Mexb .2F 67
S70: Barn .3E 31
S71: Stair .2B 32
S72: Cud .1E 19
S74: Hoyl .1A 62
Bank Ter. *S10: Shef* .*3B 118*
(off Parker's La.)
Bank Top Rd. S65: Roth .6C 98
Bank Vw. S12: Shef .5D 136
S36: Oxs .6H 177
S60: Whis .3A 112
Bank Wood Cl. S41: C'fld .1C 166
Bankwood Cl. S14: Shef .3A 134
Bankwood Cres. DN11: New R .4A 74
Bankwood La. DN11: New R .3A 74
Bankwood Rd. S14: Shef .3A 134
Bannatyne Health Club
Barnsley .2G 29
Bramley .6C 100
Banner Ct. S11: Shef .2A 132
BANNER CROSS .2A 132
Banner Cross Dr. S11: Shef .2A 132
Banner Cross Rd. S11: Shef .3A 132
Bannerdale Cl. S11: Shef .2B 132
Bannerdale Rd. S7: Shef .2B 132
S11: Shef .2B 132
Bannerdale Vw. S11: Shef .2B 132
Bannham Rd. S9: Shef .2G 121
Bannister Ho. DN2: Don .4F 41
Bar Av. S75: Mapp .6C 8
Barbados Way S66: Hel .4D 100
Barber Balk Cl. S61: Kimb P .1A 96
Barber Balk Rd. S61: Kimb P .2A 96
Barber Cl. DN3: Arm .5C 42
S26: Tod .3B 140
Barber Cres. S10: Shef .2C 118
Barber Pl. S10: Shef .2C 118
Barber Rd. S10: Shef .2C 118
Barberry Ct. S70: Barn .2G 31
Barberry Way S65: Rav .2B 100
Barber's Av. S62: P'gte, Rawm .3G 83
Barber's Cres. S62: Rawm .3H 83
Barbers La. S21: Killa .2C 152
Barber's Path S64: Mexb .1E 67
Barber St. S74: Hoyl .6B 46
Barber Wood Rd. S61: Kimb .3D 94
Barbon Cl. S40: C'fld .3F 167
Barbot Farm M. S61: Grea .6D 82
Barbot Hall Dr. S61: Grea .6D 82
Barbot Hall Ind. Est. S62: P'gte .6E 83
Barbot Hill Rd. S61: Grea .6D 82
Barclay Grange S41: C'fld .5A 168
Bar Cft. S40: C'fld .2E 167
Barcroft Flatt S75: Barn .4H 15
Barden Cres. S60: Brins .4D 110
Barden Dr. S75: Barn .5A 16
Bardolf Rd. DN4: Can .3B 58
Bardon Rd. DN3: Eden .5C 26
Bard St. S2: Shef .2H 5 (3H 119)
Bardwell Rd. S3: Shef .6E 107
Barewell Hill S72: Brier, Hems .2B 12
(not continuous)
Barfield Av. S60: Whis .3H 111
Barfield Rd. S74: Hoyl .6B 46
Barholme Cl. S41: C'fld .1C 166
Barholm Rd. S10: Shef .4G 117
Bari Cl. S73: D'fld .4H 33
Baring Rd. S61: Kimb .4E 95
Barkby Rd. S9: Shef .6D 94
Barker Fold S40: C'fld .5E 167
Barker Hades Rd. S81: Letw .4H 129
Barker La. S40: C'fld .5E 167
Barkers Cft. S61: Wing .5A 82
Barkers La. DN12: Con .5A 70
Barker's Pl. S6: Shef .3B 106
Barker's Pool S1: Shef .4D 4 (3F 119)
Barker's Rd. S7: Shef .2C 132
Barker St. S64: Mexb .2D 66
Bark Mdws. S75: Dod .3H 29
Barkston Rd. S71: Car .1H 17
Bar La. S75: Mapp, Stain .6C 8
Barlborough Rd. S73: Womb .3H 47
Barlby Gro. S12: Shef .5D 136
Barley Cl. S70: Wors .6F 31
Barley Cft. La. S25: Din .6A 128
Barley Ho. *S11: Shef* .*5D 118*
(off Napier St.)
Barley La. S42: Ash .3B 166
Barley M. S18: Dron W .2B 154
Barley Vw. S63: Thurn .3C 36
Barleywood Rd. S9: Shef .6F 109
BARLOW .4A 160
Barlow Dr. S6: Shef .6H 105
BARLOW LEES .6C 154
Barlow Lees La. S18: Dron .6D 154
Barlow Rd. S6: Shef .6H 105
S41: Up N .5A 160
S43: Stav .5B 164
Barlow Vw. S18: Dron .5G 155
Barmouth Rd. S7: Shef .3D 132
Barnabas Wlk. S71: Barn .5E 17
Barnard Av. S18: Coal A .1A 156
Barnardiston Rd. S9: Shef .1E 121
BARNBURGH .1A 52
Barnburgh Ct. S63: Gol .6D 36
Barnburgh Hall Gdns. DN5: Barnb .1A 52
Barnburgh Ho. DN12: New E .3D 70
Barnburgh La. DN5: Barnb .6D 36
S63: Gol .6D 36
BARNBY DUN .1C 26
Barnby Dun Rd. DN2: Don .3G 41
Barnby Furnace S75: Silk .4C 14
Barncliffe Cl. S10: Shef .6D 116
Barncliffe Cres. S10: Shef .5C 116
Barncliffe Dr. S10: Shef .5C 116
Barncliffe Glen S10: Shef .6D 116
Barncliffe M. S10: Shef .4E 117
Barncliffe Rd. S10: Shef .5C 116
Barn Cl. S41: C'fld .2E 167
Barnes Av. S18: Dron W .2C 154
Barnes Ct. S2: Shef .6G 5 (4G 119)
Barnes Grn. S35: Gren .5C 78
Barnes Hall Rd. S35: Burn .3C 78
Barnes Ind. Est. S66: Bram .5B 100
Barnes La. S18: Dron W .6A 146
Barnes Rd. S41: C'fld .1D 172
Barnet Av. S11: Shef .3F 131
Barnet Rd. S11: Shef .3F 131
Barnfield Av. S10: Shef .3F 117
Barnfield Cl. S10: Shef .3F 117
S43: Stav .4B 164
Barnfield Dr. S10: Shef .4F 117
Barnfield Rd. S10: Shef .3F 117
Barnfield Wlk. S43: Stav .4B 164
Barnfold Pl. S72: Shaft .4F 11
Barnham Cl. S40: W'ton .2C 170
Barn Owl Cl. S72: Bill .4G 35
Barnsbridge Gro. S70: Barn .2G 31
Barnsdale Av. S20: Mosb .6B 136
Barnside Cl. S36: Cub .5D 176
BARNSLEY .6D 16
Barnsley Av. DN12: Con .4D 68
Barnsley Bowl .2G 17
Barnsley Bus. & Innovation Cen.
S75: Barn .4A 16
Barnsley Bus. Innovation Cen.
S72: Cud .1E 19
Barnsley College Sports Academy .5D 16
Barnsley Crematorium S71: Ard .3E 33
Barnsley FC .1F 31
Barnsley Golf Course .4B 8
Barnsley Retail Pk. S70: Stair .4C 32
Barnsley Rd.
DN5: Marr, Scaws .3H 37, 3A 38
S4: Shef .4G 107
S5: Shef .5H 93
S36: H'swne, Pen .3C 176
S61: Thorpe H .1B 80
S63: Gol .5B 36
S63: Wath D .4C 48
S72: Brier, Shaft .4G 11
S72: Cud, Lund .2D 18
S73: D'fld .3A 34
S73: Womb .5E 33
(not continuous)
S74: Hoyl .4A 46
S75: Bar G, Dart .6F 7
S75: Dod .3F 29
S75: Silk .3A 28
WF4: Nott, Wool .1B 8
WF9: Hems .2B 12
Barnsley Station (Rail) .6E 17
Barnsley Trade Pk. S70: Stair .4C 32
Barnstone St. DN4: Hex .3H 55
Barnwell Cres. S73: Womb .5E 33
Baron St. S1: Shef .5F 119
Barrack La. S6: Shef .6D 106
Barrack Rd. S18: App .3D 156
Barracks Fld. Ter. S74: Els .1D 62
Barrack Vw. S18: App .3D 156
Barratt Rd. S21: Ecki .2E 159
Barrel La. DN4: Warm .6F 55
Barret Rd. DN4: Can .3C 58
Barretta St. S4: Shef .3A 108
Barrick M. S61: Kimb .3A 96
Barrie Cres. S5: Shef .1E 107
Barrie Dr. S5: Shef .1E 107
Barrie Gro. S66: Hel .6E 101
Barrie Rd. DN4: Balb .6A 56
S5: Shef .1E 107
Barron Rd. S63: Bramp B .5B 48
BARROW .5C 62
Barrow, The S62: Wentw .5C 62
Barrowby Rd. S60: Roth .1H 111
BARROWFIELD GATE .4D 62
Barrowfield La. S62: Wentw .4D 62
Barrowfield Rd. S63: Gol, Thurn .3C 36
S74: Hoyl .5A 46

BARROW HILL 3G 163
Barrow Hill S62: Wentw 5B 62
Barrow Hill Roundhouse Railway Cen.
. . . . .3F 163
Barrow Rd. S9: Shef 6E 95
Barrow St. S43: Stav 4C 164
Barrow Syke S63: Bolt D 3C 50
Barrow Way S25: Laugh C 3F 127
Barry Rd. S43: Brim C 4E 169
Bartholomew Cl. S60: Whis 2C 112
Bartholomew St. S73: Womb 1F 47
Bartin Cl. S11: Shef 3A 132
Bartle Av. S12: Shef 4C 134
Bartle Dr. S12: Shef 4C 134
Bartle Rd. S12: Shef 4C 134
Bartlett Cl. S8: Stan 1D 116
Bartlett Rd. S5: Shef 6E 93
Bartle Way S12: Shef 4C 134
Barton Cres. S40: C'fld 2B 166
Barton La. DN3: Arm 4D 42
(not continuous)
Barton Pl. DN12: Con 5E 69
Barton Rd. S8: Shef 2F 133
BARUGH GREEN 4F 15
Barugh Grn. Rd. S75: Barn, Bar G . . .3F 15
Barugh La. S75: Bar G 3F 15
BASE GREEN 5F 135
Basegreen Av. S12: Shef 5E 135
Basegreen Cl. S12: Shef 5F 135
Basegreen Cres. S12: Shef 5E 135
Basegreen Dr. S12: Shef 5E 135
Basegreen Pl. S12: Shef 5E 135
Basegreen Rd. S12: Shef 5E 135
Basegreen Way S12: Shef 5F 135
Basford Cl. S9: Shef 1E 121
Basford Dr. S9: Shef 1E 121
Basford M. S9: Shef 1F 121
Basford Pl. S9: Shef 1E 121
Basford St. S9: Shef 1E 121
Basil Av. DN3: Arm 3B 42
Basil Cl. S41: C'fld 5H 167
Basildon Rd. S63: Thurn 1B 36
Basil Griffith Ct. S3: Shef 4G 107
(off Orphanage Rd)
Baslow Cres. S75: Dod 3F 29
Baslow Pl. S60: Wav 2C 122
Baslow Rd. S17: Tot 6D 144
S42: Holy 1A 170
S71: Ath 1G 17
Bassett La. S10: Shef 2A 130
Bassett Pl. S2: Shef 4A 120
Bassett Rd. S2: Shef 4B 120
Bassey Rd. DN3: Brant 4H 59
Bassingthorpe La. S61: Grea 6C 82
Bassledene Ct. S2: Shef 6D 120
Bassledene Rd. S2: Shef 6D 120
Bass Ter. DN1: Don 1D 56
Bastock Rd. S6: Shef 3C 106
Bateman Cl. S43: New W 2C 162
S72: Cud 4E 11
Bateman Rd. S66: Hel 6D 100
(not continuous)
Bateman Sq. S63: Thurn 2B 36
BATEMOOR 4F 147
Batemoor Cl. S8: Shef 4F 147
Batemoor Dr. S8: Shef 4F 147
Batemoor Pl. S8: Shef 4F 147
Batemoor Rd. S8: Shef 4F 147
Batemoor Wlk. S8: Shef 4F 147
(off Batemoor Rd.)
Batesquire S20: Beig 6G 137
Bates St. S10: Shef 1B 118
Bate Wood Av. S43: Ink 3G 169
Bath St. S1: Shef 6B 4 (4E 119)
Battison La. S63: Wath D 2E 65
Batt St. S8: Shef 6F 119
Batty Av. S72: Cud 2D 18
Batworth Dr. S5: Shef 4F 107
Batworth Rd. S5: Shef 4F 107
Baulk Farm Cl. S61: Grea 4C 82
Bawtry Ga. S9: Tins 2H 109
Bawtry Rd. DN4: Bess, Don 2F 57
DN9: Finn 3G 77
S9: Tins 2H 109
S60: Brins 2H 109
S65: Roth 6D 98
S66: Bram, Wick, Hel 6D 98
Baxter Av. DN1: Don 6D 40
Baxter Cl. S6: Shef 6B 92
S26: Swal 1H 137
Baxter Ct. DN1: Don 6D 40

Baxter Dr. S6: Shef 6B 92
Bayardo Wlk. DN11: New R 6G 75
Baycliff Cl. S71: Monk B 2A 18
Baycliff Dr. S40: Ash 5D 166
Bay Ct. S21: Killa 5B 152
Bayford Way S73: Womb 1A 48
Baysdale Cft. S20: Mosb 3E 151
Bay Tree Av. S66: Flan 4G 99
Baytree Gro. DN9: Auck 2A 76
Bazley Rd. S2: Shef 2C 134
Beacon Cl. S9: Shef 2C 108
S75: Silk C 4B 28
Beacon Ct. S75: Silk C 5B 28
Beacon Cft. S9: Shef 2C 108
Beacon Hill S75: Silk C 4B 28
Beacon Hill Way S41: Has 3B 172
Beacon La. S66: Clftn 3G 87
Beacon Rd. S9: Shef 2C 108
Beaconsfield Rd. DN4: Hex 3H 55
S60: Roth 1H 111
Beaconsfield St. S64: Mexb 1E 67
S70: Barn 2D 30
Beacon Sq. S66: Clftn 3H 87
Beacon Vw. S74: Els 1D 62
Beacon Way S9: Shef 2C 108
Beale Way S62: P'gte 6G 83
Beancroft Cl. DN11: Wad 5F 73
Bear Tree Cl. S62: P'gte 4G 83
Bear Tree Rd. S62: P'gte 4G 83
Bear Tree St. S62: P'gte 5G 83
Beauchamp Rd. S61: Kimb P 1A 96
BEAUCHIEF 2B 146
Beauchief S8: Shef 2A 146
Beauchief Abbey La. S8: Shef 1B 146
Beauchief Abbey (remains of) 2B 146
Beauchief Cl. S36: Spink 4H 175
Beauchief Ct. S8: Shef 6D 132
Beauchief Dr. S8: Shef 3B 146
S17: Bradw 3B 146
Beauchief Golf Course 1A 146
Beauchief Ri. S8: Shef 1B 146
Beaufort Rd. DN2: Don 6G 41
S10: Shef 3C 118
Beaulieu Cl. S40: Shef 6B 8
Beaulieu Vw. S75: Mapp 6B 8
Beaumont Cl. S71: Smi 3G 17
Beaumont Av. DN6: Woodl 2A 22
S2: Shef 4D 120
S70: Barn 1A 30
Beaumont Cres. S2: Shef 4E 121
Beaumont Dr. S65: Roth 5A 98
S75: Haigh 1B 6
Beaumont M. S2: Shef 5E 121
Beaumont Nth. S2: Shef 4D 120
Beaumont Rd. S75: Kexb 1D 14
Beaumont St. S74: Hoyl 1G 61
Beaumont Way S2: Shef 4D 120
Beaver Av. S13: Shef 6C 122
Beaver Cl. S13: Shef 6C 122
Beaver Dr. S13: Shef 6C 122
BEAVER HILL 6C 122
Beaver Hill Rd. S13: Shef 6C 122
Beccles Way S66: Bram 5B 100
Beck Cl. S5: Shef 3B 94
S64: Swin 5C 66
Beck Cft. S74: Hoyl 2H 61
Becket Av. S8: Shef 4C 146
Becket Cres. S8: Shef 4C 146
S61: Kimb P 1A 96
Becket Rd. S8: Shef 4D 146
Beckett Hospital Ter. S70: Barn 2E 31
(off Dobie St.)
Beckett Rd. DN2: Don 5D 40
Beckett St. S71: Barn 6E 17
Becket Wlk. S8: Shef 4C 146
Beckfield Gro. S63: Bolt D 1A 50
Beckfield Ri. DN9: Auck 3A 76
Beckford La. S5: Shef 2A 94
Beckingham Way S40: C'fld 6H 167
Becknoll Rd. S73: Bramp 4B 48
Beck Rd. S5: Shef 3A 94
Beckton Av. S20: Water 6F 137
Beckton Cl. S20: Water 6G 137
Beckton Gro. S20: Water 6F 137
Beckwith Gro. S66: Thurc 1C 126
Beckwith Rd. S65: Roth 3C 98
Bedale Cl. S26: Swal 1B 138

Bedale Ct. S60: Roth 6G 97
Bedale Rd. DN5: Scaws 3E 39
S7: Shef 2E 133
Bedale Wlk. S72: Shaft 3F 11
Bedford Cl. S25: Nth A 1G 141
Bedford Rd. S35: Ough 2E 91
Bedford St. S6: Shef 1E 119
S66: Malt 6C 102
S70: Barn 3E 31
S72: Grim 3B 20
Bedford Ter. S71: Monk B 3F 17
Bedgebury Cl. S20: Sot 1A 152
Bedgrave Cl. S21: Killa 2E 153
Bedgreave New Mill 6B 138
Beecham Ct. S64: Swin 5B 66
Beech Av. DN9: Auck 2B 76
S62: Rawm 3A 84
S65: Roth 6D 98
S72: Cud 6E 11
S75: Silk C 5B 28
Beech Cl. S66: Malt 5G 101
S72: Brier 3B 12
S73: Hem 4F 47
WF9: Sth K 4H 13
Beech Cres. S21: Ecki 3C 158
S21: Killa 5C 152
S64: Mexb 1D 66
Beechcroft Rd. DN4: Balb 6F 55
Beechdale Cl. S40: C'fld 4E 167
Beech Dr. DN3: Brant 3H 59
S44: Ark T 5H 173
Beech en Hurst S60: Roth 6F 97
(off Reneville Cl.)
Beeches, The DN3: Kirk Sa 4C 26
S26: Swal 1C 138
S64: Swin 4B 66
S73: Hem 5G 47
Beeches Bank S2: Shef 6H 119
Beeches Dr. S2: Shef 6H 119
Beeches Gro. S20: Beig 5H 137
Beeches Hollow S2: Shef 5H 119
Beeches Rd. S26: Wales 5G 139
Beechfern Cl. S35: High G 6C 60
Beechfield Cl. S63: Bolt D 2B 50
Beechfield Rd. DN1: Don 2C 56
Beech Gro. DN4: Warm 6D 54
DN5: Bntly 2A 40
DN12: Con 5E 69
S25: Din 1A 142
S66: Wick 5H 99
S70: Barn 3C 30
Beech Hill DN12: Con 4F 69
Beech Hill Rd. S10: Shef 4B 118
Beech Ho. Cft. S66: Clftn 2G 87
Beech Ho. Rd. S73: Hem 4G 47
Beechlea S63: Thurn 1B 36
Beech Rd. DN3: Arm 4E 43
DN11: New R 6D 74
S63: Wath D 6H 49
S66: Malt 5G 101
S72: Shaft 4G 11
Beech St. S43: Hol 5F 163
S70: Barn 2E 31
Beech Tree Cl. DN3: Can 3E 59
Beech Vs. S65: Roth 2H 97
Beechville Av. S64: Swin 5B 66
Beech Way S18: Dron 1F 155
S26: Swal 6A 124
Beechwood Cl. DN3: Eden 1D 42
S62: Rawm 1A 84
S63: Wath D 3G 65
Beechwood Lodge Flats S65: Roth . .3G 97
Beechwood Rd. S6: Shef 4A 106
S18: Dron 3E 155
S35: High G 2D 78
S36: Stoc 4D 174
S60: Roth 6H 97
Beechwood Wlk. DN12: New E 5B 70
(off Grainger Cl.)
Beeden Cl. S65: Thry 5E 85
Beehive Rd. S10: Shef 2C 118
S40: C'fld 6E 167
Beehive Yd. S40: C'fld 6E 167
Beeley Cl. S43: Ink 2H 169
Beeley St. S2: Shef 5E 119
S43: Ink 3C 170
Beeley Vw. S42: W'ton 3C 170
Beeley Way S43: Ink 3H 169
Beeley Wood La. S6: Shef 5G 91
Beeley Wood Rd. S6: Shef 1B 106
Beely Rd. S35: Ough 4F 91

Beeston Cl. S18: Dron W 2B **154**
Beeston Sq. S71: Ath 6E **9**
Beeton Rd. S8: Shef 3E **133**
Beet St. S3: Shef 2B **4** (3E **119**)
Beetwell St. S40: C'fld 6H **167**
Beever Cl. S75: Barn 5H **15**
Beever La. S75: Barn 5H **15**
Beeversleigh S65: Roth 4F **97**
(off Allan St.)
Beevers Rd. S61: Kimb P 6G **81**
Beever St. S63: Gol 5E **37**
Beevor Ct. S71: Barn 1F **31**
Beevor St. S71: Barn 1G **31**
Begonia Cl. S25: Sth A 4F **141**
BEIGHTON 4H **137**
Beighton Stop (ST) 6G **137**
BEIGHTON HOLLOW 4H **151**
Beighton Rd. S12: Shef 5C **136**
S13: Shef 2D **136**
S20: Beigh 2D **136**
S64: Kiln 6D **66**
Beighton Rd. E. S20: Water 5E **137**
Beighton Sports and Leisure Club . .4H **137**
Belcourt Rd. S65: Roth 6C **98**
Beldon Cl. S2: Shef 1A **134**
Beldon Ct. S2: Shef 1A **134**
Beldon Pl. S2: Shef 1A **134**
Beldon Rd. S2: Shef 1A **134**
Belford Cl. S66: Sunn 4H **99**
Belford Dr. S66: Bram 4H **99**
Belfry Gdns. DN4: Can 5D **58**
Belfry Way S25: Din 1B **142**
Belgrave Dr. S10: Shef 5E **117**
Belgrave Pl. S26: Swal 1B **138**
Belgrave Rd. S10: Shef 5F **117**
S71: Barn 1F **31**
Belgrave Sq. S2: Shef 6F **119**
Belklane Dr. S21: Killa 3D **152**
Bella Av. S63: Gol 5F **37**
Bellamy Cl. S65: Roth 5A **98**
Bell Bank Vw. S70: Wors 5E **31**
Bellbank Way S71: Ath 6E **9**
Bellbrooke Av. S73: D'fld 3A **34**
Bellbrooke Cl. S73: D'fld 3B **34**
Bellbrooke Pl. S73: D'fld 3A **34**
Bell Butts La. DN9: Auck 2G **59**
Bellcross Gdns. S72: Cud 1F **19**
Bellcross Way S71: Monk B 2C **18**
Bellefield St. S3: Shef 1A **4** (2D **118**)
BELLE GREEN 1F **19**
Belle Grn. Cl. S72: Cud 1F **19**
Belle Grn. Gdns. S72: Cud 1F **19**
Belle Grn. La. S72: Cud 1F **19**
BELLE VUE .2F **57**
Belle Vue Av. DN4: Don 2F **57**
Belle Vue Cl. S43: Brim 6C **162**
Belle Vue Rd. S64: Mexb 1F **67**
Bellfields, The S61: Thorpe H 3B **80**
BELL HAGG 3E **117**
Bellhagg Rd. S6: Shef 6A **106**
Bellhouse La. S43: Stav 3C **164**
Bellhouse M. S5: Shef 5B **94**
Bellhouse Rd. S5: Shef 1A **108**
Bellhouse Vw. S43: Stav 3C **164**
Bellis Av. DN4: Balb 4H **55**
Bellmer Cl. S71: Monk B 3F **17**
Bellmer Cft. S70: Birdw 6E **45**
Bellows Ct. S62: Rawm 3G **83**
Bellows Rd. S62: Rawm 3G **83**
Bellrope Acre DN3: Arm 5E **43**
Bells Cl. DN9: Blax 2F **77**
Bellscroft S73: Womb 3E **47**
Bellscroft Av. S65: Thry 6D **84**
Bells Sq. S1: Shef 3D **4** (3F **119**)
Bell St. S26: Aston 1E **139**
Bellwood Ct. S65: Rav 2B **100**
Bellwood Cres. S74: Hoyl 1H **61**
Belmont S72: Cud 4F **19**
Belmont Av. DN4: Balb 3B **56**
S35: Chap 3F **79**
S71: Smi 3G **17**
Belmont Cl. DN3: Brant 4H **59**
Belmont Cres. S72: Midd 3F **35**
Belmont Dr. S36: Pen 5E **177**
S36: Stoc 3E **175**
S43: Stav 4C **164**
Belmonte Gdns. S2: Shef . . .6H **5** (4H **119**)
Belmont Pk. S42: Holy 1A **170**
Belmont St. S41: Whit M 6H **161**
S61: Roth 4B **96**
S64: Mexb 2E **67**

Belper Rd. S7: Shef 2E **133**
Belridge Cl. S75: Barn 4A **16**
Belsize Rd. S10: Shef 6F **117**
Beltoft Way DN12: Con 3H **69**
Belton Cl. S18: Dron W 3B **154**
Belvedere DN4: Balb 6G **55**
Belvedere Av. S40: W'ton 2F **171**
Belvedere Cl. S25: Nth A 3A **142**
S40: Bramp 2B **170**
S72: Shaft 4F **11**
Belvedere Dr. S73: D'fld 3A **34**
Belvedere Pde. S66: Bram 3H **99**
Belvoir Av. DN5: Barnb 1H **51**
Ben Bank Rd. S75: Dod, Silk C 5B **28**
Bence Cl. S75: Dart 1F **15**
Bence Farm Ct. S75: Dart 1F **15**
Bence La. S75: Dart, Kexb 6D **6**
Ben Cl. S6: Shef 3G **105**
Benita Av. S64: Mexb 2H **67**
Ben La. S6: Shef 3G **105**
Benmore Dr. S20: Sot 1A **152**
Bennett Cl. S62: Rawm 1A **84**
Bennett Cft. S25: Nth A 3H **141**
Bennetthorpe DN2: Don 2D **56**
Bennett St. S2: Shef 6E **119**
S61: Kimb 4H **95**
Bennimoor Way S40: W'ton 2F **171**
Benson Rd. S2: Shef 4B **120**
Bentfield Av. S60: Roth 1B **112**
Bentham Dr. S71: Monk B 4A **18**
Bentham Rd. S40: C'fld 3F **167**
Bentham Way S75: Mapp 4H **7**
Bentinck Cl. DN1: Don 2C **56**
Bentinck Rd. S44: Shut 6H **165**
Bentinck St. DN12: Con 4G **69**
Bent La. S43: Stav 3D **164**
Bent Lathes Av. S60: Roth 1B **112**
BENTLEY 2A **40**
Bentley Av. DN4: Hex 2H **55**
Bentley Business Park 1 S25: Din . . .5G **127**
Bentley Business Park 2 S25: Din . . .5G **127**
Bentley Cl. S71: Monk B 3B **18**
Bentley Comn. La. DN5: Bntly 2B **40**
BENTLEY MOOR 2G **23**
Bentley Moor La. DN6: Adw S 1E **23**
Bentley Park Station (Rail) 2H **39**
BENTLEY RISE 4A **40**
Bentley Rd. DN5: Don 3H **39**
S6: Shef 1H **117**
S35: Chap 5G **79**
S66: Bram 6B **100**
Bentley St. S60: Roth 1E **111**
Benton Ct. S61: Kimb 3A **96**
Benton Ter. S64: Swin 5C **66**
Benton Way S61: Kimb 3A **96**
Bents Cl. S11: Shef 3F **131**
S35: Chap 4D **79**
Bents Cres. S11: Shef 4G **131**
S18: Dron 3F **155**
Bents Dr. S11: Shef 3F **131**
BENTS GREEN 3G **131**
Bents Grn. Av. S11: Shef 2F **131**
Bents Grn. Pl. S11: Shef 3F **131**
Bents Grn. Rd. S11: Shef 2G **131**
Bent's La. S18: Dron 1H **155**
Bents La. S18: Dron 1H **155**
Bents Rd. S11: Shef 3G **131**
S17: Tot 6D **144**
S61: Kimb P 2A **96**
Bents St. S36: Pen 3C **176**
Bents Vw. S11: Shef 3F **131**
Benty La. S10: Shef 3G **117**
Beresford Rd. S66: Malt 6C **102**
Beresford St. DN5: Bntly 1B **40**
Beresford Way S41: C'fld 4E **161**
Berkeley Cft. S71: R'ton 2G **9**
Berkeley Pct. S11: Shef 6C **118**
Berkley Cl. S70: Wors 5E **31**
Bernard Cl. S43: Brim 6E **163**
Bernard Gdns. S2: Shef 3H **119**
(off Hyde Pk. Ter.)
Bernard Rd. DN12: New E 5C **70**
S2: Shef 2H **119**
S4: Shef 2H **119**
Bernard St. S2: Shef 2H **5** (3H **119**)
S60: Roth 5F **97**
S62: Rawm 1A **84**
Berners Cl. S2: Shef 3B **134**
Berners Dr. S2: Shef 2B **134**
Berners Pl. S2: Shef 2B **134**
Berners Rd. S2: Shef 2B **134**

Berneslai Cl. S70: Barn 6D **16**
Berne Sq. S81: Woods 4E **143**
Bernshall Cres. S5: Shef 2G **93**
Berresford Rd. S11: Shef 6C **118**
Berrington Cl. DN4: Balb 2H **71**
Berry Av. S21: Ecki 1D **158**
Berrydale S70: Wors 5G **31**
Berry Dr. S26: Kiv P 5C **140**
Berry Edge Cl. DN12: Con 5H **69**
Berry Holme Cl. S35: Chap 3F **79**
Berry Holme Ct. S35: Chap 3F **79**
Berry Holme Dr. S35: Chap 3F **79**
Berry La. S35: Howb 6A **60**
Berrywell Av. S36: Pen 5E **177**
Bertram Rd. S35: Ough 4F **91**
Berwick Av. S40: W'ton 3D **170**
Berwick Cl. S40: W'ton 3D **170**
Berwick Cl. S40: W'ton 3D **170**
Berwick Way DN2: Don 5H **41**
Berwyn Cl. S40: C'fld 3D **166**
BESSACARR 6A **58**
Bessacarr La. DN4: Bess 6B **58**
Bessemer Pk. S60: Roth 6C **96**
Bessemer Pl. S9: Shef 1B **120**
Bessemer Rd. S9: Shef 6B **108**
Bessemer Ter. S36: Stoc 2D **174**
Bessemer Way S60: Roth 5B **96**
Bessingby Rd. S6: Shef 5B **106**
Bethel Gdns. S75: Mapp 6A **8**
Bethel Rd. S65: Roth 2G **97**
Bethel Wlk. S1: Shef 4D **4**
Betjeman Gdns. S10: Shef 5B **118**
Betony Cl. S21: Killa 5A **152**
Beulah Rd. S6: Shef 3C **106**
Bevan Av. DN11: New R 5C **74**
Bevan Cl. S74: Els 6D **46**
Bevan Cres. S66: Malt 4A **102**
Bevan Dr. S43: Ink 2G **169**
Bevan Way S35: Chap 3E **79**
Bevercotes Rd. S5: Shef 1A **108**
Beverley Av. S70: Wors 4E **31**
Beverley Cl. S26: Swal 1C **138**
S71: Smi 1D **16**
Beverley Gdns. DN5: Scaws 5E **39**
Beverley Rd. DN2: Don 4F **41**
Beverleys Rd. S8: Shef 4F **133**
Beverley St. S9: Shef 6D **108**
Bevin Pl. S62: Rawm 2A **84**
Bevre Rd. DN3: Arm 2E **43**
Bewdley Cl. S71: R'ton 2A **10**
Bewicke Av. DN5: Scaws 4E **39**
Bhatia Cl. S64: Mexb 1F **67**
Bib La. S25: Brookh 5F **115**
Bickerton Rd. S6: Shef 2B **106**
Bierlow Cl. S73: Bramp 4B **48**
Bigby Way S66: Bram 3A **100**
Bignor Pl. S6: Shef 5C **92**
Bignor Rd. S6: Shef 5C **92**
Big Six S60: Tree 2G **123**
Bilby La. S43: Brim 5D **162**
Bilham La. DN5: Hoot P 1H **37**
Billam Pl. S61: Kimb P 1H **95**
Billam St. S21: Ecki 1C **158**
BILLINGLEY 4G **35**
Billingley Dr. S63: Thurn 3B **36**
Billingley Grn. La. S72: Bill 4G **35**
Billingley La. S63: Thurn 3G **35**
Billingley Vw. S63: Bolt D 2A **50**
Bilston St. S6: Shef 5C **106**
Binders Rd. S61: Kimb P 1H **95**
Binfield Rd. S8: Shef 3E **133**
Bingham Cl. S10: Shef 6H **117**
Bingham Pk. Cres. S11: Shef 1A **132**
Bingham Pk. Rd. S11: Shef 1H **131**
Bingham Rd. S8: Shef 6E **133**
Bingley Cl. S75: Barn 6C **16**
Bingley La. S6: Stan 2B **116**
Bingley St. S75: Barn 6C **16**
Binsted Av. S5: Shef 6C **92**
Binsted Cl. S5: Shef 1C **106**
Binsted Cres. S5: Shef 1C **106**
Binsted Cft. S5: Shef 1C **106**
Binsted Dr. S5: Shef 1C **106**
Binsted Gdns. S5: Shef 1C **106**
Binsted Glade S5: Shef 1C **106**
Binsted Gro. S5: Shef 1C **106**
Binsted Rd. S5: Shef 1C **106**
Binsted Way S5: Shef 1C **106**
Biram Wlk. S74: Els 2E **63**
(off Wath Rd.)
Birchall Av. S60: Whis 3A **112**

Birch Av. DN9: Auck 3B 76
S35: Chap 4F 79
Birch Cl. DN5: Sprot 3E 55
S21: Killa 5B 152
Birch Ct. S64: Swin 3B 66
Birch Cres. S66: Wick 5H 99
Birchdale Cl. DN3: Eden 1C 42
Birchen Cl. DN4: Bess 1B 74
S18: Dron W 3C 154
S40: C'fld 3E 167
Birches Fold S18: Coal A 6H 147
Birches La. S18: Coal A 6H 147
Birch Farm Av. S8: Shef 2F 147
Birchfield Cres. S75: Dod 2H 29
Birchfield Rd. S66: Malt 5C 102
Birchfield Wlk. S75: Barn 6A 16
Birch Grn. Cl. S66: Malt 4G 101
Birch Gro. DN12: Con 4G 69
S35: Ough 4F 91
Birch Hall Golf Course 1F 161
Birch Holt Gro. S18: Uns 1F 161
Birch Ho. Av. S35: Ough 4E 91
Birchin Bank S74: Els 6C 46
Birchitt Cl. S17: Bradw 5B 146
Birchitt Pl. S17: Bradw 5B 146
Birchitt Rd. S17: Bradw 5B 146
Birchitt Vw. S18: Dron 1F 155
Birch Kiln Cft. S43: Brim 1E 169
Birchlands Dr. S21: Killa 5C 152
Birch La. S43: Hol 5F 163
Birch Pk. Ct. S61: Roth 4B 96
Birch Rd. DN4: Can 4C 58
S9: Shef 6B 108
S70: Barn 3A 32
Birch Tree Cl. DN3: Barn D 1D 26
Birch Tree Rd. S36: Stoc 4D 174
Birchtree Rd. S61: Thorpe H 5C 80
Birchvale Rd. S12: Shef 5G 135
Birchwood Av. S62: Rawm 2G 83
Birchwood Cl. S20: W'fld 2F 151
S66: Malt 4G 101
Birchwood Ct. DN4: Bess 1E 75
S40: Birdh 3G 171
Birchwood Cres. S40: Birdh 3G 171
Birchwood Cft. S20: W'fld 2F 151
Birchwood Dell DN4: Bess 1E 75
Birchwood Dr. S65: Rav 2A 100
Birchwood Gdns. S20: W'fld 2F 151
S66: B'well 6B 88
Birchwood Gro. S20: W'fld 2F 151
Birchwood La. S66: Malt 3B 102
Birchwood Ri. S20: W'fld 2F 151
Birchwood Rd. S21: Mar L, Trow ..1G 157
Birchwood Vw. S20: W'fld 2F 151
Birchwood Way S20: W'fld 2F 151
Bircotes Wlk. DN11: Ross 5E 75
Bird Av. S73: Womb 2F 47
BIRDHOLME 3H 171
Birdholme Cres. S40: Birdh 2H 171
Bird La. DN5: Clay 1H 21
Bird St. S43: Stav 4C 164
BIRDWELL 4E 45
Birdwell Comn. S70: Birdw 6E 45
Birdwell Rd. S4: Shef 3C 108
S64: Kiln 6C 66
S75: Dod 4A 30
Birk Av. S70: Barn 3H 31
Birkbeck Ct. S35: High G 6C 60
Birk Cres. S70: Barn 3H 31
Birkdale Av. S25: Din 6A 128
Birkdale Cl. DN4: Can 6E 59
S72: Cud 6F 11
Birkdale Dr. S40: W'ton 2D 170
Birkdale Ri. S64: Swin 4C 66
Birkdale Rd. S71: R'ton 1G 9
BIRKENDALE 1C 118
Birkendale S6: Shef 1C 118
Birkendale Rd. S6: Shef 1C 118
Birkendale Vw. S6: Shef 1C 118
Birk Grn. S70: Barn 3A 32
Birk Ho. La. S70: Barn 3A 32
Birklands Av. S13: Shef 5H 121
Birklands Cl. S13: Shef 5H 121
Birklands Dr. S13: Shef 5H 121
Birk Rd. S70: Barn 3H 31
Birks Av. S13: Shef 2C 136
Birks Holt Dr. S66: Malt 6D 102
Birks Rd. S61: Kimb P 1H 95
Birks Wood Dr. S35: Ough 4E 91
Birk Ter. S70: Barn 3H 31
Birkwood Av. S72: Cud 4F 19

Birkwood Ter. S66: B'well 1C 102
Birley Brook Dr. S41: C'fld 1C 166
BIRLEY CARR 5B 92
Birley Cft. S41: C'fld 1C 166
BIRLEY EDGE 4A 92
BIRLEY ESTATE 5H 135
BIRLEYHAY 5G 149
Birley La. S12: Shef 6F 135
Birley Lane Stop (ST) 6H 135
Birley Moor Av. S12: Shef 5H 135
Birley Moor Cl. S12: Shef 5H 135
Birley Moor Cres. S12: Shef 5H 135
Birley Moor Dr. S12: Shef 6H 135
Birley Moor Pl. S12: Shef 5H 135
Birley Moor Rd. S12: Shef 3G 135
Birley Moor Road Stop (ST) 4A 136
Birley Moor Way S12: Shef 6H 135
Birley Ri. Cres. S6: Shef 6B 92
Birley Ri. Rd. S6: Shef 6B 92
Birley Spa 4A 136
Birley Spa Cl. S12: Shef 4C 136
Birley Spa Dr. S12: Shef 4C 136
Birley Spa La. S12: Shef 5A 136
Birley Spa Wlk. S12: Shef 4C 136
(off Carter Lodge Dr.)
Birley Va. Av. S12: Shef 4F 135
Birley Va. Cl. S12: Shef 4F 135
Birley Vw. S35: Ough 5E 91
Birley Wood Dr. S12: Shef 6A 136
Birley Wood Golf Course 6H 135
Birstall Cl. S41: C'fld 1D 166
Birthwaite Rd. S75: Kexb 5C 6
Birtley St. S66: Malt 5G 101
Bisby Rd. S62: Rawm 2H 83
Biscay La. S63: Wath D 5F 49
Biscay Way S63: Wath D 6G 49
Bishopdale Ct. S20: Mosb 1B 150
Bishopdale Dr. S20: Mosb 2B 150
Bishopdale Ri. S20: Mosb 2B 150
Bishop Gdns. S13: Shef 2B 136
Bishopgarth Cl. DN5: Don 4A 40
Bishop Hill S13: Shef 2B 136
Bishops Cl. S8: Shef 3G 133
Bishopscourt Rd. S8: Shef 3F 133
Bishopsgate La.
DN11: New R 6H 75
Bishopsholme Cl. S5: Shef 2F 107
Bishopsholme Rd. S5: Shef 2F 107
Bishop's House
Sheffield 3F 133
Bishopstoke Ct. S65: Roth 3H 97
Bishopston Wlk. S66: Malt 4H 101
Bishop St. S1: Shef 6C 4 (4E 119)
Bishops Wlk. S26: Kiv P 5B 140
Bishops Way S20: C'fld 2H 167
S71: Monk B 5H 17
Bisley Cl. S71: R'ton 3B 10
Bismarck St. S70: Barn 3E 31
Bitholmes Ga. S35: Wharn S 1A 90
Bitholmes La. S36: Spink 5H 175
Bittern Cft. S73: Bramp 3B 48
Bitterne Cft. S73: Bramp 3C 48
Bittern Vw. S61: Thorpe H 2D 80
Blackamoor S64: Swin 5F 65
Blacka Moor Cres. S17: Dore 4D 144
Blacka Moor Nature Reserve 4A 144
Blackamoor Rd. S64: Swin 5F 65
Blacka Moor Vw. S17: Dore 4D 144
Blackberry Flats S20: Half 3F 151
(off Halfway Dr.)
Blackbird Av. S60: Brins 4E 111
Blackbrook Av. S10: Shef 5A 116
Blackbrook Dr. S10: Shef 5A 116
Blackbrook Rd. S10: Shef 5A 116
BLACKBURN 4E 95
Blackburn Cres. S35: Chap 2D 78
Blackburn Cft. S35: Chap 2E 79
Blackburn Dr. S35: Chap 3D 78
Blackburne St. S6: Shef 5C 106
Blackburn La. S61: Kimb 4E 95
S70: Wors 5F 31
S75: Barn 6C 16
Blackburn Meadows Nature Reserve
...........................5A 96
Blackburn Rd. S61: Kimb 4E 95
Blackburn St. S70: Wors 5F 31
Black Carr Rd. S66: Wick 5F 99
Blackdown Av. S20: Water 6E 137
S40: C'fld 3D 166
Blackdown Cl. S20: Water 6E 137

Blacker Grange S74: Black H 4A 46
Blackergreen La. S75: Silk, Silk C ..3A 28
BLACKER HILL 3A 46
Blacker La. S70: Wors 2F 45
S72: Shaft 3F 11
S74: Black H 2F 45
Blacker Rd. S75: Mapp, Stain 5B 8
Blackheath Cl. S71: Ath 1G 17
Blackheath Rd. S71: Ath 1G 17
Blackheath Wlk. S71: Ath 1G 17
Black Hill Rd. S65: Roth 6C 98
Black Horse Cl. S75: Silk C 5B 28
Black Horse Dr. S75: Silk C 5B 28
Black La. S6: Lox 5E 105
S74: Hoyl 2E 61
S81: Woods 5G 143
Blackmoor Cres. S40: Brins 3C 110
Blackmore St. S40: Barn 1A 120
Blacksmith Cl. S61: Thorpe H 4C 80
Blacksmith La. S35: Gren 2B 92
S44: Cal 4F 169
Blacksmith Sq. S74: Els 2E 63
(off Wath Rd.)
Blackstock Cl. S14: Shef 6A 134
Blackstock Cres. S14: Shef 6A 134
Blackstock Dr. S14: Shef 6A 134
Blackstock Rd. S14: Shef 3A 134
Black Stone La. DN9: Blax 2E 77
Blackthorn Av. S66: Bram 5H 99
Blackthorn Cl. S35: High G 6C 60
S41: Has 2C 172
Blackthorne Cl. DN12: New E 5B 70
Blackthorne Ct. S70: Barn 3H 31
Blackthorn Ri. S65: Rav 2B 100
Blackwell Cl. S2: Shef ...3H 5 (3H 119)
Blackwell Ct. S2: Shef ...3H 5 (3H 119)
Blackwell Pl. S2: Shef ...3H 5 (3H 119)
Blackwood Av. DN4: Balb 6G 55
Blagden St. S2: Shef 3H 119
Blair Athol Rd. S11: Shef 2A 132
Blake Av. DN2: Don 4E 41
S63: Wath D 5D 48
Blake Cl. S66: Bram 1B 144
Blake Gro. Rd. S6: Shef 1D 118
Blakeley Cl. S71: Ath 1G 17
Blakeney M. S25: Laugh C 4F 127
(off Mountfield Way)
Blakeney Rd. S10: Shef 3B 118
Blake St. S6: Shef 1C 118
Blandford Dr. S41: C'fld 1F 167
Bland La. S6: Shef 3G 105
(not continuous)
Bland St. S4: Shef 4B 108
Blast La. S2: Shef 2H 119
(Broad St.)
S2: Shef 2H 5 (2H 119)
(Sheffield Parkway)
S4: Shef 1H 5 (2H 119)
BLAXTON 1F 77
Blaxton Cl. S20: Mosb 6B 136
Blay Ct. S43: New W 2C 162
(off High St.)
Blayton Rd. S4: Shef 4H 107
Bleachcroft Way S70: Stair 3B 32
Bleak Av. S72: Shaft 4F 11
Bleakley Av. WF4: Nott 1G 9
Bleakley Cl. S72: Shaft 4F 11
Bleakley La. WF4: Nott 1G 9
Bleakley Ter. WF4: Nott 1G 9
Bleasdale Gro. S71: Monk B 4F 17
Blenheim Av. S70: Barn 2D 30
Blenheim Cl. S25: Din 6H 127
S66: Bram 3H 99
Blenheim Ct. S66: Flan 4G 99
Blenheim Cres. S64: Mexb 1E 67
Blenheim Dr. DN9: Finn 3E 77
Blenheim Gro. S70: Barn 2C 30
Blenheim M. S11: Shef 3H 131
Blenheim Rd. S70: Barn 2C 30
Bloemfontein St. S72: Cud 2D 18
Blonk St. S1: Shef 1G 5 (2G 119)
S3: Shef 1G 5 (2G 119)
Bloomfield Ho. S75: Silk C 5B 28
Bloomfield Ri. S75: Dart 5H 7
Bloomfield Rd. S75: Dart 5G 7
BLOOMHOUSE 4H 7
Bloomhouse La. S75: Dart 4F 7
Bloomingdale Ct. S75: Wool G 3F 7
Blossom Av. S65: Thry 6D 84
Blossom Cres. S12: Shef 5E 135

Blossoms, The—Bradway Dr.

Blossoms, The S75: Barn 6C **16**
Blossom Way S63: Thurn 1C **36**
Blow Hall Riding DN12: New E 5E **71**
Blucher St. S70: Barn 1D **30**
Bluebank Vw. S43: New W 3C **162**
Bluebell Av. S36: Pen 4C **176**
Bluebell Bank S70: Barn 3F **31**
Blue Bell Cl. S43: Ink 3G **169**
Bluebell Cl. S5: Shef 1B **108**
S74: Hoyl 2H **61**
Blue Bell Ct. DN9: Blax 1F **77**
Bluebell La. S66: Thurc 1C **126**
Bluebell Rd. S5: Shef 1C **108**
S75: Dart 3F **7**
Bluebell Wood La. S66: Sunn 3G **99**
Blueberry Cl. S43: Ink 3G **169**
Blueberry Ct. S66: Sunn 3G **99**
Bluebird Hill S26: Aston 2D **138**
Blue Boy St. S3: Shef 1C **4** (2E **119**)
Bluecoat Ri. S11: Shef 1B **132**
Blue Lodge Cl. S43: Ink 3G **169**
Blue Mans Way S60: Cat 1D **122**
Blue Ridge Cl. S17: Dore 3F **145**
Blundell Cl. DN4: Can 5B **58**
Blundell Ct. S71: Monk B 3A **18**
Blunt Av. S43: Mas M 2F **165**
Blyde Rd. S5: Shef 3H **107**
Bly Rd. S73: D'fld 4A **34**
Blyth Av. S62: Rawm 3G **83**
Blyth Cl. S40: W'ton 2C **170**
S60: Whis 3C **112**
Blythe St. S73: Womb 1F **47**
Blyth Rd. S66: Malt 6A **102**
Boardman Av. S62: Rawm 6D **64**
Boat La. DN5: Sprot 4C **54**
Bobbin Mill La. S40: C'fld 6E **167**
Bochum Parkway S8: Shef 3F **147**
Bocking Cl. S8: Shef 1C **146**
Bocking Hill S36: Stoc 3F **175**
Bocking La. S8: Shef 1C **146**
Bocking Ri. S8: Shef 2D **146**
Boden La. S1: Shef 3C **4** (3E **119**)
Boden Pl. S9: Shef 1F **121**
Bodmin Ct. S71: Monk B 5G **17**
Bodmin St. S9: Shef 6C **108**
Bodmin Way S40: C'fld 3D **166**
Boggard La. S35: Ough 4D **90**
S36: Pen 5C **176**
Boiley La. S21: Killa 6A **152**
Boland Rd. S8: Shef 5C **146**
Bold St. S9: Shef 5D **108**
Bole Cl. S73: Womb 6A **34**
BOLE HILL 1G 123
BOLEHILL
S44 1G 173
S8 6F 133
Bole Hill S8: Shef 6F **133**
S44: Cal 1F **173**
S60: Tree 1F **123**
Bole Hill Cl. S6: Shef 6A **106**
Bole Hill La. S10: Shef 2H **117**
Bolehill La. S21: Ecki, Mar L 2A **158**
Bole Hill Rd. S6: Shef 2G **117**
Bolehill Vw. S10: Shef 1A **118**
Bolsover Rd. S5: Shef 2A **108**
S43: Mas M, Woodt 2G **165**
Bolsover Rd. E. S5: Shef 3A **108**
Bolsover St. S3: Shef 3A **4** (3D **118**)
BOLSTERSTONE 6E 175
Bolton Hill Rd. DN4: Bess 6B **58**
(not continuous)
Bolton-on-Dearne Station (Rail) 2C 50
Bolton Rd. S63: Wath D 6B **50**
S64: Swin 3A **66**
Bolton St. DN12: Den M 2C **68**
S3: Shef 5B **4** (4E **119**)
BOLTON UPON DEARNE 2B 50
Bond S6: Shef 1A **4** (2D **118**)
Bond Cl. DN1: Don 2B **56**
Bondfield Av. DN11: New R 6D **74**
Bondfield Cl. S73: Womb 2G **47**
Bondfield Cres. S73: Womb 2F **47**
Bondfield Cres. Flats S73: Womb 2F **47**
(not continuous)
Bondfield Rd. S43: Ink 1H **169**
Bond Rd. S75: Barn 5C **16**
Bond St. DN11: New R 6G **75**
S43: Stav 6H **163**
S73: Womb 1G **47**
Bonet La. S60: Brins 3B **110**
Bonington Ri. S66: Malt 4H **101**
Bonsall Ct. *S41: C'fld 1E* ***167***
(off Newbold Rd.)
Bonville Gdns. S3: Shef 1B **4**
Booker Cl. S43: Ink 2H **169**
Booker Rd. S8: Shef 6D **132**
Bookers La. S25: Din 4E **127**
(not continuous)
Bookers Way S25: Din 5E **127**
Booth Av. DN4: Don 3G **57**
Booth Cl. S20: Water 6E **137**
S66: Thurc 6D **114**
Booth Cft. S20: Water 6E **137**
Booth Pl. S62: Rawm 1F **83**
Booth Rd. S35: High G 1B **78**
Booth St. S61: Grea 4C **82**
S74: Hoyl 6C **46**
Bootle St. S9: Shef 6D **108**
Borough M. *S6: Shef 1E* ***119***
(off Bedford St.)
Borough Rd. S6: Shef 4B **106**
Borrowdale Av. S20: Half 4F **151**
Borrowdale Cl. S20: Half 4F **151**
S71: Ard 2D **32**
Borrowdale Cres.
S25: Din, Nth A 1A **142**
Borrowdale Dr. S20: Half 4F **151**
Borrowdale Rd. S20: Half 4F **151**
Boston Castle 6E 97
Boston Castle Gro. S60: Roth 6F **97**
Boston Castle Ter. S60: Roth 6F **97**
Boston St. S2: Shef 5E **119**
Bosville Cl. S65: Rav 5A **86**
Bosville Rd. S10: Shef 3A **118**
Bosville St. S36: Pen 5E **177**
S65: Roth 2C **98**
Boswell Cl. DN11: New R 6B **74**
S35: High G 6B **60**
S71: R'ton 2G **9**
Boswell Ct. DN4: Bess 5A **58**
Boswell Rd. DN4: Bess 5H **57**
S63: Wath D 2G **65**
Boswell St. S65: Roth 5G **97**
Bosworth Rd. DN6: Adw S 2B **22**
Bosworth St. S10: Shef 2A **118**
Botanical Rd. S11: Shef 5B **118**
Botany Bay La. DN3: Barn D 1F **27**
Botham St. S4: Shef 4B **108**
Botsford St. S3: Shef 6F **107**
Boulder Bri. La. S71: Car 4C **10**
BOULDER HILL 4A 106
Boulevard, The DN3: Eden 6B **26**
Boulton Cl. S40: C'fld 3B **166**
Boulton Dr. DN3: Can 3E **59**
Boundary Av. DN2: Don 3H **41**
Boundary Cl. DN12: New E 3D **70**
S43: Stav 3D **164**
Boundary Dr. S72: Brier 3B **12**
Boundary Grn. S62: Rawm 4H **83**
Boundary Rd. S2: Shef 4A **120**
Boundary St. S70: Barn 2G **31**
Boundary Wlk. S60: Brins 4B **110**
Bourne Cl. S43: Brim 5D **162**
Bourne Ct. S75: Stain 4B **8**
Bourne Rd. S5: Shef 6H **93**
S70: Wors 6E **31**
Bourne Wlk. S75: Stain 4B **8**
Bow Bri. Cl. S60: Roth 6D **96**
BOW BROOM 2C 66
Bowden Gro. S75: Dod 3G **29**
Bowden Housteads Wood and
Carbrook Ravine Nature Reserve
4G 121
Bowden Wood Av. S9: Shef 4F **121**
Bowden Wood Cl. S9: Shef 4F **121**
Bowden Wood Cres. S9: Shef 4F **121**
Bowden Wood Dr. S9: Shef 4F **121**
Bowden Wood Pl. S9: Shef 4F **121**
Bowden Wood Rd. S9: Shef 4F **121**
Bowdon St. S1: Shef 5C **4** (4E **119**)
Bowen Dr. S65: Thry 6E **85**
Bowen Rd. S65: Roth 2G **97**
Bower Cl. S61: Kimb P 1H **95**
Bower Farm Rd. S41: Old W 4A **162**
Bower Hill S36: Oxs 6H **177**
Bower Ho. S35: Gren 1B **92**
Bower La. S35: Gren 1A **92**
Bower Rd. S10: Shef 2C **118**
S64: Swin 1C **66**
Bowers Fold DN1: Don 1C **56**
Bower Spring S3: Shef 1E **5**
Bower Va. DN12: New E 5B **70**
Bowes Rd. DN3: Eden 1B **42**
Bowfell Vw. S71: Monk B 4F **17**
Bowfield Ct. *S5: Shef 6H* ***93***
(off Etwall Way)
Bowfield Rd. S5: Shef 6H **93**
Bowland Cl. DN5: Scawt 2G **39**
Bowland Cres. S70: Wors 6E **31**
Bowland Dr. S35: Chap 3D **78**
S42: W'ton 3C **170**
Bowlease Gdns. DN4: Can 4B **58**
Bowling Grn. St.
S3: Shef 1D **4** (1F **119**)
Bowman Cl. S12: Shef 6C **134**
Bowman Dr. S12: Shef 6C **134**
S66: Malt 3H **101**
Bowness Cl. S18: Dron W 3D **154**
S41: C'fld 1E **167**
Bowness Gro. S63: Bolt D 3B **50**
Bowness Rd. S6: Shef 5B **106**
S41: C'fld 1E **167**
Bowood Rd. S11: Shef 6C **118**
Bow Royd S73: Womb 1H **47**
BOWSHAW 6E 147
Bowshaw S18: Dron 1E **155**
Bowshaw Av. S8: Shef 5F **147**
Bowshaw Cl. S8: Shef 5F **147**
Bowshaw Vw. S8: Shef 5F **147**
Bow St. S72: Cud 1E **19**
Boyce St. S6: Shef 1C **118**
Boyd Rd. S63: Wath D 3G **65**
Boyland St. S3: Shef 6E **107**
Boynton Cres. S5: Shef 2F **107**
Boynton Rd. S5: Shef 3E **107**
(not continuous)
BOYTHORPE 1G 171
Boythorpe Av. S40: C'fld 6F **167**
Boythorpe Cres. S40: C'fld 1G **171**
Boythorpe Mt. S40: C'fld 6G **167**
Boythorpe Ri. S40: C'fld 6F **167**
Boythorpe Rd. S40: C'fld 6G **167**
Brackenbury Cl. DN5: Cad 6G **53**
Bracken Cl. DN3: Brant 3H **59**
Bracken Ct. S66: Wick 1G **113**
S70: Barn 3G **31**
Brackendale Cl. S43: Brim 1C **168**
Brackenfield Gro. S12: Shef 4G **135**
Bracken Hill S35: Burn 4C **78**
Bracken Hill La. DN10: Miss 6H **77**
BRACKEN MOOR 4E 175
Bracken Moor La. S36: Stoc 4E **175**
Bracken Rd. S5: Shef 6B **94**
(not continuous)
Brackley St. S3: Shef 6G **107**
Bradberry Balk La.
S73: Womb 6F **33**
Bradbourne Cl. S43: Stav 6H **163**
Bradbury Cl. S40: C'fld 5F **167**
Bradbury Dr. S42: W'orth 6F **171**
Bradbury Hall *S40: C'fld 5F* ***167***
(off Chatsworth Rd.)
Bradbury's Cl. S62: P'gte 5G **83**
Bradbury St. S8: Shef 2F **133**
S70: Barn 1C **30**
Bradfield Rd. S6: Shef 4B **106**
Bradfield Way S60: Wav 2C **122**
Bradford Rd. DN2: Don 2H **41**
Bradford Row DN1: Don 1C **56**
BRADGATE 3B 96
Bradgate Cl. S61: Kimb 3B **96**
Bradgate Ct. S61: Kimb 3A **96**
Bradgate Cft. S41: Has 3B **172**
Bradgate Ho. Cl. S61: Kimb 3B **96**
Bradgate La. S61: Kimb 3A **96**
Bradgate Pl. S61: Kimb 2B **96**
Bradgate Rd. S61: Kimb 2B **96**
Bradlea Ri. S62: Rawm 1H **83**
Bradley Av. S73: Womb 1F **47**
Bradley Cl. S43: Brim 1D **168**
Bradley St. S10: Shef 1A **118**
Bradley Way S43: Brim 6D **162**
Bradman Wlk. S62: Rawm 6D **64**
Bradmarsh Way S60: Roth 6D **96**
Bradshaw Av. S60: Tree 3G **123**
Bradshaw Cl. S75: Barn 6H **15**
Bradshaw Rd. S43: Ink 2G **169**
Bradshaw Way S60: Tree 3G **123**
Bradstone Rd. S65: Roth 3B **98**
BRADWAY 5A 146
BRADWAY BANK 4A 146
Bradway Cl. S17: Bradw 5A **146**
Bradway Dr. S17: Bradw 5A **146**

Bradway Grange Rd.
S17: Bradw 5B 146
Bradway Rd. S17: Bradw 5A 146
Bradwell Av. S75: Dod 4H 29
Bradwell Cl. S18: Dron W 3B 154
Bradwell Pl. S43: Ink 1H 169
Bradwell St. S2: Shef 2G 133
Braeburn Cl. S66: Malt 3G 101
Braemar Cl. S43: New W 2C 162
Braemar Rd. DN2: Don 1F 57
Braemore Rd. S6: Shef 3H 105
Braidwood Way S40: C'fld 6H 167
Brailsford Av. S5: Shef 2F 93
Brailsford Cl. S5: Shef 2F 93
Brailsford Rd. S5: Shef 2F 93
Braithwaite M. S75: Mapp 5B 8
(off Braithwaite St.)
Braithwaite St. S75: Stain 5B 8
BRAITHWELL 6B 88
Braithwell Cl. DN5: Bntly 5H 23
Braithwell Rd. DN5: Bntly 6H 23
S65: Rav 2A 100
S66: Malt 5A 102
Braithwell Wlk.
DN12: Den M 2C 68
Braithwell Way S66: Hel 3D 100
Bramah St. S71: Car 5H 9
Bramall Cl. S2: Shef 6F 119
Bramall Lane 5F 119
Bramall La. S2: Shef 5F 119
S36: Stoc 1B 174
Bramble Cl. S66: Wick 1G 113
Bramble Rd. S72: Sth H 1H 11
Brambles, The S35: Eccl 2F 93
S71: R'ton 2F 9
Bramble Way DN9: Auck 2B 76
S63: Wath D 6C 48
Brambling Cl. S41: C'fld 5B 168
Brambling La. S63: Wath D 4F 49
Bramblings, The DN4: Can 6D 58
Bramcote Av. S71: Ath 6D 8
Brameld Rd. S62: Rawm 3G 83
S64: Swin 3A 66
Bramhall Cl. S73: Womb 3E 47
Bramham Ct. S9: Shef 1E 121
(off Bramham Rd.)
Bramham Cft. S73: Womb 6A 34
Bramham Rd. DN4: Can 2C 58
S9: Shef 1E 121
BRAMLEY
S21 . . . . .6H 149
S66 . . . . .5A 100
Bramley Av. S13: Shef 6A 122
S26: Aston 6D 124
Bramley Carr S70: Barn 3A 30
Bramley Cl. S20: Mosb 3D 150
S43: Ink 3G 169
Bramley Ct. DN12: Den M 3C 68
S10: Shef 3A 118
Bramley Dr. S13: Shef 5A 122
Bramley Grange Cres. S66: Bram . .5B 100
Bramley Grange Dr. S66: Bram . .5B 100
Bramley Grange Ri. S66: Bram . .5B 100
Bramley Grange Vw. S66: Bram . .4B 100
Bramley Grange Way S66: Bram . .5C 100
Bramley Hall Rd. S13: Shef 6A 122
Bramley La. S13: Shef 5A 122
S65: Rav 2D 100
BRAMLEY LINGS 1A 114
Bramley M. S21: Ecki 1E 159
BRAMLEY MOOR 1G 157
Bramleymoor La. S21: Mar L . . .4G 157
Bramley Pk. Cl. S13: Shef 6A 122
Bramley Pk. Mobile Home Site
S21: Mar L 1A 158
Bramley Pk. Rd. S13: Shef 5A 122
Bramley Rd. S21: Mar L 3H 157
Bramley Way S66: Hel 4D 100
BRAMPTON
S40 . . . . .6C 166
S63 .5A 48
Brampton Av. S66: Thurc 6A 114
Brampton Beck S73: Bramp 3B 48
BRAMPTON BIERLOW 5B 48
Brampton Cl. DN3: Arm 5D 42
Brampton Ct. S20: Mosb 6B 136
S40: Bramp 5D 166
Brampton Cres. S73: Womb 4C 48
BRAMPTON EN LE MORTHEN 1A 126
Brampton La. DN3: Arm 5D 42
S26: Ull 2G 125

Brampton Manor Health & Fitness Club
. . . . .5D 166
Brampton Mdws. S66: Thurc . . .6A 114
Brampton Rd. S63: Wath D 5C 48
S66: Bramp M, Thurc 1H 125
S73: Bramp 5C 48
S73: Womb 3A 48
Brampton St. S73: Bramp 4C 48
Brampton Vw. S73: Womb 3A 48
Bramshill Cl. S20: Sot 1H 151
Bramshill Ct. S20: Sot 1H 151
Bramshill Ri. S40: W'ton 1E 171
Bramwell Cl. S3: Shef 2A 4 (2D 118)
Bramwell Ct. S3: Shef 2A 4 (2D 118)
Bramwell Dr. S3: Shef 2A 4 (2D 118)
Bramwell St. S3: Shef 2A 4 (2D 118)
S65: Roth 3F 97
Bramwith La. DN3: Barn D 1G 27
DN7: Sth B 1G 27
Bramwith Rd. S11: Shef 6G 117
Bramworth Rd. DN4: Hex 3G 55
Branchcroft Dr. DN4: Balb 2A 72
Brandene Cl. S44: Cal 5F 169
Brander Cl. DN4: Balb 1B 72
Brand La.
DN5: High M, Sprot 1H 53, 6A 38
Brandon St. S3: Shef 5G 107
Brandreth Cl. S6: Shef 1D 118
Brandreth Rd. S6: Shef 1D 118
Brands Cl. S81: Woods 3F 143
Brand's La. S25: Din 1C 142
S81: Gild 1C 142
Brandsmere Dr. S81: Woods . . .3F 143
Branksome Av. S70: Barn 1B 30
Branksome Chine Av. S41: Has . .3B 172
Bransby St. S6: Shef 1C 118
Branstone Rd. DN5: Sprot 2C 54
BRANTON 4G 59
Branton Cl. S40: C'fld 1G 171
Branton Ga. Rd. DN3: Brant 3H 59
Branton Ter. DN3: Brant 4G 59
(off Moor Gap)
Brantwood Cres. DN4: Can 3C 58
Brathay Cl. S4: Shef 3C 108
Brathay Rd. S4: Shef 3C 108
Brayford Rd. DN4: Balb 2A 72
Bray St. S9: Shef 1D 120
Brayton Dr. DN4: Balb 2A 72
Bray Wlk. S61: Kimb P 6F 81
Brearley Av. S36: Spink 4F 175
S43: New W 3C 162
Brearley Cen., The S9: Tins 5G 109
Brearley Dr. S5: Shef 6E 93
Brearley Hall S41: Old W 2B 162
Brearley St. S41: Old W 3B 162
Breckland Rd. S40: W'ton 2C 170
Brecklands S60: Roth 6B 98
S66: Wick 6F 99
Breck La. S25: Din 4A 128
S43: Bar H 2H 163
BRECKS 6D 98
Brecks Cres. S65: Roth 5D 98
Brecks La. DN3: Kirk Sa 4C 26
S65: Roth 3C 98
Brecon Cl. S20: Sot 6H 137
S40: C'fld 3D 166
Brendon Av. S40: C'fld 4D 166
Brendon Cl. S73: Womb 4A 48
Brent Cl. S40: C'fld 3E 167
Brentwood Av. S11: Shef 2C 132
Brentwood Cl. S74: Hoyl 2H 61
Brentwood Rd. S11: Shef 2C 132
Brentwood Vs. S65: Roth 3F 97
Bressingham Cl. S4: Shef 6H 107
Bressingham Rd. S4: Shef 6H 107
Bressingham Rd. Nth. S4: Shef . .6G 107
Bretby Cl. DN4: Can 5C 58
Bretby Rd. S40: C'fld 2B 166
Brettas Pk. S71: Monk B 3F 17
Brett Cl. S62: Rawm 6D 64
Bretton Cl. S40: Ash 3B 166
S72: Brier 4B 12
S75: Kexb 6D 6
Bretton Country Pk. 1A 6
Bretton Gro. S12: Shef 5G 135
Bretton Ho. DN1: Don 2B 56
(off St James St.)
Bretton Rd. S75: Kexb 6D 6
Bretton Vw. S72: Cud 3D 18
Brewery Rd. S63: Wath D 5G 49
Brewery St. S41: C'fld 5A 168

Brew Ho., The S11: Shef 5E 119
(off Napier St.)
Breydon Av. DN5: Cus 5F 39
Breydon Ct. DN5: Cus 5F 39
Briar Cl. DN9: Auck 2B 76
S41: C'fld 3F 167
Briar Ct. S66: Wick 1G 113
Briar Cft. DN4: Balb 4H 55
Briardene Cl. S40: C'fld 3A 166
Briarfield Av. S12: Shef 5D 134
Briarfield Cres. S12: Shef 5D 134
Briarfield Rd. S12: Shef 5D 134
Briarfields La. S35: Ough 5D 90
Briar Gro. S36: Cub 5D 176
S72: Brier 3B 12
Briar Ri. S70: Wors 6F 31
Briar Rd. DN3: Arm 2D 42
S7: Shef 2D 132
Briars Cl. S21: Killa 5C 152
Briars Fold DN9: Blax 1F 77
Briar Vw. S43: Brim 1D 168
Briarwood Gdns.
S66: Sunn 2G 99
Briary Av. S35: High G 1C 78
Briary Cl. S60: Brins 5D 110
Brick Dr. S10: Shef 2D 118
Brickhouse La. S17: Dore 2D 144
BRICK HOUSES 2D 144
Brickhouse Yd. S40: C'fld 5F 167
Brick St. S10: Shef 2A 118
Brickyard, The S72: Shaft 5F 11
Brickyard Wlk. S40: C'fld 5H 167
Bridby St. S13: Shef 2E 137
Bridge Bank Cl. S40: C'fld 2D 166
Bridge Bus. Pk. S41: C'fld 4E 161
BRIDGE END 3C 176
Bridge End La. S63: Wath D 4E 49
Bridge Gdns. S71: Barn 5E 17
Bridgegate S60: Roth 3E 97
Bridge Gro. DN5: Cus 5G 39
Bridge Hill S35: Ough 3E 91
Bridgehouses S3: Shef 1F 119
BRIDGEHOUSES RDBT. 1F 119
Bridge Inn Rd. S35: Chap 2F 79
Bridgelake Dr. DN4: Balb 2A 72
Bridge Rd. DN4: Bess 4H 57
Bridge Side S36: Pen 4E 177
Bridge St. DN4: Hex 2A 56
S3: Shef 1E 5 (1F 119)
S21: Killa 3C 152
S36: Pen 3C 176
S40: C'fld 1H 171
S60: Roth 3E 97
S63: Bolt D 1C 50
S64: Swin 3D 66
S71: Barn 5E 17
S75: Dart 5F 7
Bridgewater Way S65: Rav 2C 100
Bridge Way S41: C'fld 3E 161
Bridle Cl. S35: Chap 2F 79
Bridle Cres. S35: Chap 2F 79
Bridle La. S18: App 2E 157
Bridle Rd. S43: Woodt 5E 165
Bridle Stile S20: Mosb 3D 150
Bridle Stile Cl. S20: Mosb 3D 150
Bridle Stile Gdns.
S20: Mosb 3C 150
Bridleway, The S62: Rawm 1B 84
Bridport Rd. S9: Shef 1E 121
Bridstone Gdns. S74: Els 6D 46
Brier Cl. S20: Water 1E 151
Brierey Cl. S75: Dart 6H 7
Brierfield Cl. S75: Barn 6B 16
BRIERLEY 3A 12
Brierley Cl. S43: Stav 5B 164
BRIERLEY GAP 5E 13
Brierley Rd. DN4: Bess 5A 58
S18: Uns 6B 156
S65: Dalt 1D 98
S72: Brier, Grim 5A 12
S72: Shaft 4G 11
S72: Sth H 1G 11
Brier St. S6: Shef 4B 106
Briery Gdns. S75: Dod 3F 29
Briery Mdws. S73: Hem 4F 47
Briery Wlk. S61: Grea 5C 82
Brigadier Hargreaves Ct.
S13: Shef 2B 136
Brigantian Way WF9: Hems, Sth K . .2H 13
Briggs St. S71: Car 5H 9
Brightholmlee Ct. S35: Wharn S . .2A 90

Brightholmlee La.—Broombank Rd.

Brightholmlee La.
S35: Bright, Wharn S 1A 90
Bright Mdw. S20: Half 5H 151
Brightmore Dr. S3: Shef 3A 4 (3D 118)
Brightmore Ho. S3: Shef 2B 4
Brighton St. S72: Grim 1B 20
Brighton Ter. Rd. S10: Shef 2B 118
BRIGHTSIDE 2D 108
Brightside La. S9: Shef 5B 108
Brightside Way S9: Shef 4C 108
Brimham Cl. *DN3: Kirk Sa 4B 26*
(off Sandall La.)
BRIMINGTON 6E 163
BRIMINGTON COMMON 3E 169
Brimington Rd. S41: C'fld 4A 168
Brimington Rd. Nth.
S41: Whit M 5H 161
(not continuous)
Brimmesfield Cl. S2: Shef 1B 134
Brimmesfield Dr. S2: Shef 6B 120
Brimmesfield Rd. S2: Shef 1B 134
Brinckman St. S70: Barn 2E 31
BRINCLIFFE 1B 132
Brincliffe Cl. S40: W'ton 1C 170
Brincliffe Ct. S7: Shef 2D 132
Brincliffe Cres. S11: Shef 1B 132
Brincliffe Edge Cl. S11: Shef 2B 132
Brincliffe Edge Rd. S11: Shef 2A 132
Brincliffe Gdns. S11: Shef 1B 132
Brincliffe Hill S11: Shef 1A 132
Brindle M. S9: Shef 6E 109
Brindley Cl. S8: Shef 4F 133
Brindley Ct. S21: Killa 4B 152
Brindley Cres. S8: Shef 4F 133
Brindley Ho. S41: C'fld 2A 168
Brindley Rd. S41: C'fld 2H 167
Brindley Way S43: Stav 4C 164
S60: Shef 2B 122
Brinkburn Cl. S17: Dore 4G 145
Brinkburn Ct. S17: Dore 4G 145
Brinkburn Dr. S17: Dore 4G 145
Brinkburn Va. Rd. S17: Dore 4G 145
Brinsford Rd. S60: Brins 3C 110
BRINSWORTH 4C 110
Brinsworth Grange S60: Brins 3B 110
Brinsworth Hall Av. S60: Brins 4C 110
Brinsworth Hall Cres. S60: Brins 4C 110
Brinsworth Hall Dr. S60: Brins 4C 110
Brinsworth Hall Gro. S60: Brins 5C 110
Brinsworth La. S60: Brins 4C 110
Brinsworth Rd. S60: Brins, Cat 5B 110
(not continuous)
Brinsworth St. S9: Shef 6C 108
S60: Roth 4D 96
Bristol Gro. DN2: Don 4F 41
Bristol Rd. S11: Shef 5B 118
Britain St. S64: Mexb 2E 67
Britannia Cl. S70: Barn 2E 31
Britannia Ho. S70: Barn 2E 31
Britannia Rd. S9: Shef 2F 121
(not continuous)
S40: Birdh 3A 172
Britannia Way S60: Cat 6C 110
Britland Cl. S5: Shef 3F 93
S75: Barn 6H 15
Britnall St. S9: Shef 6D 108
(not continuous)
Briton Sq. S63: Thurn 1D 36
Briton St. S63: Thurn 1D 36
Brittain St. S1: Shef 6F 5 (4G 119)
Britten Ho. DN2: Don 4F 41
Broachgate DN5: Scawt 2F 39
Broad Bri. Cl. S26: Kiv P 6C 140
Broadcarr Rd. S74: Hoyl 4A 62
Broadcroft Cl. S20: Beig 4A 138
Broad Dyke Cl. S26: Kiv P 6C 140
Broad Elms Cl. S11: Shef 4G 131
Broad Elms La. S11: Shef 5F 131
Broadfield Cl. S8: Shef 2E 133
Broadfield Ct. S8: Shef 2E 133
Broadfield Rd. S8: Shef 2E 133
Broadfield Way S8: Shef 2E 133
Broad Gates S75: Silk 2A 28
Broadgates *DN9: Finn 3F 77*
(off Station Rd.)
Broadgorse Cl. S40: Birdh 3G 171
Broadhead Rd. S36: Spink 4F 175
Broad Inge Cres. S35: Chap 3D 78
Broadlands S66: Bram 6B 100
Broadlands Av. S20: Mosb 6B 136
Broadlands Cl. S20: Mosb 6C 136
Broadlands Cres. S66: Bram 6B 100
Broadlands Cft. S20: Mosb 6C 136
Broadlands Ri. S20: Mosb 6C 136
Broad La. DN9: Auck 3A 76
S1: Shef 3B 4 (3E 119)
S3: Shef 3E 119
WF9: Sth K 5H 13
Broad La. Ct. S1: Shef 3B 4 (3E 119)
Broadley Rd. S13: Shef 1F 135
Broad Oaks S9: Shef 2C 120
Broadoaks Cl. S25: Din 6H 127
S41: C'fld 5A 168
Broad Oaks La. S9: Shef 2C 120
Broadoaks Rd. S25: Din 5H 127
Broad Pavement S40: C'fld 5H 167
Broad Riding DN12: New E 5E 71
S66: Stain 1F 103
Broad St. S2: Shef 2H 5 (2H 119)
S62: P'gte 5G 83
S74: Hoyl 6A 46
Broad St. W. S1: Shef 2G 5 (2G 119)
Broadwater S63: Bolt D 2H 49
Broadway S60: Brins 5C 110
S64: Swin 4A 66
S65: Roth 3A 98
S70: Barn 1A 30
S75: Mapp 5A 8
Broadway, The DN4: Balb 1G 71
Broadway Av. S35: Chap 4G 79
Broadway Cl. S64: Swin 4A 66
Broadway Ct. S70: Barn 1A 30
Broadway Dr. S70: Barn 2B 30
Broadway E. S65: Roth 3A 98
Brocco Bank S11: Shef 6B 118
Brocco La. S3: Shef 2C 4 (2E 119)
Brocco St. S3: Shef 2C 4 (2E 119)
Brockfield Cl. S70: Wors 5F 31
Brockhill Ct. S43: Brim 6E 163
Brockhole Cl. DN4: Can 5C 58
Brockholes La. DN3: Brant 5G 59
S36: Cub, Pen 6A 176
Brockhurst Way S65: Thry 6E 85
Brocklehurst Av. S8: Shef 2H 147
S70: Stair 4A 32
Brocklehurst Ct. S40: C'fld 5E 167
S70: Stair 4A 32
(off Brocklehurst Av.)
Brocklehurst Piece S40: C'fld 6E 167
Brocklesby Dr. DN4: Bess 1C 74
BROCKWELL 4E 167
BROCKWELL HILL 3E 167
Brockwell La. S40: C'fld 3D 166
(Hambledon Cl.)
S40: C'fld 2C 166
(Oldridge Cl.)
S40: C'fld 2E 167
(Skiddaw Cl.)
S40: Up N 1A 166
S42: Up N 1A 166
Brockwell Pl. S40: C'fld 4F 167
Brockwell Ter. S40: C'fld 4F 167
Brockwell Wlk. S40: C'fld 3E 167
Brockwood Cl. S13: Shef 1D 136
Brodsworth Community Woodlands
. . . . 5A 22
Brodsworth Ho. *DN1: Don 2B 56*
(off Bond Cl.)
Brodsworth Way DN11: Ross 5D 74
Bromcliffe Pk. S71: Monk B 3B 18
Bromehead Way S41: C'fld 1E 167
Bromfield Ct. S71: R'ton 2A 10
BROMLEY 4A 60
Bromley Carr Rd. S35: Brom 5A 60
Brompton La. DN9: Auck 3B 76
Brompton Rd. DN5: Sprot 3D 54
S9: Shef 5D 108
Bromwich Rd. S8: Shef 6D 132
Bronte Av. DN4: Balb 6G 55
Bronte Cl. S71: Monk B 5G 17
Bronte Gro. S64: Mexb 6G 51
Bronte Pl. S62: Rawm 1A 84
Brookbank Av. S40: C'fld 4E 167
Brook Cl. S26: Aston 1D 138
S35: Gren 1B 92
S72: Grim 1B 20
Brook Ct. S61: Thorpe H 4C 80
Brook Cft. S25: Nth A 3G 141
S36: Stoc 3E 175
Brookdale Ct. S35: Chap 6F 61
Brookdale Hgts. S75: Dod 4H 29
Brookdale Rd. S35: Chap 5F 61
Brook Dr. S3: Shef 2B 4 (2E 119)
S63: Wath D 6E 49
Brooke Ct. DN9: Auck 1B 76
Brooke Dr. S43: Brim C 3E 169
Brooke St. DN1: Don 5C 40
S74: Hoyl 6A 46
Brook Farm M. S63: Wath D 5F 49
Brookfield S71: Ard 3H 33
Brookfield Av. S40: Bramp 6B 166
S64: Swin 4C 66
Brookfield Cl. DN3: Arm 5E 43
S65: Dalt 1C 98
Brookfield M. DN5: Ark 6D 24
Brookfield Rd. S7: Shef 1E 133
Brookfields Dr. S63: Wath D 5B 50
Brookfields Pk. S63: Wath D 4A 50
Brookfields Way S63: Wath D 5A 50
Brookfield Ter. S71: Car 6H 9
Brookfield Vw. Dr. S40: Bramp 6C 166
Brookfield Yd. S7: Shef 1E 133
Brook Grn. S12: Shef 5C 136
Brookhaven Way S66: Bram 6B 100
Brook Hill S3: Shef 3A 4 (3D 118)
S61: Thorpe H 3C 80
Brookhill Rd. S75: Kexb 6C 6
BROOKHOUSE 6F 115
Brookhouse Cl. S12: Shef 5C 136
Brookhouse Ct. *S12: Shef 5C 136*
(off Sheffield Rd.)
Brookhouse Dell S66: Thurc 5D 114
Brookhouse Dr. S12: Shef 5C 136
Brookhouse Hill S10: Shef 1D 130
Brookhouse La.
S25: Brookh, Laugh M 6F 115
Brookhouse Rd. S26: Aston 2C 138
Brook Ho's. S75: Cawt 4A 14
Brooklands S25: Nth A 3H 141
S66: Malt 6G 101
Brooklands Av. S10: Shef 1C 130
Brooklands Bus. Pk. *S9: Shef 5D 108*
(off Brompton Rd.)
Brooklands Cres. S10: Shef 1C 130
Brooklands Cft. S26: Wales 5G 139
Brooklands Dr. S10: Shef 1C 130
Brooklands Ho. S25: Din 5F 127
Brooklands Pk. S25: Din 5F 127
Brooklands Rd. DN6: Adw S 1D 22
Brooklands Way S25: Din 5G 127
Brook La. S3: Shef 3B 4 (3E 119)
S12: Shef 5C 136
S35: Gren 2B 92
S35: Ough 3D 90
S66: Bram 4A 100
Brook La. Cft. S66: Bram 4A 100
Brooklyn Dr. S40: C'fld 4E 167
Brooklyn Pl. S8: Shef 3F 133
Brooklyn Rd. S8: Shef 3F 133
Brooklyn Works S3: Shef 1F 119
Brook M. S25: Nth A 3G 141
Brook Rd. DN12: Con 4G 69
S8: Shef 3E 133
S35: High G 2D 78
S65: Roth 2A 98
Brook Row S36: Stoc 4E 175
BROOKSIDE 6B 166
Brookside DN12: Con 5F 69
S6: Stan 6A 104
S64: Swin 5A 66
S65: Roth 5B 98
Brookside Bank Rd. S6: Stan 6A 104
Brookside Bar S40: Bramp 6A 166
Brookside Cl. S12: Shef 5C 136
Brookside Ct. S62: P'gte 6E 83
Brookside Cres. S63: Wath D 1C 64
Brookside Dr. S70: Stair 4A 32
Brookside Glen S40: Bramp 6A 166
Brookside La. S6: Stan 6A 104
Brook Sq. DN12: Con 5F 69
Brooks Rd. S43: Bar H 2G 163
Brook St. S60: Whis 3A 112
Brook Va. S40: C'fld 6F 167
Brookvale S71: Monk B 5A 18
Brookview Ct. S18: Dron 1F 155
Brook Way DN5: Ark 6C 24
Brook Yd. S40: C'fld 5F 167
BROOM 5G 97
Broom Av. S60: Roth 6A 98
Broombank Pk. S41: C'fld 3E 161
Broombank Pk. Ind. Est.
S41: C'fld 3E 161
Broombank Rd. S41: C'fld 3D 160

190 A-Z Sheffield

Broom Bus. Pk.—Burntwood Bank

Broom Bus. Pk. S41: C'fld .3D **160**
Broom Chase S60: Roth .6G **97**
Broomcliffe Gdns.
S72: Shaft .4F **11**
Broom Cl. S2: Shef .5E **119**
S41: C'fld .1E **167**
S63: Bolt D .1A **50**
S63: Wath D .2H **65**
S66: Sunn .3H **99**
S70: Barn .4A **32**
S75: Dart .5H **7**
Broom Ct. S60: Roth .6H **97**
Broom Cres. S60: Roth .6G **97**
Broomcroft S75: Dod .4A **30**
Broomcroft Pk. S11: Shef .5G **131**
Broom Dr. S60: Roth .1A **112**
Broome Av. S64: Swin .3C **66**
BROOMFIELD .6A **4** (4C **118**)
Broomfield Av. S41: Has .3C **172**
Broomfield Cl. S70: Barn .2A **30**
Broomfield Ct. S36: Stoc .3F **175**
Broomfield Gro. S36: Stoc .4F **175**
S60: Roth .6G **97**
Broomfield La. S36: Stoc .4E **175**
Broomfield M. S71: R'ton .3A **10**
Broomfield Rd. S10: Shef .4C **118**
S36: Stoc .3F **175**
Broomfield Ter. S35: Ough .5B **90**
Broomfield Wlk. S36: Pen .5C **176**
Broom Gdns. S43: Brim .1E **169**
Broom Grange S60: Roth .6H **97**
Broom Grn. S3: Shef .5B **4** (4E **119**)
Broom Gro. S25: Sth A .5G **141**
S60: Roth .5G **97**
Broomgrove Cres. S10: Shef .4C **118**
Broomgrove Hall S10: Shef .4C **118**
Broomgrove La. S10: Shef .4C **118**
Broomgrove Rd. S10: Shef .4C **118**
Broomhall Pl. S10: Shef .6A **4** (4D **118**)
Broomhall Rd. S10: Shef .6A **4** (5C **118**)
Broomhall St. S3: Shef .6A **4** (4D **118**)
(Broomhall Pl., not continuous)
S3: Shef .5B **4** (4E **119**)
(Cavendish Ct.)
Broomhead Ct. S75: Mapp .6A **8**
Broomhead Gdns. S73: Womb .3A **48**
Broomhead Rd. S73: Womb .3A **48**
BROOMHILL
S10 .**4B 118**
S73 .**2C 48**
Broomhill DN12: Den M .2C **68**
Broomhill Cl. S21: Ecki .1C **158**
Broom Hill Dr. DN4: Can .5C **58**
Broomhill Flash Nature Reserve .2B **48**
Broomhill La. S63: Bolt D .1D **48**
Broomhill Rd. S41: Old W .4G **161**
Broomhill Vw. S63: Bolt D .3A **50**
Broomhouse La. DN4: Balb, Warm .3E **71**
DN12: New E .5C **70**
Broomhouse La. Ind. Est.
DN12: New E .3E **71**
Broom La. S60: Roth .6H **97**
Broom Riddings S61: Grea .6C **82**
Broom Rd. S60: Roth .5G **97**
Broom Royd S35: Wharn S .1A **90**
Broomroyd S70: Wors .6G **31**
Broomspring Cl. S3: Shef .5B **4** (4E **119**)
Broomspring La. S10: Shef .5A **4** (4D **118**)
(not continuous)
Broom St. S10: Shef .6A **4** (4D **118**)
Broom Ter. S60: Roth .5G **97**
Broomvale Wlk. DN12: New E .5B **70**
Broom Valley Rd. S60: Roth .5F **97**
Broomville St. S64: Swin .3D **66**
Broom Wlk. S3: Shef .5B **4**
Broomwood Cl. S20: Beig .5H **137**
Broomwood Gdns. S20: Beig .5H **137**
Brosley Av. DN3: Barn D .1H **27**
Brotherton St. S3: Shef .6G **107**
Brough Grn. S75: Dod .5H **29**
Broughton Av. DN5: Don .3H **39**
Broughton La. S9: Shef .4E **109**
Broughton Rd. DN4: Bess .6A **58**
S6: Shef .3B **106**
S41: C'fld .1E **167**
Brow, The S65: Roth .6D **98**
Brow Cl. S70: Wors .4E **31**
Brow Cres. S20: Half .3F **151**
Brow Hill Rd. S66: Malt .4H **101**
Brownell St. S3: Shef .2B **4** (2E **119**)
Brown Hills La. S10: Shef .6A **116**
Browning Av. DN4: Balb .6A **56**
(not continuous)
Browning Cl. S6: Shef .5C **92**
S71: Monk B .3G **17**
Browning Ct. S40: Bramp .5C **166**
S65: Roth .5A **98**
Browning Dr. S6: Shef .5C **92**
S65: Roth .4A **98**
Browning Rd. DN3: Barn D .1H **27**
S6: Shef .5B **92**
S63: Wath D .5D **48**
S64: Mexb .6F **51**
S65: Roth .4A **98**
Brown La. S1: Shef .5E **5** (4F **119**)
(not continuous)
S18: Coal A .1H **155**
Brownlee Cl. S60: Brins .4D **110**
Brownroyd Av. S71: R'ton .4H **9**
Browns Sq. S73: Hem .5E **47**
Brown St. S1: Shef .5F **5** (4G **119**)
S60: Roth .3C **96**
Brow Vw. S63: Bolt D .2A **50**
Broxbourne Gdns.
DN5: Bntly .1A **40**
Broxholme La. DN1: Don .6C **40**
Broxholme Rd. S8: Shef .5E **133**
Bruce Av. S70: Barn .3E **31**
Bruce Cres. DN2: Don .5G **41**
Bruce Rd. S11: Shef .6C **118**
Bruncroft Cl. DN4: Bess .6A **58**
Brunel Rd. DN5: Don .5G **39**
Brunel Way S60: Cat, Shef .2B **122**
Bruni Way DN11: New R .6G **75**
Brunswick Cl. S71: Smi .2E **17**
Brunswick Dr. S66: Sunn .3G **99**
Brunswick Gdns. S13: Shef .1E **137**
Brunswick Gdns. Village
S13: Shef .1E **137**
Brunswick Rd. S3: Shef .1G **119**
S60: Roth .6G **97**
Brunswick St. S10: Shef .4A **4** (3D **118**)
S41: C'fld .4H **167**
S63: Thurn .1D **36**
Brunt Rd. S62: Rawm .2A **84**
BRUSHES, THE .3F **161**
Brushfield Gro. S12: Shef .4G **135**
Brushfield Rd. S40: C'fld .3A **166**
Bryan Ct. S66: B'well .1A **102**
Bryn Lea S41: C'fld .5B **168**
Bryony Cl. S21: Killa .4A **152**
Bubnell Rd. S18: Dron W .2D **154**
Bubup Hill DN11: Lov .4B **72**
Bubwith Rd. S9: Shef .2E **109**
Buccaneer Dr. DN9: Finn .2C **76**
Buchanan Cres. S5: Shef .5D **92**
Buchanan Dr. S5: Shef .5D **92**
Buchanan Rd. S5: Shef .5D **92**
Buckden Cl. S40: C'fld .4E **167**
Buckden Rd. S70: Barn .6C **16**
Buckenham Dr. S4: Shef .6H **107**
Buckenham St. S4: Shef .6H **107**
Buckingham Cl. S18: Dron W .2C **154**
Buckingham Ct. S71: R'ton .2G **9**
Buckingham Rd. DN2: Don .6E **41**
DN12: Con .3E **69**
Buckingham Way S60: Brins .4D **110**
S66: Malt .4B **102**
S71: R'ton .2G **9**
Buckleigh Rd. S63: Wath D .2F **65**
Buckley Ct. S70: Barn .2E **31**
Buckley Ho. S70: Barn .2E **31**
Buckthorn Cl. S64: Swin .6B **66**
Buck Wood Vw. S14: Shef .3A **134**
Bude Ct. S71: Monk B .5H **17**
Bude Rd. DN4: Balb .4A **56**
Bullen Rd. S6: Shef .5B **92**
Bullfinch Cl. S60: Brins .4E **111**
Bull Haw La. S75: Silk .2A **28**
Bullrush Gro. DN4: Balb .1D **72**
Bungalow Rd. DN12: New E .4C **70**
Bungalows, The S21: Killa .3B **152**
S40: C'fld .5E **167**
*S41: C'fld .6A **168***
(off Piccadilly Rd.)
S41: C'fld .1F **167**
(Ringwood Av.)
S41: Whit M .5H **161**
S43: Stav .6H **163**
S60: Tree .2F **123**
S62: Rawm .1F **83**
Bunker's Hill S21: Killa .4D **152**
Bunting Cl. S8: Shef .6G **133**
S42: W'ton .1C **170**
Bunting Ho. S41: Old W .3A **162**
Bunting Nook S8: Shef .6G **133**
Burbage Cl. S18: Dron W .2C **154**
Burbage Gro. S12: Shef .3G **135**
Burbage Rd. S43: Stav .6A **164**
Burcot Rd. S8: Shef .3E **133**
BURCROFT .3G **69**
Burcroft Cl. S74: Hoyl .1G **61**
Burcroft Hill DN12: Con .3G **69**
Burden Cl. DN1: Don .2B **56**
Burford Av. DN4: Balb .1F **71**
Burford Cres. S26: Aston .1D **138**
Burgen Rd. S61: Kimb P .1H **95**
Burgess Cl. S41: Has .3C **172**
Burgess Rd. S9: Shef .6C **108**
Burgess St. S1: Shef .4E **5** (3F **119**)
Burghley Cl. S25: Din .6H **127**
Burghley Ct. DN5: Sprot .3E **55**
Burgoyne Cl. S6: Shef .6C **106**
Burgoyne Rd. S6: Shef .6C **106**
Burgundy Rd. DN4: Balb .2C **72**
Burkinshaw Av. S62: Rawm .6G **65**
Burkitt Dr. S43: Woodt .4E **165**
Burleigh Ct. S70: Barn .1E **31**
Burleigh St. S70: Barn .2E **31**
Burley Cl. S40: Birdh .3H **171**
Burlington S6: Shef .1A **4** (2D **118**)
Burlington Arc. S70: Barn .1E **31**
Burlington Cl. S17: Dore .3F **145**
Burlington Ct. S6: Shef .1D **118**
Burlington Glen S17: Dore .3F **145**
Burlington Gro. S17: Dore .3F **145**
Burlington Ho. *S40: C'fld .5H **167***
(off Burlington St.)
Burlington Rd. S17: Dore .3F **145**
Burlington St. S6: Shef .1D **118**
S40: C'fld .5H **167**
Burman Rd. S63: Wath D .1G **65**
Burnaby Ct. S6: Shef .5C **106**
Burnaby Cres. S6: Shef .6C **106**
Burnaby Grn. S6: Shef .5C **106**
Burnaby St. DN1: Don .2B **56**
S6: Shef .5C **106**
Burnaby Wlk. S6: Shef .6C **106**
Burnaston Cl. S18: Dron W .3B **154**
Burnaston Wlk. DN12: Den M .3D **68**
Burnbridge Rd. S41: Old W .3B **162**
BURNCROSS .3D **78**
Burncross Dr. S35: Chap .3E **79**
Burncross Gro. S35: Burn .3D **78**
Burncross Rd. S35: Burn, Chap .3C **78**
Burnell Rd. S6: Shef .3B **106**
Burnell St. S43: Brim .6E **163**
Burnett Cl. S36: Pen .5E **177**
BURNGREAVE .6H **107**
Burngreave Bank S4: Shef .6G **107**
Burngreave Rd. S3: Shef .5G **107**
Burngreave St. S3: Shef .6G **107**
Burn Gro. S35: Chap .4H **79**
Burngrove Pl. S3: Shef .5G **107**
Burnham Av. S75: Mapp .5A **8**
Burnham Cl. DN4: Bess .5G **57**
Burnham Gro. DN5: Scawt .2G **39**
Burnham Way S73: D'fld .5A **34**
Burn Pl. S71: Smi .1D **16**
Burnsall Cres. S60: Brins .5D **110**
Burnsall Gro. S70: Stair .4A **32**
Burns Av. WF9: Sth K .5G **13**
Burns Cl. S40: Birdh .3G **171**
Burns Ct. S35: Chap .3E **79**
Burns Dr. S18: Dron .4H **155**
S35: Chap .3E **79**
S65: Roth .4A **98**
Burnside S63: Thurn .1B **36**
Burnside Av. S8: Shef .3F **133**
Burns Rd. DN3: Barn D .1H **27**
DN4: Balb .6A **56**
S6: Shef .2C **118**
S25: Din .6B **128**
S65: Roth .4H **97**
S66: Malt .6B **102**
Burns St. DN5: Bntly .1A **40**
Burns Way DN4: Balb .4H **55**
S63: Wath D .5D **48**
Burnt Hill La. S35: Ough .5A **90**
Burnt Stones Cl. S10: Shef .4E **117**
Burnt Stones Dr. S10: Shef .4E **117**
Burnt Stones Gro. S10: Shef .4E **117**
Burntwood Bank WF9: Hems .1E **13**

Burntwood Cl. S63: Thurn 3A 36
Burntwood Court Health & Fitness Cen.
. . . . .4D 12
Burntwood Cres. S60: Tree 1F 123
Burnt Wood La. S72: Brier 6F 13
Burntwood Rd. S72: Grim 2C 20
Burrell St. S60: Roth 4E 97
Burrowlee Pk. Sq. S6: Shef 3B 106
(off Burrowlee Rd.)
Burrowlee Rd. S6: Shef 3B 106
Burrows Dr. S5: Shef 2F 107
Burrows Gro. S73: Womb 1E 47
Burrs Farm Ct. S81: Gild 6G 129
Burrs La. S81: Gild 6G 129
Burrs Wood Cft. S41: C'fld 1C 166
Bursden Cl. S41: Old W 5H 161
Burton Av. DN4: Balb 4A 56
S71: Monk B 4A 18
Burton Bank Rd. S71: Monk B 5F 17
(not continuous)
Burton Cres. S71: Monk B 3B 18
Burton La. S35: Ough 4D 90
Burtonlees Ct. DN4: Bess 5B 58
Burton Rd. S3: Shef 6E 107
S71: Monk B 5F 17
Burton Rd. Bus. Pk. S71: Monk B . . .3B 18
Burton St. S6: Shef 5C 106
S71: Barn 5D 16
Burton Ter. DN4: Balb 4A 56
S70: Barn 2G 31
Burtop Cft. S73: Hem 5F 47
Burying La. S74: Hoyl 3B 62
Bushey Wood Gro.
S17: Dore 3E 145
Bushey Wood Rd. S17: Dore 4F 145
Bushfield Rd. S63: Wath D 6E 49
Busk Knoll S5: Shef 2F 107
Busk Mdw. S5: Shef 2F 107
Busk Pk. S5: Shef 2F 107
Busley Gdns. DN5: Bntly 2H 39
(not continuous)
Butcher St. S63: Thurn 2B 36
Butchill Av. S5: Shef 2F 93
Bute St. S10: Shef 3A 118
Butler Rd. S6: Shef 5H 105
Butler Way S21: Killa 3B 152
Butterbusk DN12: Con 4H 69
BUTTERBUSK GREEN 2B 70
Buttercross Dr. S72: Lit H 2D 34
Butter Cross Pk.
S71: Monk B 3H 17
Butterfield Ct. S73: Bramp 4B 48
Butterfly Nook S65: Roth 6D 98
Butterill Dr. DN3: Arm 5G 43
Butterley Dr. S70: Stair 4A 32
Butterleys S75: Dod 3H 29
Buttermere Cl. S25: Nth A 1H 141
S41: C'fld 1E 167
S63: Bolt D 3B 50
S64: Mexb 6H 51
Buttermere Cres. DN4: Don 3G 57
Buttermere Dr. S18: Dron W 3D 154
Buttermere Rd. S7: Shef 4D 132
Buttermere Way S71: Ard 2E 33
Butterscotch Wlk.
DN5: Scawt 3G 39
BUTTERTHWAITE 1A 94
Butterthwaite Cres.
S5: Shef 3B 94
Butterthwaite La. S35: Eccl 1A 94
Butterthwaite Rd. S5: Shef 2H 93
Butterton Cl. S75: Mapp 5B 8
Butterton Dr. S40: C'fld 3B 166
Button Hill S11: Shef 4A 132
Button Row S36: Stoc 3D 174
Butts Hill S17: Tot 6E 145
Buxton Rd. S71: Ath 1F 17
Buzzard Av. S64: Mexb 6B 52
Byath La. S72: Cud 2E 19
Byford Rd. S66: Malt 5F 101
Byland Way S71: Monk B 6A 18
Byram Ct. DN4: Balb 1B 72
Byrley Rd. S61: Kimb P 1H 95
Byrne Cl. S72: Bar G 4F 15
Byron Av. DN4: Balb 6H 55
DN5: Don 6G 39
S35: Chap 4E 79
Byron Cl. S18: Dron 5H 155
Byron Cres. S63: Wath D 5D 48
Byron Dr. S65: Roth 4H 97
S71: Monk B 4G 17

Byron Rd. S7: Shef 2C 132
S20: Beig 6H 137
S25: Din 6B 128
(not continuous)
S40: Birdh 2H 171
S64: Mexb 1G 67
S66: Malt 6B 102
Byron St. S40: C'fld 1A 172
S72: Gt H 1F 35

C

CADEBY 6G 53
Cadeby Av. DN12: Con 4D 68
Cadeby Ho. DN1: Don 2B 56
(off St James's St.)
Cadeby La. DN5: Cad, Sprot 3F 53
DN12: Den M 2D 68
Cadeby Rd. DN5: Sprot 4B 54
Cadman Cl. S20: Mosb 4E 151
Cadman Rd. S12: Shef 3F 135
Cadman St. S4: Shef 2H 119
S20: Mosb 4D 150
S63: Wath D 6H 49
Cadwell Cl. S72: Cud 6F 11
Caernarvon Cl. S40: W'ton 1D 170
Caernarvon Cres. S63: Bolt D 2A 50
Caernarvon Dr. DN5: Barnb 1H 51
Caernarvon Rd. S18: Dron 4G 155
Caine Gdns. S61: Kimb 4H 95
Cairn Dr. S43: New W 2C 162
Cairngorm Cl. S43: New W 2C 162
Cairns Rd. S10: Shef 4G 117
S20: Beig 4G 137
Caister Av. S35: Chap 3E 79
Caistor Av. S70: Barn 3B 30
Calabria Gro. S70: Barn 2G 31
Calcot Gro. S64: Swin 4C 66
Calcot Pk. Av. S64: Swin 4C 66
Caldbeck Gro. S35: High G 6C 60
Caldbeck Pl. S25: Nth A 1A 142
Calder Av. S71: R'ton 3B 10
Calder Cl. S71: R'ton 3B 10
Calder Cres. S70: Barn 3A 32
Calder Rd. S61: Wing 6A 82
S63: Bolt D 3B 50
Calders Cres. S5: Shef 4E 93
Calder Ter. DN12: Con 3F 69
Caldervale S71: R'ton 2B 10
Calder Way S5: Shef 2H 107
Caldey Rd. S18: Dron 4F 155
California Cres. S70: Barn 3E 31
California St. S70: Barn 3D 30
California Gdns. S70: Barn 2E 31
California St. S70: Barn 3D 30
California Ter. S70: Barn 3D 30
Calladine Way S64: Swin 5B 66
Callander Ct. DN4: Can 5B 58
Callflex Bus. Pk. S63: Wath D 6B 50
Callis La. S36: Pen 5E 177
Callis Way S36: Cub 5D 176
Callow Dr. S14: Shef 3A 134
Callow Mt. S14: Shef 3H 133
Callow Pl. S14: Shef 3A 134
Callow Rd. S14: Shef 3H 133
Callum Ct. S62: P'gte 6F 83
Callywhite La. S18: Dron 3G 155
Calner Cft. S20: Sot 6A 138
CALOW 5E 169
Calow Brook Dr. S41: Has 2D 172
CALOW GREEN 2G 173
Calow La. S41: Has 2C 172
S44: Cal 2C 172
Calow La. Ind. Est. S41: Has 2D 172
Calstock Cl. S40: Ash 4B 166
Calver Cl. S75: Dod 4H 29
Calver Cres. S43: Stav 6A 164
Calverley Gdns. S73: Womb 1H 47
Calvert Rd. S9: Shef 6F 109
Calvert St. S74: Hoyl 1G 61
Calver Way S60: Wav 3C 122
Calvey Orchard S72: Cud 1F 19
Camborne Cl. S6: Shef 5B 92
Camborne Rd. S6: Shef 5B 92
Camborne Way S71: Monk B 5G 17
Cambourne Cl. DN6: Adw S 2C 22
Cambria Dr. DN4: Balb 6F 55
Cambrian Cl. DN5: Sprot 3B 54
S40: C'fld 2E 167

Cambridge Cl. DN5: Harl 2G 51
Cambridge Ct. S1: Shef 4D 4
(off Backfields)
Cambridge Cres. S65: Roth 3H 97
Cambridge M. S63: Wath D 4E 49
Cambridge Pl. S65: Roth 3H 97
Cambridge Rd. S8: Shef 2G 133
S36: Spink 4H 175
S43: Brim 6E 163
Cambridge St. DN11: New R 4B 74
S1: Shef 4D 4 (3F 119)
(not continuous)
S64: Mexb 1D 66
S65: Roth 4H 97
Cambron Gdns. S66: Bram 5A 100
Camdale Ri. S12: Ridg 1A 150
Camdale Vw. S12: Ridg 1A 150
Camden Gro. S66: Malt 4A 102
Camden Pl. DN1: Don 2B 56
Camelia M. S26: Swal 1B 138
Camellia Cl. DN12: Con 5G 69
Camellia Dr. DN3: Kirk Sa 5C 26
Camerory Way S43: New W 1C 162
Camlough Wlk. S41: C'fld 6A 168
Cammell Rd. S5: Shef 2A 108
Cammidge Way DN4: Bess 2C 74
Camms Cl. S21: Ecki 6E 151
Camm St. S6: Shef 6B 106
Campbell Ct. S43: New W 2C 162
(off Church Wlk.)
Campbell Dr. S43: Bar H 3F 163
S65: Roth 5A 98
Campbell St. S61: Grea 4D 82
Campbell Wlk. S60: Brins 4D 110
Campbell Way S25: Din 4G 127
Camping La. S8: Shef 6D 132
Campion Cl. S63: Bolt D 1A 50
Campion Dr. S21: Killa 4B 152
Campo La. S1: Shef 3D 4 (3F 119)
Camp Rd. WF9: Sth K 5G 13
Campsall Dr. S10: Shef 3H 117
Campsall Fld. Cl. S63: Wath D 2F 65
Campsall Fld. Rd. S63: Wath D 1F 65
Campus M. S70: Barn 3B 30
Canada St. S4: Shef 5A 108
S70: Barn 3D 30
Canal Bri. S21: Killa 4C 152
Canal M. S41: C'fld 3H 167
Canalside Vw. S64: Kiln 6D 66
Canal St. S4: Shef 1A 120
S71: Barn 5E 17
Canal Way S71: Barn 5E 17
Canal Wharf S41: C'fld 4A 168
Canal Wharfe S64: Mexb 2H 67
Canary Ct. S66: Sunn 3G 99
Canberra Ri. S63: Bolt D 2A 50
Candle Cres. S66: Thurc 1C 126
Canklow 1E 111
Canklow Hill Rd. S60: Roth 1E 111
Canklow Meadows Ind. Est.
S60: Roth 4E 111
Canklow Rd. S60: Roth 1E 111
Canning St. S1: Shef 4C 4 (3E 119)
Cannock St. S6: Shef 4B 106
Cannon Cl. S62: Rawm 2A 84
Cannon Hall Rd. S5: Shef 3H 107
Cannonthorpe Ri. S60: Tree 2G 123
Cannon Way S75: Bar G 3G 15
Canon Cl. DN11: Ross 5E 75
Canons Way S71: Monk B 5H 17
Cantelo Cl. DN11: New R 6F 75
Canterbury Av. S10: Shef 6D 116
Canterbury Cl. DN5: Scaws 4F 39
S40: C'fld 2H 171
S65: Roth 5A 98
Canterbury Cres. S10: Shef 6D 116
Canterbury Dr. S10: Shef 6D 116
Canterbury Rd. DN2: Don 4E 41
S8: Shef 3G 133
Cantilupe Cres. S26: Aston 6C 124
CANTLEY 3E 59
Cantley La. DN3: Can 3H 57
DN4: Bess, Can 3H 57
Cantley Mnr. Av. DN4: Can 5C 58
Cantrell Ct. S43: Brim 6C 162
Capel Ri. S43: Brim 6C 162
Capel St. S6: Shef 5C 106
(not continuous)
Caperns Rd. S25: Nth A 3A 142
Capitol Cl. S75: High'm 1G 29

Capitol Ct. S75: High'm 1G 29
Capitol Pk. S75: High'm 1G 29
Capri Cl. S73: D'fld 4H 33
Capthorne Cl. S40: C'fld 3A 166
Cvn. Site, The DN5: Sprot 4B 54
Caraway Gro. S64: Swin 6C 66
Carbis Cl. S71: Monk B 5G 17
CARBROOK 3E 109
Carbrook Business Pk. S9: Shef 3E 109
Carbrook Hall Rd. S9: Shef 4E 109
Carbrook Stop (ST) 3F 109
Carbrook St. S9: Shef 4E 109
Carcroft Ent. Pk. DN6: Carc 1D 22
Carcroft Ind. Est. DN6: Adw S 1E 23
Cardew Dr. S62: Rawm 3H 83
Cardigan Rd. DN2: Don 5H 41
Cardinal Cl. DN11: Ross 5E 75
Cardoness Dr. S10: Shef 4F 117
Cardoness Rd. S10: Shef 4G 117
Cardwell Av. S13: Shef 1A 136
Cardwell Cl. S66: B'well 6A 88
Cardwell Dr. S13: Shef 1A 136
Carey Av. S71: Barn 6F 17
Carfield Av. S8: Shef 3G 133
Carfield La. S8: Shef 3H 133
Carfield Pl. S8: Shef 3G 133
Car Hill S61: Grea 6D 82
Carina Dr. DN4: Balb 2C 72
Carisbrook Cl. DN5: Ark 6C 24
Carisbrooke Rd. DN2: Don 6F 41
Carlby Rd. S6: Shef 5H 105
Carley Dr. S20: W'fld 1G 151
Carlingford Rd. S60: Roth 1H 111
Carlin St. S13: Shef 2H 135
Carlisle Bus. Pk. S4: Shef 3C 108
Carlisle Cl. S41: Old W 3F 161
Carlisle Ct. S4: Shef 5B 108
Carlisle Pl. S65: Roth 3F 97
(off Wharncliffe Hill)
Carlisle Rd. DN2: Don 3G 41
S4: Shef 4B 108
Carlisle St. S4: Shef 1H 119
S64: Kiln 5C 66
S65: Roth 3F 97
Carlisle St. E. S4: Shef 4A 108
Carlisle Ter. S25: Din 5A 128
Carlthorpe Gro. S35: High G 1B 78
CARLTON 5A 10
Carlton Av. S65: Roth 4G 97
Carlton Cl. DN3: Brant 4H 59
S20: Mosb 4D 150
WF9: Hems 1D 12
Carlton Ct. S71: Ath 1G 17
Carlton Ga. Dr. S26: Kiv P 6H 139
CARLTON GREEN 6A 10
Carlton Grn. S71: Car 6H 9
Carlton Ho. DN1: Don 2B 56
(off Bond Cl.)
S72: Cud 1E 19
Carlton Ind. Est. S71: Car 1H 17
Carlton Marsh Nature Reserve 6C 10
Carlton M. S2: Shef 1B 134
S71: Car 5H 9
Carlton Ri. S35: Wharn S 1A 90
Carlton Rd. DN1: Don 5D 40
S6: Shef 2A 106
S40: Birdh 4G 171
S62: Rawm 4G 83
S71: Ath, Car, Smi 3F 17
Carlton St. S71: Barn 4D 16
S72: Cud 1E 19
S72: Grim 2B 20
Carlton Way S60: Tree 3G 123
Carlyle Cl. S66: Malt 6B 102
Carlyle Rd. S66: Malt 6B 102
Carlyle St. S64: Mexb 1F 67
Carlyon Gdns. S40: Birdh 2G 171
Carnaby Rd. S6: Shef 5B 106
Carnarvon St. S6: Shef 1D 118
Carnforth Rd. S71: Monk B 3A 18
Carnley St. S63: Wath D 5C 48
Carnoustie Av. S40: W'ton 2D 170
Carnoustie Cl. S64: Swin 4D 66
Carolina Ct. DN4: Don 5F 57
Carolina Way DN4: Don 5F 57
Carpenter Av. S43: Mas M 3E 165
Carpenter Cft. S12: Shef 2F 135
Carpenter Gdns. S12: Shef 2F 135
Carpenter M. S12: Shef 2F 135
CARR 3F 115
Carr Bank DN11: Wad 6G 73

Carr Bank Cl. S11: Shef 6G 117
Carr Bank Dr. S11: Shef 6F 117
Carr Bank La. S11: Shef 6F 117
Carr Cl. S36: Spink 4G 175
S60: Bross 4B 110
Carrcroft Ct. S36: Spink 4H 175
Carrera Ct. S25: Din 5G 127
Carrfield Cl. S75: Kexb 6E 7
Carrfield Ct. S8: Shef 2G 133
Carrfield Dr. S8: Shef 2G 133
Carr Fld. La. S63: Bolt D 1A 50
Carrfield La. S8: Shef 2G 133
Carrfield Rd. S8: Shef 2G 133
Carrfield St. S8: Shef 2G 133
Carr Fold S36: Spink 4H 175
Carr Forge Cl. S12: Shef 4B 136
Carr Forge La. S12: Shef 4B 136
Carr Forge Mt. S12: Shef 4B 136
Carr Forge Pl. S12: Shef 4C 136
Carr Forge Rd. S12: Shef 4B 136
Carr Forge Ter. S12: Shef 4B 136
Carr Forge Vw. S12: Shef 4C 136
Carr Forge Wlk. S12: Shef 4C 136
(off Carter Lodge Dr.)
Carr Furlong S71: Ath 5E 9
Carr Grange Bus. Cen. DN4: Don ...3C 56
Carr Grn. S63: Bolt D 1B 50
S75: Mapp 6B 8
Carr Grn. La. S75: Mapp 1B 16
Carr Gro. S36: Spink 4G 175
CARR HEAD 4G 175
Carr Head La. S36: Pen 1B 176
S63: Bolt D 1F 49
Carr Head Rd. S35: Howb 5A 60
Carr Hill Dr. S1: Balb 4A 56
Carr Hill Dr. DN4: Balb 4A 56
Carr Ho. S63: Gol 5D 36
(off Doncaster Rd.)
Carr Ho. Ct. S35: Brom 4A 60
Carr Ho. Rd. DN1: Don 3C 56
DN4: Don 3C 56
Carriage Dr. DN4: Don 4D 56
Carriage Way, The DN11: Ross 5E 75
Carrill Dr. S6: Shef 4B 92
Carrill Rd. S6: Shef 4B 92
Carrington Av. S75: Barn 4D 16
Carrington Rd. S11: Shef 6A 118
Carrington St. S65: Roth 5G 97
S75: Barn 5C 16
Carrington Ter. S26: Kiv P 6A 140
Carr La. DN4: Bess 1A 74
DN4: Don 3C 56
DN11: Wad 5F 73
DN12: Con 6G 69
S22: Stone D 2B 154
S25: Slade H 3F 115
S26: Ull 3E 125
S36: Bolst 6F 175
S65: Thry 2F 85
S66: Carr 3F 115
S66: Hoot L 1G 115
S75: Pil 2A 60
Carr La. M. S18: Dron W 2C 154
Carron Dr. S75: Mapp 6B 8
Carr Rd. DN12: New E 5B 70
S6: Shef 6B 106
S36: Spink 5F 175
S63: Wath D 6H 49
Carrs La. S72: Cud 3E 19
Carr St. S71: Monk B 3A 18
Carr Vw. Av. DN4: Balb 4A 56
Carr Vw. Rd. S61: Kimb 2G 95
Carrville Dr. S6: Shef 6C 92
Carrville Rd. S6: Shef 6C 92
Carrville Rd. W. S6: Shef 6B 92
Carrwell La. S6: Shef 1B 106
Carrwood Cl. S70: Wors 5G 31
Carrwood Gro. S70: Wors 6G 31
Carrwood Rd. S21: Reni 4H 159
S41: C'fld 2D 160
S31: Stair 1B 32
CARSICK 5F 117
Carsick Gro. S10: Shef 5E 117
CARSICK HILL 5E 117
Carsick Hill Cres. S10: Shef 5E 117
Carsick Hill Dr. S10: Shef 5F 117
Carsick Hill Rd. S10: Shef 5E 117
Carsick Hill Way S10: Shef 5E 117
Carsick Vw. Rd. S10: Shef 5E 117
Carsington Cl. S40: C'fld 3C 166
Carson Av. S25: Laugh C 4F 127

Carson Mt. S12: Shef 5E 135
Carson Rd. S10: Shef 3A 118
Carterhall La. S12: Shef 6F 135
Carter Hall Rd. S12: Shef 6E 135
CARTER KNOWLE 3C 132
Carter Knowle Av. S11: Shef 3A 132
Carter Knowle Rd. S7: Shef 3B 132
S11: Shef 3A 132
Carter Lodge Av. S12: Shef 4B 136
Carter Lodge Dr. S12: Shef 4C 136
Carter Lodge Pl. S12: Shef 4C 136
Carter Lodge Ri. S12: Shef 4C 136
Carter Lodge Wlk. S12: Shef 4C 136
(off Carter Lodge Dr.)
Carter Pl. S8: Shef 2G 133
Carter Rd. S8: Shef 2F 133
CARTLEDGE 5A 154
Cartledge La. S18: Holme 5A 154
Cartmel Cl. S18: Dron W 3D 154
S66: Malt 4B 102
Cartmel Ct. S71: Monk B 1A 18
Cartmel Cres. S41: C'fld 6E 161
Cartmell Ct. S8: Shef 4D 132
Cartmell Cres. S8: Shef 5E 133
Cartmell Hill S8: Shef 4D 132
Cartmell Rd. S8: Shef 4D 132
Cartmel Wlk. S25: Din 1A 142
Cart Rd. S35: Chap 1F 79
Car Vale Dr. S13: Shef 6F 121
Car Vale Vw. S13: Shef 6F 121
Carver Dr. S25: Din 6H 127
Carver La. S1: Shef 3D 4 (3F 119)
Carver St. S1: Shef 3D 4 (3F 119)
Carwood Cl. S4: Shef 5A 108
Carwood Grn. S4: Shef 5A 108
Carwood Gro. S4: Shef 5A 108
Carwood La. S4: Shef 5A 108
Carwood Pk. Ind. Units S4: Shef ..5A 108
Carwood Rd. S4: Shef 5A 108
Carwood Way S4: Shef 5A 108
Cary Gro. S2: Shef 6C 120
Cary Rd. S2: Shef 6C 120
S21: Ecki 1C 158
Castell Cres. DN4: Can 3B 58
Castle Av. DN11: Ross 6E 75
DN12: Con 4F 69
S60: Roth 1E 111
CASTLEBECK 5E 121
Castlebeck Av. S2: Shef 5E 121
Castlebeck Ct. S2: Shef 5F 121
(off Castlebeck Av.)
Castlebeck Cft. S2: Shef 5F 121
Castlebeck Dr. S2: Shef 6E 121
Castle Cl. DN5: Sprot 2F 55
S36: Pen 5E 177
S71: Monk B 5G 17
S75: Dod 4H 29
Castle Ct. S2: Shef 2A 120
Castle Cres. DN12: Con 3F 69
Castle Cft. Dr. S12: Shef 6C 5 (4H 119)
Castle Cft. La. S36: Bolst 6E 175
Castledale Cft. S2: Shef 6E 121
Castledale Gro. S2: Shef 6F 121
Castledale Pl. S2: Shef 6E 121
Castledine Ct. DN4: Balb 2A 72
Castledine Cft. S9: Shef 1E 109
Castledine Gdns. S9: Shef 2D 108
Castlegate S3: Shef 2C 5 (2G 119)
CASTLE GREEN 5E 19
Castle Grn. S3: Shef 2F 5 (2G 119)
S25: Laugh M 2G 127
Castle Gro. DN5: Sprot 3C 54
Castle Gro. Ter. DN12: Con 3G 69
Castle Hill DN12: Con 4F 69
S21: Ecki 6E 151
Castle Hill Av. S64: Mexb 2A 68
Castle Hill Cl. S21: Ecki 6E 151
Castle Hill Ct. S21: Ecki 1E 159
Castle Hill Fold DN5: Hick 3H 37
Castle Hills Rd. DN5: Scawt 1F 39
Castle Ho. S3: Shef 2F 5
Castle La. S36: Pen 5E 177
Castle M. DN5: Scawt 1G 39
Castle Pk.
Doncaster 5B 42
Castlereagh St. S70: Barn 1D 30
Castlerigg Way S18: Dron W 3D 154
Castle Row S17: Bradw 4A 146
Castlerow Cl. S17: Bradw 4A 146
Castlerow Dr. S17: Bradw 4A 146
Castlerow Vw. S17: Bradw 4A 146

Castle Sq. S1: Shef 3F 5
Castle Square Stop (ST) . . .3F 5 (3G 119)
Castle St. DN12: Con 4F 69
    S3: Shef 2F 5 (2G 119)
    S36: Pen 5E 177
    S70: Barn 2D 30
Castle Ter. DN12: Con 4F 69
Castleton Gro. S43: Ink 3G 169
Castleton Way S60: Wav 3C 122
Castle Vw. DN12: New E 5C 70
    S21: Ecki 1E 159
    S60: Roth 1E 111
    S70: Birdw 4D 44
    S75: Dod 2H 29
Castle Wlk. S2: Shef 2A 120
                        (off Castle Ct.)
Castlewell DN12: Con 4F 69
Castlewood Ct. S10: Shef 6D 116
Castlewood Cres. S10: Shef 6C 116
Castlewood Dr. S10: Shef 6D 116
Castlewood Rd. S10: Shef 6D 116
Castor Rd. S9: Shef 5C 108
Cast Theatre 2C 56
Casual Wards S11: Shef 1C 132
Catania Ri. S73: D'fld 4H 33
Catch Bar La. S6: Shef 2B 106
Catchford Vw. S41: C'fld 1C 166
CATCLIFFE 6E 111
Catcliffe Flash Local Nature Reserve
                               . . . . .1D 122
Catcliffe Glass Cone 6E 111
Catcliffe Rd. S9: Shef 2F 121
Cathedral Ct. DN7: Dunsv 4H 27
    S60: Roth 4E 97
                        (off High St.)
Cathedral Stop (ST) 3E 5 (3F 119)
Catherine Av. S26: Swal 1C 138
Catherine Ct. S40: C'fld 5F 167
Catherine Rd. S4: Shef 6G 107
Catherine St. DN1: Don 2C 56
    S3: Shef 6G 107
    S40: C'fld 5F 167
    S64: Mexb 1E 67
    S65: Roth 4F 97
Catherines Wlk. S71: Ath 1E 17
Cathill Rd. S63: Bolt D 6D 34
CATHILL RDBT. 5E 35
Cat La. S2: Shef 2H 133
    S8: Shef 3H 133
Catley Rd. S9: Shef 1F 121
Catling La. DN3: Barn D 1C 26
Cattal St. S9: Shef 1D 120
Catterick Cl. DN12: Den M 4B 68
Catterick Ho. S65: Roth 3G 97
Caudall Cl. S43: Thurn 2D 36
Cauldon Dr. S40: C'fld 3B 166
Caulk La. S70: Swai 5B 32
Causeway, The S17: Dore 3E 145
Causeway Gdns. S17: Dore 2D 144
Causeway Glade S17: Dore 2D 144
CAUSEWAY HEAD 3D 144
Causeway Head Rd. S17: Dore 2D 144
Cavalier Ct. DN4: Balb 1B 72
Cavendish Av. S6: Lox 3F 105
    S17: Dore 3G 145
Cavendish Cl. S65: Roth 6C 98
Cavendish Ct. S3: Shef . . .5B 4 (4E 119)
    S41: C'fld 3H 167
Cavendish Pl. S43: Bar H 3G 163
    S66: Malt 4B 102
Cavendish Ri. S18: Dron 4E 155
Cavendish Rd. DN5: Bntly 4H 23
    S11: Shef 1B 132
    S61: Roth 4B 96
    S75: Barn 5D 16
Cavendish Sq. S21: West H 4G 157
Cavendish St. S3: Shef 4B 4 (3E 119)
    S40: C'fld 5H 167
    S43: Stav 6H 163
Cavendish St. Nth. S41: Old W 4H 161
Cavendish Ter. DN5: Bntly 3H 23
    S21: West H 4G 157
Cavill Rd. S8: Shef 5F 133
Cawdor Rd. S2: Shef 2B 134
Cawdor St. DN5: Bntly 1A 40
Cawdron Cl. S65: Dalt 1C 98
Cawdron Ri. S60: Brins 5D 110
Cawley Pl. S71: Smi 4F 17
Cawood Dr. S63: Wath D 5G 49
Cawston Rd. S4: Shef 4H 107
CAWTHORNE 3A 14

Cawthorne Cl. S8: Shef 5D 132
    S65: Roth 3B 98
    S75: Dod 4H 29
Cawthorne Gro. S8: Shef 5D 132
Cawthorne La. S75: Cawt, Kexb 3A 14
Cawthorne Rd. S65: Roth 3B 98
    S75: Bar G 3D 14
Cawthorne Vw. S36: H'swne 1F 177
Caxton Cl. S43: New W 3C 162
Caxton La. S10: Shef 4A 118
Caxton Rd. DN6: Woodl 3C 22
    S10: Shef 4B 118
Caxton St. S70: Barn 6D 16
Caxton Way S25: Din 5G 127
Caythorpe Cl. S71: Lund 3D 18
Cayton Cl. S65: Rav 2B 100
    S71: Smi 1D 16
Cecil Av. DN4: Warm 1D 70
    S18: Dron 2F 155
Cecil Rd. S18: Dron 1F 155
Cecil Sq. S2: Shef 6E 119
Cedar Av. S40: C'fld 3E 167
    S64: Mexb 6E 51
    S66: Wick 5H 99
Cedar Cl. DN4: Balb 1F 71
    DN9: Auck 2B 76
    S21: Ecki 2C 158
    S21: Killa 5B 152
    S36: Stoc 4D 174
    S64: Swin 5B 66
    S71: R'ton 2F 9
Cedar Cres. S70: Barn 3G 31
Cedar Dr. S65: Rav 2C 100
    S66: Malt 5G 101
Cedar Gro. DN12: Con 6D 68
Cedar Nook S26: Kiv P 6H 139
Cedar Rd. DN3: Arm 3F 43
    DN4: Balb 1F 71
    S36: Stoc 4D 174
Cedars, The S10: Shef 4A 118
Cedar St. S43: Hol 5F 163
Cedar Va. S64: Swin 5B 66
Cedar Way S35: Chap 4E 79
Cedarwood Ct. S61: Scho 6F 81
Cedric Av. DN12: Con 5D 68
Cedric Cl. S66: Thurc 6B 114
Cedric Cres. S66: Thurc 6B 114
Cedric Rd. DN3: Eden 6C 26
Celandine Cl. S17: Bradw 5H 145
Celandine Gdns. S17: Bradw 5H 145
Celandine Ri. S64: Swin 6B 66
Celandine Ri. DN3: D'fld 5B 34
Celtic Ct. S61: Kimb P 6A 82
Cemetery Av. S11: Shef 5C 118
Cemetery La. S43: Stav 5B 164
Cemetery Rd. DN6: Woodl 4B 22
    S11: Shef 6D 118
    S18: Dron 4G 155
    S41: C'fld 6B 168
    S63: Bolt D 3B 50
    S63: Wath D 2F 65
    S64: Mexb 1F 67
    S70: Barn 2F 31
    S72: Grim 1B 20
    S73: Hem 5D 46
    S73: Womb 1G 47
    S74: Hem, Jum 5D 46
Cemetery Ter. S43: Brim 1D 168
Centenary Mkt. Hall S65: Roth 3F 97
Centenary Way S60: Roth 5D 96
    S65: Roth 5B 96
Centenary Works S60: Roth 4D 96
                        (off Masbrough St.)
Central Av. DN5: Bntly 2A 40
    DN6: Woodl 4B 22
    S25: Din 6A 128
    S40: C'fld 6F 167
    S64: Swin 4A 66
    S65: Roth 3A 98
    S66: Sunn 3G 99
    S72: Grim 6B 12
Central Blvd. DN2: Don 4G 41
Central Bus. Pk. S60: Roth 4D 96
Central Cl. S18: Uns 6B 156
Central Dr. DN11: New R 6B 74
    S41: Has 1B 172
    S44: Cal 5E 169
    S62: Rawm 6D 64
    S66: Thurc 6B 114
    S71: R'ton 3H 9
Central M. S25: Din 6B 128

Central Pde. S65: Roth 4A 98
Central Pavement S40: C'fld 5H 167
Central Rd. S60: Roth 4E 97
Central St. S41: Has 1B 172
    S74: Hoyl 1G 61
Central Ter. DN12: New E 4C 70
Central Wlk. S43: Brim 1C 168
Centre, The S66: Bram 5A 100
Centre in the Pk., The 6A 120
Centre Riding DN11: Wad 6H 71
    DN11: Wad, Wils 1G 89
Centurion Bus. Pk. S60: Roth 5B 96
Centurion Flds. DN4: Bess 5A 58
Centurion Retail Pk. DN5: Don 5A 40
Centurion St. S60: Roth 5B 96
Centurion Way DN5: Don 5A 40
Century Bus. Cen.
    S63: Wath D 3D 48
Century Cl. DN3: Kirk Sa 6A 26
Century Ct. DN12: New E 3D 70
Century Gdns. DN5: Bntly 1B 40
Century Pk. S63: Wath D 3D 48
Century Pk. Network Cen.
    S63: Wath D 3D 48
Century St. S9: Shef 6E 109
Century Vw. S60: Brins 4B 110
Ceramia Ct. S63: Gol 5F 37
Chadbourne Cl. DN3: Arm 5D 42
Chaddesden Cl. S18: Dron W 3B 154
Chaddesdon Wlk.
    DN12: Den M 2E 69
Chadwell Cl. S41: Has 3B 172
Chadwick Cl. S43: Stav 5A 164
Chadwick Dr. S66: Malt 4A 102
Chadwick Gdns. DN5: Ark 6D 24
Chadwick Rd. DN5: Don 5A 40
    DN6: Woodl 4B 22
    S13: Shef 1F 135
Chaff Cl. S60: Whis 3A 112
Chaffinch Av. S60: Brins 4E 111
Chaff La. S60: Whis 3A 112
Chalbury Cl. S75: Barn 4A 16
Chalfont Ct. S60: Brins 4E 111
Challands Cl. S41: Has 2B 172
Challands Way S41: Has 2B 172
Challenger Cars S63: Thurn 1B 36
Challenger Dr. DN5: Sprot 1F 55
Challiner M. S60: Cat 6D 110
Challoner Grn. S20: W'fld 2F 151
Challoner Way S20: W'fld 2F 151
Chalmers Dr. DN2: Don 1A 42
Chaloner Hgts. S74: Black H 3A 46
Chamberlain Av. DN5: Don 4H 39
Chamberlain Ct. S35: Chap 2E 79
Chamberlain Rd. DN1: Don 1C 56
Chambers Av. DN12: Con 4C 68
Chambers Dr. S35: Chap 1F 79
Chambers Gro. S35: Chap 1F 79
Chambers La. S4: Shef 3C 108
Chambers Rd. S61: Kimb P 1A 96
    S74: Hoyl 5A 46
Chambers Valley Rd. S35: Chap 1F 79
Chambers Vw. S35: Chap 1F 79
Chambers Way S35: Chap 6E 61
Chamossaire DN11: New R 6F 75
Champany Flds. S75: Dod 3E 29
Champion Cl. S5: Shef 4A 94
Champion St. S5: Shef 4A 94
Chancel Way S71: Monk B 5H 17
Chancery Pl. DN1: Don 1B 56
Chancet Ct. S8: Shef 1D 146
Chancet Wood Cl. S8: Shef 2E 147
Chancet Wood Dr. S8: Shef 2E 147
Chancet Wood Ri. S8: Shef 2E 147
Chancet Wood Rd. S8: Shef 1E 147
Chancet Wood Vw. S8: Shef 2E 147
Chandler Gro. S60: Tree 1F 123
Chandos Cres. S21: Killa 4B 152
Chandos St. S10: Shef 4B 118
Chaneyfield Way S41: C'fld 1C 166
Channing Gdns. S6: Shef 5C 106
Channing St. S6: Shef 5C 106
Chantrey Av. S41: C'fld 2G 167
Chantrey Rd. S8: Shef 5E 133
Chantry Bri. S60: Roth 3E 97
Chantry Cl. DN4: Can 5D 58
Chantry Gro. S71: R'ton 3H 9
Chantry Orchards S75: Dod 4F 29
Chantry Pl. S26: Kiv P 5C 140
Chapel Av. S73: Bramp 4B 48

Chapel Cl. DN9: Finn 3F 77
　　S10: Shef 5G 117
　　S35: Burn 3D 78
　　S61: Wing 4B 82
　　S63: Thurn 2D 36
　　S66: Thurc 5B 114
　　S70: Birdw 5D 44
　　S72: Shaft 3F 11
Chapel Cotts. S21: West H 5G 157
Chapel Ct. S63: Wath D 1F 65
　　S70: Birdw 5D 44
　　S71: Ard 2C 32
Chapel Cft. S73: Hem 5F 47
Chapelfield Cres. S61: Thorpe H 3C 80
Chapelfield Dr. S61: Thorpe H 3C 80
Chapel Fld. La. S36: Pen 5C 176
Chapelfield La. S61: Thorpe H 3C 80
Chapelfield Mt. S61: Thorpe H 3C 80
Chapelfield Pl. S61: Thorpe H 3C 80
Chapelfield Rd. S61: Thorpe H 2C 80
Chapelfields WF9: Sth K 4H 13
Chapelfield Vw. S36: Pen 5C 176
Chapel Fld. Wlk. S36: Pen 5C 176
Chapelfield Way S61: Thorpe H 3C 80
Chapel Hill S60: Whis 3A 112
　　S64: Swin 3B 66
　　S74: Black H 3A 46
　　　　　　　(off Wentworth Rd.)
Chapel Hole La. S66: Stain 5D 88
Chapel La. DN3: Brant 4H 59
　　DN9: Finn 2F 77
　　DN12: Con 5F 69
　　S9: Shef 6D 108
　　S17: Tot 6E 145
　　S18: App 3D 156
　　S35: Green M 1G 175
　　S36: Pen 5C 176
　　S60: Roth 5E 97
　　S63: Thurn 1E 37
　　S71: Car 6H 9
　　S72: Bill 4G 35
　　S72: Gt H, Lit H 2D 34
Chapel La. E. S41: Neas 3C 172
Chapel La. W. S40: Bramp 6D 166
Chapel M. S64: Swin 3B 66
　　S75: Stain 5B 8
Chapel of Our Lady 3E 97
Chapel Pl. S71: Ard 2C 32
Chapel Ri. S25: Nth A 3G 141
Chapel Rd. S35: Burn, Chap 3D 78
　　S35: High G 6D 60
　　S75: Pil 6B 44
Chapel St. DN5: Bntly 2A 40
　　S13: Shef 2C 136
　　S20: Mosb 4D 150
　　S41: Whit M 6H 161
　　　　　　　(off Station Rd.)
　　S43: Brim 6E 163
　　S61: Grea 4C 82
　　S62: Rawm 3G 83
　　S63: Bolt D 2B 50
　　S63: Thurn 2B 36
　　S63: Wath D 1F 65
　　S64: Mexb 1D 66
　　S70: Birdw 5D 44
　　S71: Ard 2C 32
　　S72: Grim 2B 20
　　S72: Shaft 3F 11
　　S74: Hoyl 1G 61
Chapel Ter. S10: Shef 5G 117
CHAPELTOWN 3F 79
Chapeltown Baths 3F 79
Chapeltown Rd. S35: Eccl 6G 79
Chapeltown Station (Rail) 3F 79
Chapel Vw. *S36: Thurl* 3A 176
　　　　　　　(off Matthew Gap)
Chapel Wlk. S1: Shef 3E 5 (3F 119)
　　S25: Sth A 4G 141
　　S60: Cat 1D 122
　　S60: Roth 4D 96
　　　　　　　(not continuous)
　　S62: Rawm 1E 83
　　S64: Mexb 2F 67
Chapel Way S26: Kiv P 6A 140
　　S62: Rawm 1E 83
Chapelwood Rd. S9: Shef 6E 109
Chapel Yd. S18: Dron 2F 155
Chapman Cl. S6: Shef 5G 105
Chapman St. S9: Shef 6E 95
Chappell Cl. S36: H'swne 1F 177
Chappell Dr. DN1: Don 5B 40

Chappell Rd. S36: H'swne 1F 177
Chapter Way S71: Monk B 5H 17
　　S75: Silk 1B 28
Charity St. S71: Monk B 2C 18
Charles Ashmore Rd. S8: Shef 2E 147
Charles Ct. DN3: Arm 3C 42
Charles Cres. DN3: Arm 3C 42
Charles Rd. S63: Wath D 1H 65
Charles Sq. S35: High G 1C 78
Charles St. DN1: Don 5D 40
　　S1: Shef 4E 5 (3F 119)
　　S25: Din 4A 128
　　S40: C'fld 5F 167
　　S62: Rawm 1A 84
　　S63: Gol 5C 36
　　S64: Kiln 1D 84
　　S64: Swin 4C 66
　　S66: Thurc 5B 114
　　S70: Barn 2D 30
　　S70: Wors 6F 31
　　S72: Cud 6F 11
　　S72: Grim 2B 20
　　S72: Midd 3F 35
　　S72: Sth H 1H 11
Charlotte Ct. S2: Shef 6G 119
Charlotte La. S1: Shef 4B 4
Charlotte Rd. S1: Shef 5F 119
　　S2: Shef 5F 119
CHARLTONBROOK 2D 78
Charlton Brook Cres.
　　S35: Chap 2D 78
Charlton Clough S35: Chap 3C 78
Charlton Dr. S35: High G 2C 78
Charlton Hill Ri. S35: Chap 3C 78
Charnell Av. S66: Malt 5B 102
Charnley Av. S11: Shef 3B 132
Charnley Cl. S11: Shef 2A 132
Charnley Dr. S11: Shef 3B 132
Charnley Ri. S11: Shef 3B 132
Charnock Av. S12: Shef 6E 135
Charnock Cres. S12: Shef 5D 134
Charnock Dale Rd. S12: Shef 6D 134
Charnock Dr. DN5: Cus 5G 39
　　S12: Shef 5E 135
Charnock Gro. S12: Shef 6E 135
CHARNOCK HALL 6E 135
Charnock Hall Rd. S12: Shef 6D 134
Charnock Vw. Rd. S12: Shef 6D 134
Charnock Wood Rd. S12: Shef 6E 135
Charnwood Ct. S20: Sot 6H 137
Charnwood Dr. DN4: Balb 1G 71
Charnwood Gro. S61: Kimb 3A 96
Charnwood Ho. S64: Swin 3C 66
Charnwood St. S64: Swin 3C 66
Charter Arc. S70: Barn 1E 31
Charter Row S1: Shef 6C 4 (4E 119)
Charter Sq. S1: Shef 5D 4 (4F 119)
Chartwell Av. S42: W'orth 5E 171
Chartwell Ri. S42: W'orth 5F 171
Chase, The S6: Lox 4E 105
　　S10: Shef 5C 118
　　　　　　　(off Clarke Dell)
　　S26: Aston 1D 138
Chasecliff Cl. S40: C'fld 3E 167
Chase Rd. S6: Lox 4E 105
Chatfield Rd. S8: Shef 6D 132
Chatham Ho. *S65: Roth* 4F 97
　　　　　　　(off Chatham St.)
Chatham St. S3: Shef 1F 119
　　S65: Roth 4F 97
Chatsworth Av. S40: Bramp 6C 166
　　S64: Mexb 6A 52
Chatsworth Bus. Pk. S40: C'fld 6F 167
Chatsworth Cl. S26: Aston 1E 139
Chatsworth Ct. S11: Shef 4G 131
　　S43: Stav 6A 164
Chatsworth Cres. DN5: Scawt 2G 39
Chatsworth Dr. DN11: Ross 6E 75
Chatsworth Pk. Av. S12: Shef 3D 134
Chatsworth Pk. Dr. S12: Shef 3D 134
Chatsworth Pk. Gro. S12: Shef 3D 134
Chatsworth Pk. Ri. S12: Shef 3D 134
Chatsworth Pk. Rd. S12: Shef 3D 134
Chatsworth Pl. S18: Dron W 2C 154
Chatsworth Ri. S60: Brins 4E 111
　　S75: Dod 3F 29
Chatsworth Rd. S17: Dore 4F 145
　　S40: Bramp, C'fld 6A 166
　　S71: Ath 2F 17
Chatterton Dr. S65: Roth 6A 98

Chaucer Cl. S5: Shef 4C 92
Chaucer Dr. S18: Dron 5H 155
Chaucer Ho. S65: Roth 5A 98
Chaucer Rd. S5: Shef 5C 92
　　S41: C'fld 6G 161
　　S64: Mexb 6G 51
　　S65: Roth 6A 98
Chauntry Av. S36: Pen 5E 177
Chavery Cl. S44: Ark T 6H 173
Cheadle St. S6: Shef 4B 106
Cheapside S70: Barn 1E 31
Checkstone Av. DN4: Bess 1B 74
Chedworth Cl. S75: Dart 1F 15
Cheedale Av. S40: C'fld 3D 166
Cheedale Cl. S40: C'fld 2E 167
Cheedale Wlk. S40: C'fld 3E 167
Cheetham Av. S18: Uns 1F 161
Cheetham Dr. S66: Malt 4B 102
Chelmsford Av. S26: Aston 6D 124
Chelmsford Dr. DN2: Don 4E 41
Chelmsford Way S43: Bar H 2G 163
Chelsea Cl. S11: Shef 1B 132
Chelsea Ri. S11: Shef 1B 132
Chelsea Rd. S11: Shef 1B 132
Cheltenham Ri. DN5: Scaws 5E 39
Cheltenham Rd. DN2: Don 5H 41
Chelwood Ct. DN4: Balb 1B 72
Chemist La. S60: Roth 3D 96
Cheney Row S1: Shef 4E 5
Chepstow Cl. S40: Birdh 2G 171
Chepstow Dr. S64: Mexb 6G 51
Chepstow Gdns.
　　DN5: Scaws 5E 39
　　S40: Birdh 3G 171
Chequer Av. DN4: Don 2D 56
Chequer Rd. DN1: Don 1C 56
Cheriton Av. DN6: Adw S 2B 22
Cherry Bank Rd. S8: Shef 5F 133
Cherry Brook S65: Roth 2A 98
Cherry Cl. S71: R'ton 2F 9
　　S72: Cud 6E 11
Cherry Gth. DN5: Bntly 5A 24
Cherry Gro. DN11: New R 6D 74
　　DN12: Con 6C 68
　　S63: Gol .5B 36
Cherry Hills S75: Dart 5H 7
Cherry La. DN5: Don 6A 40
Cherrys Rd. S71: Barn 6A 18
Cherry St. S2: Shef 6F 119
Cherry St. Sth. S2: Shef 6F 119
Cherry Tree Cl. S11: Shef 1C 132
　　S60: Brins 4E 111
　　S75: Stain 5B 8
Cherry Tree Ct. S11: Shef 1C 132
　　S63: Gol .5C 36
Cherry Tree Cres. S66: Wick 5H 99
Cherry Tree Dell S11: Shef 1C 132
Cherry Tree Dr. S11: Shef 6C 118
　　S21: Killa 5C 152
Cherry Tree Gro. S43: Mas M 3F 165
CHERRY TREE HILL 1C 132
Cherry Tree Pl. S63: Wath D 1G 65
Cherry Tree Rd. DN3: Arm 4E 43
　　DN4: Hex 2A 56
　　S11: Shef 1C 132
　　S26: Wales 6F 139
　　S66: Malt 5G 101
Cherry Tree St. S74: Els, Hoyl 6C 46
Cherry Wlk. S35: Chap 3F 79
Chertsey Cl. S40: Birdh 2G 171
Cherwell Cl. S43: Brim 5D 162
Chesham Rd. S70: Barn 1C 30
Cheshire Rd. DN1: Don 5D 40
Chessel Cl. S8: Shef 4F 133
Chester Ct. S21: Ecki 2C 158
　　WF9: Hems 1E 13
CHESTERFIELD 5H 167
Chesterfield and District Crematorium
　　S43: Brim 2C 168
Chesterfield Av. S43: New W 3D 162
Chesterfield Bowl 3A 172
Chesterfield Coach Station 6H 167
Chesterfield College
　　Infirmary Rd. 4H 167
　　Tapton House Campus 3B 168
Chesterfield Cricket Ground 6G 167
Chesterfield FC 1H 167
Chesterfield Golf Course 3E 171
Chesterfield Inner Relief Rd.
　　S41: C'fld, Whit M 4F 161
　　Chesterfield Lawn Tennis Club 4F 167

Chesterfield Mus. & Art Gallery—Church St.

Chesterfield Mus. & Art Gallery
..............................5A 168
Chesterfield Rd. S8: Shef 6E 133
S18: Dron 3F 155
S21: Ecki 3B 158
S26: Swal 2A 138
(not continuous)
S43: Brim 2B 168
S43: Hol, Stav 6F 163
S44: Ark T, Cal, Duck 6G 169
S44: Cal 6D 168
Chesterfield Rd. Sth. S8: Shef ...5F 147
Chesterfield Small Bus. Cen.
S41: Whit M 1H 167
(off Pottery La. W.)
Chesterfield Station (Rail) 5A 168
Chesterfield Trad. Est. S41: C'fld ..3D 160
Chesterhill Av. S75: Dalt 1D 98
Chester Ho. S40: C'fld 5F 167
Chester Rd. DN2: Don 4E 41
Chester St. S40: C'fld 5F 167
Chesterton Cl. S43: Brim C 4E 169
Chesterton Ct. S65: Roth 1H 97
Chesterton Rd. DN4: Balb 6B 56
S65: Roth 2G 97
Chesterton Way S65: Roth 1A 98
Chesterwood Dr. S10: Shef 4A 118
Chestnut Av. DN2: Don 3G 41
DN3: Arm 3E 43
DN11: New R 6D 74
S9: Shef 3H 121
S20: Beig 3G 137
S21: Ecki 2C 158
S21: Killa 5B 152
S26: Kiv P 5H 139
S36: Stoc 4D 174
S63: Wath D 2G 65
S65: Roth 3A 98
S72: Brier 4A 12
Chestnut Cl. S18: Dron 4H 155
S66: Flan 4G 99
Chestnut Ct. DN5: Bntly 6H 23
S35: Ough 3E 91
S65: Thry 5E 85
S70: Barn 3E 31
Chestnut Cres. S70: Barn 3G 31
Chestnut Dr. DN9: Auck 2B 76
S35: Chap 4D 78
S43: Hol 5F 163
S72: Sth H 1G 11
Chestnut Gro. DN5: Sprot 4C 54
DN12: Con 5D 68
S25: Din 4A 128
S63: Thurn 3C 36
S64: Mexb 6E 51
(not continuous)
S66: Malt 4G 101
WF9: Hems 1G 13
Chestnut M. S72: Sth H 1G 11
Chestnut Rd. S26: Swal 6A 124
Chestnut St. S72: Grim 3C 20
Chestnut Wlk. S66: Hoot L 6H 101
Cheswold La. DN5: Don 6H 39
Chevet Ho. DN1: Don 2B 56
(off Grove Pl.)
Chevet Ri. S71: R'ton 2G 9
Chevet Vw. S71: R'ton 2F 9
Cheviot Dr. DN5: Scawt 3G 39
Cheviot Wlk. S75: Barn 6A 16
Cheviot Way S40: C'fld 3D 166
Chevril Ct. S66: Wick 6F 99
Chiberworde Av. S61: Whis 4A 96
Chichester Rd. S10: Shef 2A 118
Chigwell Way S43: Bar H 3G 163
Chilcombe Pl. S70: Birdw 6E 45
Childers Dr. DN9: Auck 1H 59
Childers St. DN4: Don 3D 56
Chiltern Cl. S40: Ash 4D 166
Chiltern Ct. S40: C'fld 4D 166
(off Cuttholme Rd.)
Chiltern Cres. DN5: Sprot 3B 54
Chiltern Ri. S60: Brins 5E 111
Chiltern Rd. DN5: Scawt 3G 39
S6: Shef 4A 106
Chiltern Wlk. S75: Barn 6A 16
Chilton St. S70: Barn 2F 31
Chilwell Cl. S71: Ath 5E 9
Chilwell Gdns. S71: Ath 5E 9
Chilwell M. S71: Ath 5E 9
Chindit Ct. S25: Din 4A 128
Chinley St. S9: Shef 1D 120

Chippingham Pl. S9: Shef 6C 108
Chippingham St. S9: Shef 6C 108
(not continuous)
Chippinghouse Rd. S7: Shef 1E 133
S8: Shef 1E 133
Chiverton Cl. S18: Dron 2F 155
Chorley Av. S10: Shef 6D 116
Chorley Dr. S10: Shef 6D 116
Chorley Pl. S10: Shef 1D 130
Chorley Rd. S10: Shef 1D 130
Christchurch Av. S26: Aston ...6D 124
Christchurch Flats S63: Wath D ...5D 48
(off Masefield Rd.)
Christ Chu. Rd. DN1: Don 6C 40
S3: Shef 5G 107
Christchurch Rd. S63: Wath D ..5D 48
Christ Chu. Ter. DN1: Don 1D 56
Christian Ho. S75: Barn 5C 16
Chroma Dr. DN4: Balb 2C 72
Church Av. S62: Rawm 4F 83
Church Balk DN3: Eden 5B 26
Church Balk Gdns. DN3: Eden ...5C 26
Church Balk La. DN3: Eden 6C 26
Church Cl. DN9: Auck 2H 59
S21: Reni 4H 159
S26: Kiv P 6G 139
S35: Ough 3E 91
S42: W'orth 6H 171
S43: Stav 1H 169
S64: Swin 3B 66
S65: Rav 5H 85
S66: Malt 6A 102
S75: Dart 6F 7
Church Cnr. S25: Laugh M 1G 127
Church Cott. M. DN4: Balb 5F 55
Church Ct. DN4: Can 5C 58
S25: Sth A 4H 141
S72: Brier 3B 12
Church Cft. DN3: Eden 5B 26
S62: Rawm 4F 83
Churchdale M. S12: Shef 4G 135
Churchdale Rd. S12: Shef 4G 135
Church Dr. S36: H'swne 1F 177
S62: Wentw 5D 62
S72: Brier 4A 12
Church Farm Ct. S25: Sth A 4G 141
Churchfield S70: Barn 6D 16
Churchfield Av. S72: Cud 2E 19
S75: Kexb 6D 6
Churchfield Cl. DN5: Bntly 2H 39
S75: Kexb 6C 6
Churchfield Ct. S70: Barn 6D 16
S75: Kexb 6E 7
Churchfield Cres. S72: Cud 2E 19
Church Fld. Dr. S66: Wick 6G 99
Church Fld. Gdns. S71: Car 5A 10
Church Fld. La. S62: Wentw 6C 62
Church Fld. La. S75: Dart, Kexb ...6C 6
Church Flds. S61: Kimb 3H 95
Churchfields Cl. S70: Barn 6D 16
Church Flds. Rd. DN11: Ross ...4E 75
Churchfield Ter. S72: Cud 2E 19
Church Fld. Vw. DN4: Warm 5F 55
Church Fold S6: Shef 1H 105
S70: Barn 6D 16
Church Ga. S72: Brier 4B 12
Church Glebe S6: Shef 1H 105
Church Grn. DN5: Sprot 4C 54
S63: Wath D 6F 49
Church Gro. S66: B'well 6B 88
S71: Monk B 4H 17
Church Hgts. S36: H'swne 1F 177
Church Hill S60: Whis 3B 112
S71: R'ton 3A 10
Church Ho. M. S74: Jum 5C 46
(off Church St.)
Church Ho's. S43: Hol 5F 163
Churchill Av. DN5: Don 4H 39
S66: Malt 4B 102
Churchill Rd. DN1: Don 4D 40
S10: Shef 3B 118
S36: Stoc 2B 174
Churchill Way S35: Chap 6E 61
Church La. DN3: Barn D 1G 27
DN4: Bess, Can 6B 58
DN4: Warm, Balb 5E 55
(not continuous)
DN5: Barnb, Harl 2H 51
DN6: Adw S 2D 22

Church La. DN9: Finn 3E 77
DN11: Wad 5E 73
S9: Shef 6C 108
S12: Ridg 3H 149
S12: Shef 5D 136
S13: Shef 2C 136
S17: Dore 4E 145
S20: Beig 5H 137
S21: Killa 4D 152
S25: Din 5G 127
S26: Aston 2E 139
S36: H'swne 1F 177
S75: C'fld 5H 167
S42: Tem N 6G 173
S60: Cat 6D 110
S60: Tree 2F 123
S63: Wath D 6F 49
S65: Rav 5A 86
S66: Bram 5A 100
S66: Clftn 3G 87
S66: Malt 6A 102
S66: Wick 6G 99
S70: Barn 6D 16
S70: Wors 2E 45
S72: Sth H 1E 11
S75: Cawt 4A 14
S75: Tank 3D 60
S81: Letw 4F 129
Church La. Ct. S25: Din 6H 127
Church La. M. S66: Bram 5A 100
Church La. Nth.
S41: Old W 3H 161
Church Lea S74: Hoyl 2B 62
Church Mdw. Rd.
DN11: Ross 5E 75
Church Mdws. S25: Din 6H 127
S44: Cal 5E 169
Church M. DN5: Bntly 2H 39
S20: Mosb 3E 151
S21: Killa 3D 152
S63: Bolt D 3B 50
S64: Mexb 2H 67
Church Rein Cl.
DN4: Warm 6D 54
Church Rd. DN3: Barn D 1G 27
DN3: Kirk Sa 4C 26
DN11: Wad 2H 89
DN12: Den M 2D 68
DN12: New E 3C 70
S25: Cawt 4A 14
Churchside S41: Has 4C 172
S42: Gras 4C 172
S44: Cal 5E 169
Churchside La. S41: Has 4C 172
Church St. DN1: Don 6B 40
DN3: Arm 4D 42
DN5: Bntly 2H 39
DN12: Con 4F 69
S1: Shef 3E 5 (3F 119)
S6: Stan 1D 116
S18: Dron 3F 155
S18: Uns 5B 156
S21: Ecki 6F 151
S26: Wales 6G 139
S35: Eccl 1F 93
S35: Ough 3D 90
S36: Pen 4D 176
S43: Brim 6D 162
S43: Stav 4B 164
S44: Cal 5E 169
S60: Roth 4E 97
S61: Grea 4B 82
S61: Kimb 3H 95
S62: Rawm 4F 83
S63: Bolt D 2B 50
S63: Thurn 2B 36
S63: Wath D 6F 49
S64: Mexb 2G 67
S64: Swin 3A 66
S66: Thurc 6C 114
S70: Barn 6D 16
S71: Car 5A 10
S71: R'ton 3H 9
S72: Brier 3A 12
S72: Cud 2E 19
S72: Gt H 6F 21
S73: D'fld 5C 34
S73: Womb 2G 47
S74: Els 1D 62
S74: Jum 5C 46

Church St. S75: Barn 5H **15**
  S75: Cawt 3A **14**
  S75: Dart 6F **7**
  S75: Stain 5B **8**
Church St. Cl. S63: Thurn 2B **36**
Church St. Nth. S41: Old W 3H **161**
Church St. Sth. S40: Birdh 3G **171**
  (not continuous)
Church St. W. S40: Bramp 6D **166**
Church Ter. S75: Dod 3F **29**
CHURCH TOWN 4D **152**
Church Vw. DN1: Don 6B **40**
  DN5: Barnb 1H **51**
  DN11: Wad 6E **73**
  DN12: New E 5B **70**
  S6: Shef 1H **105**
  S13: Shef 2D **136**
  S21: Killa 3D **152**
  S26: Aston 1E **139**
  S26: Tod 3C **140**
  S40: Bramp 6D **166**
  S64: Swin 3B **66**
  S65: Thry 5E **85**
  S66: Wick 6G **99**
  S70: Wors 5G **31**
  S72: Cud 2E **19**
  S73: D'fld 5D **34**
  S74: Hoyl 1G **61**
  S75: Barn 5C **16**
Church Vw. Apartments S61: Grea . .5C **82**
  (off Fitzwilliam Wlk.)
Church Vw. Cres. S36: Pen 4D **176**
Church Vw. Rd. S36: Pen 4D **176**
Church Wlk. DN12: Den M 2D **68**
  S40: C'fld 5H **167**
  (off Stephenson Pl.)
  S43: New W 2C **162**
  S63: Thurn 2B **36**
  (off Church St.)
Church Way DN1: Don 6B **40**
  DN6: Adw S 2C **22**
  S40: C'fld 5H **167**
Churcroft S75: Barn 4H **15**
Churston Rd. S40: Ash 5E **167**
Cinder Bri. Rd. S61: Grea 4D **82**
Cinder Hill La. S35: Gren 2C **92**
Cinderhill La. S8: Shef 2G **147**
Cinderhill Rd. S61: Kimb P 6H **81**
Cinder Hills Way S75: Dod 3H **29**
Cinder La. S21: Killa 3E **153**
Cineworld Cinema
  Chesterfield 1A **172**
  Sheffield 4F **109**
Circle, The DN11: New R 5B **74**
  S2: Shef 5D **120**
  S35: High G 1D **78**
Circle Cl. S2: Shef 6E **121**
Circuit, The DN6: Woodl 2A **22**
Circular Dr. S21: Reni 4H **159**
Circular Rd. S41: Has 2A **172**
  S43: Stav 6A **164**
City Athletics Stadium 1C **120**
City Hall Stop (ST) 3D **4** (3F **119**)
City Rd. S2: Shef 4A **120**
  S32: Shef 2D **134**
City Road Crematorium S2: Shef . . .6B **120**
City Vw. S4: Shef 2D **108**
City Wharfe S3: Shef 1F **5** (2G **119**)
Civic, The .1E **31**
Civic Theatre
  Rotherham 4F **97**
Clanricarde St. S71: Barn 4D **16**
Claphouse Fold S75: Haigh 1B **6**
Clara Pl. S61: Kimb 4A **96**
Clare Ct. S60: Roth 3E **97**
Clarehurst Rd. S73: D'fld 4B **34**
Clarel Cl. S36: Pen 5C **176**
Clarel Gdns. DN4: Can 3B **58**
Clarel St. S36: Pen 5C **176**
Claremont Cres. S10: Shef 3C **118**
Claremont Gdns. S71: Lund 4C **18**
Claremont Pl. S10: Shef 3C **118**
Claremont St. S61: Kimb 4A **96**
Clarence Av. DN4: Balb 4A **56**
Clarence Ct. S6: Shef 4A **106**
Clarence La. S3: Shef 5E **119**
Clarence Pl. S66: Malt 4B **102**
Clarence Rd. S6: Shef 4A **106**
  S40: C'fld 5G **167**
  S71: Monk B 4G **17**
Clarence Sq. S25: Din 5B **128**

Clarence St. S25: Din 5B **128**
  S40: C'fld 5G **167**
  S63: Wath D 5D **48**
Clarence Ter. S63: Thurn 2D **36**
Clarendon Ct. S11: Shef 6F **117**
Clarendon Dr. S10: Shef 6F **117**
Clarendon Rd. S10: Shef 6F **117**
  S43: Ink 1H **169**
  S65: Roth 3G **97**
Clarendon St. S70: Barn 1C **30**
Clark Av. DN4: Don 2D **56**
  DN12: New E 6C **70**
Clarke Av. S25: Laugh C 3F **127**
Clarke Rd. S66: Thurc 6D **114**
Clarke Ct. S25: Din 4A **128**
Clarke Dell S10: Shef 5C **118**
Clarke Dr. S10: Shef 5C **118**
Clarkegrove Rd. S10: Shef 5C **118**
Clarkehouse Rd. S10: Shef 5B **118**
Clarkes Cft. S73: Womb 1G **47**
Clarke Sq. S2: Shef 6E **119**
Clarke St. S10: Shef 6A **4** (4D **118**)
  S75: Barn 5C **16**
Clark Gro. S6: Star 6E **105**
Clarks Ct. DN6: Adw S 2C **22**
Clarkson Av. S40: C'fld 2G **171**
Clarkson St. S10: Shef 3D **118**
  S70: Wors 5H **31**
Clark St. S74: Hoyl 5A **46**
Clarney Av. S73: D'fld 4A **34**
Clarney Pl. S73: D'fld 4B **34**
Clayburn Rd. S72: Grim 3A **20**
Claycliffe Av. S75: Barn 4G **15**
Claycliffe Bus. Pk. S75: Bar G 3G **15**
Claycliffe Rd.
  S75: Barn, Bar G, Birdw 2G **15**
Claycliffe Ter. S63: Gol 5D **36**
  S70: Barn 2C **30**
Clayfield Av. S64: Mexb 1A **68**
Clayfield Cl. S64: Mexb 1A **68**
Clayfield Ct. S64: Mexb 1A **68**
Clayfield La. S62: Wentw 5E **63**
Clayfield Rd. S64: Mexb 1A **68**
  S74: Hoyl 4A **46**
Clayfields DN4: Balb 1H **71**
Clayfield Vw. S64: Mexb 6A **52**
Clay Flat La. DN11: New R 6C **74**
Clay La. DN2: Don 1A **42**
  S1: Shef 5E **5** (4F **119**)
Claypit La. S62: Rawm 3H **83**
Clay Pits La. S36: Stoc 2A **174**
Clay Pit Way S9: Shef 6E **109**
Clayroyd S70: Wors 6G **31**
Clay St. S9: Shef 5C **108**
  (not continuous)
Clayton Av. S63: Thurn 1A **36**
Clayton Cres. S20: Water 6F **137**
Clayton Dr. S63: Thurn 2A **36**
Clayton Hollow S20: Water 6F **137**
Clayton La. S63: Thurn 1A **36**
Clayton St. S41: C'fld 6A **168**
Clayton Vw. WF9: Scth K 5H **13**
Claywheels La. S6: Shef 6A **92**
Claywood Dr. S2: Shef 6H **5** (4H **119**)
Claywood Rd. S2: Shef 5H **5** (4H **119**)
  (Claywood Dr.)
  S2: Shef 5H **119**
  (Fitzwalter Rd.)
Clayworth Dr. DN4: Bess 6G **57**
Clear Vw. S72: Grim 6B **12**
Clearwell Cft. DN5: Cus 5G **39**
Cleeve Hill Gdns. S20: Water 6E **137**
Clement M. S61: Kimb 4H **95**
Clementson Rd. S10: Shef 2B **118**
Clement St. S9: Shef 6E **109**
  S61: Kimb 4H **95**
Cleveden Way S71: R'ton 2G **9**
Clevedon Cres. DN5: Scawt 1G **39**
Clevedon Way S66: Malt 3C **102**
Cleveland Rd. DN3: Arm 4F **43**
Cleveland St. DN1: Don 2B **56**
  S6: Shef 1D **118**
Cleveland Way S40: C'fld 4C **166**
Cliff Ct. DN12: Den M 3C **68**
Cliff Cres. DN4: Warm 6D **54**
Cliff Dr. S73: D'fld 5D **34**
Cliffe Av. S70: Wors 5G **31**
Cliffe Bank S64: Swin 3C **66**
Cliffe Cl. S72: Brier 3A **12**
Cliffe Ct. S71: Monk B 5H **17**

Cliffe Cres. S75: Dod 3F **29**
Cliffedale Cres. S70: Wors 4G **31**
Cliffe Farm Dr. S11: Shef 1H **131**
Cliffefield Rd. S8: Shef 3E **133**
  (not continuous)
  S64: Swin 3C **66**
Cliffe Vw. S64: Swin 3C **66**
Cliffe Hill S6: Dung, Stan 5A **104**
  S75: Cawt 3A **14**
Cliffe Ho. Rd. S5: Shef 6G **93**
Cliffe La. S71: Monk B 5H **17**
Cliffe Rd. S6: Shef 6H **105**
  S73: Bramp 4B **48**
Cliffe Vw. Rd. S8: Shef 3F **133**
Cliff Hill S66: Malt 5G **101**
Cliff Hills Cl. S66: Malt 5H **101**
Cliff La. S72: Brier 3A **12**
Clifford Av. S65: Thry 6F **85**
Clifford Cl. S40: Bramp 6C **166**
Clifford Lister Bus. Cen., The
  S66: Wick 6F **99**
Clifford Rd. S11: Shef 1C **132**
  S61: Kimb P 1H **95**
  S66: Hel 6D **100**
  WF9: Scth K 4H **13**
Clifford St. S72: Cud 5F **11**
Clifford Wlk. DN12: Den M 3B **68**
Cliff Rd. S6: Stan 6E **105**
  S73: D'fld 5D **34**
Cliff St. S11: Shef 5E **119**
  S64: Mexb 2F **67**
Cliff Ter. S71: Barn 1F **31**
Cliff Vw. DN12: Den M 2C **68**
CLIFTON
  S65 . . . . .4G **97**
  S66 . . . . .3G **87**
Clifton Av. S9: Shef 3H **121**
  S65: Roth 4H **97**
  S71: Ath .6D **8**
Clifton Bank S60: Roth 4F **97**
Clifton Byres S66: Clftn 3G **87**
Clifton Cl. S71: Ath 6D **8**
Clifton Cres. DN2: Don 4G **41**
  S9: Shef 3G **121**
Clifton Cres. Nth. S65: Roth 4G **97**
Clifton Cres. Sth. S65: Roth 4G **97**
Clifton Dr. DN5: Sprot 2F **55**
Clifton Gdns. S72: Brier 3H **11**
Clifton Gro. S65: Roth 4G **97**
Clifton Hill DN12: Con 5F **69**
Clifton La. DN12: Con 6G **69**
  S9: Shef 4H **121**
  S65: Roth 4F **97**
Clifton Mt. S65: Roth 4F **97**
Clifton Park Mus. 4G **97**
Clifton Pk. Vw. S65: Roth 3G **97**
Clifton Ri. S66: Malt 4H **101**
Clifton Rd. S72: Grim 1B **20**
Clifton St. S9: Shef 4E **109**
  S40: C'fld 5F **167**
  S70: Barn 2F **31**
  WF9: Hems 1D **12**
Clifton Ter. DN12: Con 4G **69**
  S65: Roth 4F **97**
Clipstone Av. S71: Ath 6F **9**
Clipstone Gdns. S9: Shef 6F **109**
Clipstone Rd. S9: Shef 6F **109**
Clock Ct. S25: Din 4G **127**
Clock Tower Bus. Cen., The
  S43: Hol 4G **163**
Cloisters, The DN4: Can 5D **58**
  S70: Wors 2E **45**
Cloisters Way S71: Monk B 5A **18**
Cloister Way S72: Grim 1B **20**
Cloonmore Cft. S8: Shef 1H **147**
Cloonmore Dr. S8: Shef 1H **147**
Close, The DN3: Brant 4G **59**
  DN4: Warm 2F **71**
  S25: Din 6A **128**
  S71: Car 5H **9**
  S71: Lund 5B **18**
Cloudberry Way S75: Stain 6C **8**
Clough, The S41: C'fld 1D **172**
Clough Bank S2: Shef 6G **119**
  S61: Roth 3C **96**
CLOUGH FIELD 2G **117**
Clough Flds. S10: Shef 2G **117**

Clough Flds. Rd.—Coniston Way

Clough Flds. Rd. S74: Hoyl 1H 61
Clough Grn. S61: Roth 3D 96
Clough Gro. S35: Ough 3F 91
Clough Head S36: Cub 6D 176
Clough La. S10: Shef 2A 130
Clough Rd. S1: Shef 5F 119
S2: Shef 5F 119
S61: Roth 4C 96
(not continuous)
S74: Hoyl 1A 62
Clough St. S61: Roth 3C 96
Clough Wood Vw. S35: Ough 4E 91
Clovelly Rd. DN3: Eden 6C 26
Clover Ct. S8: Shef 6H 133
Clover Gdns. S5: Shef 1B 108
Clover Grn. S61: Kimb P 6H 81
Cloverlands Dr. S75: Stain 6B 8
Clover Wlk. S63: Bolt D 1A 50
Club Gdn. Rd. S11: Shef 6E 119
Club Gdn. Wlk. *S11: Shef* *5E 119*
(off London Rd.)
Club Grn. Rd. S11: Shef 5E 119
Club Mill Rd. S6: Shef 3D 106
Clubmill Ter. S40: C'fld 4F 167
Club St. S11: Shef 6E 119
S71: Monk B 4H 17
S74: Hoyl 1G 61
Clumber Pl. S43: Ink 2H 169
Clumber Ri. S26: Aston 2D 138
Clumber Rd. DN4: Don 3E 57
S10: Shef 5F 117
Clumber St. S75: Barn 6B 16
Clun Rd. S4: Shef 6H 107
Clun St. S4: Shef 6H 107
Clyde Rd. S8: Shef 2E 133
Clyde St. S71: Barn 1E 31
Coach Ho. Dr. DN5: Cus 6E 39
Coach Ho. La. S70: Barn 4E 31
Coach Houses, The *S10: Shef* *2C 118*
(off Moorgate Av.)
Coach Rd. S61: Grea 4C 82
S62: H'ley, Wentw 5A 62
COAL ASTON 6H 147
Coalbrook Av. S13: Shef 6E 123
Coalbrook Gro. S13: Shef 6E 123
Coalbrook Rd. S13: Shef 6E 123
Coalby Wlk. *S70: Barn* *6D 16*
(off Fitzwilliam St.)
Coal Pit La. S35: Ough 5B 90
S36: Stoc 5D 174
S66: Mick 6F 87
S72: Cud 3G 19
S72: Shaft 4G 11
Coalpit La. S26: Wales 1G 153
Coalpit Rd. DN12: Den M 3B 68
Coal Riding La. S65: Dalt M 4E 99
Coates La. S75: Silk C 6B 28
Coates St. S2: Shef 4H 119
Cobb Ct. S64: Swin 5C 66
Cobb Dr. S64: Swin 5B 66
Cobcar Av. S74: Els 1E 63
Cobcar Cl. S74: Els 6D 46
Cobcar La. S74: Els 6D 46
Cobcar St. S74: Els 1D 62
Cobden Av. S64: Mexb 1G 67
Cobden Pl. S10: Shef 2B 118
Cobden Rd. S40: C'fld 4G 167
Cobden Ter. S10: Shef 2B 118
Cobden Vw. Rd. S10: Shef 2A 118
Cobnar Av. S8: Shef 6F 133
Cobnar Dr. S8: Shef 6F 133
S41: C'fld 6E 161
Cobnar Gdns. S8: Shef 6E 133
Cobnar Rd. S8: Shef 6E 133
Cobnar Wood Cl. S41: C'fld 3C 160
COCK ALLEY 1F 173
Cockayne Pl. S8: Shef 3E 133
Cockerham Av. S75: Barn 5D 16
Cockerham La. S75: Barn 5D 16
Cockhill Fld. La. S66: B'well 6B 88
Cockhill La. S66: B'well, Stain 2B 88
Cockpit La. S36: Pen 4D 176
Cockshot La. S36: Bolst 5E 175
Cockshot Pit La. S75: Mapp 6H 7
Cockshutt Av. S8: Shef 2C 146
Cockshutt Dr. S8: Shef 2C 146
Cockshutt Rd. S8: Shef 2C 146
Cockshutts La. S35: Ough 2C 90
Coggin Mill Way S60: Roth 5B 96
COISLEY HILL 2A 136
Coisley Hill S13: Shef 2A 136
Coisley Rd. S13: Shef 3B 136
Coit La. S11: Shef 5E 131
Coke Hill S60: Roth 5E 97
Coke La. S60: Roth 5E 97
Colbeck Cl. DN3: Arm 4D 42
Colby Pl. S6: Shef 1G 117
Colchester Ct. DN5: Scaws 4F 39
Colchester Rd. S10: Shef 2A 118
Coldstream Av. DN4: Warm 6E 55
Coldwell Hill S35: Ough 3C 90
Coldwell La. S10: Shef 3F 117
Coldwell's Fold S36: Thurl 3A 176
Coleford Rd. S9: Shef 6F 109
Coleman St. S62: P'gte 5G 83
Coleridge Av. S71: Monk B 4G 17
Coleridge Gdns. S9: Shef 6E 109
Coleridge Rd. DN3: Barn D 1H 27
S9: Shef 5D 108
S63: Wath D 5D 48
S65: Roth 3G 97
S66: Malt 6B 102
Colewell Cl. S73: Womb 6F 33
Coley La. S62: Wentw 5G 63
Colister Dr. S9: Shef 2F 121
Colister Gdns. S9: Shef 3E 121
College Av. S43: Stav 5A 164
College Cl. S4: Shef 4H 107
College Ct. S4: Shef 4H 107
S64: Mexb 1G 67
College Flds. S70: Barn 3A 30
College Ho. S75: Barn 4C 16
College La. *S65: Roth* *4E 97*
(off Howard St.)
College Pk. Cl. S60: Roth 1F 111
College Rd. DN1: Don 2B 56
S60: Roth 4C 96
(not continuous)
S64: Mexb 1G 67
COLLEGE ROAD RDBT. 3D 96
College St. S10: Shef 4C 118
S65: Roth 4E 97
College Ter. S73: D'fld 5B 34
College Wlk. *S60: Roth* *3E 97*
(off Frederick St.)
College Wlk. Shop. Cen. *S60: Roth* *3E 97*
(off Frederick St.)
Collegiate Cres. S10: Shef 6A 4 (5C 118)
Colley Av. S5: Shef 4F 93
S70: Barn 4H 31
Colley Cl. S5: Shef 4F 93
Colley Cres. S5: Shef 4G 93
S70: Barn 3H 31
Colley Dr. S5: Shef 4G 93
Colley Pl. S70: Barn 3H 31
Colley Rd. S5: Shef 4F 93
Collier Ct. S63: Bramp B 5A 48
Collier Rd. S72: Shaft 5F 11
Colliers Cl. S13: Shef 2C 136
Colliery Av. S63: Wath D 4F 49
Colliery Cl. S25: Din 4H 127
S43: Stav 5C 164
Colliery Dr. S21: Killa 5C 152
Colliery La. S63: Gol 4C 36
Colliery Rd. S4: Shef 3D 108
S26: Kiv P 6A 140
Colliery Vs. S66: Thurc 4C 114
Colliery Yd. S75: Pil 2C 60
Collin Av. S6: Shef 3H 105
Collindridge Rd. S73: Womb 2G 47
Collingbourne Av. S20: Sot 1H 151
Collingbourne Dr. S20: Sot 1H 151
Collingham Rd. S26: Swal 2B 138
Collins Cl. S75: Dod 3F 29
Collinson Rd. S5: Shef 6F 93
Collins Yd. *S18: Dron* *3G 155*
(off Mill La.)
Collishaw Cl. S41: Has 2B 172
Colonel Ward Dr. S64: Swin 3D 66
Colonnades Shop. Cen. DN1: Don 1B 56
Colster Cl. S75: Barn 6H 15
Coltfield S70: Birdw 3E 45
Coltishall Av. S66: Bram 4B 100
Colton Cl. S41: C'fld 5F 161
Columbia Pl. S2: Shef 6F 5
Columbia St. S70: Barn 3D 30
Columbus Way S66: Malt 4H 101
Colver Rd. S2: Shef 6F 119
(not continuous)
Colvin Cl. DN5: Ark 1D 40
Colwall St. S9: Shef 6C 108
Colwick Gro. S61: Roth 3B 96
Combined Court
Rotherham 4E 97
Sheffield 1E 5 (2F 119)
Comelybank Dr. DN12: Den M 2A 68
S64: Mexb 2A 68
Comet Ct. DN9: Auck 2C 76
Commerce St. S35: Chap 2G 79
Commercial Rd. S63: Gol 6A 36
Commercial St. S1: Shef 3G 5 (3G 119)
S70: Barn 2F 31
Commercial Way DN4: Warm 3E 71
Common, The S35: Eccl 6G 79
S72: Sth H 1H 11
COMMON END 1G 13
Common Farm Cl. S65: Rav 2A 100
Common La. DN3: Barn D 1F 27
DN4: Warm 6E 55
DN5: Alm 3F 25
DN9: Auck 1H 59
DN11: New R 6H 75
DN12: Con 1G 87
S11: Shef 2E 131
S36: Spink 5G 175
S42: Cut 6A 160
S63: Bolt D 4C 50
S63: Wath D 6A 50
S65: Rav 1C 100
S66: Bramp M 1H 125
S66: Clftn 1G 87
S66: Thurc 1E 127
S71: R'ton 2H 9
(not continuous)
Common Rd. DN12: Con 5H 69
S25: Din 4G 127
S25: Nth A 5C 126
S63: Thurn 2A 36
S72: Brier 4B 12
WF9: Sth K 5E 13
Common Rd. Av. WF9: Sth K 5H 13
COMMON SIDE 3C 134
Commonside S10: Shef 2B 118
Common Side Cft. S12: Shef 3C 134
Commonwealth Vw. S63: Bolt D 2A 50
Companions Cl. S66: Wick 6G 99
Compass Ct. S21: Killa 6B 152
Compass Cres. S41: Old W 3B 162
Compton St. S6: Shef 6A 106
S40: C'fld 5G 167
Comrades Ho. DN5: Bntly 1B 40
Comrades Pl. S63: Gol 5E 37
Conalan Av. S17: Bradw 5A 146
CONANBY 4E 69
Conan Rd. DN12: Con 4E 69
Concept Ct. S63: Wath D 4D 48
Concorde M. DN1: Don 6C 40
Concord Pk. Golf Course 5B 94
Concord Rd. S5: Shef 4B 94
Concord Sports Cen. 6B 94
Concord Vw. Rd. S61: Kimb 5F 95
Concourse Way S1: Shef 4G 5
Conduit La. S10: Shef 2B 118
Conduit Rd. S10: Shef 2B 118
Cone La. S75: Silk, Silk C 3B 28
Conery Cl. S65: Thry 6F 85
Coney Rd. DN5: Bntly 4H 23
Congress St. S1: Shef 3C 4 (3E 119)
Coningsburgh Rd. DN3: Eden 6C 26
Coningsby Ho. S10: Shef 4E 117
Coningsby Rd. S5: Shef 3H 107
CONISBROUGH 4F 69
Conisbrough Castle 4F 69
Conisbrough Castle Vis. Cen. 4F 69
Conisbrough Station (Rail) 3E 69
Coniston Av. S75: Stain 4H 7
Coniston Cl. S25: Nth A 2A 142
S36: Pen 3D 176
Coniston Ct. S64: Mexb 6A 52
Coniston Dr. DN4: Balb 2G 71
S63: Bolt D 3B 50
Coniston Ho. *S40: C'fld* *1A 172*
(off Spinners Cft.)
Coniston Pl. DN5: Scawt 2G 39
Coniston Rd. DN2: Don 6H 41
DN3: Kirk Sa 4C 26
S8: Shef 3D 132
S18: Dron W 4C 154
S41: C'fld 6E 161
S64: Mexb 6H 51
S71: Barn 1F 31
Coniston Ter. S8: Shef 3D 132
Coniston Way S41: C'fld 6E 161

198 A-Z Sheffield

Connaught Dr. DN3: Kirk Sa 4C 26
Connelly Ct. S40: C'fld 5F 167
Conrad Dr. S66: Malt 4H 101
Constable Cl. S14: Shef 6A 134
 S18: Dron 3D 154
 S66: Flan 4G 99
Constable Dr. S14: Shef 6A 134
Constable La. S25: Din 5A 128
Constable Pl. S14: Shef 6B 134
 S63: Wath D 6F 49
Constable Rd. S14: Shef 6A 134
Constable Way S14: Shef 6A 134
 S65: Dalt 1B 98
Constitution Hill DN5: Cad 2G 69
Convent Gro. DN4: Bess 4A 58
Convent Pl.
 S3: Shef 4B 4 (3E 119)
Convent Wlk. S3: Shef 4B 4 (3E 119)
Conway Ct. DN4: Bess 1A 74
Conway Cres. S65: Roth 2B 98
Conway Dr. DN3: Brant 4G 59
 DN5: Barnb 1H 51
Conway Pl. S73: Womb 3A 48
Conway St. S3: Shef 4A 4 (3D 118)
 S70: Stair 2A 32
Conway Ter. S64: Mexb 6F 51
Conyers S26: Aston 6C 124
Conyers Rd. DN5: Don 5A 40
Coode S3: Shef 1F 5 (2G 119)
Coo Hill S13: Shef 2D 136
Cook Av. S66: Malt 4H 101
Cooke & Beard Homes S8: Shef 3G 133
Cooke St. DN5: Bntly 2H 39
Cookson Cl. S5: Shef 6C 92
Cookson Rd. S5: Shef 6C 92
Cookson St. DN4: Balb 4A 56
Cooks Rd. S20: Beig 6H 137
Cooks Wood Rd. S3: Shef 5F 107
Coole Well Cl. S43: Stav 6A 164
Coombe Pl. S10: Shef 3B 118
Coombe Rd. S10: Shef 3B 118
Co-operative Cotts. S43: Pool 6D 164
 S72: Brier 3A 12
Co-operative St. S63: Gol 5D 36
 S63: Wath D 5E 49
 S72: Cud 2D 18
Cooper Cl. S63: Bramp B 6B 48
Cooper Gallery 6D 16
Cooper Rd. S75: Kexb 6D 6
Cooper Row S75: Dod 4G 29
 (off Stainborough Rd.)
Coopers Ho. S11: Shef 5D 118
 (off Napier St.)
Coopers Ter. DN1: Don 1C 56
Cooper St. DN4: Don 3D 56
Copeland Rd. S73: Womb 2F 47
Cope St. S70: Barn 3E 31
Copley Av. DN12: Con 4D 68
Copley Cres. DN5: Scaws 4D 38
Copley Gdns. DN5: Sprot 4C 54
Copley Pl. S61: Roth 2B 96
Copley Rd. DN1: Don 6C 40
Copper Beech Cl. S20: Beig 5H 137
Copper Beech Cres. S66: Hoot L 1H 115
Copper Cl. S36: Pen 2E 31
Copper St. S3: Shef 1D 4 (4E 119)
Coppice, The S61: Kimb P 6F 81
Coppice Av. S75: Barn 4A 16
Coppice Cl. S36: Stoc 2B 174
 S41: Has 4C 172
Coppice Gdns. S61: Grea 6C 82
Coppice La. S6: Stan 2C 116
 S62: H'ley 5A 62
Coppice Ri. S35: Chap 2G 79
Coppice Rd. DN6: Highf 6C 22
 S10: Shef 3D 116
Coppice Vw. S10: Shef 3G 117
Coppicewood Ct. DN4: Balb 2B 72
Coppins St. S66: Bram 4A 100
Coppin Sq. S5: Shef 3E 93
Copse, The S66: Bram 4A 100
Coquet Av. S66: Bram 6A 100
Coral Cl. S26: Augh 4B 124
Coral Dr. S26: Augh 4B 124
Coral Pl. S26: Augh 4B 124
Coral Way S26: Augh 4B 124
Corbridge Ct. DN4: Bess 4H 57
CORBRIGGS 5E 173
Corbriggs Cvn. Pk. S41: Cor 5E 173
Corby Rd. S4: Shef 3C 108
Cordwell Av. S41: C'fld 6D 160

Cordwell Cl. S43: Stav 6A 164
Core, The .6D 16
CORKER BOTTOMS 4D 120
Corker Bottoms La. S2: Shef 3C 120
Corker Rd. S12: Shef 3D 134
Corner Pin Cl. S43: Stav 4C 164
Cornfall Pl. S70: Barn 1C 30
Cornfield Cl. S42: Ash 3B 166
Cornflower Dr. DN4: Bess 4G 57
Corn Hill DN12: Con 5G 69
Cornhill S3: Shef 3A 4
Cornish Ho. S3: Shef 1E 119
 (off Adelaide La.)
Cornish St. S6: Shef 1E 119
 (not continuous)
Cornish Way S62: P'gte 6F 83
Corn Mill Ct. S6: Shef 5A 106
Cornwall Av. S43: Brim 6E 163
Cornwall Cl. S43: Brim 6E 163
 S71: Monk B 4G 17
Cornwall Dr. S43: Brim 6E 163
Cornwall Rd. DN2: Don 5G 41
Cornwall Works S3: Shef 1D 4
Cornwell Cl. S62: Rawm 6D 64
Corona Av. DN4: Balb 1C 72
Coronach Way DN11: Harw R . .6B 74, 6F 75
Coronation Av. S25: Din 4A 128
 S71: R'ton 2B 10
 S72: Grim 2B 20
 S72: Shaft 3E 11
Coronation Bri. S60: Roth 4C 96
 S61: Roth 4C 96
Coronation Cotts. DN3: Barn D 1G 27
Coronation Ct. S64: Mexb 6F 51
Coronation Cres. S70: Birdw 3E 45
Coronation Dr. S63: Bolt D 2A 50
 S70: Birdw 3E 45
Coronation Gdns. DN4: Warm 6D 54
Coronation Rd. DN4: Balb 5A 56
 S36: Stoc 3D 174
 S43: Brim 6D 162
 S62: Rawm 2B 84
 S63: Wath D 6H 49
 S64: Swin 3D 66
 S74: Hoyl 6A 46
 S75: Bar G 4E 15
Coronation St. S63: Thurn 2D 36
 S71: Monk B 4H 17
 S73: D'fld 4C 34
Coronation Ter. S71: Ard 2C 32
 S73: Hem 4F 47
Corporation Bldgs. S3: Shef 2F 5
Corporation St. S3: Shef 1E 5 (2F 119)
 S41: C'fld 5A 168
 (not continuous)
 S60: Roth 4E 97
 S70: Barn 3F 31
Cortina Ri. S73: D'fld 4H 33
Corton Wood S73: Bramp 4A 48
Corton Wood Bus. Pk.
 S73: Bramp 4A 48
Cortonwood Dr. S73: Bramp 4A 48
Cortonwood Ho. DN1: Don 1E 119
 (off Bond Cl.)
CORTWORTH 5H 63
Cortworth La. S62: Wentw 5G 63
Cortworth Pl. S74: Els 6E 47
Cortworth Rd. S11: Shef 4H 131
Corunna Vw. S36: Pen 5E 177
Corve Way S40: C'fld 3A 166
Corwen Pl. S13: Shef 2B 136
Cosgrove Ct. DN3: Eden 6D 26
Cossey Rd. S4: Shef 6A 108
Cotefield Pl. S36: Pen 4D 176
Coterel Cres. DN4: Can 3C 58
Cotleigh Av. S12: Shef 5B 136
Cotleigh Cl. S12: Shef 5B 136
Cotleigh Cres. S12: Shef 5B 136
Cotleigh Dr. S12: Shef 5B 136
Cotleigh Gdns. S12: Shef 5B 136
Cotleigh Pl. S12: Shef 5B 136
Cotleigh Rd. S12: Shef 5B 136
Cotleigh Way S12: Shef 5B 136
Cotswold Av. S35: Chap 3D 78
Cotswold Cl. S40: C'fld 3D 165
 S75: Barn 6A 16
Cotswold Cres. S60: Whis 3B 112
Cotswold Dr. DN5: Sprot 3B 54
 S26: Aston 1D 138
 S42: Gras 6D 172
Cotswold Gdns. DN5: Scawt 3G 39

Cotswold Rd. S6: Shef 4A 106
Cottage Cl. S43: Pool 6D 164
Cottage Gro. S66: B'well 1B 102
Cottage La. S11: Shef 3D 130
Cottam Cl. S60: Shef 3B 112
Cottam Rd. S35: High G 1B 78
Cottenham Rd. S65: Roth 3G 97
Cotterdale Gdns. S73: Womb 1A 48
Cotterhill La. S43: Brim 1D 168
Cottesmore Cl. S75: Barn 5B 16
Cottingham St. S9: Shef 2C 120
Cotton Mill Row
 S3: Shef 1E 5 (1F 119)
Cotton Mill Wlk. S3: Shef 1E 119
Cotton St. S3: Shef 1E 5 (1F 119)
Coultas Av. S36: Spink 5F 175
Countess Rd. S1: Shef 5F 119
Countryside Way S64: Kiln 6D 66
County Court
 Chesterfield 5A 168
 Doncaster 2C 56
County Way S70: Barn 6E 17
Coupe St. S3: Shef 6G 107
Coupland Cl. S41: Old W 2B 162
Coupland Rd. S65: Roth 2B 98
Court Cl. DN5: Scaws 4E 39
Court Pl. S43: Stav 6H 163
Courtyard, The DN12: Old D 3H 67
 S75: Barn 1H 29
Coventry Gro. DN2: Don 3G 41
Coventry Rd. S9: Shef 1F 121
Cover Cl. S62: H'ley 5A 62
Coverdale Rd. S7: Shef 3D 132
Cover Dr. S73: D'fld 4C 34
Coverleigh Rd. S63: Wath D 2G 65
Coward Dr. S35: Ough 3E 91
Cow Ho. La. DN3: Arm 4F 43
Cow Ho. La. Residential Pk.
 DN3: Arm 4F 43
Cow La. S11: Shef 6H 117
 S43: Brim 5D 162
COWLEY 5C 154
Cowley Cl. S41: C'fld 5A 168
Cowley Dr. S35: Chap 4H 79
Cowley Gdns. S20: W'fld 2F 151
Cowley Grn. S73: Womb 2E 47
Cowley Hill S35: Eccl 4H 79
 S61: Thorpe H 4H 79
Cowley La. S18: Dron, Holme 4A 154
 S35: Chap 3G 79
Cowley Pl. DN3: Kirk Sa 4C 26
Cowley Rd. S35: Ough 4E 91
Cowley Vw. Cl. S35: Chap 4F 79
Cowley Vw. Rd. S35: Chap 5G 79
Cowley Way S35: Eccl 4H 79
Cowlishaw Rd. S11: Shef 6B 118
Cowood St. S64: Mexb 2E 67
Cowper Av. S6: Shef 4C 92
Cowper Cres. S6: Shef 4C 92
Cowper Dr. S6: Shef 4C 92
 S65: Roth 6A 98
Cowper Rd. S64: Mexb 1G 67
Cowpingle La. S43: Brim 5D 162
Cowrakes Cl. S60: Whis 3B 112
Cow Rakes La. S60: Whis 3B 112
Coxley Ct. DN11: Ross 6E 75
Coxley Mt. DN11: Ross 5F 75
Cox Pl. S6: Shef 3G 105
Cox Rd. S6: Shef 3G 105
Crabtree Av. S5: Shef 4H 107
Crabtree Cl. S5: Shef 3H 107
Crabtree Cres. S5: Shef 3G 107
Crabtree Dr. S5: Shef 3H 107
 S72: Gt H 5E 21
Crab Tree Hill La. S36: H'swne 1E 177
Crabtree La. S5: Shef 3H 107
Crabtree Pl. S5: Shef 3H 107
Crabtree Ponds Local Nature Reserve
 . . . . .4H 107
Crabtree Rd. S5: Shef 3G 107
Cracknell S3: Shef 1F 5 (1G 119)
Cradley Dr. S26: Aston 1D 138
Cradock M. S2: Shef 1B 134
Cradock Rd. S2: Shef 1B 134
Craganour Pl. DN12: Den M 3C 68
 (off Stainton St.)
Cragdale Gro. S20: Mosb 3E 151
Craggon Dr. S43: New W 2C 162
Crag Hill Cres. S6: Shef 3E 93
Craglands Gro. S40: C'fld 3B 166

Cragside Cl. S41: C'fld 5B 168
Crags Rd. DN12: Den M 3E 69
Crag Vw. Cl. S35: Ough 2E 91
Crag Vw. Cres. S35: Ough 2E 91
Craigholme Cres. DN2: Don 3H 41
Craig Wlk. S66: Bram 5B 100
Craithie Rd. DN2: Don 6E 41
Crakehall Rd. S35: Eccl 5G 79
Cramfit Cl. S25: Nth A 2G 141
Cramfit Cres. S25: Din 5G 127
Cramfit Rd. S25: Nth A 1F 141
Cramlands S75: Dod 3H 29
Cranborne Dr. S75: Dart 5G 7
Cranborne Rd. S41: C'fld 1F 167
Cranbrook Rd. DN1: Don 5D 40
Cranbrook St. S70: Barn 2C 30
Crane Dr. S61: Kimb 3H 95
Crane Moor Cl. DN5: Harl 2H 51
Crane Rd. S61: Kimb P 6H 81
Crane Well La. S63: Bolt D 2D 50
Crane Well Vw. S63: Bolt D 3D 50
Cranfield Cl. DN3: Arm 5E 43
Cranford Ct. S20: Mosb 6B 136
Cranford Dr. S20: Mosb 5B 136
Cranford Gdns. S71: R'ton 2G 9
Cranleigh Gdns. DN6: Adw S 3B 22
Cranleigh Rd. S43: Woodt 4E 165
Cranston Cl. S71: Monk B 4A 18
Cranswick Way DN12: Con 4H 69
                    (off Milner Ga.)
Cranwell Ct. S63: Gol 6B 36
Cranwell Rd. DN4: Can 5E 59
Cranworth Cl. S65: Roth 3H 97
Cranworth Pl. S3: Shef 6G 107
  S65: Roth 2G 97
Cranworth Rd. S3: Shef 6G 107
  S65: Roth 2G 97
Craven Cl. DN4: Can 4B 58
  S9: Shef 1F 121
  S71: R'ton 2G 9
Craven Ct. S72: Grim 2C 20
Craven Rd. S41: C'fld 3G 167
  WF9: Hems 1E 13
Craven St. S3: Shef 1B 4 (2E 119)
  S62: P'gte 5G 83
Craven Wood Cl. S75: Barn 5H 15
Crawford Rd. S8: Shef 4E 133
Crawshaw S3: Shef 2A 4 (2D 118)
Crawshaw Av. S6: Shef 2C 146
Crawshaw Gro. S8: Shef 2C 146
Crawshaw M. S18: Dron W 3B 154
Crawshaw Rd. DN4: Hex 2H 55
Cream St. S2: Shef 5G 119
Crecy Av. DN2: Don 6H 41
Creighton Av. S62: Rawm 3A 84
Cresacre Av. DN5: Barnb 1H 51
Crescent, The DN3: Arm 5F 43
  DN3: Eden 6D 26
  DN6: Woodl 4A 22
  DN9: Blax 1G 77
  DN12: Con 4D 68
  DN12: New E 3C 70
  S17: Tot 5F 145
  S18: Holme 4A 154
  S25: Din 5B 128
  S43: Brim 1B 168
  S60: Tree 2G 123
  S63: Bolt D 1C 50
  S64: Swin 4A 66
  S65: Roth 3F 97
  S66: Thurc 6C 114
  S72: Cud 1E 19
  S75: Barn 4A 16
Crescent E., The S66: Sunn 3H 99
Crescent End S66: Thurc 6C 114
Crescent Rd. S7: Shef 1D 132
Crescent W., The S66: Sunn 3G 99
Cressbrook Rd. S60: Wav 2C 122
Cresswell Rd. S9: Shef 2F 121
  S64: Swin 2C 66
Cresswell St. S75: Barn 6B 16
Crest Rd. S5: Shef 6G 93
Crestwood Ct. S5: Shef 6H 93
Crestwood Gdns. S5: Shef 6H 93
Creswell Rd. S64: Mexb 2E 67
Creswick Av. S5: Shef 3D 92
Creswick Cl. S40: W'ton 2C 170
  S65: Roth 2C 98
Creswick Greave S35: Gren 3D 92
Creswick Greave Cl. S5: Shef 2D 92
Creswick La. S35: Gren 2D 92

Creswick Rd. S65: Roth 2C 98
Creswick St. S6: Shef 6C 106
                    (not continuous)
Creswick Way S6: Shef 6C 106
Crewe Hall S10: Shef 5B 118
Crich Av. S71: Ath 1F 17
Crich Rd. S43: Ink 1H 169
Cricketers Wlk. S2: Shef 2A 120
                    (off Castle Ct.)
Cricket Fld. La. S26: Wales B 5E 139
Cricket Inn Cres. S2: Shef 3B 120
Cricket Inn Rd. S2: Shef 2H 5 (2H 119)
Cricket Inn Road Stop (ST) 2A 120
Cricket La. S35: Eccl 2H 93
Cricket Vw. Rd. S62: H'ley 5A 62
Crimicar Av. S10: Shef 6C 116
Crimicar Cl. S10: Shef 1D 130
Crimicar Dr. S10: Shef 6C 116
Crimicar La. S10: Shef 5C 116
CRIMPSALL 1H 55
Crimpsall Rd. DN4: Hex 2A 56
Cripps Av. DN11: New R 5D 74
Cripps Cl. S66: Malt 6C 102
Crispin Cl. S12: Shef 4D 134
Crispin Dr. S12: Shef 4D 134
Crispin Gdns. S12: Shef 4D 134
Crispin Rd. S12: Shef 4D 134
Crochley Cl. DN4: Can 3C 58
Croft, The DN5: Ark 5D 24
  DN12: Con 5F 69
  S36: H'swne 1F 177
  S60: Cat 1D 122
  S62: H'ley 5A 62
  S64: Swin 4A 66
  S74: Els .2D 62
  S75: Bar G 3F 15
Croft Av. S71: R'ton 3G 9
Croft Bldgs. S1: Shef 2D 4
Croft Cl. S11: Shef 5G 131
  S25: Laugh M 1G 127
  S73: Womb 3A 48
  S75: Mapp 5A 8
Croft Ct. DN3: Eden 5C 26
  DN9: Finn 3F 77
Croft Dr. S75: Mapp 5H 7
Crofters Cl. S21: Killa 6B 152
Crofters Ct. DN4: Balb 1B 72
Croft La. S11: Shef 5G 131
Croft Lea S18: Dron W 2B 154
Crofton Av. S6: Shef 2A 106
Crofton Cl. S18: Dron 3E 155
Crofton Dr. S63: Bolt D 1B 50
Crofton Ri. S18: Dron 3E 155
  S35: High G 2C 78
Croft Rd. DN4: Balb 1F 71
  DN9: Finn 4G 77
  S6: Stan 6E 105
  S12: Shef 3E 135
  S60: Brins 3C 110
  S70: Barn 3H 31
                    (not continuous)
  S74: Hoyl 5A 46
Crofts, The S65: Roth 4E 97
  S66: Wick 1G 113
Crofts Dr. S65: Thry 6D 84
Croft St. S61: Grea 5C 82
  S70: Wors 5F 31
Croft Vw. S43: Ink 2H 169
Cromarty Ri. S18: Dron W 2C 154
Cromdale Av. S43: New W 2C 162
Cromer Cl. S62: Rawm 2G 83
Cromer Rd. DN2: Don 6H 41
Cromford Av. S71: Ath 2G 17
Cromford Cl. DN4: Can 6D 58
Cromford Ct. S41: C'fld 1E 167
                    (off Newbold Rd.)
Cromford Dr. S43: Stav 6G 163
Cromford St. S2: Shef 5G 119
Crompton Av. DN5: Don 6G 39
  S70: Barn 2G 31
Crompton Bus. Pk. DN2: Don 2G 41
Crompton Rd. DN2: Don 2G 41
  S43: Stav 4B 164
Cromwell Dr. DN5: Don 2F 55
Cromwell Ho. DN5: Cus 5F 39
Cromwell Mt. S70: Wors 4D 30
Cromwell Rd. DN5: Don 5A 40
  S40: C'fld 4G 167
  S64: Mexb 1F 67
Cromwell St. S6: Shef 1B 118
  S63: Thurn 1D 36

Cronkhill La. S71: Car 5A 10
  S71: Car, R'ton 4B 10
Crooked La. DN12: Old D 1A 86
Crooked Spire
  St Mary & All Saints Church . .5A 168
CROOKES .3A 118
Crookes S10: Shef 2A 118
Crookes La. S71: Car 5G 9
CROOKESMOOR 2C 118
Crookesmoor Dr. S6: Shef 2C 118
Crookesmoor Rd. S6: Shef 3B 118
  S10: Shef 3B 118
Crookes Rd. DN4: Balb 6H 55
  S10: Shef 3B 118
Crookes St. S70: Barn 1C 30
Crookes Valley Rd. S10: Shef 2C 118
Crookhill Cl. DN12: New E 5B 70
Crookhill Pk. Golf Course 1A 88
Crookhill Rd. DN12: Con 4G 69
Crook Ho. La. S71: D'fld 1A 34
Cropston Cl. S41: Has 3B 172
Cropton Rd. S71: R'ton 3G 9
Crosby Av. S66: Bram 5B 100
Crosby Cl. S71: Monk B 3A 18
Crosby Rd. S8: Shef 5E 133
Crosby St. S72: Cud 6E 11
CROSS, THE 3H 93
Cross, The S75: Silk 3A 28
Cross Allen Rd. S20: Beig 6G 137
Cross Bank DN4: Balb 5A 56
Cross Bedford St. S6: Shef 1D 118
Cross Burgess St. S1: Shef . .4E 5 (3F 119)
Cross Butcher St. S63: Thurn 2B 36
Cross Chantrey Rd. S8: Shef 5F 133
Crosscourt Vw. DN4: Bess 4H 57
Cross Dr. S13: Shef 2C 136
Cross Fld. Dr. S81: Woods 5G 143
Crossfield Dr. S63: Wath D 1F 65
Crossfield Gdns. S35: High G 6C 60
Cross Ga. DN5: Don 4H 39
Crossgate S63: Thurn 3C 36
  S64: Mexb 2H 67
  S75: Mapp 5A 8
Crossgates DN11: Wad 6F 73
Cross Gilpin St. S6: Shef 6D 106
Cross Hill S35: Eccl 3H 93
  S72: Brier 3A 12
Cross Hill Cl. S35: Eccl 3H 93
Cross Ho. Cl. S35: Gren 2A 92
Cross Ho. Rd. S35: Gren 2B 92
Cross Keys La. S74: Hoyl 1F 61
Crossland Dr. S12: Shef 5D 134
Crossland Pl. S12: Shef 4D 134
Crossland St. S64: Swin 4C 66
Crossland Way DN5: Scawt 2F 39
Crossland Way Flats DN5: Scawt 3F 39
Cross La. S10: Shef 2A 118
  S17: Dore 2D 144
  S18: Coal A 1H 155
                    (Aston Towers)
  S18: Coal A 5H 147
                    (Dyche La.)
  S18: Dron 3F 155
  S35: Brom 4A 60
  S36: Cub, Thurl 4A 176
  S36: Stoc 2A 174
  S71: R'ton 3B 10
  S81: Woods 4E 143
                    (Berne Sq.)
  S81: Woods 5G 143
                    (Cross Field Dr.)
Cross La. Cl. S81: Woods 4G 143
Cross La. M. S10: Shef 3A 118
Crossley Cl. S66: Malt 4H 101
Cross London St. S43: New W 3C 162
Cross Myrtle Rd. S2: Shef 1G 133
Cross Pk. Rd. S8: Shef 3F 133
CROSSPOOL 4G 117
Cross Rd. S66: Thurc 5B 114
Cross Smithfield S3: Shef . .1C 4 (2E 119)
Cross Sth. St. S61: Grea 5D 82
Cross St. DN4: Balb 5H 55
  DN5: Bntly 1A 40
  DN11: New R 6C 74
  DN12: New E 4C 70
  S13: Shef 2C 136
  S21: Killa 3E 153
  S40: C'fld 4G 167
  S42: Gras 6D 172
  S43: Brim 6D 162
  S61: Grea 5D 82

Cross St. S61: Kimb 4B 96
  S62: P'gte 5G 83
  S63: Gol 5E 37
  S63: Wath D 6F 49
  S65: Thry 6D 84
  S66: Bram 5A 100
  S66: Malt 5B 102
  S70: Wors 4G 31
  S71: Monk B 4H 17
  S72: Grim 2C 20
  S72: Gt H 1F 35
  S73: Womb 2F 47
  S74: Hoyl 1G 61
  S75: Bar G 4E 15
  S75: Barn 5C 16
Cross Turner St. S2: Shef . . .5G 5 (4G 119)
Cross Wlk. S11: Shef 5E 119
              (off London Rd.)
Crossway S64: Swin 4A 66
Crossways DN2: Don 3G 41
  S63: Bolt D 2B 50
Crossways, The S6: Shef 5D 120
Crossways Nth. DN2: Don 3G 41
Crossways Sth. DN2: Don 4G 41
Cross Wellington St. S43: New W . .3C 162
Crowden Wlk. S75: Barn 1H 29
Crowder Av. S5: Shef 6E 93
Crowder Cl. S5: Shef 1F 107
Crowder Cres. S5: Shef 1F 107
Crowder Rd. S5: Shef 6F 93
Crowgate S25: Sth A 5F 141
Crowland Rd. S5: Shef 6G 93
Crow La. S18: Uns 5B 156
  S41: C'fld 5A 168
Crowley Dr. S63: Wath D 2F 65
Crown Av. S70: Barn 3F 31
  S72: Cud 4F 19
Crown Cl. S43: New W 3C 162
  S61: Kimb 2H 95
  S70: Barn 3F 31
Crown Court
  Doncaster 2C 56
Crownhill La. S66: Mick 1F 101
Crown Hill Rd. S70: Barn 1H 29
Crownhill Rd. S60: Brins 3B 110
Crown Pl. S2: Shef 3H 5 (3H 119)
Crown Rd. S41: C'fld 3H 167
Crown St. S64: Swin 3C 66
  S70: Barn 3F 31
  S74: Hoyl 6A 46
Crown Well Ct. S71: Ard 2C 32
          (off Crown Well Hill)
Crown Well Hill S71: Ard 2C 32
Crowther Pl. S7: Shef 6E 119
Crow Tree La. S64: Mexb 4E 51
Croydon St. S11: Shef 6E 119
Crucible Theatre, The 3F 5 (3G 119)
Cruck Cl. S18: Dron W 2D 154
Cruise Rd. S11: Shef 6G 117
Crummock Rd. S7: Shef 3D 132
Crummock Way S71: Ard 2E 33
Crumpsall Dr. S5: Shef 3E 107
Crumpsall Rd. S5: Shef 2E 107
Crumwell Rd. S61: Kimb P 6G 81
Crusader Dr. DN5: Sprot 1F 55
Crystal Peaks Shop. Cen.
  S20: Water 6F 137
Crystal Peaks Stop (ST) 6E 137
CUBLEY 6C 176
Cubley Brook Ct. S36: Cub 5C 176
Cubley Ri. Rd. S36: Cub 6C 176
CUDWORTH .1E 19
CUDWORTH COMMON 3F 19
Cudworth Parkway S72: Cud 2D 18
Cudworth Vw. S72: Grim 2B 20
Cullabine Rd. S2: Shef 1D 134
Cull Row S36: Spink 4H 175
Cumberland Av. DN2: Don 6G 41
Cumberland Cl. S70: Wors 5E 31
  S74: Hoyl 5B 46
Cumberland Cres. S35: Chap 4G 79
Cumberland Dr. S71: Ard 2C 32
Cumberland Pl. DN12: Den M 3C 68
Cumberland Rd. S74: Hoyl 5B 46
Cumberland St. S1: Shef 6D 4 (4F 119)
Cumberland Way S63: Bolt D 3B 50
Cumbrian Wlk. S75: Barn 6A 16
          (off Warner Rd.)
Cumwell La. S66: Hel 1C 114
CUNDY CROSS 1B 32
Cundy St. S6: Shef 1B 118

Cunliffe St. S18: Coal A 6H 147
Cunningham Rd. DN1: Don 2C 56
Cupola S3: Shef 1D 4 (2F 119)
Cupola La. S35: Gren 1B 92
Cupola Yd. S60: Roth 4D 96
Curbar Curve S43: Ink 2G 169
Curlew Av. S21: Ecki 1C 158
Curlew Ct. DN11: Ross 5D 74
Curlew Ridge S2: Shef 4A 120
Curlew Ri. S61: Thorpe H 2D 80
Curzen Cres. DN3: Kirk Sa 4D 26
Curzon Av. S18: Dron 4E 155
Curzon Cl. S21: Killa 4C 152
CUSWORTH .5F 39
Cusworth Gro. DN11: Ross 6E 75
Cusworth Hall 6E 39
Cusworth Ho. DN1: Don 2B 56
          (off Camden Pl.)
Cusworth La. DN5: Cus 5E 39
Cusworth Park Country Pk. 6D 38
Cusworth Rd. DN5: Don 3H 39
Cuthbert Bank Rd. S6: Shef 5C 106
Cuthbert Cooper Pl. S9: Shef 2F 121
Cuthbert Rd. S6: Shef 5C 106
Cutler Cl. S21: Killa 3A 152
Cutlers Av. S70: Barn 2C 30
Cutlers Gate S4: Shef 2H 119
Cutlers Wlk. S2: Shef 1F 133
Cuttholme Cl. S40: Ash 4C 166
Cuttholme Rd. S40: Ash 4C 166
Cuttholme Way S40: C'fld 4D 166
CUTTHORPE 1A 166
CUTTHORPE COMMON END 1A 166
Cutthorpe Grange S41: Up N 1B 166
Cutthorpe Rd. S42: Up N 1A 166
Cutts Av. S63: Wath D 1E 65
Cutts Fld. Vw. S71: R'ton 1G 9
Cutts Ter. S8: Shef 1E 133
Cutty La. S75: Barn 5C 16
Cyclops St. S4: Shef 4B 108
Cygnet Cl. S63: Bramp B 5A 48
Cygnet Dr. S64: Mexb 6B 52
Cypress Av. DN9: Auck 3A 76
  S8: Shef 1H 147
Cypress Cl. S21: Killa 5B 152
Cypress Ga. S35: Chap 4E 79
Cypress Gro. DN12: Con 6C 68
  S26: Wales 5G 139
Cypress Hgts. S71: Smi 2F 17
Cypress Rd. S70: Barn 3G 31
Cyprus Rd. S8: Shef 3F 133
Cyprus Ter. S6: Shef 6C 106

D

Dade Av. S43: Ink 2G 169
Daffodil Rd. S5: Shef 1C 108
Dagnam Cl. S2: Shef 2C 134
Dagnam Cres. S2: Shef 2C 134
Dagnam Dr. S2: Shef 1C 134
Dagnam Pl. S2: Shef 2D 134
Dagnam Rd. S2: Shef 1C 134
Daisy Bank S3: Shef 1A 4 (2D 118)
Daisy Dr. S70: Barn 3F 31
Daisy Gro. S5: Shef 1C 108
Daisy Wlk. S3: Shef 2B 4 (2E 119)
  S20: Beig 5G 137
Dakota Way DN4: Don 3F 57
Dalbury Rd. S18: Dron W 3A 154
Dalby Cft. S36: Pen 4E 177
Dalby Gdns. S20: Sot 1H 151
Dalby Gro. S20: Sot 6A 138
Dale, The S8: Shef 5E 133
Dale Av. S65: Roth 5B 98
Dale Bank Cres. S43: New W 3C 162
Dalebrook Ct. S10: Shef 5F 117
Dalebrook M. S10: Shef 5F 117
Dale Cl. S43: Stav 6H 163
  S71: Ath 1F 17
Dale Ct. S62: Rawm 3G 83
Dale Grn. Rd. S70: Wors 6E 31
Dale Gro. S63: Bolt D 3A 50
Dale Hill Cl. S66: Malt 4A 102
Dale Hill Rd. S66: Malt 4G 101
Dale Rd. DN12: Con 4F 69
  S18: Dron 4G 155
  S21: Killa 4D 152
  S62: Rawm 3G 83
  S65: Roth 6B 98
  S66: Wick 6F 99

Dale Side S10: Shef 5A 118
Dale St. S62: Rawm 2G 83
Daleswood Av. S70: Barn 1A 30
Daleswood Dr. S70: Wors 5A 32
Dale Vw. DN3: Arm 5F 43
  WF9: Hems 1G 13
Daleview Rd. S8: Shef 6C 132
Dalewood Av. S8: Shef 1B 146
Dalewood Cl. S41: C'fld 1D 172
Dalewood Dr. S8: Shef 1B 146
Dalewood Rd. S8: Shef 1B 146
Dalmore Rd. S7: Shef 3B 132
Dalroyd La. S6: Brad 1A 104
DALTON 2B 98
Dalton Ct. DN12: Den M 3C 68
  S8: Shef 1E 133
Dalton La. S65: Dalt, Roth 1C 98
DALTON MAGNA 3E 99
DALTON PARVA 2C 98
Dalton Ter. S70: Barn 2F 31
Dalvey Way S43: New W 1C 162
Damasel Cl. S35: Wharn S 1C 90
Damasel La. S35: Wharn S 1C 90
Damasel Rd. S35: Wharn S 2A 90
DAM END 1G 59
Damer St. S10: Shef 3C 118
Dam Head S61: Grea 3C 82
Dam Ings La. S26: Aston 1F 139
Damon Dr. S43: Brim 6E 163
Damson Cft. S43: Hol 5F 163
Damsteads S63: Gol 6E 37
  S75: Dod 3H 29
Danbury Cl. S42: Gras 6D 172
Danby Av. S41: Old W 4A 162
Danby Rd. S26: Kiv P 5C 140
Danebrook Cl. S2: Shef 5F 121
Danebrook Ct. S2: Shef 5F 121
Danebrook Dr. S2: Shef 5F 121
Dane Cl. S63: Thurn 2D 36
Danesthorpe Cl. DN2: Don 4H 41
Dane St. S63: Thurn 2D 36
Dane St. Nth. S63: Thurn 2D 36
Dane St. Sth. S63: Thurn 2D 36
Danesway DN5: Scawt 1G 39
Danethorpe Way DN12: Con 6D 68
Danewood Av. S2: Shef 5F 121
Danewood Cft. S2: Shef 5F 121
Danewood Gdns. S2: Shef 5F 121
Danewood Gro. S2: Shef 5F 121
Daniel Hill S6: Shef 1D 118
Daniel Hill Ct. S6: Shef 1C 118
Daniel Hill M. S6: Shef 1D 118
Daniel Hill St. S6: Shef 1C 118
Daniel Hill Ter. S6: Shef 1D 118
Daniel Hill Wlk. S6: Shef 1D 118
Daniel La. S62: Neth Hau 2C 82
Daniels Dr. S26: Augh 5B 124
Dannemora Cl. S9: Shef 5F 109
Dannemora Dr. S9: Shef 5F 109
Danum Ct. DN12: Den M 3C 68
Danum Dr. S65: Roth 3G 97
Danum Retail Pk. DN5: Don 5H 39
Danum Rd. DN4: Don 2E 57
Dara St. S9: Shef 5E 95
Darcy Cl. S26: Swal 6C 124
Darcy Rd. S21: Ecki 1D 158
Dards, The S72: Cud 5F 11
Daresbury Cl. S2: Shef 2A 134
Daresbury Dr. S2: Shef 2A 134
Daresbury Pl. S2: Shef 2A 134
Daresbury Rd. S2: Shef 2A 134
Daresbury Vw. S2: Shef 2A 134
DARFIELD 5B 34
Darfield Av. S20: Mosb 6A 136
Darfield Cl. DN11: Ross 5E 75
  S20: Mosb 6A 136
Darfield Ho. DN1: Don 2B 56
          (off Oxford Pl.)
Darfield Rd. S72: Cud 3F 19
Dargle Av. DN2: Don 5F 41
Darhaven S73: D'fld 4B 34
Dark La. S43: Brim C 4D 168
  S44: Cal 6E 169
  S70: Barn 3A 30
  S70: Wors 1G 45
Darley S70: Wors 5H 31
Darley Av. S70: Wors 4D 30
  S71: Ath 2F 17
Darley Cliff Cotts. S70: Wors 4G 31
Darley Cl. S43: Stav 5B 164
  S71: Ath 1F 17

Darley Cross S70: Wors 5G 31
Darley Gro. S6: Stan 5E 105
  S70: Wors 5H 31
Darley Pk. S61: Kimb 5A 96
Darley Ter. S75: Barn 6C 16
Darley Yd. S70: Wors 5G 31
DARNALL 2F 121
Darnall Dr. S9: Shef 1E 121
Darnall Rd. S9: Shef 6D 108
Darnall Station (Rail) 2F 121
Darnbrook Dr. S5: Shef 3E 93
Darnley Dr. S2: Shef 6D 120
Darrington Dr. DN4: Warm 1E 71
Darrington Pl. S71: Lund 5B 18
Dart Gro. DN9: Auck 1H 59
Dartmouth Rd. DN4: Can 6E 59
DARTON 5F 7
Darton Bus. Pk. S75: Dart 6C 6
Darton Common Sports Cen. 6C 6
Darton Hall Cl. S75: Dart 5G 7
Darton Hall Dr. S75: Dart 5G 7
Darton La. S75: Dart, Mapp 6G 7
Darton Rd. S75: Cawt 3A 14
Darton Station (Rail) 5F 7
Darton St. S70: Stair 2A 32
Dartree Cl. S73: D'fld 4A 34
Dartree Wlk. S73: D'fld 4A 34
Dart Sq.
  S3: Shef 2A 4 (2D 118)
Darwall Cl. S35: High G 6C 60
Darwent La. S35: Ough 6C 90
Darwent Rd. S41: C'fld 2B 168
Darwin Av. S40: C'fld 3F 167
Darwin Cl. S10: Shef 4G 117
Darwin La. S10: Shef 4G 117
Darwin Rd. S6: Shef 2A 106
  S40: C'fld 4G 167
Darwin Yd. S74: Els 2E 63
  (off Wath Rd.)
Darwynn Av. S64: Swin 3H 65
Davey Rd. S63: Gol 4C 36
Davian Way S40: W'ton 2F 171
David Cl. S13: Shef 1E 137
David La. S10: Shef 1B 130
Davids Dr. S42: W'orth 6F 171
Davies Ct. S25: Din 4A 128
Davies Dr. S64: Swin 5C 66
Davis Cl. S65: Dalt 1C 98
Davis St. S65: Roth 3H 97
Davy Dr. S66: Malt 4A 102
  S66: Sunn .3G 99
Davy Rd. DN12: Den M 3B 68
Dawber La. S21: Killa 3E 153
Dawcroft Av. S70: Wors 5F 31
Dawlands Cl. S2: Shef 4E 121
  (not continuous)
Dawlands Dr. S2: Shef 5E 121
Daw La. DN5: Bntly 6A 24
  DN11: Wad 6B 72
Dawson Av. S62: Rawm 6D 64
Dawson Cft. S61: Grea 4B 82
Dawson La. S63: Wath D 2F 65
Dawson Ter. S26: Kiv P 6A 140
Daw Wood DN5: Bntly 5B 24
Daycroft S71: Monk B 3C 18
Dayhouse Ct. S75: Barn 4A 16
Dayhouse La. S75: Barn 3A 16
Dayhouse Way S75: Barn 4A 16
Daykin Cl. S75: Kexb 6E 7
Daylands Av. DN12: Con 5D 68
Day St. S70: Barn 2D 30
Deacon Cl. DN11: Ross 5E 75
Deacon Cres. DN11: New R 5B 74
  S66: Malt .6B 102
Deacons Way S71: Monk B 5H 17
Deadman's Hole La. S9: Tins 6H 95
  S60: Roth .5B 96
Deakins Wlk. S10: Shef 5G 117
Dean Cl. DN5: Sprot 2E 55
  DN11: Ross 5E 75
Deane Fld. Vw. S20: Water 6E 137
Deanhead Cl. S20: Mosb 6B 136
Deanhead Dr. S20: Mosb 6A 136
Dean La. S65: Dalt M 4D 98
Deans Cl. S43: Brim 1C 168
Deansfield Cl. DN3: Arm 5E 43
Dean St. S70: Barn 1C 30
Deans Way S71: Monk B 4H 17
Dearden Ct. S35: Eccl 2G 93
DEARNE 5D 36
Dearne Cl. S73: Womb 3A 48

Dearne Ct. S9: Shef 2D 108
  S75: Wool G 3F 7
Dearne Hall Fold S75: Bar G 2G 15
Dearne Hall Rd. S75: Bar G 2G 15
Dearne La. S63: Wath D 4D 48
Dearne Mills S75: Dart 6F 7
Dearne Playhouse 6C 36
Dearne Rd. S63: Bolt D, Wath D 4H 49
  S73: Bramp 4B 48
Dearne Rd. Flatlets
  S63: Bolt D 3A 50
  (off Dearne Rd.)
Dearneside Leisure Cen. 6D 36
Dearne St. DN12: Con 3G 69
  S9: Shef .2D 108
  S72: Gt H .1F 35
  S75: Dart 5G 7
Dearne Valley Leisure Cen. 2B 68
Dearne Valley Parkway
  S63: Bolt D, Wath D 2D 48
  S63: Gol 5F 35
  S72: Bill 5F 35
  S73: Bramp, Womb 1E 61
  S74: Hoyl 1E 61
Dearne Vw. S63: Gol 5C 36
Dearneway S43: Wath D 6G 49
Dearnley Vw. S75: Barn 4C 16
Deben Cl. S40: W'ton 2D 170
Decoy Bank DN4: Don 4C 56
Decoy Bank Nth. DN4: Don 3C 56
Decoy Bank Sth. DN4: Don 4C 56
DEEPCAR 3H 175
Deepcar La. S72: Cud 5H 19
Deep Carrs La. S81: Work 6F 143
Deepdale Cl. S43: Stav 3B 164
Deepdale Cft. S75: Bar G 3G 15
Deepdale Rd. S61: Kimb 4H 95
Deep La. S5: Shef 3B 94
  (not continuous)
DEEP PIT 6C 120
Deepsic La. S44: Ark T 1H 173
Deeps La. DN10: Miss 6H 77
Deepwell Av. S20: Half 4G 151
Deepwell Bank S20: Half 4G 151
Deepwell Ct. S20: Half 4G 151
Deepwell Dr. S20: Half 4H 151
Deepwell M. S20: Half 4H 151
Deepwell Vw. S20: Half 4G 151
Deerlands Av. S5: Shef 4D 92
Deerlands Cl. S5: Shef 4D 92
Deerlands Mt. S5: Shef 4C 92
Deerlands Rd. S40: Ash 5C 166
Deer Pk. Cl. S6: Shef 6F 105
Deer Pk. Pl. S6: Shef 6F 105
Deer Pk. Rd. S6: Shef 6F 105
  S65: Thry 5F 85
Deer Pk. Vw. S6: Shef 6F 105
Deer Pk. Way S6: Shef 6G 105
De Houton Cl. S26: Tod 3B 140
Deightonby St. S63: Thurn 2D 36
De Lacy Dr. S70: Wors 5F 31
Delamere Cl. S20: Sot 6H 137
De La Salle Dr. S4: Shef 5H 107
Delf Gth. S75: Dod 3G 29
Delf St. S2: Shef 1G 133
Dell, The S40: Ash 5C 166
  S66: Sunn .2H 99
Della Av. S70: Barn 2C 30
Dell Av. S72: Grim 6B 12
Dell Cres. DN4: Hex 3G 55
Delmar Way S66: Flan 4G 99
Delph Bank S40: W'ton 2F 171
Delph Cl. S75: Silk 1B 28
Delph Edge S35: Green M 1G 175
Delph Ho. Rd. S10: Shef 3G 117
Delph M. S35: Green M 1G 175
Delta Cl. DN9: Finn 2D 76
Delta Pl. S65: Roth 3A 98
Delta Way S66: Malt 4C 102
Delves Av. S12: Shef 4D 136
Delves Cl. S12: Shef 4D 136
  S40: W'ton 1E 171
Delves Dr. S12: Shef 5D 136
Delves La. S26: Wales B 5C 138
Delves Pl. S12: Shef 5C 136
Delves Rd. S12: Shef 5C 136
  S21: Killa .4C 152
Delves Ter. S12: Shef 5D 136
Denaby Av. DN12: Con 5C 68
Denaby Ings Nature Reserve 6D 52

Denaby La. DN12: Old D, Den M 1F 85
  (not continuous)
Denaby La. Ind. Est. DN12: Den M . . .3B 68
  (not continuous)
DENABY MAIN 2D 68
DEN BANK 3F 117
Den Bank Av. S10: Shef 3F 117
Den Bank Cl. S10: Shef 3G 117
Den Bank Cres. S10: Shef 3F 117
Den Bank Dr. S10: Shef 3F 117
Denbrook La. DN12: Con 6G 69
Denby Rd. S43: Ink 1H 169
  S71: Smi 1E 17
Denby St. DN5: Bntly 4D 24
  S2: Shef 5E 119
Denby Way S66: Hel 5D 100
Dencombe Ter. WF9: Sth K 5H 13
Dene Cl. S66: Wick 6H 99
Dene Cres. S65: Roth 2A 98
Denehall Rd. DN3: Kirk Sa 5D 26
Dene La. S1: Shef 6B 4 (4E 119)
Dene Pl. S13: Shef 4A 122
Dene Rd. S65: Roth 2A 98
Denham Rd. S11: Shef 5D 118
Denholme Cl. S3: Shef 1G 119
Denison Ct. S70: Barn 2E 31
Denison Rd. DN4: Hex 2A 56
Denman Rd. S63: Wath D 6E 49
Denman St. S65: Roth 2F 97
Denmark Rd. S2: Shef 2G 133
Denson Cl. S2: Shef 2G 133
Dent La. S12: Shef 6A 136
Denton Rd. S8: Shef 4E 133
Dentons Grn. La. DN3: Kirk Sa 4C 26
Denton St. S71: Barn 6E 17
Derby Pl. S2: Shef 2H 133
Derby Rd. DN2: Don 2H 41
  S40: Birdh, C'fld 4H 171
  S42: W'orth 4H 171
Derbyshire Ct. DN3: Arm 3G 43
  S8: Shef 5G 133
Derbyshire La. S8: Shef 3E 133
Derby St. S2: Shef 2G 133
  S70: Barn 1C 30
Derby Ter. S2: Shef 2H 133
Derefeld Dr. S73: D'fld 5A 34
Derek Dooley Way
  S3: Shef 1G 5 (1G 119)
  S4: Shef 1G 5 (1G 119)
Derriman Av. S11: Shef 4A 132
Derriman Cl. S11: Shef 4A 132
Derriman Dr. S11: Shef 4A 132
Derriman Glen S11: Shef 4H 131
Derriman Gro. S11: Shef 4A 132
Derry Gro. S63: Thurn 3B 36
Derwent Chase S60: Wav 3D 122
Derwent Cl. S18: Dron 1G 155
  S25: Nth A 1A 142
  S71: Ath 1G 17
Derwent Cl. S17: Bradw 5H 145
  S60: Roth .2G 111
Derwent Cres. S41: C'fld 1E 167
  S60: Brins .5C 110
  S71: Ath 1G 17
Derwent Dr. DN3: Kirk Sa 5C 26
  DN4: Don .4G 57
  S35: Chap .3D 78
  S62: Rawm 4G 83
  S64: Mexb .6H 51
Derwent Gdns. S63: Gol 6D 36
Derwent Ho. S41: C'fld 1E 167
  (off Ulverston Rd.)
Derwent Pl. DN5: Sprot 3C 54
  S73: Womb .3A 48
Derwent Rd. S18: Dron 1G 155
  S61: Wing 6H 81
  S64: Mexb .6H 51
  S71: Ath 1F 17
Derwent St. S2: Shef 2A 120
Derwent Ter. S64: Mexb 6F 51
Derwent Vw. S43: Mas M 3F 165
Derwent Way S63: Wath D 4C 48
Dettori M. S25: Laugh C 4F 127
Deveron Rd. S20: Half 3G 151
Devizes Cl. S40: Birdh 2G 171
Devon Cl. DN12: Den M 4C 68
Devon Dr. S43: Brim 6E 163
Devon Pk. Vw. S43: Brim 6E 163
Devon Rd. S4: Shef 4H 107
Devonshire Av. E. S41: Has 2B 172
Devonshire Av. Nth. S43: New W 2C 162

Devonshire Bus. Pk. S1: Shef 5C **4**
Devonshire Cl. S17: Dore 4G **145**
S18: Dron 4E **155**
S41: C'fld 6G **161**
S43: Stav 4B **164**
Devonshire Ct. S17: Dore 4G **145**
S43: Brim 1C **168**
Devonshire Dr. S17: Dore 3F **145**
S25: Nth A 6H **127**
S75: Barn 4C **16**
Devonshire Glen S17: Dore 4G **145**
Devonshire Gro. S17: Dore 4F **145**
Devonshire La.
S1: Shef 4C **4** (3E **119**)
Devonshire Pl. S43: Brim 6D **162**
Devonshire Rd. DN2: Don 5G **41**
S17: Dore 3F **145**
S66: Malt 4B **102**
Devonshire Rd. E. S41: Has 2B **172**
Devonshire Rd. Nth. S43: New W . .3C **162**
Devonshire St. S3: Shef 4B **4** (3E **119**)
S41: C'fld 5H **167**
S43: Brim 6D **162**
S43: Stav 4B **164**
S61: Roth 4C **96**
(not continuous)
Devonshire Ter. Rd. S17: Dore 3E **145**
Devonshire Vs. *S41: C'fld* *6G 161*
(off Occupation Rd.)
Dewar Dr. S7: Shef 4B **132**
Dewfield Cl. S72: Grim 1B **20**
Dewhill Av. S60: Whis 3A **112**
Dial, The S5: Shef 6A **94**
Dial Cl. S5: Shef 6H **93**
Dial Ho. Ct. S6: Shef 3A **106**
Dial Ho. Rd. S6: Shef 4H **105**
Dial Way S5: Shef 6H **93**
Diamond Jubilee Way
DN12: New E 4D **70**
Diamond St. S73: Womb 1G **47**
Dickan Gdns. DN3: Arm 5G **43**
Dickens Cl. S60: Cat 6C **110**
Dickenson Ct. S35: Chap 3E **79**
Dickenson Rd. S41: C'fld 1A **172**
Dickens Rd. S62: Rawm 1A **84**
Dickey La. S6: Shef 5H **91**
Dickinson Pl. S70: Barn 3E **31**
Dickinson Rd. S5: Shef 3A **94**
S70: Barn 3E **31**
Didcot Cl. S40: Birdh 2G **171**
Digby Cl. S61: Kimb 2H **95**
Dike Hill S62: H'ley 5B **62**
Dikelands Mt. S35: High G 2C **78**
Dillington Rd. S70: Barn 3E **31**
Dillington Sq. S70: Barn 3E **31**
Dillington Ter. *S70: Barn* *3E 31*
(off Walnut Cl.)
Dingle Bank S44: Cal 1D **172**
Dingle La. S44: Cal 1D **172**
Dinmore Cl. DN4: Balb 2H **71**
DINNINGTON 5A **128**
Dinnington Bus. Cen. S25: Din 4G **127**
Dinnington Bus. Incubation Cen.
S25: Din 4G **127**
Dinnington Interchange 5A **128**
Dinnington Rd. S8: Shef 4E **133**
S26: Tod 1C **140**
S81: Woods 4D **142**
Dirleton Dr. DN4: Warm 6E **55**
Discovery Way S41: Whit M 5H **161**
S66: Malt 4G **101**
Disraeli Gro. S66: Malt 4H **101**
Distillery M. S74: Els 2E **63**
Distillery Side S74: Els 2E **63**
Ditchingham St. S4: Shef 6H **107**
Division La. S1: Shef 4D **4** (3F **119**)
Division St. S1: Shef 4C **4** (3E **119**)
S43: Stav 6H **163**
Dixon Cres. DN4: Balb 5G **55**
Dixon Dr. S35: Wharn S 2C **90**
Dixon La. S1: Shef 2G **5** (2G **119**)
Dixon Rd. DN12: New E 4B **70**
S6: Shef 3A **106**
S41: C'fld 6A **168**
Dixon St. S6: Shef 1E **119**
S65: Roth 3F **97**
Dobbin Ct. S11: Shef 1H **131**
Dobbin Hill S11: Shef 2H **131**
Dobbin La. S18: Barl 6B **154**
Dobb La. S6: Stan 2A **116**

Dobbs Cl. S21: Killa 4B **152**
Dobcroft Av. S7: Shef 5A **132**
Dobcroft Cl. S11: Shef 4H **131**
Dobcroft Rd. S7: Shef 4H **131**
S11: Shef 4H **131**
Dobie St. S70: Barn 2E **31**
Dobroyd Ter. S74: Jum 5C **46**
Dobson Pl. S43: Ink 2G **169**
Dobson Cl. S70: Wors 5A **32**
Dockin Hill Rd. DN1: Don 6C **40**
Dock Wlk. S41: C'fld 6F **167**
Doctor La. S9: Shef 6D **108**
Dodds Cl. S60: Roth 6D **96**
Dodd St. S6: Shef 5B **106**
Dodson Dr. S13: Shef 4A **122**
Dodsworth St. S64: Mexb 2E **67**
DODWORTH 3G **29**
DODWORTH BOTTOM 4G **29**
Dodworth Bus. Pk. S75: Dod 2E **29**
Dodworth Rd. S70: Barn 2H **29**
Dodworth Station (Rail) 3F **29**
Doe La. S21: Trow 6E **149**
S70: Wors 1D **44**
Doe Quarry La. S25: Din 4A **128**
Doe Quarry Pl. S25: Din 5B **128**
Doe Quarry Ter. S25: Din 5A **128**
Doe Royd Cres. S5: Shef 5C **92**
Doe Royd Dr. S5: Shef 5D **92**
Doe Royd La. S5: Shef 5C **92**
Dog Cft. La. DN5: Ark 1F **41**
Dog Hill S72: Shaft 3E **11**
Dog Hill Dr. S72: Shaft 3F **11**
Dog Kennel Hill S26: Kiv S 6E **141**
Dog Kennels La. S25: Sth A 6E **141**
S26: Kiv S 6E **141**
Dog La. S70: Barn 1D **30**
Dolcliffe Cl. S64: Mexb 1E **67**
DOLCLIFFE COMMON 2F **67**
Dolcliffe Rd. S64: Mexb 1F **67**
Doles Av. S71: R'ton 3G **9**
Doles Cres. S71: R'ton 3G **9**
Doles La. S60: Up W, Whis 4B **112**
Doleswood Dr. S25: Laugh M 2H **127**
Dome Leisure Cen., The 3G **57**
Domine La. S60: Roth 4E **97**
Domine Ct. S61: Kimb P 1H **95**
Dominoe Gro. S12: Shef 3G **135**
Don Av. S6: Shef 1H **105**
S35: Wharn S 2A **90**
DONCASTER 1B **56**
Doncaster Gate S65: Roth 4F **97**
Doncaster Golf Course 1D **74**
Doncaster Ind. Pk. DN5: Scawt 4G **39**
Doncaster Interchange 1B **56**
Doncaster Intl. Railport DN4: Don . .4C **56**
Doncaster Knights RUFC 4B **42**
Doncaster La. DN6: Adw S, Woodl . .3D **22**
(not continuous)
Doncaster Leisure & Bus. Pk.
DN4: Don 3G **57**
Doncaster Mus. & Art Gallery 1C **56**
Doncaster North (Park & Ride) 1E **39**
Doncaster Pl. S65: Roth 3H **97**
Doncaster Race Course 2G **57**
Doncaster RLFC 4F **57**
Doncaster Rd. DN3: Arm 4C **42**
DN3: Barn D, Eden, Kirk Sa . . .6A **26**
DN3: Brant 4G **59**
(Moor Gap)
DN3: Brant 4E **59**
(School La.)
DN5: Barnb 1A **52**
DN5: Bntly, Holme 3G **23**
DN5: Harl 2G **51**
DN5: Hick 4F **37**
DN5: High M 3D **52**
DN6: Highf 6D **22**
DN9: Finn 3F **77**
DN12: Con 4G **69**
DN12: Con, Den M 1B **68**
S63: Gol 5D **36**
S63: Wath D 6H **49**
S64: Mexb 2G **67**
S65: Dalt, Thry 1B **98**
S65: Hoot R, Thry 4E **85**
S65: Roth 4F **97**
S66: B'well 6B **88**
S70: Barn, Stair 1E **31**
S71: Ard, Stair 2B **32**
S73: D'fld 4C **34**
Doncaster Rovers FC 4F **57**

Doncaster South (Park & Ride) 3E **75**
Doncaster Squash Club 1E **57**
Doncaster Station (Rail) 1B **56**
Doncaster St. S3: Shef 1C **4** (2E **119**)
Doncaster Superbowl 3F **57**
Doncaster Town Moor Golf Course
. . . . .1H **57**
Don Dr. S70: Barn 3A **32**
Donetsk Way S12: Shef 5B **136**
Donetsk Way Stop (ST) 6D **136**
Don Grange S64: Kiln 6D **66**
Don Hill Height
S35: Green M 1E **175**
S36: Stoc 1E **175**
Donnington Rd. S2: Shef 5A **120**
S64: Mexb 6A **52**
Donovan Cl. S5: Shef 1D **106**
Donovan Rd. S5: Shef 1D **106**
Don Pottery Yd. S64: Swin 3E **67**
Don Rd. S9: Shef 5C **108**
Donstone Vw. S25: Din 6G **127**
Don St. DN1: Don 5C **40**
DN12: Con 3G **69**
S36: Pen 5F **177**
S60: Roth 4E **97**
Don Ter. S36: Thurl 3B **176**
Don Valley Stadium Stop (ST) 5E **109**
Don Vw. DN5: Scaws 4D **38**
S64: Mexb 1A **68**
Dorado Dr. DN4: Balb 2C **72**
Dorchester Pl. S70: Wors 5E **31**
Dorcliffe Lodge S10: Shef 6H **117**
DORE 3E **145**
Dore and Totley Golf Course 5B **146**
Dore & Totley Station (Rail) 3H **145**
Dore Cl. S17: Dore 3H **145**
Dore Ct. *S17: Dore* *3H 145*
(off Ladies Spring Dr.)
Dore Hall Cft. S17: Dore 3E **145**
Dore Ho. Ind. Est.
S13: Shef 6D **122**
Dore Lodge Gdns. S17: Dore 3G **145**
Dore Rd. S17: Dore 3E **145**
Dorking St. S4: Shef 1H **119**
Dorothy Hyman Sports & Leisure Cen.
. . . . .2F **19**
Dorothy Rd. S6: Shef 3A **106**
Dorothy Va. S40: Ash 4D **166**
Dorset Av. S43: Brim 6E **163**
Dorset Cl. S43: Brim 5E **163**
Dorset Cres. DN2: Don 5H **41**
Dorset Dr. S43: Brim 6E **163**
Dorset St. S10: Shef 4D **118**
Dorward Av. S63: Wath D 4E **49**
Douglas Rd. DN4: Balb 5F **55**
S3: Shef 6E **107**
S41: C'fld 2B **168**
Douglas St. S60: Roth 4F **97**
Douse Cft. La. S10: Shef 2A **130**
Dovebush Way S75: Bar G 3G **15**
Dovecliffe Rd. S73: Womb 1B **46**
Dovecliffe Vw. *S70: Wors* *5H 31*
(off Allendale)
Dove Cl. S63: Bolt D 2C **50**
S73: Womb 3A **48**
Dovecote La. S65: Rav 5H **85**
Dovecote M. S71: Monk B 4H **17**
Dovecott Lea S20: Sot 5A **138**
Dovedale S70: Wors 6G **31**
Dovedale Av. S43: Ink 3G **169**
Dovedale Cl. S41: C'fld 1F **167**
Dovedale Pl. S70: Wors 6G **31**
Dovedale Rd. S7: Shef 3C **132**
S65: Roth 6B **98**
Dove Hill S71: R'ton 2A **10**
Doveridge Cl. S41: Old W 4H **161**
Dove Rd. S64: Mexb 1B **68**
S73: Womb 3H **47**
Dover St. S3: Shef 1B **4** (2E **119**)
Doveside Dr. S73: D'fld 5B **34**
Dove Valley Way S73: Womb 6G **33**
Dove Vw. S73: Womb 6E **33**
Dowcarr La. S26: Wooda 5H **153**
Dowdeswell St. S41: C'fld 4H **167**

Dowfin S35: High G 1C 78
Dowland Av. S35: High G 6C 60
Dowland Cl. S35: High G 6D 60
Dowland Ct. S35: High G 6C 60
Dowland Gdns. S35: High G 6D 60
Downgate Dr. S4: Shef 4C 108
Downham Rd. S5: Shef 1H 107
Downing La. S3: Shef 1B 4 (1E 119)
Downing Rd. S8: Shef 2D 146
Downing Sq. S36: Pen 5D 176
Dowland Cl. DN4: Balb 2G 71
Downlands S43: Brim 1C 168
Downs Cres. S75: Beav 5A 16
Down's Row S60: Roth 4E 97
Dragoon Ct. S6: Shef 5C 106
Drake Cl. S35: Burn 3D 78
Drake Head La. DN12: Con 4H 69
DRAKEHOUSE 5E 137
Drake Ho. Cres. S20: Water 5E 137
Drakehouse La. S20: Beig 5G 137
Drake House Lane Stop (ST) 6G 137
Drake Ho. La. West S20: Beig 5G 137
Drake Ho. Retail Pk. S20: Water 5E 137
Drake Ho. Way S20: Water 5F 137
Drake Rd. DN2: Don 4D 40
    S66: Malt 6C 102
                                        (off Fisher Rd.)
Drake Ter. S43: Brim 6B 162
Drake Vw. S63: Bramp B 6A 48
Dransfield Av. S36: Pen 5D 176
Dransfield Cl. S10: Shef 4G 117
Dransfield Rd. S10: Shef 4F 117
Draycott Pl. S18: Dron W 4C 154
Draymans Ct. S11: Shef 5E 119
                                        (off Napier St.)
Drive, The DN3: Eden 6D 26
    S6: Shef 2A 106
Driver St. S13: Shef 6E 123
DRONFIELD 3F 155
Dronfield Civic Cen. S18: Dron 3F 155
Dronfield Ind. Est. S18: Dron 3H 155
Dronfield Rd. S21: Ecki 1B 158
Dronfield Sports Cen. 3E 155
Dronfield Station (Rail) 3F 155
DRONFIELD WOODHOUSE 3C 154
DROPPING WELL 2G 95
Droppingwell Farm Cl. S61: Kimb . .1G 95
Droppingwell Rd. S61: Kimb 4E 95
Drover Cl. S35: High G 2D 78
Droves Dale Rd. S63: Gol 4C 36
Drummond Av. DN5: Scaws 3D 38
Drummond Cres. S5: Shef 5G 93
Drummond Rd. S5: Shef 5G 93
Drummond St. S60: Roth 3E 97
    S65: Roth 3F 97
Drury Farm Ct. S75: Barn 1H 29
Drury La. S17: Dore 3E 145
    S40: Birdh 2H 171
Dryden Av. S5: Shef 6D 92
Dryden Dr. S5: Shef 6D 92
Dryden Rd. DN4: Balb 6B 56
    S5: Shef 6D 92
    S63: Wath D 5D 48
    S64: Mexb 1G 61
    S65: Roth 6A 98
    S71: Barn 6F 17
Dryden Way S5: Shef 1D 106
Dublin Rd. DN2: Don 5F 41
Duchess Rd. S2: Shef 6F 5 (5G 119)
Duckham Dr. S26: Aston 2D 138
DUCKMANTON MOOR 6H 173
Ducksett La. S21: Ecki 2E 159
Dudley Dr. S63: Gol 5A 36
Dudley Rd. DN2: Don 1G 57
    S6: Shef 2A 106
Dudley St. S62: P'gte 5G 83
Duewell Ct. S43: Bar H 3G 163
Duftons Cl. DN12: Con 3G 69
Dugdale Dr. S5: Shef 3E 93
Dugdale Rd. S5: Shef 3D 92
Duke Av. DN11: New R 5B 74
    S66: Malt 6C 102
Duke Cres. S61: Kimb P 1H 95
    S70: Barn 2E 31
Duke La. S1: Shef 6E 5 (4F 119)
Duke of Norfolk La. S66: Wick 6D 98
Dukeries Dr. S25: Nth A 1H 141
Duke's Cres. DN12: New E 3C 70
Dukes St. S41: C'fld 2F 167

Dukes La. S61: Kimb 2G 95
Dukes Pl. S65: Roth 6A 98
Duke St. DN1: Don 1B 56
    S2: Shef 3H 5 (3H 119)
    S20: Mosb 4E 151
    S25: Din 4A 128
    S41: Whit M 6H 161
    S43: Stav 4B 164
    S64: Swin 2C 66
    S70: Barn 2E 31
    S72: Grim 2B 20
    S74: Hoyl 6B 46
Dumbleton Rd. S21: Killa 5D 152
Dumble Wood Grange
    S41: C'fld 1D 166
Duncan Rd. S10: Shef 2A 118
Duncan St. S60: Brins 3D 110
Duncombe St. S6: Shef 1B 118
Dundas Rd. DN2: Don 4D 40
    S9: Tins .1H 109
Dundonald Rd. S40: C'fld 1H 171
Dunedin Glen S20: Half 4F 151
Dunedin Gro. S20: Half 4F 151
Dunella Dr. S6: Shef 3A 106
Dunella Pl. S6: Shef 3H 105
Dunella Rd. S6: Shef 3A 106
Dunford Ct. S63: Wath D 6H 49
Dungworth Grn. S6: Dung 4A 104
Dunkeld Rd. S11: Shef 3A 132
Dunkerley Rd. S6: Lox 3E 105
Dun La. S3: Shef 1E 119
Dunleary Rd. DN2: Don 6F 41
Dunlin Cl. S61: Thorpe H 2C 80
Dunlop St. S9: Shef 3E 109
Dunmere Cl. S71: Monk B 3F 17
Dunmow Rd. S4: Shef 3B 108
Dunninc Rd. S5: Shef 3A 94
Dunninc Ter. S5: Shef 3A 94
Dunniwood Av. DN4: Bess 1B 74
Dunniwood Reach DN4: Bess 6C 58
Dunns Dale S66: Malt 5C 102
Dunscroft Gro. DN11: Ross 5E 75
Dunsil Cl. S44: Ark T 6H 173
Dunsley La. S72: Brier 4F 13
    W9: Hems 2G 13
Dunsley Ter. WF9: Sth K 4H 13
Dunstan Rd. S66: Malt 6H 101
DUNSTON 6E 161
Dunston Ct. S41: Whit M 5G 161
Dunston La. S41: C'fld 5E 161
Dunston Hgts. S36: Pen 5E 177
Dunston Innovation Cen.
    S41: Whit M 5G 161
Dunston Pl. S41: Whit M 5G 161
Dunston Rd.
    S41: Up N, C'fld, Whit M 6B 160
Dunston Technology Pk.
    S41: Whit M 5G 161
Dunston Trad. Est.
    S41: C'fld 4F 161
Dunston Way S41: C'fld 5F 161
Dun St. S3: Shef 1E 119
    S64: Swin 3D 66
DUNSVILLE .4H 27
Durham Av. S43: New W 3C 162
Durham Cl. S43: New W 3C 162
Durham La. DN3: Arm 3G 43
    S10: Shef 3D 118
Durham Pl. S65: Roth 6A 98
Durham Rd. DN2: Don 3E 41
    S10: Shef 3D 118
Durham St. S66: Malt 6C 102
Durley Chine Dr. S41: Has 2B 172
Durlstone Cl. S12: Shef 3D 134
Durlstone Cres. S12: Shef 3D 134
Durlstone Dr. S12: Shef 3D 134
Durlstone Gro. S12: Shef 3D 134
Durmast Gro. S6: Stan 6D 104
Durnan Gro. S62: Rawm 6D 64
Durnford Rd. DN2: Don 5D 40
Durrant Rd. S41: C'fld 5H 167
Dursley Cl. DN9: Auck 1G 59
Durvale Ct. S17: Dore 4F 145
Dutton Rd. S6: Shef 3C 106
Duxford Cl. DN4: Can 6D 58
DVC Sports .1B 66
DW Fitness
    Barnsley .6F 17
Dyche Cl. S8: Shef 4G 147

Dyche La. S8: Shef 3F 147
    S18: Coal A 5G 147
Dyche Pl. S8: Shef 4G 147
Dyche Rd. S8: Shef 4G 147
Dycott Rd. S61: Kimb 3A 96
Dyer Rd. S74: Jum 5D 46
Dykes Hall Gdns. S6: Shef 4A 106
Dykes Hall Pl. S6: Shef 3A 106
Dykes Hall Rd. S6: Shef 3H 105
Dykes La. S6: Shef 3H 105
Dyke Vale Av. S12: Shef 4B 136
Dyke Vale Cl. S12: Shef 4B 136
Dyke Vale Pl. S12: Shef 4B 136
Dyke Va. Rd. S12: Shef 3A 136
Dyke Vale Way S12: Shef 4B 136
Dykewood Dr. S6: Shef 1G 105
Dynne Ct. S25: Din 6A 128
Dyson Holmes La.
    S35: Wharn S 2A 90
Dyson Pl. S11: Shef 6C 118
Dyson St. S70: Barn 3C 30

E

Eaden Cres. S74: Hoyl 6C 46
Eagleton Dr. S35: High G 6D 60
Eagleton Gdns. S64: Swin 3C 66
Eagleton Ri. S35: High G 6D 60
Eagle Vw. S26: Aston 2D 138
Ealands Cl. S72: Midd 3F 35
Ealand Way DN12: Con 3H 69
Eaming Vw. S71: Barn 5F 17
Earl Av. DN11: New R 5A 74
    S66: Malt 6B 102
Earldom Cl. S4: Shef 6H 107
Earldom Dr. S4: Shef 6H 107
Earldom Rd. S4: Shef 5H 107
Earldom St. S4: Shef 6H 107
Earlesmere Av. DN4: Balb 4H 55
Earl Marshal Cl. S4: Shef 3A 108
Earl Marshal Dr. S4: Shef 3H 107
Earl Marshal Rd. S4: Shef 4H 107
Earl Marshal Vw. S4: Shef 4H 107
Earls Cl. S61: Thorpe H 3C 80
Earlsmere Dr. S71: Ard 2D 32
Earlston Dr. DN5: Don 4A 40
Earl St. S1: Shef 6D 4 (4F 119)
                                     (not continuous)
Earlswood Ct. DN3: Barn D 2D 26
Earl Way S1: Shef 6D 4 (4F 119)
Earnshaw Hall S10: Shef 5A 118
Earnshaw Ter. S75: Barn 5C 16
Earsham St. S4: Shef 6H 107
Easedale Cl. S40: C'fld 3A 166
East Av. DN6: Woodl 4B 22
    S62: Rawm 2G 83
    S64: Swin 4A 66
    S73: Womb 1E 47
East Bank Cl. S2: Shef 2A 134
East Bank Pl. S2: Shef 2A 134
East Bank Rd. S2: Shef 5G 119
East Bank Vw. S2: Shef 2A 134
East Bank Way S2: Shef 2A 134
E. Bawtry Rd. S60: Roth 3H 111
East Cl. S36: Oxs 6G 177
E. Coast Rd. S9: Shef 6B 108
East Cres. S36: Stoc 3C 174
    S65: Roth 3A 98
East Cft. S63: Bolt D 2B 50
Eastcroft Cl. S20: W'fld 2G 151
Eastcroft Dr. S20: W'fld 3F 151
Eastcroft Glen S20: W'fld 2G 151
Eastcroft Vw. S20: W'fld 3G 151
Eastcroft Way S20: W'fld 2G 151
EAST DENE 3H 97
East Earsham St. S4: Shef 6A 108
East End Cres. S71: R'ton 3B 10
Eastern Av. S2: Shef 2A 134
    S25: Din 5B 128
Eastern Cl. S25: Din 6B 128
Eastern Cres. S2: Shef 2A 134
Eastern Dr. S2: Shef 1A 134
Eastern Wlk. S2: Shef 1A 134
Eastfield Av. S36: Pen 4D 176
Eastfield Cl. S75: Stain 6C 8
Eastfield Cres. S25: Laugh M 1H 127
    S75: Stain 6C 8
East Field La. S25: Laugh M 1A 128
Eastfield La. DN9: Auck 2H 59
Eastfield Pl. S62: Rawm 1B 84

Eastfield Rd. DN3: Arm 5E **43**
  S10: Shef 1B **118**
  S18: Dron 4H **155**
Eastfields S70: Wors 6G **31**
Eastgate S6: Shef 1H **105**
  S20: Barn 6D **16**
  WF9: Hems 1F **13**
Eastgate Ct. S65: Roth 4A **98**
E. Glade Av. S12: Shef 5H **135**
E. Glade Cl. S12: Shef 5H **135**
E. Glade Cres. S12: Shef 5H **135**
E. Glade Dell S12: Shef 4H **135**
E. Glade Pl. S12: Shef 5H **135**
E. Glade Rd. S12: Shef 4H **135**
E. Glade Sq. S12: Shef 5H **135**
E. Glade Way S12: Shef 4H **135**
Eastgrove Rd. S10: Shef 5C **118**
EAST HERRINGTHORPE 3B **98**
E. Laith Ga. DN1: Don 1C **56**
Eastleigh S65: Roth 3H **97**
Eastleigh Ct. S41: Has 2C **172**
E. Lodge La. S61: Grea 4D **82**
East Mall S20: Water 5F **137**
Eastmoor Gro. S71: Car 4H **9**
Eastmoor Rd. S43: Brim C 4E **169**
East Pde. S1: Shef 3E **5** (3F **119**)
East Pinfold S71: R'ton 3H **9**
East Rd. S2: Shef 1G **133**
  S36: Oxs 6G **177**
  S65: Roth 3A **98**
Eastside Cl. S41: Whit M 6A **162**
Eastside Rd. S41: Whit M 6A **162**
East St. DN1: Don 3B **56**
  S25: Din 5A **128**
  S63: Gol 4E **37**
  S72: Sth H 1H **11**
  S73: D'fld 4B **34**
East Ter. S26: Wales B 5E **139**
East Vale Dr. S65: Thry 6E **85**
East Vw. S66: Hel 5E **101**
  S72: Cud 1E **19**
  S74: Jum 5C **46**
East Vw. Av. S21: Ecki 2D **158**
East Vw. Ter. S6: Shef 3A **106**
Eastwell Gro. S73: Womb 3A **48**
EAST WHITWELL 4D **174**
EASTWOOD 2H **97**
Eastwood S6: Shef 1H **105**
Eastwood Av. S25: Nth A 3H **141**
Eastwood Cl. S41: Has 2B **172**
Eastwood Ct. S65: Roth 2H **97**
Eastwood Dr. S44: Cal 6G **169**
Eastwood Ho. *S65: Roth* *3G **97***
  (off Doncaster Rd.)
Eastwood La. S65: Roth 3F **97**
Eastwood Mt. S65: Roth 4H **97**
Eastwood Pk. Apartments
  S41: Has 3B **172**
Eastwood Pk. Dr. S41: Has 2C **172**
Eastwood Rd. S11: Shef 6C **118**
Eastwood Trad. Est. S65: Roth . .1H **97**
Eastwood Va. S65: Roth 2H **97**
Eastwood Vw. S65: Roth 2A **98**
Eaton Pl. S2: Shef 3A **120**
Eaton Sq. DN5: Barnb 1A **52**
Ebenezer Pl. S3: Shef 1D **4** (1F **119**)
  S74: Els 1D **62**
Ebenezer St. S3: Shef 1D **4** (1F **119**)
  S72: Gt H 1G **35**
Eben St. S9: Shef 2D **108**
Ebor Cl. S73: Womb 2H **47**
ECCLESALL 3A **132**
Ecclesall Rd. S11: Shef 1A **132**
Ecclesall Rd. Sth. S11: Shef 6F **131**
Eccles Dr. DN12: New E 6C **70**
ECCLESFIELD 1F **93**
Ecclesfield Cl. S35: Eccl 1G **93**
ECCLESFIELD COMMON 1G **93**
Ecclesfield Ct. S35: Eccl 1G **93**
Ecclesfield M. S35: Eccl 1G **93**
Ecclesfield Rd. S5: Shef 2A **94**
  S9: Shef 3C **94**
  S35: Chap 3G **79**
Ecclesfield Way S35: Eccl 1G **93**
Eccles St. S9: Shef 6E **95**
Eccleston Rd. DN3: Kirk Sa 3D **26**
ECKINGTON 1F **159**
Eckington Bus. Pk. S21: Ecki . . .6G **151**
Eckington Bus Station 1E **159**
Eckington Hall S20: Mosb 5E **151**
Eckington M. S20: Mosb 5E **151**

Eckington Pool 1F **159**
Eckington Rd. S18: Coal A 6H **147**
  S20: Beig, Holb 2G **151**
    (not continuous)
  S43: New W 1C **162**
  S43: Stav 3C **164**
Eckington Way S20: Half 3G **151**
  S20: Holb, Water 4E **137**
Ecton Ct. DN3: Kirk Sa 3B **26**
Edale Cl. S41: C'fld 1F **167**
Edale Ri. S75: Dod 3F **29**
Edale Rd. S11: Shef 1H **131**
  S43: Mas M 3F **165**
  S61: Kimb 4A **96**
EDDERTHORPE 2B **34**
Edderthorpe Cotts.
  S71: D'fld 2B **34**
Edderthorpe La. S71: D'fld 2B **34**
  S73: D'fld 2B **34**
Eddisons S36: Oxs 5G **177**
Eden Cl. S66: Hel 5E **101**
  S75: Bar g 3F **15**
Edencourt Dr. DN3: Eden 5D **26**
Eden Dr. S6: Lox 4F **105**
Edenfield Cl. S71: Monk B 2A **18**
Eden Fld. Rd. DN3: Eden 6D **26**
Eden Glade S26: Swal 6C **124**
Eden Gro. DN4: Hex 2H **55**
  S26: Swal 6C **124**
Eden Gro. Rd. DN3: Eden 6D **26**
Edenhall Rd. S2: Shef 1C **134**
Eden Pl. S25: Din 4H **127**
Edensor Ct. S43: Stav 6H **163**
Edensor Rd. S5: Shef 2G **107**
Eden St. S42: W'orth 6F **171**
Eden Ter. S64: Mexb 6F **51**
EDENTHORPE 6D **26**
Edenthorpe Dell S20: Mosb 6C **136**
Edenthorpe Gro. S20: Mosb 6D **136**
Edenthorpe Wlk. *S20: Mosb* *6D **136***
  (off Edenthorpe Gro.)
Edgar Allan Ho. S3: Shef 4B **4**
Edgar La. DN11: New R 5A **74**
Edgbaston Way
  DN12: New E 3D **70**
Edge Bank S7: Shef 2D **132**
Edgebrook Rd. S7: Shef 2C **132**
Edgecliffe Pl. S71: Smi 3F **17**
Edge Climbing Cen., The 5F **119**
Edge Cl. S6: Shef 4B **92**
Edgedale Rd. S7: Shef 3C **132**
Edgefield Rd. S7: Shef 3D **132**
Edge Grn. DN3: Kirk Sa 4C **26**
Edge Hill Rd. S7: Shef 2C **132**
Edgehill Rd. DN2: Don 3H **41**
  S75: Stain 4H **7**
Edgelands Ri. S72: Cud 3E **19**
Edge La. S6: Shef 4B **92**
Edgemount Rd. S7: Shef 3D **132**
Edge Well Cl. S6: Shef 4B **92**
Edge Well Cres. S6: Shef 4A **92**
Edge Well Dr. S6: Shef 5B **92**
Edge Well La. S6: Shef 4A **92**
Edge Well Pl. S6: Shef 4A **92**
Edge Well Way S6: Shef 4B **92**
Edinburgh Av. S63: Bolt D 2A **50**
Edinburgh Cl. S71: Monk B 4G **17**
Edinburgh Ct. S42: W'orth 6F **171**
Edinburgh Dr. S25: Nth A 1G **141**
Edinburgh M. S41: C'fld 4G **167**
Edinburgh Rd. S41: C'fld 3G **167**
  S42: W'orth 6F **171**
  S74: Hoyl 5B **46**
Edith Ter. DN5: Scaws 3F **39**
Edlington La. DN4: Warm 3D **70**
  DN12: New E, Old E 1B **88**
Edlington Leisure Cen. 6C **70**
Edlington Riding DN12: New E 5D **70**
Edmonton Cl. S75: Barn 6H **15**
Edmund Av. S17: Bradw 4B **146**
  S60: Brins 5E **111**
Edmund Cl. S17: Bradw 4C **146**
Edmund Ct. S2: Shef 5G **119**
Edmund Dr. S17: Bradw 4C **146**
Edmund Rd. S2: Shef 6G **119**
Edmunds Rd. S70: Wors 6H **31**
Edmund St. S41: C'fld 6G **161**
  S70: Wors 6F **31**
Edna St. S63: Bolt D 2B **50**
Edward Cl. S70: Barn 3H **31**

Edward Pl. S11: Shef 2C **132**
Edward Rd. DN6: Adw S 2E **23**
  S63: Gol 6B **36**
  S63: Wath D 4D **48**
Edward St. DN3: Arm 3C **42**
  DN5: Bntly 1A **40**
  DN11: New R 5A **74**
  S3: Shef 2B **4** (2E **119**)
  S21: Ecki 1E **159**
  S25: Din 5A **128**
  S36: Stoc 3D **174**
  S43: Stav 6H **163**
  S63: Thurn 2B **36**
  S64: Swin 2C **66**
  S72: Gt H 1F **35**
  S73: D'fld 5B **34**
  S73: Womb 1H **47**
  S74: Hoyl 6A **46**
  S75: Mapp 6B **8**
Edward St. Flats S3: Shef . . .2B **4** (2E **119**)
Edwin Av. S40: W'ton 2E **171**
Edwin Rd. DN6: Woodl 4B **22**
  S2: Shef 2H **133**
Edwins Cl. S71: Ath 1E **17**
Effingham La. S4: Shef 1H **5** (2H **119**)
Effingham Rd. S4: Shef 1A **120**
  S9: Shef 1A **120**
Effingham Sq. *S65: Roth* *3E **97***
  (off Water St.)
Effingham St. S4: Shef 1H **5** (1H **119**)
  S65: Roth 4E **97**
    (College St.)
  S65: Roth 3F **97**
    (Kenneth St.)
Egerton Cl. S3: Shef 5C **4** (4E **119**)
Egerton La. S1: Shef 6B **4** (4E **119**)
Egerton Rd. S18: Dron 2G **155**
  S26: Swal 1C **138**
Egerton St. S1: Shef 6B **4** (4E **119**)
Egerton Wlk. S3: Shef 5B **4**
Eggington Cl. DN4: Can 5E **59**
Egmanton Rd. S71: Ath 5E **9**
Egremont Cl. S66: Malt 3G **101**
Egremont Ri. S66: Malt 3G **101**
Eilam Cl. S61: Kimb P 2H **95**
Eilam Rd. S61: Kimb P 2H **95**
Eland Cl. DN11: Ross 4C **74**
Eland Rd. DN12: Den M 3A **68**
Elcroft Gdns. S20: Beig 6G **137**
Elder Av. S25: Nth A 3A **142**
Elderberry Cl. S61: Scho 6E **81**
Elder Ct. S21: Killa 5B **152**
Elder Dr. S66: Sunn 4G **99**
Elder Gro. DN9: Auck 1B **76**
  DN12: Con 5D **68**
Eldertree Rd.
  S61: Thorpe H 4C **80**
Elder Way S40: C'fld 5H **167**
  S72: Sth H 1H **11**
Eldon Arc. *S70: Barn* *1E **31***
  (off Midland St.)
Eldon Ct. S1: Shef 4C **4** (3E **119**)
Eldon Rd. S65: Roth 2G **97**
Eldon St. S1: Shef 4C **4** (3E **119**)
  S70: Barn 1E **31**
Eldon St. Nth. S71: Barn 6E **17**
Eleanor Ct. DN3: Eden 1B **42**
Eleanor St. S9: Shef 6E **109**
Elgar Dr. S66: Malt 6D **102**
Elgin Cl. S40: W'ton 3D **170**
Elgin St. S10: Shef 3A **118**
Elgitha Dr. S66: Thurc 6B **114**
Eliot Cl. S43: Brim C 3E **169**
Elizabeth Av. DN3: Kirk Sa 4D **26**
  S72: Sth H 1H **11**
Elizabeth Ct. S72: Grim 2B **20**
  WF9: Hems 1G **13**
Elizabeth Dr. S26: Aston 2C **138**
Elizabeth St. S63: Gol 5D **36**
  S72: Grim 2B **20**
Elizabeth Way *S60: Roth* *4D **96***
  (off Vine Cl.)
Elkstone Rd. S40: C'fld 3B **166**
Ellaline Cotts. S65: Rav 2D **100**
Elland Cl. S71: Smi 1D **16**
Ella Rd. S4: Shef 5H **107**
Ellavale Rd. S74: Els 6D **46**
Ellenboro Rd. S6: Shef 4A **106**
Ellen Tree Cl. S60: Brins 3C **110**
Ellerker Av. DN4: Hex 2A **56**
Ellers Av. DN4: Bess 4H **57**

Ellers Cres.—Exeter Pl.

Ellers Cres. DN4: Bess 4H 57
Ellers Dr. DN4: Bess 4H 57
Ellershaw La. DN12: Con 5D 68
Ellershaw Rd. DN12: Con 5E 69
(not continuous)
Ellers La. DN9: Auck 1H 59
Ellers Rd. DN4: Bess 4H 57
Ellerton Gdns. DN4: Can 3B 58
Ellerton Rd. S5: Shef 2A 108
Ellesmere Rd. S4: Shef 6H 107
(not continuous)
Ellesmere Rd. Nth. S4: Shef 5H 107
Ellesmere Ter. S65: Roth 4G 97
Ellesmere Wlk. S4: Shef 6H 107
Ellin Cl. S74: Jum 5C 46
Ellington Ct. S70: Barn 3B 30
Ellin St. S1: Shef 6D 4 (5F 119)
Elliott Av. S73: Womb 3G 47
Elliott Cl. S63: Wath D 5D 48
Elliott Ct. S65: Roth 3F 97
Elliott Dr. S43: Ink 2H 169
S61: Kimb P 6A 82
Elliott La. S35: Gren 4C 78
Elliott M. *S61: Kimb* *3A 96*
(off Benton Way)
Elliott Rd. S6: Shef 2C 118
Elliottville St. S6: Shef 6B 106
Ellis Av. S63: Wath D 2E 65
Ellis Ct. S73: Hem 4F 47
Ellis Cres. DN11: New R 5B 74
S73: Bramp 5B 48
Ellis Gro. S63: Wath D 5C 48
Ellisons Rd. S21: Killa 2D 152
Ellison St. S3: Shef 1B 4 (2E 119)
(not continuous)
Ellis St. S3: Shef 1C 4 (2E 119)
S60: Brins 3D 110
Elliston Av. S75: Stain 5B 8
Ellorslie Dr. S36: Stoc 3E 175
Ellwood S71: Lund 4B 18
Elmbridge Cl. S71: R'ton 3B 10
Elm Cl. DN3: Barn D 1C 26
DN11: Ross 6E 75
S21: Killa 5B 152
S41: C'fld 1G 167
Elm Cotts. S72: Gt H 6F 21
Elm Ct. S70: Wors 6G 31
Elm Cres. DN5: Bntly 6B 24
S20: Mosb 2D 150
Elmdale Cl. S64: Swin 6C 66
Elmdale Dr. DN3: Eden 1C 42
Elm Dr. DN9: Finn 3G 77
S21: Killa 5B 152
Elmfield Av. S5: Shef 6G 93
Elmfield Rd. DN1: Don 2C 56
DN11: New R 6C 74
Elm Grn. La. DN12: Con 4F 69
Elm Gro. S61: Grea 5C 82
Elmham Rd. DN4: Can 3B 58
S9: Shef 2G 121
Elmhirst Dr. S65: Roth 6C 98
Elmhirst La. S75: Silk 2E 29
(not continuous)
Elm La. S5: Shef 6G 93
Elm Lodge Farm Cl. S41: C'fld 1G 167
Elm M. *S70: Barn* *1D 30*
(off Nelson St.)
Elmore Rd. S10: Shef 3B 118
Elmore St. S66: Thurc 1D 126
Elm Pl. DN3: Arm 3D 42
S40: C'fld 6F 167
S62: Rawm 3H 83
S71: Monk B 3A 18
Elm Ri. S35: Chap 4E 79
Elm Rd. DN3: Arm 3D 42
DN9: Auck 2A 76
S20: Beig 4H 137
S21: Ecki 2D 158
S64: Mexb 6D 50
Elm Row S71: Barn 1G 31
Elmroyd Ct. S36: Pen 5E 177
Elms, The S64: Swin 5B 66
Elmsdale S70: Wors 6G 31
Elm St. S42: Tem N 6G 173
S43: Hol 5E 163
S74: Hoyl 1G 61
Elm Tree Cl. S25: Nth A 3A 142
Elm Tree Cres. S18: Dron 1F 155
Elm Tree Dr. S42: W'orth 6G 171
Elm Tree Farm Ct. S65: Hoot R 6E 67
ELM TREE HILL 2D 134
Elm Tree Rd. S66: Malt 5G 101
Elmtree Rd. S61: Thorpe H 5C 80
Elm Tree Stop (ST) 2D 134
Elmview Rd. S9: Shef 6E 95
Elmville Av. S64: Swin 5B 66
Elm Wlk. S63: Thurn 1C 36
Elm Way S63: Wath D 2H 65
Elmwood Av. DN6: Woodl 2A 22
Elmwood Cres. DN3: Arm 4D 42
Elmwood Dr. S20: Mosb 4E 151
Elmwood Ho. S43: Hol 6F 163
Elmwood Way S75: Barn 4C 16
ELSECAR 1D 62
Elsecar Heritage Cen. 2E 63
Elsecar Heritage Railway
Hemingfield Halt Station 6F 47
Rockingham Station 2E 63
Elsecar Ho. *DN1: Don* *2B 56*
(off Bond Cl.)
Elsecar Rd. S63: Bramp B, Wath D 6B 48
Elsecar Station (Rail) 1D 62
Elsham Cl. S66: Bram 3A 100
Elstead Cl. S75: Bar G 3F 15
Elstree Dr. S12: Shef 4E 135
Elstree Rd. S12: Shef 4E 135
Elsworth Cl. DN1: Don 3B 56
Elter Dr. DN4: Don 3G 57
Eltham Cft. S7: Shef 4A 132
Elton La. S66: Sunn 3G 99
Elton St. S40: C'fld 6H 167
Elton Vw. S43: Stav 6A 164
Elvaston Cl. S18: Dron W 3A 154
Elwin Ct. DN4: Balb 2A 72
Elwis St. DN5: Don 6A 40
Elwood Rd. S17: Bradw 4B 146
Ely Rd. DN2: Don 3E 41
Ely St. DN11: New R 4B 74
Embankment Rd. S10: Shef 3B 118
Emerson Cl. S5: Shef 5G 93
Emerson Cres. S5: Shef 6G 93
Emerson Dr. S5: Shef 6G 93
Emily Cl. S71: Barn 6A 18
Emily Rd. S7: Shef 2D 132
Emley Dr. DN5: Scaws 3D 38
Emley Ho. *DN1: Don* *2B 56*
(off St James St.)
Emley Vw. S71: Monk B 3F 17
Emmet Fld. Cl. S40: Birdh 2G 171
Empire Dr. S66: Malt 3G 101
Empire Rd. S7: Shef 1E 133
Empire Ter. S71: R'ton 2A 10
Emsley Av. S72: Cud 4F 19
Endcliffe Av. S10: Shef 5B 118
ENDCLIFFE CRESCENT 5A 118
Endcliffe Cres. S10: Shef 4A 118
ENDCLIFFE EDGE 5H 117
Endcliffe Edge S10: Shef 5A 118
Endcliffe Glen Rd. S11: Shef 5B 118
Endcliffe Gro. Av. S10: Shef 5H 117
Endcliffe Hall Av. S10: Shef 5H 117
Endcliffe Ri. Rd. S11: Shef 5B 118
Endcliffe Ter. Rd. S11: Shef 5B 118
Endcliffe Va. Av. S11: Shef 6B 118
Endcliffe Va. Rd. S10: Shef 5A 118
Endcliffe Way DN2: Don 3H 41
Endfield Rd. S5: Shef 3E 93
Endowood Rd. S7: Shef 6A 132
S40: Bramp 2B 170
Enfield Pl. S13: Shef 4A 122
Enfield Rd. S41: C'fld 3G 167
Engine La. S63: Gol 6E 37
S72: Shaft 5G 11
Engine La. Cl. S72: Shaft 5G 11
Ennerdale Av. S20: Half 4F 151
Ennerdale Cl. S18: Dron W 3D 154
S25: Nth A 1H 141
S64: Mexb 6H 51
Ennerdale Cres. S41: C'fld 1D 166
Ennerdale Dr. S20: Half 4F 151
Ennerdale Rd. DN2: Don 4H 41
S71: Ard 2E 33
Ennis Cres. DN2: Don 5F 41
Enterprise Cen. S63: Gol 6D 36
Enterprise Pk. S9: Shef 1B 120
Enterprise Park Ind. Est. S9: Shef 1C 120
Enterprise Way S20: Holb 2A 152
Entwhistle Rd. S35: High G 1D 78
Epping Gdns. S20: Sot 6H 137
Epping Gro. S20: Sot 6H 137
Epsom Cl. S64: Mexb 6G 51
Epsom Rd. DN4: Can 2A 58
Epworth Ct. *DN5: Bntly* *2A 40*
(off Chapel St.)
Erin Rd. S43: Pool, Stav 6C 164
Ernest Copley Ho. S35: High G 2E 79
Ernest Hardy Ct. S2: Shef 5D 120
Errington Av. S2: Shef 2B 134
Errington Cres. S2: Shef 2B 134
Errington Rd. S2: Shef 1B 134
S40: W'ton 2E 171
Errington Way S2: Shef 1B 134
Erskine Cres. S2: Shef 1H 133
Erskine Rd. S2: Shef 1H 133
S65: Roth 2F 97
Erskine Vw. S2: Shef 2H 133
Eshlands Brook S71: Monk B 3C 18
Eshton Ct. S75: Mapp 4H 7
Eshton Wlk. S70: Barn 1D 30
Eskdale Cl. S6: Shef 1B 106
S18: Dron W 3D 154
Eskdale Dr. DN5: Scawt 2G 39
Eskdale Rd. S6: Shef 2B 106
S61: Wing 5A 82
S71: Ard 2D 32
Eskdale Wlk. DN5: Scaws 3D 38
Eslaforde Ter. *S65: Roth* *2A 98*
(off Doncaster Rd.)
Esperanto Pl. S1: Shef 3F 5
Essendine Cres. S8: Shef 5G 133
Essex Av. DN2: Don 1G 57
Essex Cl. S26: Kiv P 5D 140
Essex Rd. S2: Shef 5A 120
S70: Barn 3E 31
Essoldo Chambers *S60: Roth* *4E 97*
(off High St.)
Estate Rd. S62: Rawm 1F 83
Estone Dr. S26: Swal 6C 124
Ettrick Cl. S40: C'fld 3D 166
Etwall Cl. S40: C'fld 2B 166
Etwall Way S5: Shef 6H 93
Europa Av. S9: Shef 6B 110
Europa Cl. S9: Shef 5G 109
Europa Ct. S9: Shef 6B 110
Europa Dr. S9: Shef 4G 109
Europa Link S9: Shef 5G 109
S60: Shef 6B 110
Europa Vw. S9: Shef 6A 110
Europa Way S9: Tins 4A 110
Euston Way S25: Laugh C 4F 127
Evans Bus. Cen. S25: Din 4G 127
Evans Ct. DN3: Arm 4C 42
Evans St. S3: Shef 6B 4
Evanston Gdns. DN4: Balb 4H 55
Eva Ratcliffe Ho. S5: Shef 2F 93
Eveline St. S72: Cud 2E 19
Evelyn Av. DN2: Don 6G 41
Evelyn Cl. DN2: Don 6G 41
Evelyn Rd. S10: Shef 3A 118
Evelyn St. S62: Rawm 2A 84
Evelyn Ter. S70: Barn 2F 31
Everard Av. S17: Bradw 5H 145
Everard Dr. S17: Bradw 5H 145
Everard Glade S17: Bradw 5H 145
Everett Cl. S43: Brim 1D 168
Evergreen Dr. DN5: Bntly 5A 24
Everill Cl. S73: Womb 3A 48
Everill Ga. La. S73: Womb 2A 48
(not continuous)
Everingham Cl. S5: Shef 1F 107
Everingham Cres. S5: Shef 1E 107
Everingham Pl. S5: Shef 2F 107
Everingham Rd. DN4: Can 2B 58
S5: Shef 1F 107
Everson Cl. S66: Malt 3H 101
Everton Rd. S11: Shef 6B 118
Evesham Cl. S9: Shef 1E 109
Ewden Ho. *S10: Shef* *5A 116*
(off Holyrood Av.)
Ewden Rd. S73: Womb 3A 48
EWDEN VILLAGE 6E 175
Ewden Way S75: Barn 1H 29
Ewers Rd. S61: Kimb 4A 96
Ewood Dr. DN4: Can 4B 58
Excalibur Way S41: C'fld 5A 168
Excelsior Ct. DN12: Con 4F 69
Exchange Gateway S1: Shef 3E 5
Exchange Pl. S2: Shef 2G 5 (2G 119)
Exchange St. DN1: Don 2B 56
S2: Shef 2G 5 (2G 119)
Exchange Works S1: Shef 6E 5
Exeter Dr. S3: Shef 6B 4 (5E 119)
Exeter Pl. S3: Shef 6B 4 (5E 119)

Exeter Rd. DN2: Don 4F **41**
Exeter Way S3: Shef 6A 4 (4D **118**)
Exley Av. S6: Shef 6C **106**
Experience Barnsley Mus. & Discovery Cen.
. . . . .6D **16**
Eyam Cl. S75: Dod 3F **29**
Eyam Rd. S10: Shef 3A **118**
Eyncourt Rd. S5: Shef 1A **108**
Eyre Ct. S66: Bram 6B **100**
Eyre Gdns. S35: High G 2C **78**
S41: C'fld 4G **167**
Eyre La. S1: Shef 6E 5 (4F **119**)
Eyre St. S1: Shef 6D 4 (4F **119**)
Eyre St. E. S41: Has 3B **172**

F

Fabian Way S66: Bram 6B **100**
Factory St. S40: C'fld 6E **167**
Faheem Ct. S65: Roth 1A **98**
Fairbank Rd. S5: Shef 2F **107**
Fairbank Vw. S60: Whis 3B **112**
Fairbarn Cl. S6: Shef 1F **117**
Fairbarn Dr. S6: Shef 1F **117**
Fairbarn Pl. S6: Shef 1F **117**
Fairbarn Rd. S6: Shef 1F **117**
Fairbarn Way S6: Shef 1F **117**
Fairburn Gdns. S60: Brins 4E **111**
Fairburn Gro. S74: Els 6E **47**
Fair Cl. S40: C'fld 4F **167**
Fairfax Dr. S2: Shef 6E **121**
Fairfax Ri. S2: Shef 6E **121**
Fairfax Rd. DN2: Don 6G **41**
S2: Shef 6E **121**
Fairfield S63: Bolt D 1A **50**
S70: Birdw 3E **45**
Fairfield Av. DN4: Bess 6A **58**
S43: Brim 6C **162**
S66: Bram 3H **99**
Fairfield Ct. DN3: Arm 5E **43**
S42: Ash 4A **166**
S73: Womb 6A **34**
Fairfield Dr. S42: Ash 4A **166**
Fairfield Gdns. S74: Els 6D **46**
Fairfield Hgts. S10: Shef 4A **118**
Fairfield Rd. DN5: Don 4G **39**
S40: C'fld 4G **167**
Fairford Cl. DN4: Can 6D **58**
S40: Birdh 3G **171**
Fairholme Hgts. S35: Ough 2F **91**
Fair Holme Vw. DN3: Arm 6F **43**
Fairlands Gro. DN9: Auck 3A **76**
FAIRLEIGH 6D **120**
Fairleigh S2: Shef 6D **120**
Fairleigh Dr. S60: Roth 6F **97**
Fairmount Gdns. S12: Shef 5B **136**
Fairthorn Rd. S5: Shef 6A **94**
Fair Vw. S40: C'fld 4F **167**
Fair Vw. Av. DN6: Woodl 3A **22**
Fairview Cl. DN3: Brant 5G **59**
S74: Hoyl 1H **61**
Fairview Ct. DN3: Barn S 2C **26**
Fair Vw. Dr. S26: Aston 1D **138**
Fairview Rd. S18: Dron 1F **155**
Fairview Ter. DN3: Barn D 2C **26**
Fairview Vs. DN3: Barn D 2D **26**
Fairway S75: Dod 4H **29**
Fairway, The S10: Shef 5B **116**
Fairway Vw. S75: Stain 4B **8**
Fairways S66: Wick 6G **99**
Fairwinds Cl. S18: Dron 3F **155**
Faith St. S71: Monk B 2C **18**
Falcon Cl. DN6: Adw S 2C **22**
S64: Mexb 1B **68**
Falcon Ct. DN11: Ross 5D **74**
S25: Din 6A **128**
Falcon Dr. S60: Tree 3G **123**
S70: Birdw 4E **45**
Falconer Cl. S75: Kexb 5E **7**
Falconer La. S13: Shef 6G **123**
Falconer Way S60: Tree 2G **123**
Falcon Knowle Ing S75: Kexb 5D **6**
Falcon Ri. S18: Dron 1A **156**
Falcon Rd. S18: Dron 1H **155**
Falcon St. S70: Barn 6D **16**
Falcon Way S25: Din 1H **141**
Falcon Yd. S40: C'fld 5H **167**
(off Low Pavement)
Falding St. S35: Chap 3G **79**
S60: Roth 4D **96**

Falkland Ri. S18: Dron 4F **155**
Falkland Rd. S11: Shef 2H **131**
Fall Bank Cres. S75: Dod 2E **29**
Fall Bank Ind. Est. S75: Dod 3E **29**
Fall Cl. S70: Barn 2A **30**
Fall Head La. S75: Silk 1C **28**
Fallon Cl. S25: Laugh C 4F **127**
Fallon Rd. S6: Stan 6E **105**
Fallowfield Rd.
S43: New W 3C **162**
Fall Vw. S75: Silk 2B **28**
Falmouth Cl. S71: Monk B 5G **17**
Falmouth Rd. S7: Shef 3D **132**
Falstaff Cres. S5: Shef 6E **93**
Falstaff Gdns. S5: Shef 6E **93**
Falstaff Rd. S5: Shef 5E **93**
Falthwaite Grn. La.
S75: Hood G 6E **29**
Family Court
Chesterfield 5A **168**
Fane Cres. S26: Swal 6C **124**
Fanny Av. S21: Killa 5D **152**
Fan Rd. S43: Stav 5C **164**
Fan Rd. Ind. Est. S43: Stav 5B **164**
Fanshaw Av. S21: Ecki 2D **158**
Fanshaw Bank S18: Dron 3F **155**
Fanshaw Cl. S21: Ecki 2D **158**
Fanshaw Dr. S21: Ecki 2D **158**
Fanshaw Rd. S18: Dron 2G **155**
S21: Ecki 2D **158**
Fanshaw Way S21: Ecki 2D **158**
Faraday Rd. S9: Shef 6B **108**
Faranden Rd. S9: Shef 1D **120**
Farcliff DN5: Sprot 3C **54**
Far Cres. S65: Roth 3A **98**
Far Cft. S63: Bolt D 2B **50**
Farcroft Gro. S4: Shef 3C **108**
Far Dalton La. S65: Dalt M 1D **98**
Fardell Gdns. S66: Bram 6A **100**
Far Field Cl. DN3: Eden 5D **26**
Far Field La. S63: Wath D 6A **50**
S71: Monk B 2B **18**
Farfield Pk. S63: Wath D 5A **50**
Far Field Rd. DN3: Eden 5D **26**
S65: Roth 5B **98**
Farfield Rd. S3: Shef 6D **106**
Fargate S1: Shef 3E 5 (3F **119**)
Far Golden Smithies S64: Swin 2B **66**
Farish Pl. S2: Shef 2G **133**
Far La. S6: Shef 3A **106**
S65: Roth 2A **98**
Far Lawns S71: Car 5A **10**
Farlawns Ct. DN4: Balb 2A **72**
Farlow Cft. S35: High G 6B **60**
Farlow Rd. S18: Dron W 2D **153**
Farm Bank Rd. S2: Shef 6H 5 (4H **119**)
Farm Cl. DN3: Eden 1D **42**
S12: Shef 6E **135**
S18: Coal A 6G **147**
S40: Birdh 4G **171**
S60: Brins 5C **110**
S71: Monk B 4H **17**
Farm Ct. DN6: Adw S 2D **22**
Farm Cres. S20: Mosb 4D **150**
Farm Dr. S62: Rawm 2A **84**
Farm Flds. Cl. S20: Water 1E **151**
Farm Grange DN4: Balb 2H **71**
Farmhill Cl. DN5: Cus 5F **39**
Farm Ho. La. S75: Barn 6H **15**
Farmhouse La. S35: Ough 3B **90**
Farm La. S21: Ecki 1D **158**
Far Moor Cl. DN5: Harl 2H **51**
S63: Gol 6E **37**
Farmoor Gdns. S20: Sot 6A **138**
Farm Rd. S2: Shef 5G **119**
S70: Barn 4G **31**
Farmstead Cl. S14: Shef 3A **134**
Farm Vw. Cl. S12: Shef 5C **136**
Farm Vw. Gdns. S12: Shef 5C **136**
Farm Vw. Rd. S61: Kimb 2G **95**
Farm Wlk. S20: Mosb 3D **150**
Farm Way S73: D'fld 4B **34**
Farnaby Dr. S35: High G 6C **60**
Farnaby Gdns. S35: High G 6C **60**
Farnborough Dr. DN4: Can 6D **58**
Farndale Av. S42: W'ton 2C **170**
Farndale Rd. DN5: Scaws 3E **39**

Farnham Way
S25: Laugh C 3F **127**
Farnley Av. S6: Shef 6C **92**
Farnley Rd. DN4: Balb 1B **72**
Farnon Cl. S40: C'fld 1A **172**
Farnsworth Cl. S41: Has 2C **172**
Farnsworth St. S41: Has 2B **172**
Farnworth Rd. S65: Roth 3B **98**
Far Pl. S65: Roth 3A **98**
Farquhar Rd. S66: Malt 5C **102**
(not continuous)
Farrand St. S70: Birdw 5D **44**
Farrar Rd. S7: Shef 1E **133**
Farrar St. S70: Barn 1C **30**
Farrier Cl. DN1: Don 2C **56**
Farrier Ga. S35: High G 2D **78**
Farriers Way S21: Killa 5C **152**
Farringdon Cl. WF9: Hems 1E **13**
Farringdon Dr. DN11: New R 6H **75**
Farrington Ct. S66: Wick 6H **99**
Farrow Cl. S75: Dod 3H **29**
Farthing Gale M. DN5: Cus 5G **39**
Far Townend S75: Dod 3G **29**
Far Vw. Rd. S5: Shef 6G **93**
Far Vw. Ter. S70: Barn 3D **30**
Farwater Cl. S18: Dron 4F **155**
Farwater La. S18: Dron 3E **155**
Fathers Gdns. S26: Kiv P 6A **140**
Favell Rd. S3: Shef 3A 4 (3D **118**)
S65: Roth 3C **98**
Fawcett St. S3: Shef 1A 4 (2D **118**)
(not continuous)
Fawn Cl. S42: W'orth 6G **171**
Fay Cres. S9: Shef 2E **121**
Fearnehough St. S9: Shef 1C **120**
Fearn Ho. Cres. S74: Hoyl 1H **61**
Fearnley Rd. S74: Hoyl 1H **61**
Fearn's Bldgs. S36: Pen 4C **176**
(off Stottercliffe Rd.)
Fearnville Gro. S71: R'ton 3H **9**
Felkin St. S41: C'fld 5A **168**
FELKIRK 1E **11**
Felkirk Cotts. S72: Sth H 1E **11**
Felkirk Vw. S72: Shaft 3E **11**
Fellbrigg Rd. S2: Shef 1A **134**
Fellowsfield Way S61: Kimb 3H **95**
Fellows Wlk. S73: Womb 6E **33**
Fell Rd. S9: Shef 5D **108**
Fell St. S9: Shef 4C **108**
FENCE 6G **123**
Fen Ct. DN3: Eden 6D **26**
Fenlake Wlk. S63: Wath D 4E **49**
Fenland Way S40: W'ton 2F **171**
Fenney La. S11: Shef 6F **131**
Fensome Way S73: Tank 2D **60**
Fensome Way S73: D'fld 4B **34**
Fenton Cl. DN3: Arm 5E **43**
Fenton Cft. S61: Roth 2B **96**
Fenton Dr. S12: Shef 4A **136**
Fenton Flds. S61: Roth 2B **96**
Fenton Rd.
S61: Grea, Roth, Wing 1B **96**
Fenton St. S21: Ecki 2C **158**
S61: Kimb 3A **96**
S70: Barn 1D **30**
Fentonville St. S11: Shef 6D **118**
Fenton Way DN5: Grea 6C **82**
Feoffees Rd. S35: Eccl 2G **93**
Ferguson St. S9: Shef 6C **108**
Ferham Cl. S61: Kimb 4B **96**
Ferham Pk. Av. S61: Roth 4B **96**
Ferham Rd. S61: Roth 4B **96**
Fern Av. DN5: Don 3H **39**
S20: Beig 4G **137**
S43: Stav 6H **163**
Fern Bank DN6: Adw S 2C **22**
Fernbank Cl. DN9: Blax 1G **77**
S70: Wors 4E **31**
Fernbank Dr. DN3: Arm 2E **43**
S21: Ecki 1C **158**
Fern Cl. DN2: Don 4H **41**
S21: Ecki 1C **158**
S73: D'fld 6B **34**
Fern Ct. S66: Sunn 3H **99**
Ferncroft Av. S20: Mosb 3D **150**
Ferndale Cl. S18: Coal A 1A **156**
Ferndale Dr. S66: Bram 4H **99**
Ferndale Pl. WF9: Hems 1E **13**
Ferndale Ri. S18: Coal A 1A **156**
Ferndale Rd. DN12: Con 4E **69**
S18: Coal A 1A **156**

Ferndale Vw. DN5: Cus 5G 39
Fernhall Cl. DN3: Kirk Sa 5D 26
Fernhall Ct. S73: Womb 1H 47
Fern Hollow S66: Wick 1H 113
Fernhurst Rd. DN2: Don 4H 41
Fernlea Cl. DN5: Cus 5G 39
Fern Lea Gro. S63: Bolt D 2A 50
Fernlea Gro. S35: Eccl 2G 93
Fernleigh Dr. S60: Brins 2C 110
Fern Rd. S6: Shef 6A 106
Fernvale Wlk. S64: Swin 6C 66
Fern Vw. S12: Shef 5A 136
Fern Vw. Gro. S12: Shef 5A 136
Ferny Way S21: Ecki 1C 158
Fernwood Cl. S41: Has 3D 172
Ferrara Cl. S73: D'fld 4H 33
Ferrars Cl. S9: Tins 2A 110
Ferrars Dr. S9: Tins 3A 110
Ferrars Rd. S9: Tins 1H 109
Ferrars Way S9: Tins 3A 110
Ferrers Rd. DN2: Don 5E 41
Ferriby Rd. S6: Shef 2A 106
Ferry Boat La.
 DN12: Old D 3H 67
 S64: Mexb 2H 67
Ferry La. DN12: Con 3F 69
Ferry Moor La. S72: Grim 2G 19
Ferrymoor Way S72: Grim 2H 19
Ferrymore Ho. DN1: Don 2B 56
 (off Oxford Pl.)
Ferry Ter. DN12: Con 3F 69
Fersfield St. S4: Shef 1A 120
Festival Cl. S26: Kiv P 6H 139
Festival Rd. S63: Wath D 1G 65
Fewston Way DN4: Don 4G 57
Fiddle Neck La. S26: Aston 3F 139
Fiddler's Dr. DN3: Arm 6F 43
Field Cl. S18: Dron W 2B 154
 S73: D'fld 4B 34
Field Dr. S72: Cud 3E 19
Fielder M. S5: Shef 6A 94
Fielders Way DN12: New E 3D 70
Fieldfare Gro. S63: Wath D 4F 49
Fieldfare Ho. S41: Old W 3A 162
Field Ga. DN11: Ross 4D 74
Fieldhead Ct. S74: Hoyl 6B 46
Field Head Rd. S74: Hoyl 1B 62
Fieldhead Rd. S8: Shef 1F 133
Fieldhead Way S41: C'fld 2D 166
Field Ho. Rd. DN5: Sprot 4C 54
Fieldhouse Way S4: Shef 5A 108
Fielding Dr. S66: Bram 5A 100
Fielding Gro. S62: Rawm 1G 83
Fielding Rd. S6: Shef 2B 106
Field La. DN9: Auck 2C 76
 S21: Killa 4A 152
 (Bryony Cl.)
 S21: Killa 5A 152
 (Holly Cl.)
 S60: Up W 6D 112
 S66: Mort 6D 112
 S70: Stair 3B 32
Fields End S36: Oxs 6H 177
Fields End Bus. Pk. S63: Gol 4D 36
Fieldsend Gdns. S35: Eccl 2G 93
Fields End Rd. S63: Gol 4C 36
Fieldside DN3: Eden 1C 42
Fieldside Ct. S65: Rav 1A 100
Field Sta. Rd. DN5: Bntly 1D 24
Field Vw. S40: Birdh 3H 171
 S40: C'fld 5F 167
 (off Chatsworth Rd.)
 S60: Brins 3D 110
 S71: R'ton 3H 9
Fieldview DN12: New E 5B 70
 (off Sunningdale Dr.)
Field Vw. Ct. S60: Brins 4D 110
Field Vw. Dr. DN9: Auck 3B 76
Fieldview Pl. S41: C'fld 2D 166
Field Way S60: Roth 2E 97
Fife Cl. S9: Shef 6D 94
Fife Gdns. S9: Shef 6D 94
Fife St. S9: Shef 6D 94
 S70: Barn 2C 30
Fife Way S9: Shef 6D 94
Fifth Av. DN6: Woodl 5C 22
 DN9: Finn 3C 76
Fiftyeights Rd. DN9: Finn 5H 77
Figtree La. S1: Shef 2E 5 (2F 119)
Filby Rd. DN5: Cus 5F 39
Filey Av. S71: R'ton 2A 10

Filey La. S3: Shef 5A 4 (4D 118)
Filey St.
 S10: Shef 4A 4 (3D 118)
Fillies Av. DN4: Bess 2B 74
Finch Cl. S65: Thry 6E 85
Finch Gdns. S66: Bram 6B 100
Finch Ri. S26: Aston 2D 138
Finch Rd. DN4: Balb 6G 55
Finchwell Cl. S13: Shef 4A 122
Finchwell Cres. S13: Shef 4A 122
Finchwell Ri. S13: Shef 4A 122
Finchwell Rd. S13: Shef 4A 122
Findon Cres. S6: Shef 4H 105
Findon Pl. S6: Shef 4H 105
Findon Rd. S6: Shef 4H 105
Findon St. S6: Shef 4H 106
Finkle St. DN5: Bntly 2A 40
Finlay Rd. S65: Roth 2A 97
Finlay St. S3: Shef 1A 4 (2D 118)
FINNINGLEY 3F 77
Finningley Lodge S26: Kiv P 6A 140
 (off Victoria Cl.)
Finsbury Cl. S25: Laugh C 3F 127
FIRBECK 1H 129
Firbeck Av. S25: Laugh M 2H 127
Firbeck Ho. DN1: Don 2B 56
 (off Grove Pl.)
Firbeck La. S25: Laugh M 1H 127
Firbeck Rd. DN4: Balb 2E 57
 S8: Shef 5D 132
Firbeck Way DN11: Ross 4E 75
Fir Cl. S63: Wath D 1G 65
Fircrest Way S63: Wath D 4F 49
Fircroft Av. S5: Shef 5A 94
Fircroft Rd. S5: Shef 5B 94
Firethorn Ri. S65: Rav 2B 100
Firham Cl. S71: R'ton 2F 9
Fir Pl. S6: Shef 1B 118
 S21: Killa 5B 152
Fir Rd. S21: Ecki 2D 158
Firs, The S70: Barn 4H 31
 S71: R'ton 2F 9
Firsby La. DN12: Con 2B 86
Firshill Av. S4: Shef 4G 107
Firshill Cl. S4: Shef 4G 107
Firshill Cres. S4: Shef 4F 107
Firshill Cft. S4: Shef 4F 107
Firshill Gdns. S4: Shef 4F 107
Firshill Glade S4: Shef 4F 107
Firshill M. S3: Shef 4G 107
 (off Pitsmoor Rd.)
Firshill Ri. S4: Shef 4F 107
Firshill Rd. S4: Shef 4G 107
Firshill Wlk. S4: Shef 4F 107
Firshill Way S4: Shef 4F 107
Firs La. S36: H'swne 1D 176
First Av. DN6: Woodl 4D 22
 DN9: Finn 3C 76
 S65: Roth 3H 97
 S71: R'ton 2A 10
 WF9: Stin K 5G 13
First La. S25: Sth A 5H 141
 S66: Wick 1H 113
Fir St. S6: Shef 1B 118
 S43: Hol 5G 163
Firth Av. S72: Cud 3D 18
Firth Cres. DN11: New R 5B 74
 S66: Malt 6B 102
Firth Dr. S4: Shef 6A 108
FIRTH PARK 1A 108
Firth Pk. Av. S5: Shef 1B 108
Firth Pk. Cres. S5: Shef 1A 108
Firth Pk. Rd. S5: Shef 1A 108
Firth Rd. S63: Wath D 6C 48
Firth St. DN4: Balb 3A 56
 S61: Grea 5D 82
 S71: Barn 6E 17
Firthwood Av. S18: Coal A 1A 156
Firthwood Cl. S18: Coal A 1A 156
Firthwood Rd. S18: Coal A 1A 156
Fir Tree Av. DN9: Auck 2B 76
Fir Tree Dr. S26: Wales 6F 139
Fir Tree Gdns. S70: Birdw 6D 44
Firtree Rd. S35: Chap 4F 79
FIR VALE 3H 107
Fir Vale Pl. S5: Shef 3H 107
Fir Vale Rd. S5: Shef 3H 107
Firvale Rd. S42: W'ton 2C 170

Fir Vw. Gdns. S4: Shef 4A 108
Fir Wlk. S66: Malt 5F 101
Fish Dam La. S71: Car, Monk B ..6A 10
Fisher Cl. S40: Birdh 3G 171
 S60: Roth 4D 96
Fisher La. S9: Shef 1F 121
Fisher Rd. S66: Malt 6C 102
Fisher St. DN5: Bntly 6A 24
Fisher Ter. DN5: Don 5H 39
Fish Pond La. S66: B'well 2B 102
Fishponds Rd. S13: Shef 6F 121
Fishponds Rd. W. S13: Shef 6F 121
Fishponds Vw. S13: Shef 1G 135
Fitness Village
 Balby 4A 56
Fitspace Gym
 Sheffield 1B 106
Fitzalan Rd. S13: Shef 5A 122
Fitzalan Sq. S1: Shef 3F 5 (3G 119)
Fitzalan Square Store (ST) ..2G 5 (3G 119)
Fitzalan Way S60: Tree 3G 123
Fitzgerald Rd. S10: Shef 2A 118
Fitzhubert Rd. S2: Shef 6D 120
 (not continuous)
Fitzmaurice Rd. S9: Shef 6E 109
Fitzroy Rd. S2: Shef 2G 133
Fitzwalter Rd. S2: Shef 4A 120
 (not continuous)
Fitzwilliam Av. DN12: Con 4C 68
 S63: Wath D 1F 65
Fitzwilliam Cl. S74: Hoyl 6C 46
Fitzwilliam Ct. S62: Rawm 4G 83
 S63: Wath D 6C 48
 S74: Hoyl 6C 46
 (off Fitzwilliam Cl.)
Fitzwilliam Dr. DN5: Harl 3H 51
Fitzwilliam Gate S1: Shef ..6C 4 (4F 119)
Fitzwilliam Rd. S65: Roth 3F 97
 S73: D'fld 4D 34
Fitzwilliam Sq. S61: Grea 4C 82
 S74: Els 2E 63
Fitzwilliam St. S1: Shef ...4B 4 (3E 119)
 S62: P'gte 5G 83
 S63: Wath D 1F 65
 S64: Swin 3B 66
 S70: Barn 1D 30
 S73: Hem 5E 47
 S74: Els 1D 62
 S74: Hoyl 1G 61
Fitzwilliam Wlk. S61: Grea 5C 82
Five Acres S75: Cawt 3A 14
Five Oaks DN5: Ark 5D 24
Five Trees Av. S17: Dore 4H 145
Five Trees Cl. S17: Dore 4H 145
Five Trees Dr. S17: Dore 4H 145
Five Weirs Wlk. S9: Shef 6C 108
Fixby Ho. DN1: Don 2B 56
 (off Grove Pl.)
Flamsteed Cres. S41: C'fld 1H 167
Flanders Ct. S61: Thorpe H 3C 80
FLANDERWELL 4G 99
Flanderwell Av. S66: Bram 5H 99
Flanderwell La. S66: Sunn 4H 99
Flanderwell Gdns. S66: Sunn 4H 99
Flanderwell La. S66: Bram, Sunn ..3G 99
Flash La. S6: Stan 2A 116
 S66: Bram 6B 100
Flask Vw. S6: Stan 5D 104
Flat La. S60: Whis 3A 112
 S72: Bill 5F 35
 S81: Fir 1G 129
Flat St. S1: Shef 3F 5 (3G 119)
Flatts Cl. S60: Tree 1F 123
Flatts La. S60: Tree 1F 123
 S63: Wath D 6E 49
Flaxby Rd. S9: Shef 1E 121
Flax Lea S70: Wors 5F 31
Fleet Cl. S63: Bramp B 5C 48
Fleet Hill Cres. S71: Monk B 3F 17
Fleet La. S35: Ough 6F 91
Fleetwood Av. S71: Monk B 3H 17
Fleming Gdns. S66: Flan 4G 99
Fleming Pl. S70: Barn 2D 30
Fleming Sq. S63: Wath D 6F 49
Fleming Way S66: Flan 5F 99
Fletcher Av. S18: Dron 3F 155
Fletcher Ho. S65: Roth 4F 97
 (off Wharncliffe Hill)
Fleury Cl. S14: Shef 4B 134
Fleury Cres. S14: Shef 4B 134

Fleury Pl. S14: Shef 4B 134
Fleury Ri. S14: Shef 4B 134
Fleury Rd. S14: Shef 4B 134
Flint Rd. DN2: Don 4H 41
Flintson Av. S43: New W 2C 162
Flintway S63: Wath D 3G 65
Flockton Av. S13: Shef 6D 122
Flockton Ct.
   S1: Shef 4C 4 (3E 119)
Flockton Cres. S13: Shef 6C 122
Flockton Dr. S13: Shef 6D 122
Flockton Ho. S1: Shef 4C 4
Flockton Pk. S20: Holb 1H 151
Flockton Rd. S13: Shef 6C 122
Flodden St. S10: Shef 2A 118
Floodgate Dr. S35: Eccl 2G 93
Flora St. S6: Shef 6D 106
Florence Av. DN4: Balb 4H 55
   S26: Swal 1C 138
Florence Cl. S40: Birdh 4G 171
Florence Ri. S73: D'fld 5A 34
Florence Rd. S8: Shef 6D 132
   S42: W'orth 6F 171
Flower St. S63: Gol 5E 37
Flowitt St. DN4: Hex 2A 56
   S64: Mexb 1E 67
Flying Fox Cres. DN12: New E 5D 70
Fold, The S65: Roth 2C 98
Folderings La. S36: Bolst 6E 175
Folder La. DN5: Sprot 3B 54
FOLDRINGS 2B 90
Folds Cres. S8: Shef 1B 146
Folds Dr. S8: Shef 1B 146
Folds La. S8: Shef 1B 146
Foley Av. S73: Womb 2F 47
Foley St. S4: Shef 1A 120
Foljambe Av. S40: W'ton 2E 171
Foljambe Cres. DN11: New R 5A 74
Foljambe Dr. S65: Dalt 1D 98
Foljambe Rd. S40: C'fld 5G 167
   S43: Brim 6D 162
   S65: Roth 2A 98
Foljambe St. S62: P'gte 4G 83
Folkwood Gro. S11: Shef 3F 131
Follett Rd. S5: Shef 5H 93
Folly La. S36: Thurl 2A 176
Fonteyn Ho. DN2: Don 4E 41
Fontwell Dr. S64: Mexb 6G 51
Foolow Av. S40: C'fld 1G 171
Footgate Cl. S35: Ough 3E 91
Footrill Cotts. S74: Hoyl 2B 62
Forbes Rd. S6: Shef 5B 106
FORD .5H 149
Fordoles Head La.
   S66: Malt, Mick 2F 101
Ford Rd. S11: Shef 2A 132
   S21: Mar L 5H 149
Fordstead La. DN3: Barn D . . .3E 25, 1G 27
   DN5: Alm 3E 25
Fore Hill Av. DN4: Bess 6A 58
Foremark Rd. S5: Shef 6A 94
Fore's Rd. DN3: Arm 5F 43
Forest Cl. S35: Ough 6G 91
Forest Edge S11: Shef 1H 145
Forest Grange DN4: Can 3B 58
Forest Ri. DN4: Balb 1F 71
Forest Rd. S71: Ath 6E 9
Forge, The S2: Shef 5E 119
   S18: Dron 3F 155
   S71: Smi 3E 17
Forge Dr. S40: C'fld 1H 171
Forge Hill S35: Ough 3E 91
Forge La. S21: Killa 4A 152
   S35: Ough 3E 91
   S35: Wort 1H 175
   S60: Roth 3E 97
                        (off Bridge St.)
   S74: Els 2E 63
Forge Rd. S26: Wales 5G 139
Forge Valley Sports Cen. 5G 105
Forge Way S60: Roth 1F 97
Formby Ct. S71: Monk B 2A 18
Forncett St. S4: Shef 6A 108
Fornham St. S2: Shef 6F 5 (4G 119)
                        (not continuous)
Forres Av. S10: Shef 3H 117
Forres Rd. S10: Shef 3H 117
Forrester Cl. S66: Flan 4G 99
Forrester's La. S18: Coal A 6H 147
Forster Rd. DN4: Balb 6A 56

Forth Av. S18: Dron W 2C 154
Fort Hill Rd. S9: Shef 1C 108
Fortway Rd. S60: Brins 2D 110
Forum, The S1: Shef 4C 4
Fossard Cl. DN2: Don 3F 41
Fossard Gdns. S64: Swin 4D 66
Fossard Way DN5: Scawt 1G 39
Fossdale Rd. S7: Shef 3C 132
Foster S3: Shef 1F 5
Foster Rd. S66: Wick 5G 99
Foster's Cl. S43: Swin 3B 66
Foster St. S70: Stair 2A 32
Foster Way S35: High G 6C 60
Foston Dr. S40: C'fld 3C 166
Fothergill Dr. DN3: Eden 5D 26
Foulstone Row S73: Womb 2H 47
Foundry, The S41: C'fld 6A 168
Foundry Climbing Cen., The 1F 119
Foundry Cl. S3: Shef 5G 107
Foundry Ga. S73: Womb 3E 47
Foundry Rd. DN4: Hex 3A 56
Foundry St. S41: Whit M 6H 161
   S62: P'gte 5G 83
   S70: Barn 2D 30
                        (not continuous)
   S74: Els 1D 62
Foundry St. Ind. Est.
   S41: Whit M 6H 161
                        (off Foundry St.)
Fountain Cl. S75: Dart 5F 7
Fountain Ct. DN11: Ross 6E 75
Fountain Gdns. S65: Thry 4E 85
Fountain Pde. S75: Mapp 6B 8
Fountain Pct. S1: Shef 3E 5
Fountains Cl. DN3: Kirk Sa 4B 26
Fountains Cres. S5: Shef 3E 93
Fountain Sq. S75: Dart 5F 7
Fountains Way S71: Monk B 5A 18
Fountside S7: Shef 2C 132
Four Lands Cl. S75: Bar G 3F 15
FOUR LANE ENDS 3G 135
FOURLANE ENDS 4E 133
Fourth Av. DN6: Woodl 5C 22
   DN9: Finn 3C 76
Four Wells Dr. S12: Shef 4B 136
Fowler Bri. Rd. DN5: Bntly 2B 40
Fowler Cres. DN11: New R 5B 74
Fowler St. S41: Old W 4G 161
Foxbrook Cl. S42: Ash 3A 166
Foxbrook Dr. S40: W'ton 2C 170
Fox Cl. S61: Kimb P 6G 81
Foxcote Lea S65: Thry 6F 85
Foxcote Way S42: W'ton 2C 170
Fox Ct. S64: Swin 5C 66
Foxcovert Cl. S63: Gol 1B 50
Fox Croft S8: Shef 3E 147
   S74: Hoyl 1A 62
Foxcroft Chase S21: Killa 4B 152
Foxcroft Dr. S21: Killa 4B 152
Foxcroft Gro. S21: Killa 4B 152
Foxcroft Mdws. S66: Malt 6A 102
Foxdale Av. S12: Shef 3E 135
Foxen Cft. S71: Lund 4B 18
Fox Farm Cl. S63: Bramp B 5B 48
Foxhill Cl. S12: Shef 6A 136
Fox Flds. S36: Oxs 6G 177
Foxfield Wlk. S70: Stair 4A 32
Fox Gdns. DN5: Bntly 5A 24
Fox Glen Rd. S36: Spink 4F 175
Foxglove Cl. S44: Cal 5F 169
Foxglove Rd. S5: Shef 6B 94
Fox Gro. DN4: Warm 6D 54
Foxhall La. S10: Shef 2A 130
Fox Hill S3: Shef 6G 107
Fox Hill Cl. S6: Shef 5B 92
Fox Hill Cres. S6: Shef 5B 92
                        (not continuous)
Fox Hill Dr. S6: Shef 5B 92
Fox Hill Pl. S6: Shef 4B 92
Fox Hill Rd. S6: Shef 6B 92
Fox Hill Way S6: Shef 4B 92
Foxland Av. S64: Swin 4H 65
Fox La. DN5: Barnb 1H 51
   S12: Shef 6F 135
   S17: Bradw 4C 146
Fox La. Cl. S12: Shef 4F 135
Fox La. Vw. S12: Shef 4F 135
Foxley Oaks S41: Old W 5A 162
Foxmire Gro. S75: Dod 3E 29

Foxmires Gro. S63: Gol 5E 37
Fox Rd. S6: Shef 6D 106
Foxroyd Cl. S71: Ard 2C 32
Foxshaw M. S72: Grim 2C 20
Fox's Pl. S40: C'fld 6E 167
Foxstone Cl. S43: Stav 6A 164
Foxstone Way S21: Ecki 2D 158
Fox St. S3: Shef 6F 107
   S61: Kimb 4H 95
Fox Valley Retail Pk.
   S36: Stoc 2E 175
Fox Valley Way S36: Stoc 2E 175
Fox Wlk. S6: Shef 6C 106
Foxwood Av. S12: Shef 2E 135
Foxwood Cl. S41: C'fld 5F 161
   S41: Has 4C 172
Foxwood Dr. S12: Shef 2E 135
Foxwood Gro. DN3: Eden 1B 42
   S12: Shef 3E 135
Foxwood Ind. Pk. S41: C'fld 5G 161
Foxwood Rd. S12: Shef 2E 135
   S41: C'fld 4F 161
Foxwood Way S41: C'fld 4F 161
Foyers Way S41: C'fld 5A 168
Framlingham Pl. S2: Shef 1A 134
Framlingham Rd. S2: Shef 1A 134
France Rd. S6: Lox 3E 105
Frances Dr. S42: W'orth 6F 171
Frances St. DN1: Don 1C 56
France St. S62: P'gte 5G 83
Francis Cl. S43: Brim 1C 168
Francis Cres. Nth. S60: Roth 1C 112
Francis Cres. Sth.
   S60: Roth 1C 112
Francis Dr. S60: Roth 6C 98
Francis Gro. S35: High G 1C 78
Francis St. S60: Roth 5F 97
Francus Royd S71: Car 5H 9
Frankham Cl. S25: Laugh C 4F 127
Frank Hillock Fld. S36: Spink 3G 175
Franklin Cres. DN2: Don 1E 57
Franklyn Dr. S43: Stav 3C 164
Franklyn Rd. S40: C'fld 4F 167
Frank Pl. S9: Shef 5D 108
Frank Rd. DN5: Don 4A 40
Frank Wright Cl. S2: Shef 6H 119
Fraser Cl. S8: Shef 5D 132
Fraser Cres. S8: Shef 5D 132
Fraser Dr. S8: Shef 5E 133
Fraser Rd. S8: Shef 5D 132
   S60: Roth 5G 97
Fraser Wlk. S8: Shef 6E 133
FRECHEVILLE 4G 135
Frecheville St. S43: Stav 5A 164
Fred Edwards Pk. S62: Rawm 6D 64
                        (not continuous)
Frederick Av. S70: Barn 2C 30
Frederick Dr. S35: Gren 1A 92
Frederick Rd. S7: Shef 1E 133
Frederick St. S9: Shef 1E 121
   S60: Cat 1D 122
   S60: Roth 3E 97
   S63: Gol 5D 36
   S63: Wath D 5E 49
   S64: Mexb 2E 67
   S65: Roth 3E 97
   S73: Womb 1F 47
Fred Mulley Rd. S4: Shef 1A 120
Freebirch Vw. S41: C'fld 1C 166
Freedom Ct. S6: Shef 5C 106
Freedom Rd. S6: Shef 6B 106
Freeman Gdns. S35: High G 2C 78
Freeman Rd. S66: Wick 5G 99
Freeman St. S70: Barn 2E 31
Freemans Yd. S70: Barn 1E 31
Freesia Cl. S25: Sth A 4F 141
Freeston Pl. S9: Shef 5D 108
French Ga. DN1: Don 6B 40
                        (not continuous)
Frenchgate Shop. Cen.
   DN1: Don 1B 56
French St. DN5: Bntly 6A 24
Fretson Cl. S2: Shef 6D 120
Fretson Grn. S2: Shef 6D 120
Fretson Rd. S2: Shef 6D 120
Fretson Rd. Sth. S2: Shef 1D 134
Fretwell Cl. S66: Malt 4H 101
Fretwell Rd. S65: Roth 2B 98
   S66: Hel 5E 101
Freydon Way S44: Cal 5F 169
Friar Cl. S6: Stan 6E 105

Friars Ga. DN1: Don 6B 40
Friar's Rd. S71: Lund 5B 18
Frickley Bri. La.
　S72: Brier 2H 11
Frickley Rd. S11: Shef 6G 117
Friends Cl. S66: Thurc 1D 126
Friers Cft. S62: Wentw 5E 63
Frinton Cl. S40: Birdh 3G 171
Frithbeck Cl. DN3: Arm 4E 43
Frith Cl. S12: Shef 3E 135
Frith Rd. S12: Shef 3E 135
Frithwood Dr. S18: Dron 2H 155
Frobisher Grange
　DN9: Finn 4F 77
Frobisher Gro. S66: Malt 4H 101
Froggatt Cl. S43: Ink 2H 169
Froggatt La. S1: Shef 5E 5 (4F 119)
Frogmore Cl. S66: Bram 4A 100
Frog Wlk. S11: Shef 6D 118
Front St. S60: Tree 2F 123
Frostings, The S35: Gren 1B 92
Frostings Cl. S35: Gren 1B 92
　　　　　　　　　　　(not continuous)
Fryston Ct. S63: Bramp B 5B 48
Fulford Cl. S9: Shef 1F 121
　S40: W'ton 2D 170
　S75: Dart 5H 7
Fulford Pl. S9: Shef 1F 121
Fulford Way DN12: Con 3H 69
Fuller Dr. S41: C'fld 2B 168
Fullerton Av. DN12: Con 4C 68
Fullerton Cres. S65: Thry 5D 84
Fullerton Dr. S60: Brins 4C 110
Fullerton Rd. S60: Roth 6D 96
Fullshaw Bank S36: Pen 5E 177
Fulmar Way S61: Thorpe H 2D 80
Fulmer Cl. S71: Ath 2G 17
Fulmer Cres. S5: Shef 4D 92
Fulmere Rd. S5: Shef 4D 92
Fulmer Rd. S11: Shef 1B 132
Fulney Rd. S11: Shef 6G 117
Fulton Rd. S6: Shef 1B 118
Furlong Cl. S63: Gol 1C 50
Furlong Mdws. S63: Bramp B 6A 48
Furlong Rd. DN5: Harl 3F 51
　S63: Bolt D, Gol 2C 50
Furlong Vw. DN5: Harl 2G 51
　　　　　　　　　　　(not continuous)
Furnace Hill S3: Shef 1D 4 (2F 119)
　S40: C'fld 6F 167
Furnace Hillock Way S41: Has 5D 172
　S42: Gras 5D 172
Furnace La. S13: Shef 1E 137
　S18: Barl 3A 160
　S43: Brim C 2E 169
Furnace Yd. S74: Els 2E 63
Furness Cl. S6: Stan 5E 105
　S25: Din 1A 142
Furness Dene S71: Monk B 3A 18
Furness Rd. S35: High G 1B 78
Furniss Av. S17: Dore 4E 145
Furniss M. S17: Dore 4F 145
Furnival Cl. S26: Tod 3B 140
Furnival Gate S1: Shef 5D 4 (4F 119)
Furnival Rd. DN4: Balb 4H 55
Furnival Rd. S4: Shef 2G 5 (2G 119)
　S26: Tod 3B 140
Furnival Sq. S1: Shef 5E 5 (4F 119)
Furnival St. S1: Shef 5E 5 (4F 119)
Furnival Way S60: Whis 3C 112
Fusion Magna Bus. Cen. S60: Roth . . .6B 96
Future Wlk. S40: C'fld 5G 167
Fylde Cl. S71: Monk B 2A 18

G

Gainsborough Cl. S66: Flan 5G 99
Gainsborough Dr. DN12: New E 4D 70
Gainsborough Rd. S11: Shef 1C 132
　S18: Dron 4D 154
Gainsborough Way S71: Monk B 4G 17
Gainsford Rd. S9: Shef 2F 121
Gaitskell Cl. S63: Gol 1C 50
　S66: Malt 6C 102

Gala Bingo
　Barnsley 6E 17
　Doncaster 3G 41
　Rotherham 1A 98
　Sheffield 2B 120
　Sheffield Hillsborough 1C 106
Gala Cres. S66: Malt 4G 101
Gallery, The S1: Shef 2G 5 (2G 119)
Galley Dr. S20: Water 1E 151
Gallow Tree Rd. S65: Roth 6B 98
Galpharm Way S75: Dod 2F 29
Galsworthy Av. S5: Shef 1E 107
Galsworthy Cl. DN4: Balb 1G 71
Galsworthy Rd. S5: Shef 2D 106
Galway Cl. S62: Rawm 2H 83
Galway Ct. S71: R'ton 2H 9
Gamston Rd. S8: Shef 1E 133
Gannow Cl. S21: Killa 3E 153
GANNOW HILL 3E 153
Ganton Cl. S71: Smi 1D 16
Ganton Rd. S6: Shef 2A 106
Garbroads Cres. S65: Thry 6D 84
Garbutt St. S63: Bolt D 3C 50
Garden Cl. S43: New W 3C 162
　S60: Roth 2H 111
Garden Ct. S70: Barn 1A 30
Garden Cres. S60: Roth 2H 111
Garden Dr. S73: Bramp 4B 48
Gardener La. S36: Pen 5E 177
Garden Gro. S73: Hem 4F 47
Garden Ho. Cl. S71: Monk B 3H 17
Garden Ho. Dr. S26: Kiv P 5C 140
Gardenia Rd. DN3: Kirk Sa 5B 26
Garden La. DN4: Hex 3G 55
　DN5: Cad 6G 53
　S60: Roth 3D 96
　S65: Rav 6A 86
Gardens, The S64: Bess 5A 58
　S7: Shef 6D 118
Gardens La. DN12: Con 4E 69
Garden St. S1: Shef 2C 4 (2E 119)
　S61: Roth 3C 96
　S63: Gol 5E 37
　S63: Thurn 2C 36
　S63: Wath D 5E 49
　S64: Mexb 1F 67
　S70: Barn 2E 31
　S73: D'fld 5B 34
Garden Ter. DN5: Bntly 2A 40
GARDEN VILLAGE 3C 174
Garden Wlk. S20: Beig 5H 137
　S60: Roth 2H 111
Gardom Cl. S18: Dron W 3C 154
Garfield Mt. S65: Roth 4F 97
Garland Cl. S20: W'fld 2F 151
Garland Cft. S20: W'fld 3F 151
Garland Dr. S6: Lox 3F 105
Garland M. S20: W'fld 3F 151
Garland Way S20: W'fld 3F 151
Garraby Ct. S72: Gt H 6F 21
Garry Rd. S6: Shef 3A 106
Garside's Bldgs. S36: Pen 4C 176
　　　　　　　　　(off Stottercliffe Rd.)
Garter St. S4: Shef 5A 108
Garth Cl. S9: Shef 1D 120
Garth Way S18: Dron 3E 155
Garth Way Cl. S18: Dron 3E 155
Gartrice Gdns. S20: Half 5H 151
Gartrice Gro. S20: Half 5H 151
Gashouse La. S20: Mosb 5E 151
　S21: Ecki 5E 151
Gate, The S75: Dod 2G 29
Gate Cres. S75: Dod 2G 29
Gatefield Cl. S41: C'fld 2D 166
Gatefield Rd. S7: Shef 2D 132
Gatehouse Ct. S75: Dod 2G 29
Gate Ho. La. DN9: Auck 1C 76
Gateland La. S31: Barl 6D 154, 1A 160
Gate Pk. S62: P'gte 5G 83
Gatesbridge Pk. DN9: Finn 2G 77
Gateway, The S2: Shef 2H 5
　S25: Din 4A 128
　S62: P'gte 6F 83
　S71: Ath .5D 8
Gateway Cl. S62: P'gte 1F 97
Gateway Ct. S62: P'gte 6F 83
Gateway Ind. Est., The S62: P'gte . . .6F 83
Gateway Pl. S62: P'gte 1F 97
Gateway Plaza S70: Barn 1D 30
Gatewood La. DN3: Brant, Can 2F 59
Gattison La. DN11: New R 6C 74

Gatty Rd. S5: Shef 3A 94
Gaunt Cl. S14: Shef 5A 134
　S21: Killa 4B 152
　S66: Bram 4A 100
Gaunt Dr. S14: Shef 5A 134
　S66: Bram 4A 100
Gaunt Pl. S14: Shef 4A 134
Gaunt Rd. S14: Shef 5A 134
　S66: Bram 4A 100
Gaunt Way S14: Shef 5A 134
Gawber Rd. S75: Barn 5B 16
GAWBER 4H 15
Gawtress Row S63: Wath D 6F 49
Gayle Ct. S70: Barn 6C 16
Gayton Cl. DN4: Balb 1H 71
Gayton Ct. DN4: Balb 1H 71
Gayton Rd. S4: Shef 4H 107
Geer La. S12: Ridg 5F 149
Gelderd Pl. S18: Dron 4F 155
Gell St. S3: Shef 3A 4 (3D 118)
Genn La. S70: Barn, Wors 4C 30
Genoa Cl. S73: D'fld 3H 33
Genoa St. S64: Mexb 1G 67
George Buckley Ct.
　WF9: Sth K 4H 13
George Pl. S62: Rawm 3H 83
　S64: Mexb 1H 67
Georges Cross S71: Smi 2F 17
George Sq. S70: Barn 1D 30
George St. DN3: Arm 3C 42
　DN5: Bntly 6H 23
　S1: Shef 3F 5 (3G 119)
　S41: Old W 4G 161
　S43: Brim 6D 162
　S60: Roth 3E 97
　S63: Gol 5B 36
　S63: Thurn 3E 37
　S70: Barn 1D 30
　S70: Wors 6F 31
　　　　　　　　　　　　　(John St.)
　S70: Wors 6H 31
　　　　　　　　　　　　　(Pantry Grn.)
　S72: Cud 6F 11
　S72: Midd 3E 35
　S73: Womb 2G 47
　　　　　　　　　　　　　(Hoyland St.)
　S73: Womb 6A 34
　　　　　　　　　　　　(Stonyford Rd.)
　S74: Hoyl 1B 62
　S75: Mapp 5A 8
George Woofindin Almshouses
　S11: Shef 6B 118
George Yd. S70: Barn 1D 30
Georgian M. S60: Cat 6D 110
Gerald Cl. S70: Barn 3H 31
Gerald Cres. S70: Barn 2H 31
Gerald Pl. S70: Barn 3H 31
Gerald Rd. S70: Barn 3H 31
Gerald St. S9: Shef 5D 108
Gerald Wlk. S70: Barn 3H 31
Gerard Av. S65: Thry 4D 84
Gerard Cl. S8: Shef 2G 133
　S40: W'ton 1D 170
Gerard Rd. S60: Roth 5F 97
Gerard St. S8: Shef 2G 133
Gervase Av. S8: Shef 4D 146
Gervase Dr. S8: Shef 4D 146
Gervase Pl. S8: Shef 4D 146
Gervase Rd. S8: Shef 4D 146
Gervase Wlk. S8: Shef 4D 146
Gibb Ct. S43: New W 2C 162
　　　　　　　　　　　(off Handley Rd.)
Gibbing Greaves Rd. S65: Roth 6D 98
Gibbons Dr. S14: Shef 6B 134
Gibbons Wlk. S14: Shef 6B 134
　　　　　　　　　　　(off Gibbons Dr.)
Gibraltar St. S3: Shef 1D 4 (2F 119)
Gibson La. S36: Stoc 2E 175
Gifford Dr. DN4: Warm 6E 55
Gifford Rd. S8: Shef 1F 133
Gilbert Av. S40: W'ton 2E 171
Gilbert Ct. S2: Shef 5H 5
Gilbert Gro. S70: Barn 2A 32
Gilberthorpe Ct. S65: Roth 4G 97
Gilberthorpe Pl. S65: Roth 4H 97
Gilberthorpe Rd. DN4: Balb 5G 55
Gilberthorpe St. S65: Roth 4G 97
Gilbert Row S2: Shef 3H 5 (3H 119)
Gilder Way S72: Shaft 4F 11
Gildhurst Ct. S70: Birdw 6E 45
GILDINGWELLS 1G 143

Gildingwells Rd. S81: Letw 5G 129
   S81: Woods 4F 143
Giles Av. S63: Wath D 6D 48
Gileswood Cres.
   S63: Bramp B 5B 48
Gill Cl. S66: Wick 1H 113
Gill Cft. S6: Stan 6D 104
Gilleyfield Av. S17: Dore 3F 145
Gill Mdws. S6: Stan 6D 104
Gillott Dell S66: Wick 1G 113
Gillott Ind. Est. S70: Barn 6C 16
Gillott La. S66: Wick 1G 113
Gillott Rd. S6: Shef 6B 92
Gill St. DN1: Don 2C 56
   S74: Hoyl 1C 62
Gilpin La. S6: Shef 1D 118
Gilpin St. S6: Shef 6D 106
GILROYD .5H 29
Gilroyd La. S75: Dod, Stainb 5H 29
Ginhouse La. S61: Grea 2D 96
Gipsy Grn. La. S63: Wath D 2G 65
Gipsy La. S18: App 3D 156
   S41: Old W 5A 162
Gisborne Cl. S43: Stav 5C 164
Gisborne Rd. S11: Shef 2A 132
Glade, The S10: Shef 5A 118
   S40: C'fld 5E 167
Glade Cl. S40: C'fld 3F 167
Glade Cft. S12: Shef 4D 134
Glade Lea S12: Shef 4D 134
Glade Vw. DN3: Kirk Sa 4C 26
Gladman Pk. S75: Tank 2B 60
Gladstone M. S10: Shef 5F 117
Gladstone Pl. S64: Mexb 1D 66
Gladstone Rd. DN4: Hex 3H 55
   S10: Shef 5G 117
   S40: C'fld 4G 167
   S66: Malt 4H 101
Gladwin Gdns. S40: W'ton 2E 171
Gladwin Ind. Pk. S64: Kiln 1D 84
Gladys St. S65: Roth 4H 97
Glaisdale Cl. S25: Laugh C 3F 127
Glaisdale Ct. S25: Laugh C 3F 127
Glamis Rd. DN2: Don 1F 57
Glass House Grn. S62: Wentw 4G 63
Glasshouse La. S43: New W 1C 162
   S64: Kiln 1D 84
Glasshouse Rd. S64: Kiln 1D 84
Glasshouse St. S60: Roth 3D 96
Glastonbury Ga. DN5: Scaws 5E 39
GLEADLESS 5D 134
Gleadless Av. S12: Shef 4C 134
Gleadless Bank S12: Shef 4C 134
Gleadless Comn. S12: Shef 2C 134
Gleadless Ct. S2: Shef 2G 133
Gleadless Dr. S12: Shef 4C 134
Gleadless Mt. S12: Shef 5D 134
Gleadless Ri. S12: Shef 3C 134
Gleadless Rd. S2: Shef 5D 134
   (not continuous)
   S12: Shef 3B 134
   S14: Shef 3B 134
GLEADLESS TOWNEND 5C 134
Gleadless Townend Stop (ST) . . .5D 134
GLEADLESS VALLEY 4B 134
Gleadless Vw. S12: Shef 3C 134
Glebe, The S41: Old W 4H 161
Glebe Cl. S64: Mexb 2G 67
   (off Doncaster Rd.)
   S64: Swin 5B 66
Glebe Ct. S41: Old W 4H 161
   S75: Tank 1D 60
Glebe Cres. S65: Thry 1D 98
Glebe Farm Cl. DN3: Arm 3D 42
Glebeland Cl. S62: Rawm 1F 83
Glebelands Rd. S36: Stoc 4E 175
Glebe Rd. S10: Shef 2B 118
   S64: Swin 5B 66
Glebe St. DN4: Warm 6E 55
Glebe Way, The S41: Old W 4H 161
Gledhill Av. S36: Cub 6C 176
Gledhill Cl. S18: Dron 3F 155
Glen, The S10: Shef 5A 118
   S35: Wharn S 1C 90
Glenalmond Rd. S11: Shef 1A 132
Glenavon Cl. S43: New W 1C 162
Glencairn Cl. S66: Malt 5D 102
   (off Woodside Cl.)
Glencoe Dr. S2: Shef 4H 119
Glencoe Pl. S2: Shef 4H 119
Glencoe Rd. S2: Shef 5H 5 (4H 119)

Glencoe Way S40: Ash 4C 166
Glencrest Way
   S63: Wath D 4F 49
Glencroft S11: Shef 1H 131
Glendale Cl. S75: Barn 6A 16
Glendale Rd. DN5: Sprot 3C 54
Gleneagles Cl. S40: W'ton 2D 170
Gleneagles Dr. DN4: Can 6E 59
Gleneagles Ri. S64: Swin 4C 66
Gleneagles Rd. S25: Din 6A 128
Glen Fld. Av. DN4: Hex 3H 55
Glenfield Cres. S41: C'fld 1G 167
Glen Head S17: Dore 1E 145
Glenholme Dr. S13: Shef 1H 135
Glenholme Pl. S13: Shef 1A 136
Glenholme Rd. S13: Shef 1A 136
Glenholme Way S13: Shef 6H 121
Glenmoor Av. S70: Barn 2A 30
Glenmore Cl. S43: Ink 3G 169
Glenmore Cft. S12: Shef 2E 135
Glenmore Ri. S73: Womb 3H 47
Glenorchy Rd. S7: Shef 3C 132
Glen Rd. DN3: Brant 4H 59
   S7: Shef 2D 132
   (not continuous)
Glenthorne Cl. S40: Bramp 6D 166
Glentilt Rd. S7: Shef 3C 132
Glen Va. S18: Dron W 3C 154
Glen Vw. S11: Shef 6G 117
   S64: Mexb 1G 67
Glen Vw. M. S64: Mexb 2G 67
Glen Vw. Rd. S8: Shef 2D 146
Glenville Cl. S74: Hoyl 1A 62
Glenwood Ct. S6: Shef 1G 105
Glenwood Cres. S35: Chap 3G 79
Glenwood Dr. S6: Shef 1G 105
Glenwood M. S6: Shef 1G 105
Gliwice Way DN4: Don 3G 57
Glossop La. S10: Shef 4A 4 (3D 118)
Glossop Rd. S10: Shef 4A 4 (4B 118)
Glossop Row S35: Ough 3E 91
Glossop's Cft. S41: Old W 4A 162
Gloucester Cres. S10: Shef 4D 118
Gloucester Rd. DN2: Don 5F 41
   S41: C'fld 3G 167
   S61: Kimb P 1A 96
Gloucester St. S10: Shef 4D 118
Glover Rd. S8: Shef 1F 133
   S17: Tot 6G 145
Glumangate S40: C'fld 5H 167
Glyn Av. DN1: Don 6D 40
Goals Soccer Cen.
   Doncaster 3F 41
   Sheffield 6H 5 (5H 119)
Goathland Cl. S13: Shef 1E 137
Goathland Dr. S13: Shef 1E 137
Goathland Pl. S13: Shef 1E 137
Goathland Rd. S13: Shef 1E 137
Goddard Av. S36: Stoc 2B 174
Goddard Hall Rd. S5: Shef 3H 107
Godley Cl. S71: R'ton 2A 10
Godley St. S71: R'ton 2A 10
Godric Dr. S60: Brins 3C 110
Godric Grn. S60: Brins 3C 110
Godric Rd. S5: Shef 3H 93
Goldcrest Ho. S41: Old W 3A 162
Goldcrest Wlk. S61: Thorpe H 3D 80
Gold Cft. S70: Barn 2F 31
Golden Fleece Ct. DN2: Don 3F 41
Golden Oak Dell S6: Stan 5D 104
Golden Smithies La. S63: Wath D . . .3A 66
   S64: Swin 3A 66
Goldfinch Cl. S63: Wath D 5E 49
Goldsborough Rd. DN2: Don 1F 57
Goldsmith Dr. S65: Roth 4A 98
Goldsmith Rd. DN4: Balb 6B 56
   S65: Roth 4A 98
Goldthorpe St. S70: Barn 2F 31
Goldsworthy Way S75: Wool G 3E 7
GOLDTHORPE 5D 36
Goldthorpe Grn. S63: Gol 6C 36
Goldthorpe Ind. Est. S63: Gol 6A 36
Goldthorpe Rd. S63: Gol 6D 36
Goldthorpe Station (Rail) 5C 36
Gomersal La. S18: Dron 3F 155
Gomersall Av. DN12: Con 4C 68
Gooder Av. S71: R'ton 3H 9
Goodison Blvd. DN4: Can 4B 58
Goodison Ct. DN4: Can 4B 58

Goodison Cres. S6: Shef 6G 105
Goodison M. DN4: Can 6C 58
Goodison Ri. S6: Shef 6G 105
Goodison Rd. S63: Bramp B 5B 48
Goodison Wlk. DN4: Can 6D 58
Goodman Ct. S44: Cal 5F 169
Goodwin Av. S62: Rawm 2G 83
Goodwin Cres. S64: Swin 2B 66
Goodwin Rd. S8: Shef 2F 133
   S61: Wing 4B 82
Goodwin Sports Cen. 3C 118
Goodway S61: Wing 4B 82
Goodwood Gdns. DN4: Can 2A 58
Goodyear Cres. S73: Womb 2G 47
GOOLE GREEN 1E 131
Goore Av. S9: Shef 4E 121
Goore Dr. S9: Shef 3E 121
Goore Rd. S9: Shef 4E 121
Gooseacre Av. S63: Thurn 1B 36
Goosebutt Ct. S62: P'gte 4G 83
Goosebutt Ho. S62: P'gte 4G 83
Goosebutt St. S62: P'gte 4G 83
Goosecarr La. S26: Tod 1H 139
Goose Cl. S66: Wick 6H 99
Goosecroft Av. S65: Thry 6D 84
Goosehill Ct. DN4: Balb 2A 72
Goose La. S66: Wick 6H 99
Gordon Av. S8: Shef 6F 133
Gordon Rd. DN12: New E 4C 70
   S11: Shef 6C 118
Gordon Rd. Flats
   DN12: New E 4C 70
Gordon St. DN1: Don 1B 56
   S70: Stair 2B 32
Gordon Ter. S65: Roth 4G 97
Gorehill Cl. S63: Wath D 6H 49
Gorman Cl. S41: C'fld 6F 161
Gorse, The S65: Roth 5B 98
   S66: Wick 1G 113
Gorse Cl. S63: Bramp B 6A 48
   S65: Rav 2C 100
Gorse Dr. S21: Killa 5C 152
Gorseland Ct. S66: Wick 6F 99
Gorse La. S10: Shef 1A 130
Gorse Valley Rd. S41: Has 3D 172
Gorse Valley Way S41: Has 3D 172
Gorsey Brigg S18: Dron W 3C 154
Gosber Rd. S21: Ecki 1F 159
Gosber St. S21: Ecki 1E 159
Gosforth Cl. S18: Dron 3E 155
Gosforth Cres. S18: Dron 3E 155
Gosforth Dr.
   S18: Dron, Dron W 3C 154
Gosforth Grn. S18: Dron 3E 155
Gosforth La. S18: Dron 3E 155
Gosling Ga. Rd. S63: Gol 5D 36
Gotham Rd. S60: Brins 2D 110
Gough Cl. S65: Roth 6B 98
Goulding St. S64: Mexb 2E 67
Gowdall Grn. DN5: Bntly 5H 23
Gower Cres. S40: C'fld 3D 166
Gower St. S4: Shef 6H 107
   S73: Womb 2H 47
Gower Way S62: Rawm 6D 64
Goyt Side Rd. S40: C'fld 6E 167
Goyt Ter. S40: C'fld 6F 167
Grace Rd. DN12: New E 3D 70
Grace St. S71: Monk B 2C 18
Grady Dr. DN4: Balb 1B 72
Graftdyke Cl. DN11: Ross 5E 75
Grafton St. S2: Shef 5H 5 (4H 119)
   S70: Barn 1C 30
Grafton Way S65: Roth 3F 97
Graham Av. S60: Brins 5E 111
Graham Ct. S10: Shef 6G 117
Graham Knoll S10: Shef 6G 117
Graham Ri. S10: Shef 6G 117
Graham Rd. DN3: Kirk Sa 5C 26
   S10: Shef 5F 117
Graham's Orchard
   S70: Barn 1D 30
Grainger Cl. DN12: New E 5B 70
Grainger Ct. S10: Shef 5F 117
Grammar St. S6: Shef 5C 106
   (not continuous)
Grampian Cl. DN5: Cus 5F 39
   S75: Barn 6A 16
Grampian Cres. S40: C'fld 4C 166
Granary, The S11: Shef 5E 119
   (off Napier St.)
Granary Cl. S41: Up N 6B 160

Granary Ct. S25: Nth A 2G 141
(off The Green)
Granby Ct. DN3: Arm 5F 43
Granby Cres. DN2: Don 2E 57
Granby La. DN11: New R 4A 74
Granby Rd. DN12: New E 4D 70
  S5: Shef 2A 108
Grange, The S42: Ash 4A 166
  S43: Brim 6B 162
  S61: Scho 6F 81
  S75: Barn 5H 15
  S75: Wool G 3E 7
Grange Av. DN4: Balb 5H 55
  S18: Dron W 3D 154
  S26: Augh 5B 124
  S81: Woods 5F 143
Grange Cliffe Cl. S11: Shef 4A 132
Grange Cl. DN4: Bess 6C 58
  S66: Bramp M 1A 126
  S72: Brier 3A 12
Grange Ct. DN4: Bess 6C 58
  DN5: Don 4A 40
  S66: Wick 1G 113
  S72: Brier 3A 12
(off Grange Cl.)
  S73: Womb 2H 47
Grange Cres. S11: Shef 6D 118
  S63: Thurn 1D 36
  S71: Barn 6B 18
Grange Cres. Rd. S11: Shef 6D 118
Grange Dr. S61: Kimb 1G 95
  S66: Hel 6E 101
Grange Farm Cl. S60: Brins 5E 111
Grange Farm Ct. S63: Bolt D 3B 50
  S81: Woods 5F 143
Grange Farm Dr. S26: Aston 2D 138
  S35: Ough 6E 91
Grange Farm Ri. S26: Aston 2D 138
Grangefield Av. DN4: Can 6C 58
  DN11: New R 5C 74
Grangefield Ct. DN4: Can 6C 58
Grangefield Cres. DN11: New R 5C 74
Grangefield Ter. DN11: New R 5C 74
Grange Gdns. S26: Tod 1B 140
GRANGE LANE 2C 94
Grange La. DN4: A'ley 2F 71
  DN5: Harl 2A 52
  DN11: A'ley 3G 71
  DN11: New R 6H 73
  S5: Shef 2C 94
  S13: Shef 6B 122
  S60: Brins, Roth 1B 110
  S61: Thorpe H 2C 94
  S66: Malt 5B 102
  S70: Stair 6B 18
  S71: Barn, Stair 6B 18
Grange La. Ind. Est. S71: Stair 1B 32
Grange M. S66: Wick 6G 99
Grange Mill La. S5: Shef 2C 94
  S9: Shef 2C 94
Grangemill Pl. S43: Stav 6H 163
Grange Pk. DN3: Kirk Sa 3D 26
Grange Pk. Av. S43: Brim C 4E 169
Grange Pk. Golf Course
  Rotherham 1D 94
Grange Rd. DN4: Bess, Can 6C 58
  DN5: Bntly 4H 23
  DN6: Woodl 5D 22
  DN11: New R 6B 74
  S11: Shef 6D 118
  S20: Beig 5G 137
  S60: Roth 2A 112
  S62: Rawm 1H 83
  S63: Ward 1E 65
  S64: Swin 4A 66
  S71: R'ton 3F 9
  S72: Brier 3A 12
Grange St. S63: Thurn 2D 36
Grange Vw. DN4: Balb 4H 55
  S74: Black H 3A 46
Grange Vw. Cres. S61: Kimb 2G 95
Grange Vw. Rd. S61: Kimb 2G 95
Grange Way DN12: Den M 3C 68
Grangewood Rd.
  S25: Laugh M 2H 127
  S40: Birdh 3G 171
Granham Acre S72: Shaft 4F 11
Gransden Way S40: W'ton 2D 170
Grantham St. DN11: New R 5B 74
Grantley Cl. S73: Womb 4A 48
Granville Cl. S41: Has 2C 172

Granville Rd. S2: Shef 6G 5 (4G 119)
Granville Road Stop (ST) 6G 5 (5G 119)
Granville Sq. S2: Shef 6G 5 (4G 119)
Granville St. S2: Shef 6G 5 (4G 119)
  S75: Barn 5C 16
Granville Ter. S65: Roth 4G 97
Grasby Ct. S66: Bram 3A 100
Grasmere Av. DN2: Don 6H 41
Grasmere Cl. S25: Nth A 2A 142
  S36: Pen 3D 176
  S41: C'fld 1E 167
  S64: Mexb 6A 52
Grasmere Cres. S75: Stain 4H 7
Grasmere Rd.
  DN12: Con 4E 69
  S8: Shef 3D 132
  S18: Dron W 3C 154
  S71: Barn 1F 31
Grasscroft Cl. S40: C'fld 2E 167
Grasscroft Ho. S40: C'fld 1H 171
(off Archdale Cl.)
Grasscroft Mobile Home Pk.
  S43: New W 1C 162
Grassdale Vw. S12: Shef 5A 136
GRASSHILL 6D 172
Grassholme Cl. DN4: Don 4G 57
Grassington Cl. S12: Shef 5C 136
Grassington Dr. S12: Shef 5C 136
Grassington Way
  S35: Chap 2E 79
Grassmoor Cl. S12: Shef 3C 134
Grassmoor Country Pk. 6E 173
Grassmoor Golf Course 6D 172
Grassthorpe Rd. S12: Shef 4E 135
Grattan St. S61: Kimb 4H 95
Gratton Ct. S35: Stav 3C 164
Graven Cl. S35: Gren 2A 92
Graves Art Gallery 4F 5
Graves Park Animal Farm 6G 133
Graves Tennis & Leisure Cen. 3G 147
Graves Trust Homes S8: Shef 2E 147
(Meadow Vw. Rd.)
  S8: Shef 2F 147
(Serpentine Wlk.)
  S12: Shef 3D 134
Gray Av. S26: Swal 5C 124
Gray Cl. S65: Roth 2F 97
Gray Gdns. DN4: Balb 6A 56
Grays Ct. DN12: Den M 2D 68
Grayshott Wlk. S40: Birdh 2G 171
Grayson Cl. S36: Stoc 4E 175
  S65: Rav 2A 100
Grayson Rd. S61: Wing 4B 82
Gray's Rd. S71: Car 5H 9
Gray St. S3: Shef 6G 107
  S20: Mosb 3D 150
  S74: Els 1D 62
Greasbro Rd. S9: Tins 2G 109
GREASBROUGH 5D 82
Greasbrough La. S62: Rawm 4D 82
Greasbrough Rd. S60: Roth 2E 97
(not continuous)
  S61: Grea 1E 97
  S62: P'gte 5E 83
Greasbrough St. S60: Roth 3D 96
Gt. Bank Rd. S65: Roth 6B 98
Gt. Broad Ing S75: Barn 4A 16
Gt. Central Av. DN4: Balb 4A 56
Gt. Cliffe Rd. S75: Dod 2F 29
Great Cft. S18: Dron W 2C 154
Gt. Eastern Way S62: P'gte 6G 83
GREAT HOUGHTON 1F 35
Great Nth. Rd. DN4: Bess 5A 58
  DN5: Scawt 6D 22
  DN6: Ham, Skell, Woodl, Adw S
  .... 1A 22
  DN6: Highf 6D 22
  DN11: Ross 3F 75
Great Pk. Rd. S61: Kimb P 2H 95
Great Stubbing S73: Womb 1E 47
Greaves Cl. S6: Stan 6D 104
Greaves Fold S75: Barn 6D 104
Greaves La. S6: Shef, Stan 6D 104
  S35: High G 4C 60
Greaves Rd. S5: Shef 2F 93
  S61: Roth 3B 96
Greaves Sike La. S66: Mick 1E 101
Greaves St. S6: Shef 5C 106
Greave Way S43: Brim 6B 162
Grebe Ct. S73: Bramp 3B 48
GREEN, THE 5D 176

Green, The DN5: Barnb 1A 52
  DN9: Auck 1H 59
  DN9: Finn 3F 77
  DN12: Old D 3H 67
  S9: Shef 2F 121
(off The Avenue)
  S17: Tot 6E 145
  S25: Nth A 2G 141
  S26: Wales B 5C 138
  S36: Pen 5C 176
  S36: Thurl 3A 176
  S41: Has 4B 172
  S60: Roth 1G 111
  S60: Whis 4A 112
  S63: Bolt D 1B 50
  S64: Swin 4A 66
  S66: Sunn 3H 99
  S71: R'ton 3H 9
(not continuous)
  S72: Shaft 3E 11
  S73: Hem 5F 47
Greenacre Cl. S12: Shef 4C 134
  S74: Hoyl 1C 62
Green Acres S36: Pen 4E 177
  S62: Rawm 3H 83
  S72: Grim 1B 20
  S74: Hoyl 1B 62
Greenacres Cl. S18: Dron 5H 155
Greenacres Vw. S65: Rav 2A 100
Greenacre Way S12: Shef 4C 134
Green Arbour Ct. S66: Thurc 1B 126
Green Arbour Rd. S66: Thurc 5B 114
Green Av. DN5: High M, Marr 1F 53
Green Balk S66: Clftn 3A 88
Greenbank S71: Ath 5E 9
Green Bank Dr. S66: Sunn 2H 99
Greenbank Dr. S40: Ash 4D 166
Greenbank Wlk. S72: Grim 1A 20
Green Blvd. DN4: Can 4B 58
Green Brook Pl. S36: Pen 5D 176
Green Chase S71: Ecki 1D 158
Green Cl. S18: Uns 6B 156
  S43: Ink 2H 169
Green Comn. DN3: Arm 5E 43
Green Ct. S66: Sunn 3H 99
Greencroft S60: Roth 1G 111
Greencroft Cl. S60: Roth 1G 111
Green Cross S18: Dron 2G 155
Greendale Av. S42: Holy 2A 170
Greendale Cl. S18: Dron 2G 155
Greendale Shop. Cen. S18: Dron 2G 155
Green Dyke La. DN1: Don 3B 56
Green Dyke Way S75: Barn 4H 15
Green Farm Cl. S40: C'fld 2D 166
Green Farm Hamlet S36: Stoc 3A 174
Greenfield S62: Rawm 3G 83
Greenfield Cl. DN3: Arm 5F 43
  DN3: Barn D 2D 26
  S8: Shef 3E 147
  S65: Roth 2C 98
Greenfield Cotts. S71: Car 6H 9
Greenfield Ct. DN4: Balb 4G 99
  S66: Flan 4G 99
Greenfield Dr. S8: Shef 3E 147
Greenfield Gdns. DN4: Can 5D 58
  S66: Flan 4G 99
  S71: Ath 5D 8
Greenfield La. DN4: Balb, Hex 3H 55
Greenfield M. S63: Wath D 6E 49
Greenfield Rd. S8: Shef 3E 147
  S65: Roth 2C 98
  S74: Hoyl 6B 46
  WF9: Hems 1E 13
Greenfields S21: Ecki 1D 158
Greenfield Vw. S64: Mexb 4E 51
Greenfinch Cl. S60: Brins 4E 111
Greenfoot Cl. S75: Barn 5C 16
Greenfoot La. S75: Barn 4C 16
(not continuous)
Green Gables S64: Mexb 1E 67
Green Ga. Cl. S63: Bolt D 1C 50
Greengate Cl. S13: Shef 2E 137
  S40: Bramp 6D 166
Greengate Ct. S35: High G 1D 78
Green Ga. Gdns. S70: Wors 5E 31
Greengate La. S13: Shef 2D 136
  S35: High G 2C 78
Greengate Rd. S13: Shef 2E 137
Green Glen S40: Bramp 6D 166
Greenhall Rd. S21: Ecki 1D 158
Greenhead Gdns. S35: Chap 3F 79

Greenhead La. S35: Chap 3F 79
GREENHILL 3D 146
Greenhill Av. S8: Shef 2D 146
S66: Hel 6E 101
S71: Barn .5E 17
Green Hill Gro. S36: H'swne 1G 177
Greenhill Main Rd. S8: Shef 3D 146
Greenhill Parkway S8: Shef 4C 146
Greenhill Rd. S8: Shef 6E 133
Greenhouse Ct. DN2: Don 5F 41
Greenhouse La. S10: Shef 3A 130
Green Ho. Rd. DN2: Don 4G 41
Greenhow St. S6: Shef 1E 118
Green Ings La. S63: Wath D 5H 49
GREENLAND .5F 109
Greenland S74: Black H 3A 46
Greenland Av. S66: Malt 3B 102
Greenland Av. Sth.
S66: Malt .4B 102
Greenland Cl. S9: Shef 6F 109
S25: Nth A 2G 141
Greenland Ct. S9: Shef 6F 109
Greenland Dr. S9: Shef 6F 109
Greenland Rd. S9: Shef 5F 109
Greenland Rd. Industrial & Bus. Pk.
S9: Shef 5F 109
Greenlands Av. DN11: Ross 4D 74
Greenland Vw. S9: Shef 1F 121
S70: Wors .6E 31
Greenland Wlk. S9: Shef 6F 109
Greenland Way S9: Shef 6F 109
(Greenland Dr.)
S9: Shef 5F 109
(Greenland Rd.)
S66: Malt .3B 102
Green La. DN3: Can 3E 59
DN4: Warm 3E 71
DN5: Barnb 1F 51
DN5: Scawt 6A 22
DN6: Woodl 4B 22
DN7: Dunsv, Hat 5F 27
DN11: Wad 2H 89
S3: Shef 1D 4 (1E 119)
S6: Shef 1E 119
S18: Coal A, Dron 3G 155
S21: Killa 6B 152
S21: Midd H 4A 158
S26: Aston .1F 139
S26: Ull 2C 124
S35: Eccl 2H 93
S35: Ough .2C 90
S35: Wharn S 1C 90
S36: Stoc .2A 174
S42: Cut 1A 166
S43: Brim C 4C 168
S60: Cat 5C 110
S60: Roth .2H 111
S61: Kimb .3F 95
S62: Rawm 3G 83
S63: Wath D 3E 65
S66: Carr 4F 115
S66: Thurc, Wick 3A 114
S66: Wick .5F 99
S70: Wors .5B 30
S74: Hoyl 1F 61
S75: Dod 4H 29
WF4: Nott 1F 9
WF9: Sth K 4H 13
Green Lea S18: Dron W 2B 154
Greenleafe Av. DN2: Don 3H 41
GREEN MOOR 1G 175
Green Moor Hgts. S36: Stoc 3E 175
Green Moor Rd.
S35: Green M 1F 175
Green Oak Av. S17: Tot 6F 145
Green Oak Cres. S17: Tot 6F 145
Green Oak Dr. S17: Tot 6F 145
S26: Wales 6F 139
Green Oak Gro. S17: Tot 6F 145
Green Oak Rd. S17: Tot 6F 145
Green Oak Vw. S17: Tot 6F 145
Greenock St. S6: Shef 4A 106
Green Pastures S17: Dore 3F 145
Green Ri. S62: Rawm 1E 83
Green Rd. S36: Pen 5D 176
S75: Dod 4F 29
Greenset Vw. S71: Ath 5D 8
Greenshank Dr. S64: Mexb 6B 52
GREENSIDE
S21 . . . . .1E 157
S75 . . . . .5B 8

Greenside S36: H'swne 1G 177
S61: Grea .5C 82
S72: Shaft .2E 11
S75: Mapp, Stain 5B 8
Greenside Av. S26: Kiv P 6H 139
S41: C'fld .1G 167
S75: Stain .5B 8
Greenside Cl. S63: Thurn 3C 36
Greenside Gdns.
S36: H'swne 1G 177
Greenside Ho. S75: Stain 5B 8
Greenside La. S74: Hoyl 5B 46
Greenside M. S12: Shef 5C 136
Greenside Pl. S75: Mapp 5B 8
Green Spring Av. S70: Birdw 4E 45
Greens Rd. S65: Roth 4A 98
Green St. DN4: Balb 6G 55
S36: Spink .3F 175
S41: Old W 4H 161
S61: Grea .4C 82
S70: Wors .5H 31
S74: Hoyl 6C 46
Greenway S26: Kiv P 6A 140
Greenway, The S8: Shef 2E 147
S36: Spink .4G 175
Greenways S40: W'ton 2D 170
Greenway Vw. S73: Hem 5G 47
Greenwood Av. DN4: Balb 4G 55
S9: Shef 3D 120
S70: Wors .5G 31
Greenwood Cl. S9: Shef 3E 121
Greenwood Cres. S9: Shef 3D 120
S66: Wick .5H 99
S71: R'ton .2G 9
Greenwood Dr. S9: Shef 3D 120
Greenwood La. S13: Shef 1E 137
Greenwood Rd. S9: Shef 3E 121
S35: High G 1E 79
S64: Kiln 1D 84
Greenwood Ter. S70: Barn 6D 16
Greenwood Way S9: Shef 3D 120
Greeton Dr. S35: Ough 4F 91
Gregg Ho. Cres. S5: Shef 5A 94
Gregg Ho. Rd. S5: Shef 4A 94
Gregg St. S70: Stair 3A 32
Gregory Cl. S43: Brim 6C 162
Gregory La. S43: Brim 5C 162
Gregory Rd. S8: Shef 2F 133
Gregory's Bldgs. S72: Gt H 6E 21
Grendon Vs. S65: Roth 3H 97
Grenfell Av. S64: Mexb 1G 67
Grenfolds Rd. S35: Gren 2C 92
Greno Cres. S35: Gren 2C 92
Greno Ho. S35: Gren 1B 92
Greno Ga. S35: Gren 1B 92
Grenomoor Cl. S35: Gren 2B 92
Greno Rd. S64: Swin 4C 66
GRENOSIDE .1B 92
Grenoside Crematorium S35: Gren . .3A 92
Grenoside Grange Cl. S35: Gren 2C 92
Grenoside Mt. S35: Gren 3C 92
Greno Vw. S74: Hoyl 1H 61
Greno Vw. Rd. S35: High G 1D 78
Greno Wood Cl. S35: Gren 1B 92
Grenville Pl. S75: Barn 5B 16
Grenville Rd. DN4: Balb 6F 55
Gresford Cl. S75: Wool G 3E 7
Gresham Av. S60: Brins 3D 110
Gresham Rd. S6: Shef 6B 106
Gresley Rd. DN4: Balb 3A 56
S8: Shef 5D 146
Gresley Wlk. S8: Shef 5D 146
Greyfriars S11: Shef 1H 131
Greyfriars Rd. DN1: Don 6B 40
Greystock St. S4: Shef 6B 108
GREYSTONES 1H 131
Greystones Av. S11: Shef 1A 132
S70: Wors .6E 31
GREYSTONES CLIFFE 1G 131
Greystones Cl. S11: Shef 1H 131
Greystones Ct. S11: Shef 1H 131
Greystones Cres. S11: Shef 1H 131
Greystones Dr. S11: Shef 1H 131
Greystones Grange S11: Shef 1H 131
Greystones Grange Cres.
S11: Shef .1H 131
Greystones Grange Rd.
S11: Shef .1H 131
Greystones Hall Rd. S11: Shef 6H 117

Greystones Ri. S11: Shef 1H 131
Greystones Rd. S11: Shef 1G 131
S60: Whis .3C 112
Greywood Cl. DN2: Don 2G 41
Grice Cl. DN4: Can 2C 58
Griffen Cl. S43: Stav 6B 164
Griffin Rd. S64: Swin 3A 66
Griffiths Cl. S62: P'gte 4G 83
Griffiths Rd. S35: High G 2D 78
GRIFFS 6B 104
GRIMESTHORPE 3C 108
Grimesthorpe Rd. S4: Shef 5H 107
(Ellesmere Rd., not continuous)
S4: Shef 6H 107
(Grimesthorpe Rd. Sth.)
Grimesthorpe Rd. Sth. S4: Shef 6H 107
GRIMETHORPE 2B 20
Grimsell Cl. S6: Shef 3C 92
Grimsell Cres. S6: Shef 3C 92
Grimsell Dr. S6: Shef 3C 92
Grimsell Wlk. S6: Shef 4C 92
Grinders Hill S1: Shef 5F 5
Grinders Wlk. S6: Shef 3G 105
Grindlow Av. S40: C'fld 1G 171
Grindlow Cl. S14: Shef 2H 133
Grindlow Dr. S14: Shef 2H 133
Grindon Cl. S40: C'fld 3D 166
Grinton Wlk. S40: C'fld 2G 171
Grisedale Wlk. S18: Dron W 3D 154
Grizedale Av. S20: Sot 6H 137
Grizedale Cl. S20: Sot 6H 137
Grosvenor Cres. DN4: Warm 6E 55
DN5: Ark 6C 24
Grosvenor Dr. S70: Barn 1B 30
(not continuous)
Grosvenor Gdns. S70: Barn 1B 30
Grosvenor Rd. DN6: Woodl 3C 22
S65: Roth .2G 97
Grosvenor Sq. S2: Shef 6E 119
Grosvenor Ter. DN4: Warm 6E 55
Grosvenor Wlk. S70: Barn 1A 30
Grouse Cft. S6: Shef 6C 106
Grouse St. S6: Shef 5B 106
Grove, The DN2: Don 5F 41
(not continuous)
DN3: Barn D 1G 27
S6: Lox 4F 105
S17: Tot 6E 145
S35: Wharn S 1A 90
S43: Pool 6D 164
S62: Rawm 3H 83
S65: Roth .3A 98
S66: Wick .5G 99
S72: Cud 5E 11
S75: Bar G .4F 15
Grove Av. DN5: Don 5H 39
S6: Shef 2H 105
S17: Tot 6E 145
Grove Cl. S36: Cub 6D 176
S63: Wath D 4D 48
Grove Cotts. S40: C'fld 6E 167
(off Walton Rd.)
Grove Ct. S66: Malt 5G 101
Grove Dr. WF9: Sth K 4H 13
Grove Farm Cl. S43: Brim 1D 168
Grove Gdns. S43: Brim C 4E 169
S63: Thurn 3B 36
Grove Hall Cl. DN3: Eden 6D 26
Grove Hill Rd. DN2: Don 3H 41
Grove Ho. Ct. S17: Tot 5F 145
Grove La. WF9: Sth K 4H 13
Grove Mt. WF9: Sth K 4H 13
Grove Pk. S72: Grim 3B 20
Grove Pl. DN1: Don 2B 56
Grove Rd. DN3: Kirk Sa 4A 26
S7: Shef 5B 132
S17: Tot 5F 145
S36: Spink .4H 175
S41: Whit M 1H 167
S43: Brim C 3D 168
S60: Roth .5E 97
S63: Wath D 4D 48
S75: Mapp .5H 7
Grove Sq. S6: Shef 5D 106
Grove St. S41: Has 2B 172
S70: Wors .5H 31
S71: Barn .1F 31
Grove Va. DN2: Don 3H 41
Grove Way S43: Brim C 3E 169
WF9: Sth K 4H 13
Guernsey Rd. S2: Shef 1F 133

Guest La.—Halstead Gro.

Guest La. DN4: Warm 5E 55
S75: Silk 1B 28
Guest Pl. S60: Roth 6G 97
S74: Hoyl 5B 46
Guest Rd. S11: Shef 6B 118
S60: Roth 6G 97
S75: Barn 5C 16
Guest St. S74: Hoyl 5B 46
Guilbert Av. S66: Thurc 1B 126
Guildford Av. S2: Shef 6A 120
S40: W'ton 2E 171
Guildford Cl. S2: Shef 6A 120
Guildford Dr. S2: Shef 6A 120
Guildford Ri. S2: Shef 6B 120
Guildford Rd. DN2: Don 3G 41
S71: R'ton 1G 9
Guildford Vw. S2: Shef 1B 134
Guildford Wlk. S2: Shef 6B 120
Guildford Way S2: Shef 6A 120
Guildhall Ind. Est. DN3: Kirk Sa 5B 26
Guild Rd. S65: Roth 4A 98
Guildway S26: Tod 3B 140
GUILTHWAITE 5B 112
Guilthwaite Comn. La.
S60: Up W 1B 124
Guilthwaite Cres. S60: Whis 3H 111
Guilthwaite Hill S60: Whis 6B 112
Gullane Dr. DN4: Warm 6E 55
Gullingwood Dr. S65: Thry 6F 85
Gunhills La. DN3: Arm 3F 43
Gunhills La. Ind. Est. DN3: Arm 3F 43
Gun La. S3: Shef 1G 5
Gurney Rd. DN4: Balb 6A 56
Gurth Av. DN3: Eden 6D 26
Gurth Av. Cvn. Site DN3: Eden 6D 26
Gurth Dr. S66: Thurc 1B 126
Gwendoline M. S63: Wath D 1G 65
Gwyn Reed Nature Reserve 2B 84
Gypsy La. S73: Womb 3H 47
WF4: Wool 1F 7

H

Habershon Dr. S35: Chap 2E 79
Habershon Rd. S61: Kimb P 1A 96
HACKENTHORPE 5A 136
Hackenthorpe Stop (ST) 5B 136
Hackings Av. S36: Cub 6C 176
Hackness La. S60: Brins 3C 110
Hackney La. S18: Barl 4A 160
Hackthorn Rd. S8: Shef 5E 133
Haddon Cl. S18: Dron 2G 155
S40: Bramp 6D 166
S75: Dod 3F 29
Haddon Pl. S43: Stav 6A 164
Haddon Ri. S64: Mexb 6A 52
Haddon Rd. S71: Ath 2G 17
Haddon St. S3: Shef 6E 107
Haddon Way S26: Aston 1E 139
Haden St. S6: Shef 4B 106
Hadfield Cl. S9: Shef 1D 120
Hadfield St. S6: Shef 1B 118
S73: Womb 3G 47
Hadleigh Cl. S62: Rawm 4G 83
Hadrian Rd. S60: Brins 2D 110
Hadrians Cl. DN11: New R 6H 75
HADY 6C 168
Hady Cres. S41: C'fld 6B 168
Hady Hill S41: C'fld 6A 168
Hady La. S41: C'fld 6C 168
Haggard Rd. S6: Shef 4C 106
Hagg Hill S6: Shef 1G 117
Hagg Hill La. S6: Shef 5A 92
Hagg La. S10: Shef 3D 116
Hagg La. Cotts. S10: Shef 2E 117
Haggstones Dr. S35: Ough 4D 90
Haggstones Rd. S35: Ough 4D 90
Hague Av. S21: Reni 4H 159
S62: Rawm 1F 83
Hague Cres. WF9: Hems 1F 13
Hague La. S21: Reni 5H 159, 1E 165
S35: High G 1B 78
S62: Wentw 2E 81
WF9: Sth K 4H 13
Hague Row S2: Shef 3H 5 (3H 119)
(not continuous)
Hague Ter. WF9: Hems 1F 13
Haids Cl. S66: Malt 3A 102
Haids La. S66: Malt 3A 102
Haids Rd. S66: Malt 3H 101
Haig Cres. DN11: New R 6B 74
Haigh Cl. S36: H'swne 1F 177
Haigh Ct. S63: Bramp B 6A 48
Haigh Cft. S71: R'ton 2G 9
Haigh Head Rd. S36: H'swne 1F 177
Haigh Hill S75: Haigh 1D 6
Haigh La. S36: H'swne 1G 177
S75: Haigh 1D 6
Haigh Memorial Homes
S8: Shef 3F 147
(off Meadowhead)
Haigh M. S75: Haigh 1D 6
Haigh Moor Cl. S13: Shef 5H 121
Haigh Moor Dr. S25: Din 5F 127
Haigh Moor Rd. S13: Shef 6A 122
Haigh Moor Wlk. S13: Shef 6H 121
Haigh Moor Way S26: Swal 1H 137
S71: R'ton 1H 9
Haigh Rd. DN4: Balb 5H 55
Hail Mary Dr. S13: Shef 6E 123
Haise Mt. S75: Dart 5H 7
Hakehill Cl. DN4: Bess 6A 58
Halcyon Cl. S12: Shef 5A 136
Haldane Cl. S72: Brier 3A 12
Haldane Rd. S65: Roth 2H 97
Haldene S70: Wors 6G 31
Haldynby Gdns. DN3: Arm 4F 43
Hale St. S8: Shef 2E 133
Halesworth Cl. S40: W'ton 2C 170
Halesworth Rd. S13: Shef 4H 121
Halfacre La. S18: Dron 4A 156
Half Cft. S43: Brim 1E 169
HALFWAY 3F 151
Halfway Cen. S20: Half 3F 151
Halfway Cl. S20: W'fld 3G 151
S63: Gol 5B 36
Halfway Dr. S20: Half 3F 151
Halfway Gdns. S20: Half 3F 151
Halfway (Park & Ride) 3G 151
Halfway Stop (ST) 3G 151
Halifax Av. DN12: Con 4D 68
Halifax Cres. DN5: Don 4G 39
Halifax Hall of Residence
S10: Shef 5A 118
Halifax Rd. S6: Gren, Shef 6C 92
S35: Gren 3C 92
S36: Pen 1C 176
Halifax St. S71: Barn 4D 16
Hallam Chase S10: Shef 5A 118
(Endcliffe Va. Rd.)
S10: Shef 4E 117
(Sandygate Rd.)
Hallam Cl. DN4: Bess 5H 57
S26: Augh 5B 124
S73: Womb 2H 47
Hallam Ct. *S10: Shef 5C 118*
(off Clarke Dell)
S18: Dron 4F 155
S63: Bolt D 3A 50
Hallam Dale Ct. S62: Rawm 1H 83
Hallamgate Rd. S10: Shef 4A 118
Hallam Grange Cl. S10: Shef 6D 116
Hallam Grange Cres. S10: Shef 5D 116
Hallam Grange Cft. S10: Shef 5D 116
Hallam Grange Ri. S10: Shef 5D 116
Hallam Grange Rd. S10: Shef 5D 116
HALLAM HEAD 4E 117
Hallam La. S1: Shef 6E 5 (4F 119)
Hallam Pl. S62: Rawm 3H 83
Hallam Rd. S60: Roth 2G 111
Hallam Rock S5: Shef 3G 107
Hallamshire Bus. Pk. S11: Shef 5D 118
Hallamshire Cl. S10: Shef 6C 116
Hallamshire Dr. S10: Shef 6C 116
Hallamshire Golf Course 4E 117
Hallamshire Rd. S10: Shef 6C 116
Hallamshire Vw. S10: Shef 4E 117
Hallam Way S35: Eccl 2G 93
Hall Av. S64: Mexb 1G 67
S74: Jum 5D 46
Hall Balk La. DN11: Lov 4B 72
S75: Barn 5C 16
Hall Bank S75: Barn 4C 16
Hall Broome Gdns. S63: Bolt D 1B 50
Hall Bungs. S42: W'orth 6H 171
Hallcar St. S4: Shef 1H 119
Hall Cl. S18: Dron W 2B 154
S25: Nth A 2G 141
S42: Cut 6A 160
S63: Bramp B 5C 48
S70: Wors 2F 45
Hall Cl. Av. S60: Whis 3B 112
Hall Cotts. DN5: Barnb 1A 52
S66: Mort 4G 113
Hall Ct. S13: Shef 4A 122
S25: Din 6H 127
S65: Rav 4H 85
Hall Cres. S60: Roth 2A 112
Hall Cft. S66: Wick 6H 99
S73: Womb 6A 34
Hallcroft Dr. DN3: Arm 6F 43
Hallcroft Gdns. S72: Gt H 6F 21
S74: Hoyl 6C 46
Hallcroft Ri. S71: R'ton 3G 9
Hall Cross 2D 56
Hall Cross Av. S73: Womb 3A 48
Hall Cross Hill DN1: Don 2D 56
Hall Dr. S63: Wath D 1E 65
Haller Cl. DN3: Arm 4C 42
Hall Farm Cl. S26: Augh 4B 124
S41: Has 3C 172
Hall Farm Cft. S25: Din 6A 128
Hall Farm Dr. S63: Thurn 3C 36
Hall Farm Gro. S36: H'swne 1G 177
Hall Farm Ri. S63: Thurn 3C 36
Hallfield Cl. S42: W'orth 6A 172
Hallflash La. S44: Cal 2F 173
Hall Flat La. DN4: Balb 5H 55
Hall Gdns. S72: Brier 3B 12
Hall Ga. DN1: Don 1C 56
S36: Pen 3D 176
S64: Mexb 2H 67
Hallgate S63: Thurn 3C 36
Hallgate Rd. S10: Shef 3H 117
Hall Gro. S60: Roth 5F 97
S75: Stain 5B 8
Halliwell Cl. S5: Shef 1C 106
Halliwell Cres. S5: Shef 6C 92
Hall La. S36: H'swne 1G 177
S43: Stav 2H 163
Hall Meadow Cft. S20: Half 5G 151
Hall Meadow Dr. S20: Half 4G 151
Hall Meadow Gro. S20: Half 5G 151
Hall Mews S65: Rav 4H 85
HALLOWES 4H 155
Hallowes Ct. S18: Dron 3G 155
Hallowes Dr. S18: Dron 4G 155
Hallowes Golf Course 5G 155
Hallowes La. S18: Dron 3G 155
Hallowes Ri. S18: Dron 4H 155
HALLOWMOOR 3H 105
Hallowmoor Rd. S6: Shef 3G 105
Hall Park Head S6: Shef 1E 117
Hall Park Hill S6: Shef 1F 117
Hall Park Mt. S6: Shef 1F 117
Hall Pl. S71: Monk B 4H 17
Hall Rd. S9: Shef 3H 121
S13: Shef 4H 121
S26: Augh 5B 124
S43: Brim 1D 168
S60: Roth 5F 97
S66: Malt 5F 101
Hall Royd La. S75: Silk C 4B 28
Hall Royd Wlk. S75: Silk C 5B 28
Halls Ct. S8: Shef 5E 133
Hallside Ct. DN3: Can 3E 59
S20: Mosb 4E 151
Hall's Row S40: C'fld 6E 167
Hall St. DN5: Barnb 1A 52
S60: Roth 4D 96
S63: Gol 6D 36
S73: Womb 2H 47
S74: Hoyl 6B 46
Hallsworth Av. S73: Hem 5E 47
Hall Vw. S35: Chap 2F 79
S40: C'fld 5F 167
(off Chatsworth Rd.)
S41: C'fld 2F 167
Hall Vw. Rd. DN11: New R 6H 75
Hall Villa La. DN5: Bntly 3H 23
Hallwood Ri. S35: Chap 3C 78
Hall Wood Rd. S35: Chap 3B 78
Hallworth Wlk. S21: Mar L 2H 157
Hallyburton Cl. S2: Shef 2H 133
Hallyburton Dr. S2: Shef 2H 133
Hallyburton Rd. S2: Shef 2H 133
Halmshaw Ter. DN5: Bntly 2H 39
Halsall Av. S9: Shef 3F 121
Halsall Dr. S9: Shef 3E 121
Halsall Rd. S9: Shef 3F 121
Halsbury Rd. S65: Roth 2H 97
Halstead Gro. S75: Mapp 4H 7

Halsteads S13: Shef 5G **121**
Halton Cl. S41: C'fld 5F **161**
Halton Ct. S12: Shef 5D **136**
Hamble Cl. S75: Mapp 6B **8**
Hambledon Cl. S40: C'fld 3D **166**
Hambleton Cl. S74: Els 6E **47**
S75: Barn 6A **16**
Hameline Rd. DN12: Con 4E **69**
Hamer Wlk. S65: Roth 3B **98**
Hamilton Cl. DN4: Don 3E **57**
S64: Mexb 6H **51**
Hamilton Ct. DN12: Con 4F **69**
S64: Swin 3C **66**
Hamilton M. DN4: Don 2E **57**
Hamilton Pk. Rd.
DN5: Scaws 4E **39**
Hamilton Rd. DN4: Don 3E **57**
S5: Shef 2A **108**
S63: Gol 4E **37**
S66: Malt 6C **102**
Hammerton Cl. S6: Shef 5B **106**
Hammerton Rd. S6: Shef 5B **106**
Hammond St. S3: Shef 1A **4** (2D **118**)
Hampden Rd. S64: Mexb 1F **67**
Hamper La. S36: H'swne, Pen . . .1F **177**
Hampole Dr. S63: Thurn 3B **36**
Hampson Gdns. DN3: Eden 5D **26**
Hampstead Grn. S61: Kimb P 1H **95**
Hampton Ct. S73: D'fld 5A **34**
Hampton Rd. DN2: Don 1E **57**
S5: Shef 3H **107**
Hampton St. S41: Has 3C **172**
Hanbury Cl. DN4: Balb 2H **71**
S18: Dron 3E **155**
S40: C'fld 3B **166**
S71: Monk B 4A **18**
Handby St. S41: Has 2C **172**
Handley Ct. DN9: Finn 3G **77**
S43: New W 2C **162**
Handley Cross M. DN4: Can 4D **58**
Handley Rd. S43: New W 5G **157**
Handley St. S3: Shef 1G **119**
Handleywood Golf Driving Range
. . . . .2E **163**
Hands Rd. S10: Shef 2B **118**
HANDSWORTH 5A **122**
Handsworth Av. S9: Shef 3G **121**
Handsworth Cres. S9: Shef 3G **121**
Handsworth Gdns. DN3: Arm 4F **43**
Handsworth Grange Cl. S13: Shef . .6B **122**
Handsworth Grange Cres.
S13: Shef 5B **122**
Handsworth Grange Dr. S13: Shef . .5C **122**
Handsworth Grange Rd.
S13: Shef 5B **122**
Handsworth Grange Way
S13: Shef 5C **122**
HANDSWORTH HILL 2G **121**
Handsworth Rd. S9: Shef 3G **121**
S13: Shef 4H **121**
Hanging Bank Ct. S25: Nth A 3H **141**
HANGING WATER 6G **117**
Hangingwater Cl. S11: Shef 6G **117**
Hangingwater Cotts. S11: Shef 1G **131**
(off Hangingwater Rd.)
Hangingwater Rd. S11: Shef 1G **131**
Hangman Stone La.
DN5: High M, Marr 1D **52**
Hangman Stone Rd.
DN5: Barnb, Marr 3C **52**
Hangram La. S11: Shef 4C **130**
Hangsman La.
S25: Laugh G, Laugh M 3F **127**
Hangthwaite La. DN6: Woodl 5D **22**
Hangthwaite Rd. DN6: Adw S 1E **23**
Hanley Cl. S12: Shef 4C **136**
Hanmoor Rd. S6: Stan 6D **104**
Hannah Rd. S13: Shef 1E **137**
Hannas Royd S75: Dod 3H **29**
Hanover Ct. S3: Shef 6A **4** (4D **118**)
S70: Wors 5F **31**
Hanover Sq. S3: Shef 6B **4** (4E **119**)
S63: Thurn 2D **36**
Hanover St. S3: Shef 6A **4** (4E **119**)
(not continuous)
S63: Thurn 1D **36**
Hanover Way S3: Shef 5A **4** (4D **118**)
Hanover Works S3: Shef 1C **4**
Hanslope Vw. DN3: Kirk Sa 3B **26**
Hanson Rd. S6: Lox 4E **105**
Hanson St. S70: Barn 6E **17**

Hanston Ct. S43: New W 2C **162**
(off Handley Rd.)
Hanwell Cl. S35: Eccl 2G **93**
Harborough Rd. S8: Shef 6D **132**
Harborough Av. S2: Shef 3C **120**
Harborough Cl. S2: Shef 4D **120**
Harborough Dr. S2: Shef 4D **120**
Harborough Hill Rd.
S71: Barn 1E **31**
Harborough Ri. S2: Shef 4D **120**
Harborough Rd. S2: Shef 4D **120**
Harborough Way S2: Shef 5D **120**
Harbury St. S13: Shef 6F **123**
Harcourt Cl. DN4: Bess 5H **57**
S41: Has 3B **172**
Harcourt Cres. S10: Shef 2C **118**
Harcourt Ri. S35: Chap 4G **79**
Harcourt Rd. S10: Shef 3C **118**
Harcourt Ter. S65: Roth 4G **97**
Hardcastle Dr. S13: Shef 1B **136**
Hardcastle Gdns. S13: Shef 1B **136**
Hardcastle Rd. S13: Shef 2B **136**
Harden Cl. S36: Cub 5D **176**
S75: Barn 6H **15**
Harden M. DN3: Arm 5F **43**
HARDHURST 6B **156**
Hardhurst Rd. S18: Uns 1F **161**
Hardie Cl. S66: Malt 6C **102**
Hardie Pl. S43: Stav 6A **164**
S62: Rawm 2G **83**
Hardie St. S21: Ecki 1E **159**
Harding Av. S62: Rawm 6E **65**
Harding Cl. S62: Rawm 1E **83**
Harding St. S62: Rawm 6E **65**
Hard La. S26: Hart, Kiv P 6B **140**
HARDWICK 5H **125**
Hardwick Av. S43: New W 3C **162**
Hardwick Cl. S18: Dron 2G **155**
S26: Aston 1E **139**
S70: Wors 6F **31**
S71: R'ton 2A **10**
Hardwick Cl. S43: Stav 4B **164**
(off Porter St.)
Hardwick Cres. S11: Shef 6B **118**
S71: Ath 1F **17**
Hardwick Dr. S44: Ark T 6H **173**
Hardwick Rd. S65: Roth 2F **97**
Hardwick Gro. S75: Dod 4G **29**
Hardwick La. S26: Aston 1G **139**
Hardwick St. S41: C'fld 4H **167**
S65: Roth 2C **98**
Hardwicks Yd. S40: C'fld 6F **167**
Hardy Pl. S6: Shef 6C **106**
Hardy Rd. DN2: Don 4D **40**
Hardy St. S60: Roth 3D **96**
Haredon Cl. S75: Mapp 4H **7**
Harefield Rd. S11: Shef 6C **118**
Harehill Cres.
S42: W'orth 6E **171**
Harehill Rd. S40: Birdh 3G **171**
Harehills Rd. S60: Roth 5F **97**
Harewood Av. DN3: Kirk Sa 4C **26**
DN6: Woodl 3A **22**
S70: Barn 1A **30**
Harewood Cl. DN4: Balb 2G **71**
Harewood Ct. DN11: Ross 6E **75**
Harewood Gro. S66: Bram 4A **100**
Harewood Rd. DN2: Don 1F **57**
Harewood Way S11: Shef 6H **131**
Hargrave Pl. S65: Thry 6E **85**
Harland Rd. S11: Shef 5D **118**
Harlech Cl. S35: Chap 2E **79**
Harlech Fold S10: Shef 5A **116**
Harlech Grn. S10: Shef 5A **116**
Harlech Gro. S10: Shef 5A **116**
Harlech Mead S10: Shef 5A **116**
Harleston St. S4: Shef 6A **108**
(not continuous)
HARLEY .5A **62**
Harley Rd. S11: Shef 3G **131**
S62: H'ley 5A **62**
HARLINGTON 2H **51**
Harlington DN5: Harl 2A **52**
Harlington Ct. DN12: Den M 3D **68**
Harlington Rd. S64: Mexb 1G **67**
(Addison Rd., not continuous)
S64: Mexb 4E **51**
(Crow Tree La.)
Harmer La. S1: Shef 4F **5** (3G **119**)
Harmony Way S60: Cat 6D **110**
Harney Cl. S9: Shef 1F **121**

Harold Av. DN6: Woodl 3B **22**
S71: Lund 4B **18**
Harold Cft. S61: Grea 4D **82**
Harold St. S6: Shef 6C **106**
HARPER HILL 6B **170**
Harperhill Cl. S40: Birdh 3G **171**
Harper Ri. DN12: Den M 3D **68**
Harrier Cl. DN9: Auck 2C **76**
Harriet Cl. S70: Barn 3F **31**
Harrington Ct. S71: Lund 4B **18**
Harrington Rd. S2: Shef 6F **119**
Harrington St. DN1: Don 6C **40**
S63: Wath D 4E **49**
Harris Hawk Way
S63: Wath D 4E **49**
Harrison La. S10: Shef 1A **130**
Harrison Rd. S6: Shef 5A **106**
Harrison St. S61: Roth 4B **96**
Harris Rd. DN3: Arm 4C **42**
S6: Shef 2A **106**
Harrogate Dr. DN12: Den M 3B **68**
Harrogate Rd. S26: Swal 2B **138**
Harrop Dr. S64: Swin 5B **66**
Harrop Gdn. Flats S64: Swin 3C **66**
(off Queen St.)
Harrop La. S10: Shef 2A **130**
Harrowden Ct. S9: Tins 2H **109**
Harrowden Rd. DN2: Don 4D **40**
S9: Tins 2H **109**
Harrow Rd. DN3: Arm 3F **43**
Harrow St. S11: Shef 5E **119**
Harry Firth Cl. S9: Shef 1D **120**
Harry Rd. S75: Barn 5A **16**
Hartcliff Av. S36: Pen 4C **176**
Hartcliff Hill Rd. S36: Pen 6A **176**
Hartfield Cl. S41: Has 3A **172**
Hartfield Ct. S41: Has 3A **172**
Hartford Cl. S8: Shef 5F **133**
Hartford Rd. S8: Shef 5F **133**
Hart Hill S62: Rawm 6E **65**
Harthill Rd. DN12: Con 5D **68**
S13: Shef 1E **135**
Hart Hills S73: Hem 5E **47**
Hartington Av. S7: Shef 5B **132**
Hartington Cl. S61: Roth 4B **96**
Hartington Ct. S18: Dron 2G **155**
Hartington Dr. S71: Barn 4E **17**
Hartington Ind. Est.
S43: Stav 2B **164**
Hartington Rd. S7: Shef 5B **132**
S18: Dron 2G **155**
S41: C'fld 6B **168**
S61: Roth 4B **96**
Hartington Vw. S43: Stav 2C **164**
Hartland Av. S20: Sot 6H **137**
Hartland Cl. S20: Sot 6H **137**
Hartland Cres. DN3: Eden 6C **26**
Hartland Dr. S20: Sot 6H **137**
Hartley Brook Av. S5: Shef 4H **93**
Hartley Brook Rd. S5: Shef 4H **93**
Hartley Cl. S62: Kiln 5C **66**
Hartley La. S61: Roth 3D **96**
Hartley St. S2: Shef 1F **133**
S64: Mexb 2E **67**
Hartopp Av. S2: Shef 2H **133**
Hartopp Cl. S2: Shef 2H **133**
Hartopp Dr. S2: Shef 2A **134**
Hartopp Rd. S2: Shef 2H **133**
Hartshaw S60: Roth 5F **97**
(off Moorgate Rd.)
Hartshead S1: Shef 2E **5** (2G **119**)
Hartshead Sq. S1: Shef 2F **5**
Hartside Cl. S40: C'fld 3E **167**
Harvest Av. S66: Thurc 6C **114**
Harvest Cl. DN3: Eden 5D **26**
DN4: Balb 4G **55**
S66: Malt 6F **101**
S70: Wors 6F **31**
Harvest La. S3: Shef 1F **119**
Harvest Rd. S66: Wick 5G **99**
Harvest Way S42: Ash 3B **166**
Harvey Cl. DN9: Finn 2F **77**
Harvey Clough M. S8: Shef 5G **133**
Harvey Clough Rd.
S8: Shef 5F **133**
Harvey Rd. S35: Chap 3F **79**
S41: C'fld 6D **168**
Harvey St. S36: Spink 3F **175**
S70: Barn 2C **30**
Harwell Rd. S8: Shef 1E **133**
Harwich Rd. S2: Shef 5B **120**

Harwood Cl. S2: Shef 6F 119
Harwood Dr. S20: Water 1E 151
Harwood Gdns. S20: Water 1F 151
Harwood St. S2: Shef 6F 119
Harwood Ter. S71: Lund 6B 18
Haslam Ct. S41: Shef 4H 167
Haslam Cres. S8: Shef 4C 146
Haslam Pl. S66: Malt 4C 102
Haslam Rd. DN11: New R 5C 74
HASLAND .3C 172
Hasland By-Pass
 S41: C'fld, Has 6A 168
HASLAND GREEN 3B 172
Hasland La. S44: Cal 2F 173
Hasland Rd. S41: C'fld, Has 1A 172
 (not continuous)
Haslehurst Rd. S2: Shef 4B 120
Haslemere Ct. DN5: Don 4H 39
Haslemere Gro. DN5: Don 4H 39
Hassocky La. S42: Tem N 5G 173
 S44: Cal 5G 173
Hassop Cl. S18: Dron 2H 155
 S40: C'fld 2D 166
Hassop Ct. S60: Wav 3C 122
 (off Stephenson Way)
Hassop Cft. S75: Dod 3F 29
Hassop Rd. S43: Stav 3C 164
Hastilar Cl. S2: Shef 6E 121
Hastilar Rd. S2: Shef 6E 121
Hastilar Rd. Sth. S13: Shef 6F 121
Hastings Cl. S41: C'fld 2E 167
Hastings Mt. S7: Shef 4B 132
Hastings Rd. S7: Shef 4B 132
Hastings St. S72: Grim 1B 20
Hatchell Dr. DN4: Bess 1D 74
Hatchellwood Vw. DN4: Bess 1E 75
Hatfield Cl. S71: Smi 1D 16
Hatfield Gdns. S71: R'ton 2G 9
Hatfield Gro. S25: Laugh C 3F 127
Hatfield Ho. DN1: Don 2B 56
 (off Grove Pl.)
Hatfield Ho. Ct. S5: Shef 5A 94
Hatfield Ho. Cft. S5: Shef 5A 94
Hatfield Ho. La. S5: Shef 6H 93
Hatfield La. DN3: Arm, Eden 6E 27
 DN3: Barn D 1C 26
Hathaway Ct. S26: Wales 6G 139
Hatherley Rd. S9: Tins 1H 109
 S64: Swin 1C 66
 S65: Roth 3F 97
Hathern Cl. S43: Brim C 4E 169
Hathersage Rd. S17: Dore 3A 144
Hatter Dr. DN12: New E 6C 70
Hatton Cl. S18: Dron W 4C 154
Hatton Dr. S40: C'fld 3C 166
Hatton Rd. S6: Shef 5C 106
Haugh Grn. S62: Rawm 6E 65
Haugh La. S11: Shef 4G 131
Haugh Rd. S62: Rawm 6D 64
Haughton Rd. S8: Shef 6E 133
Havelock Rd. DN4: Balb 3B 56
Havelock St. S10: Shef 5A 4 (4D 118)
 S70: Barn 2C 30
 S73: D'fld 5B 34
Haven, The S26: Kiv S 6E 141
Haven Bus. Cen. S61: Roth 3C 96
Haven Farm Ct. S25: Sth A 4H 141
Havenfield S73: D'fld 4B 34
Haven Hill Rd. S5: Shef 3F 93
Havens, The S40: Ash 4E 167
Havercroft Pl. S21: Killa 3A 152
Havercroft Ri. S72: Sth H 1H 11
Havercroft Rd. S8: Shef 4D 132
 S60: Roth 1B 112
Havercroft Ter. S21: Killa 3A 152
Haverdale Ri. S75: Barn 5C 16
Haverhill Gro. S73: Womb 1H 47
Haverlands La. S70: Wors 6C 30
Haverlands Ridge S70: Wors 6E 31
Haw Ct. S75: Silk 1A 28
Hawes Cl. S64: Mexb 6H 51
Hawfield Cl. DN4: Hex 3H 55
Hawke Cl. S62: Rawm 1D 82
Hawke Rd. DN2: Don 4E 41
Hawke St. S9: Shef 4D 108
Hawk Hill La. S66: Bramp M 2A 126
Hawkhills S6: Shef 6G 105
Hawking Ho's. S40: C'fld 3E 167
Hawkins Av. S35: Burn 3D 78
Hawks Cliff Vw. S75: Dod 3E 29
Hawkshead Av. S18: Dron W 3C 154

Hawkshead Cres. S25: Nth A 2A 142
Hawkshead Rd. S4: Shef 3C 108
Hawksley Av. S6: Shef 4B 106
 S40: C'fld 3F 167
Hawksley Cl. DN3: Arm 4E 43
Hawksley Ct. DN3: Arm 3E 43
Hawksley M. S6: Shef 4B 106
Hawksley Ri. S35: Ough 4E 91
Hawksley Rd. S6: Shef 4B 106
Hawksway S21: Ecki 1C 158
Hawksworth Cl. S65: Roth 3B 98
Hawksworth Rd. S6: Shef 6C 106
 S65: Roth 3B 98
Hawkwell Bank S71: Ard 2C 22
Hawley St. S1: Shef 2D 4 (2F 119)
 S18: App 3D 156
 S62: Rawm 3G 83
Haworth Bank S60: Roth 3G 111
Haworth Cl. S71: Monk B 5G 17
Haworth Cres. S60: Roth 3G 111
Haw Royd S70: Barn 3F 31
Hawshaw Bank S74: Hoyl 5H 45
Hawshaw La. S74: Hoyl 6H 45
Hawthorn Av. DN3: Arm 2E 43
 S20: Water 1E 151
 S66: Malt 5G 101
Hawthorne Av. DN7: Dunsv 4H 27
 S18: Dron 1F 155
 S25: Sth A 5G 141
 S36: Stoc 2B 174
 S43: Mas M 2F 165
 S62: Rawm 3H 83
 S71: Lund 6A 18
Hawthorne Chase S64: Swin 3B 66
Hawthorne Cl. S21: Killa 5C 152
Hawthorne Ct. S65: Roth 3A 98
 S75: Kexb 6C 6
Hawthorne Cres. S64: Mexb 1D 66
 S75: Dod 2F 29
Hawthorne Dr. S63: Bolt D 2C 50
Hawthorne Farm Ct. S63: Bolt D 2C 50
 (off Station Rd.)
Hawthorne Flats S63: Thurn 1C 36
Hawthorne Gro. DN5: Bntly 6A 24
Hawthorne Pl. S26: Swal 1D 138
Hawthorne Rd. DN9: Auck 2B 76
 S63: Wath D 1H 65
Hawthornes, The S20: Beig 4G 137
 S66: B'well 2B 102
Hawthorne St. S6: Shef 6A 106
 S40: C'fld 1A 172
 S70: Barn 2D 30
 S72: Shaft 3F 11
Hawthorne Way S72: Shaft 3F 11
Hawthorn Gro. DN12: Con 6D 68
 S75: Silk 1A 28
Hawthorn Hill S43: Stav 1C 164
Hawthorn M. S35: High G 6C 60
Hawthorn Rd. S6: Shef 4A 106
 S21: Ecki 2C 158
 S35: High G 1D 78
Hawthorn Ter. S10: Shef 3B 118
 (off Parker's La.)
Hawthorn Way S42: Ash 3A 166
Hawtop La. WF4: Wool 1G 7
Haxby Cl. S13: Shef 2H 135
Haxby Pl. S13: Shef 2H 135
Haxby St. S13: Shef 2H 135
Haybrook Ct. S17: Tot 5F 145
Haycraft Gdns. S43: Mas M 2E 165
Haydn Rd. S66: Malt 6C 102
Haydock Av. S25: Laugh C 4F 127
Haydock Chase S25: Laugh C 4F 127
Haydock Cl. S64: Mexb 6G 51
Haydon Gro. S66: Flan 4G 99
Hayes Cl. S20: Half 4F 151
Hayes Ct. S70: Barn 1E 31
Hayes Dr. S20: Half 4F 151
Hayfield Cl. DN3: Barn D 1D 26
 S18: Dron W 3C 154
 S42: W'orth 6G 171
 S43: Stav 3C 164
 S75: Dod 3F 29
Hayfield Cres. S12: Shef 5G 135
Hayfield Dr. S12: Shef 5G 135
Hayfield La. DN9: Auck, Finn 3F 75
Hayfield La. Bus. Pk. DN9: Auck 2B 76
Hayfield M. DN9: Auck 2B 76
Hayfield Pl. S12: Shef 5G 135

Hayfield Vw. S21: Ecki 1C 158
Hayfield Wlk. S61: Kimb P 1H 95
 (off Byrley Rd.)
Hayford Way S43: Stav 5B 164
HAY GREEN 5E 45
Hay Grn. Ct. S70: Birdw 5E 45
Hay Grn. La. S70: Birdw 5E 45
Hayhurst Cres. S66: Malt 6B 102
Hayland St. S9: Shef 2E 109
Haylock Cl. S75: High'm 5F 15
Haymarket S1: Shef 2F 5 (2G 119)
Haythorne Way S64: Swin 5C 66
Haywagon Mobile Home Pk.
 DN6: Adw S 1D 10
Haywood Av. S36: Spink 3F 175
Haywood Cl. S65: Roth 3B 98
Haywood La. S36: Spink 3F 175
 (not continuous)
Hazel Av. DN9: Auck 2B 76
 S21: Killa 5B 152
Hazelbadge Cres.
 S12: Shef 5H 135
Hazel Cl. S18: Dron 4H 155
Hazel Ct. S18: Dron 4G 155
 S65: Rav 2B 100
Hazel Cft. S17: Dore 2D 144
Hazel Dr. S40: W'ton 2E 171
 S42: W'orth 6A 172
Hazel Gdns. S70: Wors 4G 31
 (off Overdale Av.)
Hazel Gro. DN3: Arm 3F 43
 DN11: New R 6C 74
 DN12: Con 5E 69
 S35: Chap 4F 79
 S43: Mas M 5D 154
 S66: Wick 5H 99
Hazel Ho. S8: Shef 4D 132
 (off Archer Rd.)
Hazelhurst S41: Has 4C 172
Hazelhurst Cl. S65: Dalt 1C 98
Hazelhurst La. S8: Shef 2C 148
Hazelmeres, The S40: W'ton 2E 171
Hazel Rd. DN12: New E 4C 70
 S21: Ecki 2D 158
 S66: Malt 5G 101
Hazelshaw S75: Dod 4H 29
Hazelshaw Gdns. S35: High G 1C 78
Hazelwood S71: Monk B 3F 17
Hazelwood Cl. S18: Dron W 3B 154
Hazelwood Dr. S64: Swin 6C 66
 S71: Lund 5A 18
Hazelwood Way S60: Wav 2D 122
Hazlebarrow Cl. S8: Shef 4G 147
Hazlebarrow Cres. S8: Shef 4G 147
Hazlebarrow Dr. S8: Shef 3G 147
Hazlebarrow Gro. S8: Shef 3H 147
Hazlebarrow Rd. S8: Shef 4G 147
Hazledene Cres. S72: Shaft 5G 11
Hazledene Rd. S72: Shaft 5F 11
Hazlehurst Av. S41: C'fld 3H 167
Hazlehurst La. S41: C'fld 3H 167
Headford Gdns. S3: Shef 5B 4 (4E 119)
Headford Gro. S3: Shef 5B 4 (4E 119)
Headford M. S3: Shef 6B 4 (4E 119)
Headford Pde. S3: Shef 4E 119
Headford St. S3: Shef 5B 4 (4E 119)
Headingley Cl. DN3: Kirk Sa 3C 26
Headingley Way DN12: New E 3D 70
Headland Cl. S43: Brim 1D 168
Headland Dr. S10: Shef 3H 117
Headland Rd. S10: Shef 3H 117
 S43: Brim 1D 168
Headlands Rd. S74: Hoyl 6A 46
Heads La. S36: Bolst 6B 174
Healaugh Way S40: C'fld 2A 172
Healthy Living Cen.
 Upperthorpe 1D 118
Healthy Living Cen., The
 Staveley 5B 164
Heartswood Rd. DN5: Bntly 5B 24
Heath Av. S21: Killa 5C 152
Heath Bank Rd. DN2: Don 3H 41
Heathcote Cl. S75: Wool G 3F 7
Heathcote Dr. S41: Has 2D 172
Heathcote Ho. S41: C'fld 2A 168
 (off Tapton Lock Hill)
Heathcote St. S4: Shef 3A 108
Heath Cl. DN4: Warm 5E 55
 S40: C'fld 2H 171
Heathcroft Chase S71: Ard 2E 33

Heatherbank Rd.—High Fld. Knoll

Heatherbank Rd. DN4: Bess 5B **58**
Heathercliff Way S36: Pen 4E **177**
Heather Cl. S44: Cal 5F **169**
S60: Roth 6F **97**
Heather Ct. DN2: Don 2A **42**
S63: Bolt D 1A **50**
S66: Bram 6A **100**
Heatherdale Rd. S66: Malt 5C **102**
Heatherfields Cres.
DN11: New R 4H **73**
Heather Gdns. S41: Has 3D **172**
Heather Knowle S75: Dod 3H **29**
Heather Lea Av. S17: Dore 3D **144**
Heather Lea Pl. S17: Dore 3D **144**
Heather Rd. S5: Shef 1B **108**
Heather Va. Cl. S41: Has 3D **172**
Heather Va. Rd. S41: Has 3C **172**
Heather Wlk. S63: Bolt D 1A **50**
Heatherwood Cl. DN2: Don 4H **41**
Heathfield Av. S40: C'fld 5E **167**
Heathfield Cl. DN3: Barn D 2D **26**
S18: Dron 4E **155**
S42: W'orth 6A **172**
Heathfield Rd. S12: Shef 4G **135**
Heathfields S70: Barn 2G **31**
Heath Gro. S63: Bolt D 3A **50**
Heath Ho. *DN1: Don 2B **56***
(off Grove Pl.)
Heathland Ct. S71: Lund 6A **18**
Heath Rd. S6: Shef 6C **92**
S36: Spink 4F **175**
Heaton Cl. S18: Dron W 3C **154**
Heaton Gdns. DN12: New E 4D **70**
Heatons Bank S62: Rawm 2H **83**
Heaton St. S40: Bramp 6D **166**
Heavens Wlk. DN4: Don 3C **56**
Heavygate Av. S10: Shef 6A **106**
Heavygate Rd. S10: Shef 6B **106**
Hedge Hill Rd. S36: Thurl 4A **176**
Hedge La. S75: Dart 1E **15**
(not continuous)
Hedgerows, The S64: Mexb 4F **51**
Hedley Dr. S43: Brim 6C **162**
HEELEY 2G **133**
Heeley Bank Rd. S2: Shef 1G **133**
Heeley City Farm 1F **133**
Heeley Grn. S2: Shef 2G **133**
Heeley Retail Pk. S8: Shef 2E **133**
Heeley Swimming Pool 2E **133**
Heelis St. S70: Barn 2E **31**
Heighton Vw. S26: Augh 5C **124**
Helena Cl. S70: Barn 2C **30**
Helena St. S64: Mexb 1F **67**
HELLABY 6E **101**
Hellaby (Euroway) Ind. Est.
S66: Hel 4D **100**
Hellaby Hall Rd. S66: Hel 6E **101**
Hellaby La. S66: Hel 5E **101**
Hellaby Vw. S65: Rav 3A **100**
Helliwell Ct. S36: Spink 5G **175**
Helliwell Cft. *S36: Spink 4G **175***
(off Helliwell La.)
Helliwell La. S36: Spink 4G **175**
Helmsley Av. S20: Half 3E **151**
Helmsley Cl. S26: Swal 2B **138**
S41: C'fld 1D **166**
Helmton Dr. S8: Shef 6F **133**
Helmton Rd. S8: Shef 6E **133**
Helston Cl. S41: Has 2A **172**
Helston Cres. S71: Monk B 5G **17**
Helston Ri. S7: Shef 4B **132**
HEMINGFIELD 5F **47**
Hemingfield Halt Station
Elsecar Heritage Railway 6F **47**
Hemingfield Rd. S73: Hem, Womb 3E **47**
Hemmingway Cl. S60: Tree 2F **123**
Hemper Gro. S8: Shef 3C **146**
Hemper La. S8: Shef 4C **146**
Hemp Pits Rd. DN5: Ark 1C **40**
HEMSWORTH
S14 6A **134**
WF9 1D **12**
Hemsworth By-Pass S72: Brier 2C **12**
WF9: Hems 1G **13**
Hemsworth Rd. S8: Shef 6F **133**
WF9: Hems, Sth K 1F **13**
Henderson Ct. S60: Roth 1E **111**
Henderson Glen S71: R'ton 3F **9**
Hendon St. S13: Shef 5A **122**
Hengist Rd. DN5: Don 2G **55**
Henley Av. S8: Shef 2G **147**
Henley Gro. Rd. S61: Roth 3C **96**
(not continuous)
Henley La. S61: Roth 2B **96**
Henley Ri. S61: Roth 2B **96**
Henley Rd. DN2: Don 5H **41**
Henley Way S61: Roth 2B **96**
Hennings Cl. DN4: Bess 5G **57**
Hennings La. DN4: Bess 4G **57**
Hennings Rd. DN4: Bess 1H **73**
Henry Adams Memorial Church
*S73: Womb 1G **47***
(off Barnsley Rd.)
Henry Cl. S72: Shaft 3F **11**
Henry Ct. S62: P'gte 5G **83**
S65: Roth 3E **97**
Henry La. DN11: New R 4A **74**
Henry Moore Ct.
S75: Wool G 3E **7**
Henry Pl. S64: Mexb 1H **67**
Henry Rd. S63: Wath D 6H **49**
Henry St. S3: Shef 1B **4** (1E **119**)
S21: Ecki 1E **159**
S35: High G 1B **78**
S41: Whit M 6A **162**
S65: Roth 3E **97**
(not continuous)
S70: Wors 5F **31**
S73: Womb 6A **34**
Henshall Ho. *S41: C'fld 2A **168***
(off Tapton Lock Hill)
Henshall St. S70: Barn 2F **31**
Henson St. S9: Shef 6E **109**
Heppenstall La. S9: Shef 6C **108**
Heptinstall St. S70: Wors 5G **31**
Hepworth Cl. S75: Wool G 3F **7**
Hepworth Dr.
S26: Aston, Swal 1C **138**
Hepworth Rd. DN4: Balb 5G **55**
Herald Rd. DN3: Eden 1B **42**
Herbert Cl. DN5: Don 5H **39**
Herbert Rd. DN5: Don 5H **39**
S7: Shef 2D **132**
Herbert St. S61: Kimb 3H **95**
S64: Mexb 1G **67**
HERDINGS 5B **134**
Herdings Ct. S12: Shef 5D **134**
Herdings Stop (ST) 5C **134**
Herdings Park Stop (ST) 6B **134**
Herdings Rd. S12: Shef 5D **134**
Herdings Vw. S12: Shef 5C **134**
Hereford Dr. S43: Brim 6E **163**
Hereford Rd. DN2: Don 3G **41**
Hereford St. S1: Shef 6D **4** (5F **119**)
(not continuous)
Hereward Ct. DN12: Con 4H **69**
Hereward Rd. S5: Shef 6G **93**
Hereward's Rd. S8: Shef 1A **148**
Heritage Ct. *S73: Hem 4G **47***
(off Beech Ho. Rd.)
Heritage M. S74: Els 2D **62**
Hermitage St. S2: Shef 5E **119**
Hermit Hill S35: Wort 6A **44**
Hermit La. S75: Barn, High'm 6F **15**
Heron Ct. DN2: Don 3F **41**
DN12: Con 4A **70**
Heron Dr. S63: Bramp B 5A **48**
S64: Mexb 1B **68**
Heron Hill S26: Aston 2D **138**
Heron Mt. S2: Shef 4B **120**
Herons Way DN4: Balb 5C **56**
S70: Birdw 4E **45**
Herrick Gdns. DN4: Balb 6B **56**
Herrick Rd. DN3: Barn D 1H **27**
Herries Av. S5: Shef 2F **107**
Herries Dr. S5: Shef 2F **107**
Herries Pl. S5: Shef 2F **107**
Herries Rd. S5: Shef 2C **106**
S6: Shef 2B **106**
Herries Rd. Sth. S6: Shef 2B **106**
HERRINGTHORPE 5A **98**
Herringthorpe Av. S65: Roth 6A **98**
Herringthorpe Cl. S65: Roth 5A **98**
Herringthorpe Gro. S65: Roth 6B **98**
Herringthorpe La. S65: Roth 5B **98**
Herringthorpe Stadium 5H **97**
Herringthorpe Valley Rd.
S60: Roth 2B **98**
S65: Roth 2B **98**
Herriot Dr. S40: C'fld 1A **172**
Herschell Rd. S7: Shef 1E **133**
(not continuous)
Herten Way DN4: Don 3G **57**
Hesketh Dr. DN3: Kirk Sa 4D **26**
Hesley Bar S61: Thorpe H 4B **80**
Hesley Ct. DN12: Den M 3C **68**
S64: Swin 5B **66**
Hesley Grange S61: Scho 6F **81**
Hesley Gro. S35: Chap 4H **79**
Hesley La. S61: Thorpe H 4B **80**
Hesley M. S61: Scho 6F **81**
Hesley Rd. DN11: New R 6C **74**
S5: Shef 3A **94**
Hesley Ter. S5: Shef 3A **94**
Heslow Gro. S61: Thorpe H 3B **80**
Hessey St. S13: Shef 2A **136**
Hessle Rd. S6: Shef 2A **106**
Hethersett Way DN11: New R 6F **75**
Hewitt St. S64: Mexb 1H **67**
HEXTHORPE 2A **56**
Hexthorpe Bus. Pk.
DN4: Hex 3A **56**
Hexthorpe Rd. DN4: Hex 2A **56**
Heyhouse Dr. S35: Chap 1E **79**
Heyhouse Way S35: Chap 1E **79**
Heysham Grn. S71: Monk B 2A **18**
Heywood St. S43: Brim 6D **162**
Hibberd Pl. S6: Shef 4H **105**
Hibberd Rd. S6: Shef 4H **105**
Hibbert Ter. *S70: Barn 3E **31***
(off Walnut Cl.)
HICKLETON 3H **37**
Hickleton Ct. S63: Thurn 3B **36**
Hickleton Golf Course 2G **37**
Hickleton Rd. DN5: Barnb 6H **37**
Hickleton St. DN12: Den M 3C **68**
Hickleton Ter. *S63: Thurn 3D **36***
(off Lidget La.)
Hickmott Rd. S11: Shef 6C **118**
Hickson Dr. S71: Lund 4B **18**
Hicks St. S3: Shef 6F **107**
Hides St. S9: Shef 4E **109**
High Alder Rd. DN4: Bess 4H **57**
HIGHAM 5F **15**
Higham Comn. Rd.
S75: Bar G, High'm 5F **15**
Higham Ct. S75: High'm 5F **15**
Higham La. S75: Dod, High'm 6F **15**
(not continuous)
Higham Rd. S63: Bramp B 5B **48**
Higham Vw. S75: Kexb 1E **15**
High Ash Dr. S25: Sth A 5G **141**
High Balk S75: Barn 4C **16**
High Bank S36: Thurl 3A **176**
S65: Thry 6D **84**
High Bank La. S36: Thurl 4A **176**
Highbury Av. DN4: Can 4B **58**
Highbury Cres. DN4: Can 4B **58**
Highbury Gro. S41: C'fld 3G **167**
Highbury Rd. S41: C'fld 3G **167**
Highbury Va. DN12: New E 5B **70**
Highbury Way S75: Barn 5C **16**
Highcliffe Ct. S11: Shef 1H **131**
S64: Swin 3C **66**
Highcliffe Dr. S11: Shef 2G **131**
S35: Ough 4E **91**
S64: Swin 3C **66**
Highcliffe Pl. S11: Shef 2G **131**
Highcliffe Rd. S11: Shef 1G **131**
High Cl. S75: Kexb 5E **7**
High Ct. S1: Shef 2F **5** (2G **119**)
High Cft. S74: Hoyl 6B **46**
Highcroft S11: Shef 1H **131**
High Cft. Dr. S71: Ath 6E **9**
Highdale Fold S18: Dron 3F **155**
Higher Albert St. S41: C'fld 4H **167**
HIGHER STUBBIN 1C **82**
HIGHFIELD
S1 5F **119**
WF9 1E **13**
Highfield S63: Wath D 6G **49**
Highfield Av. S26: Kiv P 5B **140**
S41: C'fld 2F **167**
S63: Gol 5C **36**
S70: Wors 4E **31**
S71: Ath 2F **17**
Highfield Cen. WF9: Hems 1E **13**
Highfield Cl. DN3: Barn D 1D **26**
Highfield Cotts. S75: Silk 1B **28**
Highfield Ct. S64: Swin 3B **66**
S73: Womb 1F **47**
Highfield Gro. S63: Wath D 5B **48**
High Fld. Knoll S36: Pen 5E **177**

Highfield La. S13: Shef 4C 122
S41: C'fld 2F 167
S60: Wav 2D 122
Highfield M. S60: Wav 3D 122
Highfield Pk. S66: Malt 4C 102
(not continuous)
Highfield Pl. S2: Shef 6F 119
WF9: Hems 1D 12
Highfield Range S73: D'fld 3B 34
Highfield Ri. S6: Stan 6C 104
Highfield Rd. DN1: Don 6D 40
DN12: Con 4G 69
S41: C'fld 3G 167
S61: Grea 6D 82
S64: Swin 3A 66
S73: D'fld 4B 34
WF9: Hems 1D 12
HIGHFIELDS 6D 22
Highfields S36: H'swne 1F 177
Highfields Country Pk. 5C 22
Highfields Cres. S18: Dron 4F 155
High Field Spring
S13: Wav 2B 122
S60: Cat 2B 122
Highfield Sq. S13: Wav 3D 122
Highfields Rd. S18: Dron 4F 155
S75: Kexb 6C 6
Highfield Ter. S41: C'fld 3G 167
Highfield Vw. S60: Cat 6D 110
Highfield Vw. Rd. S41: C'fld 3G 167
(not continuous)
High Fisher Ga. DN1: Don 6C 40
HIGHGATE 5B 36
Highgate S9: Tins 2H 109
(not continuous)
S73: Womb 2C 48
Highgate Cl.
DN11: New R 6D 74, 6H 75
S43: New W 3C 162
High Gate Ct. S70: Stair 2A 32
Highgate Cl. S63: Gol 6B 36
Highgate Dr. S18: Dron 5H 155
Highgate Greyhound Racing Track . . .4B 36
Highgate La. S18: Dron 5G 155
S63: Bolt D, Gol 1B 50
High Gate Way S72: Shaft 4F 11
High Greave S71: Smi 3F 17
Highgreave S5: Shef 3H 93
High Greave Av. S5: Shef 3G 93
High Greave Ct. S5: Shef 3H 93
High Greave Pl. S65: Roth 3B 98
High Greave Rd. S65: Roth 2B 98
HIGH GREEN 6C 60
High Gro. DN4: Bess 1D 74
Highgrove Cl. S41: Whit M 6H 161
Highgrove Dr. DN4: Can 6D 58
S71: Car 6A 10
High Hazel Ct. S60: Tree 2F 123
High Hazel Cres. S60: Cat 6D 110
High Hazel Rd. S60: Tree 2F 123
High Hazels 2G 121
High Hazels Cl. S9: Shef 2G 121
High Hazels Mead S9: Shef 2G 121
High Hooton Rd. S25: Slade H 4H 115
S66: Hoot L 4H 115
High Ho. Farm Ct. S26: Wales 6G 139
High Ho. Ter. S6: Shef 5C 106
Highland Rd. S43: New W 1C 162
HIGHLANE 1H 149
High La. S12: Ridg 1H 149
S42: W'ton 5A 170
S66: Bramp M 4G 125
High Lee La. S36: H'swne 2F 177
Highlow Cl. S40: C'fld 3D 166
Highlow Vw. S60: Brins 3D 110
High Matlock Av. S6: Stan 6E 105
High Matlock Rd. S6: Stan 5E 105
HIGH MELTON 3E 53
High Melton Golf Course 4E 53
Highmill Av. S64: Swin 3H 65
HIGH MOOR 5E 153
Highmoor Av. S26: Kiv P 6H 139
Highnam Cres. Rd. S10: Shef 3B 118
High Nook Rd. S25: Din 6B 128
High Pavement Row S2: Shef 2H 119
High Ridge S70: Wors 5E 31
Highridge Cl. DN12: Con 5G 69
High Rd. DN4: Balb 5H 55
DN4: Warm 6D 54
DN12: New E 5C 70
High Royd Av. S72: Cud 2E 19

High Royd La. S36: H'swne 2G 177
S74: Hoyl 4G 45
Highroyds S70: Wors 4E 31
Highstone Av. S70: Barn 3D 30
Highstone Cnr. S70: Wors 4E 31
Highstone Ct. S70: Barn 3E 31
Highstone Cres. S70: Barn 3D 30
Highstone La. S70: Wors 4E 31
Highstone Pk. S70: Barn 3D 30
Highstone Rd. S70: Barn 3E 31
High Stones Pl. S5: Shef 3F 93
Highstone Va. S70: Barn 3D 30
Highstone Vw. S70: Barn 3E 31
High Storrs Cl. S11: Shef 2G 131
High Storrs Cres. S11: Shef 1H 131
High Storrs Dr. S11: Shef 2G 131
High Storrs Ri. S11: Shef 1H 131
High Storrs Rd. S11: Shef 2G 131
High St. DN1: Don 1B 56
DN3: Barn D 1B 26
DN5: Ark 6C 24
DN5: Barnb 1H 51
DN5: Bntly 3A 40
DN7: Dunsv 5G 27
DN11: Wad 5E 73
DN12: Con 4F 69
S1: Shef 3E 5 (3B 119)
S9: Shef 2F 109
S17: Dore 3E 145
S18: App 3D 156
S18: Dron 2E 155
S20: Beig 4H 137
S20: Mosb 3D 150
S21: Ecki 1D 158
S21: Killa 4C 152
S25: Laugh M 1G 127
S25: Sth A 4G 141
S26: Swal 1B 138
S35: Eccl 2F 93
S36: Pen 4D 176
S40: C'fld 5H 167
S41: Old W 4H 161
(not continuous)
S43: Brim 1E 169
(not continuous)
S43: New W 3B 162
S43: Stav 4B 164
S60: Roth 4E 97
S60: Whis 1B 112
S61: Kimb 3H 95
S62: Rawm 4G 83
S63: Bolt D 2B 50
S63: Gol 5D 36
S63: Thurn 2A 36
S63: Wath D 6G 49
S64: Mexb 2F 67
S66: B'well 1F 101
S66: Malt 5B 102
S70: Barn 6D 16
S70: Wors 5G 31
S71: Monk B 4H 17
S71: R'ton 3F 9
S72: Bill 3G 35
S72: Grim 2A 20
S72: Gt H 6E 21
S72: Shaft 3F 11
S72: Sth H 1H 11
S73: Womb 1G 47
S74: Hoyl 6B 46
S75: Dod 3G 29
S75: Silk 3A 28
S75: Stain 4H 7
High St. La. S2: Shef 3H 5 (3H 119)
High St. Mews S20: Mosb 3D 150
Highthorn Rd. S64: Kiln 5C 66
High Thorns S75: Silk 2A 28
Highthorn Vs. S64: Kiln 5D 66
Highthorn Way S26: Kiv P 5C 140
Highton St. S6: Shef 6B 106
High Trees S17: Dore 3E 145
S60: Roth 1A 112
High Vw. S5: Shef 4F 107
S71: R'ton 3G 9
High Vw. Cl. S41: C'fld 6C 168
S73: D'fld 4C 34
HIGH WINCOBANK 6D 94
Highwood Cl. S75: Kexb 6D 6
Highwood Pl. S21: Ecki 1D 158
HIGHWOODS 1D 66
Highwoods Cres. S64: Mexb 1D 66
Highwoods Rd. S64: Mexb 1D 66

High Wray Cl. S11: Shef 4A 132
Hilary Way S26: Swal 1C 138
Hilda Ter. S72: Grim 2A 20
Hild Av. S72: Cud 4G 19
Hillary Ho. DN2: Don 4E 41
Hillberry Ri. S40: Birdh 4G 171
Hill Cl. S6: Stan 6D 104
S65: Roth 6D 98
Hillcote Cl. S10: Shef 5E 117
Hillcote Dr. S10: Shef 5E 117
Hillcote M. S10: Shef 5E 117
Hillcote Ri. S10: Shef 5E 117
Hill Crest S65: Thry 5D 84
S74: Hoyl 1H 61
Hillcrest S63: Thurn 3B 36
Hillcrest Dr. DN3: Brant 4G 59
S25: Sth A 5G 141
S35: Ough 4D 90
Hillcrest Gro. S43: Stav 2C 164
Hillcrest Ri. S36: Spink 4H 175
Hill Crest Rd. S35: Chap 3E 79
S36: Spink 4G 175
S41: Has 3C 172
Hillcrest Way S66: Sunn 2G 99
Hill End Rd. S75: Mapp 1B 16
Hill Farm Cl. S63: Thurn 3A 36
HILLFOOT
S17 .6E 145
S6 . . . . .5C 106
Hillfoot Cl. S17: Tot 6E 145
Hillfoot Rd. S3: Shef 6D 106
S17: Tot 5D 144
Hill Gro. S43: Bar H 2G 163
Hillman Dr. S43: Ink 2H 169
Hill Rise Cl. S66: Sunn 4H 99
HILLSBOROUGH 4B 106
Hillsborough 2B 106
Hillsborough Arc., The S6: Shef 4B 106
Hillsborough Barracks Bus. & Shop. Cen.
S6: Shef 4C 106
Hillsborough Golf Course 1G 105
Hillsborough Gro. S6: Shef 2B 106
Hillsborough Interchange 4B 106
(off Langsett Rd.)
Hillsborough Leisure Cen. 3C 106
Hillsborough Park Stop (ST) 4B 106
Hillsborough Pl. S6: Shef 4B 106
S6: Shef 4B 106
Hillsborough Rd. DN4: Can 4B 58
S6: Shef 4B 106
Hills Cl. DN5: Sprot 2F 55
S64: Mexb 1F 67
Hillscroft Rd. DN9: Blax 1F 77
HILLSIDE 4B 12
Hill Side S60: Whis 3A 112
S61: Thorpe H 4C 80
S65: Thry 6D 84
Hillside S20: Mosb 3D 150
S25: Nth A 2G 141
S71: Ard 2D 32
Hillside Av. S5: Shef 4G 93
S18: Dron 4F 155
Hillside Cl. S36: H'swne 1F 177
Hillside Ct. DN5: Sprot 4C 54
S61: Grea 1E 97
Hillside Cres. S72: Brier 4B 12
Hillside Dr. DN12: New E 5B 70
S40: W'ton 6E 167
S43: Mas M 3F 165
S74: Hoyl 1C 62
Hillside Gro. S72: Brier 4A 12
Hill Side La. S36: Thurl 5A 176
Hillside Mt. S72: Brier 4B 12
Hillside Rd. DN2: Don 3H 41
Hills Rd. S36: Spink 3F 175
Hill St. S2: Shef 5E 119
S71: Stair 2B 32
S73: D'fld 5B 34
S74: Els 1D 62
HILL TOP
DN12 . . . . .1C 86
S11 .3F 131
S18 .5F 155
S35 .2C 90
S6 . . . . .5A 104
S61 .4F 95
S71 .1E 17
Hill Top S75: Cawt 3A 14
Hilltop S72: Brier 3A 12

Hill Top Av. S71: Ath 5D 8
Hill Top Cl. S60: Brins 3C 110
  S61: Kimb 4G 95
  S66: Malt 4G 101
Hill Top Cres. DN2: Don 3H 41
  DN12: New E 6C 70
  S20: Water 1E 151
Hill Top Dr. S35: Wharn S 2C 90
Hill Top Est. WF9: Sth K 5G 13
Hilltop Gdns. DN12: Den M 4C 68
Hilltop Grn. S6: Shef 1E 107
Hill Top La. S35: Green M 1F 175
  S35: Gren 2A 92
  S61: Kimb 4G 95
  S65: Dalt M 3E 99
  S66: Dalt M 3E 99
  S75: Barn 5A 16
Hill Top Ri. S35: Gren 3C 92
Hill Top Rd.
  DN12: Con, Den M 3B 68
  S35: Gren 3C 92
  S70: Birdw 4E 45
Hilltop Rd. S18: Dron 4F 155
  S41: Old W 4H 161
  S42: W'orth 6E 171
Hilltops S62: Rawm 4G 83
Hill Top Smithies S71: Smi 2E 17
Hilltop Way S18: Dron 5F 155
Hill Turrets Cl. S11: Shef 4G 131
Hill Vw. E. S61: Kimb 2G 95
Hill Vw. Rd. S43: Brim 6D 162
  S61: Kimb 2G 95
Hilmian Way WF9: Hems 1G 13
Hilton Dr. S35: Eccl 2C 90
Hilton St. S75: Barn 6C 16
Hindburn Cl. DN4: Bess 5G 57
Hinde Ho. Cres. S4: Shef 2B 108
Hinde Ho. Cft. S4: Shef 2B 108
Hinde Ho. La. S4: Shef 3A 108
Hinde St. Shef 3B 108
Hindewood Cl. S4: Shef 2B 108
Hindle St. S70: Barn 1C 30
Hind Rd. S60: Whis 2B 112
Hipley Cl. S40: C'fld 2C 166
Hipper St. S40: C'fld 6H 167
Hipper St. Sth. S40: C'fld 6H 167
Hipper St. W. S40: C'fld 6F 167
Hirst Comn. La. S6: Shef 4A 92
Hirst Dr. S65: Roth 3C 98
Hirst Ga. S64: Mexb 2H 67
Hirst La. S66: Stain 1F 103
HMP Doncaster DN5: Don 1A 56
Hoades Av. S81: Woods 4F 143
Hobart St. S11: Shef 6E 119
Hobner La. S43: Stav 6H 163
Hobson Av. S6: Shef 5D 106
Hobson Pl. S6: Shef 5D 106
Hockley La. S42: W'orth 6H 171
Hodder Ct. S35: Chap 2E 79
Hodgkinson Av. S36: Pen 4D 176
Hodgson St. S3: Shef 6C 4 (4E 119)
Hodroyd Cl. S72: Shaft 5G 11
Hodroyd Cotts. S72: Brier 4B 12
Hodroyd La. S72: Shaft 5G 11
Hodster La. S72: Gt H 4D 20
Hogarth Ri. S18: Dron 4E 155
Holbeach Dr. S40: W'ton 2F 171
Holbeck Cl. S41: C'fld 4A 168
Holbein Cl. S18: Dron 4E 155
Holberry Cl. S10: Shef 5A 4 (4D 118)
Holberry Gdns. S10: Shef ...5A 4 (4D 118)
Holborn Av. S18: Dron 2F 155
Holbourne Gro. S35: High G 5C 60
HOLBROOK 2H 151
Holbrook Av. S20: Holb 2G 151
Holbrook Cl. S20: Holb 1G 151
  S40: W'ton 1F 171
Holbrook Dr. S13: Shef 2E 135
Holbrook Ent. Pk. S20: Holb 2H 151
Holbrook Ind. Est. S20: Holb 2H 151
Holbrook Pl. S43: Ink 1H 169
Holbrook Ri. S20: Holb 1G 151
Holbrook Rd. S13: Shef 1E 135
Holden Ct. S70: Barn 1D 30
Holderness Dr. S26: Aston, Swal ..6C 124
Holdings Rd. S2: Shef 5A 120
Holdroyds Yd. S75: Dod 4G 29
HOLDWORTH 6A 90
Holdworth La. S6: Brad 6A 90
Hole Ho. La. S36: Stoc 3D 174

Holgate S73: Womb 5E 33
Holgate Av. S5: Shef 5E 93
Holgate Cl. S5: Shef 4E 93
Holgate Cres. S5: Shef 4F 93
Holgate Dr. S5: Shef 4F 93
Holgate Hospital
  WF9: Hems 1B 12
Holgate Mt. S70: Wors 4E 31
Holgate Rd. S5: Shef 4E 93
                    (not continuous)
Holgate Vw. S72: Brier 3B 32
Holiwell Cl. S66: Malt 4C 102
Holkham Rd. S11: Shef 6G 131
Holland Cl. S62: Rawm 1G 83
Holland Pl. S2: Shef 6F 119
Holland Rd. S2: Shef 6F 119
  S35: High G 1C 78
  S41: Old W 4G 161
Holland St. S1: Shef 3C 4 (3E 119)
Hollens Way S40: C'fld 3A 166
Hollies Cl. S18: Dron 4H 155
Hollinberry La. S35: Howb 5A 60
HOLLIN BUSK 5D 174
Hollin Busk La. S36: Spink 5E 175
Hollin Busk Rd. S36: Spink 4E 175
Hollin Cl. DN11: Ross 4E 75
  S41: C'fld 6D 160
Hollin Cft. S75: Dod 2H 29
Hollindale Dr. S12: Shef 3F 135
Hollin Edge La. S36: Bolst 6H 175
Holling Cft. S36: Spink 3G 175
Holling Hill La. S66: Wick 6E 99
Holling Moor La. S66: Wick 6F 99
Holling's La. S65: Rav, Thry 6E 85
Hollingsworth Way S66: Sunn 3H 99
HOLLINGWOOD 5F 163
Hollingwood Cres. S43: Hol 4F 163
Hollingwood Est. S43: Hol 5F 163
Hollingworth Cl. S64: Mexb 6A 52
Hollin Ho. La. S6: Lox 1A 104
Hollin La. S36: Bolst 6E 175
  S75: Cawt 3A 14
Hollin Rd. S35: Ough 4D 90
Hollins, The S75: Dod 4H 29
Hollins Cl. S6: Shef 1G 117
Hollins Ct. S6: Shef 6G 105
Hollins Dr. S6: Shef 1H 117
HOLLINS END 3F 135
Hollinsend Av. S12: Shef 3F 135
Hollinsend Pl. S12: Shef 3F 135
Hollinsend Rd. S12: Shef 4D 134
Hollinsend Stop (ST) 3D 134
Hollins La. S6: Shef 6G 105
Hollins Spring Av. S18: Dron 4F 155
Hollins Spring Rd. S18: Dron 4F 155
Hollins Wood Gro. S72: Cud 4G 19
Hollis Cl. S62: Rawm 2H 83
Hollis Cft. S1: Shef 2C 4 (2E 119)
  S13: Shef 2B 136
Hollis La. S41: C'fld 6A 168
                    (not continuous)
Hollowdene S75: Barn 5A 16
Hollow Ga. DN5: Cad 1F 69
  S35: Chap 3C 78
  S60: Whis 3A 112
Hollowgate DN5: Harl, Barnb 2G 51
  S60: Roth 5F 97
Hollowgate Av. S63: Wath D 4D 48
Hollow La. S20: Half 4E 151
Hollows, The DN4: Bess 6B 58
  DN9: Auck 2H 59
Holly Av. DN5: Don 3H 39
Hollybank Av. S12: Shef 2F 135
Hollybank Cl. S12: Shef 2G 135
Hollybank Cres. S12: Shef 2F 135
Hollybank Dr. S12: Shef 2F 135
Hollybank Rd. S12: Shef 2G 135
Hollybank Way S12: Shef 2G 135
Holly Barn Fold S65: Hoot R 2H 85
Holly Bush Dr. S63: Thurn 2C 36
Holly Bush La. DN3: Kirk Sa 5C 26
Hollybush St. S62: P'gte 5G 83
Holly Cl. S21: Killa 5B 152
  S35: Chap 4E 79
  S41: Old W 5A 118
  S70: Barn 3E 31
                    (off Hornby St.)
Holly Cres. S66: Sunn 4H 99
Hollycroft Av. S71: R'ton 3G 9
Holly Dene DN3: Arm 2D 42

Holly Dr. DN5: Bntly 6A 24
Holly Farm S72: Shaft 3F 11
Holly Fld. Cres. DN3: Eden 5C 26
Holly Gdns. S12: Shef 2F 135
Hollygate S70: Wors 5H 31
Holly Gro. DN11: Ross 4D 74
  S12: Shef 2F 135
  S63: Gol 5B 36
  S63: Wath D 2G 65
  S72: Brier 3B 12
  S73: D'fld 5B 34
                  (off Snape Hill Rd.)
Holly Hall La.
  S35: Green M 1H 175
Holly Ho. La. S35: Gren 2H 91
Holly La. S1: Shef 3D 4 (3F 119)
Holly Mt. S66: Wick 6H 99
Holly Rd. DN9: Auck 2B 76
Holly's Ho. Rd. S65: Rav 1B 100
Holly St. DN1: Don 3B 56
  S1: Shef 3D 4 (3F 119)
                    (not continuous)
Holly Ter. DN4: Balb 5G 55
  S26: Swal 6B 124
Hollythorpe Cl. S41: Has 2C 172
Hollythorpe Cres. S8: Shef 4F 133
Hollythorpe Ri. S8: Shef 4G 133
Hollythorpe Rd. S8: Shef 4G 133
Hollytree Av. S66: Malt 4G 101
Hollywell Cl. S62: Rawm 1A 84
Hollywell Dr. DN4: Bess 1E 75
Hollywood Bowl
  Sheffield 4F 109
Holmbrook Wlk. S40: C'fld 3D 166
Holm Cl. S18: Dron W 2C 154
Holme, The S18: Dron 1G 155
Holmebank Cl. S40: C'fld 4F 167
Holmebank E. S40: C'fld 4F 167
Holmebank Vw. S40: C'fld 4F 167
Holmebank W. S40: C'fld 4F 167
Holmebrook Vw. S40: C'fld 2D 166
Holme Cl. S6: Shef 4B 106
Holme Ct. S63: Gol 6B 36
Holmefield Cl. DN3: Arm 5F 43
Holme Hall Cres. S40: C'fld 2C 166
Holme Hall La. S66: Stain 2F 103
Holme La. S6: Shef 5A 106
  S35: Gren 3C 92
Holme Oak Way S6: Stan 5D 104
Holme Pk. Av. S41: C'fld 1C 166
Holme Rd. S41: C'fld 2H 167
Holmeroyd Rd. DN6: Adw S 1F 23
HOLMES 5B 96
Holmes, The DN1: Don 6C 40
Holmes Carr Cres.
  DN11: New R 5A 74
Holmes Carr Rd. DN4: Bess 6A 58
  DN11: New R 5A 74
Holmes Cl. S61: Roth 4C 96
Holmes Cres. S60: Tree 2F 123
HOLMESDALE 1H 155
Holmesdale Cl. S18: Dron 1H 155
Holmesdale Rd. S18: Dron 1G 155
HOLMESFIELD 4A 154
Holmesfield S61: Roth 4F 97
                  (off Rosebery St.)
Holmesfield Gro. S60: Wav 2C 122
Holmesfield Rd. S18: Dron W 3A 154
  S35: Ough 4E 91
Holmes La. DN12: Old D 6G 67
  S61: Roth 4B 96
  S65: Hoot R 6G 67
Holmes Mkt., The DN1: Don 6D 40
                    (off Kings Rd.)
Holmes Rd. S66: Bram 6A 100
Holme Vw. Rd. S75: Kexb 6C 6
Holme Wood Ct. DN3: Eden 6D 26
Holme Wood Gdns. DN4: Bess 5B 58
Holme Wood La. DN3: Arm 4G 43
                    (not continuous)
Holm Flatt St. S62: P'gte 5F 83
Holmhirst Cl. S8: Shef 6D 132
Holmhirst Dr. S8: Shef 5D 132
Holmhirst Rd. S8: Shef 5D 132
Holmhirst Way S8: Shef 5D 132
Holmley Bank S18: Dron 1F 155
HOLMLEY COMMON 1F 155
Holmley La.
  S18: Coal A, Dron 1F 155
Holmoak Cl. S64: Swin 5C 66

Holmshaw Cl. DN3: Eden 5D **26**
Holmshaw Dr. S13: Shef 6H **121**
Holmshaw Gro. S13: Shef 6H **121**
Holmsley Av. WF9: Sth K 4H **13**
Holmsley Gro. WF9: Sth K 4H **13**
Holmsley La. S72: Brier 5F **13**
  WF9: Sth K 5F **13**
Holmsley Mt. WF9: Sth K 4H **13**
Holt Ho. Gro. S7: Shef 4C **132**
Holtwood Rd. S4: Shef 5G **107**
Holwick Cl. S75: Silk 2A **28**
Holwick Ct. S70: Barn 1D **30**
Holy Grn. S1: Shef 6D **4** (4F **119**)
Holymoor Rd. S42: Holy 1A **170**
Holyoake Av. S13: Shef 5H **121**
Holyrood Av. S10: Shef 5A **116**
Holyrood Ri. S66: Bram 3A **100**
Holyrood Rd. DN2: Don 1F **57**
Holyrood Vw. S10: Shef 5A **116**
Holywell Cotts. S66: B'well 2B **102**
Holywell Ct. S4: Shef 2D **108**
Holywell Cres. S66: B'well 1B **102**
Holywell Ga. S4: Shef 2D **108**
Holywell Hgts. S4: Shef 2D **108**
Holywell La. DN12: Con 5F **69**
  S66: B'well 1B **102**
Holywell Pl. S65: Roth 3F **97**
  (off Wharncliffe Hill)
Holywell Rd. S4: Shef 3C **108**
  S9: Shef 3C **108**
  S64: Kiln 5C **66**
Holywell St. S41: C'fld 4H **167**
Homecroft Rd. S63: Gol 5C **36**
Home Farm Ct. DN5: Hick 3H **37**
Homefield Cres.
  DN5: Scawt 2F **39**
Homeport M. S41: C'fld 4H **167**
Homestead Cl. S5: Shef 5A **94**
Homestead Dr. S60: Brins 3C **110**
  S62: Rawm 1G **83**
Homestead Rd. S5: Shef 5H **93**
Honeymere Ct. S70: Barn 2G **31**
Honeysuckle Cl. DN4: Bess 4H **57**
  S73: D'fld 6B **34**
Honeysuckle Ct. DN9: Finn 3F **77**
Honeysuckle Gdns. S70: Barn 3G **31**
Honeysuckle Rd. S5: Shef 1C **108**
  S41: Has 3D **172**
HONEYWELL 5E **17**
Honeywell Cl. S71: Barn 5E **17**
Honeywell Gro. S71: Barn 4E **17**
Honeywell La. S71: Barn 5D **16**
  S75: Barn 5D **16**
Honeywell Pl. S71: Barn 5E **17**
Honeywell St. S71: Barn 5E **17**
Honister Cl. S63: Bramp B 5B **48**
HOOBER 5B **64**
Hoober Av. S11: Shef 3G **131**
Hoober Ct. S62: Rawm 6E **65**
Hoober Fld. Rd.
  S62: Wentw 5B **64**
  S63: Wath D 5B **64**
Hoober Hall La.
  S62: Wentw 3H **63**
  S63: Wath D 3H **63**
Hoober La. S62: Wentw 5B **64**
Hoober Stand 4A **64**
Hoober St. S63: Wath D 5C **48**
Hoober Vw. S62: Rawm 6E **65**
  S73: Womb 3A **48**
Hoodhill Rd. S62: H'ley 6A **62**
Hoole La. S10: Shef 4B **118**
Hoole Rd. S10: Shef 3B **118**
Hoole St. S6: Shef 6B **106**
  S41: Has 2C **172**
Hooley Rd. S13: Shef 2E **137**
Hooton Cl. S25: Laugh M 1H **127**
Hooton La.
  S25: Laugh M, Slade H 1H **127**
  S65: Rav 5H **85**
  S66: Hoot L 6H **101**
HOOTON LEVITT 6H **101**
Hooton Rd. S64: Kiln 1D **84**
HOOTON ROBERTS 2A **86**
Hope Av. S25: Din 4A **128**
  S63: Gol 5C **36**
Hopedale Rd. S12: Shef 4G **135**
Hopefield Av. S12: Shef 4G **135**
Hope Rd. S35: Ough 4F **91**

Hope St. S36: Stoc 3E **175**
  S40: C'fld 5F **167**
  S60: Roth 3D **96**
  S64: Mexb 2F **67**
  S71: Monk B 2C **18**
  S73: Womb 1H **47**
  (Gower St.)
  S73: Womb 1H **47**
  (Providence St.)
  S75: Barn 6C **16**
  S75: Stain 6B **8**
Hope St. Ind. Est. S60: Roth 2D **96**
Hopewell St. S70: Stair 2A **32**
Hopwood La. S6: Stan 2C **116**
Hopwood St. S70: Barn 6D **16**
Horace St. S60: Roth 5F **97**
Horbiry End S26: Tod 3B **140**
Horbury La. S35: Burn 4D **78**
Horbury Rd. S72: Cud 6E **11**
Hornbeam Cl. S35: Chap 4E **79**
  S43: Hol 4F **163**
Hornbeam Rd. S66: Flan 4G **99**
Hornby Ct. S11: Shef 1H **131**
Hornby M. S70: Barn 3F **31**
  (off Hornby St.)
Hornby St. S70: Barn 3E **31**
  (not continuous)
Horncroft S75: Cawt 3A **14**
Horndean Rd. S5: Shef 3A **108**
Horner Cl. S36: Stoc 3D **174**
Horner Rd. S7: Shef 1E **133**
Hornes La. S75: Stain 5B **8**
Horninglow Cl. DN4: Can 5D **58**
  S5: Shef 1H **107**
Horninglow Mt. S5: Shef 1H **107**
Horninglow Rd. S5: Shef 1H **107**
Hornsby Rd. DN3: Arm 5F **43**
Hornthorpe Rd. S21: Ecki 2C **158**
Hornthwaite Cl. S36: Thurl 4A **176**
Hornthwaite Hill Rd. S36: Thurl ...5A **176**
Horse Carr Vw. S71: Ard 2D **32**
Horse Chestnut Cl. S40: C'fld 1H **171**
Horse Cft. La. S35: Wharn S 2C **90**
Horsefair Cl. S64: Swin 3C **66**
Horsehills La. DN3: Arm 5D **42**
Horsemoor Rd. S63: Thurn 2A **36**
Horseshoe Cl. S26: Wales 5H **139**
Horse Shoe Ct. DN4: Balb 5G **55**
Horseshoe Gdns. S26: Wales 5G **139**
Horsewood Cl. S70: Barn 2A **30**
Horsewood Rd. S13: Shef 6E **123**
  S42: W'ton 2C **170**
Horsley Cl. S40: C'fld 3B **166**
Horton Cl. S20: Half 3F **151**
Horton Dr. S20: Half 3F **151**
Horton Vw. DN3: Kirk Sa 3B **26**
Hough Cl. S40: C'fld 1H **171**
Hough La. S73: Womb 3E **47**
Houghton Rd. S25: Nth A 5E **127**
  S63: Thurn 2H **35**
Houldsworth Dr. S41: C'fld 6C **168**
Hound Hill La. S64: Mexb 4C **50**
  S70: Wors 6C **30**
Houndhill Pk. S63: Wath D 6B **50**
Houndkirk Rd. S11: Dore, Shef 1A **144**
Hounsfield Cres. S65: Roth 3C **98**
Hounsfield La. S3: Shef 4A **4**
Hounsfield Rd. S3: Shef 3A **4** (3D **118**)
  S65: Roth 3C **98**
House Carr La. S75: Hood G 6C **28**
Housley La. S35: Chap 3E **79**
Housley Pk. S35: Chap 2E **79**
Houstead Rd. S9: Shef 3G **121**
Hoveringham Ct. S26: Swal 2B **138**
Howard Dr. S41: Old W 4H **161**
HOWARD HILL 1B **118**
Howard La. S1: Shef 5F **5** (4G **119**)
Howard Rd. S6: Shef 1B **118**
  S66: Bram 5A **100**
  S66: Malt 6C **102**
Howards Cl. S66: Thurc 6D **114**
Howard St. S1: Shef 5F **5** (4G **119**)
  S25: Din 5B **128**
  S60: Roth 3E **97**
  S65: Roth 4F **97**
  S70: Barn 3E **31**
  S73: D'fld 5D **34**
Howarth Dr. S60: Brins 5E **111**
Howarth La. S60: Brins 4F **111**
  (not continuous)
Howarth Rd. S60: Brins 4E **111**

Howbeck Cl. DN12: New E 5B **70**
Howbeck Dr. DN12: New E 5B **70**
HOWBROOK 5A **60**
Howbrook Cl. S35: High G 6B **60**
Howbrook La. S35: Wort, Howb ...5A **60**
  (not continuous)
Howden Cl. DN4: Bess 6H **57**
  S43: Stav 3C **164**
  S75: Dart 5G **7**
Howden Rd. S9: Shef 5D **108**
Howdike La. S65: Hoot R 1G **85**
Howe La. S25: Slade H 4H **115**
Howell Gdns. S63: Thurn 3B **36**
Howell La. DN5: Clay 2F **21**
  S72: Brier 2F **21**
Howell M. WF9: Sth K 4G **13**
Howells Pl. S43: Mas M 2E **165**
Howlett Wood Country Pk. 1G **21**
Howlett Cl. S60: Whis 3C **112**
Howlett Dr. S60: Brins 5D **110**
Howse St. S74: Els 6E **47**
Howson Cl. S65: Rav 2B **100**
Howson Rd. S36: Spink 3F **175**
Hoylake Av. S40: W'ton 3D **170**
Hoylake Dr. S64: Swin 5C **66**
HOYLAND 6B **46**
HOYLAND COMMON 1G **61**
Hoyland Leisure Cen. & Swimming Pool
  ....6A **46**
HOYLAND LOWE 6A **46**
Hoyland Rd. S3: Shef 6D **106**
  S74: Hoyl 1G **61**
Hoyland St. S66: Malt 5C **102**
  S73: Womb 2G **47**
HOYLANDSWAINE 1G **177**
Hoyland Ter. WF9: Sth K 4H **13**
Hoy La. S64: Mexb 5D **50**
Hoyle Cft. La. S66: B'well 1H **101**
HOYLE MILL 1G **31**
Hoyle Mill La. S36: Thurl 3B **176**
Hoyle Mill Rd. S70: Stair 2A **32**
Hoyle St. S3: Shef 1C **4** (1E **119**)
HUBS, The 5F **5**
Hucklow Av. S40: C'fld 2G **171**
  S43: Ink 1H **169**
Hucklow Dr. S5: Shef 1A **108**
Hucklow Rd. S5: Shef 2A **108**
Hucknall Av. S40: Ash 4D **166**
Huddersfield Rd.
  S36: Ingb, Pen 1A **176**
  S70: Barn 4B **16**
  S75: Barn 4B **16**
  S75: Dart, Haigh, Kexb 2C **6**
  S75: Haigh 1B **6**
Hudson Haven S73: Womb 6E **33**
  (off Upton Cl.)
Hudson Rd. S13: Shef 6F **123**
  S61: Kimb P 6H **81**
Hudson's M. DN1: Don 1B **56**
Hughes Way S63: Wath D 5C **48**
Humberside Way S71: Car 2A **18**
Hummingbird Wlk. S63: Wath D ...5G **49**
Humphrey Rd. S8: Shef 2D **146**
Humphries Av. S62: Rawm 1E **83**
HUNDALL 5E **157**
Hundall La. S18: Uns 5C **156**
  S41: Old W 2H **161**
Hungerhill Cl. S61: Kimb P 2G **95**
Hunger Hill La. S60: Whis 3B **112**
Hungerhill La. DN3: Eden 6A **26**
Hunger Hill Rd. S60: Whis 2A **112**
Hungerhill Rd. S61: Kimb 1G **95**
Hunloke Av. S40: C'fld, W'ton 1E **171**
Hunloke Cres. S40: C'fld 1F **171**
Hunloke Vw. S42: W'orth 6A **172**
Hunningley Cl. S70: Stair 3A **32**
Hunningley La. S70: Stair 4A **32**
  (Burnsall Gro.)
  S70: Stair 2A **32**
  (Greggs Ct.)
Hunsdon Rd. S21: Ecki 1D **158**
HUNSHELF BANK 1D **174**
Hunshelf La. S35: Eccl 6G **79**
Hunshelf Pk. S36: Stoc 2E **175**
Hunshelf Rd. S35: Chap 3E **79**
  S36: Stoc 2D **174**
  (Pea Royd La.)
  S36: Stoc 1B **174**
  (Underbank La.)
Hunsley St. S4: Shef 4B **108**
Hunster Cl. DN4: Can 5C **58**

Hunster Flat La.
DN11: New R 6G 75
Hunster Gro. DN11: New R 6C 74
Hunstone Av. S8: Shef 3F 147
Hunt Cl. S71: Monk B 4H 17
Hunter Ct. S11: Shef 1A 132
Hunter Hill Rd. S11: Shef 6B 118
Hunter Ho. Rd. S11: Shef 6B 118
Hunter Rd. S6: Shef 4A 106
Hunter's Av. S70: Barn 2H 29
Hunters Bar S11: Shef 6B 118
Hunters Chase S25: Din 3A 128
Hunters Cl. S25: Din 3A 128
Hunters Ct. S25: Din 3A 128
Hunters Dr. S25: Din 3A 128
Hunters Gdns. S6: Lox 3E 105
S25: Din 3A 128
Hunters Grn. S25: Din 3A 128
Hunters La. S13: Shef 2F 135
Hunters Pk. S25: Din 3A 128
Hunters Ri. S75: Barn 1H 29
Hunters Way S25: Din 3A 128
Huntingdon Cres. S11: Shef 6D 118
Huntingdon Rd. DN2: Don 5H 41
Huntington St. DN5: Bntly 6H 23
Huntington Way S66: Malt 3H 101
Huntingtower Rd.
S11: Shef 1A 132
Hunt La. DN5: Don 5A 40
Huntley Cl. S43: Ink 6G 163
Huntley Gro. S11: Shef 2G 131
Huntley Rd. S11: Shef 2H 131
Huntsman Rd. S9: Shef 2G 121
S43: Stav 4B 164
Hunt St. S74: Hoyl 1G 61
Hurl Dr. S12: Shef 3C 134
Hurley Cft. S63: Bramp B 5B 48
(not continuous)
HURL FIELD 3B 134
Hurlfield Av. S12: Shef 3C 134
Hurlfield Ct. S12: Shef 2D 134
Hurlfield Dr. S12: Shef 3C 134
S65: Rav 3A 100
Hurlfield Rd. S12: Shef 3B 134
Hurlfield Vw. S12: Shef 2C 134
Hurlingham Cl. S11: Shef 3B 132
Hurlstone Cl. DN3: Eden 5D 26
Hursley Cl. S20: Sot 1H 151
Hursley Dr. S20: Sot 1H 151
Hurst Grn. S35: High G 1C 78
Hurst La. DN9: Auck 2H 59, 5G 75
Huskar Cl. S75: Silk 2A 28
Hutchinson Cl. S60: Roth 5F 97
Hutchinson La. S7: Shef 5C 132
Hutchinson Rd. S7: Shef 5C 132
S62: Rawm 2H 83
Hutcliffe Dr. S8: Shef 6C 132
Hutcliffe Wood Crematorium
S8: Shef 6C 132
Hutcliffe Wood Rd. S8: Shef 6C 132
Hutcliffe Wood Vw. S8: Shef 1C 146
Hut La. S21: Killa 6D 152
Hutton Bank S66: Bram 6B 100
Hutton Ct. DN3: Arm 3C 42
Hutton Cft. S12: Shef 5C 136
Hutton Rd. S61: Kimb P 1H 95
Hut Yd. DN11: Lov 4B 72
Huxterwell Dr. DN4: Balb 2A 72
Hyacinth Cl. S5: Shef 1C 108
Hyacinth Rd. S5: Shef 1C 108
HYDE PARK 3C 56
Hyde Pk. Ind. Est. DN4: Don 4D 56
Hyde Park Stop (ST) 2A 120
Hyde Pk. Ter. S2: Shef 3H 119
Hyde Pk. Wlk. S2: Shef 3H 119
(not continuous)
Hydra Way S35: Eccl 6G 79
Hyland Cres. DN4: Balb 6F 55
Hyman Cl. DN4: Warm 5E 55
Hyperion Way DN11: New R 6B 74

I

Ians Way S40: Ash 4D 166
Ibberson Av. S75: Mapp 6A 8
Ibbotson Rd. S6: Shef 6B 106
Ibsen Cl. DN3: Barn D 1H 27
iceSheffield 5D 108
ICKLES 6C 96
ICKLES RDBT. 5D 96

Ickles Way S60: Roth 6C 96
Icknield Way S60: Brins 4D 110
Ida Gro. S66: Malt 4G 101
Ida's Rd. S21: Ecki 6E 151
Idsworth Rd. S5: Shef 2A 108
Ilam Cl. S43: Ink 2H 169
Ilford Ct. S43: New W 2C 162
(off Bamford St.)
Ilkley Cres. S26: Swal 2B 138
Ilkley Rd. S5: Shef 6A 94
Illsley Rd. S73: D'fld 4F 49
Immingham Gro. S43: Stav 5A 164
Imperial Bldgs. S60: Roth 4E 97
Imperial Cres. DN2: Don 6E 41
Imperial M. S70: Birdw 4D 44
Imperial St. S70: Barn 3E 31
Imrie Pl. S26: Kiv P 6A 140
Inchburn Cres. S36: Pen 4E 177
Industry Rd. S9: Shef 1E 121
S71: Car 1H 17
Industry St. S6: Shef 6B 106
(not continuous)
Infield La. S9: Shef 2G 121
Infirmary Rd. S6: Shef 6D 106
S41: C'fld 4H 167
S62: P'gte 5H 83
Infirmary Road Stop (ST) 1D 118
Ingbirchworth Rd.
S36: Thurl 3A 176
Ingelow Av. S5: Shef 5G 93
Ingfield Av. S9: Tins 2H 109
Ingleborough Cft. S35: Chap 2E 79
Ingleborough Dr. DN5: Don 2F 55
Ingleby Cl. S18: Dron W 3B 154
Ingledene M. DN3: Barn D 1C 26
Ingle Gro. DN5: Don 2F 55
Inglenook Ct. S66: Malt 6D 102
(off Sousa St.)
Ingleton M. S71: Smi 2F 17
Ingleton Rd. S41: Has 3A 172
Ingleton Wlk. S70: Barn 6C 16
Inglewood S75: Dart 5H 7
Inglewood Av. S20: Sot 1H 151
Inglewood Ct. S20: Sot 1H 151
Inglewood Dell S20: Sot 1H 151
Ingram Cl. S2: Shef 4A 120
Ingram Rd. S2: Shef 4A 120
Ingsfield Cl. S63: Bolt D 2A 50
Ingsfield La. S63: Bolt D 2F 49
(not continuous)
Ingshead Av. S62: Rawm 3G 83
Ings La. DN5: Ark 6E 25
(Arksey Comn. La.)
DN5: Ark 6D 24
(Chadwick Gdns.)
DN5: Sprot 2F 55
S72: Lit H 3C 34
Ings Rd. DN5: Bntly, Don 5A 40
DN5: Cad 6G 53
S73: Womb 6A 34
(not continuous)
Ings Way DN5: Ark 6C 24
Inkerman Cotts. S40: Ash 4D 166
Inkerman Rd. S73: D'fld 5B 34
Inkersall Dr. S20: W'fld 2F 151
INKERSALL GREEN 1H 169
Inkersall Grn. Rd. S43: Ink 6G 163
Inkersall Rd. S43: Ink, Stav 6B 164
Innovate Pk. S63: Wath D 1C 66
Innovation Way S13: Shef 6G 123
S75: Barn 4B 16
Insall Way DN9: Auck 3A 76
Insley Gdns. DN4: Bess 5B 58
Institute of Sports 5D 108
INTAKE
DN2 ....6F 41
S12 ....3D 134
Intake Cres. S75: Dod 4G 29
Intake Gdns. S75: Barn 6A 16
(off Wade St.)
Intake La. S72: Cud 6F 11
S75: Barn 5A 16
Interchange Way S70: Barn 6E 17
S71: Barn 6E 17
Iport DN11: New R 4G 73
Iquarter S3: Shef 1G 5
Ireland Bus. Pk. S43: Stav 5C 164
Ireland Cl. S43: Stav 5C 164
Ireland Ind. Est. S43: Stav 6B 164
Ireland St. S43: Stav 4C 164

Irongate S40: C'fld 5H 167
(off High St.)
Ironside Cl. S14: Shef 6A 134
Ironside Pl. S14: Shef 5B 134
Ironside Rd. S14: Shef 6A 134
Ironside Wlk. S14: Shef 6A 134
Ironstone Cres. S35: Chap 1E 79
Ironstone Dr. S35: Chap 1E 79
Ironworks Pl. S74: Els 2E 63
(off Wath Rd.)
Ironworks Row S74: Els 2E 63
(off Wath Rd.)
Irving St. S9: Shef 2F 121
Irwell Gdns. DN4: Can 2A 58
Isinglass Dr. DN12: New E 4D 70
Island Cl. S60: Roth 1B 112
Islay St. S10: Shef 3A 118
Islington Dr. DN4: Bess 6C 58
Issott St. S71: Barn 5E 17
Ivanbrook Cl. S18: Dron W 3B 154
Ivanhoe Av. S26: Kiv P 5B 140
Ivanhoe Cl. DN5: Don 6G 39
Ivanhoe M. S26: Swal 6B 124
Ivanhoe Rd. DN3: Eden 1C 42
DN4: Balb 6F 55
DN12: Con 4E 69
DN12: New E 5C 70
S6: Shef 6H 105
S66: Thurc 6B 114
Ivanhoe Way DN5: Don 6G 39
Ivor Gro. DN4: Balb 4H 55
Ivy Cl. DN11: Ross 5D 74
S41: Old W 4H 161
Ivy Cott. La. S11: Shef 2E 131
Ivy Cotts. S11: Shef 1F 131
S71: R'ton 2A 10
S74: Black H 3A 46
Ivy Ct. DN12: Old D 4B 90
S8: Shef 6H 133
S72: Cud 2E 19
Ivy Dr. S10: Shef 2C 118
Ivy Farm Cl. S71: Car 5A 10
Ivy Farm Ct. DN5: Barnb 1H 51
Ivy Farm Cft. S65: Dalt 1C 98
Ivy Gro. S10: Shef 2C 118
(off Ivy Dr.)
Ivy Hall Rd. S5: Shef 4B 94
Ivy Ho. Ct. DN9: Auck 1G 59
Ivy Ho. Farm La. S43: Brim 1D 168
Ivy La. S20: Beig 4H 137
Ivy Pk. Ct. S10: Shef 5F 117
Ivy Pk. Rd. S10: Shef 4F 117
Ivy Side Cl. S21: Killa 4C 152
Ivy Side Gdns. S21: Killa 4C 152
Ivy Spring Cl. S42: W'orth 6A 172
Ivy Ter. S70: Barn 2F 31

J

Jack Cl. Orchard S71: R'ton 2H 9
Jackdaw Dr. S63: Wath D 4F 49
Jackey La. S35: Ough 3C 90
Jackson Cres. S62: Rawm 1F 83
Jackson St. S63: Gol 5D 36
S72: Cud 2D 18
Jackson Way S61: Grea 5D 82
Jacobs Cl. S5: Shef 6B 94
Jacobs Dr. S5: Shef 6B 94
Jacobs Hall Ct. S75: Kexb 6D 6
Jacques Pl. S71: Barn 6A 18
Jamaica St. S4: Shef 5A 108
James Andrew Cl. S8: Shef 3E 147
James Andrew Cres.
S8: Shef 3D 146
James Andrew Cft. S8: Shef 3E 147
James Rd. DN6: Adw S 1E 23
James St. S9: Shef 3F 121
S41: C'fld 2H 167
S60: Roth 3D 96
(not continuous)
S64: Mexb 1A 68
S70: Wors 5H 31
S71: Barn 6E 17
S72: Sth H 1A 12
James Walton Ct. S20: Half 3G 151
James Walton Rd. S20: Half 3G 151
James Walton Pl. S20: Half 3G 151
James Walton Vw. S20: Half 3G 151
Janet's Wlk. S73: Womb 6D 32
Janson St. S9: Shef 4D 108

Jardine Cl. S9: Shef 6D 94
Jardine St. S9: Shef 6E 95
  S73: Womb 2G 47
Jarratt St. DN1: Don 2C 56
Jarrow Rd. S11: Shef 6C 118
Jasmine Av. S20: Beig 5G 137
Jasmine Cl. DN12: Con 5G 69
Jasmine Gdns. S66: Swal 6B 124
Jaunty Av. S12: Shef 5E 135
Jaunty Cl. S12: Shef 5E 135
Jaunty Cres. S12: Shef 4E 135
Jaunty Dr. S12: Shef 5E 135
Jaunty La. S12: Shef 4E 135
Jaunty Mt. S12: Shef 5E 135
Jaunty Pl. S12: Shef 5E 135
Jaunty Rd. S12: Shef 5F 135
Jaunty Vw. S12: Shef 5F 135
Jaunty Way S12: Shef 4E 135
Jawbones Hill S40: C'fld 2H 171
Jay La. S26: Aston 2D 138
Jebb Gdns. S40: Bramp 6D 166
Jebb La. S75: Haigh 3A 6
Jedburgh Dr. S9: Shef 6D 94
Jedburgh St. S9: Shef 6D 94
Jeffcock Pl. S35: High G 1D 78
Jeffcock Rd. S61: Shef 2F 121
  S35: High G 1D 78
Jefferson Av. DN2: Don 1A 42
Jeffery Cres. S36: Spink 4F 175
Jeffery Grn. S10: Shef 1A 130
Jeffery St. S2: Shef 2G 133
Jenkin Av. S9: Shef 1D 108
Jenkin Cl. S9: Shef 1D 108
Jenkin Dr. S9: Shef 2D 108
Jenkin Rd. S5: Shef 1C 108
  S9: Shef 1D 108
Jenkinson Gro. DN3: Arm 4C 42
Jenkin Wood Cl. S66: Sunn 3H 99
Jennings Cl. S65: Roth 2F 97
Jenny La. S72: Cud 2E 19
Jepson Rd. S5: Shef 6C 94
  S41: Has 3B 172
Jericho St. S3: Shef 1A 4 (2E 119)
Jermyn Av. S12: Shef 4H 135
Jermyn Cl. S12: Shef 5A 136
Jermyn Cres. S12: Shef 5A 136
Jermyn Cft. S75: Dod 3G 29
Jermyn Dr. S12: Shef 5A 136
Jermyn Sq. S12: Shef 5A 136
Jermyn Way S12: Shef 5A 136
Jersey Rd. S2: Shef 1F 133
Jervis Pl. S43: Ink 2G 169
Jesmond Av. S71: R'ton 3G 9
Jessamine Rd. S5: Shef 6B 94
Jessell St. S9: Shef 1C 120
Jessop Ct. S25: Din 4A 128
Jessop St. S1: Shef 6D 4 (4F 119)
Jetstream Dr. DN9: Finn 2C 76
Jewitt Rd. S61: Kimb P 6H 81
Jew La. S1: Shef 3G 5
Joan La. S66: Hoot L 6H 101
Joan Royd La. S36: Cub 6B 176
Jockell Dr. S62: Rawm 3G 83
Jockey Rd. S36: Oxs 5H 177
John Calvert Rd. S13: Shef 2E 137
John Eaton's Almshouses
  S8: Shef 6G 133
John Hartop Pl. S74: Els 2E 63
            (off Wath Rd.)
John Hibbard Av. S13: Shef 1F 137
John Hibbard Cl. S13: Shef 1F 137
John Hibbard Cres. S13: Shef ...1F 137
John Hibbard Ri. S13: Shef 1F 137
John La. DN11: New R 5B 74
Johnson Ct. DN12: New E 3D 70
  S65: Roth 5G 97
         (off Johnson St.)
Johnson Gdns. S63: Wath D 5E 49
Johnson La. S3: Shef 1F 5 (2G 119)
  S35: Eccl 1G 93
Johnson St. S3: Shef 1F 5 (1G 119)
  S36: Stoc 3D 174
  S65: Roth 5G 97
  S75: Barn 6C 16
Johnstone Cl. S40: C'fld 1G 171
John St. S2: Shef 5E 119
  S21: Ecki 1E 159
  S40: C'fld 5F 167
  S43: Brim 6D 162
  S60: Roth 4D 96
  S66: Thurn 2C 36

John St. S64: Mexb 2F 67
  S66: Thurc 5B 114
  S70: Barn 2E 31
  S70: Wors 6F 31
  S72: Gt H 1F 35
  S72: Midd 3F 35
  S73: Womb 1F 47
John St. Ct. S73: Womb 6F 33
John St. Way S73: Womb 6F 33
John Trickett Ho. S35: Chap 2E 79
          (off Bevan Way)
John Ward St. S13: Shef 1E 137
John West St. S36: Stoc 4D 174
Joiner St. S3: Shef 1F 5 (2G 119)
Jones Av. S73: Womb 1E 47
Jons Av. WF9: Sth K 4H 13
JORDAN 5A 96
Jordan Cres. S61: Kimbgham 5H 95
Jordan Hill S75: Barn 5C 16
JORDANTHORPE 4G 147
Jordanthorpe Cen. S8: Shef 4G 147
Jordanthorpe Grn. S8: Shef 4H 147
Jordanthorpe Parkway S8: Shef ..3G 147
Jordanthorpe Vw. S8: Shef 3H 147
Joseph Ct. S70: Barn 2E 31
Josephine Rd. S61: Roth 4B 96
Joseph Rd. S6: Shef 1B 118
Joseph Stone Ct. S20: Mosb 3E 151
Joseph St. S21: Ecki 1E 159
  S70: Barn 2E 31
  S72: Grim 2B 20
Joshua Rd. S7: Shef 2D 132
Josselin Ct. S35: Chap 3E 79
Jossey La. DN5: Bntly, Scawt ...2E 39
Jowitt Cl. S66: Malt 6C 102
Jowitt Rd. S11: Shef 2A 132
Jubb Cl. S65: Roth 6C 98
Jubilee Cl. DN12: New E 4C 70
  WF9: Hems 1G 13
Jubilee Cotts. S44: Cal 1F 173
  S60: Brins 3C 110
  S74: Hoyl 1F 61
         (off Sheffield Rd.)
Jubilee Ct. DN2: Don 4H 41
Jubilee Cres. S21: Killa 3D 152
Jubilee Gdns. S71: R'ton 2A 10
Jubilee Rd. DN1: Don 5D 40
  S9: Shef 6E 109
Jubilee St. S60: Roth 6E 97
Jubilee Ter. S70: Barn 2G 31
Judith Rd. S26: Aston 2C 138
Judy Row S71: Monk B 4H 17
Juggernaut Trade Cen. S71: Smi ..3F 17
Julian Rd. S9: Shef 1E 109
Julian Way S9: Shef 1E 109
Jumble La. S35: Eccl 1A 94
Jumble Rd. S11: Shef 6A 130
JUMP 5D 46
Junction 34 Ind. Est. S9: Tins ..3G 109
Junction Cl. S73: Womb 3B 48
Junction Rd. DN11: New R 6A 74
  S11: Shef 6B 118
  S13: Shef 1E 137
Junction St. S70: Barn 2G 31
  S73: Womb 3A 48
Junction Ter. S70: Barn 2G 31
June Rd. S13: Shef 1E 137
Jungle, The 5G 161
Juniper Cl. S43: Hol 4F 163
Juniper Ri. S21: Killa 5B 152

Keats Gro. S36: Pen 3D 176
Keats Rd. DN4: Balb 6A 56
  S6: Shef 4C 92
  S41: C'fld 6G 161
Keats Way S42: Gras 6D 172
Keble Martin Way
  S63: Wath D 6E 49
Kedleston Cl. S41: C'fld 1D 166
Kedleston Ct. S43: Stav 4B 164
         (off Porter St.)
Keeper La. WF4: Nott 1C 8
Keepers Cl. DN11: Ross 4E 75
  S5: Shef 6A 94
Keepers La. S18: Barl 3A 160
Keemoat Stadium 4F 57
Keeton Hall Rd. S26: Kiv P 5C 140
Keeton's Hill S2: Shef 6E 119
Keighley Vw. DN12: Con 5C 68
Keilder Ct. S40: W'ton 1E 171
Keir Pl. S62: Rawm 2A 84
Keir St. S70: Barn 6C 16
Keir Ter. S70: Barn 6C 16
Kelburn Av. S40: W'ton 1D 170
Kelby Cft. S75: Bar G 3G 15
Kelgate S20: Mosb 4E 151
KELHAM BANK 3B 56
Kelham Ct. DN1: Don 3B 56
KELHAM ISLAND 1F 119
Kelham Island S3: Shef 1F 119
Kelham Island Mus. 1F 119
Kelham Sq. S3: Shef 1F 119
Kelham St. DN1: Don 3B 56
Kelley La. S63: Gol 5D 36
Kelsey Gdns. DN4: Bess 1B 74
Kelsey Ter. S70: Barn 3E 31
Kelso Dr. DN4: Warm 5E 55
Kelvin Cl. S65: Scho 6F 81
Kelvin Gro. S73: Womb 2H 47
Kelvin St. S64: Mexb 1F 67
Kemp Cl. S21: Killa 4B 152
Kempton Dr. DN7: Dunsv 4H 27
Kempton Gdns. S64: Mexb 6H 51
Kempton Pk. Rd. DN5: Scaws 4E 39
Kempton St. DN4: Can 2A 58
Kempwell Dr. S62: Rawm 6G 65
Kenbourne Gro. S7: Shef 1D 132
Kenbourne Rd. S7: Shef 1D 132
Kendal Av. S25: Nth A 2A 142
Kendal Cl. DN5: Sprot 3B 54
Kendal Cres. DN12: Con 4G 69
  S70: Wors 6F 31
Kendal Dr. S18: Dron W 3C 154
  S63: Bolt D 3B 50
Kendal Grn. S70: Wors 6D 30
Kendal Grn. Rd. S70: Wors 6D 30
Kendal Gro. S71: Ard 2D 32
Kendal Pl. S6: Shef 4A 106
Kendal Rd. DN5: Scawt 3H 39
  S6: Shef 4A 106
  S41: C'fld 6F 161
Kendal Va. S70: Wors 6F 31
KENDRAY 3A 32
Kendray St. S70: Barn 1E 31
Kenilworth Cl. DN5: Scaws 4E 39
Kenilworth Pl. S11: Shef 4G 131
Kenilworth Pl. S11: Shef 6B 118
Kenilworth Rd. DN4: Balb 5F 55
Kenmare Cres. DN2: Don 5F 41
Kennedy Ct. S10: Shef 3A 118
Kennedy Dr. S63: Gol 1C 50
Kennedy Rd. S8: Shef 6D 132
Kennels, The S62: Wentw 5F 63
Kenneth Av. DN7: Dunsv 4H 27
Kenneth St. S65: Roth 3F 97
Kennet Va. S40: C'fld 3E 167
Kenninghall Cl. S2: Shef 1A 134
Kenninghall Dr. S2: Shef 1A 134
Kenninghall Rd. S2: Shef 1A 134
Kenninghall Vw. S2: Shef 1A 134
Kennington Av. DN6: Woodl 3A 22
Kennington Gro. DN12: New E ...3D 70
Kenrock Cl. DN5: Ark 1D 40
Kensington Av. S36: Thurl 3A 176
Kensington Chase S10: Shef 6A 116
Kensington Cl. S25: Laugh C ...4F 127
Kensington Ct. S10: Shef 5A 116
Kensington Dr. S10: Shef 6A 116
Kensington Pk. S10: Shef 6A 116
Kensington Pl. DN4: Bess 6C 58
Kensington Rd. S75: Barn 5C 16
Kent Av. S62: Rawm 1F 83

Kaldo Ct. S60: Roth 1F 97
Kariba Cl. S41: C'fld 5A 168
Kashmir Gdns. S9: Shef 1E 121
Katherine Ct. S66: Thurc 6B 114
Katherine Rd. S66: Thurc 5B 114
Katherine St. S66: Thurc 6C 114
Kathleen Gro. S63: Gol 4E 37
Kathleen St. S63: Gol 4E 37
Kay Cres. S62: Rawm 6D 64
Kaye Pl. S10: Shef 2C 118
Kaye St. S71: Barn 6E 17
Kay's Ter. S70: Stair 3B 32
Kay's St. S74: Hoyl 1G 61
Kea Pk. Cl. S66: Hel 5D 100
Kearsley La. DN12: Con 6C 69
Kearsley Rd. S2: Shef 6F 119
Keats Dr. S25: Din 6C 128

Kent Cl. S41: C'fld 3G **167**
  S71: R'ton 2H **9**
Kent Ho. Cl. S12: Ridg 2H **149**
Kentmere Cl. S18: Dron W 3D **154**
Kentmere Dr. DN4: Don 5G **57**
Kentmere Way S43: Stav 6H **163**
Kent Rd. DN4: Balb 5A **56**
  S8: Shef 2G **133**
  S61: Kimb P 1H **95**
Kents Gro. S63: Gol 5F **37**
Kent St. S41: Has 2B **172**
Kenwell Dr. S17: Bradw 5A **146**
Kenwood Av. S7: Shef 1D **132**
Kenwood Bank S7: Shef 6D **118**
Kenwood Chase S7: Shef 6E **119**
        (off Wostenholm Rd.)
Kenwood Cl. S70: Stair 2A **32**
Kenwood Ct. S7: Shef 1C **132**
Kenwood Pk. Rd. S7: Shef 1D **132**
Kenwood Ri. S66: Bram 4H **99**
Kenwood Rd. S7: Shef 1C **132**
Kenworthy Rd. S36: Stoc 4D **174**
  S70: Barn 3E **31**
Kenyon All. S3: Shef 2B **4**
Kenyon Rd. S41: C'fld 1D **172**
Kenyon St. S1: Shef 2B **4** (2E **119**)
Keppel Dr. S61: Scho 6E **81**
Keppel Hgts. S61: Scho 6E **81**
Keppel Pl. S5: Shef 4B **94**
Keppel Rd. S5: Shef 4C **94**
  S61: Scho 6E **81**
Keppel's Column 6E **81**
Keppel Vw. Rd. S61: Kimb 2G **95**
Keppel Wharf S60: Roth 4E **97**
Kepple Cl. DN11: New R 6G **75**
Keresforth Cl. S71: Barn 2B **30**
Keresforth Ct. S70: Barn 2B **30**
Keresforth Hall Dr. S70: Barn 3B **30**
Keresforth Hall Rd. S70: Barn 3C **30**
Keresforth Hill Rd.
  S70: Barn 4A **30**
Keresforth M. S70: Barn 3A **30**
Keresforth Rd. S75: Dod 4G **29**
Kerwin Cl. S17: Dore 2D **144**
Kerwin Dr. S17: Dore 2D **144**
Kerwin Rd. S17: Dore 2D **144**
Kestrel Av. S61: Thorpe H 3D **80**
Kestrel Cl. S21: Killa 3A **152**
Kestrel Dr. DN6: Adw S 2C **22**
  DN11: Ross 5D **74**
  S21: Ecki 1C **158**
  S64: Mexb 6E **51**
Kestrel Grn. S2: Shef 4B **120**
Kestrel Ri. S26: Swal 1H **137**
  S70: Birdw 4E **45**
Keswick Cl. DN5: Scawt 2H **39**
  S6: Lox 4F **105**
Keswick Cres. S60: Brins 5C **110**
Keswick Dr. S41: C'fld 1D **166**
Keswick Pl. S18: Dron W 3C **154**
Keswick Rd. S75: Stain 3H **7**
Keswick Wlk. S71: Ard 2D **32**
Keswick Way S25: Nth A 2A **142**
Ket Hill La. S72: Brier 3A **12**
Kettlebridge Rd. S9: Shef 3D **120**
Ketton Av. S8: Shef 5G **133**
Ketton Wlk. S75: Barn 5B **16**
Kevin Gro. S66: Hel 6E **101**
Kew Ct. S64: Swin 5B **66**
Kew Cres. S12: Shef 6C **134**
KEXBROUGH 6D **6**
Kexbrough Dr. S75: Kexb 6C **6**
Key Av. S74: Hoyl 6C **46**
Keyworth Pl. S13: Shef 2B **136**
Keyworth Rd. S6: Shef 3B **106**
Khartoum Rd. S11: Shef 5C **118**
Kibroyd Dr. S75: Kexb 1D **14**
Kibworth Cl. S41: Has 3B **172**
Kidd La. S81: Fir 1H **129**
Kidsley Cl. S40: C'fld 3B **166**
Kieran Cl. S25: Laugh C 4F **127**
Kier Hardie Av. DN11: New R 6C **74**
Kilburn Rd. S18: Dron W 3B **154**
Kildale Gdns. S20: Mosb 3E **151**
Kildonan Gro. S12: Shef 5F **135**
Kilham La. DN3: Brant 3H **59**
KILLAMARSH 4C **152**
Killamarsh La. S26: Wooda 5F **153**
Killamarsh Leisure Cen. 3C **152**
Kiln Ct. DN3: Barn D 3C **26**
Kilncroft S73: Womb 3F **47**

Kilner Ct. DN12: Den M 2E **69**
Kilner Way S6: Shef 1C **106**
Kiln Hill S18: Coal A 1H **155**
KILNHURST 1D **84**
Kilnhurst Bus. Pk. S64: Kiln 2D **84**
Kilnhurst Rd. S62: Rawm 2H **83**
  S64: Kiln 2H **83**
  S65: Hoot R 1E **85**
Kiln Rd. S61: Kimb P 2A **96**
Kilnsea Wlk. S70: Barn 1D **30**
        (off Fitzwilliam St.)
Kiln St. S8: Shef 1E **133**
Kilton Hill S3: Shef 6G **107**
Kilton Pl. S3: Shef 6G **107**
Kilvington Av. S13: Shef 1E **135**
Kilvington Cres. S13: Shef 2E **135**
Kilvington Rd. S13: Shef 2E **135**
Kimberley St. S9: Shef 6C **108**
KIMBERWORTH 3H **95**
KIMBERWORTH PARK 1H **95**
Kimberworth Pk. Rd.
  S61: Kimb, Kimb P 6G **81**
        (not continuous)
Kimberworth Rd. S61: Kimb, Roth . . .3A **96**
Kinder Gdns. S5: Shef 5G **93**
Kinder Rd. S43: Ink 2G **169**
King Av. DN11: New R 5B **74**
  S66: Malt 6C **102**
Kingdom Cl. S66: Thurc 1D **126**
King Edward Rd. S17: Dore 5F **145**
King Edward Rd. DN4: Balb 4A **56**
King Edwards App. S6: Shef 3C **116**
King Edwards Gdns. S70: Barn 2D **30**
King Edwards Swimming Pool 4C **118**
King Edward St. S1: Monk B 2A **18**
Kingfield Ct. S11: Shef 1C **132**
Kingfield Rd. S11: Shef 1C **132**
Kingfisher Cl. DN2: Don 3G **41**
Kingfisher Cl. DN11: Ross 5D **74**
  DN12: Con 4A **70**
Kingfisher Dr. S64: Mexb 1B **68**
  S73: Bramp 3B **48**
Kingfisher Ho. S41: Old W 3A **162**
Kingfisher M. S73: Bramp 3C **48**
Kingfisher Ri. S61: Thorpe H 2D **80**
Kingfisher Rd. DN6: Adw S 2C **22**
King Georges Cl. DN11: New R 6A **74**
King George Sq. DN3: Kirk Sa 4C **26**
King George's Rd. DN11: New R 4A **74**
King George Ter. S70: Barn 2G **31**
King James St. S2: Shef 6C **106**
Kings Arc. DN1: Don 1B **56**
        (off St Sepulchre Ga.)
Kingsbrook Chase S63: Wath D 4E **49**
Kingsbury Ct. DN5: Scawt 1E **39**
Kingsclere Wlk. S40: Birdh 3G **171**
Kings Coppice S17: Dore 4E **145**
Kings Ct. S1: Shef 6B **4**
  S36: Pen 3C **176**
  S60: Roth 2H **111**
King's Cres. DN12: New E 3C **70**
Kings Cft. S70: Barn 2B **30**
  S70: Wors 6H **31**
Kingscroft Cl. S17: Dore 2F **145**
Kingsforth La. S66: Thurc 4B **114**
Kingsforth Rd. S66: Thurc 5B **114**
Kings Ga. S60: Roth 2H **111**
Kingsgate DN1: Don 1C **56**
Kingsgate Flats DN1: Don 1C **56**
        (off Cleveland St.)
Kingsland Cl. S71: R'ton 2A **10**
Kingsley Av. DN5: Don 6G **39**
  S40: Birdh 2G **171**
        (not continuous)
Kingsley Cl. S71: Ath 2F **17**
Kingsley Ct. S60: Roth 1E **111**
Kingsley Cres. DN3: Arm 4F **43**
Kingsley Dr. S65: Rav 2C **100**
Kingsley Pk. Av. S7: Shef 4A **132**
Kingsley Pk. Gro. S11: Shef 4A **132**
Kingsley Rd. DN6: Adw S 3B **22**
Kingsmark Way S63: Gol 5E **37**
Kingsmead Dr. DN3: Brant 4G **59**
Kingsmead Av. S40: W'ton 1E **171**
Kings M. DN1: Don 1C **56**
  S21: Ecki 1F **159**
King's Rd. DN1: Don 6D **40**
  S64: Mexb 1G **67**
  S72: Cud 5F **11**

Kings Rd. S73: Womb 2H **47**
King's Stocks S72: Bill, Midd 4F **35**
King's St. S72: Grim 2B **20**
Kings St. DN1: Don 1C **56**
Kingston Cl. DN3: Brant 3H **59**
KINGSTONE 3C **30**
Kingstone Pl. S70: Barn 3C **30**
Kingston Rd. DN2: Don 6G **41**
Kingston St. S4: Shef 5A **108**
King St. DN3: Arm 3C **42**
  S3: Shef 2F **5** (2G **119**)
  S26: Swal 6B **124**
  S35: Chap 2F **79**
  S43: Brim 5E **163**
  S63: Gol 5D **36**
  S63: Thurn 3D **36**
  S64: Swin 3C **66**
  S70: Barn 2E **31**
  S74: Hoyl 6B **46**
King St. Nth. S41: Whit M 1H **167**
King St. Sth. S40: Birdh 3H **171**
Kings Way S60: Roth 2H **111**
Kingsway S63: Thurn 2B **36**
  S72: Grim 1B **20**
  S73: Womb 2G **47**
  S75: Mapp 5H **7**
Kingsway Cl. DN11: New R 6H **75**
Kingsway Complex S25: Din 5A **128**
Kingsway Gro. S63: Thurn 2B **36**
Kingsway Ho. DN1: Don 1C **56**
Kingswood S6: Shef 6G **91**
  S11: Shef 2C **132**
Kingswood Av. S20: Mosb 6B **136**
  S25: Laugh M 2F **127**
Kingswood Cl. S20: Mosb 6B **136**
  S41: C'fld 5E **161**
  S81: Fir 1H **129**
Kingswood Ct. S81: Fir 1H **129**
Kingswood Cres. S74: Hoyl 5B **46**
Kingswood Cft. S20: Mosb 6B **136**
Kingswood Dearne Valley Outdoor
  Educational & Activity Centres
  . . . . .2E **69**
Kingswood Gro. S20: Mosb 6B **136**
Kingswood Hall S6: Shef 6G **91**
Kings Wood La.
  S25: Laugh M 1E **129**
  S66: Malt 1E **129**
Kingwell Cres. S70: Wors 4E **31**
Kingwell Cft. S70: Wors 5F **31**
Kingwell M. S70: Wors 5F **31**
Kingwell Rd. S70: Wors 5E **31**
Kingwood Cl. S71: Monk B 2C **18**
Kinharvie Rd. S5: Shef 1E **107**
Kinnaird Av. S5: Shef 5H **93**
Kinnaird Pl. S5: Shef 5H **93**
Kinnaird Rd. S5: Shef 5H **93**
Kinsey Rd. S35: High G 1B **78**
Kipling Av. DN4: Balb 6G **55**
Kipling Cl. S18: Dron 5H **155**
Kipling Rd. DN3: Barn D 1H **27**
  S6: Shef 4B **106**
  S41: C'fld 6G **161**
Kirby Cl. S9: Shef 2F **121**
  S41: Has 3B **172**
Kirby Dr. S12: Shef 4D **134**
Kirby La. S35: Chap 6A **62**
Kirby Row S61: Thorpe H 3C **80**
Kirby St. S64: Mexb 1F **67**
Kirk Balk S74: Hoyl 6A **46**
Kirk Cft. Rd.
  S25: Laugh M 2H **127**
Kirk Cross Cres. S71: R'ton 4H **9**
Kirkdale Cl. S40: C'fld 2A **172**
Kirkdale Cres. S13: Shef 5C **122**
Kirkdale Dr. S13: Shef 5C **122**
Kirk Edge Av. S35: Ough 6E **91**
Kirk Edge Dr. S35: Ough 6D **90**

Kirk Edge Rd. S6: Brad 5A 90
  S35: Ough 5A 90
Kirkers Cl. S63: Gol 6E 37
Kirkfield Cl. S75: Cawt 4A 14
Kirkfield Way S71: R'ton 4H 9
Kirkgate La. S72: Sth H 1E 11
Kirkham Cl. S71: Monk B 5H 17
Kirkham Pl. S71: Monk B 1A 18
Kirkhill Bank S36: Cub 6C 176
Kirkhill Cl. DN3: Arm 5F 43
Kirk Ho. S65: Roth 5A 98
  (off Browning Rd.)
Kirkland Gdns. S71: Monk B 3F 17
Kirklands Dr. S62: Rawm 2F 83
Kirk La. DN3: Kirk Sa 5B 26
KIRK SANDALL 4C 26
Kirk Sandall Ind. Est.
  DN3: Kirk Sa 4A 26
  (not continuous)
Kirk Sandall Network Cen.
  DN3: Kirk Sa 5A 26
Kirk Sandall Station (Rail) 4B 26
Kirkstall Cl. DN5: Scaws 5E 39
  S25: Sth A 5G 141
  S60: Brins 3B 110
Kirkstall Rd. S11: Shef 6B 118
  S71: Smi 1D 16
Kirkstead Abbey M.
  S61: Thorpe H 6D 80
Kirkstead Gdns. S13: Shef 1F 137
Kirkstead Rd. S61: Kimb 3D 94
Kirkstone Cl. DN5: Don 2H 39
Kirkstone Rd. S6: Shef 5B 106
  S41: C'fld 6D 160
Kirk St. DN4: Hex 2A 56
  S4: Shef 6H 107
Kirk Vw. S74: Hoyl 6A 46
Kirk Way S71: Monk B 5A 18
Kirkwood Cl. S36: Pen 5F 177
Kirstead Ct. DN4: Bess 1E 75
Kirton Rd. S4: Shef 5H 107
Kitchen Wood La.
  S18: Dron W, Holme 4A 154
Kitchin Rd. S73: Womb 1E 47
Kitson Ct. S63: Bramp B 5B 48
Kitson Dr. S71: Monk B 5A 18
Kiveton Bridge Station (Rail) 6A 140
Kiveton Gdns. S26: Kiv P 5C 140
Kiveton La. S26: Kiv P, Tod 3C 140
KIVETON PARK 5B 140
Kiveton Park Station (Rail) 6E 141
Knabbs La. S75: Silk C 5A 28
Knab Cl. S7: Shef 3B 132
Knab Cft. S7: Shef 3B 132
Knab Ri. S7: Shef 3B 132
Knab Rd. S7: Shef 3B 132
Knapton Av. S62: Rawm 2F 83
Knaresborough Cl. S26: Swal 1B 138
Knaresborough Rd.
  DN12: Con 5C 68
  S7: Shef 5B 132
Knavesmire Av. S25: Laugh C 4F 127
Knavesmire Gdns. DN4: Can 2A 58
Knifesmithgate S40: C'fld 5H 167
Knighton Cl. S41: Has 3A 172
Knightsbridge Ct. S40: C'fld 5G 167
Knoll, The S18: Dron 1A 156
  S40: Bramp 6A 166
Knollbeck Av. S73: Bramp 4B 48
Knoll Beck Cl. S63: Gol 6B 36
Knollbeck Cres.
  S73: Bramp 4B 48
Knollbeck La. S73: Bramp 4B 48
Knoll Cl. S36: Stoc 3E 175
Knoll M. S75: Wool G 3F 7
KNOLL TOP 3E 175
Knowle Cl. S6: Stan 6D 104
Knowle Cl. S11: Shef 3A 132
Knowle Cft. S11: Shef 3H 131
Knowle Grn. S17: Dore 3D 144
Knowle La. S11: Shef 3G 131
Knowle Rd. S5: Shef 4G 93
  S70: Barn, Wors 4G 31
Knowles Av. S36: Spink 4F 175
Knowles St. S36: Pen 5F 177
KNOWLE TOP 6D 104
Knowle Top S20: Half 3F 151
Knowsley St. S70: Barn 1C 30
Knutton Cres. S5: Shef 4D 92
Knutton Ri. S5: Shef 3D 92
Knutton Rd. S5: Shef 4D 92

Kyle Cl. S5: Shef 6D 92
Kyle Cres. S5: Shef 6D 92
Kynance Cres. S60: Brins 5C 110

L

Laburnum Av. S66: Sunn 4G 99
Laburnum Cl. S25: Sth A 4G 141
  S35: Chap 4F 79
Laburnum Ct. S44: Cal 5F 169
  S75: Bar G 4E 15
Laburnum Dr. DN3: Arm 3F 43
  S63: Bolt D 2B 50
Laburnum Gro. DN12: Con 5D 68
  S21: Killa 5B 152
  S36: Stoc 4D 174
  S70: Wors 6G 31
Laburnum Pde. S66: Malt 5G 101
Laburnum Pl. DN5: Bntly 6A 24
Laburnum Rd. DN4: Balb 6G 55
  S64: Mexb 4E 57
  S66: Malt 5G 101
Laburnum St. S43: Hoyl 5G 163
Laburnum Vw. S75: Bar G 4E 15
Laceby Cl. S66: Bram 3A 100
Laceby Ct. S70: Barn 3B 30
Ladies Spring Ct. S17: Dore 3H 145
  (off Ladies Spring Dr.)
Ladies Spring Dr. S17: Dore 3H 145
Ladies Spring Gro. S17: Dore 3H 145
Ladock Cl. S71: Monk B 5G 17
Lady Bank Dr. DN4: Don 3D 56
Ladybank Rd. S20: Mosb 4E 151
Lady Bank Vw. S21: Ecki 6E 151
Ladybower Cl. S17: Bradw 5H 145
Ladybower La. S43: Stav 6A 164
Lady Cft. S63: Wath D 6F 49
Ladycroft S63: Bolt D 2B 50
Lady Cft. La. S73: Hem 5F 47
Ladycroft Rd. DN3: Arm 6E 43
Lady Ida's Dr. S21: Ecki 6B 150
  (not continuous)
Lady Mary's Wlk. DN5: Hick 4H 37
Lady Mary Vw. DN5: Hick 3G 37
Ladymead S71: Monk B 4G 17
Lady Oak Rd. S65: Roth 1B 98
Lady Oak Way S65: Roth 1B 98
Ladyroyd S75: Silk C 5A 28
Ladyroyd Cft. S72: Cud 2E 19
Lady's Bri. S3: Shef 1F 5 (2G 119)
Ladyshaw Cres. S36: Pen 5E 177
Ladysmith Av. S7: Shef 2C 132
Ladywood Dr. S41: C'fld 1D 166
Ladywood Rd. S72: Grim 2C 20
Laird Av. S6: Shef 3H 105
Laird Dr. S6: Shef 3H 105
Laird Rd. S6: Shef 3H 105
Lairds Way S36: Pen 4E 177
Laithe Cft. S75: Dod 3G 29
Laithes Cl. S71: Ath 1G 17
Laithes Cres. S71: Ath 1E 17
Laithes La. S71: Ath 1E 17
Laithes Shop. Cen. S71: Ath 1E 17
Lake Cl. DN12: New E 5B 70
Lake Ct. DN6: Woodl 4D 22
Lakeen Rd. DN2: Don 6F 41
Lakeland Cl. S72: Cud 3E 19
Lakeland Dr. S25: Din, Nth A 2H 141
Lake Rd. DN6: Woodl 5D 22
Lakeside S6: Shef 5G 105
  S20: Holb 1A 152
Lakeside Blvd. DN4: Don 5F 57
Lakeside Cl. S41: Old W 2B 162
  S66: Sunn 2H 99
Lakeside Ct. S63: Bramp B 5A 48
Lakeside Vw. S36: Pen 1A 176
Lakeside Village DN4: Don 4E 57
Lake Vw. Av. S40: W'ton 1D 170
Lambcote Way S66: Malt 4C 102
Lambcroft La. S13: Shef 2D 136
Lambcroft Vw. S13: Shef 2D 136
Lamb Dr. S5: Shef 1C 106
Lambcroft S71: Car 5H 9
Lambe Flatt S75: Kexb 6D 6
Lambert Fold S75: Dod 3H 29
Lambert Rd. S70: Barn 3H 31
Lamberts La. S65: Thry 5E 85
Lambert St. S3: Shef 2D 4 (2F 119)
Lambert Wlk. S63: Wath D 4D 48
  S70: Barn 2H 31

Lambeth Rd. DN4: Balb 5A 56
Lambeth Rd. Cvn. Pk.
  DN4: Balb 5A 56
Lamb Hill Cl. S13: Shef 1G 135
Lamb La. S71: Monk B 3H 17
  S81: Fir 3D 128
Lambourne Ct. S41: Has 3B 172
Lambra Rd. S70: Barn 1E 31
Lambrell Av. S26: Kiv P 6H 139
Lambrell Grn. S26: Kiv P 6H 139
Lamb Rd. S5: Shef 1C 106
Lambs Flat La. S75: Kexb 1D 14
Lamp Post La. S25: Din 5A 128
Lanark Gdns. DN2: Don 5H 41
Lancar Ct. S71: Monk B 4F 17
Lancaster Av. DN2: Don 6H 41
  DN3: Kirk Sa 4C 26
Lancaster Cl. DN9: Auck 2B 76
Lancaster Ga. S70: Barn 1D 30
Lancaster Rd. S36: Stoc 3D 174
  S41: C'fld 6F 161
Lancaster St. S3: Shef 1E 119
  S63: Thurn 1D 36
  S70: Barn 1C 30
Lancelot Cl. S40: W'ton 2E 171
Lancing Rd. S2: Shef 6F 119
  (not continuous)
Landon Cl. S42: W'ton 3C 170
Landsdown Av. WF9: Sth K 5H 13
Landseer Cl. S14: Shef 6A 134
  S18: Dron 3D 154
Landseer Dr. S14: Shef 6B 134
Landseer Pl. S14: Shef 6B 134
Landseer Wlk. S14: Shef 6B 134
Lane, The S71: R'ton 2H 9
Lane Cotts. S71: R'ton 3H 9
LANE END 1F 79
Lane End M. S63: Thurn 2A 36
Lane End Rd. S60: Roth 2H 111
Lane End Vw. S60: Roth 1H 111
Laneham Cl. DN4: Bess 6A 58
Lane Head S35: Gren 2A 92
Lane Head Ct. S62: Rawm 2H 83
  S75: Stain 4H 7
Lane Head Ri. S75: Stain 4H 7
Lane Head S17: Tot 6D 144
  S75: Cawt 4A 14
Lanes, The S65: Roth 3A 98
Laneside Cl. DN4: Hex 3H 55
Langar Cl. DN5: Bntly 4H 23
Lang Av. S71: Lund 6B 18
Lang Cres. S71: Lund 6B 18
Langdale Cl. S40: C'fld 3A 166
Langdale Ct. S71: Barn 1E 31
Langdale Dr. DN5: Scawt 2G 39
  S18: Dron 1H 155
Langdale Rd. S8: Shef 3D 132
  S71: Barn 1F 31
  S75: Bar G 3F 15
Langdale Sq. S43: Brim 6C 162
Langdale Way S25: Din 1A 142
Langdon Rd. S61: Kimb P 2H 95
Langdon St. S11: Shef 6E 119
Langdon Wlk. S61: Kimb P 2H 95
  S70: Barn 6D 16
Langer Fld. Av. S40: Birdh 3H 171
Langer La. S40: Birdh 6F 171
  S42: W'orth 6F 171
Langer St. DN4: Hex 3H 55
Langford Cl. S75: Dod 3H 29
Langford Cft. S40: C'fld 1H 171
Langham Ind. Pk. S41: Cor 6F 173
Langhurst Cl. S40: Ash 4E 167
Langhurst Rd. S40: Ash 4E 167
Langley Cl. S40: C'fld 3B 166
  S65: Roth 3C 98
Langmere Cl. S70: Barn 1B 30
Langsett Av. S6: Shef 2H 105
Langsett Cl. S6: Shef 5C 106
Langsett Ct. DN4: Don 4G 57
  S71: Smi 1D 16
Langsett Cres. S6: Shef 5C 106
Langsett Gro. S6: Shef 6C 106
Langsett Ri. S6: Shef 5C 106
Langsett Rd. S6: Shef 4B 106
  S71: Smi 1D 16

Langsett Rd. Nth. S35: Ough 1D 90
Langsett Road Stop (ST) 6D 106
Langsett Rd. Sth. S35: Ough 3E 91
Langsett Wlk. S6: Shef 5C 106
Langthwaite La. DN5: Scawt 6E 23
Langthwaite Rd. DN5: Scawt 1E 39
Langton Gdns. DN3: Brant 4H 59
Langtree Av. S41: Old W 5H 161
Lansbury Av. DN11: New R 5D 74
   S35: Chap 3E 79
   S43: Mas M 2E 165
   S66: Malt 6C 102
Lansbury Ct. S21: Ecki 1E 159
Lansbury Pl. S62: Rawm 2B 84
Lansbury Rd. S21: Ecki 1E 159
Lansdowne Av. S41: C'fld 1F 167
Lansdowne Cl. S63: Thurn 2B 36
Lansdowne Cres. S64: Swin 4C 66
   S75: Dart 1E 15
Lansdowne Rd. DN2: Don 5H 41
   S43: Brim 1C 168
Lantern M. S73: Womb 6A 34
Lantern Theatre 1D 132
Lanyon Way S71: Monk B 5G 17
Lapwater Rd. S61: Wing 5A 82
Lapwater Wlk. S61: Wing 5A 82
Lapwing Va. S61: Thorpe H 2D 80
Larch Av. DN9: Auck 3A 76
   S21: Killa 5B 152
   S64: Wick 5G 99
Larch Cl. S73: D'fld 5B 34
Larch Dr. DN3: Arm 4E 43
   (not continuous)
Larches, The S64: Swin 3B 66
Larchfield Pl. S71: Monk B 3A 18
Larchfield Rd. DN4: Balb 5G 55
Larch Gro. DN12: Con 6D 68
   S26: Aston 6D 124
   S35: Chap 4F 79
Larch Hill S9: Shef 3H 121
Larch M. S65: Roth 2A 98
Larch Pl. S70: Barn 4G 31
Larch Rd. S21: Ecki 2C 158
   S66: Malt 4G 101
Larch Sq. DN9: Auck 2B 76
Larch Way S40: C'fld 3E 167
Lark Av. S60: Brins 4E 111
Larkhill Cl. S62: P'gte 5G 83
Larkin Gro. S5: Shef 5G 93
Larkspur Cl. DN3: Eden 1C 42
   S66: Swin 6A 66
Lark St. S6: Shef 6A 106
Larwood Gro. DN12: New E 3D 70
Latchmoor Cl. S75: Barn 4C 16
Latham Sq. DN3: Kirk Sa 3D 26
   S11: Shef 3F 131
Lathe Rd. S60: Roth 2B 112
Lathkill Av. S43: Ink 2G 169
Lathkill Cl. S13: Shef 1F 135
Lathkill Rd. S13: Shef 1F 135
Latimer Cl. S26: Kiv P 6C 140
Latin Gdns. DN5: Scaws 3D 38
Lauder Rd. DN4: Don 4H 39
Lauder St. S4: Shef 2A 108
Laudsdale Cl. S65: Roth 3C 98
Laudsdale Rd. S65: Roth 2B 98
LAUGHTON COMMON 3F 127
Laughton Comn. Rd.
   S66: Thurc 2D 126
LAUGHTON EN LE MORTHEN 1G 127
Laughton Mdws. S25: Laugh C 3F 127
Laughton Rd. DN4: Hex 2A 56
   S9: Shef 1E 109
   S25: Din 4A 128
   S66: Thurc 6C 114
Launce Rd. S5: Shef 6E 93
Laurel Av. DN5: Cus 5F 39
   S44: Ark T 5H 173
   S66: Bram 5A 100
   S70: Barn 3A 32
Laurel Cl. DN9: Finn 2G 77
   S21: Ecki 2D 158
   S25: Sth A 5G 141
Laurel Ct. S10: Shef 5A 118
Laurel Cres. S43: Hol 5F 163
Laurel Dr. S21: Killa 6B 152
Laurel Gth. Cl. S41: Old W 3A 162
Laurel Rd. DN3: Arm 3E 43
Laurel Sq. DN9: Auck 2B 76
Laurel Ter. DN4: Balb 5H 55
Laurence Cl. S41: Old W 4H 161

Lavender Cl. DN12: Con 5G 69
Lavender Ct. S70: Barn 3H 31
Lavender Way S5: Shef 1C 108
Laverack St. S13: Shef 5A 122
Laverdene Av. S17: Tot 6G 145
Laverdene Cl. S17: Tot 6F 145
Laverdene Dr. S17: Tot 6G 145
Laverdene Rd. S17: Tot 6F 145
Laverdene Way S17: Tot 6G 145
Laverock Way S5: Shef 5A 94
Lavinia Rd. S35: Gren 2D 92
Law Courts
   Barnsley 6D 16
Lawn, The S18: Dron 2G 155
   (not continuous)
Lawn Av. DN1: Don 1D 56
   DN6: Woodl 2A 22
Lawndale Fold S75: Dart 5G 7
Lawn Rd. DN1: Don 1D 56
Lawns, The S11: Shef 2A 132
Lawnswood Ct. DN4: Bess 4H 57
Lawns Wood Gdns.
   S65: Thry 4E 85
Lawn Vs. S44: Cal 5F 169
Lawnwood Dr. S63: Gol 5B 36
Lawrence Cl. S66: Rawm 5G 99
   S75: High'm 4F 15
Lawrence Ct. S60: Roth 3D 96
   S64: Swin 5B 66
Lawrence Dr. S64: Swin 4B 66
Lawrence St. S9: Shef 6C 108
Lawson Rd. S10: Shef 4A 118
Lawton La. S60: Roth 1F 111
Lawton Ter. S6: Shef 4A 106
Laxey Rd. S6: Shef 1F 117
Laxfield Cl. S40: W'ton 2D 170
Laxton Cl. S66: Malt 4G 101
Laxton Rd. S71: Ath 6E 9
Laycock Av. S26: Aston 1D 138
Layden Ct. S66: Malt 6H 101
Layden Dr. DN5: Scaws 2D 38
Layton Dr. S41: Old W 5A 162
Lazarus Exhibition Hall 1G 57
Lea, The S20: Water 6E 137
   S64: Swin 4A 66
LEA BROOK 3H 63
Lea Brook La. S62: Wentw 3H 63
Leabrook Rd.
   S18: Dron W 3B 154
Leach La. S64: Bess 2C 67
Leadbeater Dr. S12: Shef 3D 134
Leadbeater Rd. S12: Shef 4C 134
Leader Ct. S6: Shef 3A 106
Leader Rd. S6: Shef 3A 106
Leadhill Rd. S40: Ash 4B 166
Leadmill Rd. S63: Gol 5D 36
Leadmill Ct. S1: Shef 6F 5
Leadmill Point S1: Shef 6F 5
Leadmill Rd. S1: Shef 5F 5 (4G 119)
   S2: Shef 6F 5 (4G 119)
Leadmill St. S1: Shef 6F 5 (4G 119)
Leaf Cl. S66: Malt 4C 102
Leake Rd. S6: Shef 2B 106
Leamington Gdns. DN2: Don 5G 41
Leamington St. S10: Shef 2B 118
Leander Ct. S43: Stav 4C 164
Leapings La. S36: Thurl 4A 176
   (not continuous)
Lea Rd. S18: Dron 3F 155
   S71: Ath 1G 17
Leas, The DN5: Cus 5G 39
Lease Gate Rd. S60: Whis 2A 112
Leatham Av. S61: Roth 3B 96
Leaton Cl. S6: Lox 3E 105
Leavy Greave S3: Shef 4A 4 (3D 118)
Leavygreave Rd. S3: Shef 3A 4 (3D 118)
Leawood Pl. S6: Stan 6E 105
Ledbury Gdns. DN5: Scaws 5E 39
Ledbury Rd. S71: Ath 2E 17
Ledsham Ct. S74: Els 5E 47
Ledsham Rd. S60: Roth 6H 97
Ledstone Rd. S8: Shef 4D 132
Lee Av. S36: Spink 3F 175
Leebrook Av. S20: Mosb 1C 150
Leebrook Ct. S20: Mosb 1C 150
Leebrook Dr. S20: Mosb 1C 150
Leebrook Pl. S20: Mosb 1C 150
Lee Cft. S1: Shef 2E 5 (2F 119)
   S66: Malt 6C 102
Leedham Cl. S5: Shef 6C 94

Leedham Rd. S5: Shef 6C 94
   S65: Roth 6B 98
Leeds Av. S25: Nth A 1H 141
Leeds Rd. S9: Shef 6D 108
Lee Ho. La. S36: Stoc 4B 174
Lee La. S71: R'ton, Stain 4C 8
Lee Moor La. S6: Stan 5A 104
Lee Rd. S6: Lox 3E 105
   S6: C'fld 6D 168
Lees, The S8: Shef 5F 133
   S71: Ard 2E 33
Lees Av. S36: Pen 4D 176
Lees Comn. S18: Barl 6B 154
Lees Hall Av. S8: Shef 3G 133
Lees Hall Golf Course 6H 133
Lees Hall Pl. S8: Shef 3G 133
Lees Hall Rd. S8: Shef 3G 133
Lees Ho. Ct. S8: Shef 4F 133
Lees Nook S8: Shef 3F 133
Leeswood Cl. S41: C'fld 6E 161
Leewood Cl. S63: Bramp B 6A 48
Leger Ct. DN2: Don 1D 56
Leger Retail Cen. DN2: Don 2A 42
Leger Way DN2: Don 2F 57
Legion Dr. S26: Aston 1D 138
Leicester Av. DN2: Don 1F 57
Leicester Rd. S25: Din 5B 128
Leigh St. S9: Shef 5D 108
Leigh St. Ind. Est.
   S9: Shef 5D 108
Leighton Cl. S71: Barn 5E 17
Leighton Dr. S14: Shef 5C 134
Leighton Pl. S14: Shef 5C 134
Leighton Rd. S14: Shef 3B 134
Leighton Road Stop (ST) 5C 134
Leighton Vw. S14: Shef 3B 134
Leinster Av. DN2: Don 5F 41
Lemont Rd. S17: Tot 6F 145
Lengdale Ct. S62: Rawm 3G 83
Lennox Rd. DN2: Don 5G 41
   S6: Shef 3A 106
Lenthall's Back Row S40: Ash 5E 167
Lenton St. S2: Shef 6F 5 (5G 119)
Leonard Cl. S2: Shef 1D 134
Leopold Av. S25: Din 6A 128
Leopold Sq. S1: Shef 3D 4
Leopold St. S1: Shef 3E 5 (3F 119)
   S25: Din 5A 128
   S70: Barn 2C 30
Leppings La. S6: Shef 2B 106
Leppings Lane Stop (ST)
   Middlewood Rd. (North) 2B 106
   Middlewood Rd. (South) 3B 106
Lepton Gdns. S70: Stair 4A 32
Lescar La. S11: Shef 6B 118
Lescar Rd. S60: Wav 2C 122
Lesley Rd. S63: Gol 5D 36
Leslie Av. DN12: Con 4D 68
   S66: Malt 5G 101
Leslie Rd. S6: Shef 3A 106
   S70: Barn 2A 32
Lesmond Cres. S72: Midd 4F 35
Lestermoor Av. S26: Kiv P 6H 139
Letard Dr. S60: Brins 3D 110
Letsby Av. S9: Shef 6H 109
LETWELL 4H 129
Letwell Cl. DN4: Bess 1E 75
Levens Way S41: C'fld 6F 161
Leverick Dr. S62: Rawm 1B 84
Leverton Dr. S11: Shef 5E 119
Leverton Gdns. S11: Shef 5E 119
Leverton Way S65: Dalt 1D 98
Levet La. S4: Shef 1A 120
Levet Rd. DN4: Can 3C 58
Levett Cl. S66: Thurc 1C 126
Levett Dr. S66: Thurc 1C 126
Levick Cft. S74: Els 6C 46
Lewdendale S70: Wors 6F 31
Lewden Farm La. S70: Wors 6A 32
Lewden Gth. S70: Wors 6A 32
Lewes Rd. DN12: Con 5E 69
Lewis Rd. S13: Shef 1F 135
   S71: Lund 1B 18
Lewyns Dr. DN4: Can 3C 58
Leybourne Rd. S61: Kimb P 1H 95
Leyburn Cl. DN4: Can 2C 58
   S40: C'fld 3E 167
Leyburn Dr. S26: Swal 6B 124
Leyburn Gro. S35: Chap 2F 79
Leyburn Rd. S8: Shef 2E 133
Ley End S70: Wors 6E 31

Leyfield Ct. DN3: Arm 5F **43**
Leyfield Pl. S73: Womb 6A **34**
Leyfield Rd. S17: Dore 3E **145**
Leylands, The
    S75: Barn 4A **16**
Leyland Wlk. S75: Barn 4A **16**
Leys, The WF9: Sth K 5H **13**
Leys Cl. DN4: Balb 2G **71**
Leys La. S25: Din 5C **128**
Liberty Cl. S6: Shef 1F **117**
Liberty Dr. S6: Shef 1F **117**
LIBERTY HILL 1F **117**
Liberty Hill S6: Shef 1F **117**
Liberty Pl. S6: Shef 1F **117**
Liberty Rd. S6: Shef 1F **117**
Libra Dr. DN4: Balb 2C **72**
Library Cl. S61: Wing 5B **82**
Library Pk. S70: Barn 2A **30**
Lichen Cl. DN3: Eden 1C **42**
Lichfield Gdns.
    DN12: New E 5B **70**
Lichfield Rd. DN2: Don 4E **41**
    S40: W'ton 2D **170**
Lichfield Way
    S60: Brins 4E **111**
Lichford Rd. S2: Shef 2H **133**
Lidgate La. S72: Shaft 3E **11**
LIDGET 2H **59**
Lidget Cl. DN4: Bess 5B **58**
    S26: Swal 2A **138**
    S63: Thurn 3D **36**
Lidget La. DN5: Hick 3D **36**
    S63: Thurn 3D **36**
    S65: Bram 4A **100**
Lidget La. Ind. Est.
    S63: Thurn 2E **37**
Lidgett Gdns. DN9: Auck 2H **59**
Lidgett Grange S74: Hoyl 4H **61**
Lidgett La. S25: Din 6A **128**
    S75: Pil 1C **60**
Lidgett Way S71: R'ton 2H **9**
Lidster La. S25: Sth A 4H **141**
Lifestyle Ho. S10: Shef 4B **118**
Liffey Av. DN2: Don 5F **41**
Lifford Pl. S74: Els 1E **63**
Lifford Rd. DN2: Don 5E **41**
Lifford St. S9: Tins 1H **109**
LIGHTWOOD
    S21 . . . . .2A **158**
    S8 . . . . .1C **148**
Lightwood La. S8: Shef 1B **148**
    S21: Midd H 3H **157**
Lightwood Rd. S21: Mar L 3H **157**
Lilac Av. S36: Stoc 4D **174**
Lilac Cl. S25: Sth A 4G **141**
Lilac Cres. DN12: New E 5C **70**
    S74: Hoyl 5B **46**
Lilac Farm Cl. S66: Wick 6G **99**
Lilac Gro. DN4: Can 4C **58**
    DN9: Auck 2B **76**
    DN12: Con 5D **68**
    S66: Bram 5H **99**
    S66: Malt 5G **101**
Lilac Rd. DN3: Arm 3F **43**
    S5: Shef 1B **108**
    S20: Beig 5G **137**
Lilacs, The S71: R'ton 2B **10**
Lilac St. S43: Hol 5F **163**
Lilac Way S72: Brier 4B **12**
Lilian St. S60: Roth 5F **97**
Lilian St. Sth. S60: Roth 5F **97**
Lilleymede Cl.
    S40: Birdh 4G **171**
Lillford Rd. DN3: Brant 4H **59**
Lilly Hall Cl. S66: Malt 4G **101**
Lilly Hall Rd. S66: Malt 4G **101**
Lilydene Av. S72: Grim 1A **20**
Lily Ter. S74: Jum 5C **46**
Limb La. S17: Dore 2E **145**
Limbreck Cl. DN5: Bntly 1H **39**
Limbrick Cl. S6: Shef 5B **106**
Limbrick Rd. S6: Shef 5B **106**
Lime Av. DN9: Auck 2B **76**
    S43: Stav 5B **164**
    S81: Fir .1H **129**
Lime Cl. S44: Cal 5F **169**
    S65: Rav 6A **86**
Lime Ct. DN5: Sprot 3E **55**
Limecroft Vw. S42: W'orth 6H **171**
Limedale Vw.
    DN3: Barn D 2D **26**

Lime Gro. S35: Chap 4F **79**
    S36: Stoc 4D **174**
    S60: Roth 6H **97**
    S64: Swin 4C **66**
    S66: Malt 5C **102**
    S71: Car .5H **9**
Limekiln La. S66: Stain 2F **103**
              (Stainton La.)
    S66: Stain 6F **89**
              (Tickhill Bk. La.)
Limekilns S25: Nth A 2G **141**
Limelands Rd. S25: Din 5H **127**
Lime Rd. S21: Ecki 3C **158**
Limes, The S60: Roth 6H **97**
Limes Av. S75: Barn 5A **16**
    S75: Stain 4B **8**
Limes Cl. S75: Stain 4B **8**
Limestone Cl. S81: Woods 5F **143**
Limestone Cott. La. S6: Shef 6A **92**
Lime St. S6: Shef 6D **106**
    S20: Beig 4G **137**
Limesway S66: Malt 5A **102**
    S75: Barn 5A **16**
Lime Tree Av. DN3: Arm 3E **43**
    DN4: Don 2D **56**
    S21: Killa 5B **152**
Limetree Av. S26: Kiv P 5H **139**
    S66: Thurc 6C **114**
Lime Tree Cl. S72: Cud 1E **19**
Limetree Cl. S43: Brim C 3E **169**
Lime Tree Ct. DN4: Don 3E **57**
Lime Tree Cres. DN11: New R 6D **74**
Limetree Cres. S62: Rawm 2A **84**
Lime Tree Gro. S44: Ark T 5H **173**
Lime Tree Wlk. DN12: Den M 2C **68**
Limpool Cl. DN4: Can 6C **58**
Limpsfield Rd. S9: Shef 2D **108**
Linacre Ho. S40: C'fld 1H **171**
            (off Archdale Cl.)
Linacre Rd. S40: Ash, C'fld 4B **166**
LINACRE WOODS 3B **166**
Linaker Rd. S6: Shef 6H **105**
Linburn Cl. S71: R'ton 2F **9**
Linburn Rd. S8: Shef 6E **133**
Linby Rd. S71: Ath 6E **9**
Lincoln Cl. DN12: Den M 4C **68**
Lincoln Gdns. S63: Gol 5C **36**
Lincoln Rd. DN2: Don 4E **41**
Lincolnshire Way DN3: Arm 3H **43**
Lincoln St. DN11: New R 4B **74**
    S9: Shef 2E **109**
    S40: Birdh 2H **171**
    S60: Roth 2E **97**
    S66: Malt 6B **102**
Lincroft Cl. S63: Gol 6C **36**
Lincroft Dr. S62: P'gte 5G **83**
Lindale Cl. S25: Nth A 3A **142**
Lindale Gdns. S63: Gol 6E **37**
Lindale Gro. WF9: Hems 1F **13**
Lindale Rd. S41: C'fld 5E **161**
Lindales, The S75: Barn 6B **16**
Linden Av. S8: Shef 6D **132**
    S18: Dron 1G **155**
    S40: Bramp 1C **170**
    S66: Wick 4H **99**
Linden Ct. S10: Shef 5A **118**
    S35: Eccl 1G **93**
Linden Cres. S36: Stoc 3D **174**
Linden Dr. S41: Has 4C **172**
Linden Gro. DN12: New E 5C **70**
    S66: Malt 5G **101**
Linden Pk. Gro. S40: C'fld 5F **167**
Linden Rd. S35: Eccl 1G **93**
    S63: Wath D 6C **48**
Linden Wlk. DN5: Bntly 4H **23**
Lindholme Dr. DN11: Ross 4E **75**
Lindholme Gdns. S20: Mosb 6D **136**
Lindhurst Lodge S71: Ath 6E **9**
Lindhurst Rd. S71: Ath 6D **8**
Lindisfarne Cl. S40: W'ton 1D **170**
Lindisfarne Rd. S18: Dron 4G **155**
Lindley Cl. DN9: Finn 3F **77**
Lindley Cres. S63: Thurn 3C **36**
Lindley Rd. DN9: Finn 3F **77**
    S5: Shef 2A **108**
Lindley's Cft. S26: Tod 3C **140**
Lindley St. S65: Roth 2F **97**
Lindrick Av. S64: Swin 4D **66**
Lindrick Cl. DN4: Bess 6H **57**
    DN12: Con 3H **69**
    S72: Cud 5F **11**

Lindrick Ct. S81: Woods 5G **143**
Lindrick Dr. DN3: Arm 5E **43**
Lindrick Gdns. S40: W'ton 2D **170**
Lindrick Golf Course 6F **143**
Lindrick Rd. S81: Woods 5F **143**
Lindsay Av. S5: Shef 5F **93**
Lindsay Cres. S5: Shef 5G **93**
Lindsay Dr. S5: Shef 5G **93**
Lindsay Pl. S26: Swal 1C **138**
Lindsay Rd. S5: Shef 5G **93**
Lindsey Cl. DN4: Bess 1A **74**
Lindum Dr. S66: Wick 6H **99**
Lindum St. DN4: Hex 2A **56**
Lindum Ter. S65: Roth 4F **97**
Lindup Rd. S18: Dron W 2D **154**
Lineside La. S71: R'ton 2B **10**
Lingamoor Leys S63: Thurn 1C **36**
Lingard La. S35: Ough 5E **91**
Lingard St. S75: Barn 5C **16**
Lingfield Cl. S66: Bram 6B **100**
Lingfield Dr. DN5: Scaws 5E **39**
Lingfield Wlk. S64: Mexb 6H **51**
Lingfoot Av. S8: Shef 4G **147**
Lingfoot Cl. S8: Shef 4G **147**
Lingfoot Cres. S8: Shef 4G **147**
Lingfoot Dr. S8: Shef 4G **147**
Lingfoot Pl. S8: Shef 4G **147**
Lingfoot Wlk. S8: Shef 4H **147**
Lingmoor Cl. DN4: Balb 6F **55**
Lingodell Cl. S25: Laugh M 2A **128**
Ling Rd. S40: W'ton 2E **171**
Lings, The DN3: Arm 5G **43**
    S66: Bram 6A **100**
Lings La. S66: Wick 6H **99**
Lingthwaite S75: Dod 3H **29**
Link, The S75: Dod 4H **29**
Link Rd. S65: Thry 6F **85**
Link Row S2: Shef 2H **119**
            (off Hyde Pk. Ter.)
Links Rd. S18: Dron 4G **155**
Links Vw. S75: Stain 4A **8**
Linkswood Av. DN2: Don 3H **41**
Linkswood Rd. S65: Dalt 1C **98**
Linkway DN2: Don 4G **41**
Linley La. S12: Shef 3G **135**
    S13: Shef 3G **135**
Linnet Ho. S41: Old W 3H **161**
Linnet Mt. S61: Thorpe H 3C **80**
Linscott Cl. S41: C'fld 1E **167**
Linscott Rd. S8: Shef 6D **132**
Linthwaite La. S62: Wentw 2F **63**
    S74: Els .2F **63**
Linton Cl. S70: Barn 2A **30**
Linton Rd. S40: W'ton 2D **170**
Lipp Av. S21: Killa 3B **152**
Liskeard Pl. DN6: Adw S 3B **22**
Lisle Rd. S60: Roth 6H **97**
Lismore Rd. S8: Shef 3G **133**
Lister Av. DN4: Balb 4A **56**
    S12: Shef 4E **135**
    S62: Rawm 1F **83**
Lister Cl. S12: Shef 5E **135**
    S41: C'fld 4H **167**
Lister Ct. DN2: Don 5F **41**
Lister Cres. S12: Shef 5D **134**
LISTERDALE 6F **99**
Listerdale Shop. Cen. S65: Roth 6D **98**
Lister Pl. S12: Shef 5E **135**
Lister Rd. S6: Shef 5B **106**
Lister Row S72: Gt H 5E **21**
Lister St. S65: Roth 4G **97**
Lister Way S12: Shef 5E **135**
Little Bri. Rd. S60: Roth 1F **97**
Lit. Brind Rd. S41: C'fld 1C **166**
Lit. Cockhill La. DN12: Old E 1C **88**
LITTLE COMMON 5H **131**
Little Comn. La. S11: Shef 5G **131**
    S60: Whis 3D **112**
    S61: Kimb 3G **95**
Littledale Rd. S9: Shef 4F **121**
Lit. Fell Rd. S5: Shef 3E **93**
Littlefield La. S73: Womb 1G **47**
            (not continuous)
Littlefield Rd. S25: Din 5H **127**
Lit. Haynooking La.
    S66: Malt 5A **102**
Littlehey Cl. S66: Malt 4G **101**
LITTLE HOUGHTON 2D **34**
Lit. Houghton La. S73: D'fld 4C **34**

Little La. DN2: Long S 1H 41
 DN5: Sprot 6B 38
 S4: Shef .3B 108
 S12: Shef 2E 135
 S61: Scho 4E 81
 S61: Thorpe H 2B 80
Little La. Ind. Est. DN2: Long S 1G 41
Little Leeds S74: Hoyl 6B 46
Lit. London Pl. S8: Shef 2E 133
Lit. London Rd. S8: Shef 4D 132
Lit. Matlock Gdns. S6: Stan 6E 105
Lit. Matlock Way S6: Stan 6E 105
Littlemoor S21: Ecki 1F 159
 S41: C'fld 2E 167
Littlemoor Av. S26: Kiv P 6H 139
Littlemoor Bus. Cen. S21: Ecki 6F 151
Littlemoor Cen. S41: C'fld 1E 167
Littlemoor Cres. S41: C'fld 1E 167
Littlemoor La. DN4: Balb 3A 56
Littlemoor St. DN4: Balb 3A 56
Little New Cl. S75: Barn 5A 16
LITTLE NORTON 2F 147
Lit. Norton Av. S8: Shef 3F 147
Lit. Norton Dr. S8: Shef 2F 147
Lit. Norton La. S8: Shef 2F 147
Lit. Norton Way S8: Shef 3F 147
Little Pear Tree Nature Reserve 4F 107
LITTLE SHEFFIELD 5E 119
Little Stubbing S73: Womb 6E 33
Little Westfields S71: R'ton 2F 9
Lit. Wood Dr. S12: Shef 5D 134
Lit. Wood Rd. S12: Shef 5D 134
Littlewood St. DN4: Hex 2A 56
Littlewood Way S66: Malt 4C 102
LITTLEWORTH 5E 75
Littleworth Av. S71: Lund 6B 18
Littleworth Cl. DN11: Ross 5E 75
Littleworth La. DN11: Ross 4E 75
 S71: Lund, Monk B 4A 18
Littleworth M. DN11: Ross 4E 75
 S71: Monk B 4A 18
Litton Cl. S43: Stav 6H 163
 S72: Shaft 3F 11
Litton Wlk. S72: Barn 6C 16
 S72: Shaft 3F 11
Liverpool Av. DN2: Don 4E 41
Liverpool St. S9: Shef 5C 108
Livesey St. S6: Shef 4C 106
Livingstone Av. DN2: Don 1A 42
Livingstone Cres. S71: Monk B 3G 17
Livingstone Rd. S35: Chap 3D 78
Livingstone Ter. S70: Barn 2D 30
Livingston Rd. S42: W'orth 6B 108
LivingWell Health Club
 Sheffield 2G 5
Lloyd St. S4: Shef 3A 108
 S62: P'gte 5G 83
Loakfield Dr. S5: Shef 3E 93
Lobelia Cl. S25: Sth A 4G 141
Lobelia Cres. DN3: Kirk Sa 5C 26
Lobwood S70: Wors 5F 31
Lobwood La. S70: Wors 5G 31
Lock Av. S70: Wors 4E 31
Lockeaflash Cres. S70: Stair 3A 32
Lockeaflash Gdns. S70: Stair 3A 32
Locke Av. S70: Barn 2D 30
Locke Dr. S9: Shef 2E 121
Locke Rd. S75: Dod 4H 29
Lockesley Av. DN12: Con 4D 68
Locke St. S70: Barn 3C 30
Lock Ho. Rd. S9: Tins 3F 109
Lock Ho. Wlk. S9: Tins 4F 109
Locking Dr. DN3: Arm 5F 43
Lock Keepers Vw. DN5: Sprot 4D 54
Lock La. S9: Tins 6H 95
Lockoford La. S41: C'fld 2A 168
 (Muirfield Cl.)
 S41: C'fld 2H 167
 (William St., not continuous)
Lockoford Rd. S41: C'fld 2H 167
Locksley Dr. S66: Thurc 6B 114
Locksley Gdns. S70: Birdw 6E 45
Lock St. S6: Shef 6D 106
Lockton Cl. S35: High G 6B 60
Lockton Way DN12: Con 3G 69
Lockwood Av. S25: Sth A 4G 141
Lockwood Cl. S65: Roth 3B 98
Lockwood Gdns. S36: H'swne 1G 177
Lockwood La. S63: Thurn 3D 36
 S70: Barn 3E 31

Lockwood Rd. DN1: Don 5D 40
 S63: Gol .5D 36
 S65: Roth 3B 98
Lodge, The S11: Shef 3H 131
Lodge Cl. S26: Aston 1D 138
 S43: Brim C 4F 169
Lodge Dr. S42: W'orth 6H 171
 S62: H'ley 5A 62
Lodge Farm Cl. S25: Nth A 2G 141
 S42: W'ton 3D 170
Lodge Farm M.
 S25: Nth A 2G 141
Lodge Hill Dr. S26: Wales 6G 139
Lodge La. S6: Shef 3B 116
 S10: Shef 3B 116
 S25: Din .5C 128
 S26: Aston 2C 138
 S61: Thorpe H 5C 80
LODGE MOOR 5B 116
Lodge Moor Rd. S10: Shef 6A 116
Lodge Pl. S43: Ink 2H 169
Lodge Wlk. S43: Ink 2H 169
Lodge Way S60: Brins 3D 110
Loganberry Cl. S66: Sunn 3G 99
Logan Rd. S9: Shef 2G 121
Loicher La. S35: Eccl 1H 93
Lomas Cl. S6: Stan 5D 104
Lomas Lea S6: Stan 6C 104
Lombard Cl. S75: Barn 5D 16
Lombard Cres. S73: D'fld 5H 33
London Rd. S2: Shef 5E 119
London St. S43: New W 3C 162
London Way
 S61: Thorpe H 4B 80
Long Acre S71: Car 5G 9
Longacre Cl. S20: Holb 1H 151
Longacre Ct. S18: Dron 5F 155
Longacre Rd. S18: Dron 5F 155
Long Acre Vw. S20: Holb 2H 151
Longacre Way S20: Holb 2H 151
Longcar La. S70: Barn 2C 30
Long Causeway
 S71: Monk B 4H 17
Long Cliffe Cl. S72: Shaft 4F 11
Longcliff Wlk. S40: C'fld 2E 167
Long Cl. DN4: Bess 1A 74
Long Cft. S75: Mapp 5A 8
Longcroft Av. S18: Dron W 2B 154
Longcroft Cl. S40: Birdh 3G 171
Longcroft Cres. S18: Dron W 2B 154
Longcroft Rd. S18: Dron W 2B 154
Longdale Cft. S71: Monk B 4G 17
Longedge Gro. S42: W'orth 6A 172
Long Edge La. DN5: Scawt 1F 39
Longedge La. S42: W'orth 6F 171
Longedge Ri. S42: W'orth 6H 171
Longfellow Dr. S65: Roth 5A 98
Longfellow Fold S65: Roth 5A 98
Longfellow Rd. DN4: Balb 6B 56
Longfield Cl. S73: Womb 6E 33
Longfield Dr. DN3: Eden 6D 26
 DN4: Bess 6A 58
 S65: Rav .2A 100
 S75: Mapp 5A 8
Long Fld. Grange S41: C'fld 2D 166
Long Fld. Rd. DN3: Eden 5D 26
Longfield Rd. S10: Shef 1A 118
Longfields Cres. S74: Hoyl 6A 46
Longfields Rd. S74: Hoyl 6C 9
Long Fold S63: Wath D 6D 48
Longford Cl. S17: Bradw 5H 145
Longford Cres. S17: Bradw 5H 145
Longford Dr. S17: Bradw 6G 145
Longford Rd. S17: Bradw 5H 145
Longford Spinney S17: Bradw 6G 145
Long Furlong S36: Pen 5E 177
Long Gate DN11: Wils 4E 89
Long Henry Row S2: Shef 3H 5 (3H 119)
 (not continuous)
Longlands Av. S26: Kiv P 6H 139
Longlands Dr. S65: Thry 5F 85
 S75: Mapp 6A 8
Long Lands La.
 DN5: Brod 3A 22
Long La. DN5: Sprot 3D 104
 S6: Lox 3D 104
 S6: Stan .1E 117
 S10: Shef 2F 117
 S21: Killa .4D 152
 S21: Mar L, West H 3F 157

Long La. S35: Ough 3C 90
 (Jackey La.)
 S35: Ough 3D 104
 (Loxley Rd.)
 S36: Pen .6F 177
 (Castle La.)
 S36: Pen .2B 176
 (Huddersfield Rd.)
 S36: Stoc 4A 174
 S60: Tree, Whis 4G 111
Longley Av. W. S5: Shef 2D 106
Longley Cl. S5: Shef 2G 107
 S75: Bar G 4F 15
Longley Cres. S5: Shef 1G 107
Longley Dr. S5: Shef 2G 107
Longley Farm Vw. S5: Shef 2H 107
Longley Hall Gro. S5: Shef 2H 107
Longley Hall Ri. S5: Shef 1G 107
Longley Hall Rd. S5: Shef 1H 107
Longley Hall Way S5: Shef 2H 107
Longley Ings S36: Pen 5G 177
Longley La. S5: Shef 2G 107
Long Leys La. S66: B'well 3B 88
Longley Spring S74: Hoyl 4H 61
Longley St. S75: Bar G 4F 15
Long Line S11: Shef 6B 130
Longman Rd. S70: Barn 5D 16
Long Meadows S66: Bram 6A 100
Long Plantation DN3: Eden 6D 26
Long Pye Cl. S75: Wool G 3F 7
Longridge Rd. S71: Monk B 2A 18
Long Rd. S66: Bramp M 3A 126
Long Royd S72: Grim 2A 20
LONG SANDALL 6A 26
Long Sandall Bri. DN2: Long S 5H 25
Long Shambles S40: C'fld 3H 167
 (off Central Pavement)
Longshaw Cl. S43: Stav 6A 164
Longside Way S75: Barn 6H 15
Longsight Rd. S75: Mapp 5H 7
Longstone Cres. S12: Shef 4G 135
Longthwaite Cl.
 S25: Laugh M 2H 127
Longton Rd. DN3: Kirk Sa 4D 26
Long Wlk. S10: Shef 2H 117
Longwood Cl. S66: Sunn 2G 99
Longworth Rd. WF9: Hems 1E 13
Lonsdale Av. DN2: Don 1G 57
 S71: Ard .2E 33
Lonsdale Cl. S25: Nth A 2A 142
Lonsdale Ho. DN2: Don 5H 41
Lonsdale Rd. S6: Shef 5B 106
Loosemore Dr. S12: Shef 3C 134
Lopham Cl. S3: Shef 1G 119
Lopham St. S3: Shef 6G 107
 (not continuous)
Lordens Hill S25: Din 5B 128
Lord Roberts Rd. S40: C'fld 1H 171
Lords Cl. DN4: Don 3H 57
 DN12: New E 3D 70
Lord's Head La. DN4: Warm 1D 70
Lordsmill Ga. S41: C'fld 6A 168
Lordsmill St. S41: C'fld 6A 168
 (not continuous)
Lord St. S65: Roth 3H 97
 S71: Barn 6H 17
Loretta Cotts. S74: Hoyl 6A 46
Lorna Rd. S64: Mexb 1F 67
Lorne Cl. S18: Dron W 2C 154
Lorne Rd. S63: Thurn 2A 36
Loscoe Gro. S63: Gol 5B 36
Lothian Rd. DN2: Don 5H 41
Louden Cl. S61: Scho 6E 81
Louden Rd. S61: Scho 6E 81
Lounde Cl. DN5: Sprot 3D 54
Lounde Rd. S18: Uns 6B 156
Loundeswood Av. S41: C'fld 6D 160
Lound Rd. S9: Shef 3G 121
Lound Side S35: Chap 2F 79
Loundsley Cl. S42: Ash 4A 166
LOUNDSLEY GREEN 3D 166
Loundsley Grn. Rd.
 S40: C'fld 4C 166
Lousy Busk La. S64: Mexb 6D 50
Louth Rd. S11: Shef 1A 132
Lovell St. S4: Shef 1A 120
LOVERSALL 4B 72
Loversall Cl. DN4: Balb 1A 72
Love St. S3: Shef 1E 5 (2F 119)
Lovetot Av. S26: Aston 6C 124

Lovetot Rd. S9: Shef 1B 120
(Bacon La.)
S9: Shef 1B 120
(Stoke St.)
S61: Kimb P 6H 81
LOW BARUGH 2G 15
Lowburn Rd. S13: Shef 1F 135
Low Comn. Rd. S25: Din 5G 127
Low Cft. S71: R'ton 3A 10
S73: Womb 1H 47
Low Cronkhill La. S71: Car 4B 10
Low Cudworth S72: Cud 3E 19
Low Cudworth Grn. S72: Cud 3E 19
Low Deeps La. DN10: Miss 5H 77
LOWEDGES 4E 147
Low Edges S8: Shef 4F 147
Lowedges Cl. S8: Shef 4D 146
Lowedges Cres. S8: Shef 4E 147
Lowedges Dr. S8: Shef 4E 147
Lowedges Pl. S8: Shef 4E 147
Lowedges Rd. S8: Shef 5C 146
Lowe La. S75: Hood G, Stainb 6G 29
Lowell Av. DN4: Balb 6A 56
Lower All. S44: Cal 1F 173
Lwr. Boundary Rd. DN5: Bntly 1E 25
LOWER BRADWAY 4B 146
Lwr. Castlereagh St. S70: Barn 1D 30
Lwr. Collier Fold S75: Cawt 3A 14
LOWER CRABTREE 4H 107
Lwr. Dolcliffe Rd. S64: Mexb 1E 67
Lower Gro. Rd. S40: C'fld 5G 167
Lwr. Haigh Head S36: H'swne 1F 177
Lwr. High Royds S75: Dart 6H 7
LOWER LEWDEN 6A 32
Lwr. Limes, The S70: Wors 6G 31
Lwr. Malton Rd. DN5: Scaws 3F 39
Lwr. Mill Cl. S63: Gol 6B 36
Lower Pasture DN9: Blax 2F 77
LOWER PILLEY 1D 60
Lwr. Thomas St. S70: Barn 2D 30
Lwr. Unwin St. S36: Pen 5D 176
LOWER WALKLEY 5B 106
Lwr. York St. S73: Womb 1G 47
Low Farm Ct. S71: D'fld 2B 34
LOWFIELD .6F 119
Lowfield Av. S12: Ridg 1H 149
S61: Grea .5D 82
Lowfield Cl. DN3: Barn D 2E 27
Lowfield Ct. S2: Shef 1F 133
Lowfield Farm Cl. S63: Bolt D 2D 50
Lowfield Gro. S63: Bolt D 3D 50
Lowfield La. S63: Bolt D 2D 50
Lowfield Mdws. S63: Bolt D 3C 50
Lowfield Rd. DN2: Don 3H 41
S63: Bolt D 2C 50
Lowfields S43: Stav 4D 164
Lowfield Wlk. DN12: Den M 2C 68
Low Folds S71: Monk B 3C 18
Lowgate DN5: Scawt 3F 39
Lowgates S43: Stav 4C 164
Low Golden Smithies S64: Swin . . .2B 66
Low Grange Rd. S63: Thurn 2B 36
Low Grange Sq. S63: Thurn 2B 36
Lowgreave S65: Roth 2B 98
Lowhouse Rd. S5: Shef 3B 94
LOW LAITHES 4E 33
Low Laithes Vw. S73: Womb 6E 33
Low Laithes Village S71: Low L 4F 33
Lowland Cl. S71: Monk B 3A 18
Low Lands Cl. DN5: Bntly 5A 24
Low La. DN4: Bess 6H 57
S61: Kimb, Roth 2B 96
S66: Carr, Hoot L 2F 115
Low Lathe La. S36: Spink 2H 175
Low Matlock La. S6: Lox 5E 105
Low Pasture Cl. S75: Dod 3H 29
Low Pavement S40: C'fld 5H 167
Low Riddings S66: Sunn 4G 99
Low Rd. DN4: Balb 5H 55
DN12: Con 3F 69
S6: Shef .6H 105
S35: Ough 3E 91
Low Rd. E. DN4: Warm 6E 55
Low Rd. W. DN4: Warm 1D 70
Low Row S75: Dart 3F 7
Lowry Dr. S18: Dron 3E 155
Low St. S75: Dod 4A 30
LOW STUBBIN 6D 64
Lowther Rd. DN1: Don 5D 40
S6: Shef .3C 106
Lowton Way S66: Hel 5D 100

LOW VALLEY 6A 34
Low Vw. S75: Dod 3G 29
LOW WINCOBANK 5D 94
Low Wood Cl. S64: Swin 5B 66
Loxdale Gdns. S70: Barn 6C 16
LOXLEY 4F 105
Loxley Av. S73: Womb 2F 47
LOXLEY BOTTOM 4H 105
Loxley Cl. S40: Ash 5C 166
Loxley Ct. S6: Shef 3G 105
(Ben La.)
S6: Shef .5B 106
(Limbrick Cl.)
S60: Roth 2G 111
Loxley New Rd. S6: Shef 5A 106
Loxley Pk. S6: Shef 5H 105
Loxley Rd. S6: Brad, Lox, Shef 2A 104
S60: Wav .3D 122
S71: Lund .5C 18
Loxley Vw. Rd. S10: Shef 1A 118
Loy Cl. S61: Wing 5B 82
Lucas Rd. S41: C'fld 2F 167
Lucas St. S4: Shef 5H 107
Lucknow Ct. S7: Shef 2D 132
Ludgate Cl. DN11: New R 6H 75
Ludham Cl. S41: C'fld 1G 167
Ludham Gdns. S41: C'fld 1G 167
Ludwell Cl. DN5: Barnb 2B 52
Ludwell Hill DN5: Barnb 2B 52
Lugano Gro. S73: D'fld 4H 33
Luke La. S6: Shef 3G 105
Lulworth Cl. S70: Barn 2G 31
Lumb La. S35: Ough 2B 90
Lumley Cl. S66: Malt 5D 102
Lumley Cres. S66: Malt 6D 102
Lumley Dr. S66: Malt 6C 102
Lumley St. S4: Shef 2A 120
S9: Shef .2C 120
Lump La. S35: Gren 1B 92
Lumsdale Rd. S43: Stav 6H 163
Luna Cft. S12: Shef 6C 134
Lunbreck Rd. DN4: Warm 1D 70
Lund Av. S71: Lund 5C 18
Lund Cl. S71: Lund 5C 18
Lund Cres. S71: Lund 5C 18
Lundhill Cl. DN5: Womb 3H 47
Lundhill Farm M. S73: Hem 4G 47
Lundhill Gro. S73: Womb 3H 47
Lund Hill La. S71: R'ton 2C 10
Lundhill Rd. S73: Womb 4H 47
Lund La. S71: Lund 5C 18
Lund Rd. S35: Ough 5E 91
LUNDWOOD 5B 18
Lundwood Cl. S20: Mosb 6D 136
Lundwood Dr. S20: Mosb 6D 136
Lundwood Gro. S20: Mosb 6D 136
Lundwood Ho. DN1: Don 2B 56
(off Bond Cl.)
Lundy Rd. S18: Dron 4F 155
Lunn Rd. S72: Cud 2E 19
Lupin Way S44: Cal 5F 169
Lupton Cres. S8: Shef 4E 147
Lupton Dr. S8: Shef 4E 147
Lupton Rd. S8: Shef 4E 147
Lupton Wlk. S8: Shef 4F 147
Luterel Dr. S26: Swal 6C 124
Lutterworth Dr. DN6: Adw S 2B 22
Lutyens Cl. S40: Bramp 6A 166
Lyceum Theatre
Sheffield 4F 5 (3G 119)
Lych Ga. Cl. DN4: Can 5D 58
Lydden Cl. S43: Brim 6D 162
Lydford Av. S41: Old W 5A 162
LYDGATE 3H 117
Lydgate Ct. S10: Shef 3A 118
Lydgate Dr. S42: W'orth 6F 171
Lydgate Hall Cres. S10: Shef 3H 117
Lydgate La. S10: Shef 3H 117
Lyle Cl. S66: Thurc 1C 126
Lyle M. S66: Thurc 1D 126
Lymegate S63: Bramp B 6A 48
Lyme St. S60: Roth 4D 96
Lyminster Rd. S6: Shef 5B 92
Lyminton La. S60: Tree 2F 123
Lymister Av. S60: Roth 2G 111
Lyncroft Cl. S60: Brins 4E 111
Lyndale Av. DN3: Eden 1B 42
Lynden Av. DN6: Adw S 3B 22
Lyndhurst Bank S36: Pen 5D 176
Lyndhurst Cl. S11: Shef 1B 132
Lyndhurst Cres. DN3: Eden 5B 26

Lyndhurst Rd. S11: Shef 1B 132
Lynham Av. S70: Birdw 6E 45
Lynmouth Rd. S7: Shef 3D 132
Lynn Pl. S9: Shef 4E 109
Lynthwaite Cl.
S63: Bramp B 5A 48
Lynton Av. S60: Roth 1H 111
Lynton Dr. DN3: Eden 6B 26
Lynton Pl. S75: Kexb 6E 7
Lynton Rd. S11: Shef 6C 118
Lynwood Cl. S18: Dron W 3C 154
Lynwood Dr. S64: Mexb 6F 51
S71: Car 5H 9
Lyons Cl. S4: Shef 5H 107
Lyons Rd. S4: Shef 5H 107
Lyons St. S4: Shef 5H 107
Lytham Av. S25: Din 1A 142
S71: Monk B 2A 18
Lytham Cl. DN4: Can 6E 59
Lyttleton Ct. S36: Cub 6C 176
Lyttleton Cres. S36: Cub 6C 176
Lytton Av. S5: Shef 5D 92
Lytton Cl. DN4: Balb 6A 56
Lytton Cres. S5: Shef 5D 92
Lytton Dr. S5: Shef 5D 92
Lytton Rd. S5: Shef 5D 92

M

Mabel St. S60: Roth 5G 97
Macaulay Cres. DN3: Arm 4F 43
McConnel Cres. DN11: New R 5A 74
Macdonald Cl. S42: Gras 6E 173
McGregor's Way S40: Birdh 3A 172
Machin Dr. S62: Rawm 6D 64
Machin La. S36: Stoc 2A 174
Machins Ct. S18: Dron 2F 155
Machon Bank S7: Shef 2D 132
Machon Bank Rd. S7: Shef 1C 132
McIntyre Rd. S36: Stoc 3D 174
Mackenzie Cres. S10: Shef . .6A 4 (4D 118)
S35: Burn .4C 78
Mackenzie St. S11: Shef 6D 118
McKenzie Way S26: Kiv P 6A 140
Mackey Cres. S72: Brier 3H 11
Mackey La. S72: Brier 3H 11
Mackinnon Av. S26: Kiv P 6A 140
McLaren Cres. S66: Malt 6B 102
McLintock Way S70: Barn 1C 30
McLoughlin Way S26: Kiv P 6A 140
McMahon Av. S43: Ink 2G 169
McManus Av. S62: Rawm 6G 65
Macmillan M. S40: Bramp 5C 166
Macnaghten Rd. S75: Tank 1E 61
Macro Rd. S73: Womb 2H 47
Madam La. DN3: Barn D 1G 27
Madehurst Gdns. S2: Shef 1G 133
Madehurst Ri. S2: Shef 1G 133
Madehurst Rd. S2: Shef 1G 133
Madehurst Vw. S2: Shef 1G 133
Madin Dr. S43: Ink 2G 169
Madingley Cl. DN4: Balb 4H 57
Madin St. S41: C'fld 4H 167
Madison Ct. DN9: Finn 3F 77
Mafeking Pl. S35: Chap 2F 79
Magdalene Gdns. S63: Gol 5E 37
S71: Lund .4B 18
Magellan Rd. S66: Malt 4H 101
Magenta Cres. DN4: Balb 2C 72
Magistrates' Court
Chesterfield 5A 168
Doncaster 5C 40
Sheffield 2F 5 (2G 119)
Magna 34 Business Pk.
S60: Roth 6B 96
Magna Cl. S66: Flan 4G 99
Magna Cres. S66: Flan 4F 99
Magna La. S65: Dalt 1C 98
Magna Science Adventure Cen. 6A 96
Magna Way S60: Roth 6A 96
Magnolia Cl. DN3: Kirk Sa 5C 26
S25: Sth A 5G 141
S72: Shaft 4G 11
Magnolia Ct. S10: Shef 6F 117
Magpie Gro. S2: Shef 4B 120
Mahon Av. S62: Rawm 2G 83
Maidstone Rd. S6: Shef 6C 92
Maidwell Way DN3: Kirk Sa 4B 26
Main Av. DN12: New E 3C 70
S17: Tot 6F 145

Main Rd. S9: Shef 1F **121**
  S12: Ridg 2H **149**
  S18: Barl 4A **160**
  S18: Holme 4A **154**
  S18: Uns 5B **156**
  S21: Mar L 2H **157**
  S21: Reni 3H **159**
  S21: West H 5G **157**
  S35: Wharn S 1A **90**
  S42: Cut 1A **166**
  S42: Old B 4A **166**
Main St. DN3: Can 3E **59**
  DN5: Sprot 4C **54**
  DN9: Auck 1G **59**
  DN11: Wad 5E **73**
  S12: Shef 4C **136**
  S25: Nth A 3G **141**
  S26: Augh 5B **124**
  S26: Swal 1B **138**
  S26: Ull 3D **124**
  S35: Gren 1B **92**
  S60: Cat 1E **123**
  S60: Roth 4D **96**
  S61: Grea 4D **82**
  S62: Rawm 2H **83**
  S62: Wentw 5D **62**
  S63: Gol 5D **36**
           (not continuous)
  S64: Mexb 1E **67**
  S65: Rav 5A **86**
  S66: Bram 5A **100**
  S72: Sth H 1G **11**
  S73: Womb 1F **47**
Main St. Shop. Cen.
  S66: Bram 5A **100**
Mair Ct. S60: Roth 3H **111**
Majestic Ct. S75: Dart 5F **7**
Majuba St. S6: Shef 6C **106**
Makin St. S64: Mexb 2H **67**
Malcolm St. S70: Barn 2A **32**
Malham Cl. S40: C'fld 3E **167**
  S72: Shaft 3F **11**
Malham Ct. S70: Barn 6C **16**
Malham Gdns. S20: Half 3E **151**
Malham Gro. S20: Half 3F **151**
Malham Pl. S35: Chap 2E **79**
Malham Tarn Ct.
  DN4: Don 4G **57**
Malia Rd. S41: C'fld 2B **168**
MALINBRIDGE 5A **106**
Malin Bridge (Park & Ride) 5A **106**
Malin Bridge Stop (ST) 5A **106**
Malincroft S75: Mapp 4F **7**
Malinda St.
  S3: Shef 1B **4** (1E **119**)
Malin Rd. S6: Shef 5H **105**
  S65: Roth 2C **98**
Malkin St. S41: C'fld 5A **168**
Mallard Av. DN3: Barn D 2C **26**
  DN5: Scawt 3G **39**
Mallard Cl. DN4: Balb 6G **55**
  S61: Thorpe H 2D **80**
Mallard Ct. DN11: Ross 5D **74**
  S43: Stav 4C **164**
Mallard Dr. S21: Killa 3A **152**
Mallard Way DN4: Don 6E **57**
Mallin Cft. S74: Hoyl 6B **46**
Mallinder Cl. S21: Killa 4C **152**
Mallin Dr. DN12: New E 6C **70**
Mallory Av. S62: Rawm 2F **83**
Mallory Cl. S41: Old W 3F **161**
Mallory Dr. S64: Mexb 6A **52**
Mallory Rd. S65: Roth 2B **98**
Mallory Way S72: Cud 1F **19**
Malon Way S13: Shef 5C **122**
Malsin Gdns. S73: Womb 3F **47**
Malson Way S41: C'fld 2G **167**
Maltas Ct. S70: Wors 5H **31**
MALTBY .5A **102**
Maltby Av. S75: Wool G 4F **7**
Maltby Ho. DN1: Don 2B **56**
           (off Burden Cl.)
Maltby La. S66: B'well 1B **102**
Maltby Leisure Cen. 5A **102**
Maltby Low Common Nature Reserve
  . . . . .6E **103**
Maltby St. S9: Shef 5D **108**
Malthouse Cotts. S26: Kiv S 6E **141**
Malthouse Ct. S41: C'fld 4H **167**
Malthouse La. S32: W'orth 6C **170**
Malthouse Rd. S71: Barn 1E **31**

Malting La. S4: Shef 1H **5** (2H **119**)
Maltings, The S11: Shef 5E **119**
           (off Napier St.)
  S36: Cub 5C **176**
           (off Mortimer Rd.)
  S60: Roth 5E **97**
Maltings Ct. DN3: Kirk Sa 3C **26**
Maltkiln Cotts. DN3: Barn D 3C **26**
Maltkiln Farm Ct. S66: B'well 6A **88**
Malt Kiln Row S75: Cawt 3A **14**
           (off Hill Top)
Maltkiln St. S60: Roth 5E **97**
Malton Dr. S26: Aston 1D **138**
Malton Pl. S71: Smi 1D **16**
Malton Rd. DN2: Don 5G **41**
  DN5: Scaws 3E **39**
Malton St. S4: Shef 5H **107**
Malton Wlk. S40: Birdh 3G **171**
Malton Way DN6: Woodl 1A **22**
Maltravers Cl. S2: Shef 4B **120**
Maltravers Cres. S2: Shef 3A **120**
Maltravers Pl. S2: Shef 3B **120**
Maltravers Rd. S2: Shef 2A **120**
Maltravers Ter. S2: Shef 4B **120**
           (not continuous)
Maltravers Way S2: Shef 3B **120**
Malvern Av. DN5: Cus 5F **39**
Malvern Cl. S75: Barn 6A **16**
Malvern Dr. S66: Sunn 3G **99**
Malvern Rd. DN2: Don 6H **41**
  S9: Shef 1E **121**
  S40: C'fld 4F **167**
Malvern Way S66: Sunn 3G **99**
Malwood Way S66: Malt 4C **102**
Manchester Rd. S6: Shef 4A **116**
  S10: Shef 4A **116**
  S36: Spink, Stoc 1A **174**
  S36: Thurl 4A **176**
Mandale Rd. DN3: Barn D 1H **27**
Mandeville St. S9: Shef 1F **121**
Mangham Rd. S61: Grea 1E **97**
  S62: P'gte 1E **97**
Mangham Way S61: Grea 1E **97**
Manifold Av. S43: Stav 6A **164**
Manknell Rd. S41: Whit M 6H **161**
Mannering Rd. DN4: Balb 6F **55**
Manners St. S3: Shef 6E **107**
MANOR 6D **120**
Manor App. S61: Kimb 3H **95**
Manor Av. S43: Brim 1E **169**
  S63: Gol 5D **36**
Manor Bungs. S18: Dron 3E **155**
Manor Cl. DN3: Barn D 1B **26**
  S26: Tod 3C **140**
  S62: Rawm 6D **64**
  S63: Bramp B 5C **48**
  S66: Malt 5A **102**
Manor Ct. DN5: Harl 2H **51**
  DN12: Den M 3C **68**
  S65: Roth 2C **98**
  S70: Wors 5E **31**
  S71: R'ton 3F **9**
  S72: Grim 2C **20**
Manor Cres. S18: Dron 3E **155**
  S40: Ash 5E **167**
  S60: Brins 4C **110**
  S72: Grim 6B **12**
Manor Cft. S72: Sth H 1G **11**
Manor Development Cen.
  S2: Shef 5E **121**
Manor Dr. DN2: Don 2E **57**
  DN5: Cad 1G **69**
  S25: Din 4H **127**
  S26: Tod 3C **140**
  S40: Ash 5D **166**
  S43: Brim 1E **169**
  S60: Whis 3B **112**
  S71: R'ton 3G **9**
  S72: Sth H 1G **11**
Manor End S70: Wors 5E **31**
Manor Est. DN5: Bntly 4G **23**
Mnr. Farm Cl. DN6: Adw S 2C **22**
  S26: Augh 4C **124**
  S71: Car 6A **10**
Mnr. Farm Ct. DN9: Finn 3F **77**
Mnr. Farm Ct. S20: Beig 5H **137**
  S21: Killa 5C **152**
  S65: Thry 4E **85**
  S71: Ard 1D **15**
           (off Doncaster Rd.)
  S72: Cud 2E **19**

Mnr. Farm Cft. S81: Woods 4F **143**
Mnr. Farm Dr. S64: Swin 4B **66**
Mnr. Farm Est. S62: Rawm 1D **82**
Mnr. Farm Gdns.
  S25: Sth A 4G **141**
Mnr. Farm M. S20: Beig 5H **137**
Manor Flds. S61: Kimb 2H **95**
  S72: Gt H 6F **21**
Manor Fields Cl.
  S61: Kimb 2H **95**
Manor Gdns. DN5: Sprot 3C **54**
  S71: Ard 2E **33**
  S72: Shaft 4F **11**
Manor Gro. S71: R'ton 3G **9**
  S72: Grim 6A **12**
  WF9: Sth K 5H **13**
Manor Ho. S6: Stan 6D **104**
Manor Ho. Cl. S74: Hoyl 6B **46**
Manor Ho. Ct. DN5: Scawt 1G **39**
  S41: C'fld 3H **167**
Manor Ho. Rd. S61: Kimb 2H **95**
Manor Laith Rd. S61: Kimb 4A **120**
Manor La. S2: Shef 2C **120**
  S25: Din 3B **128**
  S36: Oxs 6H **177**
  S64: Mexb 4E **51**
Manor Oaks Cl. S2: Shef 3B **120**
Manor Oaks Ct. S2: Shef 3A **120**
Manor Oaks Dr. S2: Shef 3A **120**
Manor Oaks Gdns. S2: Shef 3H **119**
Manor Oaks Pl. S2: Shef 4B **120**
Manor Oaks Rd. S2: Shef 3H **119**
Mnr. Occupation Rd.
  S71: R'ton 2G **9**
MANOR PARK 4D **120**
Manor Pk. S75: Silk 3A **28**
Manor Pk. Av. S2: Shef 5C **120**
Manor Pk. Cen. S2: Shef 4C **120**
Manor Pk. Cl. S2: Shef 5C **120**
Manor Pk. Cres. S2: Shef 5C **120**
Manor Pk. Dr. S2: Shef 5C **120**
Manor Park Ind. Est.
  S9: Shef 2D **120**
Manor Pk. Pl. S2: Shef 4C **120**
Manor Pk. Ri. S2: Shef 4C **120**
Manor Pk. Rd. S2: Shef 4C **120**
Manor Pk. Way S2: Shef 4C **120**
Manor Pl. S62: Rawm 3H **83**
Manor Ri. S74: Hoyl 6C **46**
Manor Rd. DN3: Barn D 1G **27**
  DN5: Bntly 4H **23**
  DN5: Harl 3H **51**
  S21: Killa 5D **152**
  S25: Din 3A **128**
  S26: Hart, Kiv S 6E **141**
  S26: Wales 5G **139**
  S40: Ash 5E **167**
           (Ash Tree Cl.)
  S40: Ash 5E **167**
           (Lenthall's Back Row)
  S43: Brim, Brim C 1E **169**
  S60: Brins 4C **110**
  S61: Kimb 4H **95**
  S63: Bramp B 5B **48**
  S63: Thurn 2B **36**
  S64: Swin 4C **66**
  S66: Malt 5B **102**
  S72: Cud 2D **18**
Manor Sq. S63: Thurn 2B **36**
Manor St. S71: Car 6A **10**
Manor Top Stop (ST) 2D **134**
Manor Vw. S20: Half 3F **151**
  S72: Shaft 4F **11**
Manor Wlk. DN11: Wad 6E **73**
Manor Way S2: Shef 2B **120**
  S26: Tod 3C **140**
  S63: Bolt D 2C **50**
  S74: Hoyl 6B **46**
Manse Cl. DN4: Can 4D **58**
Manse Farm M. S72: Cud 1E **19**
Mansel Av. S5: Shef 4D **92**
Mansel Cl. S5: Shef 4D **92**
Mansel Cres. S5: Shef 4C **92**
Mansel Rd. S5: Shef 4D **92**
Mansfeldt Cres. S41: C'fld 2F **167**
Mansfeldt Rd. S41: C'fld 2F **167**
Mansfield Cres. DN3: Arm 3B **42**
Mansfield Dr. S12: Shef 2E **135**

Mansfield Rd.—Masefield Flats

Mansfield Rd. DN4: Balb 3A 56
S12: Shef 2D 134
S21: Killa 3E 153
S26: Aston, Swal, Wales B 1B 138
(not continuous)
S41: Has, Cor 3C 172
S60: Roth 4F 97
S71: Ath 6E 9
Mansfield Vw. S12: Shef 2E 135
Manton Ho. DN1: Don 2B 56
(off Oxford Pl.)
Manton St. S2: Shef 6F 5 (5G 119)
Manvers Cl. S25: Nth A 1H 141
S26: Swal 1C 138
Manvers Ct. S41: C'fld 4H 167
(off Nightingale Cl.)
Manvers Rd. S6: Shef 5B 106
S20: Beig 4G 137
S26: Swal 1B 138
S44: Cal 4F 169
S64: Mexb 1D 66
Manvers Waterfront Boat Club 4H 49
Manvers Way S63: Wath D 3D 48
Maori Av. S63: Bolt D 2H 49
Maple Av. DN4: Can 4C 58
DN9: Auck 2B 76
S66: Malt 5G 101
Maplebeck Dr. S9: Tins 2A 110
Maplebeck Rd. S9: Tins 2A 110
Maple Cl. S70: Barn 3G 31
Maple Cl. S62: Rawm 3H 83
S75: Tank 3B 60
Maple Cft. Cres. S9: Shef 1C 108
Maple Cft. Rd. S9: Shef 1C 108
Maple Dr. DN9: Auck 1H 59
S21: Killa 5B 152
S66: Flan 4G 99
Maple Est. S75: Mapp 1B 30
Maple Gro. DN3: Arm 3E 43
DN12: Con 6C 68
S9: Shef 3H 121
S26: Aston 6E 125
S36: Stoc 4D 174
Maple Pl. S35: Chap 4F 79
Maple Rd. S26: Kiv P 5H 139
S64: Mexb 1E 67
S75: Mapp 5H 7
S75: Tank 3C 60
Maple St. S43: Hol 6G 163
Maplewood Av. S66: Sunn 2G 99
Mapperley Rd. S18: Dron W 3B 154
Mappin Ct. S1: Shef 4B 4
(off Mappin St.)
Mappin's Rd. S60: Cat 1D 122
Mappin St. S1: Shef 3B 4 (3E 119)
Mapplebeck Rd. S35: High G 1D 78
MAPPLEWELL 6H 7
Mapplewell Dr. S75: Mapp 6B 8
Maran Av. S73: D'fld 5D 34
Marbeck Cl. S25: Din 5G 127
Marcham Dr. S20: Beig 4H 137
March Bank S65: Thry 5F 85
March Flatts Rd. S65: Thry 6F 85
March Ga. DN12: Con 5F 69
March St. DN12: Con 4F 69
S9: Shef 5E 109
(not continuous)
March Va. Ri. DN12: Con 5F 69
Marchwood Av. S6: Shef 6F 105
Marchwood Cl. S40: C'fld 4G 167
Marchwood Dr. S6: Shef 5F 105
Marchwood Rd. S6: Shef 6F 105
Marcliff Cl. S66: Wick 6E 99
Marcliff Cres. S66: Wick 6E 99
Marcliff La. S66: Wick 6E 99
Mardale Cl. S41: C'fld 5F 161
Mardale Ct. S41: C'fld 5F 161
Mardale Wlk. DN2: Don 4H 41
Marden Rd. S7: Shef 2D 132
Margaret Cl. S26: Aston 2C 138
S73: D'fld 5A 34
Margaret Ct. S73: Womb 2H 47
Margaret Rd. S73: D'fld 5A 34
S73: Womb 2H 47
Margaret St. S1: Shef 5F 119
S66: Malt 6C 102
Margate Dr. S4: Shef 4A 108
Margate St. S4: Shef 4B 108
Margerison Rd. S8: Shef 1F 133
Margetson Cres. S5: Shef 4E 93
Margetson Dr. S5: Shef 4E 93

Margetson Rd. S5: Shef 4E 93
Marian Rd. DN3: Eden 5B 26
Marigold Cl. S5: Shef 1B 108
Marina Ri. S73: D'fld 5H 33
Marine Dr. S41: C'fld 5B 168
Marion Cl. WF9: Sth K 4H 13
Marion Rd. S6: Shef 2A 106
Markbrook Dr.
S35: High G 6B 60
Market Cl. S71: Barn 1F 31
Market Hall S40: C'fld 5H 167
Market Hill S70: Barn 1D 30
Market La. S36: Pen 4C 176
Market Pde. S70: Barn 1E 31
Market Pl. DN1: Don 1C 56
S1: Shef 2F 5 (2G 119)
S25: Din 5A 128
S35: Chap 3G 79
S36: Pen 4D 176
S40: C'fld 5H 167
S43: Stav 4B 164
S60: Roth 4E 97
S63: Gol 5D 36
S72: Cud 1E 19
S73: Womb 2H 47
S74: Els 1D 62
Market Rd. DN1: Don 6C 40
Market Sq. S13: Shef 2D 136
S60: Roth 4E 97
(off Market Pl.)
S63: Gol 5D 36
S65: Roth 3F 97
Market St. DN6: Highf 6C 22
S9: Shef 2F 109
S13: Shef 2D 136
S21: Ecki 1E 159
S35: Chap 3G 79
S36: Pen 4D 176
S43: Stav 4B 164
S60: Roth 4E 97
S63: Gol 5D 36
S63: Thurn 2B 36
S64: Mexb 2F 67
(Bank St.)
S64: Mexb 2G 67
(Leach La.)
S64: Swin 3D 66
S70: Barn 1D 30
S72: Cud 1E 19
S74: Hoyl 5B 46
Markfield Dr. S66: Flan 4G 99
Mark Gro. S66: Flan 5G 99
Markham Av. DN3: Arm 3D 42
DN12: Con 4D 68
Markham Cotts. DN12: Con 4D 68
(off Leslie Av.)
Markham Ct. DN12: Con 4D 68
Markham Cres. S43: Stav 4C 164
Markham Ho. DN1: Don 2B 56
(off Burden Cl.)
Markham Quay S41: C'fld 6A 168
(off Camlough Wlk.)
Markham Rd. DN12: New E 4C 70
S40: C'fld 6G 167
Markham Sq. DN12: New E 4D 70
Markham Ter. DN12: New E 4C 70
S8: Shef 2E 133
Mark La. S10: Shef 2B 130
Mark St. S70: Barn 1D 30
Marlborough Av. DN5: Don 6G 39
Marlborough Cl. S25: Nth A 1G 141
S63: Thurn 2B 36
Marlborough Ri. S26: Aston 2D 138
Marlborough Rd. DN2: Don 6E 41
S10: Shef 3B 118
Marlborough Ter. S70: Barn 2D 30
Marlcliffe Rd. S6: Shef 1H 105
Marles Cl. S73: Womb 3F 47
Marlfield Cft. S35: Eccl 2G 93
Marlow Cl. DN2: Don 5H 41
Marlowe Cl. S66: Bram 6A 100
Marlowe Dr. S65: Roth 5A 98
Marlowe Rd. DN3: Barn D 1C 26
S65: Roth 5A 98
Marlow Rd. DN2: Don 5H 41
Marmion Rd. S11: Shef 6A 118
(Kenilworth Pl.)
S11: Shef 1A 132
(Psalter La.)
Marples Cl. S8: Shef 1E 133
Marples Dr. S8: Shef 1E 133

Marquis Gdns. DN3: Barn D 1C 26
Marr Grange La. DN5: Marr 3A 38
Marrian Av. S66: Thurc 1C 126
Marrick Ct. S35: Chap 3E 79
Marrion Rd. S62: Rawm 2H 83
Marriott La. S7: Shef 5C 132
Marriott Pl. S62: Rawm 1E 83
Marriott Rd. S7: Shef 5C 132
S64: Swin 2D 66
Marrison Dr. S21: Killa 4B 152
Marr Ter. S10: Shef 5G 117
Marsala Wlk. S73: D'fld 4A 34
Marsden Gdns.
DN3: Kirk Sa 4B 26
(off Sandall La.)
Marsden Ind. Est. S13: Shef 4A 122
Marsden La. S3: Shef 2B 4 (2E 119)
Marsden M. WF9: Hems 1E 13
Marsden Pl. S40: C'fld 6E 167
(South Pl.)
S40: C'fld 4H 167
(Spencer St.)
Marsden Rd. S36: Stoc 3E 175
Marsden St. S40: C'fld 5H 167
Marshall Av. DN4: Balb 5H 55
Marshall Cl. S62: P'gte 5G 83
Marshall Gro. S63: Wath D 1G 65
Marshall Hall S10: Shef 5C 118
Marshall Rd. S8: Shef 6D 132
Marsh Av. S18: Dron 1G 155
Marsh Cl. S20: Mosb 4D 150
Marshfield S70: Birdw 3E 45
Marshfield Gro. S43: Stav 4D 164
Marsh Ga. DN5: Don 6A 40
Marsh Hill S66: Mick 1F 101
Marsh Ho. Rd. S11: Shef 3G 131
MARSH LANE 2H 157
Marsh La. DN3: Barn D 1H 25
DN5: Ark 5C 24
DN5: Bntly 3C 24
S10: Shef 3G 117
Marsh Quarry S21: Ecki 3B 158
Marsh Rd. DN5: Don 5B 40
Marsh St. S36: Spink 3F 175
S60: Roth 5D 96
S73: Womb 1H 47
Marsh Vw. S21: Ecki 2C 158
Marsh Wlk. S2: Shef 2A 120
(off Castle Ct.)
Marson Av. DN6: Woodl 3A 22
Marston Cl. S18: Dron W 4C 154
Marston Cres. S71: Smi 2E 17
Marstone Cres. S17: Tot 5F 145
Marston Rd. S10: Shef 2A 118
Martin Cl. S6: Shef 1D 118
Martin Cl. S6: Shef 1D 118
S26: Augh 4B 124
S70: Birdw 4E 45
Martin Ct. S21: Ecki 1D 158
Martin Cres. S5: Shef 4G 93
Martin Cft. S75: Silk 2A 28
Martindale Cl. S43: Stav 6H 163
Martin La. S74: Black H 3A 46
Martin Ri. S21: Ecki 1D 158
S61: Thorpe H 2D 80
Martin's Rd. S71: Lund 5C 18
Martin St. S6: Shef 1A 4 (2D 118)
(not continuous)
Martin Well's Rd. DN12: New E 5D 70
Marton Rd. DN5: Bntly 3G 23
Marvell Rd. DN5: Scaws 4E 39
Marvell Way S63: Wath D 5G 49
Mary Ann Cl. S71: Barn 6A 18
Mary Ann St. S41: Old W 2F 161
Maryhill Cl. S60: Tree 2G 123
Mary La. S73: D'fld 5C 34
Mary's Pl. S75: Barn 6B 16
Mary St. S1: Shef 6E 5 (5F 119)
S21: Ecki 1E 159
S60: Roth 3D 96
S72: Midd 3F 35
S75: Bar G 4E 15
Marys Wlk. S2: Shef 2A 120
(off Castle Ct.)
Mary Tozer Ho. S10: Shef 3A 118
MASBROUGH 4B 96
Masbrough St. S60: Roth 4C 96
(not continuous)
Masefield Cl. S25: Din 6B 128
Masefield Flats S63: Wath D 5D 48
(off Masefield Rd.)

Masefield Rd. DN2: Don 3H **41**
S13: Shef 1F **135**
S63: Wath D 5D **48**
Masham Ct. DN4: Can 4B **58**
Masham Rd. DN4: Can 5B **58**
Mason Av. S26: Swal 5C **124**
Mason Cres. S13: Shef 1G **135**
Mason Dr. S26: Swal 5C **124**
Mason Gro. S13: Shef 1G **135**
Mason Lathe Rd.
S5: Shef 5B **94**
Mason St. S63: Gol 5D **36**
Masons Way S70: Barn 4H **31**
Mason Way S74: Hoyl 5A **46**
Massey Rd. S13: Shef 3E **137**
Masson Cl. S40: C'fld 3E **167**
Mastall La. DN5: Ark 6D **24**
Masters Cres. S5: Shef 5G **93**
Masters Rd. S5: Shef 5G **93**
MASTIN MOOR 2F **165**
Mather Av. S9: Shef 3E **121**
Mather Ct. S9: Shef 3E **121**
Mather Cres. S9: Shef 3E **121**
Mather Dr. S9: Shef 3E **121**
Mather Rd. S9: Shef 3E **121**
Mather Wlk. S9: Shef 3E 121
(off Mather Rd.)
Matilda La. S1: Shef 6F **5** (4G **119**)
Matilda St. S1: Shef 5D **4** (4F **119**)
(not continuous)
Matilda Way S1: Shef 5D **4** (4F **119**)
Matlock Dr. S43: Ink 3H **169**
Matlock Rd. S6: Shef 1B **118**
S40: W'ton 6A **170**
S42: W'ton 6A **170**
S45: Ston E 6A **170**
S71: Ath 2G **17**
Matlock Way S60: Wav 3C **122**
Mattersey Cl. DN4: Bess 1B **74**
Matthew Gap S36: Thurl 3A **176**
Matthew Ho. S75: Barn 5C **16**
Matthews Av. S63: Wath D 6E **49**
Matthews Cl. S63: Wath D 1E **65**
Matthews Dr. S66: Wick 1G **113**
Matthews Fold S8: Shef 1H **147**
Matthews La. S8: Shef 1H **147**
Matthew St. S3: Shef 1C **4** (1E **119**)
Maudesley Av. S40: C'fld 1H **171**
Mauds Ter. S71: Monk B 3H **17**
Maugerhay S8: Shef 1H **147**
Maulays Ct. DN11: Ross 6E **75**
Mauncer Cres. S13: Shef 1C **136**
Mauncer Dr. S13: Shef 1C **136**
Mauncer La. S13: Shef 2C **136**
Maun Way S5: Shef 1H **107**
Maurice Dobson Mus. & Heritage Cen., The
. . . . .5C **34**
Maurice St. S62: P'gte 5G **83**
Mawfa Av. S14: Shef 6A **134**
Mawfa Cres. S14: Shef 6A **134**
Mawfa Dr. S14: Shef 6A **134**
Mawfa La. S14: Shef 6A **134**
(Constable Rd.)
S14: Shef 5A **134**
(Ironside Cl.)
Mawfa Rd. S14: Shef 1A **148**
Mawfa Wlk. S14: Shef 6A **134**
Mawfield Rd. S75: Barn 4G **15**
Maxey Pl. S8: Shef 2F **133**
Maxfield Av. S10: Shef 3B **118**
Maxwell St. S4: Shef 6H **107**
Maxwell Way S4: Shef 6H **107**
May Av. DN4: Balb 6H **55**
S41: Old W 3B **162**
Mayberry Dr. S75: Silk 2A **28**
May Cl. S63: Thurn 2C **36**
Maycock Av. S61: Kimb P 6G **81**
Maydal Dr. S75: Wool G 3E **7**
May Day Grn. S70: Barn 1E **31**
May Day Grn. Arc. S70: Barn 1E 31
(off Cheapside)
Mayfield S36: Oxs 6H **177**
S71: Monk B 4G **17**
Mayfield Alpacas 4A **130**
Mayfield Ct. S10: Shef 6D **116**
S36: Oxs 6H **177**
S75: Dod 2G **29**
Mayfield Cres.
DN11: New R 6C **74**
S70: Wors 4D **30**
Mayfield Hgts. S10: Shef 1E **131**

Mayfield Rd. DN5: Don 5H **39**
S10: Shef 1A **130**
S40: Bramp 6D **166**
Mayfields DN5: Scawt 1E **39**
Mayflower Cl. S12: Shef 2E **135**
Mayflower Cres. DN4: Warm 1D **70**
Mayflower Rd. DN4: Warm 1D **70**
Mayflower Way S73: Womb 2H **47**
Maynard Rd. S40: C'fld 1G **171**
S60: Roth 1B **112**
May Rd. S6: Shef 4A **106**
May Ter. S70: Barn 1B **30**
Maythorne Cl. S75: Stain 6B **8**
May Tree Cl. S20: Water 1F **151**
Maytree Cl. S73: D'fld 5B **34**
May Tree Cft. S20: Water 1F **151**
May Tree La. S20: Water 1F **151**
Mead, The S41: Has 2B **172**
Meadow Av. S62: Rawm 1E **83**
S72: Cud 4G **19**
Meadow Bank Av. S7: Shef 1C **132**
Meadowbank Cl. S61: Kimb 4B **96**
Meadow Bank Ind. Est.
S61: Kimb 5A **96**
Meadow Bank Rd. S11: Shef 1C **132**
S61: Kimb 6F **95**
Meadow Bank Works S61: Kimb 5G **95**
Meadowbrook Ind. Est.
S20: Half 2H **151**
Meadowbrook Pk. S20: Half 3H **151**
Meadow Cl. S18: Coal A 6H **147**
S26: Kiv P 5C **140**
S43: New W 4C **162**
S65: Dalt 1D **98**
Meadow Ct. DN3: Arm 4F **43**
DN6: Adw S 2D **22**
DN11: New R 6B **74**
S43: New W 2C 162
(off Bamford St.)
S71: Lund 5A **18**
S71: R'ton 3A **10**
Meadowcourt S9: Shef 2E **109**
Meadow Cres. S20: Mosb 3C **150**
S71: R'ton 2A **10**
S72: Grim 1A **20**
Meadow Cft. DN3: Eden 6D **26**
DN5: Sprot 4E **55**
S63: Bolt D 3C **50**
S64: Swin 6B **66**
S72: Shaft 3F **11**
WF9: Hems 1F **13**
Meadowcroft Cl. S60: Whis 4A **112**
Meadowcroft Gdns. S20: W'fld 2F **151**
Meadowcroft Glade S20: W'fld 2F **151**
Meadowcroft Ri. S20: W'fld 2F **151**
Meadow Dr. S35: Chap 3D **78**
S64: Swin 4B **66**
S71: Monk B 4A **18**
S73: D'fld 5C **34**
Meadowfield Dr. S74: Hoyl 2B **62**
Meadow Fld. Rd. DN3: Barn D 2D **26**
Meadow Ga. S73: Womb 3B **48**
Meadowgate S63: Bramp B 6A **48**
Meadow Gate Av. S20: Sot 5A **138**
Meadow Gate Cl. S20: Sot 4A **138**
Meadowgate Lake Nature Reserve
. . . . .2C **152**
Meadow Gate La. S20: Sot 1A **152**
Meadowgate Pk. S21: Killa 3C **152**
Meadowgate S63: Bolt D 1B **50**
Meadow Gro. S17: Tot 6F **145**
Meadow Gro. Rd. S17: Tot 6E **145**
MEADOWHALL 1F **109**
Meadowhall Cen. S9: Shef 2F **109**
Meadowhall Dr. S9: Shef 3E **109**
Meadowhall Interchange (Bus) 1F 109
Meadowhall Interchange Stop (ST)
. . . . .1F **109**
Meadowhall (Park & Ride) 6E 95
Meadowhall Retail Pk. S9: Shef 4F **109**
Meadowhall Rd. S9: Shef 2E **109**
S61: Kimb 5F **95**
Meadowhall South Stop (ST) 2G 109
Meadowhall Station (Rail) 1E 109
Meadowhall Way S9: Shef 1F **109**
MEADOW HEAD 6E **133**
Meadowhead S8: Shef 1E **147**
Meadow Head Av. S8: Shef 3D **146**
Meadow Head Cl. S8: Shef 3D **146**

Meadow Head Dr. S8: Shef 2E **147**
Meadowhill Rd. S41: Has 2C **172**
Meadow Ho. Dr. S10: Shef 5E **117**
Meadowland Ri. S72: Cud 3F **19**
Meadow La. DN9: Auck 3A **76**
DN12: Old D 3F **67**
S62: Rawm 6E **65**
S66: Malt 6B **102**
S75: Dart 1F **15**
Meadowpark Cft. S25: Din 6H **127**
Meadow Rise DN3: Barn D 1D **26**
DN11: Wad 6F **73**
S42: Ash 4A **166**
Meadow Rd. S71: R'ton 3A **10**
Meadows, The S21: Killa 4C **152**
S26: Tod 3B **140**
S42: Ash 3A **166**
S75: Bar G 4F **15**
S75: Silk C 5A **28**
Meadows Ct. DN11: Ross 6E **75**
Meadows Dr. S43: Stav 5B **164**
Meadowside Cl. S42: W'orth 6H **171**
Meadows Rd. S63: Wath D 5H **49**
Meadow St. S3: Shef 1B **4** (1E **119**)
S25: Laugh C 4F **127**
(not continuous)
S61: Roth 4B **96**
S71: Barn 6E **17**
Meadow Ter. S11: Shef 6B **118**
MEADOW VIEW 6C **66**
Meadow Vw. S36: H'swne 1F **177**
S40: Bramp 2B **170**
S70: Wors 5F **31**
S71: Lund 6B **18**
Meadow Vw. Cl. S74: Hoyl 1A **62**
Meadow Vw. Dr. S65: Rav 2B **100**
Meadow Vw. Rd. S8: Shef 2E **147**
S64: Kiln 6C **66**
Meadow Wlk. DN3: Eden 5D **26**
Meadow Way S64: Swin 3E **67**
Meads, The S8: Shef 2G **147**
Meadstead Dr. S71: R'ton 3G **9**
Meadstead Fold S71: R'ton 3G **9**
Meadway, The S17: Dore 3E **145**
Meadway Dr. S17: Dore 3D **144**
Meakin St. S41: Has 2C **172**
Mears Cl. S36: Pen 4E **177**
MEASBOROUGH DIKE 3G **31**
Mecca Bingo
Chesterfield 5G **167**
Doncaster 4E **97**
Rotherham 4E **97**
Sheffield, Flat St. 3F **5** (3G **119**)
Sheffield, Langsett Rd. 6D **106**
Mede, The DN6: Woodl 3A **22**
Medina Way S75: Bar G 3F **15**
Medlar Cft. S75: Barn 6C **16**
Medlock Cl. S13: Shef 5B **122**
S42: W'ton 3C **170**
Medlock Ct. S25: Din 6A **128**
Medlock Cres. S13: Shef 4B **122**
Medlock Cft. S13: Shef 4B **122**
Medlock Dr. S13: Shef 5B **122**
Medlock Rd. S13: Shef 5B **122**
S40: W'ton 2D **170**
Medlock Way S13: Shef 4B **122**
Medway Cl. S75: Bar G 3G **15**
Medway Pl. S73: Womb 3A **48**
MEERSBROOK 3G **133**
Meersbrook Av. S8: Shef 3E **133**
MEERSBROOK BANK 3E **133**
Meersbrook Ent. Cen. S8: Shef 2F **133**
Meersbrook Pk. Rd. S8: Shef 2F **133**
Meersbrook Rd. S8: Shef 3G **133**
Meetinghouse Cft. S13: Shef 2D **136**
Meetinghouse La. S1: Shef . . .2F **5** (2G **119**)
S13: Shef 2D **136**
Mekyll Cl. S66: Sunn 4G **99**
Melbeck Dr. S35: Chap 3D **78**
Melbourne Av. S10: Shef 4B **118**
S18: Dron W 3A **154**
S26: Aston 6D **124**
S63: Bolt D 2A **50**
Melbourne Ct. S43: Stav 4B 164
(off Duke St.)
Melbourne Rd. DN4: Balb 6F **55**
S36: Stoc 3C **174**
Melbourn Rd. S10: Shef 2B **118**
Melciss Rd. S66: Wick 6F **99**
Meld Cl. DN11: New R 6G **75**

Melford Cl. S75: Mapp 5A 8
Melford Dr. DN4: Balb 2H 71
Melfort Glen S10: Shef 3G 117
Melhaven Way S66: Bram 6A 100
Mell Av. S74: Hoyl 6B 46
Melling Av. DN5: Don 1G 55
Melling Cl. S40: Birdh 2G 171
Melling Ct. S40: Birdh 2G 171
Mellington Cl. S8: Shef 6H 133
Mellor La. S18: Barl 5A 160
Mellor Lea Farm Chase S35: Eccl . . .6G 79
Mellor Lea Farm Cl. S35: Eccl 6G 79
          (off Mellor Lea Farm Dr.)
Mellor Lea Farm Dr. S35: Eccl 6G 79
Mellor Lea Farm Gth. S35: Eccl 6G 79
          (off Mellor Lea Farm Dr.)
Mellor Rd. S73: Womb 2G 47
Mellor Way S40: Birdh 3H 171
Mellow Flds. Rd. S25: Laugh M 2G 127
Mellwood Gro. S73: Hem 4F 47
Melrose Cl. DN4: Balb 5F 55
     S40: Ash 5D 166
     S66: Thurc 6A 114
Melrose Cotts. S60: Whis 3B 112
Melrose Gro. S60: Roth 2H 111
Melrose M. DN9: Auck 3A 76
Melrose Rd. S3: Shef 5G 107
Melrose Way S71: Monk B 6A 18
Meltham La. S41: C'fld 2A 168
Melton Av. S63: Gol 5D 36
     S73: Bramp 4C 48
MELTON BRAND 1H 53
Melton Cl. DN11: New R 6B 74
Melton Ct. DN12: Den M 2C 68
     S26: Aston 1F 139
Meltonfield S63: Gol 5E 37
Meltonfield Cl. DN3: Arm 5F 43
Melton Gdns. DN5: Sprot 3C 54
Melton Grn. S63: Wath D 6D 48
Melton Gro. S20: Mosb 6B 136
Melton High St. S63: Wath D 6D 48
Melton Mill La. DN5: High M 3C 52
Melton Rd. DN5: Sprot 3G 53
Melton St. S64: Mexb 2H 67
     S73: Bramp 4C 48
Melton Ter. S70: Wors 5H 31
Melton Vw. DN5: Barnb 1H 51
Melton Way S71: R'ton 1H 9
Melton Wood Gro. DN5: Sprot 3C 54
Melville Av. DN4: Balb 5H 55
Melville Cres. S43: Brim C 4E 169
Melville Dr. S2: Shef 6D 120
Melville St. S73: Womb 1G 47
Melvinia Cres. S75: Barn 4C 16
Melwood Ct. DN3: Arm 6F 43
Memoir Gro. DN11: New R 6F 75
Memory La. S25: Nth A 2G 141
Mendip Cl. DN5: Cus 5F 39
     S75: Barn 6A 16
Mendip Cres. S40: Ash 4C 166
Mendip Ri. S60: Brins 5E 111
Merbeck Dr. S35: High G 5D 60
Merbeck Gro. S35: High G 6D 60
Mercaston Cl. S40: C'fld 3B 166
Mercel Av. DN3: Arm 2F 43
Merchant Cft. S71: Monk B 3A 18
Merchants Cres. S2: Shef 2G 5 (2H 119)
Merchant Way DN2: Don 1H 41
Mercia Dr. S17: Dore 4F 145
Meredith Cres. DN4: Balb 6A 56
Meredith Rd. S6: Shef 4A 106
Mere Gro. DN3: Arm 2D 42
Mere La. DN3: Arm, Eden 3D 42
          (not continuous)
Mere Vw. S63: Wath D 5F 49
Merlin Cl. DN6: Adw S 2C 22
     S70: Birdw 4E 45
Merlin Dr. DN9: Auck 3B 76
Merlin Theatre 1D 132
Merlin Way S5: Shef 1H 107
     S61: Thorpe H 2D 80
Merrick Cl. S40: C'fld 3E 167
Merrill Rd. S63: Thurn 2B 36
Merryton Cres. S5: Shef 3F 93
Merton La. S9: Shef 6E 95
Merton Ri. S9: Shef 6E 95
Merton Rd. S9: Shef 6E 95
Metcalfe Av. S21: Killa 4B 152
Methley Cl. S12: Shef 2C 134
Methley Ho. DN1: Don 2B 56
          (off Grove Pl.)

Methley St. S72: Cud 2E 19
Metrodome Leisure Complex, The . .6F 17
Metro Trad. Cen. S75: Bar G 3F 15
Mews, The DN5: Hick 4F 15
          (off Castle Hill Fold)
Mews Ct. DN3: Arm 3F 43
MEXBOROUGH 2F 67
Mexborough Bus. Cen. S64: Mexb . .1G 67
Mexborough Interchange 2F 67
          (off John St.)
Mexborough Rd. S63: Bolt D 3C 50
Mexborough Station (Rail) 2F 67
Meynell Cl. S40: Bramp 6D 166
Meynell Cres. S5: Shef 6C 92
Meynell Rd. S5: Shef 6C 92
Meynell Way S21: Killa 4B 152
          (off Marrison Dr.)
Meyrick Dr. S75: Dart 1E 15
MFA Bowl
     Sheffield .6A 94
Michael Cl. S42: W'orth 5H 171
Michael Cft. S63: Wath D 6E 49
Michael Rd. S71: Lund 6B 18
Michael's Est. S72: Grim 1B 20
MICKLEBRING 6G 87
Micklebring La. DN12: Con 6D 68
Micklebring La.
     S66: B'well, Mick 6G 87
Micklebring Way S66: Hel 3E 101
Mickleden Way S75: Barn 1H 29
MICKLEY 1A 154
Mickley La. S17: Tot 6F 145
     S18: Dron W 6F 145, 1A 154
Middle Av. S62: Rawm 3G 83
Middle Bank DN4: Don 4D 56
Middleburn Cl. S70: Barn 3F 31
Middlecliff Cl. S20: Water 1F 151
Middlecliff Cotts. S72: Midd 3F 35
Middlecliff Ct. S20: Water 1F 151
MIDDLECLIFFE 3F 35
Middlecliffe M. S72: Midd 3E 35
Middlecliff La. S72: Lit H, Midd 2D 34
Middlecliff Ri. S20: Water 1F 151
Middle Cl. S75: Kexb 5D 6
MIDDLECROFT 6H 163
Middlecroft Rd. S43: Stav 1H 169
Middle Dr. S60: Roth 3G 111
Middle Farm Ct. S71: D'fld 2A 34
Middlefield Cl. S17: Dore 3D 144
Middlefield Cft. S17: Dore 3D 144
Middle Fld. La. WF4: Wool 1F 7
Middle Fld. Rd. S75: Silk 5E 29
Middlefield Rd. DN4: Bess 5A 58
     S60: Roth 2H 111
Middlefields Dr. S60: Whis 3B 112
Middlegate DN5: Scawt 1F 39
          (not continuous)
Middleham Rd. DN4: Can 5B 58
MIDDLE HANDLEY 4A 158
Middle Hay Cl. S14: Shef 3B 134
Middle Hay Pl. S14: Shef 4B 134
Middle Hay Ri. S14: Shef 4B 134
Middle Hay Vw. S14: Shef 4B 134
Middle La. DN4: Warm 2E 71
     S6: Shef .6H 105
     S35: Gren 1A 92
     S65: Roth 3G 97
Middle La. Sth. S65: Roth 4H 97
Middle Ox Cl. S20: Half 4G 151
Middle Ox Gdns. S20: Half 4G 151
Middle Pavement S40: C'fld 5H 167
          (off Central Pavement)
Middlepeak Way S13: Shef 4A 122
Middle Pl. S65: Roth 3A 98
Middlesex St. S70: Barn 3E 31
Middle Shambles S40: C'fld 5H 167
          (off High St.)
Middleton Av. S25: Din 6H 127
Middleton Dr. S43: Ink 3G 169
Middleton Gro. S75: Dod 2F 29
Middleton La. S35: Gren 2C 92
Middleton Rd. S65: Roth 4G 97
MIDDLEWOOD 6G 91
Middlewood Chase S6: Shef 1H 105
Middlewood Dr. S6: Shef 1G 105
     S61: Scho 6F 81
Middlewood Dr. E. S6: Shef 1G 105
Middlewood Lodge S6: Shef 1H 105
Middlewood (Park & Ride) 1A 106
Middlewood Ri. S6: Shef 1H 105
Middlewood Rd. S6: Shef 6H 91

Middlewood Rd. Nth.
     S35: Ough 4F 91
Middlewoods S75: Dod 3H 29
Middlewood Stop (ST) 1A 106
Middlewoods Way S71: Ath 6G 9
Midfield Rd. S10: Shef 2H 117
Midhill Cres. S2: Shef 1G 133
Midhill Rd. S2: Shef 1G 133
Midhope Way S75: Barn 1H 29
Midhurst Gro. S75: Bar G 3F 15
Midhurst Rd. S6: Shef 4A 92
Midland Cotts. S41: Has 3A 172
Midland Rd. S41: Has 2G 172
     S60: Roth 4C 96
     S61: Roth 4B 96
Midland Rd. S61: Roth 4B 96
     S64: Swin 3D 66
     S71: R'ton 2H 9
Midland St. S1: Shef 5F 119
     S62: P'gte 6G 83
     S70: Barn 1E 31
Midland Ter. S41: Has 3A 172
     S43: Bar H 2G 163
Midvale Av. S6: Shef 6D 106
Midvale Cl. S6: Shef 6D 106
Milano Ri. S73: D'fld 5A 34
Milbanke St. DN1: Don 6C 40
Milburn Ct. S20: Sot 1H 151
Milburn Gro. S20: Sot 1H 151
Milden Pl. S70: Barn 3F 31
Milden Rd. S6: Shef 2H 105
Milefield Ct. S72: Grim 1A 20
Milefield La. S72: Grim, Shaft 1H 19
Milefield Vw. S72: Grim 1A 20
MILEHILL 5E 173
Mile Oak Rd. S60: Roth 1G 111
Miles Cl. S6: Shef 3F 107
Miles Rd. S6: Shef 3E 107
     S35: High G 1D 78
Milestone Ct. DN4: Bess 5B 58
Milestone Dr. DN2: Don 3F 41
Mileswood Cl. S72: Gt H 5E 21
Milethorn La. DN1: Don 5C 40
Milford Av. S74: Els 6E 47
Milford Rd. S43: Ink 3H 169
Milford St. S9: Shef 4E 109
Milgate St. S71: R'ton 3E 9
Milgrove Cres. S35: High G 6C 60
Milking La. S73: Bramp 5B 48
Millais Ri. S66: Flan 3G 99
Millard La. S66: Malt 5B 102
Millars Wlk. WF9: Sth K 5H 13
Millbank Cl. S35: High G 2C 78
Mill Cl. S25: Brookh 6G 115
     S26: Tod .4C 140
     S60: Roth 6D 96
     WF9: Sth K 4H 13
Mill Ct. S35: Eccl 1G 93
     S70: Wors 5F 31
Millcross La. S18: Barl 3A 160
Milldale Cl. S40: C'fld 3D 166
Milldale Rd. S17: Tot 5G 145
Milldyke Cl. S60: Whis 3C 112
Millennium Gallery 4F 5 (3G 119)
Millennium Sq. S1: Shef 4E 5 (3F 119)
Millennium Way S41: Shef 5F 161
Miller Av. S43: Mas M 2F 165
Miller Cft. S13: Shef 2B 136
Miller Dale Dr. S60: Brins 5E 111
Miller Rd. S7: Shef 1E 133
Millers Cft. S71: R'ton 2H 9
Millers Dale S70: Wors 6F 31
Mill Fld. Cl. DN3: Barn D 2D 26
Millfield Ind. Est. DN5: Bntly 1B 40
Millfield Rd. DN5: Bntly 2B 40
Mill Flds. S26: Tod 4B 140
Mill Ga. DN5: Bntly 2A 40
Mill Grn. S43: Stav 4B 164
Mill Haven S25: Nth A 3G 141
Mill Hill S60: Whis 3B 112
     S73: Womb 6E 33
Mill Hill Cl. DN5: Don 1G 55
Millhill Cl. DN3: Arm 6F 43
Mill Hills S26: Tod 3C 140
Millhouse Ct. S65: Dalt 1B 98
Mill Ho. M. S43: Stav 4B 164
MILLHOUSES
     S7 . . . . .5C 132
     S73 . . . . .4D 34
Millhouses Ct. S11: Shef 4A 132

Millhouses Glen S11: Shef 4A 132
Millhouses La. S7: Shef 3H 131
   S11: Shef 3H 131
Millhouses St. S74: Hoyl 1B 62
Millicent Sq. S66: Malt 6B 102
Millindale S66: Malt 6B 102
Mill La. DN3: Brant 4F 59
   DN4: Warm 4C 54
   DN5: Harl 3H 51
   DN6: Adw S 2C 22
   S17: Tot 5G 145
   S18: Dron 3G 155
   S21: Reni 2H 159
   S25: Sth A 3G 141
   S36: Spink 3H 175
   S36: Thurl 4A 176
   S40: C'fld 6E 167
   S42: Tem N 6G 173
   S44: Stan 6H 165
   S60: Tree 2E 123
   S62: Wentw 4C 62
   S63: Wath D 1D 64
   S75: Dart 5F 7
   WF9: Sth K 5H 13
Mill Mdw. Cl. S20: Sot 1A 152
Mill Mdw. Gdns. S20: Sot 1A 152
Millmoor Ct. S73: Womb 6A 34
Millmoor La. S60: Roth 4C 96
Millmoor Rd. DN4: Can 4B 58
   S73: Womb 6A 34
Millmount Rd. S8: Shef 3E 133
   S74: Hoyl 1C 62
Millrace Dr. S63: Gol 6B 36
Mill Rd. S21: Ecki 6E 151
   S35: Eccl 1G 93
   S60: Tree 2E 123
Mill Rd. Cl. S35: Eccl 1G 93
Millsands S3: Shef 1F 5 (1G 119)
Millside S72: Shaft 3F 11
Millside Cl. DN5: Bnty 2A 40
Millside Wlk. S72: Shaft 3F 11
Millstone Cl. S18: Dron W 2C 154
Millstone Dr. S26: Aston 6C 124
Millstones S36: Oxs 6H 177
Mill Stream Cl. S40: W'ton 1D 170
Millstream Cl. DN5: Sprot 3E 55
Mill St. DN3: Arm 4E 43
   S41: C'fld 5A 168
   S60: Roth 5E 97
   S61: Grea 4C 82
   WF9: Sth K 4H 13
Millthorpe Rd. S5: Shef 6A 94
Millua S3: Shef 1F 119
          (off Kelham Island)
Mill Vw. S63: Bolt D 3A 50
Millwood Rd. DN4: Balb 1G 71
Millwood Vw. S6: Stan 5D 104
Milner Av. S36: Pen 3B 176
Milner Cl. S66: Bram 4B 100
Milner Ga. Ct. DN12: Con 4H 69
Milner Ga. La. DN12: Con 4G 69
Milner Rd. DN4: Balb 5G 55
Milnes St. S70: Barn 2F 31
Milne St. S75: Bar G 4F 15
Milnrow Cres. S5: Shef 4E 93
Milnrow Dr. S5: Shef 4E 93
Milnrow Rd. S5: Shef 4E 93
Milnrow Vw. S5: Shef 4E 93
MILTON 2B 62
Milton Av. DN5: Don 6G 39
Milton Cl. S61: Grea 4C 82
   S63: Wath D 4C 48
   S74: Jum 5C 46
Milton Ct. DN1: Don 2C 56
   S64: Swin 3B 66
Milton Cres. S40: Birdh 2H 171
   S74: Hoyl 5C 46
Milton Cft. S74: Hoyl 5C 46
Milton Dr. DN3: Arm 4E 43
   DN3: Eden 6C 26
   S73: Womb 2H 47
Milton La. S3: Shef 6C 4 (4E 119)
Milton Pl. S43: Stav 4C 164
Milton Rd. DN3: Brant 3H 59
   S7: Shef 1D 132
   S25: Din 6B 128
   S35: Burn 3C 78
   S64: Mexb 1F 67
   S65: Roth 2G 97
   S74: Hoyl 6B 46

Milton St. S1: Shef 6B 4 (4E 119)
   S3: Shef 6B 4 (4E 119)
   S60: Roth 2D 96
   S64: Swin 3B 66
   S66: Malt 6A 102
   S72: Gt H 6E 21
Milton Wlk. DN1: Don 2B 56
Minden Cl. S66: Wick 6G 99
Minden Ct. DN5: Bntly 1H 39
Miners Cl. S66: Sunn 3G 99
Miners Row S63: Thurn 3D 36
Minimum Ter. S40: C'fld 6F 167
Minna Rd. S3: Shef 5G 107
Minneymoor Hill DN12: Con 3G 69
Minneymoor La. DN12: Con 4G 69
Minster Cl. DN4: Can 5D 58
   S35: Eccl 2H 93
Minster Rd. S35: Eccl 2G 93
Minster Way S71: Monk B 5A 18
Minto Rd. S7: Shef 3A 106
Miriam Av. S40: Bramp 2B 170
Mission Cir. S75: Wool G 3F 7
          (off Wooley Edge La.)
Mission Fld. S73: Bramp 4B 48
Mitchell Av. S73: Womb 6F 33
Mitchell Cl. S73: Wors 5A 32
Mitchell Rd. S8: Shef 6E 133
   S73: Womb 5F 33
Mitchells Ct. S73: Womb 6G 33
Mitchells Ent. Cen. S73: Womb 5F 33
Mitchells M. S73: Womb 6F 33
Mitchells Ter. S3: Shef 2A 4 (2D 118)
   S70: Swai 5B 32
Mitchells Way S73: Womb 6F 33
Mitchell Way S43: New W 3D 162
   S60: Wav 2B 122
Mitchelson Av. S73: Dod 3F 29
Moat Cft. S66: Sunn 3H 99
Moat Cft. DN5: Scawt 1G 39
Moat Dr. DN9: Auck 3A 76
Moat Hills Ct. DN5: Bntly 1A 40
Moat Ho. Way DN12: Con 3F 69
Moatlands S66: Wick 2H 113
Moat La. S66: Wick 3H 113
Mobray Dr. S75: Wool G 3F 7
Modena Ct. S73: D'fld 4H 33
Moffat Gdns. DN2: Don 1A 42
Moffatt Rd. S2: Shef 1G 133
Molineaux Cl. S5: Shef 5A 94
Molineaux Rd. S5: Shef 4H 93
Molineux Av. S43: Stav 5A 164
Molloy Pl. S8: Shef 2F 133
Molloy St. S8: Shef 2F 133
Momentum Leisure Cen. 2B 4
Mona Av. S10: Shef 2B 118
Mona Rd. DN4: Balb 4A 56
   S10: Shef 2B 118
Mona St. S75: Barn 6C 16
Monckton Rd. S5: Shef 1C 108
Moncrieffe Rd. S7: Shef 2D 132
MONK BRETTON 4G 17
Monk Bretton Priory (remains) 6B 18
Monksbridge Trad. Est. . . . .
   S25: Laugh C 4G 127
Monks Cl. S61: Kimb P 6F 81
Monkspring S70: Wors 5H 31
Monks Way S71: Monk B 5A 18
Monk Ter. S71: Monk B 3B 18
Monkton Way S71: R'ton 1H 9
MONKWOOD 3B 160
Monkwood Rd. S41: C'fld 6E 161
   S62: Rawm 1E 83
Monmouth Rd. DN2: Don 4F 41
Monmouth St. S3: Shef 5A 4 (4D 118)
Monsal Cres. S43: Ink 2G 169
   S71: Ath 1F 17
Monsal St. S63: Thurn 2B 36
Montague Av. DN12: Con 4D 68
Montague St. DN1: Don 6C 40
   S6: Shef 5C 106
   S11: Shef 5D 118
   S72: Cud 6F 11
Montagu Rd. DN5: Don 2F 55
Montagu Sq. S64: Mexb 2F 67
Montagu St. S64: Mexb 2G 67
Monteney Cres. S5: Shef 2F 93
Monteney Gdns. S5: Shef 3F 93
Monteney Rd. S5: Shef 3F 93
Montfort Dr. S3: Shef 6G 107

Montgomery Av. S7: Shef 1D 132
Montgomery Cl. S60: Tree 3G 123
Montgomery Ct. S11: Shef 3H 131
Montgomery Dr. S7: Shef 1D 132
Montgomery Gdns. DN2: Don 4H 41
Montgomery M. S63: Wath D 6E 49
Montgomery Rd. S7: Shef 2D 132
   S63: Wath D 6F 49
Montgomery Sq. S63: Wath D 6G 49
Montgomery Ter. Rd. . . . .
   S6: Shef 1E 119
Montgomery Theatre 4E 5 (3F 119)
Montrose Av. DN2: Don 5G 41
   S75: Dart 5G 7
Montrose Ct. S11: Shef 4G 131
Montrose Pl. S18: Dron W 2C 154
Montrose Rd. S7: Shef 3B 132
Mont Wlk. S73: Womb 6D 32
Monument Dr. S72: Brier 4A 12
Monyash Cl. S43: Stav 1H 169
Moonpenny Way S18: Dron 3F 155
Moonshine La. S5: Shef 1E 107
Moonshine Way S5: Shef 2E 107
Moor, The S1: Shef 6D 4 (4F 119)
Moorbank Cl. S10: Shef 4E 117
   S73: Womb 6E 33
   S75: Barn 4B 16
Moorbank Ct. S10: Shef 3E 117
Moorbank Dr. S10: Shef 3F 117
Moorbank Rd. S10: Shef 3E 117
   S73: Womb 5E 33
Moorbank Vw. S73: Womb 5E 33
Moorbridge Cres. . . . .
   S73: Bramp 3C 48
Moor Cres. S20: Mosb 3D 150
Moorcrest Ri. S75: Stain 4A 8
Moorcroft Av. S10: Shef 1C 130
Moorcroft Cl. S10: Shef 1C 130
Moorcroft Dr. S10: Shef 1C 130
Moorcroft Ho. S40: C'fld 1H 171
          (off Archdale Cl.)
Moorcroft Rd. S10: Shef 1C 130
Moordale Vw. S62: Rawm 1B 84
Moor End Ho's. S75: Silk C 5C 28
Moorend La. S75: Silk C 5B 28
Moor End Rd. S10: Shef 2B 118
Moore St. S3: Shef 6B 4 (5E 119)
Moor Farm Av. S20: Mosb 2C 150
Moor Farm Gth. S20: Mosb 2D 150
Moor Farm Ri. S20: Mosb 2C 150
Moorfield Av. S10: Shef 3A 100
Moorfield Cl. S65: Rav 3A 100
Moorfield Dr. DN3: Arm 5E 43
Moorfield Gro. S65: Rav 3A 100
Moorfield Pl. WF9: Hems 1D 12
Moorfields S3: Shef 1D 4 (2F 119)
Moorfields Flats S3: Shef 1D 4
          (off Moorfields)
Moor Gap DN3: Brant 4G 59
MOORGATE 2H 111
Moorgate Av. S10: Shef 2C 118
   S60: Roth 6F 97
Moorgate Bus. Cen. . . . .
   S60: Roth 5F 97
          (off Moorgate Rd.)
Moorgate Chase S60: Roth 5F 97
Moorgate Ct. S60: Roth 5F 97
Moorgate Cres. S18: Dron 4G 155
Moorgate Gro. S60: Roth 6G 97
Moorgate La. S60: Roth 6F 97
Moorgate Rd. S60: Roth 5F 97
Moorgate St. S60: Roth 4E 97
Moorgate Vw. S60: Roth 1G 111
Moorgate Wlk. S60: Roth 6F 97
Moor Grn. Cl. S75: Barn 1H 29
Moorhay Cl. S41: C'fld 1C 166
Moorhead S1: Shef 5D 4
Moorhead Way S66: Bram 5C 100
Moorhouse Cl. . . . .
   S60: Whis 3C 112
Moorhouse Dr. S66: Thurc 1C 126
Moorhouse La. S60: Whis 3B 112
   S75: Haigh 1D 6
Moorings, The S64: Swin 3D 66
Moorland Av. S70: Barn 2A 30
   S75: Stain 4A 8
Moorland Cl. DN1: Don 1D 56
   S71: Lund 6B 18
Moorland Cres. S75: Stain 4A 8
Moorland Dr. S36: Stoc 3C 174
Moorland Gro. DN4: Bess 3H 57

Moorland Pl. S6: Stan 6D 104
S75: Silk C 5B 28
Moorlands S66: Wick 6E 99
Moorlands Ct. S63: Wath D 4D 48
Moorlands Cres. S60: Whis 3B 112
Moorland Ter. S72: Cud 3F 19
Moorland Vw. S12: Shef 6D 134
S18: App 3D 156
S26: Aston 1D 138
S63: Wath D 4D 48
Moorland Vw. Rd. S40: W'ton 2D 170
Moor La. DN3: Kirk Sa 3A 26
S44: Ark T, Cal 3H 173
S66: Mick 1E 101
S70: Birdw 1E 61
S72: Brier, Gt H 5E 13
Moor La. Nth. S65: Rav 6A 86
Moor La. Sth. S65: Rav 2A 100
Moor Ley S70: Birdw 3E 45
Moor Mkt., The S1: Shef 6D 4 (4F 119)
Moor Oaks Rd. S10: Shef 3B 118
Moor Pk. Av. S40: W'ton 2D 170
Moor Rd. S6: Brad 1A 104
S63: Wath D 6G 49
(not continuous)
S65: Roth 4A 98
Moorshutt Rd. WF9: Hems 1D 12
Moorside S10: Shef 6B 116
Moorside Av. S36: Cub 5D 176
Moorside Cl. S20: Mosb 2D 150
S75: Mapp 6A 8
Moorsyde Av. S10: Shef 1A 118
Moorsyde Cres. S10: Shef 1A 118
Moorthorpe Bank S20: Mosb 6C 136
Moorthorpe Cl. S20: Mosb 6C 136
Moorthorpe Gdns. S20: Mosb 6B 136
Moorthorpe Grn. S20: Mosb 6A 136
Moorthorpe Ri. S20: Mosb 1C 150
Moorthorpe Vw. S20: Mosb 1B 150
Moorthorpe Way S20: Mosb 6C 136
(Moorthorpe Bank)
S20: Mosb 6A 136
(Sheffield Rd.)
Moor Top Dr. WF9: Hems 1E 13
Moortop Rd. S18: App 3E 157
Moortown Av. S25: Din 1B 142
Moor Valley S20: Mosb 6A 136
Moor Valley Cl. S20: Mosb 1B 150
Moor Vw. DN3: Brant 4G 59
Moorview S61: Kimb 4G 95
Moorview Cl. S42: W'orth 6A 172
S43: Brim 1C 168
Moorview Ct. S17: Bradw 5A 146
S61: Kimb 4G 95
Moor Vw. Crt. S10: Shef 3G 117
Moor Vw. Dr. S8: Shef 6D 132
Moor Vw. Rd. S8: Shef 6D 132
S43: Stav 4D 164
Moor Vw. Ter. S11: Shef 3F 131
Moorwinstow Cft. S17: Dore 3F 145
Moorwoods Av. S35: Chap 3F 79
Moorwoods La. S35: Chap 3F 79
Moray Pl. S18: Dron W 2C 154
Mordaunt Rd. S2: Shef 2C 134
More Hall La. S36: Bolst 6G 175
More Hall Vw. S35: Wharn S 1A 90
Morgan Av. S5: Shef 2E 107
Morgan Cl. S5: Shef 1E 107
Morgan Rd. DN2: Don 6H 41
S5: Shef 2E 107
Morland Bank S14: Shef 5B 134
Morland Cl. S14: Shef 5C 134
Morland Dr. S14: Shef 5C 134
Morland Pl. S14: Shef 5C 134
Morland Rd. S14: Shef 5B 134
Morley Av. S40: Ash 4D 166
Morley Cl. S18: Dron W 3B 154
Morley Pl. DN12: Con 5E 69
Morley Rd. DN1: Don 5D 40
S61: Kimb P 1H 95
Morley St. S6: Shef 5A 106
S62: P'gte 4G 83
Morpeth Gdns. S3: Shef 1B 4
Morpeth St. S3: Shef 1B 4 (2E 119)
S65: Roth 4F 97
Morrall Rd. S5: Shef 3E 93
Morrell St. S66: Malt 6B 102
Morris Av. S41: C'fld 3F 167
S62: Rawm 6G 65
Morris Dr. S41: C'fld 3F 167
Morrison Av. S66: Malt 4B 102

Morrison Dr. DN11: New R 6D 74
Morrison Pl. S73: D'fld 4B 34
Morrison Rd. S73: D'fld 4A 34
Morse Way S60: Cat, Shef 2B 122
Morston Claycliffe Office Pk.
S75: Barn 4H 15
Mortain Rd. S60: Roth 2G 111
Mortains S26: Tod 2C 140
MORTHEN 5G 113
Morthen Cotts. S66: Mort 5F 113
Morthen Gdns. S66: Wick 6G 99
Morthen Hall La. S66: Mort 5G 113
Morthen La. S60: Up W 6D 112
S66: Mort 4F 113
Morthen Rd. S66: Thurc, Wick 6G 99
Morthen Vw. S66: Wick 3H 113
Mortimer Dr. S36: Cub 6C 176
Mortimer Hgts. S36: Cub 6C 176
Mortimer Rd.
S36: Cub, Midh, Pen 6C 176
S66: Malt 6D 102
Mortimer St. S1: Shef 6F 5 (4G 119)
Mortlake Rd. S5: Shef 2A 108
MORTOMLEY 1D 78
Mortomley Cl. S35: High G 1D 78
Mortomley Cft. S35: Chap 1E 79
Mortomley Hall Gdns.
S35: High G 1D 78
Mortomley La. S35: High G 6D 60
Morton Cl. S71: Monk B 3A 18
Morton Gdns. S20: Half 4G 151
Morton La. S21: West H 3F 157
Morton Mt. S20: Half 3G 151
Morton Pl. S35: Gren 2B 92
Morton Rd. S64: Mexb 1G 67
MOSBOROUGH 3E 151
Mosborough Hall Dr. S20: Half 5F 151
Mosborough Moor S20: Mosb 2C 150
Mosborough Parkway S12: Shef 3A 136
S13: Shef 5G 121
S20: Beig 3F 137
Mosborough Rd. S13: Shef 1E 135
Moscar Cotts. S7: Shef 4C 132
Moscrop Cl. S13: Shef 1D 136
Mosham Cl. DN9: Blax 1E 77
Mosham Rd. DN9: Auck, Blax 2H 59
Moss Beck Ct. S21: Ecki 1D 158
Moss Cl. S66: Wick 6G 99
Mossdale Av. S20: Mosb 3E 151
Mossdale Cl. DN5: Scawt 3F 39
Moss Dr. S21: Killa 5C 152
Moss Gro. S12: Shef 5E 137
Moss Ho. Ct. S20: Mosb 4E 151
Mossley Pl. S36: Pen 4E 177
Moss Ri. Pl. S21: Ecki 1D 158
Moss Rd. S17: Tot 6B 144
Moss Vw. S20: Mosb 4D 151
Moss Way S20: Water, W'fld 5D 136
Moss Way Stop (ST) 5D 136
Moston Wlk. S40: Birdh 4F 171
Motehall Dr. S2: Shef 5D 120
Motehall Pl. S2: Shef 5E 121
Motehall Rd. S2: Shef 5D 120
Motehall Wlk. S2: Shef 5E 121
Motehall Way S2: Shef 5D 120
Motorpoint Arena
Sheffield 5E 109
Motte, The S61: Kimb 2A 96
Mottram St. S71: Barn 6E 17
Mottram Way S71: Barn 6E 17
Mound Rd. S40: C'fld 1H 171
Mount, The DN3: Eden 1D 42
S41: Old W 3H 161
S66: Sunn 3G 99
Mount Av. S72: Grim 6B 12
S72: Gt H 1F 35
Mountbatten Dr. S35: Burn 3C 78
Mountcastle St. S41: C'fld 6G 161
Mountcastle Wlk. S41: C'fld 6G 161
Mount Cl. S70: Barn 3E 31
Mount Cres. S74: Hoyl 5A 46
Mountenoy Rd. S60: Roth 5E 97
Mountfield Way S25: Laugh C 4F 127
Mountford Cft. S17: Tot 5F 145
Mount Olive S36: Stoc 3D 174
Mt. Osborne Ind. Pk. S71: Barn 2G 31
Mt. Pleasant DN4: Balb 5H 55
S35: Chap 2F 79
S70: Wors 6G 31
S72: Grim 6B 12
Mt. Pleasant Cl. S35: Chap 2F 79

Mt. Pleasant Rd. S7: Shef 6E 119
S61: Roth 3C 96
S63: Wath D 2G 65
Mount Rd. S3: Shef 5E 107
S35: Chap 3D 78
S72: Grim 6B 12
Mount St. S11: Shef 5E 119
S61: Roth 3C 96
S70: Barn 2D 30
S71: Ard 2C 32
Mount Ter. S63: Wath D 6D 48
S73: Womb 1F 47
Mt. Vernon Av. S70: Barn 3E 31
Mt. Vernon Cres. S70: Barn 4F 31
Mt. Vernon Rd. S70: Barn, Wors 3F 31
Mount Vw. DN12: New E 5C 70
Mount Vw. Av. S8: Shef 5F 133
Mount Vw. Gdns. S8: Shef 5F 133
Mount Vw. Rd. S8: Shef 6F 133
Mousehole Cl. S65: Dalt 1D 98
Mousehole La. S65: Dalt 1D 98
Mouse Pk. Ga. S35: Gren 1G 91
Mowbray Gdns. S65: Roth 2B 98
Mowbray Pl. S65: Roth 2B 98
Mowbray St. S3: Shef 1F 119
S65: Roth 2A 98
Mowson Cres. S35: Ough 5E 91
Mowson Dr. S35: Ough 5E 91
Mowson Hollow S35: Ough 5E 91
Mowson La. S35: Ough 5E 91
Moxon Cl. S36: Spink 4G 175
Mucky La. S36: Stoc 1C 174
(Hunshelf Rd.)
S36: Stoc 5B 174
(Lee Ho. La.)
S71: Ard 1D 32
Muglet La. S66: Malt 5B 102
Muirfield Av. DN4: Can 6E 59
S64: Swin 4D 66
Muirfield Cl. S41: C'fld 2A 168
S72: Cud 5F 11
Muirfields, The S75: Dart 5H 7
Mulberry Cl. DN5: Cus 5E 39
S42: W'orth 6H 171
S62: P'gte 5G 83
S63: Gol 5B 36
S73: D'fld 5B 34
Mulberry Ct. DN4: Warm 5E 55
DN9: Auck 2B 76
(off Fir Tree Av.)
Mulberry Cft. S43: Hol 5F 163
Mulberry Rd. S21: Ecki 2C 158
S25: Nth A 5A 152
Mulberry St. S1: Shef 3F 5 (3G 119)
Mulberry Way DN3: Arm 6E 43
S21: Killa 5A 152
Mulehouse Rd. S10: Shef 2H 117
Mundella Pl. S8: Shef 5F 133
Muneeb Ct. S62: Rawm 3G 83
Mungy La. S65: Thry 6C 84
Munro Cl. S21: Killa 4C 152
Munsbrough La. S61: Grea 6C 82
(not continuous)
Munsbrough Ri. S61: Grea 5C 82
Murdoch Pl. S71: Smi 1D 16
Murdock Rd. S5: Shef 6E 93
Murfin Cl. S25: Laugh C 3F 127
Murrayfield Dr. S20: Half 4F 151
Murray Rd. S11: Shef 2A 132
S21: Killa 3D 152
S62: Rawm 2H 83
Musard Pl. S43: Stav 5A 164
Musard Way S21: Killa 4B 152
Musgrave Cres. S5: Shef 3F 107
Musgrave Dr. S5: Shef 3F 107
Musgrave Pl. S5: Shef 3F 107
Musgrave Rd. S5: Shef 3E 107
Musgrove Av. S65: Thry 6F 85
Mushroom La. S3: Shef 2A 4 (3C 118)
S10: Shef 3C 118
Muskoka Av. S11: Shef 3F 131
Muskoka Dr. S11: Shef 3F 131
Mutual St. DN4: Hex 2A 56
Muxlow S11: Shef 2C 132
Myers Av. S35: Ough 2E 91
Myers Gro. La. S6: Shef 5F 105
(not continuous)
Myers La. S6: Lox 1B 104
Mylnhurst Rd. S11: Shef 3A 132
Mylor Ct. S71: Monk B 5H 17
Mylor Rd. S11: Shef 2H 131

Myndon Wlk. DN12: Den M 3D 68
Myrtle Cl. S2: Shef 2H 133
Myrtle Cres. S2: Shef 1H 133
S66: Wick .5H 99
Myrtle Dr. S2: Shef 2H 133
Myrtle Gro. DN9: Auck 1H 59
S26: Kiv P 6H 139
S43: Hol .5F 163
Myrtle Rd. S2: Shef 6F 119
S73: Womb 1F 47
Myrtle Springs S12: Shef 3B 134
(not continuous)
Myrtle Springs Dr. S12: Shef 3C 134
Myrtle St. S75: Barn 6B 16
Mysten Clt. S75: Barn 4C 16
Myton Rd. S9: Shef 2D 120

N

Nabeel Ct. S60: Roth 5F 97
Nairn Ct. S18: Dron W 3C 154
Nairn St. S10: Shef 3A 118
Nancy Cres. S72: Grim 2C 20
Nancy Rd. S72: Grim 2C 20
Nanny Hill S36: Stoc 3E 175
Nanny Marr Rd. S73: D'fld 5B 34
Napier Mt. S70: Wors 5E 31
Napier St. S11: Shef 5D 118
Narrow La. S25: Nth A 3H 141
Narrow Twitchell S60: Roth 4F 97
(off Hollowgate)
Narrow Wlk. S10: Shef 3B 118
Nascot Cl. S66: Bram 1C 114
Nascot Gdns. S26: Augh 4B 124
Naseby Av. DN5: Scaws 4E 39
Naseby St. S9: Shef 2D 108
Nasmyth Row S74: Els 2E 63
(off Wath Rd.)
Nathan Ct. S20: Water 1G 151
Nathan Dr. S20: Water 6G 137
Nathan Gro. S20: Water 6F 137
National Emergency Services Mus.
. . . . .1E 5 (2F 119)
Navan Rd. S2: Shef 1D 134
Navigation Way S73: Bramp 3B 48
Naylor Gro. S35: Ough 4D 90
S75: Dod .3G 29
Naylor Rd. S35: Ough 3D 90
Naylor St. S62: P'gte 5G 83
Neale Bank S43: Brim 1C 168
Neale Rd. DN2: Don 2G 41
Nearcroft Rd. S61: Kimb P 2A 96
Nearfield Rd. DN4: Bess 6A 58
Needham Way S7: Shef 3B 132
Needle's Eye 4G 63
Needlewood S75: Dod 4G 29
NEEPSEND 6E 107
Neepsend Ind. Est. S3: Shef 5E 107
Neepsend La. S3: Shef 6D 106
Neill Rd. S11: Shef 6B 118
Nellie Stagles Way DN1: Don 2C 56
Nelson Av. S71: Monk B 4F 17
Nelson Cl. S60: Brins 4E 111
Nelson Mandela Wlk. S2: Shef 5E 121
(off Castlebeck Av.)
Nelson Pl. S35: Burn 3C 78
Nelson Rd. DN11: New R 5A 74
DN12: New E 4C 70
S6: Shef .6G 105
S66: Malt .5C 102
(not continuous)
Nelson Rd. Flats DN12: New E 4C 70
(off Nelson Rd.)
Nelson St. DN4: Don 3C 56
S41: C'fld 2H 167
S65: Roth .3F 97
S70: Barn .1D 30
S72: Sth H 1H 11
Nemesia Cl. S25: Sth A 4F 141
Nene Gro. DN9: Auck 1H 59
NESFIELD .5A 160
Nesfield Cl. S41: C'fld 6E 161
Nesfield Way S5: Shef 6A 94
Nether Av. S21: Killa 4B 152
S35: Gren .1C 92
NETHER CANTLEY 2E 59
Nether Cantley La. DN3: Can 2E 59
Nether Cres. S35: Gren 1C 92
Nethercroft S75: Bar G 3F 15
Nether Cft. Cl. S43: Brim 1D 168

Nether Cft. Rd. S43: Brim 1D 168
Netherdene Rd. S18: Dron 3F 155
(not continuous)
NETHER EDGE 2D 132
Nether Edge Rd. S7: Shef 2D 132
Nether Farm Cl. S43: Brim C 3E 169
Netherfield S36: Pen 2C 176
S74: Els 6C 46
Netherfield Cl. S36: Spink 4H 175
S43: Stav 4C 164
Netherfield Ct. S65: Roth 2F 97
Netherfield Cft. S72: Shaft 4F 11
Netherfield Farm Cl.
S36: Pen 3C 176
Netherfield La. S62: P'gte 4G 83
Netherfield Rd. S10: Shef 1A 118
S40: Bramp 2B 170
Netherfields Cres. S18: Dron 4F 155
Netherfield Vw. S65: Dalt 2C 98
NETHERGATE 1D 116
Nethergate S6: Stan 1C 116
NETHER GREEN 6F 117
Nethergreen Av. S21: Killa 3C 152
Nethergreen Ct. S21: Killa 3C 152
Nethergreen Gdns.
S21: Killa 3C 152
Nethergreen Rd. S11: Shef 6G 117
NETHER HANDLEY 5A 158
NETHER HAUGH 2C 82
Nether La. S35: Eccl 6G 79
Netherleigh Ct. S40: Bramp 5C 166
Netherleigh Rd. S40: Ash 5C 166
Nether Ley Av. S35: Chap 3F 79
Nether Ley Ct. S35: Chap 3F 79
Nether Ley Cft. S35: Chap 3F 79
Nether Ley Gdns.
S35: Chap 3F 79
Nethermoor Av. S21: Killa 3C 152
Nethermoor Cl. S21: Killa 3C 152
Nethermoor Dr. S21: Killa 3C 152
S66: Wick 2H 113
Nethermoor La. S21: Killa 3C 152
Nether Oak Cl. S20: Sot 6A 138
Nether Oak Dr. S20: Sot 6A 138
Nether Oak Vw. S20: Sot 6A 138
Nether Rd. S35: Eccl 1G 93
S75: Silk .1B 28
Nether Royd Vw. S75: Silk C 5B 28
Nether Shire La. S5: Shef 3H 93
NETHERTHORPE
S21 . . . . .3B 152
S26 . . . . .3F 155
S3 . . . . .2A 4 (2D 118)
S43 . . . . .4C 164
Netherthorpe S43: Stav 4C 164
Netherthorpe Cl. S21: Killa 3C 152
S43: Stav 5C 164
Netherthorpe Flash Nature Reserve
. . . . .4E 165
Netherthorpe La. S21: Killa 4H 152
Netherthorpe Pl. S3: Shef . .1B 4 (1E 119)
Netherthorpe Rd. S3: Shef . .3A 4 (3D 118)
S43: Stav 4C 164
Netherthorpe Road Stop (ST)
. . . . .2B 4 (2E 119)
Netherthorpe St. S3: Shef . .1B 4 (2E 119)
Netherthorpe Wlk. S3: Shef . .1B 4 (2E 119)
Netherthorpe Way S25: Nth A 1H 141
Nether Wheel Row S13: Shef 3A 136
Netherwood Av. S12: Shef 3H 135
Netherwood Country Pk. 5F 33
Netherwood Rd. S73: Womb 5G 33
Nettlecroft S71: Monk B 3C 18
Nettleham Rd. S8: Shef 5E 133
Network Cen. S75: Barn 3H 15
Neville Av. S70: Barn 3A 32
Neville Cl. S3: Shef 1G 119
S70: Barn .3A 32
S73: Womb 6E 33
Neville Ct. S73: Womb 6E 33
Neville Cres. S70: Barn 3A 32
Neville Dr. S3: Shef 6G 107
Neville Rd.
S61: Kimb P 1A 96
Nevill St. S60: Roth 3E 97
Nevis Cl. S40: C'fld 4E 167
Newark S20: W'fld 2F 151
(off Shortbrook Rd.)
Newark Cl. S75: Stain 4A 8
Newark Rd. S64: Mexb 1D 66

Newark St. DN11: New R 4B 74
S9: Shef .5D 108
New Beetwell St. S40: C'fld 5H 167
Newbiggin Cl. S62: P'gte 4F 83
Newbiggin Dr. S62: P'gte 4F 83
NEWBOLD 1F 167
Newbold Av. S41: C'fld 2F 167
Newbold Bk. La. S40: C'fld 2E 167
Newbold Ct. S41: C'fld 1E 167
Newbold Dr. S41: C'fld 2F 167
NEWBOLD MOOR 6G 161
Newbold Rd.
S41: Up N, C'fld 6B 160
Newbold Ter. DN5: Cus 5G 39
NEWBOLD VILLAGE 2E 167
Newbold Village S41: C'fld 2E 167
Newbolt Rd. DN4: Balb 6A 56
Newbould Cres. S20: Beig 5H 137
Newbould La. S10: Shef 4B 118
Newbridge Ct. S41: Old W 5H 161
Newbridge Dr. S43: Brim 6C 162
Newbridge Gro.
DN12: New E 4D 70
S71: Monk B 5G 17
Newbridge La. S41: Old W 4H 161
S43: Brim .4H 161
Newbridge St. S41: Old W 5H 161
NEW BRIMINGTON 5E 163
Newburn Dr. S9: Tins 2H 109
Newburn Rd. S9: Tins 2G 109
(off Town St.)
Newbury Rd. S10: Shef 2A 118
Newbury Way DN5: Scaws 4E 39
Newby Cres. DN4: Balb 1H 71
Newby Rd. S41: C'fld 6D 160
Newcastle Cl. S20: Sot 5A 138
Newcastle St. S1: Shef 3C 4 (3E 119)
New Chapel Av. S36: Cub 6C 176
New Cl. S75: Silk 2A 28
Newcomen Rd. DN5: Don 5H 39
Newcroft Cl. S20: Sot 5A 138
New Cross Dr. S13: Shef 2B 136
New Cross Wlk. S13: Shef 2B 136
New Cross Way S13: Shef 2B 136
Newdale Av. S72: Cud 3D 18
New Droppingwell Rd.
S61: Kimb .4E 95
NEW EDLINGTON 4C 70
New Edlington Way DN4: Warm 2E 71
Newent La. S10: Shef 2A 118
Newfield Av. S71: Monk B 4A 18
Newfield Cl. DN3: Barn D 1E 27
Newfield Ct. S10: Shef 6E 117
Newfield Cres. S17: Dore 3D 144
S63: Wath D 1E 65
Newfield Cft. S17: Dore 2D 144
Newfield Farm Cl. S14: Shef 3B 134
NEWFIELD GREEN 3A 134
Newfield Grn. Rd. S2: Shef 2A 134
Newfield La. S17: Dore 3D 144
Newfield Pl. S17: Dore 3D 144
Newgate Cl. S35: High G 1C 78
NEWHALL 4D 108
Newhall Av. S66: Wick 2H 113
New Hall Cres. S36: Stoc 2B 174
Newhall Grange S66: Carr 1D 114
New Hall La. S36: Stoc 3A 174
S71: Ard 3E 33
Newhall La. S66: Carr 1D 114
New Hall Rd. DN3: Kirk Sa 5D 26
S9: Shef .4B 108
Newhaven Cl. S40: W'ton 1C 170
New Haven Gdns. S17: Shef 6F 145
NEWHILL 1E 65
New Hill DN12: Con 4F 69
Newhill S63: Wath D 1E 65
Newhill Grange S63: Wath D 1E 65
Newhill La. S12: Shef 4A 136
Newhill Rd. S63: Wath D 1E 65
S71: Monk B 3F 17
New Houses S41: C'fld 5B 168
New Ings DN3: Arm 4D 42
Newington Av. S72: Cud 6E 11
Newington Cl. DN4: Can 5C 58
Newington Dr. S26: Aston 1D 138
Newington Rd. S11: Shef 6B 118
Newland Av. S66: Malt 4A 102
S72: Cud 3D 18

Newland Dale. S41: C'fld 4H 167
Newland Gdns. S41: C'fld 3F 167
Newland Rd. S71: Smi 1D 16
Newlands Av. S12: Shef 2D 134
S40: Ash 5D 166
Newlands Cl. DN4: Can 5C 58
Newlands Dr. DN5: Cus 5G 39
S12: Shef 2D 134
Newlands Gro. S12: Shef 2E 135
Newlands Rd. S12: Shef 2D 134
Newlands Way S73: Womb 3B 48
New La. DN5: Sprot 3B 54
DN11: Ross 5D 74
S63: Bolt D 6E 35
(not continuous)
NEW LODGE 1E 17
New Lodge Cres. S71: Smi 1D 16
Newlyn Dr. S71: Monk B 5G 17
Newlyn Pl. S8: Shef 5E 133
Newlyn Rd. S8: Shef 5E 133
Newman Av. S71: Car 5H 9
Newman Cl. S9: Shef 6E 95
Newman Ct. S9: Shef 6E 95
S60: Roth 2H 111
Newman Dr. S9: Shef 6D 94
Newman Rd. S9: Shef 1C 108
S60: Roth 2H 111
Newmarch St. S9: Tins 1H 109
Newmarket Rd. DN4: Can 2A 58
New Mdws. S62: Rawm 6E 65
New Mill Bank S36: Bolst 6E 175
New Orchard La. S66: Thurc 5B 114
New Orchard Rd. S66: Thurc 5B 114
New Oxford St. S64: Mexb 2G 67
New Queen St. S41: C'fld 4G 167
New Rd. DN3: Brant 4H 59
DN11: Wad 6F 73
S18: App 3D 156
S25: Din 6A 128
S25: Nth A 2F 141
S36: Spink 3F 175
S42: W'orth 6F 171
S61: Kimb 5E 95
S63: Wath D 6G 49
S66: B'well 5H 87
S73: Hem 5G 47
S75: Mapp, Stain 4H 7
S75: Pil, Tank 1C 60
S81: Fir 1G 129
NEW ROSSINGTON 5B 74, 6F 75
New Row Cl. S72: Cud 1E 19
Newsam Rd. S64: Kiln 5C 66
New School Cl. S20: Mosb 3D 150
New School Ct. S20: Mosb 3D 150
New School Rd. S20: Mosb 3D 150
Newsham Rd. S8: Shef 4E 133
New Smithy Av. S36: Thurl 3A 176
New Smithy Dr. S36: Thurl 3A 176
Newsome Av. S73: Womb 1E 47
New Sq. S40: C'fld 5H 167
New Station Av. S64: Swin 3D 66
Newstead Av. S12: Shef 6H 135
S35: Ough 2E 91
Newstead Cl. S12: Shef 5H 135
S18: Dron W 3B 154
Newstead Dr. S12: Shef 6H 135
Newstead Gro. S12: Shef 5H 135
Newstead Rd. DN5: Scawt 2G 39
S12: Shef 5H 135
(not continuous)
S71: Ath 6D 8
Newstead Way S12: Shef 6H 135
(not continuous)
New St. DN1: Don 3B 56
DN5: Bntly 2H 39
DN9: Blax 1F 77
S1: Shef 2E 5 (2F 119)
S20: Holb 3H 151
S25: Din 5A 128
S25: Laugh M 2H 127
S35: High G 6C 60
S36: Spink 3G 175
S40: C'fld 6H 167
S60: Cat 6E 111
S61: Grea 4C 82
S61: Thorpe H 4C 80
S62: Rawm 3G 83
S63: Bolt D 3C 50
S64: Mexb 1A 68
S70: Barn 2D 30
(not continuous)

New St. S70: Wors 6H 31
(Edmunds Rd.)
S70: Wors 6F 31
(West St.)
S71: R'ton 3H 9
S71: Stair 2B 32
S72: Grim 2B 20
S72: Gt H 1F 35
S72: Sth H 1G 11
S73: D'fld 5B 34
S73: Hem 5E 47
S73: Womb 1H 47
S75: Dod 4G 29
S75: Mapp 5A 8
New St. La. S2: Shef 2H 5 (2H 119)
NEWTON 1G 55
Newton Av. S36: Stoc 2B 174
Newton Chambers Rd.
S35: Chap 6E 61
Newton Cl. S35: Chap 1F 79
Newton Ct. S70: Barn 6C 16
(off Newton St.)
Newton Cft. S13: Shef 2C 136
Newton Dr. DN5: Don 1G 55
S65: Roth 4H 97
Newton Gdns. S35: Chap 1F 79
Newton La. DN5: Don 1G 55
S1: Shef 6E 5 (4F 119)
S36: Stoc 2B 174
Newton Pl. S61: Thorpe H 5C 80
Newton Rd. S35: High G 1D 78
Newton St. S65: Roth 4H 97
S70: Barn 6C 16
Newton Va. S35: Chap 1F 79
NEW TOTLEY 6F 145
Newtown Av. S71: R'ton 2G 9
S72: Cud 3D 18
Newtown Grn. S72: Cud 3E 19
Newtree Dr. DN11: Wad 6E 73
Newven Ho. S65: Roth 3G 97
(off St Leonard's Rd.)
NEW VILLAGE 6A 24
NEW WHITTINGTON 3C 162
New Winterwell S63: Wath D 5E 49
New Wortley Rd. S60: Roth 3B 96
S61: Roth 3B 96
NEW YORK 5D 96
New York Stadium 5D 96
New York Way S60: Roth 4D 96
Niagara Dr. S6: Shef 1B 106
Niagara Rd. S6: Shef 1B 106
Nicholas La. S63: Gol 5B 36
Nicholas St. S41: Has 3C 172
S70: Barn 1C 30
Nicholson Av. S63: Wath D 1E 65
S75: Bar G 4F 15
Nicholson Pl. S8: Shef 2G 133
Nicholson Rd. DN4: Hex 3H 55
S8: Shef 2F 133
Nichols Rd. S6: Shef 1H 117
Nickerwood Dr. S26: Aston 2C 138
Nickleby Ct. S60: Cat 6C 110
Nidderdale Pl. S66: Sunn 4H 99
Nidderdale Rd. S81: Wing 5A 82
Nidd Cl. S9: Shef 1D 120
Nidd Rd. E. S9: Shef 1E 121
Nightingale Cl. S41: C'fld 4H 167
S60: Roth 5E 97
Nightingale Ct. S60: Roth 5E 97
Nightingale Cft. S61: Thorpe H 2D 80
Nightingale Rd. S35: Gren 2C 92
Nightingales, The S63: Wath D 4F 49
Nile St. S10: Shef 4B 118
Nine Acre La. S36: Stoc 1D 174
Nine Trees Trad. Est. S66: Thurc . . .4A 114
Ninian Gro. DN4: Can 4B 58
Nobel Way S25: Din 4G 127
Noble St. S74: Hoyl 1C 62
Nodder Rd. S13: Shef 6F 121
Noehill Pl. S2: Shef 5E 121
Noehill Rd. S2: Shef 5E 121
Nook, The S8: Shef 4E 133
S10: Shef 2C 118
S36: H'swne 1G 177
NOOK END 6E 105
Nookery Cl. S66: Malt 4C 102
Nooking Cl. DN3: Arm 3F 43
Nook La. S6: Stan 6D 104
S36: Pen 6E 177
S44: Cal 5G 169
Nora St. S63: Gol 4E 37

Norborough Rd. DN2: Don 5E 41
S9: Tins 2H 109
Norbreck Cres. DN4: Warm 2D 70
Norbreck Rd. DN4: Warm 1D 70
NORBRIGGS 3E 165
Norbriggs Rd. S43: Woodt 3E 165
Norbrook Way S60: Whis 3C 112
Norburn Dr. S21: Killa 4C 152
Norbury Cl. S18: Dron W 3C 154
S40: C'fld 3C 166
Norcroft S70: Wors 4E 31
Norcroft La. S75: Cawt 5A 14
Norcross Gdns. S73: D'fld 5C 34
Norfolk Cl. S42: W'ton 2C 170
S71: Monk B 4G 17
Norfolk Ct. S65: Roth 3F 97
(off Norfolk St.)
Norfolk Dr. S25: Nth A 2H 141
Norfolk Gdns. S43: Ink 2G 169
Norfolk Hill S35: Gren 1B 92
Norfolk Hill Cft. S35: Gren 1B 92
Norfolk Park Av. S2: Shef 5H 119
Norfolk Park Dr. S2: Shef 5H 119
Norfolk Park Rd. S2: Shef 5G 119
Norfolk Park Students' Residence
S2: Shef 5A 120
Norfolk Pl. S66: Malt 5B 102
Norfolk Rd. DN4: Balb 6A 56
S2: Shef 5H 5 (4H 119)
S72: Gt H 1F 35
Norfolk Row S1: Shef 3E 5 (3F 119)
Norfolk St. S1: Shef 4E 5 (3F 119)
(not continuous)
S65: Roth 3F 97
Norfolk Way S60: Roth 2H 111
Norgreave Way S20: Half 3F 151
Norman Cl. S70: Wors 5F 31
S71: Monk B 4H 17
Norman Ct. S71: Carl 6H 9
Norman Cres. DN5: Scaws 3E 39
DN11: New R 5B 74
Normancroft Ct. S2: Shef 5E 121
Normancroft Cres.
S2: Shef 5F 121
Normancroft Dr. S2: Shef 5E 121
Normancroft Way S2: Shef 5F 121
NORMANDALE 3F 105
Normandale Av. S6: Lox 4F 105
Normandale Rd. S6: Shef 5C 106
S72: Gt H 6F 21
Norman St. S9: Shef 5C 108
S63: Thurn 2D 36
Normanton Gdns. S4: Shef 5H 107
Normanton Gro. S13: Shef 2A 136
Normanton Hill S13: Shef 2F 135
NORMANTON SPRING 1H 135
Normanton Spring Cl. S13: Shef 3A 136
Normanton Spring Ct. S13: Shef 2A 136
Normanton Spring Rd. S13: Shef . . .3H 135
Normanville Av. S60: Brins 3C 110
Norrel's Cft. S60: Roth 6G 97
Norrels Dr. S60: Roth 6G 97
Norris Rd. S6: Shef 4A 106
Norroy St. S4: Shef 6A 108
Norstead Cres. S66: Bram 5B 100
Northampton Rd. DN2: Don 5H 41
NORTH ANSTON 3H 141
Nth. Anston Bus. Cen. S25: Nth A . . .6F 127
Nth. Anston Trad. Est. S25: Nth A . . .6E 127
North Bank S3: Shef 1G 5 (2G 119)
North Bri. Rd. DN5: Don 6A 40
Nth. Carr La. S71: D'fld 2B 34
Nth. Church St. S1: Shef 2E 5 (2F 119)
Nth. Cliff Rd. DN12: Con 3E 69
North Cl. S18: Uns 6B 156
S71: R'ton 3H 9
Northcote Av. S2: Shef 2G 133
Northcote Rd. S2: Shef 2G 133
Northcote Ter. S75: Barn 6B 16
North Cres. S21: Killa 2D 152
S65: Roth 3H 97
Northcroft S72: Shaft 4F 11
North Dr. S60: Roth 2E 97
North End Dr. DN5: Harl 2G 51
Northern Av. S2: Shef 1B 134
Northern Comn.
S18: Dron W 1A 154
Nth. Farm Ct. S26: Aston 1E 139
NORTHFIELD 2E 97
North Fld. S75: Dod 2G 29
S75: Silk 2A 28

Northfield Av. DN5: Bntly 3G 23
  S10: Shef 1A 118
  S62: Rawm 1G 83
Northfield Cl. S10: Shef 1B 118
Northfield Ct. S10: Shef 1A 118
  S66: Wick .5G 99
Northfield Dr. S81: Woods 4F 143
Northfield Ind. Est.
  S60: Roth .2E 97
North Fld. La. DN7: Sth B 1G 27
Northfield La. S66: Wick 5F 99
Northfield Rd. DN5: Don 5H 39
  S10: Shef 2A 118
  S60: Roth .3E 97
North Ga. S21: Ecki 1E 159
  S64: Mexb 1H 67
Northgate S72: Sth H 1H 11
  S75: Barn .5B 16
North Hill Rd. S5: Shef 6E 93
Northlands DN6: Adw S 2B 22
  S71: R'ton 2H 9
Northlands Rd. S5: Shef 6E 93
North La. S75: Cawt, Silk 6B 14
North Mall DN1: Don 1B 56
      (off French Ga.)
Northmoor Cl. S43: Brim 1E 169
Northmoor Vw. S43: Brim 1E 169
Northorpe S75: Dod 4A 30
Nth. Pitt St. S61: Kimb 4A 96
North Pl. S65: Roth 3H 97
  S75: Barn .5A 16
Northpoint Ind. Est. S9: Shef 1E 109
North Quad. S5: Shef 6A 94
North Quay Dr. S2: Shef 1H 5 (2H 119)
North Rd. S44: Cal 5E 169
  S65: Roth .3H 97
  S71: R'ton .1A 10
  S75: Dod 2G 29
Nth. Royds Wood S71: Ath 5E 9
Northside Rd. S63: Wath D 6G 49
North Sq. DN12: New E 4D 70
North St. DN4: Don 3D 56
  DN12: New E 4D 70
  S60: Roth .3D 96
  S62: Rawm 1H 83
  S64: Swin .3D 66
  S73: D'fld 4B 34
Nth. Swaithe Cl. DN5: Bntly 6H 23
North Ter. S41: Has 3A 172
Northumberland Av. DN2: Don 5G 41
  S74: Hoyl .5B 46
Northumberland La. DN12: Den M . . .3B 68
Northumberland Rd. S10: Shef 3C 118
Northumberland Way S71: Ard 2C 32
North Vw. S72: Grim 1A 20
Nth. Wingfield Rd. S42: Gras 5C 172
Northwood S6: Shef 6H 91
Northwood Dr. S6: Shef 6G 91
Northwood Pl. S6: Shef 1H 105
NORTON 1H 147
Norton Av. S8: Shef 1A 148
  S12: Shef 6B 134
  S14: Shef 6B 134
  S40: Bramp 2B 170
Norton Church Glebe S8: Shef 1G 147
Norton Chu. Rd. S8: Shef 1G 147
Norton Grn. Cl. S8: Shef 1H 147
NORTON HAMMER 4D 132
Norton Hammer La. S8: Shef 4D 132
Norton La. S8: Shef 3F 147
      (not continuous)
Norton Lawns S8: Shef 1H 147
      (off School La. Cl.)
NORTON LEES 4F 133
Norton Lees Cl. S8: Shef 5F 133
Norton Lees Cres. S8: Shef 4F 133
Norton Lees Glade S8: Shef 4F 133
Norton Lees La. S8: Shef 4F 133
Norton Lees Rd. S8: Shef 3E 133
Norton Lees Sq. S8: Shef 4F 133
Norton M. S8: Shef 1H 147
Norton Pk. Av. S8: Shef 2G 147
Norton Pk. Cres. S8: Shef 2F 147
Norton Pk. Dr. S8: Shef 2F 147
Norton Pk. Rd. S8: Shef 3F 147
Norton Pk. Vw. S8: Shef 2F 147
Norton Rd. DN2: Don 5G 41
  S63: Wath D 5E 49
NORTON WOODSEATS 5G 133
Norville Cres. S73: D'fld 4C 34
Norwich Rd. DN2: Don 3F 41

Norwich Row S2: Shef 3H 5 (3H 119)
      (not continuous)
Norwith Rd. DN4: Bess 6A 58
NORWOOD .2E 153
Norwood Av. DN9: Auck 1H 59
  S5: Shef .2G 107
  S41: Has .3C 172
  S66: Malt .4A 102
Norwood Cl. S5: Shef 3G 107
  S41: Has .4D 172
  S66: Malt .4A 102
Norwood Cres. S21: Killa 3E 153
  S26: Kiv P 6H 139
Norwood Dr. DN5: Bntly 5A 24
  S5: Shef .3G 107
  S72: Brier .3B 12
  S75: Bar G .3F 15
Norwood Grange Dr.
  S5: Shef .2G 107
Norwood Ind. Est. S21: Killa 2D 152
Norwood La. S36: Thurl 2A 176
Norwood Pl. S21: Killa 3E 153
Nor Wood Rd. WF9: Hems 1E 13
Norwood Rd. DN12: Con 4E 69
  S5: Shef .3G 107
Norwood St. S65: Dalt 1C 98
Nostel Ho. DN1: Don 2B 56
      (off Grove Pl.)
Nostell Fold S75: Dod 4G 29
Nostell Pl. DN4: Bess 6A 58
Nottingham Cliff S3: Shef 6G 107
Nottingham Cl. DN5: Scaws 4E 39
  S25: Sth A 4G 141
  S42: W'orth 6A 172
  S71: Ard 3D 32
Nottingham Dr. S42: W'orth 6A 172
Nottinghamshire Way DN3: Arm 4G 43
Nottingham St. S3: Shef 5G 107
  S65: Roth .3F 97
Novara Cl. S70: Barn 2G 31
Novello St. S66: Malt 6D 102
      (not continuous)
Nowill Ct. S8: Shef 2F 133
Nowill Pl. S8: Shef 2F 133
Nuffield Health
  Chesterfield 1A 172
  Doncaster 4D 56
  Sheffield 5E 119
Nunnery Cres. S60: Cat 6D 110
Nunnery Dr. S2: Shef 2C 120
Nunnery Square (Park & Ride) 2A 120
Nunnery Square Stop (ST) 2B 120
Nunnery Ter. S2: Shef 3C 120
Nunnington Way DN3: Kirk Sa 4B 26
Nursery Cres. S25: Nth A 1G 141
Nursery Dr. S35: Eccl 2G 93
  S60: Cat .6D 110
Nursery Gdns. DN3: Eden 6C 26
  S70: Stair .3B 32
Nursery Gro. S35: Eccl 2H 93
Nursery La. DN5: Sprot 5B 54
  S3: Shef 1F 5 (1G 119)
Nursery Rd. S25: Din, Nth A 2H 141
      (not continuous)
  S26: Swal 3A 124
Nursery St. S3: Shef 1F 5 (1G 119)
  S70: Barn .2D 30
Nuttall Pl. S2: Shef 3A 120
NUTWELL 6F 43
Nutwell Cl. DN4: Bess 6B 58
Nutwell La. DN3: Arm, Can 4F 43
Nutwood Trad. Est.
  S6: Shef 5A 92

O

O2 Academy
  Sheffield 3F 5 (3G 119)
Oadby Dr. S41: Has 3B 172
Oakamoor Cl. S40: C'fld 3C 166
Oak Apple Wlk. S6: Stan 5D 104
Oak Av. S63: Wath D 1H 65
Oak Bank Av. S41: Old W 3A 162
Oakbank Cl. S64: Swin 6C 66
Oakbank Ct. S17: Tot 5F 145
Oakbrook Cl. S10: Shef 6G 117
Oakbrook Rd. S11: Shef 6G 117
Oakbrook Wlk.
  S65: Roth .2A 98
Oakburn Ct. S10: Shef 5C 118

Oak Cl. S21: Killa 5B 152
  S43: Brim .1C 168
  S63: Wath D 2H 65
  S64: Mexb .1D 66
  S66: Flan 4G 99
  S74: Hoyl 1H 61
Oak Ct. DN4: Balb 1B 72
  DN5: Sprot 3E 55
  S64: Mexb .1D 66
Oak Cres. S42: W'orth 6G 171
Oak Crest DN4: Bess 2E 75
Oakdale S70: Wors 5G 31
Oakdale Cl. DN3: Eden 1C 42
  S70: Wors .6G 31
Oakdale Pl. S61: Kimb 4A 96
Oak Dale Rd. DN4: Warm 2D 70
Oakdale Rd. S7: Shef 2C 132
  S25: Nth A 3A 142
  S61: Kimb 4A 96
Oakdell S18: Dron 1A 156
Oakdene DN11: New R 6C 74
Oak Dene Way S60: Wav 3D 122
Oakenroyd Cft. S74: Els 6E 47
Oaken Wood Cl. S61: Thorpe H 3D 80
Oaken Wood Rd.
  S61: Thorpe H 3C 80
Oakes Grn. S9: Shef 6B 108
Oakes Pk. Vw. S14: Shef 1A 148
Oakes St. S9: Shef 6E 95
Oakfern Gro. S35: High G 6C 60
Oakfield Av. S40: Bramp 1C 170
Oakfield Ct. S75: Mapp 5H 7
Oakfield Wlk. S75: Barn 6A 16
Oak Gro. DN3: Arm 2D 42
  DN12: Con 5D 68
  S66: Thurc 5C 114
Oakham Dr. S3: Shef 6E 107
Oakham Pl. S75: Barn 5B 16
Oak Haven Av. S72: Gt H 1F 35
Oak Head Cl. S71: Smi 3G 17
Oak Hill Cl. S7: Shef 2D 132
Oakhill Ct. S71: Ard 2C 32
Oak Hill Rd. S7: Shef 2C 132
Oakhill Rd. DN2: Don 4G 41
  S18: Dron 2H 155
Oakholme M. S10: Shef 5B 118
Oakholme Rd. S10: Shef 4B 118
Oakland Av. S71: Monk B 4A 18
Oakland Cl. S81: Woods 3F 143
Oakland Ct. S6: Shef 4A 106
Oakland Rd. S6: Shef 4A 106
Oaklands DN4: Bess 2F 75
  S66: Wick 1H 113
Oaklands Dr. DN4: Bess 4A 58
Oaklands Gdns. DN4: Bess 5A 58
Oaklands Pl. S63: Wath D 1F 65
  DN12: New E 4C 70
Oak Lea S61: Grea 5C 82
  S70: Wors .6H 31
Oaklea S63: Thurn 2D 36
Oak Lea Av. S63: Wath D 5D 48
Oaklea Cl. S75: Stain 4A 8
Oak Leigh S75: Cawt 4A 14
Oakley Av. S40: C'fld 4F 167
Oakley Rd. S13: Shef 4H 121
Oak Lodge Rd.
  S35: High G 1B 78
Oak Mdws. S65: Roth 2A 98
Oak M. S66: Bram 5A 100
Oak Pk. S10: Shef 4A 118
Oak Pk. Ri. S70: Barn 3F 31
Oak Rd. DN3: Arm 2D 42
  S12: Shef 6D 134
  S20: Beig .4G 137
  S63: Thurn .2C 36
  S63: Wath D 1H 65
  S64: Mexb .1D 66
  S66: Malt .5G 101
  S72: Shaft .4G 11
Oakroyd Cres. S72: Grim 2B 20
Oaks, The S10: Shef 4A 118
Oaks Av. S36: Stoc 3C 174
Oaks Bus. Pk. S71: Stair 1H 31
Oaks Cres. S70: Barn 2H 31
Oaks Farm Cl. S75: Dart 5G 7
Oaks Farm Dr. S75: Dart 5G 7
Oaks Farm La. S44: Cal 6F 169
Oaks Fold S5: Shef 4B 94
Oaks Fold Av. S5: Shef 5B 94
Oaks Fold Rd. S5: Shef 5B 94

Oaks La. S5: Shef 5B 94
　S36: Midh 2A 174
　S61: Kimb P 1F 95
　S70: Barn 2H 31
　S71: Barn, Stair 1H 31
Oak St. S8: Shef 1F 133
　S20: Mosb 2D 150
　S43: Hol 5F 163
　S70: Barn 1C 30
　S72: Grim 2C 20
Oaks Wood Dr. S75: Dart 6G 7
Oak Ter. DN1: Don 3B 56
　S26: Swal 6A 124
Oak Tree Av. DN9: Auck 2A 76
　S72: Cud 1E 19
Oak Tree Cl. S44: Ark T 5H 173
　S66: Wick 5H 99
　S75: Kexb 6E 7
Oak Tree Cotts. S44: Cal 1F 173
Oak Tree Ct. S60: Roth 1E 111
Oak Tree Gro. WF9: Hems 1G 13
Oak Tree Rd. DN3: Brant 3H 59
Oak Vw. S17: Dore 5F 145
Oakwell 1F 31
Oakwell Bus. & Youth Enterprise Cen.
　S71: Barn 1G 31
Oakwell Cl. S66: Malt 4B 102
Oakwell Ct. S70: Barn 2F 31
Oakwell La. S71: Barn 1F 31
Oakwell Ter. S71: Barn 2F 31
Oakwell Va. S71: Barn 1F 31
Oakwell Vw. S71: Barn 2F 31
Oakwood Av. S5: Shef 3E 93
　S71: R'ton 2H 9
Oakwood Cl. S70: Wors 6H 31
Oakwood Cres. S35: Ough 5E 91
　S62: Rawm 1F 83
　S71: R'ton 2G 9
Oakwood Dr. DN3: Arm 5D 42
　DN3: Brant 4G 59
　S60: Roth 6H 97
　WF9: Hems 1F 13
Oakwood Flats S5: Shef 3G 107
Oakwood Gro. S60: Roth 6H 97
Oakwood Hall Dr. S60: Roth 2G 111
Oakwood Rd. DN4: Balb 5G 55
　S71: R'ton 2G 9
Oakwood Rd. E. S60: Roth 1H 111
Oakwood Rd. W. S60: Roth 1G 111
Oakwood Sq. S75: Kexb 6C 6
Oakwood Way S43: Mas M 2E 165
　S75: Barn 5A 16
Oakworth Cl. S20: Half 4F 151
Oakworth Dr. S20: Half 4E 151
Oakworth Gro. S20: Half 4E 151
Oakworth Vw. S20: Half 4E 151
Oasis, The S9: Shef 2F 109
Oates Av. S62: Rawm 3G 83
Oates Cl. S61: Roth 3B 96
Oates Orchard S20: Mosb 4E 151
Oates St. S61: Roth 3B 96
Oberon Cres. S73: D'fld 4A 34
Oborne Cl. S65: Rav 2B 100
Occupation La. S6: Lox 3E 105
　S12: Shef 5H 135
Occupation Rd. S41: C'fld 6G 161
　S62: H'ley 5A 62
　S62: P'gte 4F 83
Ochre Dike Cl. S20: Water 6F 137
Ochre Dike La. S20: Water 6E 137
Ochre Dike Wlk. S61: Wing 4A 82
Octagon Cen. S10: Shef 3D 118
　　　　　　　　　　　　(off Durham Rd.)
Octavia Cl. S60: Brins 2D 110
Odeon Cinema
　Sheffield 3F 5 (3G 119)
Odom Ct. S2: Shef 2G 133
Ogden Pl. S8: Shef 2F 147
Ogden Rd. DN2: Don 2A 42
Oil Mill Fold S60: Roth 4E 97
Oldale Cl. S13: Shef 3D 136
Oldale Ct. S13: Shef 2D 136
Oldale Gro. S13: Shef 3D 136
Old Anna La. S36: Thurl 3A 176
Old Bakery Cl. S41: Old W 4H 161
Old Bawtry Rd. DN9: Finn 5E 77
Old Brewery Ter. S6: Shef 6D 106
Old Brick Pl. S9: Shef 6E 109
Old Brick Works La. S41: C'fld 2H 167
Old Clifton La. S65: Roth 4G 97
Old Colliery Way S20: Swal 2A 138

Oldcotes Cl. S25: Din 4A 128
Oldcotes Rd. S25: Din 3A 128
Old Cottage Cl. S13: Shef 1E 137
Old Cross La. S63: Wath D 6G 49
Old Crown Gdns. S72: Gt H 6F 21
OLD CUBLEY 6C 176
Old Cubley S36: Cub 6D 176
OLD DENABY 3H 67
Old Denaby Wetlands Nature Reserve
　 . . . . .3H 67
Old Doncaster Rd. S63: Wath D 6A 50
OLD EDLINGTON 1B 88
Old Farm Ct. S64: Mexb 6D 50
Old Farm La. S71: Low L 4E 33
　S73: Low L, Womb 4E 33
Oldfield Av. DN12: Con 4C 68
　S6: Stan 6E 105
Oldfield Cl. DN3: Barn D 1E 27
　S6: Stan 6E 105
　S74: Hoyl 6B 46
Oldfield Gro. S6: Stan 6E 105
Oldfield Rd. S6: Stan 1C 116
　S65: Roth 3C 98
Old Field Shutt La.
　S65: Dalt M 2E 99
Oldfield Ter. S6: Stan 1E 117
Old Forge Bus. Pk. S2: Shef 1F 133
　　　　　　　　　　　　　(off Sark Rd.)
Old Fulwood Rd. S10: Shef 1E 131
Old Garden Dr. S65: Roth 3H 97
Old Gate La. S65: Thry 1C 98
Old Guildhall Yd. DN1: Don 1B 56
Old Hall Cl. DN5: Sprot 3D 54
　S25: Laugh M 2G 127
　S26: Tod 2B 140
　S66: Bram 5A 100
Old Hall Cres. DN5: Bntly 2A 40
Old Hall Dr. S66: Bram 5A 100
Old Hall Farm S61: Kimb 3H 95
Old Hall La. S66: Bram 5A 100
　　　　　　　　　　　(off Old Hall Dr.)
Old Hall M. S8: Shef 3E 147
　S66: Bram 5A 100
Old Hall Pl. DN5: Bntly 2A 40
Old Hall Rd. DN5: Bntly 2A 40
　S9: Shef 5D 108
　S40: C'fld 6E 167
　S70: Wors 2D 44
　S75: Wors 2C 44
Old Hall Wlk. S72: Gt H 1F 35
Old Hay Cl. S17: Dore 4E 145
Old Hay Gdns. S17: Dore 4D 144
Old Hay La. S17: Dore 5D 144
OLD HAYWOODS 3G 175
Old Hellaby La. S66: Hel 5E 101
Old Hexthorpe DN4: Hex 3G 55
Old Hill DN12: Con 4F 69
Old Hill La. S65: Dalt M 3E 99
Old House Cl. S13: Shef 5F 47
Old House Rd. S40: C'fld 2E 167
Old Houses S41: C'fld 5B 168
OLD KIRK SANDALL 3B 26
Old La. S20: Half 3H 151
　S35: Ough 4B 90
Old Manor Dr. S36: Oxs 6H 177
Old Market Pl. S73: Womb 2G 47
OLD MILL 5F 17
Old Mill Dr. S41: Up N 1B 166
Old Mill La. S70: Barn 5F 17
　S71: Barn 5F 17
Old Mill Rd. DN12: Con 5G 69
Old Moor La. S73: Wath D 3D 48
Old Moor Nature Reserve 3E 49
Old Moor Nature Reserve Vis. Cen.
　 . . . . .3D 48
Old Oaks Vw. S70: Barn 2H 31
Old Park Av. S8: Shef 3C 146
Old Pk. Rd. S8: Shef 3C 146
Old Pheasant Ct. S40: Bramp 6B 166
Old Quarry Av. S26: Wales 5G 139
Old Retford Rd. S13: Shef 6D 122
Oldridge Cl. S40: C'fld 2C 166
Old Rd. DN12: Con 6C 68
　S40: Bramp, C'fld 5C 166
　S42: Bramp 5B 166
　S71: Smi 3F 17
Old Row S74: Els 1E 63
Oldroyd Av. S72: Grim 2B 20
Oldroyd Row S75: Dod 4G 29
　　　　　　　　　　(off Stainborough Rd.)
Old Royston Av. S71: R'ton 2H 9

Old School Cl. DN3: Arm 4E 43
　S61: Grea 4D 82
　S74: Hoyl 5B 46
Old School Cft. S35: Wharn S 1C 90
Old School Dr. S5: Shef 5G 93
Old School Ho., The
　DN5: Bntly 2A 40
　　　　　　　　　　　　　(off Chapel St.)
Old School La. DN11: Wad 5E 73
　S44: Cal 6E 169
　S60: Cat 6E 111
Old School Rd. DN2: Don 5D 40
Old School Wlk. S25: Din 4A 128
Old Scotch Spring La. S66: Stain . . .2F 103
Old Sheffield Rd. S60: Roth 5E 97
Old Ship La. S40: C'fld 6H 167
Old Stables, The S62: Rawm 1E 83
Old Station Dr. S7: Shef 5C 132
Old Station Yd. S43: Brim 6B 162
Old St. S2: Shef 2H 5 (2H 119)
Old Tannery Rd.
　S71: Barn, Monk B 5F 17
OLD TOWN 5C 16
Old Town Hall S60: Roth 3E 97
　　　　　　　　　　　　(off Effingham St.)
Old Warren Vale S62: Rawm 1G 83
Oldwell Cl. S17: Tot 6E 145
OLD WHEEL 3C 104
OLD WHITTINGTON 4H 161
Old Whittington La. S18: Uns 3B 156
Old Works La. S44: Cal 6G 169
Old Wortley Rd. S61: Kimb 2H 95
Old Yew Ga. S35: Ough, Wort 1E 91
Olive Cl. S26: Swal 1C 138
Olive Cres. S12: Shef 6D 134
Olive Gro. Rd. S2: Shef 1G 133
Oliver Ho. S41: C'fld 5A 168
Olive Rd. S20: Mosb 3E 151
　S36: Stoc 3D 174
Oliver Rd. DN4: Balb 5H 55
　S7: Shef 4B 132
Olivers Dr. S9: Shef 2G 121
Olivers Mt. S9: Shef 2G 121
Oliver St. S64: Mexb 1E 67
Olivers Way S60: Cat 5C 110
Olive Ter. S6: Lox 5E 105
Olivet Rd. S8: Shef 5E 133
Ollerton Rd. S71: Ath 6E 9
Onchan Rd. S6: Shef 1F 117
ONESACRE 3C 90
Onesacre S35: Ough 3C 90
Onesmoor Bottom S6: Brad 3A 90
　S35: Brad 3A 90
Onslow Rd. S11: Shef 1A 132
Onyx Retail Pk. S63: Wath D 4E 49
Opal One S1: Shef 5C 4 (4E 119)
Orange St. S1: Shef 3C 4 (3E 119)
Orchard, The S25: Nth A 2H 141
　S63: Thurn 3B 36
　S66: Stain 5A 100
　S66: Wick 6H 99
Orchard Av. S25: Nth A 1H 141
Orchard Cl. DN3: Kirk Sa 4B 26
　S5: Shef 3G 93
　S25: Laugh M 1H 127
　S60: Cat 6E 111
　S64: Mexb 1F 67
　S71: Monk B 3H 17
　S75: Silk C 5B 28
　S75: Stain 5A 8
Orchard Cres. S5: Shef 3G 93
Orchard Cft. S18: Dron 3G 155
　S26: Wales 5G 139
　S75: Dart 6F 7
　S75: Dod 4H 29
Orchard Dr. S71: R'ton 3F 9
　S72: Sth H 1G 11
Orchard Flatts Cres. S61: Wing 6B 82
Orchard Gdns. S25: Sth A 4G 141
Orchard Gro. S66: Malt 4G 101
　S71: R'ton 2G 9
Orchard La. DN5: Cus 5E 39
　S1: Shef 3D 4 (3H 119)
　S20: Beig 6G 137
　S26: Wales 6G 139
Orchard Lea Dr. S26: Swal 1C 138
Orchard M. DN5: Cus 5G 39
　S25: Nth A 2H 141
　S63: Bolt D 2C 50
　S75: Barn 5D 16

Orchard Pl. S21: Killa 4C 152
S60: Roth 4D 96
S63: Wath D 6E 49
S72: Cud 3F 19
Orchard Rd. S6: Shef 6B 106
Orchard Sq. S1: Shef 3E 5 (3F 119)
S18: Dron W 2C 154
Orchard Square Shop. Cen.
S1: Shef 3E 5 (3F 119)
Orchard St. DN4: Balb 3A 56
S1: Shef 3E 5 (3F 119)
S35: Ough 3E 91
S36: Spink 4H 175
S63: Gol 6D 36
S73: Womb 1G 47
Orchards Way S40: W'ton 1D 170
Orchard Ter. S75: Cawt 4A 14
Orchard Vw. Rd. S40: Ash 4D 166
Orchard Vs. S65: Thry 6E 85
S71: Barn 5E 17
Orchard Way S60: Brins 5D 110
S63: Thurn 2C 36
Orchard Wells S66: Wick 6H 99
Orchid Cl. S44: Cal 5F 169
Orchid Cres. S5: Shef 1C 108
Orchid Way S25: Sth A 4F 141
Ordnance Ter. S61: Kimb 4A 96
(off Up. Clara St.)
ORGREAVE 4C 122
Orgreave Cl. S13: Shef 5D 122
Orgreave Cres. S13: Shef 5D 122
Orgreave Dr. S13: Shef 5D 122
Orgreave Ho. DN1: Don 2B 56
(off Burden Cl.)
Orgreave La. S13: Shef 5B 122
Orgreave Pl. S13: Shef 4C 122
Orgreave Ri. S13: Shef 6E 123
Orgreave Rd. S13: Shef 5C 122
S60: Cat 1D 122
Orgreave Way S13: Shef 6D 122
Oriel Mt. S10: Shef 1D 130
Oriel Rd. S10: Shef 1E 131
Oriel Way S71: Monk B 5A 18
Orion Way DN4: Balb 2C 72
Ormesby Cl. S18: Dron W 3B 154
Ormesby Cres. DN5: Cus 5F 39
Ormesby Way S66: Bram 5B 100
Ormes Mdw. S20: Mosb 6D 136
Ormond Cl. S8: Shef 4G 147
S42: W'ton 3C 170
Ormond Dr. S8: Shef 4G 147
Ormonde Av. DN12: New E 4D 70
Ormonde Way DN11: New R 6B 74
Ormond Rd. S8: Shef 4G 147
Ormond Way S8: Shef 3G 147
Ormsby Cl. DN4: Balb 2H 71
Ormsby Rd. S41: C'fld 1G 167
Orpen Dr. S14: Shef 6B 134
Orpen Way S14: Shef 6B 134
Orphanage Rd. S3: Shef 4G 107
Orwell Cl. S73: Womb 3A 48
Orwins Cl. S41: C'fld 1E 167
Osbert Dr. S66: Thurc 5B 114
Osberton Pl. S11: Shef 6C 118
S62: Rawm 2A 84
Osberton St. DN11: Wad 5F 73
S62: Rawm 2A 84
Osberton Way S65: Dalt 1B 98
Osbert Rd. S60: Roth 1A 112
Osborne Av. DN6: Woodl 3A 22
S26: Aston 6D 124
Osborne Cl. S11: Shef 1B 132
Osborne Ct. S11: Shef 1B 132
S71: Monk B 4A 18
Osborne Dr. S26: Tod 3C 140
Osborne M. S11: Shef 1C 132
S70: Barn 2F 31
Osborne Rd. DN2: Don 6E 41
S11: Shef 1B 132
S26: Kiv P 6C 140
S26: Tod 3C 140
Osborne St. S70: Barn 2F 31
Osborne Wlk. S11: Shef 2C 132
Osgathorpe Cres. S4: Shef 4H 107
Osgathorpe Dr. S4: Shef 4H 107
Osgathorpe Rd. S4: Shef 4H 107
(not continuous)
Osmaston Rd. S8: Shef 6E 133
Osmond Dr. S70: Wors 5F 31
Osmond Pl. S70: Wors 5F 31
Osmond Way S70: Wors 5F 31

Osmund Ct. S21: Ecki 1D 158
Osmund Rd. S21: Ecki 1C 158
Osprey Av. S70: Birdw 4E 45
Osprey Cl. DN6: Adw S 2C 22
Osprey Gdns. S2: Shef 4B 120
Osprey Rd. S26: Aston 2D 138
Oswestry Rd. S5: Shef 6H 93
Oswin Av. DN4: Balb 4G 55
Otley Cl. DN12: Con 4G 69
Otley Wlk. S6: Shef 6C 106
Otter St. S9: Shef 6C 108
OUGHTIBRIDGE 3E 91
Oughtibridge S35: Ough 3E 91
Oughtibridge La.
S35: Gren, Ough 3F 91
Oughton Way S4: Shef 5A 108
Oulton Av. S66: Bram 4B 100
Oulton Dr. S72: Cud 1F 19
Oulton Ri. S64: Mexb 6A 52
Ouseburn Cft. S9: Shef 1D 120
Ouseburn Rd. S9: Shef 2D 120
Ousebürn St. S9: Shef 1D 120
Ouse Rd. S9: Shef 1D 120
Ouse Ter. DN12: Con 3F 69
Ouslethwaite Ct. S70: Wors 4D 30
Ouson Gdns. S71: Car 5H 9
Outgang La. S25: Din 4H 127
S25: Din, Laugh C 3F 127
S66: Malt 6C 102
Outram Rd. S2: Shef 4B 120
S41: C'fld 2G 167
Oval, The DN4: Bess 3H 57
DN6: Woodl 2A 22
DN12: Con 3H 69
S5: Shef 1H 107
S25: Nth A 2H 141
Oval Rd. S65: Roth 3A 98
Overcroft Ri. S17: Tot 6E 145
Overdale Av. S70: Wors 4G 31
Overdale Gdns. S17: Dore 4D 144
Overdale Ri. S17: Dore 4D 144
Overdale Rd. S73: Womb 3H 47
Overend Cl. S14: Shef 4A 134
Overend Dr. S14: Shef 4A 134
Overend Rd. S14: Shef 4A 134
Overend Way S14: Shef 4A 134
Oversley Rd. DN2: Don 4E 41
Oversley St. S9: Tins 1H 109
Overton Cl. S43: Stav 3C 164
Overton Rd. S6: Shef 2A 106
Owday La. S81: Work 6H 143
Owen Cl. S6: Shef 4C 92
S65: Roth 2F 97
Owen Falls Av. S41: C'fld 5B 168
Owen Pl. S6: Shef 4C 92
Owen Wlk. S6: Shef 4C 92
Owler Car La. S18: Coal A 6B 148
S21: Trow 5C 148
Owler Cl. S73: Womb 6E 33
Owler La. S35: Wharn S 2B 90
Owler La. S4: Shef 4B 108
(Firth Pk. Rd.)
S4: Shef 3B 108
(Upwell St.)
OWLERTON .3C 106
Owlerton Grn. S6: Shef 4C 106
Owlerton Stadium (Greyhound & Speedway)
. . . . .3C 106
Owlet La. S4: Shef 3B 108
Owlings Pl. S6: Shef 4H 105
Owlings Rd. S6: Shef 3H 105
OWLTHORPE 6C 136
Owlthorpe Av. S20: Mosb 2C 150
Owlthorpe Cl. S20: Mosb 2C 150
Owlthorpe Dr. S20: Mosb 2C 150
Owlthorpe Greenway
S20: Holb, Water 1E 151
Owlthorpe Gro. S20: Mosb 2C 150
Owlthorpe La. S20: Mosb 2C 150
Owlthorpe Ri. S20: Mosb 2C 150
Owram St. S73: D'fld 5B 34
Ox Carr DN3: Arm 4G 25
OXCLOSE 4G 151
Ox Cl. Av. S17: Bradw 5H 145
S61: Kimb P 1H 95
Oxclose Dr. S18: Dron W 3B 154
Oxclose La. S18: Dron W 3B 154
Oxclose Pk. Gdns. S20: Half 4G 151
Oxclose Pk. Ri. S20: Half 4G 151
Oxclose Pk. Rd. S20: Half 3G 151
Oxclose Pk. Rd. Nth. S20: Half 3G 151

Oxclose Pk. Vw. S20: Half 4G 151
Oxclose Pk. Way S20: Half 4G 151
Oxford S6: Shef 2D 118
Oxford Cl. S43: Brim 6E 163
S61: Grea 5D 82
Oxford M. S63: Wath D 4E 49
Oxford Pl. DN1: Don 2B 56
S71: Stair 2B 32
Oxford Rd. S43: Brim 6E 163
Oxford St. DN11: New R 5B 74
S6: Shef 2C 118
S64: Mexb 1D 66
S65: Roth 3H 97
S70: Barn 3F 31
S71: Stair 2B 32
Oxford Vs. S65: Roth 3H 97
(off Oxford St.)
Ox Hill S20: Half 5H 151
Oxley Cl. S36: Stoc 3C 174
Oxley Ct. S60: Roth 6G 97
Oxley Gro. S60: Roth 6G 97
OXSPRING 6H 177
Oxspring Bank S5: Shef 2C 106
Oxspring La. S36: Oxs 3G 177
Oxted Rd. S9: Shef 2D 108
Oxton Dr. DN4: Warm 6E 55
Oxton Rd. S71: Ath 6E 9

P

Packers Row S40: C'fld 5H 167
Pack Horse Grn. S75: Silk 2A 28
Pack Horse La. S35: High G 6D 60
Packington Rd. DN4: Can 5D 58
Packman Rd. S62: Wentw 5D 64
S63: Wath D 5C 48
(Brampton Rd.)
S63: Wath D 1D 64
(Mill La.)
Packmans Cl. S35: Gren 1B 92
Packmans Way S35: Gren 1B 92
Packman Way S63: Wath D 6C 48
Packwood Cl. S66: Malt 4C 102
Paddington Cl.
S25: Laugh C 4F 127
Paddock, The DN3: Barn D 1G 27
DN6: Adw S 2D 22
S61: Scho 4E 81
S66: Stain 2F 103
S73: D'fld 4B 34
S73: Hem 4F 47
Paddock Cl. DN5: Cus 5F 39
S75: Stain 5B 8
Paddock Cres. S2: Shef 3B 134
Paddock Cft. S64: Swin 3A 66
Paddock Dr. S66: Sunn 3H 99
Paddock Gro. S72: Cud 1F 19
Paddock La. DN11: Wils 3F 89
Paddock Rd. S75: Stain 5B 8
Paddocks, The DN5: Cad 6G 53
DN5: Cus 5E 39
DN9: Auck 2H 59
S26: Aston 1D 138
S43: Woodt 3F 165
S65: Rav 2B 100
S65: Thry 6F 85
Paddock Vw. DN1: Don 2C 56
S26: Tod 3B 140
Paddock Way S18: Dron 1G 155
(Holmesdale Rd.)
S18: Dron 2G 155
(Stonelow Grn.)
Padley Cl. S75: Dod 3F 29
Padley Wlk. S5: Shef 6A 94
Padley Way S5: Shef 6H 93
Padua Ri. S73: D'fld 5A 34
Page Hall Rd. S4: Shef 3A 108
Pagenall Dr. S26: Swal 6C 124
Paget St. S9: Shef 5C 108
Pagnell Av. S63: Thurn 3A 36
Paisley Cl. S43: Stav 6H 163
Palermo Fold S73: D'fld 4A 34
Palgrave Cres. S5: Shef 6D 92
Palgrave Rd. S5: Shef 6C 92
Palington Gro. DN4: Can 3B 58
Pall Mall S70: Barn 1E 31
Palm Av. DN3: Arm 3F 43
Palmer Cl. S36: Cub 6C 176
Palmer Cres. S18: Dron 3G 155
Palmer Rd. S9: Shef 6F 109

Palmersgate—Parsley Hay Gdns.

Palmersgate *S40: C'fld 5H 167*
(off Central Pavement)
Palmerston Av. S66: Malt 4H **101**
Palmerston Rd. S10: Shef 3C **118**
Palmer St. DN4: Don 3D **56**
S9: Shef 1C **120**
Palmers Way S66: Thurc 6A **114**
Palm Gro. DN12: Con 5D **68**
Palm Hollow Cl. S66: Wick 6E **99**
Palm La. S6: Shef 6B **106**
Palm St. S6: Shef 6B **106**
S75: Barn 5C **16**
Pamela Dr. DN4: Warm 6D **54**
Pangbourne Rd. S63: Thurn 1B **36**
Panthers Pl. S41: C'fld 3H **167**
Pantry Grn. S70: Wors 6H **31**
Pantry Hill S70: Wors 5H **31**
Pantry Well S70: Wors 6H **31**
Paper Mill Rd. S5: Shef 3B **94**
Parade, The S12: Shef 2D **134**
S62: Rawm 1F **83**
S74: Hoyl 1A **62**
Paradise La. S1: Shef 2E **5**
Paradise Sq. S1: Shef 2E **5** (2F **119**)
Paradise St. S1: Shef 2E **5** (2F **119**)
S3: Shef 2E **5** (2F **119**)
Paramount Cinema 4D **176**
Parish Way S71: Monk B 5A **18**
Park, The DN6: Woodl 5B **22**
Park & Ride
Abbeydale 4C **132**
Doncaster North 1E **39**
Doncaster South 3E **75**
Halfway 3G **151**
Malin Bridge 5A **106**
Meadowhall 6E **95**
Middlewood 1A **106**
Nunnery Square 2A **120**
Valley Centertainment 5E **109**
White Rose Way 1D **72**
Park Av. DN3: Arm 3C **42**
DN5: Sprot 3D **54**
DN12: Con 5F **69**
S10: Shef 6A **118**
S18: Dron 2G **155**
S25: Din, Nth A 1H **141**
S35: Chap 4F **79**
S36: Pen 4C **176**
S60: Tree 2G **123**
S60: Whis 2B **112**
S64: Mexb 1F **67**
S70: Barn 1D **30**
S71: Ath 1E **17**
S71: R'ton 3A **10**
S72: Brier 3C **12**
S72: Cud 1E **19**
S72: Grim 6B **12**
Park Cl. DN3: Arm 4E **43**
DN5: Sprot 3D **54**
S40: Birdh 3H **171**
S64: Swin 3B **66**
S65: Thry 6E **85**
S75: Stain 6B **8**
Park Cotts. S70: Wors 1F **45**
Park Ct. S35: Gren 2B **92**
S63: Thurn 2C **36**
Park Cres. DN4: Warm 1D **70**
S10: Shef 4C **118**
S35: Eccl 2G **93**
S63: Bolt D 2C **50**
S71: R'ton 3A **10**
Park Dr. DN5: Sprot 3C **54**
S26: Swal 1A **138**
S36: Stoc 3D **174**
S41: C'fld 1A **172**
S75: Stainb 6A **30**
Park Dr. Way S36: Stoc 2D **174**
(not continuous)
Park End Rd. S63: Gol 6C **36**
Parker Av. S44: Cal 4E **169**
Parker's La. S10: Shef 3B **118**
Parkers La. S17: Dore 2E **145**
Parker's Rd. S10: Shef 3B **118**
Parker's Ter. S70: Birdw 5D **44**
Parker St. S70: Barn 1C **30**
Parkers Yd. S41: C'fld 5A **168**
Parker Way S9: Shef 2E **121**
Park Farm S18: Dron W 2B **154**
Parkfield Ct. S62: P'gte 5G **83**
Parkfield Pl. S2: Shef 6F **119**
Parkfield Rd. S65: Roth 4G **97**
PARKGATE 5G **83**
Parkgate S18: Dron 2H **155**
S63: Gol 5E **37**
Parkgate Av. DN12: Con 4D **68**
Parkgate Bus. Pk. S62: P'gte 6G **83**
Parkgate Cl. S20: Mosb 2B **150**
Parkgate Ct. *S62: P'gte 6F 83*
(off The Gateway)
Parkgate Cft. S20: Mosb 1B **150**
Parkgate Dr. S20: Mosb 1B **150**
Parkgate La. S21: Neth Han 1D **162**
Park Grange Ct. S2: Shef 6A **120**
Park Grange Cft. S2: Shef 5H **119**
Park Grange Croft Stop (ST) 5H **119**
Park Grange Dr. S2: Shef 6H **119**
Park Grange Mt. S2: Shef 6H **119**
Park Grange Ri. S2: Shef 6H **119**
Park Grange Rd. S2: Shef 5H **119**
Park Grange Road Stop (ST) 6H **119**
Park Grange Vw. S2: Shef 1A **134**
Park Gro. S36: Stoc 2D **174**
S62: Rawm 1G **83**
S66: Bram 5A **100**
S70: Barn 1D **30**
Park Hall Av. S42: W'ton 2B **170**
Park Hall Cl. S42: W'ton 3C **170**
Park Hall Gdns. S42: W'ton 2C **170**
PARK HEAD 1E **117**
PARKHEAD 4G **131**
Parkhead Cl. S71: R'ton 2F **9**
Parkhead Ct. S11: Shef 4G **131**
Parkhead Cres. S11: Shef 4G **131**
Parkhead Rd. S11: Shef 5F **131**
PARK HILL 3A **120**
Park Hill DN3: Barn D 3D **26**
S21: Ecki 1F **159**
S26: Swal 1A **138**
S73: D'fld 4C **34**
Parkhill Cres. DN3: Barn D 1D **26**
Park Hill Dr. S81: Fir 1H **129**
Park Hill Gdns. S26: Swal 1A **138**
Park Hill Gro. S75: Dod 2G **29**
Park Hill Rd. S73: Womb 1H **47**
Parkhill Rd. DN3: Barn D 1D **26**
Park Hollow S73: Womb 2H **47**
Park Homes S64: Mexb 2H **67**
Parkhouse Ct. S5: Shef 3F **93**
Park Ho. La. S9: Tins 3A **110**
Parkin Ct. S65: Rav 2C **100**
Parkinson St. DN1: Don 5C **40**
Parkland Cres. DN5: Bntly 5B **24**
S12: Shef 6H **135**
(not continuous)
Parkland Dr. DN11: Ross 5E **75**
Parklands DN3: Eden 1C **42**
S66: Thurc 1D **126**
Parklands Av. S25: Din 6H **127**
Parklands Cl. DN11: Ross 5D **74**
Parklands Vw. S26: Aston 3D **138**
Parkland Vw. S71: Lund 3C **18**
Parkland Wlk. DN9: Blax 1G **77**
Park La. DN4: Bess 2H **57**
DN7: Dunsv, Hat 5H **27**
DN9: Blax 1F **77**
DN12: Con 1D **86**
S9: Shef 1F **109**
S10: Shef 4C **118**
S25: Laugh C 4F **127**
S35: High G 5F **61**
S36: Pen 4C **176**
S36: Spink, Stoc 2E **175**
S41: C'fld 1G **167**
S65: Rav 6D **86**
S65: Thry 6E **85**
S72: Gt H, Grim 4C **20**
Park La. Ct. S65: Thry 5E **85**
Park La. Rd. DN7: Dunsv 4H **27**
Park Mdws. S72: Shaft 3G **11**
Park Mt. S65: Roth 4F **97**
Park Nook S65: Thry 6D **84**
Park Pl. S65: Roth 3A **98**
Park Ri. S18: Holme 4A **154**
Park Rd. DN1: Don 1C **56**
DN5: Bntly 1H **39**
DN12: Con 5E **69**
S6: Shef 6G **105**
S40: C'fld 1G **171**
(not continuous)
S63: Thurn 2B **36**
S63: Wath D 1F **65**
S64: Mexb 1F **67**
Park Rd. S64: Swin 4A **66**
S65: Roth 3A **98**
S70: Barn 3C **30**
S70: Wors 1F **45**
S72: Brier 3C **12**
S72: Grim 1B **20**
PARK SIDE 1D **116**
Parkside S41: C'fld 1H **167**
S71: Car 5A **10**
Parkside Cl. S12: Shef 6A **136**
Parkside La. S6: Stan 1E **117**
Park Side M. S12: Shef 5A **136**
Parkside M. S70: Wors 5F **31**
Parkside Rd. S6: Shef 3B **106**
S74: Hoyl 2G **61**
Parkside Shop. Cen. S21: Killa 3C **152**
Parkside Vw. S41: C'fld 2C **166**
Parkside Way S75: Kexb 5E **7**
Parkson Rd. S60: Roth 2A **112**
Park Spring Cl. S2: Shef 6H **119**
Park Spring Dr. S2: Shef 6H **119**
Park Spring Gro. S2: Shef 6H **119**
Park Spring Rd.
S72: Grim, Lit H, Midd 2A **20**
Park Springs Ind. Est.
S72: Grim 2A **20**
Park Spring Way S2: Shef 6H **119**
Park Sq. S2: Shef 2G **5** (3G **119**)
S35: Chap 1F **79**
Parkstone Ct. S25: Sth A 5F **141**
Parkstone Cres. S66: Hel 6E **101**
Parkstone Delph S12: Shef 6D **134**
Parkstone Way DN2: Don 3H **41**
Park St. S26: Swal 1B **138**
S40: Birdh 3H **171**
S61: Roth 3C **96**
S62: Rawm 2G **83**
S70: Barn 2D **30**
S73: Womb 2H **47**
Park Ter. DN1: Don 1C **56**
S35: Chap 4G **79**
S65: Thry 6D **84**
Park Vale Dr. S65: Thry 6E **85**
Park Vw. DN6: Adw S 3D **22**
S26: Kiv P 5B **140**
S41: Has 3C **172**
S61: Grea 5C **82**
S61: Thorpe H 4B **80**
S64: Mexb 1D **66**
S66: Malt 5C **102**
(not continuous)
S70: Barn 3C **30**
S70: Wors 5G **31**
S71: R'ton 2A **10**
S72: Brier 3C **12**
S72: Shaft 4F **11**
S74: Hoyl 1C **62**
S75: Dod 3G **29**
Park Vw. Av. S20: Half 3F **151**
Park Vw. Ct. S63: Wath D 5G **49**
Parkview Ct. S8: Shef 6F **133**
Park Vw. Rd. S6: Shef 3B **106**
S35: Chap 4F **79**
S61: Kimb 5F **95**
S75: Stain 5C **8**
Park Wlk. *S2: Shef 2A 120*
(off Castle Ct.)
Park Way DN6: Adw S 2C **22**
S63: Thurn 2C **36**
Parkway DN3: Arm 5E **43**
Parkway Av. S9: Shef 2C **120**
Parkway Centre Retail Pk.
S2: Shef 2B **120**
Parkway Cinema
Barnsley 6E **17**
Parkway Cl. S9: Shef 2C **120**
Parkway Dr. S9: Shef 3D **120**
Parkway Nth. DN2: Don 4E **41**
Parkway Ri. S9: Shef 3D **120**
Parkway Sth. DN2: Don 4E **41**
Parkwood Ind. Est. S3: Shef 6F **107**
Parkwood Karting 5D **106**
Parkwood Ri. DN3: Barn D 3D **26**
Parkwood Rd. S3: Shef 5D **106**
Parkwood Rd. Nth. S5: Shef 2E **107**
PARKWOOD SPRINGS 5E **107**
Parliament St. S11: Shef 5D **118**
Parma Ri. S73: D'fld 5H **33**
Parsley Hay Cl. S13: Shef 5A **122**
Parsley Hay Dr. S13: Shef 5A **122**
Parsley Hay Gdns. S13: Shef 5A **122**

Parsley Hay Rd. S13: Shef 5A 122
Parsonage Cl. S20: Mosb 4E 151
Parsonage Ct. S6: Shef 6B 106
(off Parsonage Cres.)
Parsonage Cres. S6: Shef 6B 106
Parsonage St. S6: Shef 6B 106
PARSON CROSS 4E 93
Parson Cross Rd. S6: Shef 6B 92
Parson La. S75: Dod 4E 29
Partridge Cl. S21: Ecki 1C 158
Partridge Flatt Rd.
DN4: Bess 6C 58
Partridge Pl. S26: Aston 2D 138
Partridge Ri. DN4: Bess 6C 58
Partridge Rd. DN3: Barn D 1C 26
Partridge Vw. S2: Shef 4B 120
Parwich Cl. S40: C'fld 3B 166
Parwich Ct. S60: Wav 3C 122
Parwich Wlk. S75: Dod 3F 29
Pashley Cft. S73: Womb 2E 47
Passfield Rd.
DN11: New R 6D 74
Passhouses Rd. S4: Shef 4G 107
Pasture Cl. DN3: Arm 5D 42
Pasture Cft. S66: Thurc 5C 114
Pasture Gro. S21: Ecki 1D 158
Pasture La. DN5: Cad 5D 52
S63: Bolt D 6E 35
Pastures, The S26: Tod 3B 140
S71: R'ton 3F 9
Pastures Ct. DN11: Ross 6E 75
S64: Mexb 1A 68
Pastures M. S64: Mexb 1A 68
Pastures Rd. S64: Mexb 1A 68
Paternoster Row S1: Shef . .5F 5 (4G 119)
Paterson Cl. S36: Stoc 2C 174
Paterson Ct. S36: Stoc 2C 174
Paterson Cft. S36: Stoc 2C 174
Paterson Gdns. S36: Stoc 2C 174
Paterson Rd. S25: Din 5B 128
Patmore Rd. S5: Shef 6A 94
Paton Gro. S43: Brim 6C 162
Patrick Stirling Ct. DN4: Hex 3H 55
Patrick Tobin Bus. Pk. S63: Wath D . .5C 50
Patterdale Cl. S18: Dron W 3D 154
Patterdale Gro. S66: Wick 6E 99
Patterdale Way S25: Nth A 2A 142
Pavement, The S2: Shef 3H 5 (3H 119)
Pavements Shop. Cen., The
S40: C'fld 5H 167
Pavilion Cl. S43: Ink 1H 169
S72: Brier 3B 12
Pavilion Ct. S10: Shef 6F 117
Pavilion Dr. S43: Stav 6B 164
Pavilion La. S60: Brins 2C 110
Pavilion Way S5: Shef 6A 94
Pavillion Cl. DN12: New E 3D 70
Paxton Ct. S14: Shef 4C 134
Paxton Cres. DN3: Arm 3C 42
Paxton La. S10: Shef 4C 118
Paxton Rd. S41: C'fld 3B 168
Payler Cl. S2: Shef 6D 120
Payne Cres. S62: Rawm 1F 83
Peace Garden 4E 5
Peacehaven DN3: Barn D 1C 26
Peacock Cl. S21: Killa 4B 152
S61: Thorpe H 2C 80
Peacock La. S25: Nth A 3G 141
Peacock Trad. Est. S6: Shef 4D 106
Peak Chase S72: Brier 4A 12
Peak Cl. S66: Sunn 3G 99
Peakdale Cres. S12: Shef 3H 135
Peak Dale Dr. S60: Wav 3C 122
Peak District National Pk. 4A 144
Peake Av. DN12: Con 4D 68
Peak La. S66: Hoot L 1H 115
PEAKLEY HILL 6B 154
Peak Pl. S43: Ink 1H 169
Peak Rd. S71: Shef 1F 17
Peaks Mt. S20: Water 5F 137
Peak Sq. S20: Water 6F 137
Peakstone Cl. DN4: Balb 5G 55
Peakstone M. S62: Rawm 3G 83
Peak Vw. Rd. S40: C'fld 4E 167
Pearce Av. S9: Shef 3F 121
Pearce Wlk. S9: Shef 2F 121
Pearl St. S11: Shef 6D 118
Pearmain Dr. S66: Malt 4G 101
Pea Royd La. S36: Stoc 2E 175
Pearson Cres. S73: Womb 5E 33
Pearson Cft. S41: C'fld 2D 166

Pearson Pl. S8: Shef 3E 133
Pearson's Cl. S65: Roth 6B 98
Pearson's Fld. S73: Womb 1G 47
Pearson St. S36: Stoc 2D 174
Pearson Trad. Est.
S41: Old W 5A 162
Pear St. S11: Shef 5D 118
Pear Tree Av. S42: W'orth 6F 171
S66: Bram 5A 100
Peartree Av. S63: Thurn 2B 36
Pear Tree Cl. S21: Killa 5B 152
S43: Hol 6F 163
S60: Brins 4E 111
S72: Gt H 6E 21
S81: Woods 4F 143
Pear Tree Ct. S63: Thurn 2B 36
Pear Tree M. DN11: Lov 4B 72
Peartree Orchard S71: R'ton 1A 10
Pear Tree Rd. S5: Shef 4A 94
Pearwood Cl. S63: Gol 5F 37
Pearwood Cres. DN4: Balb 1G 71
Peasehill Cl. S70: Barn 2D 30
Peashill St. S62: Rawm 3G 83
Peatfield Rd. S21: Killa 3E 153
Peckham Rd. S35: High G 2E 79
Pedley Av. S20: W'fld 1F 151
Pedley Cl. S20: W'fld 1F 151
Pedley Dr. S20: W'fld 2F 151
Pedley Gro. S20: W'fld 1F 151
Peel Cen. Retail Pk., The
S71: Barn 6F 17
Peel Cl. S66: Malt 4H 101
Peel Gdns. S18: Dron 3E 155
Peel Pde. S70: Barn 1D 30
Peel Pl. S71: Barn 5F 17
Peel Sq. S70: Barn 1D 30
Peel St. S10: Shef 4B 118
S70: Barn 3E 31
(Rowan Cl.)
S70: Barn 1D 30
(West Way)
Peel St. Arc. S70: Barn 1D 30
Peel Ter. S10: Shef 4A 4 (3D 118)
Pegasus Way DN4: Balb 2C 72
Peg Folly S36: Stoc 3A 174
Peggy La. S35: Eccl 1B 94
S35: Gren 1C 92
Pell's Cl. DN1: Don 1B 56
Pembrey Ct. S20: Sot 6H 137
Pembridge Ct. S71: R'ton 2H 9
(off Strawberry Gdns.)
Pembroke Av. DN4: Balb 6H 55
Pembroke Cl. S40: W'ton 1D 170
Pembroke Ct. S41: C'fld 1F 167
Pembroke Cres. S35: High G 2C 78
Pembroke Ri. DN5: Scaws 4E 39
S25: Sth A 4G 141
Pembroke Rd. S18: Dron 4F 155
Pembroke St. S11: Shef 5D 118
S61: Kimb 4A 96
Pencil La. S25: Din 5A 128
Pendeen Rd. S11: Shef 6G 117
Pendlebury Dr. S74: Hoyl 1H 61
Pendle Cft. S20: Sot 1A 152
Pendon Ho. S36: Pen 4D 176
Pengeston Rd. S36: Pen 4B 176
PENISTONE 4D 176
Penistone Cl. S36: Pen 4E 177
Penistone Ho. S3: Shef 1E 119
(off Adelaide La.)
Penistone Rd. S6: Shef 2B 106
S35: Chap, Gren 2A 78
Penistone Rd. Nth. S6: Shef 1B 106
Penistone Station (Rail) 4E 177
Penistone St. DN1: Don 6C 40
Penley St. S11: Shef 6E 119
Penlington Cl. WF9: Hems 1E 13
Penmore Cl. S41: Has 2B 172
Penmore Gdns. S41: Has 1B 172
Penmore La. S41: Has 2B 172
Penmore Rd. S41: Has 2B 172
Pennine Cen., The S1: Shef 2D 4
Pennine Cl. S75: Dart 4H 7
Pennine Ct. S36: Pen 5F 177
Pennine Gdns. S66: Malt 4G 101
Pennine Vw. S36: Stoc 1D 174
S74: Black H 3A 46
Pennine Way S40: C'fld 3D 166
S75: Barn 6A 16
Pennington Cl. S66: Malt 6H 101

Pen Nook Cl. S36: Spink 5F 175
Pen Nook Ct. S36: Spink 5G 175
Pen Nook Dr. S36: Spink 5G 175
Pen Nook Gdns. S36: Spink 5G 175
Pen Nook Glade S36: Spink 5G 175
(Pen Nook Ct.)
S36: Spink 4G 175
(The Greenway)
Penns Rd. S2: Shef 2H 133
Penny Engine La. S21: Ecki 6F 151
Pennyfields S63: Bolt D 2A 50
Penny Hill S81: Fir 2F 129
Penny Hill La. S26: Ull 2E 125
S66: Bramp M 2E 125
Pennyholme Cl. S26: Kiv P 6C 140
Penny La. S17: Tot 6D 144
Penny Piece La. S25: Nth A 2G 141
Penny Piece Pl. S25: Nth A 2G 141
Penrhyn Rd. S11: Shef 1B 132
Penrhyn Wlk. S71: Ard 2D 32
Penrith Cl. S5: Shef 2D 106
Penrith Cres. S5: Shef 2D 106
Penrith Gro. S71: Ard 2C 32
Penrith Rd. DN2: Don 6H 41
S5: Shef 2D 106
Penrose Cres. S44: Ark T 5H 173
Penrose Pl. S13: Shef 2B 136
Penthorpe Cl. S12: Shef 2E 135
Pentland Chase DN9: Auck 3A 76
Pentland Cl. S40: C'fld 3D 166
Pentland Gdns. S20: Water 6E 137
Pentland Rd. S18: Dron W 3C 154
Penton St. S1: Shef 3D 4 (3F 119)
Penwood Wlk. S66: Sunn 2G 99
Penyghent Cl. S35: Chap 2E 79
Pepper Cl. S61: Kimb P 6G 81
Pepper St. S74: Hoyl 4B 46
Percy St. S3: Shef 1E 119
S65: Roth 4F 97
Peregrine Dr. S70: Birdw 4E 45
Perigree Rd. S8: Shef 5D 132
Periwood Av. S8: Shef 5D 132
Periwood Cl. S8: Shef 5D 132
Periwood Dr. S8: Shef 5D 132
Periwood Gro. S8: Shef 5D 132
Periwood La. S8: Shef 5D 132
Perkyn Rd. S5: Shef 3A 94
Perkyn Ter. S5: Shef 3A 94
Perran Gro. DN5: Cus 5G 39
Perrot Ct. S64: Swin 4D 68
Perseverance St. S70: Barn 1C 30
Persimmon Cl.
DN11: New R 6G 75
Perth Cl. S64: Mexb 6H 51
Petal Cl. S66: Malt 4C 102
Peterborough Cl. S10: Shef 6B 116
Peterborough Dr. S10: Shef 5B 116
Peterborough Rd. S10: Shef 5B 116
Peterdale Cl. S43: Brim 6D 162
Peterdale Rd. S43: Brim 6D 162
Peterfoot Way S71: Car 5G 9
Petersgate DN5: Scawt 1G 39
Peter's Rd. DN12: New E 5C 70
Peter St. S61: Kimb 3H 95
S66: Thurc 5B 114
Peters Yd. S61: Kimb 3H 95
(off Peter St.)
Petre Dr. S4: Shef 4B 108
Petre St. S4: Shef 5A 108
Pettyclose La. S41: C'fld 3C 168
Petunia Rd. DN3: Kirk Sa 5C 26
Petworth Cft. S71: R'ton 2G 9
Petworth Dr. S11: Shef 6G 131
Pevensey Av. S41: C'fld 2F 167
Pevensey Cl. S41: C'fld 1F 167
Peveril Cl. S26: Kiv P 5B 140
Peveril Cres. S71: Ath 1F 17
Peveril Rd. DN4: Balb 6F 55
S11: Shef 1A 132
S21: Ecki 6F 151
S41: C'fld 1G 167
Pexton Rd. S4: Shef 4H 107
Pheasant Bank DN11: Ross 5D 74
PHILADELPHIA 6E 107
Philadelphia Dr. S6: Shef 1D 118
Philadelphia Gdns. S6: Shef 1D 118
Philadelphia Gro. S6: Shef 1D 118
Philip La. S35: Howb 6A 60
Philip Rd. S70: Barn 3A 32
Phillimore Rd. S9: Shef 6E 109
Phillips Rd. S6: Lox 3E 105

Phoenix Ct. S1: Shef 4D 4
  S12: Ridg 1H 149
Phoenix Dr. DN4: Balb 2C 72
Phoenix Golf Course 2C 110
Phoenix Gro. S60: Brins 2C 110
Phoenix La. S63: Thurn 3D 36
Phoenix Riverside S60: Roth 6C 96
Phoenix St. S12: Ridg 1H 149
PICCADILLY 5C 66
Piccadilly DN5: Bntly 2H 39
Piccadilly Hgts. S41: C'fld 6A 168
    (off Piccadilly Rd.)
Piccadilly Rd. S41: C'fld 6A 168
  S64: Swin 5B 66
Pickard Cres. S13: Shef 6G 121
Pickard Dr. S13: Shef 6H 121
Pickering Cres. S26: Swal 2A 138
Pickering Rd. DN5: Bntly 5H 23
  S3: Shef 5E 107
Pickhill's Av. S63: Gol 5E 37
Pickhills Gro. S63: Gol 6E 37
Picking La. S35: Eccl 2G 93
Pickle Gro. DN11: New R 4B 74
Pickle Wood Ct. DN9: Finn 2F 77
Pickmere Rd. S10: Shef 2A 118
Pickton Cl. S40: W'ton 6E 167
Pickup Cres. S73: Womb 3G 47
Pickwick Dr. S60: Cat 6C 110
Piece End S35: High G 1C 78
    (Alma Rd.)
  S35: High G 6C 60
    (Piece End Cl.)
Piece End Cl. S35: High G 6C 60
Pieces Nth., The S60: Whis 4A 112
Pieces Sth., The S60: Whis 4A 112
Pigeon Bri. Way S26: Aston 2D 138
Pighills La. S18: Coal A 6G 147
Pike Cl. S40: C'fld 3C 166
Pike Lowe Gro. S75: Stain 6C 8
Pike Rd. S60: Brins 3D 110
Pilgrim St. S3: Shef 5G 107
Pilkingtons Yd. S21: Ecki 1F 159
    (off Station Rd.)
PILLEY 6C 44
PILLEY GREEN 1C 60
Pilley Grn. S75: Pil 1C 60
PILLEY HILLS 6B 44
Pilley La. S75: Pil 6C 44
Pilley La. End S75: Pil 5B 44
Pinchfield Ct. S66: Wick 1G 113
Pinchfield Holt S66: Wick 2G 113
Pinchfield La. S66: Wick 1G 113
PINCHMILL 3F 113
Pinchmill Hollow S66: Wick 2G 113
Pinch Mill La. S60: Whis 3D 112
Pinchwell Vw. S66: Wick 1G 113
Pindale Av. S43: Ink 1H 169
Pindar Oaks S70: Barn 3F 31
Pindar Oaks Cotts. S70: Barn 2G 31
Pindar Oaks St. S70: Barn 2F 31
Pindar St. S70: Barn 2G 31
Pine Av. S25: Sth A 5G 141
Pine Cl. S21: Killa 5B 152
  S66: Sunn 4H 99
  S70: Barn 4H 31
  S74: Hoyl 1B 62
Pine Cft. S35: Chap 4F 79
Pinecroft Way S35: Chap 4F 79
Pinefield Av. DN3: Barn D 2D 26
Pinefield Rd. DN3: Barn D 2D 26
Pine Gro. DN12: Con 6D 68
Pine Hall Dr. S71: Monk B 4A 18
Pine Hall Rd. DN3: Barn D 2C 26
Pinehurst Ri. S64: Swin 4C 66
Pine Rd. DN4: Can 4C 58
Pines, The S10: Shef 6B 116
  S66: Wick 1H 113
Pine St. S43: Hol 6F 163
Pine Vw. S40: Ash 5C 166
Pine Wlk. S64: Swin 6C 66
Pinewood Av. DN3: Arm 2E 43
  DN4: Balb 1F 71
Pinewood Cl. S65: Dalt 1C 98
  S72: Gt H 5E 21
Pinfield Cl. S72: Gt H 6F 21
Pinfold S63: Wath D 6F 49
Pinfold, The DN5: Barnb 6H 37
Pinfold Ct. DN9: Finn 3F 77
  S64: Swin 4B 66
  S71: Stair 2B 32
Pinfold Cotts. S72: Cud 2F 19
Pinfold Ct. DN3: Barn D 2C 26
Pinfold Gdns. S72: Cud 3F 19
Pinfold Hill S70: Wors 4F 31
Pinfold Lands S64: Mexb 2G 67
Pinfold La. S3: Shef 5F 107
  S60: Roth 5F 97
  S71: R'ton 3H 9
  S73: D'fld 5C 34
Pinfold St. S1: Shef 3D 4 (4F 119)
  S21: Ecki 1E 159
Pingle Av. S7: Shef 5B 132
Pingle Grange S43: Shef 1D 168
Pingle Rd. S7: Shef 5A 132
  S21: Killa 3D 152
Pinnacles, The S2: Shef . .2H 5 (2H 119)
Pinner Rd. S11: Shef 6B 118
Pinsent S7: Shef 1F 5
Pinstone St. S1: Shef 5E 5 (4F 119)
Pioneer Cl. S63: Wath D 6B 50
Pipe Ho. La. S62: Rawm 6G 65
    (not continuous)
Piper Cl. S5: Shef 1F 107
Piper Cl. S5: Shef 1F 107
Piper Cres. S5: Shef 6F 93
Pipering La. E. DN5: Scawt 3G 39
Pipering La. W. DN5: Scawt 3F 39
Piper La. S26: Aston 1E 139
  S42: Ash 5A 166
Piper Rd. S5: Shef 1G 107
  S44: Ark T 6H 173
Pipeyard La. S21: Ecki 1D 158
Pippin Cl. S66: Malt 4G 101
Pipworth Gro. S2: Shef 5F 121
Pipworth La. S21: Ecki 6G 151
Pipworth Rd. S2: Shef 5E 121
Pisgah Ho. Rd. S10: Shef 3B 118
PISMIRE HILL 6A 94
Pitchford La. S10: Shef 5E 117
Pit Fld. Cl. S71: Ath 6E 9
Pithouse La. S26: Wales B 1D 152
Pit La. DN4: Warm 3E 71
  S12: Shef 2D 134
  S60: Tree 2G 123
  S61: Thorpe H 4C 80
  S73: Womb 2D 46
Pitman Rd. DN12: Den M 3B 68
Pit Row S73: Hem 6F 47
PITSMOOR 5G 107
Pitsmoor Rd. S3: Shef 6F 107
    (not continuous)
Pittam Cl. DN3: Arm 4E 43
Pitt Cl. S1: Shef 4B 4
Pitt La. S1: Shef 4B 4
  S75: Mapp 5H 7
Pitt St. S1: Shef 4B 4 (3E 119)
  S21: Ecki 2D 158
  S61: Kimb 4A 96
  S64: Mexb 1H 67
  S70: Barn 1D 30
  S73: Womb 5H 33
Pitt St. W. S70: Barn 1C 30
Planation Gro. DN5: Sprot 3D 54
Plane Cl. DN4: Can 4C 58
Plane Dr. S66: Wick 5H 99
Plane Tree Way DN9: Auck 3A 76
Planet Rd. DN6: Adw S 1D 22
Plank Ga. S35: Ough 1D 92
Plantation Av. DN4: Bess 2E 75
  S25: Din 5A 128
  S25: Nth A 2H 141
  S71: R'ton 3A 10
Plantation Cl. DN5: Bntly 5B 24
  S40: Ash 3B 166
  S66: Malt 4A 102
Plantation Ct. S25: Din 5A 128
Plantation Rd. DN4: Balb 2B 72
  DN5: Bntly 1F 25
  S8: Shef 2F 133
Plantation Wlk. S25: Din 5A 128
    (off Plantation Av.)
Plantin, The S20: Half 3F 151
Plantin Ri. S20: Half 3F 151
Plaster Pits La. DN5: Sprot 6C 38
PLATTS COMMON 5B 46
Platts Comn. Ind. Est. S74: Hoyl 5A 46
Platts Dr. S20: Beig 4H 137
Platts La. S35: Ough 3F 91
Platt St. S3: Shef 6F 107
Playford Yd. S74: Hoyl 4A 46
Plaza Quarter S70: Barn 1D 30
Pleasance Cl. DN12: New E 6B 70
Pleasant Av. S72: Gt H 6F 21
Pleasant Cl. S12: Shef 2E 135
Pleasant Pl. S40: C'fld 5E 167
Pleasant Rd. S12: Shef 2E 135
Pleasant Vw. S72: Cud 4F 19
Pleasant Vw. Cft. S71: Barn 4D 16
Pleasley Rd. S26: Augh 3H 111
  S60: Whis 3H 111
Ploughmans Cft. S63: Bramp B 5A 48
Plover Ct. DN11: Ross 5D 74
  S2: Shef 4B 120
Plover Cft. S61: Thorpe H 2D 80
Plover Dr. S70: Birdw 4E 45
Plover Way S44: Cal 5E 169
Plowmans Way S61: Wing 5A 82
Plowright Cl. S14: Shef 3A 134
Plowright Dr. S14: Shef 3A 134
Plowright Mt. S14: Shef 3A 134
Plowright Way S14: Shef 3A 134
Plumber St. S70: Barn 1C 30
PLUMBLEY 4D 150
Plumbley Hall M. S20: Mosb 4D 150
Plumbley Hall Rd. S20: Mosb 3D 150
Plumbley La. S20: Mosb 4C 150
Plumb Leys S60: Tree 2F 123
Plumbleywood La. S12: Ridg 4A 150
  S20: Mosb 4A 150
Plum La. S3: Shef 1E 5 (2F 119)
Plumpers Rd. S9: Tins 2G 109
Plumpton Av. S64: Mexb 6H 51
Plumpton Cl. S36: Thurl 4A 176
Plumpton Gdns. DN4: Can 6D 58
Plumpton Pk. S72: Shaft 4F 11
Plumpton Pk. Rd.
  DN4: Bess, Can 1D 74
Plum St. S3: Shef 1E 5 (2F 119)
Plunket Rd. DN2: Don 6E 41
Plymouth Rd. S7: Shef 3D 132
Pocket Handkerchief La.
  S26: Tod 5C 126
Poggy La. S66: B'well 1C 102
POGMOOR 6A 16
Pogmoor La. S75: Barn 6H 15
    (Farm Ho. La.)
  S75: Barn 1H 29
    (The Courtyard)
Pogmoor Rd. S70: Barn 6A 16
  S75: Barn 6A 16
Pog Well La. S75: High'm 5F 15
    (not continuous)
Point, The S60: Roth 6D 96
Polka Ct. S3: Shef 5F 107
Pollard Av. S5: Shef 1D 106
Pollard Cres. S5: Shef 1D 106
Pollard Rd. S5: Shef 1D 106
Pollard St. S61: Kimb 4H 95
Pollitt Cl. S9: Shef 2E 121
Pollitt St. S75: Barn 5C 16
Pollyfox Way S75: Dod 3G 29
Pomegranate Theatre 5A 168
Pommern Dr. DN12: New E 4D 70
Pomona St. S11: Shef 5D 118
Pond Cl. S6: Stan 6E 105
Pond Hill S1: Shef 3F 5 (3G 119)
Pond La. S42: W'orth 4F 167
Pond Rd. S6: Stan 6E 105
Ponds Forge Stop (ST) 2G 5 (3G 119)
Ponds Forge International Sports Cen.
  . . . . .3G 5 (3G 119)
Pond Sq. S1: Shef 3G 5
Pond St. S1: Shef 3F 5 (3G 119)
    (not continuous)
  S40: C'fld 6H 167
  S70: Barn 2D 30
    (not continuous)
Pondwell Dr. S43: Brim 1E 169
Pontefract Rd. S70: Barn 1E 31
  S71: Barn, Lund 1E 31
  S72: Cud, Shaft 6E 11
  S73: Bramp 5C 48
Pool Dr. DN4: Bess 1E 75
Poole Pl. S9: Shef 2E 121
Poole Rd. S9: Shef 2E 121
POOLSBROOK 6D 164
Poolsbrook Av. S43: Pool 6D 164
Poolsbrook Cvn. Club
  S43: Stav 6B 164
Poolsbrook Country Pk. 6B 164
Poolsbrook Cres. S43: Pool 6D 164

Poolsbrook Sq. S43: Pool 6D 164
Poolsbrook Vw. S43: Pool 6D 164
Pool's La. S21: West H 5F 157
Pools La. S71: R'ton 3B 10
Pool Sq. S1: Shef 4E 5 (3F 119)
Pop Av. DN12: Con 4C 68
Pop La. DN12: Con 4F 69
Poplar Av. S20: Beig 3G 137
  S36: Stoc 4D 174
  S40: Bramp 6C 166
  S63: Gol 5D 36
  S65: Thry 6D 84
  S72: Shaft 4F 11
Poplar Cl. DN3: Brant 3G 59
  S18: Dron 5H 155
  S21: Killa 5B 152
  S35: Ough 3D 90
  S64: Mexb 6E 51
Poplar Dr. DN2: Don 4H 41
  S60: Brins 4C 110
  S63: Wath D 2G 65
Poplar Glade S66: Wick 6G 99
Poplar Gro. DN4: Warm 2D 70
  DN12: Con 6E 69
  S64: Swin 3C 66
  S65: Rav 2B 100
  S71: Lund 4B 18
Poplar Nook S26: Kiv P 5H 139
Poplar Pl. DN3: Arm 4E 43
  S41: C'fld 6G 161
Poplar Ri. S66: Malt 4G 101
Poplar Rd. S21: Ecki 2D 158
  S35: Ough 3D 90
  S73: Womb 2H 47
Poplars, The DN5: Barnb 1H 51
  DN12: Con 5E 69
  S25: Laugh C 3F 127
  S42: Cut 6A 160
Poplars Ind. Est., The S60: Cat ...1C 122
Poplars Rd. S70: Barn 3G 31
Poplar St. S72: Grim 2C 20
Poplar Ter. DN5: Bntly 2A 40
  S71: R'ton 2A 10
Poplar Vw. S25: Nth A 2G 141
Poplar Way DN9: Auck 1B 76
  S60: Cat 1B 122
Popple St. S4: Shef 3A 108
Poppyfields Way DN3: Brant 5F 59
Poppy Pl. S5: Shef 1C 108
Porter Av. S75: Barn 6B 16
Porter Brook Vw. S11: Shef 6C 118
  (not continuous)
Porter St. S43: Stav 4B 164
Porter Ter. S11: Shef 6B 118
  S75: Barn 6A 16
Portland Av. S26: Aston 1D 138
Portland Bldgs. S6: Shef 1D 118
  (off Portland St.)
Portland Bus. Pk. S13: Shef 4H 121
Portland Cl. S25: Nth A 6H 127
  S41: C'fld 4H 167
Portland Ct. S6: Shef 6D 106
Portland La. S1: Shef 4B 4 (3E 119)
Portland Pl. DN1: Don 1B 56
  S66: Malt 5B 102
Portland Rd. DN4: Bess 1C 74
  DN11: New R 6G 73
  S20: Beig 6H 137
Portland St. S6: Shef 1D 118
  (Cross Bedford St.)
  S6: Shef 1D 118
  (Straw La.)
  S64: Swin 3C 66
  S70: Barn 2G 31
Portobello S1: Shef 3B 4 (3E 119)
Portobello La. S1: Shef 3B 4 (3E 119)
Portobello St. S1: Shef ...3C 4 (3E 119)
Portsea Rd. S6: Shef 4A 106
Portway Cl. S12: Shef 3H 135
Pot House La. S36: Stoc 3D 174
Potterdyke Av. S62: Rawm 6G 65
POTTER HILL 1B 78
Potter Hill S61: Grea 5D 82
Potter Hill La. S35: High G 1B 78
Potteric Carr Nature Reserve 1G 73
Potteries, The DN11: New R 5C 74
Potteries Acre S64: Swin 3C 66
Potters Cl. S41: Old W 4A 162
Potters Ga. S35: High G 1B 78
  (not continuous)
Potters Way S64: Kiln 5D 66

Pottery Cl. S62: Rawm 3G 83
Pottery La. S62: Rawm 3A 84
Pottery La. E. S41: Whit M 1A 168
Pottery La. W. S41: Whit M 1H 167
Pottery Row S61: Roth 5B 96
Potts Cres. S72: Gt H 6F 21
Poucher St. S61: Kimb 4G 95
Poulton St. S71: Monk B 2A 18
Powder Mill La. S70: Wors 1H 45
Powell Dr. S21: Killa 4B 152
Powell St. S3: Shef 2A 4 (2D 118)
  S70: Wors 6G 31
Powerhouse Sq. S74: Els 2E 63
  (off Wath Rd.)
Powerleague Soccer Cen.
  Sheffield 1C 120
Power Sta. Rd. DN5: Don 6A 40
Powley Rd. S6: Shef 5C 92
Poynton Av. S26: Ull 3D 124
Poynton Dr. S25: Din 4A 128
Poynton Way S26: Ull 3D 124
Poynton Wood Cres. S17: Bradw ...4H 145
Poynton Wood Glade S17: Bradw ..4H 145
Prefect Cl. S70: Barn 2B 30
Prescott Rd. S6: Shef 2H 105
President Way S4: Shef 6A 108
Preston Av. S74: Jum 5D 46
Preston St. S8: Shef 1F 133
Preston Way S71: Monk B 2A 18
Prestwich St. S9: Shef 6E 95
Prestwold Way S41: Has 3B 172
Prestwood Gdns. S35: Chap 3D 78
Priest Cft. La. S71: D'fld 2A 34
Priestfield Gdns. S41: C'fld 1C 166
Priestley Av. S62: Rawm 1A 84
  S75: Kexb 6D 6
Priestley Cl. DN4: Balb 1G 71
Priestley St. S2: Shef 5G 119
Priest Royd S75: Dart 5H 7
Primrose Av. S5: Shef 6B 94
  S60: Brins 5E 111
  S73: D'fld 5A 34
Primrose Bank S71: Smi 2E 17
Primrose Circ. DN11: New R 6D 74
Primrose Cl. S21: Killa 3D 152
  S63: Bolt D 1A 50
Primrose Cres. S20: Beig 5G 137
Primrose Dr. S35: Eccl 2G 93
Primrose Hill S6: Shef 6C 106
  (not continuous)
  S60: Roth 2D 96
  S74: Hoyl 1B 62
Primrose La. S21: Killa 2D 152
  S60: Roth 2D 96
Primrose Pl. DN4: Bess 4G 57
Primrose View Stop (ST) 6D 106
Primrose Wlk. S8: Shef 2E 133
Primrose Way S74: Hoyl 2B 62
Primulas Cl. S25: Sth A 4F 141
Prince Arthur St. S75: Barn 6C 16
Princegate DN1: Don 1C 56
Prince of Wales Rd. S2: Shef 1D 134
  S9: Shef 4F 121
Prince's Cres. DN12: New E 3C 70
Prince's Rd. DN4: Bess 3G 57
Princess Cl. S63: Bolt D 2A 50
Princess Ct. S2: Shef 6E 121
Princess Dr. S36: Spink 4E 175
  S63: Thurn 3D 36
Princess Gdns. S73: Womb 2G 47
Princess Gro. S75: Pil 1B 60
Prince's Sq. DN3: Kirk Sa 4C 26
Princess Rd. S18: Dron 2F 155
  S63: Gol 5D 36
  S64: Mexb 1G 67
Princess St. DN6: Woodl 4C 22
  S4: Shef 1A 120
  S25: Laugh C 4F 127
  S41: C'fld 4G 167
  S43: Brim 5E 163
  S63: Wath D 5E 49
  S70: Barn 1D 30
  S72: Cud 5F 11
  S72: Grim 2B 20
  S73: Womb 1F 47
  S74: Hoyl 1G 61
  S75: Mapp 5H 7
Prince's St. DN1: Don 1C 56
Princes St. S60: Roth 4C 96
Prince St. S64: Swin 2C 66
Pringle La. S41: Old W 2G 161

Pringle Rd. S60: Brins 3C 110
Printing Office St. DN1: Don 1B 56
Prior Cft. S63: Bolt D 3C 50
Prior Rd. DN12: Con 5E 69
Prior Way S63: Bolt D 3C 50
Priory, The S18: Dron 2F 155
Priory Av. S7: Shef 6E 119
Priory Cl. DN12: Con 3F 69
  S35: Eccl 1F 93
  S42: W'ton 3C 170
  S64: Mexb 2H 67
  S70: Wors 2E 45
Priory Ct. S71: Monk B 3A 18
Priory Cres. S71: Lund 5B 18
Priory Gro. DN9: Finn 3F 77
Priory Pl. DN1: Don 1B 56
  S7: Shef 6E 119
  S71: Lund 4B 18
Priory Rd. S7: Shef 1D 132
  S35: Eccl 1F 93
  S63: Bolt D 2B 50
  S71: Lund 4B 18
  (not continuous)
Priory Ter. S7: Shef 6E 119
Priory Wlk. DN1: Don 1C 56
  (off High St.)
Priory Way S26: Aston 1D 138
Pritchard Cl. S12: Shef 5C 136
Private Dr. S43: Hol 6F 163
Proact Stadium 1H 167
Probert Av. S63: Gol 5C 36
Proctor Pl. S6: Shef 4B 106
Progress Dr. S66: Bram 6A 100
Prominence Way S66: Sunn 2G 99
Prospect S36: Thurl 4A 176
Prospect Cl. S66: Bram 6A 100
Prospect Ct. S17: Bradw 5H 145
  S62: P'gte 4G 83
Prospect Dr. S17: Bradw 5G 145
Prospect Ho. S43: Stav 5C 164
Prospect Pl. DN1: Don 2B 56
  S17: Bradw 4H 145
  S74: Hoyl 1A 62
Prospect Rd. DN5: Bntly 4H 23
  S2: Shef 1F 133
  S17: Bradw 5H 145
  S18: Dron 1H 155
  S41: Old W 4G 161
  S63: Bolt D 1B 50
  S72: Cud 2E 19
Prospect St. S70: Barn 1C 30
  S72: Cud 1E 19
Prospect Ter. S40: C'fld 4F 167
Providence Ct. S70: Barn 2D 30
  S73: Womb 6A 34
  (off Providence St.)
Providence Rd. S6: Shef 6A 106
Providence St. S60: Roth 4D 96
  S61: Grea 5D 82
  S73: Womb 6A 34
Provincial Ho. S1: Shef ...2C 4 (2E 119)
Psalter Cl. S11: Shef 1B 132
Psalter Cft. S11: Shef 1A 132
Psalter La. S11: Shef 1A 132
Psalters Dr. S36: Oxs 6H 177
Psalters La. S61: Kimb 3A 96
Pudding Poke S6: Dung 4A 104
Pullman Cl. S43: Stav 3C 164
Pump Riding DN12: New E 5E 71
Purbeck Av. S40: C'fld 4E 167
Purbeck Cl. S20: Water 6E 137
Purbeck Gro. S20: Water 6E 137
Purbeck Rd. S20: Water 6E 137
Purcell Cl. S66: Malt 6D 102
PureGym
  Millhouses 5D 132
  Sheffield City Centre 6F 5 (5H 119)
  Sheffield North 1H 119
Purslove Cl. S66: Bram 6B 100
Pye Av. S75: Mapp 6H 7
Pye Bank Cl. S3: Shef 6F 107
Pye Bank Dr. S3: Shef 6F 107
Pye Bank Rd. S3: Shef 1F 119
Pym Rd. S64: Mexb 1F 67
Pynot Rd. S41: Old W 4A 162

Q

Quadrant, The S17: Tot 5F 145
Quail Ri. S2: Shef 4B 120

Quaker Cl. S63: Wath D 1E **65**
Quaker La. DN4: Warm 6E **55**
S71: Ard 2C **32**
(Crown Well Hill)
S71: Ard 2D **32**
(Top Fold)
S71: Monk B 4G **17**
Quantock Way S40: C'fld 3C **166**
Quantum Ct. DN6: Adw S 1D **22**
Quarry Bank S63: Wath D 6C **48**
Quarry Bank Cl. S72: Cud 3E **19**
Quarry Bank Ho. S70: Barn 5D **16**
Quarry Bank Rd. S41: C'fld 6B **168**
Quarry Cl. S60: Brins 4B **110**
S75: Kexb 6E **7**
Quarry Field La. S66: Wick 1G **113**
(not continuous)
Quarryfield La. S66: Malt 4A **102**
Quarryfield Rd. S9: Shef 6E **109**
Quarry Flds. S66: Wick 1G **113**
Quarry Hill S20: Mosb 2B **150**
S21: Trow 1F **157**
S60: Roth 4E **97**
Quarry Hill Ct. S63: Wath D 2F **65**
Quarry Hill Rd. S63: Wath D 2F **65**
QUARRY HILLS 5D **34**
Quarry La. DN3: Brant 4G **59**
DN6: Woodl 4B **22**
S11: Shef 2B **132**
S25: Nth A 2G **141**
S40: Bramp 6D **166**
S61: Grea 2D **96**
S64: Mexb 5E **51**
S73: D'fld 5D **34**
Quarry Pl. S71: Monk B 3F **17**
Quarry Rd. S13: Shef 4A **122**
S17: Tot 5F **145**
S18: App 3D **156**
S21: Killa 3B **152**
S74: Black H 3A **46**
Quarry St. S62: Rawm 2G **83**
S64: Mexb 2G **67**
S70: Barn 2E **31**
S71: Smi 3F **17**
S72: Cud 1E **19**
Quarry Va. S72: Cud 2E **19**
Quarry Va. Gro. S12: Shef 4F **135**
Quarry Va. Rd. S12: Shef 4F **135**
Quayside, The S2: Shef 1H **5** (2H **119**)
Queen Av. DN11: New R 5B **74**
S66: Malt 6B **102**
Queen Mary Cl. S2: Shef 1D **134**
S2: Shef 6D **120**
Queen Mary Gro. S2: Shef 1C **134**
Queen Mary M. S2: Shef 1D **134**
Queen Mary Ri. S2: Shef 6D **120**
Queen Mary Rd. S2: Shef 6C **120**
(not continuous)
S40: Bramp 1C **170**
Queen Mary's Rd. DN11: New R 5B **74**
Queen Mary St. S66: Malt 6C **102**
Queen Rd. S72: Grim 2C **20**
Queen's Av. S64: Swin 2C **66**
S72: Midd 3E **35**
S75: Barn 6C **16**
Queens Av. S26: Kiv P 6H **139**
Queensberry Rd. DN2: Don 5H **41**
Queen's Ct. DN5: Don 4H **39**
Queen's Cres. DN12: New E 3C **70**
Queens Cres. S74: Hoyl 1F **61**
Queen's Dr. DN5: Don 4H **39**
S72: Cud 5F **11**
S72: Shaft 3E **11**
S75: Dod 3G **29**
Queens Dr. S75: Barn 5B **16**
Queens Gdns. S2: Shef 6H **119**
S73: Womb 2G **47**
S74: Hoyl 1G **61**
S75: Barn 5B **16**
Queensgate DN1: Don 1C **56**
S35: Gren 2C **92**
Queens Ho. S71: Barn 6F **17**
Queens M. S2: Shef 6H **119**
Queens Pk. DN12: New E 3C **70**
Queen's Park Miniature Railway 6G **167**
(off Boythorpe Rd.)
Queen's Pk. Sports Cen. 6G **167**
Queens Retail Pk. S2: Shef 6G **119**

Queen's Rd. DN1: Don 6D **40**
S26: Swal 1B **138**
S71: Barn 1E **31**
S72: Cud 5F **11**
Queens Rd. S2: Shef 6G **5** (1F **133**)
S20: Beig 4G **137**
Queen's Row S3: Shef 1C **4** (2E **119**)
Queens Stables S2: Shef 6H **119**
Queen's Ter. S64: Mexb 1F **67**
Queen St. DN4: Balb 4A **56**
(not continuous)
S1: Shef 2E **5** (2F **119**)
S20: Mosb 3D **150**
S21: Ecki 1F **159**
S25: Din 4A **128**
S35: Chap 3F **79**
S36: Pen 4E **177**
S40: C'fld 4G **167**
S43: Brim 5E **163**
S43: Stav 6A **164**
S62: Rawm 1H **83**
S63: Gol 5D **36**
S63: Thurn 3D **36**
S64: Swin 3C **66**
S65: Roth 3H **97**
S70: Barn 1D **30**
S73: D'fld 4C **34**
S74: Hoyl 1F **61**
Queen St. M. S20: Mosb 3D **150**
Queen St. Nth. S41: Whit M 6H **161**
Queen St. Sth. S70: Barn 1E **31**
Queens Vw. S2: Shef 6H **119**
Queensway S60: Roth 2G **111**
S70: Wors 5G **31**
S71: R'ton 2H **9**
S72: Grim 2B **20**
S74: Hoyl 6C **46**
S75: Barn 5B **16**
Queensway Ct. S60: Roth 2G **111**
Queenswood Cl. S6: Shef 1H **105**
Queenswood Ct. S6: Shef 1G **105**
Queenswood Dr. S6: Shef 1G **105**
Queenswood Ga. S6: Shef 1G **105**
Queenswood Rd. S6: Shef 1G **105**
Queen Victoria Rd. S17: Bradw 6G **145**
Quern Way S73: D'fld 4B **34**
Quest Av. S73: Hem 4F **47**
Quiet La. S10: Shef 2C **130**
Quilter Rd. S66: Malt 6D **102**
Quintec Ct. S61: Grea 1F **97**
QUOIT GREEN 3G **155**
Quoit Grn. S18: Dron 3G **155**
Quorn Dr. S40: C'fld 3B **166**

R

Rabbit La. S21: Spink 2H **159**
Raby Rd. DN2: Don 5E **41**
Raby St. S9: Tarn 1H **109**
Race Comn. Av. S36: Cub 6C **176**
Racecommon La. S70: Barn 3C **30**
(not continuous)
Racecommon Rd. S70: Barn 3C **30**
Racecourse Cl. S64: Swin 3H **65**
Racecourse Mt. S41: C'fld 6G **161**
Racecourse Rd.
S41: C'fld, Whit M 6G **161**
S64: Swin 3H **65**
Race La. S36: Bolst 6F **175**
Race St. S70: Barn 1D **30**
Racker Way S6: Shef 5A **106**
Rackford La. S25: Nth A 4A **142**
S81: Work 4A **142**
Rackford Rd. S25: Nth A 3H **141**
Radbourne Comn. S18: Dron W 3C **154**
Radburn Rd. DN11: New R 6B **74**, 6F **75**
Radcliffe Cl. DN5: Scawt 1F **39**
Radcliffe La. DN5: Scawt 1F **39**
Radcliffe Mt. DN5: Bntly 6H **23**
Radcliffe Rd. DN5: Bntly 6H **23**
S71: Ath 6E **9**
Radford Cl. S65: Rav 2B **100**
Radford Pk. Av. WF9: Sth K 5H **13**
Radford St. S3: Shef 2B **4** (2E **119**)
Radiance Rd. DN1: Don 5D **40**
Radley Av. S66: Wick 5G **99**
Radnor Cl. S20: Sot 6H **137**
Radnor Way DN2: Don 5H **41**

Raeburn Cl. S14: Shef 6B **134**
Raeburn Pl. S14: Shef 5B **134**
Raeburn Rd. S14: Shef 6B **134**
Raeburn Way S14: Shef 6B **134**
Ragusa Dr. DN11: New R 6G **75**
Raikes St. S64: Mexb 2E **67**
Rail Mill Way S62: P'gte 6G **83**
RAILS 2B **116**
Rails Rd. S6: Shef, Stan 2B **116**
Railway Av. S60: Cat 1D **122**
Railway Cotts. S41: Cor 5E **173**
S60: Cat 6D **110**
S75: Dod 3F **29**
Railway Ct. DN4: Don 3C **56**
DN5: Scawt 3H **39**
S71: R'ton 2F **9**
(off High St.)
Railway Ter. S41: Has 3A **172**
S60: Roth 4D **96**
S63: Gol 5C **36**
Railway Vw. S63: Gol 5D **36**
Rainborough Ct. S63: Bramp B 6A **48**
Rainborough M. S63: Bramp B 5C **48**
Rainborough Rd.
S63: Wath D 6C **48**
Rainboro Vw. S73: Hem 5F **47**
Rainbow Av. S12: Shef 4C **136**
Rainbow Cl. S12: Shef 4C **136**
Rainbow Cres. S12: Shef 4D **136**
Rainbow Dr. S12: Shef 4D **136**
Rainbow Gro. S12: Shef 4D **136**
Rainbow Pl. S12: Shef 4D **136**
Rainbow Rd. S12: Shef 4D **136**
Rainbow Wlk. S12: Shef 4C **136**
(off Carter Lodge Dr.)
Rainbow Way S12: Shef 4C **136**
Rainford Dr. S71: Monk B 2A **18**
Rainford Sq. DN3: Kirk Sa 3C **26**
RAINSTORTH 6B **80**
Rainton Gro. S75: Barn 5A **16**
Rainton Rd. DN1: Don 2D **56**
Raintree Ct. DN5: Cus 5G **39**
Raisen Hall Pl. S5: Shef 2F **107**
Raisen Hall Rd. S5: Shef 1E **107**
Rake Bri. Rd. DN7: Hat 1H **43**
Rakes La. DN11: Lov 4B **72**
DN12: Old E 5D **88**
Raleigh Cl. DN2: Don 1G **57**
Raleigh Dr. S35: Burn 3C **78**
Raleigh Rd. S2: Shef 2G **133**
Raleigh Ter. DN4: Balb 6F **55**
Raley St. S70: Barn 3C **30**
(not continuous)
Ralph Ellis Dr. S36: Stoc 4D **174**
Ralph Rd. S43: Stav 4D **164**
Ralston Cl. S20: Half 4E **151**
Ralston Cft. S20: Half 4F **151**
Ralston Gro. S20: Half 4E **151**
Ralston Pl. S20: Half 4E **151**
Ramper La. DN3: Barn D 1B **26**
Ramper Rd. S66: Carr 3E **115**
S81: Letw 3H **129**
Rampton Rd. S7: Shef 1E **133**
Ramsay Cres. DN5: Don 4G **39**
Ramsden Rd. DN4: Hex 2H **55**
S60: Roth 5F **97**
Ramsey Av. S40: W'ton 1E **171**
Ramsey Rd. S10: Shef 2B **118**
Ramshaw Cl. S41: C'fld 1D **166**
Ramshaw Rd. S18: Uns 6B **156**
Ramsker Dr. DN3: Arm 5E **43**
Ranby Rd. S11: Shef 1A **132**
Randall Pl. S2: Shef 5F **119**
Randall St. S2: Shef 5F **119**
S21: Ecki 2C **158**
Randerson Dr. S64: Kiln 5D **66**
Rands La. DN3: Arm 3F **43**
Rands La. Ind. Est. DN3: Arm 3G **43**
Ranelagh Dr. S11: Shef 3A **132**
Raneld Mt. S40: W'ton 2D **170**
Ranfield Ct. S65: Rav 2B **100**
Rangeley Rd. S6: Shef 1H **117**
Range Rd. S4: Shef 3C **108**
RANMOOR 5G **117**
Ranmoor Chase S10: Shef 5A **118**
Ranmoor Cliffe Rd. S10: Shef 5F **117**
Ranmoor Ct. S41: Has 2B **172**
Ranmoor Cr. S10: Shef 6H **117**
Ranmoor Cres. S10: Shef 5G **117**

Ranmoor Gdns. S10: Shef 5H 117
Ranmoor Pk. Rd. S10: Shef 5G 117
Ranmoor Ri. S10: Shef 5G 117
Ranmoor Rd. S10: Shef 5G 117
Ranmoor Vw. S10: Shef 5G 117
Ranmoor Village, The S10: Shef . . .4H 117
Ranskill Ct. S9: Shef 5F 109
Ranulf Ct. S7: Shef 5B 132
Ranworth Cl. DN5: Cus 5F 39
Ranworth Rd. S66: Bram 5B 100
Ranyard Rd. DN4: Balb 5G 55
Raseby Av. S20: Water 6F 137
Raseby Cl. S20: Water 6F 137
Raseby Pl. S20: Water 6F 137
Rasen Cl. S64: Mexb 6H 51
Ratcliffe Cl. S41: Has 3B 172
Ratcliffe Rd. S11: Shef 6C 118
Ratten Row DN11: Wad 5F 73
S75: Dod 4F 29
Rattigan Ho. DN2: Don 4F 41
(off Parkway Nth.)
Ravencar Rd. S21: Ecki 1C 158
Ravencarr Pl. S2: Shef 5D 120
Ravencarr Rd. S2: Shef 5D 120
Raven Dr. S61: Thorpe H 2D 80
Raven Edge S65: Rav 4A 100
RAVENFIELD 5A 86
Ravenfield Cl. S20: Mosb 6B 136
RAVENFIELD COMMON 2A 100
Ravenfield Ct. DN12: Con 5C 68
Ravenfield Dr. S71: Smi 2F 17
Ravenfield La. S65: Hoot R, Rav 2H 85
Ravenfield Rd. DN3: Arm 5F 43
Ravenfield St. DN12: Den M 2C 68
Ravenholt S70: Wors 6F 31
Raven La. S72: Sth H 1D 10
Raven Mdws. S64: Swin 5B 66
Ravenna Cl. S70: Barn 2G 31
Raven Rd. S7: Shef 2C 132
Raven Royd S71: Ath 5E 9
Ravenscar Cl. DN12: Den M 3B 68
Ravens Cl. S75: Mapp 6A 8
Ravenscourt S70: Wors 6G 31
Ravenscroft Av. S13: Shef 6H 121
Ravenscroft Cl. S13: Shef 6H 121
Ravenscroft Ct. S13: Shef 6H 121
Ravenscroft Cres. S13: Shef 6H 121
Ravenscroft Dr. S13: Shef 6H 121
Ravenscroft Oval S13: Shef 6H 121
Ravenscroft Pl. S13: Shef 6H 121
Ravenscroft Rd. S13: Shef 6G 121
Ravenscroft Way S13: Shef 6H 121
Ravensdale Cl. S43: Ink 2H 169
Ravensdale Rd. S18: Dron W 3B 154
Ravenshaw Cl. S75: Barn 5A 16
Ravenside Retail Pk. S40: C'fld 6H 167
Ravensmead Ct. S63: Bolt D 3B 50
Ravens Wlk. DN12: Con 4H 69
Ravenswood Dr. DN9: Auck 1H 59
S66: Sunn .2G 99
Ravenswood Rd. S40: C'fld 3B 166
Ravensworth Rd. DN1: Don 2D 56
Ravine, The S5: Shef 3B 94
Raw La. S66: Stain 1F 103
Rawlins Ct. S18: Coal A 6H 147
RAWMARSH 3G 83
Rawmarsh Hill S62: P'gte 4G 83
Rawmarsh Ho. S62: P'gte 4G 83
(off Ryan Pl.)
Rawmarsh Rd. S60: Roth 3E 97
Rawmarsh Shop. Cen. S62: Rawm . .3G 83
Rawson Cl. DN4: Can 3C 58
Rawson Rd. S65: Roth 3F 97
Rawsons Bank S35: Eccl 2G 93
Rawson Spring Av. S6: Shef 2C 106
Rawson Spring Rd. S6: Shef 2C 106
Rawson Spring Way S6: Shef 2C 106
Rawson St. S6: Shef 5D 106
Raybould Rd. S61: Kimb P 1A 96
Rayleigh Av. S43: Brim 6C 162
Rayls Ri. S26: Tod 3C 140
Rayls Rd. S26: Tod 3C 140
Raymond Av. S72: Grim 2B 20
Raymond Rd. DN5: Scawt 4G 39
S70: Barn .2A 32
Raynald Rd. S2: Shef 5D 120
Raynor Sike La. S35: Ough 2B 90
Reader Cres. S64: Swin 2C 66
Reaper Cres. S35: High G 2D 78

Reasbeck Ter. S71: Smi 3E 17
Reasby Av. S65: Rav 2A 100
Reaton M. S75: Barn 5A 16
Reavill Cl. S25: Din 4A 128
Rebecca M. S70: Barn 2E 31
Rebecca Row S70: Barn 2E 31
Recreation Av. S66: Thurc 6C 114
S71: Ath 6D 8
Recreation La.
DN11: New R 5B 74
Recreation Rd. DN6: Woodl 4C 22
S43: Brim C 3E 169
S63: Wath D 5G 49
Rectory Cl. S21: Ecki 6F 151
S36: Stoc 3E 175
S63: Thurn 2A 36
S71: Car .5A 10
S73: Womb 2G 47
Rectory Ct. S25: Laugh M 1G 127
Rectory Dr. S42: W'orth 6F 171
S60: Whis 4B 112
Rectory Gdns. DN1: Don 6D 40
DN12: Old E 1B 88
S21: Killa 4C 152
S26: Tod .4C 140
Rectory La. DN9: Finn 3E 77
S63: Thurn 2A 36
Rectory M. DN5: Sprot 4C 54
Rectory Rd. S21: Killa 4C 152
S43: Stav 4B 164
Rectory St. S62: Rawm 4G 83
Rectory Way S71: Monk B 5A 18
Redbourne Rd. DN5: Bntly 1A 40
REDBROOK .3A 16
Redbrook Av. S41: Has 2A 172
Redbrook Bus. Pk. S75: Barn 3A 16
Redbrook Cft. S75: Barn 4B 16
Redbrook Cft. S20: Mosb 5B 136
Redbrook Gro. S20: Mosb 5B 136
Redbrook Mill Cl. S75: Barn 4H 15
Redbrook Rd. S75: Barn 4H 15
Redbrook Vw. S75: Barn 4B 16
Redbrook Wlk. S75: Barn 4B 16
Redcar Cl. DN12: Den M 4B 68
Redcar Rd. S10: Shef 3B 118
Redcliffe Cl. S75: Barn 4A 16
Red Dike La. DN11: Wils 5F 89
Redfearn St. S71: Barn 6E 17
Redfern Av. S20: Water 1E 151
Redfern Cl. S20: Water 1E 151
Redfern Dr. S20: Water 1E 151
Red Fern Gro. S36: Stoc 4D 174
Redfern Gro. S20: Water 1E 151
Redgrave S3: Shef 1F 5
Redgrave Pl. S66: Flan 4G 99
Redgrove Way S40: W'ton 2D 170
Redhall Cl. DN3: Kirk Sa 4D 26
Red Hill S1: Shef 2C 4 (3E 119)
S26: Kiv P, Kiv S 6C 140
Redhill Av. S70: Barn 3H 31
Redhill Ct. DN11: Wad 5E 73
S75: Barn 4H 15
Red Hill La. DN5: Hick 3H 37
Redholme S10: Shef 4F 117
Red Ho. Cl. S43: New W 2C 162
Red Ho. La. DN6: Adw S 1A 22
Red Kite Av. S63: Wath D 4F 49
Red Kite M. S63: Wath D 4F 49
Redland Gro. S75: Stain 4A 8
Redland La. S7: Shef 5C 132
Redland Way S66: Malt 4H 101
Red La. S10: Shef 5B 118
S41: Old W 5B 162
Red Lion Yd. S60: Roth 4E 97
(off Effingham St.)
Redmarsh Av. S62: Rawm 1F 83
Redmires La. S10: Shef 5A 116
Redmires Way S10: Shef 5A 116
Rednall Cl. S40: C'fld 3B 166
Red Oak La. S6: Stan 5D 104
Red Quarry La. S25: Din 6E 129
S81: Gild 6E 129
Redrock Rd. S60: Roth 2H 111
Redscope Cres. S61: Kimb P 6G 81
Redscope Rd. S61: Kimb 1G 95
Redshank Pl. S73: Bramp 3C 48
Redshank Rd. S63: Wath D 4E 49

Redthorne Way S72: Shaft 3E 11
Redthorn Rd. S13: Shef 6A 122
Redthorpe Crest S75: Barn 4H 15
Redvers Buller Rd.
S40: C'fld 1H 171
Redwall Cl. S25: Laugh C 4F 127
Redwood Av. S21: Killa 5B 152
S71: R'ton .3H 9
Redwood Cl. S43: Hol 6F 163
S74: Hoyl .1A 62
Redwood Ct. S25: Din 4H 127
Redwood Dr. S66: Malt 5F 101
Redwood Glen S35: Chap 4E 79
Reed Cl. S73: D'fld 5B 34
Reedham Dr. S66: Bram 5B 100
Reed Wlk. S63: Wath D 4E 49
Reeves Way DN3: Arm 4C 42
Regency Rd. S63: Wath D 5C 48
Regent Av. DN3: Arm 5F 43
Regent Ct. DN1: Don 1D 56
S1: Shef 3B 4
S6: Shef .4C 106
S74: Hoyl .1F 61
S75: Barn .4B 16
Regent Cres. S71: Ath 1E 17
S72: Sth H 1H 11
Regent Gdns. S70: Barn 5D 16
Regent Gro. DN5: Cus 5G 39
DN11: New R 6D 74, 6D 75
Regent Sq. DN1: Don 1D 56
Regent St. DN4: Balb 5H 55
S1: Shef 3B 4 (3E 119)
S61: Kimb .4A 96
S70: Barn .6D 16
S72: Sth H 1H 11
S74: Hoyl .1F 61
Regent St. Sth. S70: Barn 6E 17
Regents Way S26: Aston 1D 138
Regent Ter. DN1: Don 1D 56
S3: Shef 3B 4 (3E 119)
Regina Cres. S72: Brier 4H 11
Reginald Rd. S70: Barn 3A 32
S73: Womb 2A 48
Rembrandt Dr. S18: Dron 3D 154
Remington Av. S5: Shef 3E 93
Remington Dr. S5: Shef 3E 93
Remington Rd. S5: Shef 4E 93
Remount Rd. S61: Kimb P 6G 81
Remount Way
S61: Kimb P 6G 81
Rempstone Dr. S41: Has 3A 172
Renald La. S36: H'swne 1E 177
Renathorpe Rd. S5: Shef 4A 94
Rencliffe Av. S60: Roth 1G 111
Reneville Cl. S5: Shef 2F 93
S60: Roth .6F 97
Reneville Ct. S60: Roth 6E 97
Reneville Cres. S5: Shef 2F 93
Reneville Dr. S5: Shef 2F 93
Reneville Rd. S60: Roth 6E 97
Reney Av. S8: Shef 4C 146
Reney Cres. S8: Shef 4C 146
Reney Dr. S8: Shef 4C 146
Reney Rd. S8: Shef 3D 146
Reney Wlk. S8: Shef 4C 146
RENISHAW .4H 159
Renishaw Av. S60: Roth 2A 112
Renishaw Hall & Gardens 2G 159
Renishaw Pk. 3G 159
Renishaw Pk. Golf Course 2H 159
Renishaw Rd. S43: Mas M 1F 165
Renshaw Cl. S35: High G 6B 60
Renshaw Rd. S11: Shef 2H 131
Renville Cl. S62: Rawm 1F 83
Renville Rd. S60: Roth 1H 111
Repton Cl. S40: C'fld 3B 166
Repton Pl. S18: Dron W 3B 154
Reresby Cres. S60: Whis 2B 112
Reresby Dr. S60: Whis 2B 112
Reresby Rd. S60: Whis 2A 112
S65: Thry .6F 85
Reresby Wlk.
DN12: Den M 2C 68
S26: Ull 2B 124
Reservoir Rd. S10: Shef 3B 118
Reservoir Ter. S40: C'fld 4F 167
Retail World S60: Roth 6G 83
Retford Rd. S13: Shef 5C 122
Retford Wlk. DN11: Ross 5E 75

Revell Cl. S65: Roth 3C **98**
Revill Cl. S66: Malt 4A **102**
Revill La. S13: Shef 2D **136**
Revolution House (Mus.) 3H **161**
Rex Av. S7: Shef 4A **132**
Reynard Cres. S21: Reni 4H **159**
Reynard La. S6: Stan 1C **116**
Reynolds Cl. S18: Dron 4D **154**
  S66: Flan 4G **99**
Rhodes Av. S41: C'fld 3F **167**
  S61: Kimb P 6G **81**
Rhodes Dr. S60: Whis 2B **112**
Rhodesia Ct. DN4: Bess 4A **58**
Rhodesia Rd. S40: Bramp 6C **166**
Rhodes St. S2: Shef 4H **5** (3H **119**)
Rhodes Ter. S70: Barn 2F **31**
Rialto S3: Shef 1F **119**
  (off Kelham Island)
Ribble Cft. S35: Chap 2F **79**
Ribblesdale Dr. S12: Ridg 1A **150**
Ribble Way S5: Shef 1H **107**
Riber Av. S71: Ath 1F **17**
Riber Cl. S6: Stan 6E **105**
  S43: Ink .3H **169**
Riber Ter. S40: C'fld 6F **167**
Ribston Ct. S9: Shef 1D **120**
Ribston M. S9: Shef 2E **121**
Ribston Pl. S9: Shef 2E **121**
Ribston Rd. S9: Shef 2D **120**
Ribston Wlk. S9: Shef 2E **121**
Richard Av. S71: Smi 2F **17**
Richard La. DN11: New R 5B **74**
Richard Rd. S60: Roth 5F **97**
  S71: Smi .2F **17**
  S75: Dart .6E **7**
Richards Ct. S2: Shef 2G **133**
Richardson Wlk.
  S73: Womb 6E **33**
Richards Rd. S2: Shef 1F **133**
  (not continuous)
Richard St. S70: Barn 1C **30**
Richards Way S62: Rawm 2H **83**
Rich Farm Cl. DN5: Ark 5C **24**
RICHMOND 1G **135**
Richmond Av. S13: Shef 6H **121**
  S75: Dart .1E **15**
Richmond Bus. Pk. DN4: Don 4D **56**
Richmond Cl. S40: W'ton 2F **171**
Richmond Ct. S13: Shef 1G **135**
Richmond Farm M. S13: Shef 1G **135**
Richmond Gro. S13: Shef 6H **121**
Richmond Hall Av. S13: Shef 6G **121**
Richmond Hall Cres. S13: Shef . . .6G **121**
Richmond Hall Dr. S13: Shef 6G **121**
Richmond Hall Rd. S13: Shef 6G **121**
Richmond Hall Way S13: Shef 1G **135**
Richmond Hill Ho. S13: Shef 1G **135**
Richmond Hill Rd. DN5: Don 2F **55**
  S13: Shef 1H **135**
RICHMOND PARK 4G **95**
Richmond Pk. Av. S13: Shef 4H **121**
  S61: Kimb 4G **95**
Richmond Pk. Cl. S13: Shef 5H **121**
Richmond Pk. Cres. S13: Shef 4H **121**
Richmond Pk. Cft. S13: Shef 4H **121**
Richmond Pk. Dr. S13: Shef 5H **121**
Richmond Pk. Gro. S13: Shef 5H **121**
Richmond Pk. Ri. S13: Shef 4G **121**
Richmond Pk. Rd. S13: Shef 4H **121**
Richmond Pk. Vw. S13: Shef 5H **121**
Richmond Pk. Way S13: Shef 5H **121**
Richmond Pl. S13: Shef 1G **135**
Richmond Rd. DN5: Scaws 3E **39**
  S13: Shef 2F **135**
  S61: Kimb 4H **95**
  S63: Thurn 2B **36**
Richmond St. S3: Shef 6G **107**
  S70: Barn 1C **30**
Richmond Way S61: Kimb 4H **95**
Richworth Rd. S13: Shef 6A **122**
Ricknald Cl. S26: Augh 5C **124**
Ridal Av. S36: Stoc 2C **174**
Ridal Cl. S36: Stoc 2C **174**
Ridal Cft. S36: Stoc 2C **174**
Riddings Cl. S2: Shef 1D **134**
  S66: Thurc 6C **114**
  WF9: Hems 1E **13**
Riddings Cft. S41: C'fld 2D **166**
Rider Rd. S6: Shef 4B **106**

Ridge, The DN6: Woodl 4A **22**
  S10: Shef .5D **116**
Ridge Balk La. DN6: Woodl 3A **22**
Ridge Cl. S10: Shef 4D **116**
  S65: Roth .3G **97**
Ridgehill Av. S12: Shef 2D **134**
Ridgehill Gro. S12: Shef 3E **135**
Ridge Rd. DN6: Highf 6C **22**
  S21: Mar L 2H **157**
  S65: Roth .3F **97**
Ridge Vw. Cl. S9: Shef 1D **108**
Ridge Vw. Dr. S9: Shef 1D **108**
Ridgewalk Way S70: Wors 4E **31**
RIDGEWAY 2H **149**
Ridgeway S65: Roth 3B **98**
Ridgeway, The S18: Coal A 1A **156**
Ridgeway Cl. S65: Roth 3C **98**
Ridgeway Cott. Industry Cen.
  S12: Ridg .2H **149**
Ridgeway Cres. S12: Shef 3D **134**
  S71: Car 5H **9**
Ridgeway Dr. S12: Shef 2D **134**
RIDGEWAY MOOR 4H **149**
Ridgeway Moor S12: Ridg 4H **149**
Ridgeway Moor Farm Ct.
  S12: Ridg .4H **149**
Ridgeway Rd. S12: Shef 2D **134**
  S60: Brins 4D **110**
Ridgewood Av. DN3: Eden 1C **42**
Ridgway Av. S73: D'fld 4B **34**
Ridgway Cl. S66: Hel 5D **100**
Riding Cl. DN4: Bess 6E **59**
  S66: Flan .5F **99**
Ridings, The
  S71: Monk B 3G **17**
Ridings Av. S71: Smi 3G **17**
Rig Cl. S61: Kimb P 1A **96**
Rig Dr. S64: Swin 3H **65**
Riggotts La. S42: W'ton 3E **171**
Riggotts Way S42: Cut 6A **160**
Riggs High Rd. S6: Stan 1A **116**
Riggs Low La. S6: Stan 1A **116**
Riggs Low La. S6: Stan 1B **116**
Rig La. S62: Neth Hau 2D **82**
Riley Av. DN4: Balb 6G **55**
Riley Dr. DN3: Arm 3D **42**
Riley Rd. S63: Wath D 1G **65**
Rimington Rd. S73: Womb 1G **47**
Rimini Ri. S73: D'fld 5H **33**
RINGINGLOW 4B **130**
Ringinglow Cl. S11: Shef 3F **131**
Ringinglow Gdns. S11: Shef 3F **131**
Ringinglow Rd. S11: Shef 4A **130**
Ringstead Av. S10: Shef 4F **117**
Ringstead Cres. S10: Shef 4F **117**
Ringstone Gro. S72: Brier 3B **12**
Ringway S63: Bolt D 2A **50**
Ringwood Av. S41: C'fld 1F **167**
  S43: Stav 6H **163**
Ringwood Cres. S20: Sot 6H **137**
Ringwood Dr. S20: Sot 6H **137**
Ringwood Gro. S20: Sot 6H **137**
Ringwood Rd. S20: Sot 6H **137**
  S43: Brim 6E **163**
Ringwood Vw. S43: Brim 1E **169**
Ripley Gro. S75: Barn 4A **16**
Ripley St. S6: Shef 5B **106**
Ripon Av. DN2: Don 4E **41**
Ripon St. S9: Shef 1C **120**
  (not continuous)
Ripon Way S26: Swal 1B **138**
Rippon Ct. S62: Rawm 1G **83**
Rippon Cres. S6: Shef 4A **106**
Rippon Rd. S6: Shef 4A **106**
Rise, The DN4: Warm 2E **71**
  S25: Nth A 3H **141**
  S64: Swin 4A **66**
  S72: Brier 4B **12**
Risedale Rd. S63: Gol 6E **37**
Rising St. S3: Shef 6G **107**
Rivelin Bank S6: Shef 5A **106**
Rivelin Cl. S6: Shef 3C **116**
Rivelin Glen S6: Shef 2F **117**
Rivelin Glen Cotts. S6: Shef 2F **117**
Rivelin Pk. Cl. S6: Shef 6H **105**
Rivelin Pk. Cres. S6: Shef 6H **105**
Rivelin Pk. Dr. S6: Shef 6G **105**
Rivelin Pk. Rd. S6: Shef 1H **117**
Rivelin Rd. S6: Shef 6H **105**

Rivelin St. S6: Shef 6A **106**
Rivelin Ter. S6: Shef 6H **105**
Rivelin Valley Rd. S6: Shef 3A **116**
Rivelin Way S60: Wav 3D **122**
River Bank S35: Ough 3F **91**
River Ct. S17: Dore 3H **145**
  (off Ladies Spring Dr.)
Riverdale Av. S10: Shef 6H **117**
Riverdale Dr. S10: Shef 6H **117**
Riverdale M. S10: Shef 6G **117**
Riverdale Pk. S43: Stav 3D **164**
Riverdale Rd. DN5: Scawt 2F **39**
  S10: Shef .5H **117**
Riverhead DN5: Sprot 3C **54**
Riverside S6: Shef 5H **105**
Riverside, The S60: Roth 5D **96**
Riverside Cl. DN4: Hex 3G **55**
  DN12: Con 3F **69**
  S6: Shef 4G **105**
  S73: D'fld .5D **34**
Riverside Ct. S9: Shef 5C **108**
  S25: Laugh C 3F **127**
  S64: Mexb 2H **67**
Riverside Dr. DN5: Sprot 4D **54**
Riverside Gdns.
  DN9: Auck 1G **59**
  S63: Bolt D 3C **50**
Riverside Ho. S60: Roth 4D **96**
Riverside M. S6: Shef 4B **106**
  (off off Rudyard Rd.)
Riverside Pk. S2: Shef 5G **119**
Riverside Pct. S60: Roth 4E **97**
  (off Corporation St.)
Riverside Way S60: Roth 5D **96**
River Ter. S6: Shef 4B **106**
River Vw. S75: Wool G 3F **7**
River Vw. Rd. S35: Ough 3E **91**
River Way DN9: Auck 1G **59**
Riviera Mt. DN5: Don 5A **40**
Riviera Pde. DN5: Don 5A **40**
Rix Ct. S64: Kiln 6C **66**
Rix Rd. S64: Kiln 6C **66**
Roache Dr. S63: Gol 6B **36**
Roach Rd. S11: Shef 1B **132**
Robart Av. S71: Barn 6A **18**
Robert Cl. S18: Uns 1F **161**
Robert Rd. S8: Shef 3E **147**
Roberts Av. DN12: Con 5G **69**
Roberts Gro. S26: Aston 1D **138**
Robertshaw S3: Shef 2A **4**
Robertshaw Cres. S36: Spink 3F **175**
Robertson Dr. S6: Shef 6H **105**
Robertson Rd. S6: Shef 1H **117**
Roberts Rd. DN4: Balb 3A **56**
  DN12: New E 5D **70**
Roberts St. S72: Cud 1E **19**
  S73: Womb 2F **47**
Robert St. S60: Roth 4C **96**
Robey St. S4: Shef 3A **108**
Robinbrook La. S12: Shef 2F **149**
Robin Cft. S40: Birdh 3G **171**
Robincroft Rd. S42: W'orth 6E **171**
Robinets Rd. S61: Wing 5B **82**
ROBIN HOOD AIRPORT
  DONCASTER SHEFFIELD 4C **76**
Robin Hood Av. S71: R'ton 2A **10**
Robin Hood Chase S6: Stan 5D **104**
Robin Hood Cres. DN3: Eden 1D **42**
Robin Hood Rd. DN3: Eden 1D **42**
  S9: Shef 6D **94**
Robin La. S20: Beig 3G **137**
  S71: R'ton 2A **10**
  WF9: Hems 1A **12**
Robin Pl. S26: Aston 2D **138**
Robins Cl. S26: Aston 1D **138**
Robinson Av. S9: Shef 2E **121**
Robinson Ct. S61: Kimb 3A **96**
Robinson Rd. S2: Shef 4H **119**
Robinson's Sq. S70: Birdw 5D **44**
Robinson St. S60: Roth 6E **97**
Robinson Way S21: Killa 4B **152**
Rob Royd S70: Wors 5B **30**
  S75: Dod .4G **29**
Rob Royd La. S70: Barn, Wors 5C **30**
  (not continuous)
Roche S20: W'fld 2F **151**
  (off Shortbrook Dr.)
Roche Cl. S71: Monk B 5G **17**
Roche End S26: Tod 3B **140**

Rocher Av. S35: Gren 3D **92**
Rocher Cl. S35: Gren 3D **92**
Rocher Gro. S35: Gren 3D **92**
Rochester Cl. S10: Shef 5B **116**
Rochester Dr. S10: Shef 5B **116**
Rochester Rd. S10: Shef 5B **116**
    S25: Sth A 5G **141**
    S71: Monk B 4G **17**
Rochester Row DN5: Scaws 5E **39**
Rockcliffe Cl. DN11: Wad 5E **73**
Rockcliffe Dr. DN11: Wad 5E **73**
Rockcliffe Ho's. S62: Rawm 4G **83**
                                    (off High St.)
Rockcliffe Rd. S62: Rawm 4G **83**
Rockfield Dr. S81: Woods 5F **143**
ROCKINGHAM 5A **82**
Rockingham S20: W'fld 2F **151**
                            (off Shortbrook Dr.)
Rockingham Bus. Pk. S70: Birdw 6E **45**
Rockingham Cl. S1: Shef 6D **4**
    S18: Dron W 3B **154**
    S40: Ash 5D **166**
    S70: Birdw 6E **45**
Rockingham Ct. S64: Swin 3A **66**
    S71: Barn 1F **31**
Rockingham Gdns. S60: Roth 2H **111**
Rockingham Gate
    S1: Shef 5D **4** (4F **119**)
Rockingham Ho. DN1: Don 2B **56**
                            (off Elsworth Cl.)
    DN2: Don 2E **57**
    S1: Shef 3C **4**
    S62: Rawm 2H **83**
Rockingham La. S1: Shef 4D **4** (3F **119**)
Rockingham Mausoleum 1B **82**
Rockingham M. S70: Birdw 6D **44**
Rockingham Rd. DN2: Don 5D **40**
    S62: Rawm 2H **83**
    S64: Swin 4H **65**
    S75: Dod 4H **29**
Rockingham Row S70: Birdw 6E **45**
Rockingham Station
    Elsecar Heritage Railway 2E **63**
Rockingham St. S1: Shef . . .3C **4** (3E **119**)
    S70: Birdw 6E **45**
    S71: Barn 4D **16**
    S74: Hoyl 6G **45**
Rockingham Way S61: Wing 5A **82**
Rockland Dr. S65: Thry 6D **84**
                                (off Poplar Av.)
Rockland Vs. S65: Thry 6D **84**
Rocklea Cl. S64: Swin 4B **66**
Rockley Av. S70: Birdw 4D **44**
    S73: Womb 3E **47**
Rockley Cl. S40: Birdh 3F **171**
Rockley Cres. S70: Birdw 5D **44**
Rockley La. S70: Birdw 4C **44**
    S75: Wors 1B **44**
Rockley Mdws. S70: Barn 3B **30**
Rockley Nook DN2: Don 3G **41**
Rockley Rd. S6: Shef 2A **106**
Rockleys S75: Dod 4H **29**
Rockley Vw. S75: Pil 6C **44**
Rockley Vw. Ct. S70: Birdw 6D **44**
Rockliffe Av. DN4: Balb 6F **55**
Rock Mt. S74: Hoyl 6C **46**
Rockmount Rd. S9: Shef 6E **95**
Rock Pl. S36: Spink 3F **175**
Rocksand Dr. DN12: New E 4D **70**
Rockside Rd. S36: Thurl 4A **176**
Rock St. S3: Shef 1F **119**
    S70: Barn 6C **16**
Rock Ter. DN12: Con 5E **69**
Rockwood Cl. S35: Chap 3D **78**
    S75: Dart 5G **7**
Roddis Cl. S25: Din 5G **127**
Roden Way S62: Rawm 6D **64**
Rodes Av. S72: Gt H 6F **21**
Rodge Cft. S41: Old W 3H **161**
Rodger Rd. S13: Shef 1E **137**
Rodger St. S61: Roth 3C **96**
Rodman Dr. S13: Shef 6E **123**
Rodman St. S13: Shef 6E **123**
Rod Moor Rd. S18: Dron W 6A **146**
Rodney Hill S6: Lox 4E **105**
Rodsley Cl. S40: C'fld 3C **166**
Rodwell Cl. S60: Tree 7F **123**
Roebuck Chase S63: Wath D 5E **49**
Roebuck Hill S74: Jum 4C **46**

Roebuck Ridge S74: Jum 4C **46**
Roebuck Rd. S6: Shef 2C **118**
Roebuck St. S73: Womb 2H **47**
Roeburn Cl. S75: Mapp 4H **7**
Roecar Cl. S41: Old W 4A **162**
Roe Cft. DN5: Sprot 2C **54**
Roehampton Ri.
    DN5: Scaws 5E **39**
    S60: Brins 3B **110**
    S71: Ard 2C **32**
Roe La. S3: Shef 4G **107**
Roewood Cl. S3: Shef 4G **107**
                            (off Orphanage Rd.)
Roger Rd. S71: Lund 6B **18**
Rojean Rd. S35: Gren 2C **92**
Rokeby Dr. S5: Shef 4F **93**
Rokeby Rd. S5: Shef 4F **93**
Rolands Cl. S61: Kimb 3H **95**
Rolleston Av. S66: Malt 6H **101**
ROLLESTONE 4A **134**
Rolleston Rd. S5: Shef 6H **93**
Rollin Dr. S6: Shef 3A **106**
Rolling Dales Cl. S66: Malt 4H **101**
Rolls Cres. S62: Rawm 6D **64**
Roman Ct. S61: Kimb 4H **95**
Roman Cres. S60: Brins 2D **110**
    S62: Rawm 2F **83**
Romandale Gdns. S2: Shef 5F **121**
Roman Ridge DN5: Scaws 3F **39**
    S5: Shef 1C **108**
Roman Ridge Rd. S9: Shef 1E **109**
Roman Rd. DN4: Don 2D **56**
    S75: Kexb 1E **15**
Roman St. S63: Thurn 1D **36**
ROMAN TERRACE 2D **66**
Romford Way S43: Bar H 3G **163**
Romney Cl. S66: Flan 4G **99**
Romney Dr. S18: Dron 3D **154**
Romney Gdns. S2: Shef 2G **133**
Romsdal Rd. S10: Shef 2A **118**
Romwood Av. S64: Swin 3H **65**
Ronald Rd. DN4: Balb 5H **55**
    S9: Shef 2F **121**
Ronksley Cres. S5: Shef 4A **94**
Ronksley Rd. S5: Shef 3A **94**
Rookdale Cl. S75: Barn 4A **16**
Rookery, The S36: Spink 4H **175**
Rookery Bank S36: Spink 4H **175**
Rookery Chase S36: Spink 4H **175**
Rookery Cl. S26: Wales 5H **139**
    S36: Spink 4H **175**
Rookery Dell S36: Spink 4H **175**
Rookery Ri. S36: Spink 5H **175**
Rookery Rd. S64: Swin 4A **66**
Rookery Vale S36: Spink 4H **175**
Rookery Vw. S70: Barn 3F **31**
Rook Hill S70: Wors 5H **31**
Rosamond Av. S17: Bradw 4H **145**
Rosamond Cl. S17: Bradw 4H **145**
Rosamond Ct. S17: Bradw 4H **145**
Rosamond Dr. S17: Bradw 4H **145**
Rosamond Glade S17: Bradw 4H **145**
Rosamond Pl. S17: Bradw 4H **145**
Rosa Rd. S10: Shef 2B **118**
Roscoe Bank S6: Shef 2E **117**
Roscoe Ct. S6: Shef 6G **105**
Roscoe Dr. S6: Shef 1G **117**
Roscoe Mt. S6: Shef 1G **117**
Roscoe Rd. S3: Shef 1E **119**
Roscoe Vw. S6: Shef 2E **117**
Rose Av. DN4: Balb 4A **56**
    S20: Beig 5G **137**
    S44: Cal 5F **169**
    S73: D'fld 3A **34**
Roseberry Cl. S74: Hoyl 2B **62**
Rosebery St. S61: Roth 4B **96**
    S70: Stair 2A **32**
Rosebery Ter. S70: Barn 2E **31**
Rose Cl. S60: Brins 5E **111**
Rose Cott. DN3: Barn D 1H **27**
Rose Cotts. S41: C'fld 6B **168**
Rose Ct. DN4: Balb 4H **55**
    S66: Wick 6F **99**
Rose Cres. DN5: Scawt 3F **39**
    S43: Mas M 2F **165**
    S62: Rawm 2A **84**
Rosedale Av. S40: C'fld 2A **172**
    S62: Rawm 2G **83**
Rosedale Cl. S26: Aston 6D **124**

Rosedale Gdns. S11: Shef 6C **118**
    S70: Barn 1B **30**
Rosedale Rd. DN5: Bntly 6H **23**
    DN5: Scaws 3E **39**
    S11: Shef 6C **118**
    S26: Aston 6C **124**
Rosedale Vw. S42: W'ton 3C **170**
Rosedale Way S66: Sunn 4H **99**
Rosedene Cl. S70: Stair 2A **32**
Rose Dr. S66: Wick 5H **99**
Rosefield Av. S75: Wool G 3F **7**
Rose Gdns. S44: Ark T 6H **173**
Rose Gth. Cl. S41: C'fld 1B **172**
Rosegarth Cl. DN5: Scawt 3G **39**
Rosegreave S63: Gol 5C **36**
Rose Gro. DN3: Arm 4D **42**
    S73: Womb 6E **33**
Rose Hill DN4: Bess 3H **57**
    S20: Mosb 2C **150**
    S40: C'fld 5G **167**
Rosehill S62: Rawm 1G **83**
Rose Hill Av. S20: Mosb 2C **150**
    S62: Rawm 1H **83**
Rose Hill Cl. S20: Mosb 2C **150**
    S36: Cub 5D **176**
Rosehill Cotts. S62: H'ley 5B **62**
Rose Hill Ct. DN4: Bess 2H **57**
Rosehill Ct. S70: Barn 6D **16**
Rose Hill Crematorium
    DN4: Can 3B **58**
Rose Hill Dr. S20: Mosb 2C **150**
    S75: Dod 3G **29**
Rose Hill E. S40: C'fld 5H **167**
Rose Hill M. S20: Mosb 2C **150**
Rose Hill Ri. DN4: Bess 3H **57**
Rosehill Rd. S62: Rawm 2G **83**
Rose Hill Vw. S20: Mosb 2C **150**
Rose Hill W. S40: C'fld 5G **167**
Rose Ho. DN3: Arm 4D **42**
Rose La. S25: Brookh 1E **127**
Roselle St. S6: Shef 4B **106**
Rosemary Cl. DN4: Can 5B **58**
Rosemary Ct. S10: Shef 1B **118**
                            (off Bank Ho. Rd.)
Rosemary Gro. DN5: Cad 1G **69**
Rosemary Rd. S20: Beig 4G **137**
    S66: Wick 5F **99**
Rose Mead S26: Swal 6B **124**
Rose Pl. S73: Womb 6F **33**
Rose Tree Av. S72: Cud 1E **19**
Rose Tree Ct. S72: Cud 1E **19**
Rose Way S21: Killa 5C **152**
Rosewell Ct. S65: Roth 2A **98**
Rose Wood Cl. S41: C'fld 6E **161**
Rosewood Dr. DN3: Barn D 1B **26**
    S60: Wav 2D **122**
Rosling Way S44: Ark T 6H **173**
Roslin Rd. S10: Shef 3B **118**
Ross Ct. S21: Killa 6C **152**
Rossendale Cl. S40: W'ton 2F **171**
Rosser Av. S12: Shef 6C **134**
Rossetti Mt. S66: Flan 4G **99**
ROSSINGTON 5D **74**
Rossington Community Sports Village
                                    . . . . . .6G **75**
Rossington Ho. DN1: Don 3B **56**
                            (off Elsworth Cl.)
Rossington Leisure Cen. 5C **74**
Rossington Rd. S11: Shef 6B **118**
Rossington St. DN12: Den M 2C **68**
Rossiter Rd. S61: Grea 4D **82**
Rosslyn Av. S26: Aston 6D **124**
Rosslyn Cres. DN5: Bntly 6A **24**
Rossmoor Cl. DN9: Auck 1H **59**
Rosston Rd. S66: Malt 5C **102**
ROSTHOLME 6H **23**
Rostholme Sq. DN5: Bntly 6A **24**
Roston Cl. S18: Dron W 3C **154**
Rotary Dr. S63: Wath D 4E **49**
Rothay Cl. S18: Dron W 4D **154**
Rothay Rd. S4: Shef 3C **108**
Rothbury Cl. S20: Sot 6H **137**
Rothbury Ct. S20: Sot 6H **137**
Rothbury Way S60: Brins 3D **110**
Rother Av. S43: Brimn 6C **162**
Rother Cl. S40: W'ton 2F **171**

Rother Ct. S62: P'gte 6F 83
Rother Cres. S60: Tree 2F 123
Rother Cft. S74: Hoyl 6B 46
ROTHERHAM .4E 97
Rotherham Baulk S81: Gild 1G 143
Rotherham Central Station (Rail) . . .4E 97
Rotherham Cl. S21: Killa 2E 153
Rotherham College of Arts & Technology
. . . . .4E 97
(off Howard St.)
Rotherham Crematorium S65: Roth . .4B 98
Rotherham Gateway S60: Cat 1C 122
Rotherham Golf Course 3E 85
Rotherham Health Village 3E 97
Rotherham Interchange 3E 97
Rotherham La. S35: Laugh M 1F 127
Rotherham Leisure Complex 2F 97
Rotherham Minster 4E 97
Rotherham Pl. S13: Shef 5C 122
Rotherham Rd. S13: Shef 4C 122
S20: Beig 4H 137
S20: Half 6F 151
S21: Ecki 6F 151
S21: Killa 3E 153
S21: Killa, Barl 6F 153
S25: Laugh C 4F 127
S26: Swal 1B 138
S43: Barl 6F 153
S60: Cat 6E 111
S60: Roth 1F 97
S62: P'gte 1F 97
S63: Wath D 6C 48
S66: Malt 5F 101
S71: Ath, Barn, Monk B, Smi . . .2E 17
S72: Gt H, Midd 6F 21
Rotherham Rd. Nth. S20: W'fld 3G 151
Rotherham St. S9: Shef 5D 108
Rotherham Titans RUFC 5G 97
Rotherham United 4D 96
Rotherhill Cl. S65: Roth 3H 97
Rother M. S74: Hoyl 6B 46
Rothermoor Av. S21: Kiv P 6H 139
Rother Rd. S60: Roth 1E 111
Rotherside Ct. S21: Ecki 6G 151
Rotherside Rd. S21: Ecki 6G 151
Rotherstoke Cl. S60: Roth 5D 110
Rother St. S73: Bramp 4B 48
Rother Ter. S60: Roth 1E 111
Rothervale Cl. S20: Beig 4H 137
Rothervale Rd. S40: Birdh 3H 171
S40: C'fld 2H 171
Rother Valley Country Park 5C 138
Rother Valley Country Park Visitors Cen.
. . . . .6B 138
Rother Valley Golf Course 1E 153
Rother Valley Way S20: Holb 3A 152
Rother Vw. Cl. S26: Swal 1H 137
Rother Vw. Gdns. S26: Swal 1H 137
Rother Vw. Rd. S60: Roth 1E 111
Rother Way S41: C'fld 2A 168
S66: Hel 4D 100
Rotherway S60: Roth 4F 111
Rotherwood Av. S13: Sher 6E 123
Rotherwood Cl. DN5: Scaws 4E 39
Rotherwood Cres. S66: Thurc 6B 114
Rotherwood Rd. S21: Killa 2D 152
Rothesay Cl. DN5: Cus 5G 39
Rothey Gro. S40: C'fld 3A 166
Rotunda Bus. Cen. S35: Chap 1F 79
Roughbirchworth S36: Oxs 6H 177
Rough La. S35: Green 1A 92
Roughwood Grn. S61: Wing 5B 82
Roughwood Rd. S61: Kimb P, Wing . .6H 81
Roughwood Way
S61: Kimb P, Wing 6H 81
Roundacre S75: Barn 4C 16
Roundel St. S9: Shef 1C 120
Round Grn. La. S75: Stainb, Wors . . .6A 30
Round Hill S75: Dart 5H 7
Roundhill Ct. DN4: Don 4G 57
Roundwood Ct. S70: Wors 6F 31
Roundwood Golf Course 4H 83
Roundwood Gro. S62: Rawm 3H 83
Roundwood Way S73: D'fld 4A 34
Row, The DN3: Can 3E 59
Rowan Cl. DN9: Auck 2B 76
S35: Chap 4F 79
S63: Gol 5B 36
S70: Barn 3E 31

Rowan Ct. DN2: Son 4H 41
Rowan Dr. S66: Bram 5H 99
S75: Barn 5A 16
Rowan Gth. DN5: Don 4H 39
Rowan La. S72: Sth H 1H 11
Rowan Mt. DN2: Don 4G 41
Rowan Ri. S66: Malt 5G 101
Rowan Rd. S21: Ecki 3D 158
S43: Mas M 3F 165
Rowan Tree Cl. S21: Killa 5B 152
Rowan Tree Dell S17: Tot 6F 145
Rowan Tree Rd. S21: Killa 4B 152
Rowborn Dr. S35: Ough 6G 91
Rowdale Cres. S12: Shef 3G 135
Rowell La. S6: Lox 4C 104
Rowena Av. DN3: Eden 1C 42
Rowena Dr. DN5: Scaws 4E 39
S66: Thurc 5B 114
Rowena Rd. DN12: Con 4E 69
Rowenfields S25: Din 1C 142
Rowland Pl. DN1: Don 2B 56
Rowland Rd. S2: Shef 6F 119
S75: Barn 5B 16
Rowland St. S3: Shef 1F 119
S71: R'ton 2A 10
Rowley Way S66: Sunn 2G 99
Rowms La. S64: Swin 3D 66
Rowsley Cres. S43: Stav 6H 163
Rowsley Dr. S60: Wav 3C 122
Rowsley St. S2: Shef 5G 119
Roxby Cl. DN4: Bess 6A 58
Roxton Av. S8: Shef 2E 147
Roxton Rd. S8: Shef 1D 146
Royal Av. DN1: Don 6D 40
Royal Cl. S41: C'fld 4H 167
S74: Hoyl 6C 46
S75: Bar G 2F 15
Royale Cl. S21: Ecki 1F 159
Royal Oak Ct. S43: Mas M 2G 165
Royal Plaza S1: Shef 4C 4
Royal St. S70: Barn 1D 30
Royalty La. DN3: Barn D 1G 25
ROYD 5G 175
Royd, The S36: Spink 5F 175
Royd Av. S72: Cud 2E 19
S75: Mapp 5A 8
Royd Cl. S70: Wors 6E 31
Royd Ct. S36: Spink 5F 175
Roydfield Cl. S20: Water 6E 137
Roydfield Dr. S20: Water 6E 137
Roydfield Gro. S20: Water 6E 137
Royd Fld. La. S36: Cub 6D 176
Royd La. S36: Spink 5F 175
S75: High'm, Silk 5D 14
Royd Moor Cl. S36: Thurl 3A 176
Royd Moor Rd. S36: Thurl 3A 176
Royds Av. S60: Whis 2B 112
Royds Cl. Cres. S65: Thry 6D 84
Royds La. S74: Els 1F 63
ROYDS MOOR 3E 113
Royds Moor Hill S60: Whis 3E 113
Royd Vw. S72: Brier 3B 12
Roy Kilner Rd. S73: Womb 6E 33
ROYSTON 3H 9
Royston Av. DN5: Don 3H 39
S20: Mosb 6B 136
Royston Cl. S20: Mosb 6B 136
S42: W'ton 3C 170
Royston Cotts. S74: Hoyl 6A 46
Royston Cft. S20: Mosb 6B 136
Royston Gro. S20: Mosb 6B 136
(off Royston Cl.)
Royston Hill S74: Hoyl 6A 46
Royston La. S71: Car, R'ton 4H 9
Royston Leisure Cen.
Barnsley 2H 9
Royston Rd. S72: Cud 5D 10
Rubens Cl. S18: Dron 3E 155
Rubens Row S2: Shef 2H 119
(off Hyde Pk. Ter.)
Rud Broom Cl. S36: Pen 5C 176
Rud Broom La. S36: Pen 4B 176
Ruddle La. S66: Clftn, Mick 6G 87
Ruddle Mill La. S66: Stain 1D 102
(not continuous)
Rudyard M. S6: Shef 4B 106
Rudyard Rd. S6: Shef 4B 106
Rufford Av. S71: Ath 6F 9
Rufford Cl. S40: C'fld 1F 171

Rufford Ct. S20: Sot 6H 137
Rufford Gro. S64: Swin 4D 66
Rufford Ri. S20: Sot 6H 137
S63: Gol 6B 36
Rufford Rd. DN4: Don 3E 57
Rufus La. DN11: New R 5A 74
Rugby Dr. S41: C'fld 3H 167
Rugby St. S3: Shef 6F 107
Rundle Dr. S7: Shef 1D 132
Rundle Rd. S7: Shef 1D 132
S36: Stoc 3D 174
Runnymede Rd. DN2: Don 6G 41
Rupert Rd. S7: Shef 3D 132
Rural Cres. DN3: Brant 4A 42
Rural La. S6: Shef 2G 105
Ruscombe Pl. S71: Car 5H 9
Rushby St. S4: Shef 3A 108
Rushdale Av. S8: Shef 3F 133
Rushdale Mt. S8: Shef 3F 133
Rushdale Rd. S8: Shef 3F 133
Rushdale Ter. S8: Shef 3F 133
Rushen Mt. S40: Birdh 4G 171
Rushey Cl. S62: Rawm 6F 65
Rushleigh Ct. S17: Dore 2E 145
Rushley Av. S17: Dore 2E 145
Rushley Cl. DN9: Auck 2H 59
S17: Dore 2E 145
Rushley Dr. S17: Dore 2E 145
Rushley Rd. S17: Dore 2E 145
Rushworth Cl. S75: Kexb 6D 6
Ruskin Av. S64: Mexb 6G 51
Ruskin Cl. S63: Wath D 5D 48
Ruskin Dr. DN3: Arm 4F 43
Ruskin Rd. DN4: Balb 6H 55
Ruskin Sq. S8: Shef 2F 133
Russell Cl. S26: Swal 1A 138
S71: Monk B 3G 17
Russell Ct. S11: Shef 6H 131
Russell Ho. S25: Sth A 3G 141
Russell Pl. S66: Malt 4B 102
Russell Rd. S64: Kiln 1D 84
Russell St. S3: Shef 1D 4 (1F 119)
S65: Roth 2F 97
Russett Ct. S66: Malt 4G 101
Rustic Ct. S9: Shef 6E 109
Rustlings Ct. S10: Shef 6G 117
Rustlings Rd. S11: Shef 6H 117
Ruston Cl. S40: C'fld 2C 166
Ruston Dr. S71: R'ton 2H 9
Ruthin St. S4: Shef 4B 108
Ruth Sq. S10: Shef 4D 118
Ruthven Dr. DN4: Warm 5E 55
Rutland Av. S25: Nth A 1G 141
Rutland Ho. S3: Shef 1E 119
(off Adelaide La.)
Rutland La. DN11: New R 5A 74
Rutland Pk. S10: Shef 4B 118
Rutland Pl. S73: Womb 2E 47
Rutland Rd. S3: Shef 1E 119
S40: C'fld 5G 167
Rutland St. DN1: Don 6D 40
S3: Shef 6F 107
S41: Old W 4H 161
Rutland Way S3: Shef 6E 107
S75: Barn 5B 16
Ryan Dr. S13: Shef 1F 137
Ryan Pl. S62: P'gte 4G 83
Ryburn Rd. S60: Wav 3D 122
Rydal Cl. S18: Dron W 3C 154
S25: Din 1A 142
S36: Pen 3D 176
S63: Bolt D 3B 50
Rydal Ct. DN4: Balb 6H 71
Rydal Cres. S8: Shef 3D 132
(off Langdale Rd.)
Rydal Dr. DN4: Don 3G 57
Rydalhurst Av. S6: Shef 2H 105
Rydall Pl. DN5: Scawt 2G 39
Rydal Rd. S8: Shef 3D 132
S25: Din 1A 142
Rydal Ter. S71: Shef 1F 31
Rydal Way S64: Mexb 6H 51
Rye Bank S60: Whis 3C 112
RYECROFT 2A 84
Rye Cft. DN12: Con 4H 69
S71: Smi 2F 17
Ryecroft Bank S74: Hoyl 5A 46
Ryecroft Glen Rd. S17: Dore 2H 145

Ryecroft Rd. S62: Rawm 2B 84
Ryecroft Vw. S17: Dore 2E 145
Ryedale Wlk. DN5: Scaws 3D 38
Ryefield Gdns. S11: Shef 3H 131
Rye Flatt La. S40: Bramp 6C 166
Ryegate Cres. S10: Shef 3A 118
Ryegate Rd. S10: Shef 4A 118
Ryehill Av. S40: Bramp 6B 166
Rye La. S6: Stan 5A 104
Ryeview Gdns. S61: Grea 6C 82
Ryhill Dr. S20: Mosb 6B 136
Rykneld Sq. S40: C'fld 5H 167
(off Church Way)
Ryle Rd. S7: Shef 1D 132
Rylstone Ct. S12: Shef 5C 136
Rylstone Gro. S12: Shef 6C 136
Rylstone Wlk. S70: Stair 4A 32
Ryton Av. S73: Womb 3A 48
Ryton Cl. S66: Malt 5B 102
Ryton Rd. S25: Nth A, Sth A 4G 141
Ryton Way DN4: Can 6D 58

S

Sackerville Ter. S21: Killa 4A 152
Sackup La. S75: Dart, Stain 5G 7
Sackville Cl. S42: W'ton 2C 170
Sackville Hgts. S70: Barn 6D 16
(off Sackville St.)
Sackville Rd. S10: Shef 2A 118
Sackville St. S70: Barn 6C 16
Saddler Av. S20: Water 1E 151
Saddler Cl. S20: Water 1E 151
Saddler Grn. S20: Water 1E 151
Saddler Gro. S20: Water 1E 151
Saddletree Vw. S43: Mas M 2E 165
Sadler Ga. S70: Barn 6D 16
Sadler's Ga. S73: Womb 6F 33
Saffron Ct. S73: Womb 2H 47
Saffron Dr. DN4: Balb 2C 72
St Agnes' Rd. DN4: Don 2F 57
St Aidan's Av. S2: Shef 6A 120
St Aidan's Dr. S2: Shef 5B 120
St Aidan's Pl. S2: Shef 6B 120
St Aidan's Ri. S2: Shef 5B 120
St Aidan's Rd. S2: Shef 5A 120
St Aidan's Way S2: Shef 6B 120
St Albans Cl. S10: Shef 5D 116
St Alban's Ct. S66: Wick 6G 99
St Albans Dr. S10: Shef 5C 116
St Albans Rd. S10: Shef 5C 116
St Alban's Way S66: Wick 6F 99
St Andrew Rd. S36: Spink 4G 175
St Andrew's Cl. S11: Shef 1C 132
S64: Swin 5C 66
S66: Sunn 3H 99
St Andrews Cl. DN4: Can 6E 59
S25: Din 6A 128
St Andrews Cres. S74: Hoyl 6B 46
St Andrews Dr. S75: Dart 5H 7
St Andrews Ri. S40: W'ton 2D 170
St Andrew's Rd. DN12: Con 5E 69
S11: Shef 1C 132
St Andrews Rd. S74: Hoyl 6B 46
St Andrew's Sq. S63: Bolt D 2B 50
St Andrew's Ter. DN4: Don 3C 56
St Andrew's Wlk. S60: Brins 3B 110
St Andrew's Way DN3: Barn D 2D 26
St Andrews Way S71: Ard 3D 32
St Anne's Cl. S43: Stav 6A 164
St Anne's Dr. S71: Monk B 1A 18
St Anne's Rd. DN4: Don 2F 57
ST ANN'S 2F 97
St Ann's Rd. S36: Spink 3F 175
S65: Roth 2F 97
ST ANN'S RDBT. 3F 97
St Anthony Rd. S10: Shef 2H 117
ST AUGUSTINES 2H 171
St Augustines Av. S40: C'fld 2H 171
St Augustines Cres. S40: C'fld 2H 171
St Augustines Dr. S40: C'fld 1H 171
St Augustines Mt. S40: C'fld 2H 171
St Augustines Ri. S40: C'fld 2H 171
St Augustine's Rd. DN4: Bess 3H 57
St Augustines Rd. S40: C'fld 2G 171
St Austell Dr. S75: Bar G 4F 15
St Barbara's Cl. S66: Hoot L 6H 101
St Barbara's Rd. S73: D'fld 5A 34

St Barnabas La. S2: Shef 6F 119
St Barnabas Rd. S2: Shef 6F 119
St Bartholomew's Cl. S66: Malt 6H 101
St Bartholomews Ri.
DN4: Bess 4A 58
St Bart's Ter. S70: Barn 2E 31
(off Dobie St.)
St Bede's Rd. S60: Roth 4D 96
St Benedicts Ct. S2: Shef 6A 120
St Catherine's Av. DN4: Balb 4A 56
St Catherine's Dr.
DN7: Dunsv 4H 27
St Catherine's Way S75: Barn 1A 30
St Cecilia's Rd. DN4: Don 3F 57
St Chad's Sq. DN12: Den M 2C 68
St Chad's Way DN5: Sprot 3D 54
S41: Whit M 6H 161
St Charles St. S9: Shef 6B 108
St Christophers Cl. S71: Ard 3D 32
St Christopher's Cres.
DN5: Scaws 4F 39
St Christopher's Flats
DN4: Balb 5H 55
(off Ashfield Rd.)
St Clement's Cl. DN5: Scaws 4E 39
St Clements Cl. S71: Ard 3D 32
St David Rd. S36: Spink 4G 175
St David's Dr. DN5: Scaws 4E 39
S25: Sth A 5G 141
S60: Brins 3B 110
S71: Ard 2C 32
St David's Ri. S40: W'ton 2E 171
St David's Rd. DN12: Con 4E 69
St Dominic's Cl. DN5: Sprot 4C 54
St Edmund's Av. S66: Thurc 1B 126
St Edward's Av. S70: Barn 2C 30
St Elizabeth Cl. S2: Shef 6G 119
St Eric's Rd. DN4: Bess 4A 58
St Francis Blvd.
S71: Monk B 1A 18
St Francis Cl. S10: Shef 4F 117
S66: Sunn 3H 99
St George Ga. DN1: Don 1B 56
St George Rd. S36: Spink 4G 175
St George's Av. DN7: Dunsv 4H 27
S64: Swin 3A 66
St George's Cl. S3: Shef 2A 4 (2D 118)
St Georges Cl. S81: Woods 4F 143
St George's Ct. S3: Shef 3B 4
St George's Dr. S60: Brins 3B 110
St George's Rd. DN4: Bess 3G 57
S70: Barn 1D 30
St George's Ter. S1: Shef 3B 4 (3E 119)
St George's Wlk. S3: Shef 2B 4 (2E 119)
St Giles Cl. S40: C'fld 2A 172
St Giles Ga. DN5: Scaws 5E 39
St Giles Sq. S35: Chap 3E 79
St Helen Rd. S36: Spink 5G 175
ST HELEN'S 3A 18
St Helen's Av. S71: Smi 3G 17
St Helen's Blvd. S71: Smi 2G 17
St Helen's Cl. S41: C'fld 4H 167
S60: Tree 3G 123
St Helens Cl. S63: Thurn 2A 36
St Helens Ct. S74: Els 6D 46
St Helen's La. DN5: Barnb 2B 52
St Helens Pl. S71: Smi 3G 17
St Helen's Rd. DN4: Don 2F 57
St Helen's Sq. DN3: Kirk Sa 4C 26
St Helen's St. S41: C'fld 4H 167
S74: Els 6D 46
St Helen's Way S71: Monk B 3A 18
St Helier Dr. S75: Barn 6A 16
St Hilda Av. S70: Barn 1B 30
St Hilda Cl. S36: Spink 5G 175
St Hildas Cl. S63: Thurn 1D 36
St Hilda's Rd. DN4: Don 2F 57
St James Av. DN7: Dunsv 3H 27
S25: Sth A 4G 141
St James Cl. DN3: Kirk Sa 4C 26
S41: Has 1B 172
S63: Wath D 6H 49
St James' Cl. S70: Wors 6F 31
St James Ct. DN1: Don 2C 56
S8: Shef 1H 147
St James Dr. S65: Rav 5A 86
St James' Gdns. DN4: Balb 3A 56
St James' Row S1: Shef 2E 5 (2F 119)
St James Rd. DN4: Don 2B 56

St James Sq. S40: C'fld 5H 167
(off Vicar La.)
S74: Hoyl 6B 46
(off West St.)
St James St. DN1: Don 2B 56
St James Wlk. S11: Shef 3E 5 (3F 119)
St James' Vw. S65: Rav 5A 86
St James Wlk. S13: Shef 6E 123
St Joan Av. S36: Spink 5G 175
St Johns Av. S60: Roth 4C 96
S66: Sunn 4H 99
S75: Bar G 4F 15
St John's Cl. S2: Shef 2H 119
S36: Pen 5C 176
S65: Roth 2H 97
S75: Dod 3F 29
St Johns Cl. S42: W'ton 3C 170
St Johns Cl. S25: Laugh M 2H 127
S41: Whit M 1F 167
(off St John's Rd.)
S66: Sunn 4H 99
St Johns Cft. S60: Roth 3C 96
St John's Cft. DN11: Wad 6E 73
St Johns Grn. S61: Kimb P 1H 95
St John's Mt. S41: C'fld 6G 161
St Johns Pl. S43: Stav 5A 164
St John's Rd. DN4: Balb 4H 55
DN12: New E 4C 70
S2: Shef 2A 120
S18: Uns 4B 156
S25: Laugh M 2H 127
S36: Spink 3H 175
S41: C'fld, Whit M 1F 167
(not continuous)
S64: Swin 3B 66
S65: Roth 2H 97
S70: Barn 2D 30
S72: Cud 2E 19
St Johns Rd. S43: Stav 5H 163
St John's Row S25: Din 5B 128
St John's Wlk. S64: Mexb 4F 51
S71: R'ton 3A 10
St Joseph's Cl. S25: Din 5A 128
St Joseph's Gdns. S70: Barn 2G 31
St Joseph's Rd. S13: Shef 4A 122
St Julien's Mt. S75: Cawt 4A 14
St Julien's Way S75: Cawt 4A 14
St Laurence Cl. DN6: Adw S 2B 22
St Lawrence Glebe S9: Tins 2H 109
St Lawrence Rd. S9: Tins 1H 109
St Lawrence's Ter.
DN6: Adw S 2D 22
St Leger Cl. S25: Laugh C 4F 127
St Leger Way S25: Din 4A 128
St Leonard's Av. S65: Thry 6E 85
St Leonard's Cl. S25: Din 6H 127
St Leonards Ct. S5: Shef 1G 107
St Leonard's Cft. S65: Thry 5E 85
St Leonards Dr. S41: C'fld 1B 172
St Leonard's La. S65: Roth 3G 97
St Leonard's Lea DN5: Scaws 4F 39
St Leonard's Pl. S65: Roth 3G 97
St Leonard's Rd. S65: Roth 3F 97
St Leonards Way S71: Ard 3D 32
St Luke's Cl. DN7: Dunsv 4H 27
St Lukes Cl. S41: C'fld 6G 161
St Lukes Rd. S72: Grim 2B 20
St Lukes Way S71: Monk B 5H 17
St Margaret Av. S36: Spink 4G 175
St Margaret's Av. DN5: Barnb 1H 51
St Margaret's Dr. S40: C'fld 5G 167
S64: Swin 3A 66
St Margaret's Rd. DN4: Don 2F 57
St Margarets Rd. S35: Eccl 3G 93
St Marie's RC Cathedral 3E 5 (3F 119)
St Mark Rd. S36: Spink 4G 175
St Mark's Cres. S10: Shef 4C 118
St Mark's Rd. S40: C'fld 5F 167
St Martin Cl. S36: Spink 4G 175
St Martin's Av. DN5: Cus 4F 39
St Martin's Cl. S41: C'fld 2E 167
S75: Barn 1A 30
S81: Fir 1H 129
St Mary & All Saints Church
Crooked Spire 5A 168
St Mary Cres. S36: Spink 5G 175
St Mary's S71: Lund 6B 18
St Mary's Cl. S72: Cud 1E 19

St Marys Cl. S35: Eccl 1F 93
St Marys Ct. DN1: Don 6D 40
St Mary's Cres. DN1: Don 6D 40
   S64: Swin .2B 66
St Mary's Dr. DN3: Arm 4F 43
   DN7: Dunsv 4H 27
   S60: Cat .6D 110
St Marys Gdn. S70: Wors 2F 45
St Mary's Ga. S2: Shef 6C 4 (5E 119)
   S41: C'fld 5A 168
   S70: Barn .6D 16
St Marys La. S35: Eccl 1F 93
St Mary's Pl. S41: C'fld 5A 168
            (off St Mary's Ga.)
   S70: Barn .6D 16
St Mary's Rd. DN1: Don 5D 40
   DN7: Dunsv 3H 27
   DN12: New E 5D 70
   S2: Shef 6E 5 (5F 119)
   S62: Rawm 3H 83
   S63: Gol 4E 37
   S73: D'fld .5C 34
   S73: Womb 2F 47
St Mary's Sq. S1: Shef 6C 4 (5E 119)
St Mary's St. S36: Pen 4D 176
St Mary's Ter. S36: Bolst 6E 175
            (off Heads La.)
St Mary's Vw. S61: Grea 5C 82
St Mary's Wlk. DN5: Sprot 4C 54
St Matthew's Cl. S21: Reni 3H 159
St Matthew's Ct. S73: Womb 5A 34
St Matthews Way
   S71: Monk B 5H 17
St Matthias Rd. S36: Spink 5G 175
St Michael's Av. S64: Swin 2C 66
   S71: Monk B 2A 18
St Michaels Av. DN11: Ross 4D 74
St Michaels Cl. S35: Eccl 2G 93
   S63: Gol 5C 36
St Michaels Cres. S35: Eccl 2G 93
St Michael's Rd. DN4: Bess 3G 57
St Michaels Rd. S35: Eccl 2G 93
St Nicholas Cl. DN3: Eden 6B 26
St Nicolas Rd. S62: Rawm 2H 83
St Nicolas Wlk. S62: Rawm 2A 84
St Oswalds Cl. DN9: Finn 3E 77
St Oswald's Dr. DN3: Eden 6C 26
   DN9: Finn .3F 77
St Owens Dr. S75: Barn 6A 16
St Pancras Cl. S25: Laugh C 4E 127
St Patrick Rd. S36: Spink 4G 175
St Patrick's Rd. DN2: Don 5F 41
St Patrick's Way
   DN5: Scaws 4E 39
St Paul Cl. S26: Tod 3B 140
   S36: Spink 4G 175
St Pauls Av. S41: Has 4C 172
St Pauls Cl. S25: Laugh C 3F 127
St Paul's Pde. DN5: Scaws 5E 39
   S1: Shef 4E 5
   S71: Ard 2C 32
St Pauls Rd. S75: Barn 5B 16
St Paul's Sq. S1: Shef 4E 5
St Peter & St Paul's Cathedral
   .2E 5 (2F 119)
St Peter Av. S36: Spink 4H 175
St Peter's Cl. DN3: Barn D 1G 27
   DN5: Barnb 6H 37
   S1: Shef 2E 5 (2F 119)
   S60: Brins 4B 110
St Peter's Dr. DN12: Con 5E 69
St Peters Ga. S63: Thurn 1B 36
St Peters Hgts. DN12: New E 6C 70
St Peters Pl. S65: Thry 6D 84
St Peter's Rd. DN4: Balb 5F 55
   DN12: Con 5E 69
St Peter's Ter. S70: Barn 2F 31
St Philip's Cl. S66: Malt 6H 101
St Philip's Dr. S41: Has 2A 172
St Philip's La. S3: Shef 1E 119
St Philip's Rd. S3: Shef 2A 4 (2D 118)
            (not continuous)
St Quentin Cl. S17: Bradw 5A 146
St Quentin Dr. S17: Bradw 5A 146
St Quentin Mt. S17: Bradw 5A 146
St Quentin Ri. S17: Bradw 5A 146
St Quentin Vw. S17: Bradw 5A 146
St Ronan's Rd. S7: Shef 1E 133
St Sepulchre Ga. DN1: Don 1B 56

St Sepulchre Ga. W. DN1: Don 2B 56
   DN4: Don .2B 56
St Stephens Dr. S26: Aston 6C 124
St Stephen's Rd. S3: Shef 1A 4 (2D 118)
   S65: Roth .3F 97
St Stephen's Wlk.
   S3: Shef 2A 4 (2D 118)
St Stephens Wlk. DN5: Scaws 5F 39
St Thomas' Ct. DN4: Bess 6A 58
St Thomas' Rd. S10: Shef 3A 118
St Thomas's Cl. DN4: Balb 6F 55
St Thomas's Rd. S75: Barn 4H 15
St Thomas St. S1: Shef 3C 4 (3E 119)
   S40: Bramp 6D 166
St Ursula's Rd. DN4: Don 2F 57
St Veronica Rd. S36: Spink 4H 175
St Vincent Av. DN1: Don 6D 40
   DN6: Woodl 2A 22
St Vincent Rd. DN1: Don 6D 40
St Vincent's Av. DN3: Brant 5F 59
St Wandrilles Cl. S35: Eccl 1G 93
St Wilfrids Ct. DN4: Can 5B 58
           (off Middleham Rd.)
St Wilfrid's Rd. DN4: Bess, Can 3H 57
   S2: Shef .6F 119
St Withold Av. S66: Thurc 6B 114
St Withold Cl. S66: Thurc 6B 114
Salcey Sq. S40: W'ton 1E 171
Salcombe Cl. S75: Mapp 6B 8
Sale Hill S10: Shef 4A 118
Sale St. S74: Hoyl 1F 61
Salerno Way S73: D'fld 4H 33
Salisbury Av. S18: Dron 4F 155
   S41: C'fld 1F 167
Salisbury Cres. S41: C'fld 1G 167
Salisbury Rd. DN4: Hex 3H 55
   S10: Shef 2A 118
   S18: Dron 5G 155
   S66: Malt .4A 102
Salisbury St. S75: Barn 5C 16
Salmon Pastures Nature Reserve . . .1B 120
Salmon St. S11: Shef 6E 119
Salt Box Gro. S35: Gren 2B 92
Salt Box La. S35: Gren 3B 92
Saltergate S40: C'fld 5G 167
Salter Oak Cft. S71: Car 5H 9
Saltersbrook S63: Gol 5C 36
Saltersbrook Rd. S73: D'fld 3A 34
Salters Ri. S70: Barn 1B 30
Salters Way S36: Cub 5D 176
Salt Hill S81: Fir 1H 129
Salutations Gdns. S35: High G 6C 60
Samson St. S2: Shef 4H 119
Samuel Cl. S2: Shef 1A 134
Samuel Ct. S72: Cud 6F 11
Samuel Dr. S2: Shef 1A 134
Samuel Fox Av. S36: Stoc 2E 175
Samuel Pl. S2: Shef 6A 120
Samuel Rd. S2: Shef 1A 134
   S75: Barn 5A 16
Samuel Sq. S75: Barn 5A 16
Sanctuary Flds. S25: Nth A 1G 141
Sandal Ct. S61: Roth 3C 96
Sandall Beat La. DN2: Don 4A 42
Sandall Beat Rd. DN2: Don 1G 57
Sandall Beat Vis. Cen. 6B 42
Sandall Beat Wood (Nature Reserve)
   . . . . .6B 42
Sandall Carr Rd. DN3: Kirk Sa 5B 26
Sandall La. DN3: Kirk Sa 3A 26
Sandall Pk. Dr. DN2: Don 3H 41
Sandall Ri. DN2: Don 4G 41
Sandall Stones Rd. DN3: Kirk Sa 5A 26
Sandall Vw. S25: Laugh C 3F 127
Sandall Wood Rd. DN12: Con 5D 68
Sandalwood Cl. DN2: Don 2H 41
Sandalwood Ri. S64: Swin 6C 66
Sandbeck Cl. S71: Barn 5E 17
Sandbeck Ct. DN11: Ross 6D 74
   DN12: Den M 3C 68
Sandbeck Ho. DN1: Don 2B 56
            (off Grove Pl.)
Sandbeck La. S66: Malt 6G 103
Sandbeck Pl. S11: Shef 6C 118
Sandbeck Rd. DN4: Don 2E 57
Sandbeck Way S66: Hel 5D 100
Sandbed Rd. S3: Shef 5D 106

Sandbergh Rd. S61: Kimb P 6H 81
Sandby Ct. S14: Shef 6B 134
Sandby Cft. S14: Shef 6B 134
Sandby Dr. S14: Shef 6B 134
Sandcliffe Rd. DN2: Don 4G 41
Sandcroft Cl. S74: Hoyl 1H 61
Sandeby Dr. S65: Rav 3A 100
Sanderson St. S9: Shef 5C 108
Sanderson Way S64: Swin 4D 66
Sanders Way S25: Laugh C 4F 127
Sandford Ct. DN4: Balb 5H 55
   S70: Barn .1C 30
Sandford Gro. Rd. S7: Shef 3D 132
            (not continuous)
Sandford Rd. DN4: Balb 6H 55
SANDHILL
   S62 . . . . .1A 84
   S72 . . . . .1G 35
Sandhill Cl. S62: Rawm 1A 84
Sandhill Ct. S72: Gt H 1G 35
Sandhill Golf Course 2E 35
Sandhill Gro. S72: Grim 5B 12
Sandhill M. S72: Gt H 1G 35
Sandhill Ri. DN9: Auck 1G 59
Sandhill Rd. S62: Rawm 1A 84
Sandhills Way DN3: Brant 4G 59
Sandhurst Pl. S10: Shef 2B 118
Sandhurst Rd. DN4: Can 5D 58
Sandiron Ho. S7: Shef 1A 146
Sandiway S40: W'ton 2D 170
Sandon Vw. S10: Shef 6A 4
Sandown Cl. S21: Ecki 1C 158
Sandown Gdns. DN4: Can 2A 58
Sandown Rd. S64: Mexb 6G 51
Sandpiper Ct. S41: Uns 2F 161
Sandpiper Rd.
   S61: Thorpe H 2C 80
Sandpit Hill DN3: Brant 4G 59
Sandringham Av. S60: Whis 3A 112
Sandringham Cl. S36: Thurl 3A 176
   S41: Whit M 6H 161
   S44: Cal 4F 169
Sandringham Pl. S10: Shef 5A 116
   S65: Rav .2A 100
Sandringham Rd. DN2: Don 1F 57
   S9: Shef .6D 94
   S44: Cal 4F 169
Sandrock Dr. DN4: Bess 5B 58
Sands Cl. S14: Shef 4B 134
Sandstone Av. S9: Shef 2C 108
   S42: W'ton 2C 170
Sandstone Cl. S9: Shef 1D 108
Sandstone Dr. S9: Shef 2C 108
Sandstone Rd. S9: Shef 2C 108
Sandwith Rd. S26: Tod 3B 140
Sandy Acres Cl. S20: Water 1G 151
Sandy Acres Dr. S20: Water 1G 151
Sandybridge La. S72: Shaft 1D 10
Sandybridge La. Ind. Est.
   S72: Shaft .2E 11
Sandycroft Cres. DN4: Balb 5F 55
Sandy Flat La. S66: Wick 3F 113
SANDYGATE .4E 117
Sandygate S63: Wath D 6G 49
            (not continuous)
Sandygate Ct. S10: Shef 4E 117
Sandygate Cres. S63: Wath D 2G 65
Sandygate Grange Dr. S10: Shef 4F 117
Sandygate Gro. S10: Shef 4E 117
Sandygate La. S10: Shef 4F 117
   S71: Stair .2B 32
Sandygate Pk. S10: Shef 4D 116
Sandygate Pk. Cres. S10: Shef 4E 117
Sandygate Pk. Rd. S10: Shef 4E 117
Sandygate Rd. S10: Shef 4E 117
Sandy Hill La. S25: Din 1B 142
Sandy La. DN4: Don 3F 57
   S35: Chap 4B 78
   S66: Bram 1B 114
   S66: Thurc 5C 114
   S73: Womb 2B 46
Sandymount Rd. S63: Wath D 1H 65
Sanforth St. S41: C'fld 2H 167
Sankey Sq. S63: Gol 5C 36
Sarah Ct. DN3: Arm 3H 43
Sarah St. S61: Roth 4C 96
   S64: Mexb 2F 67
Sargeson Rd. DN3: Arm 4C 42
Sark Rd. S2: Shef 1F 133

Sarrius Ct. DN4: Can 4B 58
Saundby Cl. DN4: Bess 5H 57
Saunderson Rd. S36: Pen 3B 176
Saunders Pl. S2: Shef 3B 120
Saunders Rd. S2: Shef 3B 120
Saunder's Row
  S73: Womb 2F 47
Savage La. S17: Dore 3E 145
Savile St. S3: Shef 1G 119
  S4: Shef 1G 119
Savile St. E. S4: Shef 1A 120
Savile Wlk. S72: Brier 3C 12
Saville Ct. S74: Hoyl 1G 61
Saville Hall La. S75: Dod 4G 29
Saville La. S36: Thurl 4A 176
Saville Rd. S60: Whis 3A 112
  S63: Wath D 6F 49
  S75: Dod 4G 29
Saville St. S65: Dalt 1B 98
  S72: Cud 1F 19
Saville Ter. S70: Barn 2D 30
Sawdon Rd. S11: Shef 5D 118
Sawmill Cl. S36: Pen 5D 176
Sawn Moor Av. S66: Thurc 6C 114
Sawn Moor Rd.
  S66: Thurc 1C 126
Sawston Cl. DN4: Balb 2H 71
Saxon Av. WF9: Sth K 4G 13
Saxon Cl. DN3: Eden 6B 26
  DN4: Bess 6C 58
  DN5: Scawt 3G 39
Saxon Cres. S70: Wors 5F 31
Saxon Gro. WF9: Sth K 5H 13
Saxonlea Av. S2: Shef 5F 121
Saxonlea Ct. S2: Shef 5F 121
Saxonlea Cres. S2: Shef 5F 121
Saxonlea Dr. S2: Shef 5E 121
Saxon M. DN3: Barn D 1C 26
Saxon Mt. WF9: Sth K 4G 13
Saxon Rd. S8: Shef 2F 133
  S26: Kiv P 6C 140
  S61: Kimb 4G 95
Saxon Row DN12: Con 5H 69
Saxon St. S63: Thurn 2D 36
  S72: Cud 2E 19
Saxton Av. DN4: Bess 4H 57
Saxton Cl. S41: Has 2B 172
  S74: Els 6E 47
Saxton Dr. S60: Roth 3G 111
Sayers Cl. DN5: Harl 2H 51
Scafell Pl. S25: Nth A 2A 142
Scaftworth Cl. DN4: Bess 5H 57
Scammadine Cl. S60: Brins 4E 111
Scamming La. S25: Laugh M 1A 128
Scampton Lodge S5: Shef 2G 107
Scarborough Cl. S25: Nth A 1H 141
Scarborough La. DN11: New R 5A 74
Scarborough Rd. S9: Shef 1F 121
  S66: Wick 5G 99
Scarbrough Cres. S66: Malt 6B 102
Scarbrough Farm Ct. S66: Malt 5A 102
Scarfield Cl. S71: Ard 2C 32
Scargill Cft. S1: Shef 2E 5 (2F 119)
Scar La. S71: Ard 2C 32
Scarlett Oak Mdw. S6: Stan 6D 104
Scarll Rd. DN4: Hex 3H 55
Scarsdale Cl. S18: Dron 4G 155
Scarsdale Cres. S43: Brim 1C 168
Scarsdale Cross S18: Dron 3G 155
Scarsdale Dr. S8: Shef 5E 133
  S18: Dron 3F 155
  S41: Whit M 6H 161
Scarsdale St. S25: Din 5B 128
Scarth Av. DN4: Balb 4A 56
SCAWSBY 4E 39
Scawsby La. DN5: Scaws 2C 38
SCAWTHORPE 2F 39
Scawthorpe Av. DN5: Scawt 2E 39
Scawthorpe Cotts. DN5: Scawt 2D 38
Sceptone Gro. S72: Shaft 3F 11
Sceptre Av. DN4: Bess 1C 74
Sceptre Gro. DN11: New R 6F 75
Schofield Dr. S73: D'fld 4B 34
Schofield Pl. S73: D'fld 4B 34
Schofield Rd. S36: Spink 3F 175
  S73: D'fld 4B 34
Schofield St. S64: Mexb 1E 67
Scholar's Ga. S72: Cud 6E 11
Schole Av. S36: Pen 4C 176

Schole Hill La. S36: Cub 5B 176
                              (not continuous)
SCHOLES 5F 81
Scholes Fld. Cl. S61: Scho 6F 81
Scholes Grn. S61: Scho 5F 81
Scholes La. S61: Scho 5D 80
Scholes Ri. S35: Eccl 2G 93
Scholes Vw. S35: Eccl 1G 93
  S61: Thorpe H 5D 80
  S74: Hoyl 1B 62
  S74: Jum 5C 46
Scholes Village S61: Scho 2E 81
Scholey Av. S81: Woods 5F 143
Scholey Rd. S66: Wick 5G 99
Scholey St. S3: Shef 1G 119
Scholfield Cres. S66: Malt 6C 102
School Board La.
  S40: C'fld 5F 167
School Cl. S20: Half 3G 151
  S26: Wales 5G 139
  DN3: Wath D 1F 65
School Ct. DN1: Don 6C 40
                          (off Dockin Hill Rd.)
Schoolfield Dr. S62: Rawm 1G 83
School Gdns. S70: Barn 2B 30
School Grn. La. S10: Shef 1C 130
School Gro. S26: Aston 1D 138
School Hill S60: Whis 3B 112
  S72: Cud 1E 19
School Ho. M. DN1: Don 2C 56
School La. DN3: Can 4E 59
  DN9: Auck 1C 92
  S2: Shef 4H 5 (3H 119)
  S6: Stan 1D 116
  S8: Shef 3E 147
                        (James Andrew Crt.)
  S8: Shef 1H 147
                          (School La. Cl.)
  S18: Dron 3F 155
  S21: Mar L 1H 157
  S35: Gren 1B 92
  S35: Wharn S 2A 90
                            (not continuous)
  S44: Ark T 5H 173
  S62: P'gte 5F 83
  S65: Thry 5E 85
  S66: Stain 2F 103
School La. Cl. S8: Shef 1H 147
School Rd. S10: Shef 3A 118
  S20: Beig 5H 137
  S25: Laugh M 2G 127
  S26: Wales 6F 139
  S35: High G 1D 78
  S41: Whit M 1H 167
  S66: Thurc 6C 114
School St. S20: Mosb 3E 151
  S21: Ecki 1E 159
  S25: Din 5A 128
  S26: Swal 1B 138
  S63: Bolt D 2B 50
  S63: Thurn 2C 36
  S65: Thry 6D 84
  S70: Stair 2A 32
  S72: Cud 6E 11
  S72: Gt H 6E 21
  S73: D'fld 4C 34
  S73: Hem 5F 47
  S73: Womb 1G 47
  S75: Barn 5C 16
  S75: Dart 5F 7
  S75: Stain 5B 8
School Ter. DN12: Con 4E 69
School Wlk. DN12: Den M 2C 68
  DN12: Old E 1B 88
  S66: Malt 5A 102
Scorah's La. S64: Swin 3H 65
Scotch Spring La. S66: Malt 3F 103
Scotia Cl. S2: Shef 6C 120
Scotia Dr. S2: Shef 6C 120
Scotland St. S3: Shef 1C 4 (2E 119)
Scot La. DN1: Don 1C 56
Scotsman Dr. DN5: Scawt 3G 39
Scott Av. DN5: Barnb 2H 51
  DN12: Con 4D 68
Scott Cl. S40: Gras 6D 172
  S66: Thurc 6B 114
Scott Cres. DN3: Eden 5B 26
Scott Hill DN5: Sprot 4C 54

Scott Rd. S4: Shef 4G 107
Scott Wlk. S66: Malt 4G 101
Scott Way S35: Chap 4E 79
SCOUT DIKE 1B 176
Scovell Av. S62: Rawm 1E 83
Scovell Ho. S62: Rawm 1E 83
Scowerdons Cl. S12: Shef 3A 136
Scowerdons Dr. S12: Shef 3A 136
Scraith Wood Dr. S5: Shef 2C 106
Scrooby Dr. S61: Grea 5D 82
Scrooby La. S62: P'gte 5E 83
Scrooby Pl. S61: Grea 5D 82
Scrooby St. S61: Grea 5D 82
Sea Breeze Ter. S13: Shef 6G 121
Seabrook Rd. S2: Shef 4A 120
Seagrave Cl. S12: Shef 4E 135
Seagrave Cres. S12: Shef 5D 134
Seagrave Dr. S12: Shef 4E 135
  S41: Has 3B 172
Seagrave Rd. S12: Shef 4D 134
Sea King Dr. DN9: Finn 2C 76
Searby Rd. S66: Bram 3A 100
Seaton Cl. S2: Shef 4C 120
Seaton Cres. S2: Shef 4C 120
Seaton Gdns.
  DN11: New R 6G 75
Seaton Pl. S2: Shef 4C 120
Seaton Way S2: Shef 4C 120
Sebastian Vw. S60: Brins 2D 110
Second Av. DN6: Woodl 4D 22
  DN9: Finn 2C 76
  WF9: Sth K 5G 13
Second La. S25: Sth A 5H 141
  S66: Wick 2H 113
Sedan St. S4: Shef 5H 107
Sedbergh Cres. S41: C'fld 1E 167
Sedge Cl. S66: Bram 6B 100
Sedgefield Way S64: Mexb 6G 51
Sedgemoor Cl. S40: C'fld 4C 166
Sedgley Rd. S6: Shef 4C 106
Sefton Ct. S10: Shef 1F 131
Sefton Rd. S10: Shef 1E 131
Selborne Rd. S10: Shef 4H 117
Selborne Cl. S75: Bar G 3F 15
Selby Cl. S26: Swal 1B 138
  S40: W'ton 2D 170
Selby Rd. DN2: Don 5F 41
  S4: Shef 3A 108
  S71: Smi 1E 17
Selhurst Cres. DN4: Bess 5B 58
Selhurst Rd. S41: C'fld 3G 167
Selig Pde. S12: Shef 6F 135
                              (off White La.)
Selkirk Av. DN4: Warm 6E 55
Selkirk Rd. DN2: Don 4H 41
Sellars Rd. S61: Kimb P 1H 95
Sellars Row S35: High G 6C 60
Sellers St. S8: Shef 1E 133
Selly Oak Gro. S8: Shef 4H 147
Selly Oak Rd. S8: Shef 4H 147
Selmer Cl. S43: Brim 6C 162
Selwood Flats S65: Roth 3G 97
Selwyn St. S65: Roth 2F 97
Senior Rd. DN4: Hex 2H 55
  S9: Shef 2G 121
Seniors Pl. S35: Chap 2E 79
Sennen Cft. S71: Monk B 5G 17
Serlby Ho. DN1: Don 2B 56
                              (off Grove Pl.)
Serpentine Wlk. S8: Shef 2F 147
Setcup La. S21: Ecki 2D 158
Seth Ter. S70: Barn 2F 31
Setts Way S42: W'orth 6A 172
Sevenairs Fold S20: Beig 5F 137
Sevenairs Rd. S20: Beig 5F 137
Sevenairs Vw.
  S20: Beig 5F 137
Sevenfields Cl. S6: Shef 3H 105
Sevenfields La. S6: Shef 3H 105
Seven Yards Rd. DN3: Can 6H 43
Severn Cl. S10: Shef 3C 118
Severn Rd. S10: Shef 3C 118
Severnside Dr. S13: Shef 1B 136
Severnside Gdns.
  S13: Shef 1B 136
Severnside Pl. S13: Shef 1B 136
Severnside Wlk. S13: Shef 1B 136
Sewell Rd. S20: Half 4G 151

Sexton Dr. S66: Bram 6A **100**
Seymore Rd. S26: Aston 2C **138**
Seymour La. S43: Woodt 5F **165**
Seymour Rd. S66: Malt 5C **102**
Shackleton Rd. DN2: Don 1A **42**
Shackleton Vw. S36: Cub 5D **176**
Shady Side DN4: Hex 2H **55**
Shadyside DN4: Hex 3H **55**
Shaftesbury Av. DN2: Don 1G **57**
   S40: C'fld 5E **167**
Shaftesbury Dr. S74: Hoyl 1A **62**
Shaftesbury Ho. DN2: Don 5H **41**
Shaftesbury Sq. S65: Roth 3F **97**
Shaftesbury St. S70: Stair 2B **32**
SHAFTHOLME 3C **24**
Shaftholme La. DN5: Bntly 2A **24**
Shaftholme Rd. DN5: Bntly 3C **24**
SHAFTON .3F **11**
Shafton Ga. S63: Gol 5E **37**
Shafton Hall Dr. S72: Shaft 3E **11**
Shafton Rd. S60: Roth 2A **112**
SHAFTON TWO GATES 5F **11**
Shaftsbury Av. DN6: Woodl 2A **22**
Shakespeare Av. DN5: Don 6G **39**
Shakespeare Cres. S18: Dron 4H **155**
Shakespeare Dr. S25: Din 6B **128**
Shakespeare Rd. DN5: Bntly 1A **40**
   S63: Wath D 5E **49**
   S65: Roth 2G **97**
Shakespeare St. S42: Gras 6D **172**
Shaldon Gro. S26: Aston 1C **138**
Shalesmoor S3: Shef 1D **4** (2F **119**)
                (Gibraltar St.)
   S3: Shef 1C **4** (1E **119**)
                 (Hoyle St.)
SHALESMOOR RDBT. 1E **119**
            (off Shalesmoor)
Shalesmoor Stop (ST) 1E **119**
Shambles, The S40: C'fld 5H **167**
           (off Packers Row)
Shambles St. S70: Barn 1D **30**
Shamrock Pl. S43: Mas M 2F **165**
Shap Cl. S40: C'fld 3D **166**
Shardlow Ct. DN4: Bess 6C **58**
Shardlow Gdns. DN4: Bess 6C **58**
Sharlston Gdns. DN11: Ross 5E **75**
Sharman Cl. S18: App 3D **156**
Sharman Wlk. S18: App 3D **156**
Sharpe Av. S8: Shef 2D **146**
Sharpfield Av. S62: Rawm 6F **65**
Sharrard Cl. S12: Shef 3E **135**
Sharrard Dr. S12: Shef 3E **135**
Sharrard Gro. S12: Shef 2E **135**
Sharrard Rd. S12: Shef 3E **135**
SHARROW 1C **132**
SHARROW HEAD 6D **118**
Sharrow La. S11: Shef 6D **118**
Sharrow Mt. S11: Shef 1C **132**
Sharrow St. S11: Shef 6E **119**
SHARROW VALE 6C **118**
Sharrow Vale Rd. S11: Shef 6B **118**
Sharrow Vw. S7: Shef 6D **118**
Shaw Ct. DN3: Arm 5F **43**
Shawfield Cl. DN3: Barn D 2D **26**
Shawfield Rd. S71: Car 1A **18**
SHAW LANDS 1B **30**
Shawlands Ct. S63: Wath D 5D **48**
Shaw La. DN2: Don 2A **42**
   S70: Barn 1B **30**
   S71: Car 5A **10**
   S75: Stain 4B **8**
Shaw La. Ind. Est. DN2: Don 2B **42**
Shaw Rd. DN12: New E 3D **70**
   S65: Roth 2H **97**
Shawsfield Rd. S60: Roth 6G **97**
Shaw's Row S40: C'fld 6E **167**
Shaw St. S18: Coal A 6H **147**
   S41: Whit M 6H **161**
   S70: Barn 1C **30**
Shaw Wood Way DN2: Don 3A **42**
Shay, The DN4: Bess 5B **58**
SHAY HOUSE 3E **175**
Shay Ho. La. S36: Stoc 4D **174**
Shay Rd. S36: Stoc 3D **174**
Sheaf Av. S7: Shef 2D **132**
Sheaf Bank S2: Shef 1F **133**
Sheaf Cl. DN12: Con 5G **69**
Sheaf Ct. S70: Barn 3A **32**
Sheaf Cres. S63: Bolt D 3C **50**

Sheaf Gdns. S2: Shef 5G **119**
Sheaf Gdns. Ter. S2: Shef 5G **119**
Sheaf Sq. S1: Shef 5G **5** (4G **119**)
Sheaf St. S1: Shef 5F **5** (4G **119**)
Sheardown St. DN4: Hex 2A **56**
Sheards Cl. S18: Dron W 2E **155**
Sheards Dr. S18: Dron W 3D **154**
Sheards Way S18: Dron W 3E **155**
Shearman Av. S61: Kimb P 6G **81**
Shearwood Rd. S10: Shef 3C **118**
Shed La. S75: Stainb 6G **29**
SHEEPBRIDGE 4F **161**
Sheepbridge Bus. Cen.
   S41: Old W 3G **161**
Sheep Bri. La. DN11: Ross 5D **74**
Sheepbridge La. S41: C'fld 3F **161**
Sheepbridge Trad. Est. S41: C'fld . . .3D **160**
Sheepbridge Works S41: C'fld 4F **161**
Sheepcote Hill S21: Killa 4C **152**
Sheep Cote Rd. S60: Roth 1C **112**
Sheepcote Rd. S21: Killa 4B **152**
Sheepcote Wlk. S70: Stair 2A **32**
Sheep Dike La. S66: Mort 4H **113**
Sheephill Rd. S11: Shef 4B **130**
Sheep La. DN5: High M 3F **53**
Sheep Wlk. La. DN5: Scaws 3C **38**
Sheerien Cl. S71: Ath 6D **8**
SHEFFIELD 3G **119**
Sheffield Airport Bus. Pk.
   S9: Shef 5G **109**
                (Europa Link)
   S9: Shef 6A **110**
              (Europa Vw.)
   S9: Tins 4G **109**
Sheffield Botanical Gdns. 5B **118**
Sheffield College, The Stop (ST)
   . . . . .6G **5** (5G **119**)
Sheffield Hallam University
   City Campus 4F **5** (3G **119**)
   Collegiate Crescent Campus
   . . . . .5C **118**
Sheffield Hallam University Stop (ST)
   . . . . .5G **5** (3G **119**)
Sheffield Interchange 4F **5** (3G **119**)
Sheffield La. S60: Cat 1D **122**
SHEFFIELD LANE TOP 6H **93**
Sheffield Manor Lodge 4C **120**
Sheffield Outer Ring Rd. S8: Shef . .3G **147**
SHEFFIELD PARK 5B **120**
Sheffield Pk. Academy Leisure Cen.
   . . . . .4E **121**
        (off Beaumont Rd. Nth.)
Sheffield Parkway S2: Shef . .2H **5** (2H **119**)
   S9: Shef 4G **121**
Sheffield Rd. DN4: Warm 2C **70**
   DN12: Con 6C **68**
   S9: Tins 3F **109**
             (not continuous)
   S12: Shef 6A **136**
   S13: Shef 6F **123**
             (Furnace La.)
   S13: Shef 2B **136**
            (Wolverley Rd.)
   S18: Dron 1E **155**
             (Bowshaw)
   S18: Dron 5F **147**
         (Jordanthorpe Parkway)
   S18: Uns 5B **156**
   S21: Ecki 5F **151**
   S21: Killa 3A **152**
   S25: Sth A 2D **140**
   S26: Sth A, Tod 1A **140**
   S26: Swal 6H **123**
   S35: Wort 1A **78**
   S36: Oxs, Pen 4E **177**
   S41: C'fld, Whit M 6H **161**
             (not continuous)
   S41: Old W, Whit M 3F **161**
   S60: Roth 6C **96**
   S70: Barn 2E **31**
   S70: Birdw, Wors 3D **44**
   S74: Hoyl 1F **61**
Sheffield Station (Rail) 5G **5** (4G **119**)
Sheffield Station Stop (ST)
   . . . . .5G **5** (3G **119**)
Sheffield Technology Pk. S9: Shef . .6D **108**
Sheffield Transport Sports Club 3E **147**
Sheffield United FC 5F **119**
Sheffield United FC Academy 4G **107**

Sheffield Wednesday FC 2B **106**
Sheldon Av. DN12: Con 5G **69**
Sheldon La. S6: Stan 6D **104**
Sheldon Rd. S7: Shef 2D **132**
   S36: Stoc 3E **175**
   S40: C'fld 3C **166**
Sheldon Row S3: Shef 1G **5** (2G **119**)
Sheldon St. S2: Shef 5F **119**
Sheldrake Cl. S61: Thorpe H 2C **80**
Shelley Av. DN4: Balb 6A **56**
Shelley Cl. S36: Pen 3D **176**
Shelley Dr. DN3: Arm 4F **43**
   S18: Dron 5H **155**
   S25: Din 6C **128**
   S65: Roth 5A **98**
   S71: Monk B 5F **17**
Shelley Gro. DN5: Don 1G **55**
Shelley Ri. DN6: Adw S 3B **22**
Shelley Rd. S65: Roth 4A **98**
Shelley Way S63: Wath D 5D **48**
Shenstone Dr. S65: Roth 6A **98**
Shenstone Rd. S6: Shef 2B **106**
   S65: Roth 6A **98**
Shepcote Business Village
   S9: Shef 5F **109**
Shepcote Enterprise Pk. 1
   S9: Shef 5G **109**
Shepcote Enterprise Pk. 2
   S9: Tins 4G **109**
Shepcote La. S9: Shef, Tins 5F **109**
Shepcote Way S9: Shef 5F **109**
Shephard's Cl. DN12: Den M 3C **68**
Shepherd Dr. S35: Chap 2D **78**
Shepherd La. S63: Thurn 3C **36**
Shepherd St. S3: Shef 1C **4** (2E **119**)
Shepherd Way S71: R'ton 2H **9**
Shepherd Wheel (Water Mill) . . .1G **131**
Shepley Cft. S35: High G 2D **78**
Shepley St. S40: C'fld 6E **167**
Shepleys Yd. S40: C'fld 5H **167**
Sheppard Rd. DN4: Balb 5H **55**
Shepperson Rd. S6: Shef 3A **106**
Sherbourne Av. S41: C'fld 6F **161**
   S66: Bram 1B **114**
Sherburn Ga. S35: Chap 2E **79**
Sherburn Rd. S71: Smi 1D **16**
Sherde Rd. S6: Shef 1D **118**
Sheridan Av. DN4: Balb 6B **56**
Sheridan Ct. S71: Monk B 5G **17**
Sheridan Dr. S65: Roth 4B **98**
Sheridan Rd. DN3: Barn D 1H **27**
Sheringham Cl. S35: High G 1C **78**
Sheringham Gdns. S35: High G 1C **78**
        (off Sheringham Cl.)
Sherwood Av. DN3: Eden 6C **26**
   DN5: Scaws 4E **39**
   DN12: Con 5D **68**
Sherwood Chase S17: Dore 5F **145**
Sherwood Cres. S60: Roth 4F **97**
Sherwood Dr. DN4: Balb 1F **71**
Sherwood Glen S7: Shef 1A **146**
Sherwood Pl. S18: Dron W 3C **154**
Sherwood Rd. DN11: New R 6D **74**
   S18: Dron W 3C **154**
   S21: Killa 3D **152**
Sherwood St. S40: C'fld 1A **172**
   S71: Barn 1E **31**
Sherwood Way S72: Cud 5D **10**
Shetland Gdns. DN2: Don 5G **41**
Shetland Rd. S18: Dron 4G **155**
Shield Av. S70: Wors 5F **31**
Shining Bank S13: Shef 4A **122**
Shinwell Av. S43: Ink 1G **169**
Shipcroft Cl. S73: Womb 2H **47**
Ship Hill S60: Roth 4E **97**
Shipman Balk S66: Clftn 3H **87**
Shipman Ct. S20: Mosb 3E **151**
Shippen Rural Bus. Cen., The
   S18: Barl 4A **160**
Shipton St. S6: Shef 1D **118**
Shirburn Gdns. DN4: Can 3C **58**
Shirebrook Rd. S8: Shef 2F **133**
Shire Brook Valley Nature Reserve
   . . . . .3B **136**
Shire Brook Vis. Cen. 3B **136**
SHIRECLIFFE 2F **107**
Shirecliffe Cl. S3: Shef 4G **107**
Shirecliffe La. S3: Shef 5F **107**
Shirecliffe Rd. S5: Shef 2F **107**

SHIREGREEN 4A 94
Shiregreen La. S5: Shef 6B 94
Shiregreen Ter. S5: Shef 5A 94
Shirehall Cres. S5: Shef 3A 94
Shirehall Rd. S5: Shef 4A 94
Shire Oak Dr. S74: Els 1E 63
Shireoaks Rd. S18: Dron 2H 155
Shireoaks Way S72: Grim 1A 20
Shires Cl. DN5: Sprot 3C 54
Shirewood Cl.
  S63: Bramp B 6B 48
Shirland Av. S71: Ath 2F 17
Shirland Cl. S9: Shef 6C 108
Shirland Ct. S9: Shef 1E 121
Shirland La. S9: Shef 6C 108
Shirland M. S9: Shef 1D 120
Shirland Pl. S9: Shef 1E 121
Shirland St. S41: C'fld 4H 167
Shirle Hill S11: Shef 1C 132
Shirley Cl. S40: C'fld 3C 166
Shirley Rd. DN4: Hex 3H 55
  S3: Shef 5G 107
Shooters Hill Dr. DN11: Ross 6E 75
Shop. Mall, The S36: Stoc 3E 175
Shore Ct. S10: Shef 4H 117
Shoreham Av. S60: Roth 3H 111
Shoreham Dr. S60: Roth 3G 111
Shoreham Rd. S60: Roth 3G 111
Shoreham St. S1: Shef 6F 5 (4G 119)
  S2: Shef 6E 5 (6F 119)
              (not continuous)
Shore La. S10: Shef 4H 117
Shorland Dr. S60: Tree 2G 123
Shortbrook Bank S20: W'fld 2F 151
Shortbrook Cl. S20: W'fld 2F 151
Shortbrook Cft. S20: W'fld 2F 151
Shortbrook Dr. S20: W'fld 2F 151
Shortbrook Rd. S20: W'fld 2F 151
Shortbrook Wlk. S20: W'fld 2F 151
              (off Eastcroft Way)
Shortbrook Way S20: W'fld 2F 151
Shortfield Ct. S71: Ath 6D 8
Short Ga. DN11: Wils 2G 89
Short La. DN4: Don 5G 57
Shortridge St. S9: Shef 6C 108
Short Rd. DN2: Don 6H 41
Short Row S71: Smi 3E 17
Shorts La. S17: Dore 4C 144
Short St. S74: Hoyl 1G 61
Shortwood Bus. Pk. S74: Hoyl 5F 45
Short Wood Cl. S70: Birdw 3E 45
Shortwood Ct. S74: Hoyl 5G 45
Shortwood La. DN5: Clay 4H 21
Shortwood Vs. S74: Hoyl 5F 45
Shortwood Way S74: Hoyl 4G 45
Shotton Wlk. DN1: Don 2B 56
Showroom Cinema, The 5F 5 (4G 119)
Shrewsbury Almshouses
  S2: Shef 5H 5 (4H 119)
Shrewsbury Cl. S36: Pen 4D 176
  S64: Mexb 1E 67
Shrewsbury Rd. S2: Shef ...6G 5 (4G 119)
  S36: Pen 4D 176
Shrewsbury Ter. S17: Tot 6E 145
  S61: Kimb 5A 96
Shroggs Head Cl. S73: D'fld 4C 33
Shrogswood Rd. S60: Roth 1C 112
Shubert Cl. S13: Shef 6C 122
Shude Hill S1: Shef 2G 5 (2G 119)
Shuttle Cl. DN11: Ross 6E 75
SHUTTLEWOOD 6H 165
Shuttleworth Cl. DN11: Ross 6D 74
Sibbering Row S36: Spink 4H 175
Sicey Av. S5: Shef 2A 94
Sicey La. S5: Shef 4A 94
Sicklebrook La. S18: Coal A 6B 148
Sickleworks Cl. DN12: Con 5E 69
Sidcop Rd. S72: Cud 5D 10
Siddall St. S1: Shef 3B 4 (3E 119)
Sidings, The S73: Womb 2C 48
Sidings Ct. DN4: Don 4D 56
Sidlaw Cl. S40: C'fld 3D 166
Sidney Rd. DN2: Don 6G 41
Sidney St. S1: Shef 6E 5 (4F 119)
  S64: Swin 3C 66
Sidons Cl. S61: Kimb P 6H 81
Siemens Cl. S9: Tins 2H 109
Siena Cl. S73: D'fld 4H 33
Sike Cl. S75: Kexb 5D 6

Sike La. S36: Cub 6A 176
Sikes Rd. S25: Nth A 3G 141
Silk Rd. DN2: Don 4D 40
SILKSTONE 2A 28
Silkstone Cl. S12: Shef 4H 135
  S75: Pil 1C 60
SILKSTONE COMMON 5B 28
Silkstone Common Station (Rail) ..5A 28
Silkstone Cres. S12: Shef 4H 135
SILKSTONE CROSS 3A 28
Silkstone Dr. S12: Shef 4G 135
Silkstone Golf Course 2D 28
Silkstone La. S75: Cawt, Silk 4A 14
Silkstone Pl. S12: Shef 4H 135
Silkstone Rd. S12: Shef 4G 135
Silkstone Vw. S74: Hoyl 4B 46
Silver Birch Av. S10: Shef 1D 130
Silver Birch Gro. DN9: Finn 3G 77
Silverdale Cl. DN3: Brant 4H 59
  S11: Shef 4H 131
  S41: C'fld 5F 161
Silverdale Ct. S11: Shef 3A 132
              (off Silverdale Rd.)
Silverdale Cres.
  S11: Shef 3H 131
Silverdale Cft. S11: Shef 4H 131
Silverdale Dr. S11: Monk B 3A 18
Silverdale Gdns. S11: Shef 4A 132
Silverdale Glade S11: Shef 4A 132
Silverdale Rd. S11: Shef 4H 131
Silverdales S25: Din 5B 128
Silver Hill Rd. S11: Shef 3A 132
Silver Jubilee Cl. DN2: Don 4H 41
Silver Mill Rd. S2: Shef 6F 119
Silvermoor Dr. S65: Rav 2A 100
Silverstone Av. S72: Cud 1F 19
Silver St. DN1: Don 1C 56
  S1: Shef 2E 5 (2F 119)
  S65: Thry 6D 84
  S70: Barn 2D 30
  S75: Dod 4G 29
Silver St. Head S1: Shef 2D 4 (2F 119)
Silver Well Dr. S43: Stav 6A 164
Silverwood Cl. S66: Sunn 3G 99
Silverwood Ct. S63: Wath D 6A 50
Silverwood Ho. DN1: Don 3B 56
              (off St James St.)
Silverwood Rd. S75: Wool G 3E 7
Silverwood Vw. DN12: Con 4E 69
Silverwood Wlk. S66: Flan 4G 99
Simcrest Av. S21: Killa 5C 152
Simmonite Rd. S61: Kimb P 6H 81
Simon Cl. S10: Shef 6G 117
Simons Ct. S73: Womb 5E 33
Simons Way S73: Womb 5E 33
Simply Gym
  Chesterfield 1H 167
Simpson Pl. S64: Mexb 1E 67
Sims Cft. S41: Old W 3B 162
Sims St. S1: Shef 2D 4 (2F 119)
Sincil Way DN4: Can 5B 58
Singleton Cres. S6: Shef 5B 106
Singleton Gro. S6: Shef 5B 106
Singleton Rd. S6: Shef 5B 106
Site Gallery 5F 5 (4G 119)
Sitka Cl. S71: R'ton 4G 9
Sitwell S20: W'fld 2F 151
              (off Shortbrook Way)
Sitwell Av. S36: Stoc 3C 174
  S40: C'fld 1G 171
Sitwell Dr. S60: Roth 1H 111
Sitwell Gro. S60: Roth 2H 111
  S64: Swin 4C 66
Sitwell La. S66: Wick 1G 113
Sitwell Pk. Golf Course 1D 112
Sitwell Pk. Rd. S60: Roth 1C 112
Sitwell Pl. S7: Shef 6E 119
Sitwell Rd. S7: Shef 6E 119
              (not continuous)
Sitwell St. S21: Ecki 2C 158
Sitwell Ter. S66: Wick 1G 113
Sitwell Va. S60: Roth 1G 111
Sitwell Vw. S60: Whis 3C 112
Sivilla Rd. S64: Kiln 6C 66
Sixth Av. DN9: Finn 3C 76
Skate Central 5G 119
Skeldale Dr. S40: C'fld 2A 172
Skelton Av. S75: Mapp 5A 8

Skelton Cl. S13: Shef 3C 136
Skelton Dr. S13: Shef 2C 136
Skelton Gro. S13: Shef 2C 136
Skelton La. S13: Shef 2C 136
  S20: Beig 5G 137
Skelton Ri. S35: Ough 4E 91
Skelton Rd. S8: Shef 3F 133
Skelton Wlk. S13: Shef 2D 136
Skelton Way S13: Shef 2C 136
Skelwith Cl. S4: Shef 3C 108
  S41: C'fld 6E 161
Skelwith Dr. S4: Shef 2C 108
Skelwith Rd. S4: Shef 3C 108
Skew Hill S35: Gren 3B 92
Skew Hill La. S35: Gren 2A 92
Skiddaw Cl. S40: C'fld 2E 167
Skiers Vw. Rd. S74: Hoyl 1H 61
Skiers Way S74: Hoyl 1H 61
Skinnerthorpe Rd. S4: Shef 3A 108
Skinpit La. S36: H'swne 1G 177
              (not continuous)
Skipton Cl. DN12: Den M 3B 68
Skipton Rd. S4: Shef 4H 107
  S26: Swal 1B 138
Skipwith Cl. DN11: Lov 4B 72
Skipwith Gdns.
  DN11: New R 6B 74
Sky Bus. Pk. DN9: Finn 2C 76
Skye Cft. S71: R'ton 1H 9
Skye Edge Av. S2: Shef 4A 120
Skye Edge Rd. S2: Shef 4A 120
Skylark Vw. S63: Wath D 5E 49
Slackfields La.
  S35: Wharn S 1C 90
Slack La. S40: Ash 5C 166
  S72: Sth H 1E 11
Slacks La. S66: Bram 1B 114
SLADE HOTON 5H 115
Slade Rd. S64: Swin 4B 66
Slade Vw. S25: Slade H 5H 115
Slag La. S21: Neth Han 6G 157
Slaidburn Av. S35: Chap 2E 79
SLATEPIT DALE 5A 170
Slate St. S2: Shef 1G 133
Slayleigh Av. S10: Shef 6D 116
Slayleigh Delph S10: Shef 6E 117
Slayleigh Dr. S10: Shef 6E 117
Slayleigh La. S10: Shef 6D 116
Sleaford St. S9: Shef 6C 108
Sledgate Dr. S66: Wick 1E 113
Sledgate La. S66: Wick 1E 113
Sledmere Rd. DN5: Scaws 4F 39
Slinn St. S10: Shef 2B 118
Slitting Mill La. S9: Shef 6C 108
Sloade La. S12: Ridg 3G 149
SLOADLANE 3G 149
Smallage La. S13: Shef 5G 123
SMALL BRIDGE 3H 57
Smallbridge Cl. S71: Monk B 2C 18
Smalldale Rd. S12: Shef 4G 135
Smeaton Cl. S65: Rav 2A 100
Smeaton St. S7: Shef 6E 119
Smeckley Wood Cl. S41: C'fld 3D 160
SMEE Model Railway 2H 145
Smelter Wood Av. S13: Shef 1H 135
Smelter Wood Cl. S13: Shef 1H 135
Smelter Wood Ct. S13: Shef 1H 135
              (off Smelter Wood Way)
Smelter Wood Cres.
  S13: Shef 1A 136
Smelter Wood Dr. S13: Shef 1H 135
Smelter Wood La. S13: Shef 1H 135
Smelter Wood Pl. S13: Shef 1A 136
Smelter Wood Ri. S13: Shef 1A 136
Smelter Wood Rd. S13: Shef 1H 135
Smelter Wood Way S13: Shef 1H 135
Smeltinghouse La. S18: Barl 3A 160
Smillie Rd. DN11: New R 6D 74
Smith Av. S43: Ink 1G 169
Smith Cres. S41: C'fld 1C 172
Smithey Cl. S35: High G 2C 78
Smithfield S3: Shef 1D 4 (2F 119)
Smithfield Apartments
  S1: Shef 4C 4
Smithfield Av. S41: Has 3B 172
Smithfield Rd. S12: Shef 6D 134
SMITHIES 3F 17
Smithies La. S71: Barn, Smi 4D 16
  S75: Barn 4D 16

Smithies Rd.—Spa Vw. Rd.

Smithies Rd. S64: Swin 2C **66**
Smithies St. S71: Barn 4D **16**
SMITHLEY 1C 46
Smithley La. S73: Womb 1C **46**
Smith Rd. S36: Stoc 3D **174**
Smith Sq. DN4: Balb 5G **55**
Smith St. DN4: Balb 5G **55**
S35: Chap 3F **79**
S73: Womb 1H **47**
Smithy Bri. La. S63: Bramp B 5H **47**
S73: Hem 5G **47**
(not continuous)
Smithy Carr Av. S35: Chap 3E **79**
Smithy Carr Cl. S35: Chap 3E **79**
Smithy Cl. S61: Kimb P 1A **96**
Smithy Cft. S18: Dron W 2B **154**
S63: Bolt D 2C **50**
SMITHY GREEN 3E 17
Smithy Grn. Rd. S71: Smi 3E **17**
SMITHY MOOR 2B 174
Smithy Moor Av. S36: Stoc 1A **174**
Smithy Moor La. S36: Stoc 2A **174**
Smithy Wood Bus. Pk.
S35: Eccl 5H **79**
Smithy Wood Cres. S8: Shef 4D **132**
(not continuous)
Smithy Wood Dr. S35: Eccl 5H **79**
Smithy Wood La. S75: Dod 4G **29**
Smithy Wood Rd. S8: Shef 4D **132**
S61: Thorpe H 4A **80**
Snail Hill S60: Roth 4E **97**
Snailsden Way S75: Stain 6C **8**
Snaithing La. S10: Shef 5F **117**
Snaithing Pk. Cl. S10: Shef 5F **117**
Snaithing Pk. Rd. S10: Shef 5F **117**
Snake La. DN12: Con 5G **69**
SNAPE HILL
S18 2F 155
S73 5A 34
Snape Hill S18: Dron 2F **155**
Snape Hill Cl. S18: Dron 1F **155**
Snape Hill Cres. S18: Dron 1F **155**
Snape Hill Dr. S18: Dron 1F **155**
Snape Hill Gdns. S18: Dron 1G **155**
Snape Hill La. S18: Dron 2F **155**
Snape Hill Rd. S73: D'fld 5A **34**
Snelston Cl. S18: Dron W 3B **154**
Snetterton Cl. S72: Cud 1F **19**
Snig Hill S3: Shef 2F **5** (2G **119**)
Snowberry Cl. S41: Has 3D **172**
S64: Swin 6B **66**
Snowden Ter. S73: Womb 1G **47**
Snowdon La. S18: Coal A 1D **156**
S21: Mar L, Trow 1D **156**
Snowdon Way S60: Brins 5E **111**
Snow Hill S75: Dod 4G **29**
Snow La. S3: Shef 1D **4** (2F **119**)
Snuff Mill La. S11: Shef 6C **118**
Snydale Rd. S72: Cud 1E **19**
Soaper La. S18: Dron 2F **155**
Soap Ho. La. S13: Shef 1F **137**
(not continuous)
Society St. DN1: Don 1C **56**
Sokell Av. S73: Womb 2F **47**
Solario Way DN11: New R 6F **75**
Solly St. S1: Shef 3B **4** (3E **119**)
Solway Ri. S18: Dron W 2C **154**
Somercotes Rd. S12: Shef 3G **135**
Somersall Cl. S40: Bramp 1B **170**
Somersall Hall Dr. S40: Bramp 2B **170**
Somersall La. S40: Bramp 2B **170**
Somersall Pk. Rd. S40: Bramp 1B **170**
Somersall Willows S40: Bramp 1B **170**
Somersby Av. DN5: Don 6G **39**
S42: W'ton 3C **170**
Somerset Ct. S72: Cud 2E **19**
Somerset Dr. S43: Brim 5E **163**
Somerset Rd. DN1: Don 2C **56**
S3: Shef 6G **107**
Somerset St. S3: Shef 6G **107**
S66: Malt 6C **102**
S70: Barn 6C **16**
S72: Cud 2E **19**
Somerton Dr. DN4: Bess 5B **58**
Somerville Ter. S6: Shef 6C **106**
Somin Ct. DN4: Balb 1B **72**
Songthrush Way S63: Wath D 5E **49**
Sopewell Rd. S61: Kimb 4G **95**
Sorby Hall S10: Shef 5A **118**
Sorby Rd. S26: Swal 1A **138**
Sorby St. S4: Shef 1H **119**
Sorby Way S66: Wick 1F **113**
Soresby St. S40: C'fld 5H **167**
Sorrel Rd. S66: Sunn 4H **99**
Sorrelsykes Cl. S60: Whis 4A **112**
Sorrento Way S73: D'fld 3A **34**
SOTHALL 6H 137
Sothall Cl. S20: Beig 5G **137**
Sothall Ct. S20: Beig 5G **137**
Sothall Grn. S20: Beig 5G **137**
Sothall M. S20: Beig 5G **137**
Sough Hall Av. S61: Thorpe H 3C **80**
Sough Hall Cl. S61: Thorpe H 3C **80**
Sough Hall Cres.
S61: Thorpe H 3C **80**
Sough Hall Rd. S61: Thorpe H 4C **80**
Sousa St. S66: Malt 6D **102**
Southall St. S8: Shef 2F **133**
SOUTH ANSTON 4G 141
South Av. S64: Swin 4A **66**
Southbourne Ct. S17: Dore 4E **145**
Southbourne Hall S10: Shef 4C **118**
Southbourne M. S10: Shef 5B **118**
Southbourne Rd. S10: Shef 4B **118**
South Cl. S18: Uns 6C **156**
S71: R'ton 4H **9**
Southcote Dr. S18: Dron W 3C **154**
South Ct. S17: Dore 3F **145**
South Cres. S21: Killa 3D **152**
S65: Roth 3A **98**
S75: Dod 3G **29**
South Cft. S72: Shaft 3F **11**
Southcroft Gdns. S7: Shef 2E **133**
Southcroft Wlk. *S7: Shef 2E 133*
(off Southcroft Gdns.)
Southdown Av. S40: C'fld 4D **166**
South Dr. S63: Bolt D 3A **50**
S71: R'ton 4H **9**
South Dr. Vw. S63: Bolt D 3A **50**
Southend Pl. S2: Shef 4B **120**
Southend Rd. S2: Shef 4B **120**
Southey Av. S5: Shef 1F **107**
Southey Cl. S5: Shef 1E **107**
(not continuous)
Southey Cres. S5: Shef 1E **107**
S66: Malt 5B **102**
Southey Dr. S5: Shef 1F **107**
SOUTHEY GREEN 6D 92
Southey Grn. Cl. S5: Shef 1E **107**
Southey Grn. Rd. S5: Shef 6C **92**
Southey Hall Dr. S5: Shef 1F **107**
Southey Hall Rd. S5: Shef 1E **107**
Southey Hill S5: Shef 6D **92**
Southey Pl. S5: Shef 1E **107**
Southey Ri. S5: Shef 1E **107**
Southey Rd. S66: Malt 5B **102**
Southey Wlk. S5: Shef 1E **107**
Southfield Av. S41: Has 4C **172**
Southfield Cotts. S71: Car 5H **9**
Southfield Cres. S63: Thurn 3A **36**
Southfield Dr. S18: Dron 4H **155**
Southfield La. S63: Thurn 4A **36**
(not continuous)
Southfield Mt. S18: Dron 4H **155**
Southfield Rd. DN3: Arm 4D **42**
S72: Cud 4F **19**
Southgate S21: Ecki 1F **159**
S36: Pen 5E **177**
S72: Shaft 4G **11**
S72: Sth H 1H **11**
S74: Hoyl 6B **46**
S75: Barn 5B **16**
Southgate Ct. S21: Ecki 1F **159**
Southgate Way S43: Bar H 2G **163**
South Gro. S60: Roth 5E **97**
South Gro. Dr. S74: Hoyl 1A **62**
Southgrove Rd. S10: Shef 5C **118**
SOUTH HIENDLEY 1H 11
SOUTH KIRKBY 4H 13
Sth. Kirkby Bus. Pk. WF9: Hems 1H **13**
Sth. Kirkby Ind. Est. WF9: Sth K 2H **13**
Southlands Way S26: Aston 1D **138**
South La. S1: Shef 6C **4** (5E **119**)
Southlea Av. S74: Hoyl 1C **62**
Southlea Cl. S74: Hoyl 1C **62**
Southlea Dr. S74: Hoyl 1B **62**
Southlea Rd. S74: Hoyl 1C **62**
Sth. Lodge Ct. S40: Bramp 5C **166**
South Mall DN1: Don 1B **56**
Southmoor Av. DN3: Arm 4D **42**
Southmoor Cl. S43: Brim C 4E **169**
Southmoor La. DN3: Arm 5D **42**
Southmoor Rd. S72: Brier 4E **13**
WF9: Hems 1E **13**
South Pde. DN1: Don 1C **56**
S3: Shef 1D **4** (1F **119**)
South Pl. S40: C'fld 6H **167**
(Beetwell St.)
S40: C'fld 6E **167**
(Hall's Row)
S73: Womb 1E **47**
S75: Barn 5A **16**
Sth. Quay Dr. S2: Shef 1H **5** (2H **119**)
South Rd. DN3: Barn D 1H **25**
S6: Shef 6B **106**
S35: High G 1C **78**
S61: Kimb 3H **95**
S75: Dod 3G **29**
Southsea Rd. S13: Shef 2B **136**
South St. DN4: Don 3C **56**
DN6: Highf 6C **22**
S2: Shef 3H **5** (3H **119**)
S20: Mosb 4E **151**
S25: Din 5A **128**
S40: C'fld 6H **167**
S61: Grea 5D **82**
S61: Kimb 5H **95**
S62: Rawm 2H **83**
S66: Thurc 5C **114**
S70: Barn 1C **30**
S73: D'fld 5B **34**
S75: Dod 4G **29**
WF9: Hems 1F **13**
South St. Nth. S43: New W 3C **162**
South Ter. S26: Wales B 5E **139**
S60: Roth 4E 97
(off Moorgate St.)
South Va. Dr. S65: Thry 6E **85**
South Vw. DN12: New E 5B **70**
S20: Holb 3H **151**
S26: Kiv P 6A **140**
S72: Grim 2A **20**
S73: D'fld 5B **34**
South Vw. Cl. S6: Lox 3F **105**
South Vw. Cres. S7: Shef 1E **133**
South Vw. Ri. S6: Lox 3F **105**
South Vw. Rd. S7: Shef 6E **119**
S74: Hoyl 1A **62**
South Vw. Ter. S60: Cat 1D **122**
Southwell Gdns. S26: Swal 1H **137**
(not continuous)
Southwell Ri. S64: Mexb 6G **51**
Southwell Rd. DN2: Don 4E **41**
S4: Shef 3C **108**
S62: Rawm 2A **84**
Southwell St. S75: Barn 6C **16**
Southwood S6: Shef 1H **105**
Southwood Av. S18: Dron 5F **155**
Southwood Gro. S6: Shef 1H **105**
Southworth Pl. S9: Shef 6E **109**
Sth. Yorkshire Bldgs. S75: Silk C 5B **28**
Sth. Yorkshire Fresh Produce & Flower Cen.
S9: Shef 2E **121**
Sth. Yorkshire (Redbrook) Ind. Est.
S75: Barn 3H **15**
South Yorkshire Transport Mus. 1H 97
Sovereign Ct. DN5: Don 1G **55**
Sowters Row *S40: C'fld 5H 167*
(off High St.)
Spa Brook Cl. S12: Shef 4A **136**
Spa Brook Dr. S12: Shef 3A **136**
(not continuous)
SPA HOUSES 1G 123
Spa La. S13: Shef 3D **136**
S41: C'fld 5A **168**
(not continuous)
Spa La. Cft. S13: Shef 2D **136**
Spalton Rd. S62: P'gte 4G **83**
Spansyke St. DN4: Hex 2A **56**
Sparkfields S75: Mapp 6A **8**
Spark La. S75: Mapp 1H **15**
Sparrowhawk Way S63: Wath D 5F **49**
Spartan Vw. S66: Malt 3G **101**
Spa Vw. Av. S12: Shef 5A **136**
Spa Vw. Dr. S12: Shef 5A **136**
Spa Vw. Pl. S12: Shef 5A **136**
Spa Vw. Rd. S12: Shef 5A **136**

Spa Vw. Ter. S12: Shef 5A 136
Spa Vw. Way S12: Shef 5A 136
Spa Well Cres. S60: Tree 1F 123
Spa Well Gro. S72: Brier 3B 12
Spa Well Ter. S71: Barn 6E 17
Speedwell Ind. Est. S43: Stav 5B 164
(Hayford Way)
S43: Stav 4C 164
(Telford Cres.)
Speeton Rd. S6: Shef 5B 106
Speighthill Cres. S42: W'orth 6F 171
Spencer Av. DN1: Don 6D 40
S43: Woodt 4E 165
Spencer Ct. S60: Whis 3C 112
Spencer Cft. S75: Cawt 3A 14
Spencer Dr. S65: Rav 2A 100
Spencer Grn. S60: Whis 3C 112
Spencer Pk. S60: Roth 2D 96
Spencer Rd. S2: Shef 1F 133
Spencer St. S40: C'fld 4H 167
S64: Mexb 2D 66
S70: Barn 2D 30
Spenser Rd. S65: Roth 5A 98
Spey Cl. S75: Mapp 1B 16
Spey Dr. DN9: Auck 1H 59
Spilsby Cl. DN4: Can 6D 58
SPINK HALL 4D 174
Spink Hall Cl. S36: Stoc 4E 175
Spink Hall La. S36: Stoc 4D 174
Spinkhill Av. S13: Shef 6F 121
Spinkhill Dr. S13: Shef 6G 121
Spinkhill La.
S21: Reni, Spink 3H 159
Spinkhill Rd. S13: Shef 1F 135
S21: Killa 6C 152
Spinner Cft. S40: C'fld 1H 171
Spinners Rd. DN2: Don 4D 40
Spinners Wlk. S60: Roth 5F 97
(off Warwick St.)
Spinney, The DN3: Barn D 2D 26
DN4: Balb 1G 71
S17: Dore 3D 144
S43: Brim 6C 162
Spinney Cl. DN5: Bntly 5B 24
S60: Roth 1H 111
Spinneyfield S60: Roth 2H 111
Spinney Hill DN5: Sprot 4C 54
Spire Hgts. S40: C'fld 4G 167
Spire Lodge S41: C'fld 3H 167
Spire Wlk. S40: C'fld 6H 167
Spire Wlk. Bus. Pk. S40: C'fld 6A 168
Spital S3: Shef 1B 172
Spital Brook Cl. S41: C'fld 1B 172
Spitalfields S3: Shef 1G 119
Spital Gdns. S41: C'fld 1B 172
Spital Gro. DN11: New R 6H 75
Spital Hill S4: Shef 1H 119
Spital La. S3: Shef 1H 119
S41: C'fld 6A 168
Spital St. S3: Shef 1G 119
S4: Shef 1H 119
Spitfire Way DN9: Auck 2C 76
Spofforth Rd. S9: Shef 1D 120
Spooner Dr. S21: Killa 4B 152
Spooner Rd. S10: Shef 4B 118
Spoon Glade S6: Stan 6D 104
Spoonhill Rd. S6: Shef 6G 105
Spoon La. S6: Stan 6B 104
Spoon M. S6: Stan 6D 104
Spoon Oak Lea S6: Stan 6D 104
Spoon Way S6: Stan 6D 104
Spotswood Cl. S14: Shef 4B 134
Spotswood Dr. S14: Shef 3B 134
Spotswood Mt. S14: Shef 4A 134
Spotswood Pl. S14: Shef 4A 134
Spotswood Rd. S14: Shef 4A 134
Spout Copse S6: Stan 6C 104
Spout La. S6: Stan 5C 104
Spout Spinney S6: Stan 6C 104
Spreadeagle Yd. S40: C'fld 6H 167
(off Beetwell St.)
Springbank S18: Uns 4B 156
S73: D'fld 5C 34
Springbank Cl. S71: Car 6H 9
Spring Bank Rd. DN12: Con 6E 69
S40: C'fld 5G 167
Springbrook Cl. S63: Thurn 1C 36
Spring Cl. S60: Whis 3B 112
Spring Cl. Ct. S14: Shef 4C 134

Spring Cl. Dell S14: Shef 4C 134
Spring Cl. Dr. S14: Shef 4C 134
Spring Cl. Mt. S14: Shef 4C 134
Spring Cl. Vw. S14: Shef 4B 134
Spring Cres. DN5: Sprot 3C 54
Spring Ct. S61: Kimb P 1A 96
Springcroft Dr. DN5: Scawt 2F 39
Spring Dr. S73: Bramp 4B 48
Springfield S63: Bolt D 2H 49
Springfield Av. S7: Shef 3B 132
S40: C'fld 5E 167
WF9: Hems 1F 13
Springfield Cl. DN3: Arm 5F 43
S7: Shef 4B 132
S21: Ecki 1D 158
S61: Grea 1E 97
S73: D'fld 5C 34
S81: Woods 4F 143
Springfield Ct. DN5: Cus 5F 39
Springfield Cres. S73: D'fld 5C 34
S74: Hoyl 1H 61
Springfield St. S70: Barn 1B 30
Springfield Ter. S25: Nth A 1F 141
S70: Barn 1C 30
Springfield Way S35: Burn 3C 78
Spring Gdns. DN1: Don 1B 56
DN3: Can 3F 59
S70: Barn 2C 30
S71: Monk B 4H 17
S74: Hoyl 6B 46
Spring Gro. S71: Car 5A 10
Spring Gro. Gdns. S35: Wharn S 1C 92
Spring Hill S10: Shef 2B 118
S75: Wool G 3F 7
Springhill Av. S73: Bramp 4B 48
Spring Hill Cl. DN5: Sprot 3C 54
Spring Hill Rd. S10: Shef 2B 118
S72: Grim 3A 20
Spring Ho. Cl. S42: Ash 3A 166
Spring Ho. Rd. S10: Shef 2B 118
Spring La. DN5: Sprot 6C 38
S2: Shef 6B 120
S71: Car 6A 10
WF4: Wool 2B 8
Spring Lane Stop (ST) 6B 120
Spring Pl. S40: C'fld 5H 167
Spring Ram Bus. Pk. S75: Kexb 4D 6
Springs Leisure Cen. 2C 134
Spring St. S3: Shef 1E 5 (2F 119)
S65: Roth 3F 97
S70: Barn 2D 30
SPRING VALE 4E 177
Spring Va. Av. S70: Wors 6E 31
Spring Va. Rd. S43: Brim 6C 162
Springvale Rd. S6: Shef 2C 118
S10: Shef 2A 118
S72: Grim 3A 20
Springvale Wlk. S6: Shef 1C 118
Spring Vw. Rd. S10: Shef 2B 118
Spring Wlk. S65: Roth 3F 97
(off Carlisle St.)
S73: Womb 6E 33
Spring Water Av. S12: Shef 5B 136
Spring Water Cl. S12: Shef 5A 136
Spring Water Dr. S12: Shef 5B 136
Springwell S20: Beig 4F 137
Springwell Av. S20: Beig 4F 137
Springwell Cl. S66: Malt 4C 102
Springwell Ct. WF9: Hems 1F 13
Springwell Cres. S20: Beig 4F 137
Springwell Gdns. DN4: Balb 6G 55
Springwell Gro. S20: Beig 4F 137
Springwell Hill S21: Neth Han 6H 157

Springwell La. DN4: Balb 6G 55
DN11: A'ley 6G 55
Springwell Pk. Dr. S43: Ink 1H 169
Springwood S5: Shef 2D 106
Springwood Av. S26: Augh 5B 124
Spring Wood Cl. S41: C'fld 6D 160
Springwood Cl. DN3: Brant 5G 59
Springwood Ct. S26: Aston 5C 124
S43: New W 2C 162
Springwood Gro. S63: Thurn 3B 36
Springwood Ho. DN1: Don 2B 56
(off Elsworth Cl.)
Springwood La. S35: High G 1B 78
Springwood Rd. DN5: Scawt 2F 39
S8: Shef 2F 133
S74: Hoyl 1H 61
Springwood St. S42: Tem N 6G 173
Springwood Vw. S36: Pen 4F 177
SPROTBROUGH 3C 54
Sprotbrough Flash Nature Reserve . . .6B 54
SPROTBROUGH PARK 3E 55
Sprotbrough Rd. DN5: Don 1G 55
Spruce Av. S66: Wick 5H 99
S71: R'ton 3G 9
Spruce Cl. S40: Bramp 6C 166
Spruce Cres. DN9: Auck 3B 76
Spruce Ri. S21: Killa 5B 152
Spry La. DN5: Clay 4H 21
Spurley Hey Gro. S36: Stoc 4E 175
Spurr St. S2: Shef 6G 119
Square, The S26: Wales 6G 139
S42: Cut 1A 166
(not continuous)
S62: H'ley 5A 62
S70: Barn 2C 30
S72: Grim 2C 20
Square W., The
S66: Sunn 3H 99
Square W., The
S66: Sunn 3G 99
Squirrel Cft. S61: Wing 4A 82
Stable Gdns. DN5: Sprot 4D 54
Stables, The S64: Swin 3A 66
Stables La. DN5: Barnb 6H 37
Stables Way S63: Wath D 5G 49
Stacey Bank S6: Lox 2A 104
Stacey Cres. S72: Grim 1A 20
Stacey Dr. S65: Thry 5E 85
Stacey La. S6: Lox 2A 104
Stackyard, The S71: Ard 2E 33
Stacye Av. S13: Shef 2E 137
Stacye Ri. S13: Shef 2E 137
Stadium Ct. S62: P'gte 6F 83
Stadium Way DN4: Don 3D 56
S9: Shef 1C 120
S60: Roth 1G 97
Stafford Cl. S18: Dron W 2B 154
Stafford Cres. S60: Roth 3G 111
Stafford Dr. S60: Roth 3G 111
Stafford La. S2: Shef 4A 120
Stafford M. S2: Shef 4A 120
Stafford Pl. DN12: Den M 3C 68
Stafford Rd. DN6: Woodl 4D 22
S2: Shef 4A 120
Staffordshire Cl. S66: Malt 5C 102
Stafford St. S2: Shef 5H 5 (4H 119)
Stafford Way S35: Chap 3E 79
Stag Cl. S60: Roth 1B 112
Stag Cres. S60: Roth 1B 112
Stag La. S60: Roth 1A 112
Stag Willow Cl. S60: Roth 1A 112
STAINBOROUGH 6H 29
Stainborough Cl. S75: Dod 4G 29
Stainborough Rd. S75: Dod 4G 29
Stainborough Vw. S70: Wors 5E 31
S75: Pil 6C 44
STAINCROSS 4A 8
Staincross Comn. S75: Stain 3A 8
Staindrop Cl. S35: Chap 2E 79
Staindrop Vw. S35: Chap 2F 79
Stainforth Rd.
DN3: Barn D 1C 26, 1H 27
Stainley Cl. S75: Barn 4A 16
Stainmore Av. S20: Sot 6H 137
Stainmore Cl. S75: Silk 2A 28
STAINTON 2F 103
Stainton Cl. S71: Smi 2D 16
Stainton La. DN11: Wils 6F 89
S66: Malt, Stain 3C 102
Stainton Rd. S11: Shef 6A 118

Stainton St.—Stoneacre Dr.

Stainton St. DN12: Den M 3C **68**
STAIRFOOT 2B 32
Stairfoot Bus. Pk. S70: Stair 3B **32**
Stairfoot Way S70: Stair 3B **32**
Stair Rd. S4: Shef 4H **107**
Staithes Wlk. DN12: Den M 2D **68**
Stalker Lees Rd. S11: Shef 6C **118**
Stalker Wlk. S11: Shef 5D **118**
Stambers Cl. S81: Woods 5F **143**
Stamford Rd. S66: Sunn 2G **99**
Stamford St. S9: Shef 5C **108**
Stamford Way S75: Stain 4A **8**
Stanage Ri. S12: Shef 3H **135**
Stanage Way S40: C'fld 3A **166**
Stanbury Cl. S75: Barn 4A **16**
Standall Cl. S18: Dron W 1A **154**
Standhill Cres. S71: Smi 1D **16**
Standish Av. S5: Shef 4F **107**
Standish Bank S5: Shef 4F **107**
Standish Cl. S5: Shef 3F **107**
Standish Dr. S5: Shef 3F **107**
Standish Gdns. S5: Shef 3F **107**
Standish Rd. S5: Shef 3F **107**
Standish Way S5: Shef 4F **107**
Standon Cres. S9: Shef 5D **94**
Standon Dr. S9: Shef 5D **94**
Standon Rd. S9: Shef 5D **94**
Stand Pk. Ind. Est.
S41: C'fld 1H **167**
Stand Rd. S41: C'fld 6G **161**
Staneford Ct. S20: Water 1E **151**
Stanford Cl. S66: Malt 6D **102**
Stanford Rd. S18: Dron W 3B **154**
Stanford Way S42: W'ton 2C **170**
Stanhope Av. S75: Cawt 3A **14**
Stanhope Gdns. S75: Barn 5B **16**
Stanhope Mdws. S75: Cawt 3A **14**
Stanhope Rd. DN1: Don 5D **40**
S12: Shef 3F **135**
Stanhope St. S70: Barn 1C **30**
Stanier Ct. S41: Has 3B **172**
Staniforth Av. S21: Ecki 1C **158**
Staniforth Cres. S26: Tod 3B **140**
Staniforth Rd. S9: Shef 1C **120**
Stanley Av. S43: Ink 2G **169**
Stanley Ct. *S66: Malt 5G **101***
(off Leslie Av.)
Stanley Gdns. DN4: Balb 3A **56**
Stanley Gro. S26: Aston 6D **124**
(not continuous)
Stanley La. S3: Shef 1G **5** (1G **119**)
Stanley Rd. DN5: Scaws 3E **39**
S8: Shef 3G **133**
S35: Chap 2C **78**
S36: Stoc 4E **175**
S70: Stair 2B **32**
Stanley Sq. DN3: Kirk Sa 4C **26**
Stanley St. S3: Shef 1F **5** (1G **119**)
S21: Killa 3C **152**
S41: C'fld 6B **168**
S60: Roth 4E **97**
S70: Barn 1C **30**
S72: Cud 3F **19**
Stanley Ter. S66: Malt 5G **101**
STANNINGTON 6D 104
Stannington Glen S6: Stan 6F **105**
Stannington Ri. S6: Shef 5H **105**
Stannington Rd. S6: Shef, Stan 6C **104**
Stannington Vw. Rd. S10: Shef 2H **117**
Stanton Cres. S12: Shef 4G **135**
Stanwell Av. S9: Shef 6D **94**
Stanwell Cl. S9: Shef 6D **94**
Stanwell St. S9: Shef 6D **94**
Stanwell Wlk. S9: Shef 6D **94**
Stanwood Av. S6: Shef 6G **105**
Stanwood Cres. S6: Shef 6G **105**
Stanwood Dr. S6: Shef 6G **105**
S42: W'ton 2C **170**
Stanwood M. S6: Shef 6G **105**
Stanwood Rd. S6: Shef 6G **105**
Staple Grn. S65: Thry 6F **85**
Stapleton Rd. DN4: Warm 1E **71**
Star La. DN12: Con 4F **69**
S70: Barn 1D **30**
Starling Cl. S63: Wath D 4F **49**
Starling Mead S2: Shef 4A **120**
Starnhill Cl. S35: Eccl 1H **93**
Station App. *DN1: Don 1B **56***
(off Factory La.)
Station Bk. La. S41: C'fld 5A **168**
Station Cl. DN9: Blax 2E **77**
Station Cotts. S75: Dart 5F **7**
Station Ct. DN1: Don 1B **56**
S25: Sth A 3G **141**
Station La. DN9: Blax 2F **77**
S9: Shef 2D **108**
S18: App 3D **156**
S35: Ough 3E **91**
S41: Old W 4H **161**
S43: New W 4H **161**
Station La. Ind. Est.
S41: Old W 4A **162**
Station Rd. DN3: Barn D 2C **26**
DN5: Ark 1C **40**
DN6: Adw S, Carc 1E **23**
DN9: Blax 3F **77**
DN11: Ross 5D **74**
DN12: Con 3F **69**
S9: Shef 2F **121**
S13: Shef 2D **136**
S20: Half, Mosb 3E **151**
S21: Ecki, Reni 1F **159**
S21: Killa 4A **152**
S25: Laugh C 3F **127**
S26: Kiv P 6A **140**
S35: Chap 3G **79**
S35: Eccl 1H **93**
S36: Spink 3H **175**
S41: C'fld 5A **168**
S41: Whit M 5H **161**
S43: Bar H 3G **163**
S43: Brim 6B **162**
S43: Hol 5E **163**
S60: Cat 6D **110**
S60: Roth 4C **96**
S60: Tree 2F **123**
S63: Bolt D 2B **50**
S63: Thurn 2C **36**
S63: Wath D 6G **49**
S64: Mexb 2F **67**
(not continuous)
S70: Barn 6C **16**
S70: Wors 6H **31**
S71: Lund 3C **18**
S71: R'ton 1G **9**
S73: Womb 1H **47**
(not continuous)
S75: Dart 5F **7**
S75: Dod 3F **29**
Station Rd. Ind. Est. S73: Womb 6H **33**
Station St. S64: Swin 3C **66**
Station Ter. S43: Brim 6B **162**
S71: R'ton 2B **10**
Station Way S25: Laugh C 3F **127**
Staton Av. S20: Beig 4H **137**
Statutes, The S60: Roth 4E **97**
Staunton Cl. S40: Birdh 4H **171**
Staunton Rd. DN4: Can 5D **58**
STAVELEY 4B 164
Staveley La. S21: Ecki 2F **159**
S21: Neth Han 5A **158**
S43: Bar H 5A **158**
S43: Stav 2F **159**
Staveley Northern Loop Rd.
S43: Stav 3B **164**
Staveley Rd. S8: Shef 1F **133**
S43: New W 3D **162**
S43: Pool 6C **164**
Staveley St. DN12: New E 3C **70**
Stayers Rd. DN4: Bess 2C **74**
Steade Rd. S7: Shef 1E **133**
Steadfield Rd. S74: Hoyl 2G **61**
Steadfolds Cl. S66: Thurc 6D **114**
Steadfolds Gdns. S66: Thurc 6D **114**
Steadfolds La. S66: Thurc 5C **114**
Steadfolds Ri. S66: Thurc 6D **114**
Steadlands, The S62: Rawm 6E **65**
Stead La. S74: Hoyl 1G **61**
Stead M. S21: Ecki 1E **159**
Stead St. S21: Ecki 1E **159**
STEEL BANK 1B 118
Steel City Plaza S1: Shef 3D **4** (3F **119**)
Steele Av. S43: Ink 2G **169**
Steele St. S74: Hoyl 1F **61**
Steelhouse La. S3: Shef 1E **5**
Steel Rd. S11: Shef 6B **118**
Steel St. S61: Roth 5B **96**
Steeping Cl. S43: Brim 6D **162**
Steep La. S36: H'swne 3F **177**
S42: W'orth 6B **170**
Steeplegate S40: C'fld 5H **167**
Steeple Grange S41: C'fld 1C **172**
Steeton Ct. S74: Els 6D **46**
Stella Ho. S65: Dalt 1B **98**
Stemp St. S11: Shef 6E **119**
Stenson Ct. DN4: Balb 4H **55**
Stenton Rd. S8: Shef 3E **147**
Stentons Ter. S64: Mexb 2G **67**
Stephen Dr. S10: Shef 3G **117**
S35: Gren 2A **92**
STEPHEN HILL 3G 117
Stephen Hill S10: Shef 3G **117**
Stephen Hill Rd. S10: Shef 3G **117**
Stephen La. S35: Gren 2A **92**
Stephenson Ct. S40: Bramp 6C **166**
Stephenson Hall of Residence
S10: Shef 5B **118**
Stephenson Pl. S40: C'fld 5H **167**
S64: Swin 2C **66**
Stephenson Rd. S43: Stav 5B **164**
Stephenson Way
S60: Wav 3C **122**
Stepney St. S2: Shef 2H **5** (2H **119**)
Stepping La. S35: Gren 1A **92**
Sterland St. S40: C'fld 5F **167**
Sterndale Rd. S7: Shef 5B **132**
Steven Cl. S35: Chap 4E **79**
Steven Cres. S35: Chap 3E **79**
Steven Mangle Cl. S12: Shef 6H **135**
Steven Pl. S35: Chap 4E **79**
Stevenson Dr. S65: Roth 5A **98**
S75: High'm 4F **15**
Stevenson Ho. *S41: C'fld 2A **168***
(off Tapton Lock Hill)
Stevenson Rd. DN4: Balb 6A **56**
S9: Shef 5C **108**
(Alfred Rd.)
S9: Shef 6B **108**
(St Charles St.)
Stevenson Way S9: Shef 6C **108**
Stevens Rd. DN4: Balb 3A **56**
Steventon Rd. S65: Thry 6F **85**
Stewart Rd. S11: Shef 6C **118**
Stewarts Rd. S62: Rawm 2A **84**
Stewart St. DN1: Don 2B **56**
STICKING HILL 5D 50
Sticking La. S64: Mexb 5C **50**
Stillman Cl. S41: Has 2B **172**
Stirling Cl. S74: Els 6D **46**
Stirling Ct. S41: C'fld 4H **167**
Stirling La. DN5: Scawt 3G **39**
Stirling St. DN1: Don 2B **56**
Stirling Way S2: Shef 6D **120**
Stockarth La. S35: Ough 5F **91**
Stockarth Pl. S35: Ough 6G **91**
STOCKBRIDGE 1B 40
Stockbridge Av. DN5: Don 3H **39**
Stockbridge Cvn. Site DN5: Bntly 1B **40**
Stockbridge La. DN5: Bntly 1B **40**
Stockil Rd. DN4: Don 2D **56**
Stockingate WF9: Sth K 5H **13**
Stock Rd. S2: Shef 5B **120**
STOCKSBRIDGE 3E 175
Stocksbridge & District Golf Course
5F 175
Stocksbridge Leisure Cen. 3C 174
Stocks Grn. Ct. S17: Tot 6E **145**
Stocks Grn. Dr. S17: Tot 6E **145**
Stocks Hill S35: Eccl 1F **93**
Stockshill Cl. S71: Car 5H **9**
Stock's La. S62: Rawm 3G **83**
S75: Barn 6B **16**
Stockton Cl. S3: Shef 1G **119**
Stockwell Av. S26: Kiv P 1H **153**
Stockwell Ct. S75: Wool G 3E **7**
Stockwell Grn. S71: Monk B 3G **17**
Stockwell La. S26: Wales 1G **153**
Stockwith La. S74: Hoyl 4G **45**
Stocthorn Gap S35: Ough 1D **90**
Stoddart Way S62: P'gte 6G **83**
Stokes Ho. S18: Dron 2D **154**
Stoke St. S9: Shef 1B **120**
Stoket La. S26: Ull 1E **125**
Stokewell Rd. S63: Wath D 5D **48**
Stoneacre Av. S12: Shef 5C **136**
Stoneacre Cl. S12: Shef 5C **136**
Stoneacre Dr. S12: Shef 6C **136**

Stoneacre Ri. S12: Shef 5C 136
Stone Bank Ct. S18: Dron 3G 155
Stonebridge La. S72: Gt H 1F 35
Stonechat Mead S63: Wath D 4F 49
Stonecliffe Cl. S2: Shef 5D 120
Stonecliffe Dr. S36: Stoc 5D 174
Stonecliffe Pl. S2: Shef 5D 120
Stonecliffe Rd. S2: Shef 5D 120
Stonecliffe Wlk. S2: Shef 5E 121
Stonecliff Wlk.
 DN12: Den M 2D 68
Stone Cl. S18: Coal A 1H 155
 S26: Kiv P 6B 140
 S65: Rav 3A 100
Stone Cl. Av. DN4: Hex 2A 56
Stone Cotts. DN5: Bntly 3G 23
Stone Cl. S72: Sth H 1H 11
Stone Cres. S66: Wick 5G 99
Stone Cft. DN4: Bess 6C 58
 S70: Barn 2A 30
Stonecroft Ct. S75: Silk C 5A 28
Stonecroft M. S66: B'well 1B 102
Stonecroft Rd. S17: Tot 5G 145
Stone Cross Dr. DN5: Sprot 2C 54
Stonecross Gdns. DN4: Can 4D 58
Stone Dell S10: Shef 5D 116
Stone Font Gro. DN4: Can 5C 58
Stonefont Gro. S72: Grim 1B 20
Stonegarth Cl. S72: Cud 2E 19
Stonegate M. DN4: Balb 4A 56
STONEGRAVELS 3H 167
Stonegravels Cft. S20: Half 4F 151
Stonegravels La. S41: C'fld 3H 167
Stonegravels Way S20: Half 4G 151
Stone Gro. S10: Shef 3C 118
Stonehill Cl. S74: Hoyl 5H 45
Stone Hill Dr. S26: Swal 1C 138
Stonehill Ri. DN5: Scawt 2F 39
 S36: Cub 6C 176
 S72: Cud 2E 19
Stone La. S13: Shef 3B 136
 S43: New W 2C 162
Stonelea Cl. S75: Silk 2A 28
Stone Leigh S75: Pil 1C 60
Stoneleigh Cl. S25: Din 1C 142
Stoneleigh Cft. S70: Barn 3E 31
Stoneley Cl. S12: Shef 1E 149
Stoneley Cres. S13: Shef 1E 149
Stoneley Dell S12: Shef 1E 149
Stoneley Dr. S70: Shef 1E 149
Stonelow Rd. S18: Dron 2G 155
 (off Stonelow Rd.)
Stonelow Cres. S18: Dron 2H 155
Stonelow Grn. S18: Dron 2G 155
Stonelow Rd. S18: Dron 2G 155
Stonely Brook S65: Rav 4A 100
Stone Moor Rd. S36: Bolst, Stoc 4C 174
Stone Pk. Cl. S66: Malt 5C 102
Stone Riding DN12: New E 1E 89
Stone Ridings DN12: New E 5B 70
Stone Rd. S18: Coal A 6H 147
Stone Row S40: C'fld 6F 167
Stone Row Ct. S75: Pil 2C 60
Stonerow Way S60: Roth 1F 97
Stonesdale Cl. S20: Mosb 3E 151
Stones Inge S35: High G 1C 78
Stone St. S20: Mosb 3E 151
 S71: Barn 4D 16
Stoneway M. S35: Green M 1G 175
Stonewood Ct. S10: Shef 4E 117
Stonewood Gro. S10: Shef 4E 117
 S74: Hoyl 2B 62
Stoney Bank Dr. S26: Kiv P 6B 140
Stoney Cft. S74: Hoyl 1G 61
Stoneycroft La. S42: W'orth 6B 170
Stoneycroft Rd. S13: Shef 4A 122
Stoney Ga. S35: High G 6C 60
Stoney Royd S71: Ath 5E 9
Stoney Well La. S66: Malt 6F 103
Stonyford Rd. S73: Womb 6A 34
Stony La. S6: Brad 1A 104
Stony Wlk. S6: Shef 5B 106
Stoops Cl. S40: C'fld 2E 167
Stoops La. DN4: Bess 5G 57
Stoops Rd. DN4: Bess 5A 58
Stopes Rd. S6: Stan 6A 104
Stoppard Row S40: Bramp 6D 166
Store St. S2: Shef 5G 119
Storey's Ga. S73: Womb 1E 47

Storey St. S64: Swin 3B 66
Storforth La.
 S40: Birdh, Has 3H 171
 S41: Has 3H 171
Storforth La. Ter. S41: Has 2B 172
Storforth La. Trad. Est.
 S41: Has 2A 172
Stormont Gro. S43: Ink 1H 169
Storrs Bri. La. S6: Shef 3B 104
STORRS 5B 104
Storrs Carr S6: Stan 4A 104
Storrs Grn. S6: Stan 4A 104
Storrs Hall Rd. S6: Shef 6A 106
Storrs La. S6: Stan 5B 104
 S35: Brom 4A 60
 S36: Oxs 4H 177
Storrs Mill La. S72: Cud 6H 19
Storrs Rd. S40: Bramp 6C 166
Storrs Wood Vw. S72: Cud 4G 19
Storth Av. S10: Shef 6F 117
Storth Hollow Cft. S10: Shef 5F 117
Storth La. S10: Shef 5F 117
 S26: Kiv P, Tod 5G 139
 S35: Wharn S 1B 90, 2A 90
Stortholme M. S10: Shef 5F 117
Storth Pk. S10: Shef 1E 131
Storthwood Ct. S10: Shef 5F 117
Stotfold Dr. S63: Thurn 2B 36
Stotfold Rd. DN5: Clay, Hoot P 1E 37
Stothard Cl. S10: Shef 2A 118
Stothard Rd. S10: Shef 2A 118
Stottercliffe Rd.
 S36: Pen, Thurl 4B 176
Stour Cl. S43: Brim 6D 162
Stour La. S6: Shef 2G 105
Stovin Cl. S9: Shef 5E 109
Stovin Dr. S9: Shef 6E 109
Stovin Gdns. S9: Shef 6E 109
Stow Bri. La. S60: Up W 6D 112
Stowe Av. S7: Shef 4B 132
Stradbroke Av. S13: Shef 1G 135
Stradbroke Cl. S13: Shef 1H 135
Stradbroke Cres. S13: Shef 1H 135
Stradbroke Dr. S13: Shef 1H 135
Stradbroke Pl. S13: Shef 1H 135
Stradbroke Ri. S40: W'ton 2D 170
Stradbroke Rd. S13: Shef 1G 135
Stradbroke Wlk. S13: Shef 1G 135
Stradbroke Way S13: Shef 1H 135
Strafford Av. S70: Wors 4E 31
 S74: Els 6D 46
Strafford Gro. S70: Birdw 1E 61
Strafford Ind. Pk. S75: Dod 5H 29
Strafford Pl. S61: Thorpe H 3B 80
Strafford Rd. DN2: Don 5D 40
 S61: Kimb P 6H 81
Strafford St. S75: Kexb 6D 6
Strafforth Wlk. S75: Dod 4G 29
Strafforth Ho. DN12: Den M 3B 68
 (off Ravenscar Cl.)
Straight La. S63: Gol 5D 36
Straight Riding DN12: New E 6D 70
Strait La. S63: Wath D 6F 49
Stratford Rd. S10: Shef 5E 117
Stratford Way S66: Bram 6B 100
Strathmore Gro. S63: Wath D 6G 49
Strathmore Rd. DN2: Don 1F 57
Strathtay Rd. S11: Shef 1A 132
Strauss Cres. S66: Malt 6C 102
Strawberry Av. S5: Shef 4G 93
Strawberry Gdns. S71: R'ton 2H 9
Strawberry Lee La. S17: Tot 5C 144
Straw La. S6: Shef 1D 118
Streatfield Cres. DN11: New R 6B 74
STREET 4H 63
Streetfield Cres. S20: Mosb 4E 151
Streetfield La. S20: Half 4F 151
Streetfields S20: Half 4F 151
Street La. S62: Wentw 4G 63
Strelley Av. S8: Shef 1D 146
Strelley Rd. S8: Shef 1D 146
 S71: Ath 6D 8
Stretton Cl. DN4: Can 4D 58
Stretton Rd. S11: Shef 1B 132
 S71: Monk B 3F 17
Stride, The S6: Birdh 3G 171
Strines Ho. S10: Shef 5A 116
 (off Holyrood Av.)
Stringers Cft. S60: Whis 3C 112

Stripe Rd.
 DN11: New R, Ross, Tick
 . . . . .5D 74, 6H 75
Struan Rd. S7: Shef 3B 132
Strutt Rd. S3: Shef 5F 107
Stuart Cl. S41: C'fld 2B 168
Stuart Gro. S35: Chap 4G 79
Stuart Rd. S35: Chap 4G 79
Stuart St. S63: Thurn 2D 36
STUBBIN 3G 175
Stubbin Cl. S62: Rawm 1E 83
STUBBING .1D 104
Stubbing Ho. La. S6: Shef 3H 91
Stubbing La. S35: Ough 1D 104
Stubbing Riding DN12: New E 5D 70
Stubbing Rd. S40: Birdh 3G 171
Stubbin La. S5: Shef 6H 93
 S62: Rawm 6D 64
 (not continuous)
Stubbin Rd. S62: Neth Hau, Rawm . . .1C 82
Stubbins Hill DN12: New E 4C 70
Stubbs Cres. S61: Kimb P 1A 96
Stubbs Rd. S73: Womb 2F 47
Stubbs Wlk. S61: Kimb P 1A 96
Stubley Cl. S18: Dron W 1D 154
Stubley Cft. S18: Dron W 2C 154
Stubley Hollow S18: Dron 1D 154
Stubley La. S18: Dron, Dron W 2C 154
Stubley Pl. S18: Dron 2D 154
Studfield Cres. S6: Shef 4G 105
Studfield Dr. S6: Shef 3G 105
Studfield Gro. S6: Shef 4G 105
STUDFIELD HILL 4G 105
Studfield Hill S6: Lox, Shef 4F 105
Studfield Ri. S6: Shef 3G 105
Studfield Rd. S6: Shef 3G 105
Studios, The S40: C'fld 5F 167
 (off School Board La.)
Studley Ct. S9: Shef 2F 121
Studley Gdns. DN3: Kirk Sa 4B 26
Studmoor Rd. S61: Kimb P 6G 81
Studmoor Wlk. S61: Kimb P 6G 81
STUMP CROSS 4G 63
Stump Cross Ct. S63: Wath D 1F 65
 (off Stump Cross Rd.)
Stump Cross Gdns. S63: Bolt D 2A 50
Stump Cross Rd. S63: Wath D 1F 65
STUMPERLOWE 6E 117
Stumperlowe Av. S10: Shef 6F 117
Stumperlowe Cl. S10: Shef 6F 117
Stumperlowe Cres. Rd.
 S10: Shef 6E 117
Stumperlowe Cft. S10: Shef 5E 117
Stumperlowe Hall Chase
 S10: Shef 5E 117
Stumperlowe Hall Rd.
 S10: Shef 6E 117
Stumperlowe La. S10: Shef 6E 117
Stumperlowe Mans. S10: Shef 6E 117
Stumperlowe Pk. Rd. S10: Shef 6E 117
Stumperlowe Vw. S10: Shef 5E 117
Stupton Rd. S9: Shef 2D 108
Sturge Cft. S2: Shef 2G 133
Sturton Cl. DN4: Bess 6H 57
Sturton Cft. S65: Dalt 1D 98
Sturton Rd. S4: Shef 4H 107
Sub Station La. S41: Whit M 6H 161
 (off Sheffield Rd.)
Sudbury Cl. S40: C'fld 3C 166
Sudbury Dr. S26: Aston 1D 138
Sudbury St. S3: Shef 1B 4 (1E 119)
Sudhall Cl. S41: C'fld 6E 161
Sudhall Dr. S41: C'fld 6E 161
Suffolk Cl. S25: Nth A 2H 141
Suffolk La. S2: Shef 6G 5 (4G 119)
Suffolk Rd. DN4: Balb 6A 56
 S2: Shef 5F 5 (4G 119)
Suffolk Vw. DN12: Den M 4C 68
Sulby Gro. S70: Stair 4A 32
Summerdale Rd. S72: Cud 2D 18
SUMMERFIELD 4B 118
Summerfield S10: Shef 4B 118
 S65: Roth 4F 97
Summerfield Cres. S43: Brim 6C 162
Summerfield Rd. S18: Dron 1G 155
 S40: C'fld 1G 171
Summerfields Dr. DN9: Blax 1F 77
Summerfield St. S11: Shef 5D 118

Summer La.—Tap La.

Summer La. S17: Tot 6E 145
S70: Barn 6B 16
S71: R'ton 2G 9
S73: Womb 1E 47
S75: Barn 6B 16
SUMMERLEY 2B 156
Summerley Lwr. Rd. S18: App 2B 156
Summerley Rd. S18: App 2B 156
Summerley Wlk. S40: C'fld 3E 167
Summer Rd. S71: R'ton 2G 9
Summerskill Grn. S43: Ink 1H 169
Summer St. S3: Shef 2A 4 (2D 118)
S70: Barn 6C 16
(not continuous)
Summer Vw. S71: R'ton 3G 9
Summerwood Cft. S18: Dron 2E 155
Summerwood La. S18: Dron 1E 155
Summerwood Pl. S18: Dron 2E 155
Summit Dr. DN4: Bess 2C 74
Sumner Rd. S65: Roth 2G 97
Sunbury Ct. S10: Shef 4B 118
Sunderland St. S11: Shef 5D 118
Sunderland Ter. S70: Barn 2F 31
Sundew Cft. S35: High G 6C 60
Sundew Gdns. S35: High G 6C 60
Sundown Pl. S13: Shef 6A 122
Sundown Rd. S13: Shef 6A 122
Sunflower Gdns. DN4: Bess 4G 57
Sunflower Gro. S5: Shef 1C 108
Sunlea Flats *S65: Roth* *3G 97*
(off Ridge Rd.)
Sunningdale Av. S75: Dart 5H 7
Sunningdale Cl. DN4: Can 6E 59
S40: W'ton 2F 171
S64: Swin 5C 66
Sunningdale Dr. DN12: New E 5B 70
S72: Cud 6F 11
Sunningdale Mt. S11: Shef 3A 132
Sunningdale Ri. S40: W'ton 2D 170
Sunningdale Rd. DN2: Don 5F 41
DN4: Balb 5A 56
S25: Din 6A 128
Sunny Bank S10: Shef 6A 4 (5D 118)
S35: High G 1C 78
S74: Jum 5C 46
Sunnybank DN3: Eden 1D 42
Sunnybank Cres. S60: Brins 4D 110
Sunny Bank Dr. S72: Cud 3E 19
Sunnybank Nature Reserve
....6A 4 (5D 118)
Sunny Bank Ri. S74: Els 6D 46
Sunny Bank Rd. S36: Bolst 6E 175
S75: Silk 2A 28
Sunny Bar DN1: Don 1C 56
Sunnybrook Cl. S74: Hoyl 2B 62
SUNNYFIELDS 3E 39
SUNNYSIDE
DN3 ....5C 26
S66 ....2G 99
Sunnyside DN3: Brant 4H 59
DN3: Eden 5B 26
Sunnyside Cl. S25: Nth A 2H 141
Sunny Springs S41: C'fld 4H 167
Sunnyvale Av. S17: Tot 6E 145
Sunnyvale Rd. S17: Tot 6E 145
Sunnyview Pk. DN11: A'ley 2G 71
Sunrise Mnr. S74: Hoyl 5B 46
Superbowl 2000
Rotherham 2H 95
Surbiton St. S9: Shef 4E 109
Surrey Cl. S70: Barn 3E 31
Surrey La. S1: Shef 5F 5 (4G 119)
Surrey Pl. S1: Shef 4F 5 (3G 119)
Surrey St. DN4: Balb 5A 56
S1: Shef 4E 5 (3F 119)
Surtees Cl. S66: Malt 3H 101
Sussex Gdns. DN12: Den M 3C 68
Sussex Rd. S4: Shef 1H 119
S35: Chap 3F 79
Sussex St. DN4: Balb 5A 56
S4: Shef 1H 5 (1H 119)
Suthard Cross Rd. S10: Shef 2A 118
Sutherland Ho. DN2: Don 4F 41
Sutherland Rd. S4: Shef 6H 107
Sutherland St. S4: Shef 6A 108
Sutton Av. S71: Ath 6E 9
Sutton Cres. S43: Ink 1H 169
Sutton La. S44: Ark T, Sut S 6H 173
Sutton Rd. DN3: Kirk Sa 3D 26
SUTTON SPRING WOOD 4G 173
Sutton St. DN4: Hex 3H 55
S3: Shef 3A 4 (3D 118)
Sutton Vw. S42: Tem N 6G 173
Swaddale Av. S41: C'fld 2A 168
Swaddale Cl. S41: C'fld 2A 168
Swaith Av. DN5: Scawt 3G 39
SWAITHE 5B 32
Swaithedale S70: Wors 5H 31
Swaithe Vw. S70: Wors 5A 32
S75: Wool G 4F 7
Swalebank Cl. S40: C'fld 2A 172
Swale Cl. S63: Bolt D 2C 50
Swale Ct. S60: Roth 2G 111
Swaledale Dr. S73: Womb 1H 47
Swaledale Rd. S7: Shef 3C 132
Swale Dr. S35: Chap 3D 78
Swale Gdns. S9: Shef 2F 121
Swale Rd. S61: Wing 5B 82
Swallow Cl. S70: Birdw 4E 45
S75: Kexb 6E 7
Swallow Ct. DN11: Ross 5D 74
Swallow Cres. S62: Rawm 2A 84
Swallow Dale DN12: New E 4C 70
SWALLOW HILL 1H 15
Swallow Hill Rd. S75: Bar G 1H 15
Swallow La. S26: Aston 2D 138
SWALLOWNEST 1B 138
Swallownest Ct. S26: Swal 6B 124
Swallowood Ct. S63: Bramp B 6A 48
Swallow's La. S20: Mosb 2D 150
Swallow Wood Cl. S60: Tree 2F 123
Swallow Wood Ct. S13: Shef 2B 136
Swallow Wood Rd. S26: Swal 1H 137
Swamp Wlk. S6: Shef 5C 106
Swanbourne Cl. S41: Has 1B 172
Swanbourne Pl. S5: Shef 6H 93
Swanbourne Rd. S5: Shef 5H 93
Swanee Rd. S70: Barn 3G 31
Swangate S63: Bramp B 5A 48
Swannington Cl. DN4: Can 5E 59
Swan Rd. S26: Aston 2D 138
Swan St. DN5: Bntly 1A 40
S60: Roth 5E 97
Swanwick St. S41: Old W 4H 161
Swarcliffe Rd. S9: Shef 1D 120
SWATHWICK 6F 171
Swathwick Cl. S42: W'orth 6F 171
Swathwick La. S42: W'orth 6A 170
Sweeney Ho. S36: Stoc 3C 174
Sweet La. DN11: Wad 5F 73
Sweyn Cft. S70: Wors 5F 31
Swifte Rd. S60: Roth 1H 111
Swift Ri. S61: Thorpe H 2D 80
Swift Rd. S35: Gren 2C 92
Swift St. S75: Barn 5C 16
Swift Way S2: Shef 5B 120
Swim School, The *2C 162*
(off Red Ho. Cl.)
Swinburne Av. DN4: Balb 6A 56
(not continuous)
DN6: Adw S 3B 22
Swinburne Cl. DN3: Barn D 1H 27
Swinburne Pl. S65: Roth 5A 98
Swinburne Rd. S65: Roth 5A 98
Swinnock La. S35: Bright 1B 90
Swinscoe Way S40: C'fld 3B 166
Swinston Hill Gdns. S25: Din 6B 128
Swinston Hill Mdws. S25: Din 1B 142
Swinston Hill Rd. S25: Din, Nth A 6A 128
SWINTON 3C 66
SWINTON BRIDGE 3E 67
Swinton Meadows Bus. Pk.
S64: Swin 3E 67
Swinton Meadows Ind. Est.
S64: Swin 3E 67
Swinton Rd. S64: Mexb 2E 67
(not continuous)
Swinton Station (Rail) 3D 66
Swinton St. S3: Shef 1F 119
Swithen Farm S75: Haigh 3C 6
Swithland Cl. S41: Has 3B 172
Sycamore Av. DN3: Arm 3F 43
S18: Dron 1F 155
S26: Kiv P 6G 139
S40: C'fld 1F 171
S66: Wick 5H 99
S72: Cud 1E 19
S72: Grim 3C 20
Sycamore Cen. S65: Roth 1A 98
Sycamore Ct. S11: Shef 1B 132
S35: Ough 3E 91
S64: Mexb 1D 66
S71: R'ton 2F 9
Sycamore Cres. S63: Wath D 1H 65
Sycamore Dr. DN9: Auck 1B 76
S21: Killa 5B 152
S44: Cal 5C 168
S66: Thurc 5C 114
S71: R'ton 3F 9
Sycamore Farm Cl. S66: Wick 1G 113
Sycamore Gro. DN4: Can 4C 58
DN12: Con 5D 68
Sycamore Ho. Rd.
S5: Shef 4B 94
Sycamore La. S36: H'swne 1G 177
S43: Hol 5F 163
Sycamore Rd. DN3: Barn D 1C 26
S35: Eccl 2G 93
S36: Stoc 4C 174
S43: Hol 5E 163
S64: Mexb 1D 66
S65: Roth 1A 98
WF9: Hems 1D 12
Sycamores, The DN5: Scawt 2E 39
Sycamore St. S20: Beig 4G 137
S20: Mosb 2D 150
S75: Barn 6B 16
Sycamore Vw. DN5: Sprot 3E 55
Sycamore Wlk. S36: Pen 4D 176
S63: Thurn 2C 36
Sydney Rd. S6: Shef 2C 118
Sydney St. S40: C'fld 5F 167
Sykes Av. S75: Barn 6C 16
Sykes Ct. S64: Swin 5C 66
Sykes St. S70: Barn 3C 30
Sylvan Cl. S41: C'fld 1A 172
S66: Malt 4C 102
Sylvester Av. DN4: Balb 3B 56
Sylvester Gdns. S1: Shef 6E 5 (4F 119)
Sylvester St. S1: Shef 6D 4 (4F 119)
Sylvestria Ct. DN11: Ross 5D 74
Sylvia Cl. S13: Shef 1E 137
Sylvia Rd. S18: Uns 6A 156
Symes Gdns. DN4: Can 3C 58
Symonds Av. S62: Rawm 6D 64
Symons Cres. S5: Shef 6E 93

T

Tadcaster Cl. DN12: Den M 4B 68
Tadcaster Cres. S8: Shef 4E 133
Tadcaster Rd. S8: Shef 4E 133
Tadcaster Way S8: Shef 4E 133
Taddington Rd. S40: C'fld 3C 166
Tait Av. DN12: New E 6C 70
Talbot Av. DN3: Barn D 1C 26
Talbot Circ. DN3: Barn D 1D 26
Talbot Cres. S2: Shef 5H 5 (4H 119)
S41: Has 3C 172
Talbot Gdns. S2: Shef 5H 5 (4H 119)
Talbot Pl. S2: Shef 5H 5 (4H 119)
Talbot Rd. S2: Shef 5H 5 (4H 119)
S36: Pen 3C 176
S64: Swin 3E 67
Talbot St. S2: Shef 5H 5 (4H 119)
S41: Has 3C 172
Talmont Rd. S11: Shef 2A 132
Tamar Cl. S75: High'm 5F 15
Tanfield Cl. S71: R'ton 2F 9
Tanfield Rd. S6: Shef 3C 106
Tanfield Way S66: Wick 6G 99
TANKERSLEY 2E 61
Tankersley La. S74: Hoyl 2E 61
Tankersley Pk. Golf Course 5F 61
Tank Row S71: Stair 1A 32
Tannery Cl. S13: Shef 2C 136
Tannery Ct. S75: Dod 3G 29
Tannery St. S13: Shef 2C 136
Tan Pit La. S63: Gol 1C 50
Tansley Dr. S9: Shef 6E 95
S40: Ash 3B 166
Tansley St. S9: Shef 6E 95
Tansley Way S43: Ink 2H 169
Tanyard S75: Dod 4F 29
Tanyard Cft. S72: Brier 3B 12
Tap La. S40: C'fld 5F 167

Taplin Rd. S6: Shef 4A 106
TAPTON 2B 168
Tapton Bank S10: Shef 4H 117
Tapton Ct. S10: Shef 4A 118
Tapton Cres. Rd. S10: Shef 4H 117
Tapton Grange
 S43: Brim C 3D 168
Tapton Gro. S43: Brim C 3D 168
Tapton Hall of Residence
 . . . . .3B 118
TAPTON HILL 4H 117
Tapton Mnt. Rd. S10: Shef 3H 117
Tapton Ho. Rd. S10: Shef 4A 118
Tapton La. S41: C'fld 5A 168
Tapton Lock Hill S41: C'fld 2A 168
Tapton Lock Vis. Cen. 2A 168
Tapton M. S10: Shef 3A 118
Tapton Mt. Cl. S10: Shef 4A 118
Tapton Pk. Gdns. S10: Shef 5H 117
Tapton Pk. Mt. S10: Shef 5H 117
Tapton Pk. Municipal Golf Course
 . . . . .4B 168
Tapton Pk. Rd. S10: Shef 5G 117
Tapton Ter. S41: C'fld 4A 168
Tapton Va. S41: C'fld 3B 168
Tapton Vw. Rd. S41: C'fld 3F 167
Taptonville Cres.
 S10: Shef 4B 118
Taptonville Head S10: Shef 3B 118
Taptonville Rd. S10: Shef 3B 118
Tapton Wlk. S10: Shef 4A 118
 S41: C'fld 5A 168
 (off Tapton La.)
Tapton Way S44: Cal 5E 169
Tarleton Cl. DN3: Kirk Sa 4D 26
Tarn Rd. S70: Barn 2E 31
 (off Union St.)
Tasker Rd. S10: Shef 2A 118
Tasman Gro. S66: Malt 4H 101
Tatenhill Gdns. DN4: Can 5D 58
Taunton Av. S9: Shef 1E 109
Taunton Gdns. S66: Mexb 6H 51
Taunton Gro. S9: Shef 6E 95
Taverner Cl. S35: High G 5C 60
Taverner Cft. S35: High G 6D 60
Taverner Way S35: High G 6C 60
Tavistock Rd. S7: Shef 2E 133
Tavy Cl. S75: Bar G 3F 15
Tay Cl. S18: Dron W 2C 154
 S75: Mapp 1B 16
Taylor Cres. S41: C'fld 1C 172
 S72: Grim 2C 20
 S81: Woods 5F 143
Taylor Dr. S81: Woods 5F 143
Taylor Hill S75: Cawt 4A 14
Taylor Row S63: Wath D 2E 65
 S70: Barn 2E 31
Taylor's Cl. S62: P'gte 6F 83
Taylor's Cl. S62: P'gte 6G 83
Taylor's La. S62: P'gte 6F 83
Taylor St. DN12: Con 4H 59
Tay St. S6: Shef 2C 118
Teal Cl. S73: Bramp 3B 48
Teal Dr. DN4: Balb 2C 72
Teasdale Rd. S12: Ridg 2A 150
 S61: Wing 5A 82
Teeside Cl. DN5: Scaws 5E 39
Telford Cres. S43: Stav 4C 164
Telford Rd. DN5: Don 5H 39
Telson Cl. S64: Swin 3H 65
Temperance St. S64: Swin 3C 66
Tempest Av. S73: D'fld 3B 34
Templar Cl. S66: Thurc 6A 114
TEMPLEBOROUGH 1B 110
Templeborough Bus. Cen.
 S60: Roth 6D 96
Temple Cl. S60: Roth 6B 96
Temple Cres. S66: Bram 6A 100
Temple Gdns. DN4: Can 5D 58
TEMPLE NORMANTON 6G 173
Temple Normanton By-Pass
 S42: Tem N 6A 170
Temple Rd. S60: Roth 1A 110
Templestowe Ga.
 DN12: Con 4H 59
Temple Way S71: Monk B 5A 18
Templing Cl. S70: Barn 3F 31
Ten Acre Rd. S61: Kimb P 2A 96
Tenby Gdns. DN4: Balb 5H 55

Tennyson Av. DN3: Arm 4E 43
 DN5: Don 6G 39
 S40: C'fld 5G 167
 S64: Mexb 6G 51
Tennyson Cl. S25: Din 6B 128
 S36: Pen 3D 176
Tennyson Ri. S63: Wath D 4D 48
Tennyson Rd. DN5: Bntly 1A 40
 S6: Shef 6C 106
 S65: Roth 5H 97
 S66: Malt 6B 102
 S71: Monk B 4G 17
Tennyson Way S42: Gras 6D 172
Ten Pound Wlk. DN4: Don 4B 56
Tenter Balk La. DN6: Adw S 3B 22
Tenterden Rd. DN5: Shef 6C 94
Tenter Hill S36: Thurl 3A 176
Tenter La. DN4: Warm 6D 54
Tenter Rd. DN4: Warm 6D 54
Tenters Grn. S70: Wors 6E 31
Tenter St. S1: Shef 2D 4 (2F 119)
 S60: Roth 3D 96
Terminus Rd. S7: Shef 5B 132
Terrace, The S5: Shef 1B 108
Terrace Rd. S62: P'gte 4G 83
Terrace Wlk. S11: Shef 6B 118
Terrey Rd. S17: Tot 5F 145
Terry St. S9: Shef 4E 109
Tetney Rd. S10: Shef 4G 117
Tewitt Rd. DN5: Bntly 4H 23
Teynham Dr. S5: Shef 2E 107
Teynham Rd. S5: Shef 2D 106
Thackeray Av. S62: Rawm 1A 84
Thames St. S60: Roth 3D 96
Thatch Pl. S61: Wing 5B 82
The . . . .
 Names prefixed with 'The' for example
 'The Acorn Cen.' are indexed under the
 main name such as 'Acorn Cen., The'
Thealby Gdns. DN4: Bess 5H 57
Theatre La. S41: C'fld 5A 168
Theatre Yd. S40: C'fld 5A 168
 (off Low Pavement)
Thellusson Av. DN5: Scaws 4D 38
Theobald Av. DN4: Don 3E 57
Theobald Cl. DN4: Don 3D 56
Thicket Dr. S66: Malt 4C 102
Thicket La. S41: C'fld 6H 31
Thickett La. S36: Pen 6E 177
Third Av. DN6: Woodl 4D 22
 DN9: Finn 2C 76
Thirlmere Ct. S64: Mexb 6A 52
Thirlmere Dr. S18: Dron 2F 155
 S25: Nth A 2A 142
Thirlmere Gdns. DN3: Kirk Sa 5C 26
Thirlmere Rd. S8: Shef 3D 132
 S41: C'fld 1D 166
 S71: Barn 1F 31
Thirwall Av. DN12: Con 4D 68
Thirlwell Rd. S8: Shef 2F 133
Thirsk Cl. DN12: Den M 4B 68
Thistley Cl. S72: Grim 6A 12
Thomas St. DN12: New E 5C 70
 S1: Shef 5C 4 (4E 119)
 S26: Kiv P 6A 140
 S64: Kiln 1E 85
 S64: Swin 2C 66
 S70: Barn 2E 31
 S70: Wors 5F 31
 S73: D'fld 5C 34
Thompson Av. DN12: New E 4C 70
Thompson Cl. S41: Whit M 6H 161
 S62: Rawm 6D 64
 S66: Malt 3H 101
Thompson Dr. S64: Swin 5B 66
Thompson Gdns. S35: High G 6B 60
Thompson Hill S35: High G 1B 78
Thompson Rd. S11: Shef 5C 118
 S73: Womb 2G 47
Thompson St. S41: Whit M 5H 161
 (not continuous)
Thomson Av. DN4: Balb 5G 55
Thomson Cl. S63: Wath D 6G 49
Thoresby Av. DN4: Don 3E 57
 S71: Monk B 5H 17
Thoresby Cl. S26: Aston 1E 139
Thoresby Pl. S43: Ink 2H 169
Thoresby Rd. S6: Shef 5B 106

Thornborough Cl. S2: Shef 1H 133
Thornborough Pl. S2: Shef 1H 133
Thornborough Rd. S2: Shef 1G 133
Thornbridge Av. S12: Shef 5G 135
Thornbridge Cl. S12: Shef 5G 135
Thornbridge Cres. S12: Shef 5H 135
 S40: Birdh 4G 171
Thornbridge Dr. S12: Shef 5G 135
Thornbridge Gro. S12: Shef 5G 135
Thornbridge La. S12: Shef 5H 135
Thornbridge Pl. S12: Shef 5G 135
Thornbridge Ri. S12: Shef 5H 135
Thornbridge Rd. S12: Shef 6G 135
Thornbridge Way S75: Tank 1D 60
Thorndale Ri. S60: Brins 4E 111
Thorndene Cl. S41: C'fld 2G 167
Thorndon Way S40: W'ton 2D 170
Thorne Cl. S42: Ash 4A 166
 S71: Smi 1D 16
Thorne End Rd. S75: Stain 4A 8
Thornely Av. S75: Dod 2G 29
Thornely Sq. S75: Dod 3G 29
Thorne Rd. DN1: Don 1C 56
 DN2: Don 6E 41
 DN3: Eden 1B 42
 DN9: Blax 1F 77
 S7: Shef 3D 132
Thornfield Av. S40: Bramp 1C 170
Thornfield Ct. S41: C'fld 3H 167
Thorn Gth. DN5: Don 4H 39
Thornham Cl. DN3: Arm 5E 43
Thornham Mdws. S63: Gol 5E 37
THORN HILL 2D 96
Thornhill Av. DN2: Don 4G 41
 S60: Brins 5C 110
Thornhill Dr. S70: Barn 3E 31
Thornhill Edge S60: Roth 3D 96
Thornhill Pl. S63: Wath D 6F 49
Thorn La. DN2: Long S 6A 26
Thornlea Ct. DN12: New E 5B 70
Thornley Brook S63: Thurn 2A 36
Thornley Cotts. S75: Dod 3G 29
Thornley Sq. S63: Thurn 2A 36
Thornley Vs. S70: Birdw 5D 44
Thorn Rd. S64: Kiln 5C 66
Thornsett Ct. S11: Shef 6D 118
Thornsett Gdns. S17: Dore 3G 145
Thornsett Rd. S7: Shef 6D 118
Thornton Cl. WF9: Hems 1E 13
Thorntondale Rd. DN5: Scaws 3E 39
Thornton Pl. S18: Dron W 3B 154
Thornton Rd. S70: Barn 3H 31
Thornton St. S61: Kimb 5H 95
Thornton Ter. S61: Kimb 5H 95
 S70: Barn 3H 31
Thorntree Cl.
 S61: Thorpe H 4C 80
Thorntree Ct. S40: Birdh 3G 171
Thorntree La. S75: Barn 5C 16
Thorntree Rd. S61: Thorpe H 5C 80
Thorntree Rd. S72: Cud 2D 18
Thornwell La. S61: Thorpe H 2C 80
Thornwood Cl. S63: Thurn 1B 36
Thornwood Ct. S63: Thurn 1C 36
Thorogate S62: Rawm 1F 83
Thorold Pl. DN3: Kirk Sa 3C 26
Thorp Cl. S2: Shef 6F 119
Thorpe Av. S18: Coal A 6H 147
Thorpe Bank DN3: Barn D 1A 26
Thorpe Bridle Rd. S25: Sth A 6G 141
Thorpe Cl. S41: C'fld 6G 161
THORPE COMMON 5C 80
Thorpe Dr. S20: Water 1F 151
Thorpe Fid. M. S61: Thorpe H 3C 80
Thorpefield Dr. S61: Thorpe H 3C 80
Thorpe Fld. M. S61: Thorpe H 3C 80
Thorpe Grn. S20: Water 1E 151

Thorpehall Rd. DN3: Kirk Sa 5D 26
THORPE HESLEY 3C 80
Thorpe Ho. Av. S8: Shef 4G 133
Thorpe Ho. Ri. S8: Shef 4F 133
Thorpe Ho. Rd. S8: Shef 4F 133
Thorpe La. DN5: Sprot 3C 54
THORPE MARSH 1H 25
Thorpe Marsh Nature Reserve 1E 25
Thorpe Mere Rd. DN5: Bntly 1F 25
Thorpe Mere Vw. DN5: Bntly 1F 25
Thorpe St. S61: Thorpe H 3B 80
Thorpleigh Rd. S43: Woodt 4E 165
Three Hills Cl. S65: Thry 5E 85
Three Nooks La. S72: Cud 5E 11
Threshfield Way S12: Shef 5C 136
THROAPHAM 3A 128
Thrush Av. S60: Brins 4E 111
Thrush St. S6: Shef 6A 106
Thruxton Cl. S72: Cud 6F 11
THRYBERGH 6E 85
Thrybergh Country Pk. & Reservoir
. . . . .4G 85
Thrybergh Country Pk. Visitors Cen.
. . . . .3F 85
Thrybergh Ct. DN12: Den M 3E 69
Thrybergh Hall Rd. S62: Rawm 2A 84
Thrybergh La. S65: Thry 5F 85
Thrybergh Sports Cen. 6E 85
Thrybergh Vw. S65: Thry 6D 84
Thundercliffe Rd. S61: Kimb 3E 95
Thurbrook Gdns. S66: Thurc 5D 114
THURCROFT 5B 114
Thurcroft Ho. DN1: Don 2B 56
(off St James St.)
Thurcroft Ind. Est. S66: Thurc 4B 114
THURLSTONE 3A 176
Thurlstone Rd. S36: Pen 4B 176
THURNSCOE 3B 36
Thurnscoe Bri. La. S63: Thurn 4C 36
Thurnscoe Bus. Cen. S63: Thurn . . .3D 36
Thurnscoe Bus. Pk. S63: Thurn 3D 36
THURNSCOE EAST 2D 36
Thurnscoe Hall M. S63: Thurn 3B 36
Thurnscoe La. S72: Gt H 1F 35
Thurnscoe Rd. S63: Bolt D 2B 50
Thurnscoe Station (Rail) 2C 36
Thurstan Av. S8: Shef 2D 146
Tiber Vw. S60: Brins 3D 110
Tickhill Bk. La. DN11: Wils 6F 89
Tickhill Rd. DN4: Balb 5H 55
DN11: Lov 6H 55
S66: Malt 5C 102
Tickhill Sq. DN12: Den M 3C 68
Tickhill St. DN12: Den M 2C 68
Tickhill Way DN11: Ross 6E 75
Tideswell Cl. S43: Stav 6G 163
Tideswell Ct. S5: Shef 1H 107
Tideswell Rd. S5: Shef 1H 107
Tideswell Wlk. S60: Wav 3C 122
Tiercel M. S25: Din 5H 127
Tilford Rd. S13: Shef 2D 136
Tillotson Cl. S8: Shef 2F 133
Tillotson Ri. S8: Shef 2F 133
Tillotson Rd. S8: Shef 2F 133
TILTS 1B 24
TILTS HILLS .1H 23
Tiltshills La. DN5: Bntly 1H 23
Tilts La. DN5: Bntly 1B 24
(not continuous)
Timothy Wood Av. S70: Birdw 4E 45
Tinglebridge S73: Hem 5F 47
Tingle Bri. Av. S73: Hem 5F 47
Tingle Bri. Cres. S73: Hem 5F 47
Tingle Bri. La. S73: Hem 5F 47
Tingle Cl. S73: Hem 5F 47
Tinker La. S6: Shef 1A 118
S10: Shef 1A 118
S74: Hoyl 6F 45
Tinker Rd. S62: Rawm 2H 83
TINSLEY 2H 109
Tinsley Ind. Est. S9: Shef 6F 109
Tinsley Link Rd. S9: Shef 1G 109
Tinsley Pk. Cl. S9: Shef 5F 109
Tinsley Pk. Golf Course 2G 121
Tinsley Pk. Rd. S9: Shef 6E 109
(not continuous)
Tinsley Rd. S74: Hoyl 5A 46
Tinsley Stop (ST) 2G 109
Tippit La. S72: Cud 2F 19

Tipsey Ct. S75: Stain 5C 8
Tipsey Hill S75: Stain 5C 8
Tipton St. S9: Shef 1D 108
Tissington Cl. S40: C'fld 3C 166
Tissington Dr. S60: Wav 3C 122
Tithe Barn Av. S13: Shef 1C 136
Tithe Barn Cl. S13: Shef 1D 136
Tithe Barn Ct. S64: Mexb 4E 51
Tithe Barn La. S13: Shef 2C 136
Tithe Barn Way S13: Shef 1C 136
Tithe Laithe S74: Hoyl 6B 46
Titterton Cl. S9: Shef 6D 108
Titterton St. S9: Shef 6D 108
Tiverton Cl. S64: Swin 4C 66
Tivy Dale Cl. S75: Cawt 4A 14
Tivydale Dr. S75: Dart 1F 15
Toad Holes La. DN11: Ross 3C 74
Toad La. S66: Bramp M 1A 126
Toch Yd. S40: C'fld 6E 167
Tockwith Rd. S9: Shef 1E 121
Todmorden Cl. DN12: Den M 3B 68
TODWICK 3B 140
Todwick Grange S26: Tod 1B 140
Todwick Ho. Gdns. S26: Tod 2B 140
Todwick Rd. S8: Shef 5D 132
S25: Din, Nth A 6D 126
S26: Tod 6D 126
Todwick Rd. Ind. Est. S25: Din 5E 127
Todwick Vs. S26: Tod 3B 140
Toecroft La. DN5: Sprot 3A 54
Tofield Rd. DN11: Wad 6H 71
TOFTS 2D 116
Tofts La. S6: Stan 2D 116
Toftstead DN3: Arm 5E 43
Toftwood Av. S10: Shef 2H 117
Toftwood Rd. S10: Shef 2A 118
Togo Bldgs. S63: Thurn 3B 36
Togo St. S63: Thurn 3B 36
TOLL BAR 4H 23
Toll Bar Av. S12: Shef 3B 134
Toll Bar Cl. S12: Shef 3B 134
Toll Bar Dr. S12: Shef 3C 134
Toll Bar Rd. S12: Shef 3B 134
S64: Swin 4A 66
S65: Roth 5D 98
Tollbridge Rd. S43: Woodt 4E 165
Tollgate Cl. S72: Shaft 4G 11
Tollgate Ct. S3: Shef 5G 107
Toll Ho. Mead S20: Mosb 3D 150
Tolson Wlk. S63: Wath D 5G 49
Tom La. S10: Shef 5E 117
Tomlinson Rd. S74: Els 6D 46
Tontine Rd. S40: C'fld 6H 167
Tooker Rd. S60: Roth 5F 97
Topcliffe Rd. S71: Monk B 3F 17
Top Fld. La. S65: Roth 2C 98
Top Fold S71: Ard 2D 32
Top Fold Cotts. DN12: Old D 4H 67
Top Hall Rd. DN4: Bess 6C 58
Top La. DN4: Bess 5G 57
S66: B'well 2D 102
Toppham Dr. S8: Shef 4E 147
Toppham Rd. S8: Shef 4E 147
Toppham Way S8: Shef 4E 147
Top Pingle Cl. S43: Brim 1D 168
Top Rd. DN3: Barn D 1C 26
S35: Ough 5E 91
S44: Cal 6E 169
Top Row S75: Dart 3F 7
Tops, The S62: Neth Hau, Rawm 2D 82
Top Side S35: Gren 1A 92
Top Ter. S10: Shef 3B 118
(off Parker's La.)
Top Tree Way S65: Thry 5E 85
Top Vw. Cres. DN12: New E 6C 70
Top Warren S35: Chap 6G 61
Torbay Rd. S4: Shef 5A 108
Tor Cl. S71: Monk B 3G 17
Torksey Cl. DN4: Bess 1B 74
Torksey Rd. S5: Shef 6A 94
Torksey Rd. W. S5: Shef 6A 94
Torne Cl. DN4: Can 6D 58
Torne Vw. DN9: Auck 1H 59
Torrington Cl. DN6: Adw S 2B 22
Torry Ct. S13: Shef 2D 136
Tortmayns S26: Tod 3B 140
Torver Dr. S63: Bolt D 3B 50
Tor Way S60: Brins 4E 111

Torwood Dr. S8: Shef 3D 146
TOTLEY 6E 145
TOTLEY BROOK 5F 145
Totley Brook Cl. S17: Dore 5E 145
Totley Brook Cft. S17: Dore 5E 145
Totley Brook Glen S17: Dore 4E 145
Totley Brook Gro. S17: Dore 5E 145
Totley Brook Rd. S17: Dore 5E 145
Totley Brook Way S17: Dore 5E 145
Totley Cl. S71: Ath 1G 17
Totley Grange Cl. S17: Tot 6E 145
Totley Grange Dr. S17: Tot 6E 145
Totley Grange Rd. S17: Tot 6E 145
Totley Hall Cft. S17: Tot 6E 145
Totley Hall Dr. S17: Tot 6E 145
Totley Hall La. S17: Tot 6E 145
Totley Hall Mead S17: Tot 6E 145
Totley La. S17: Bradw 6H 145
S17: Tot 6G 145
(not continuous)
Totley M. S17: Tot 6E 145
Totley Mt. S43: Brim 6C 162
TOTLEY RISE 5G 145
Tourist Info. Cen.
Chesterfield 5H 167
Doncaster 1B 56
Rotherham 6E 97
Sheffield 4F 5 (3F 119)
Towcester Way S64: Mexb 6H 51
Tower Cl. DN5: Scawt 1E 39
Tower Ho. S2: Shef 6H 119
Tower Ri. S2: Shef 6H 119
Tower St. S70: Barn 3D 30
TOWN END
S36 . . . . .4H 175
S6 . . . . .1F 117
Town End DN5: Don 6A 40
S18: App 3C 156
Town End Av. S26: Aston 6D 124
Townend Av. S65: Dalt 1D 98
Townend Cl. S60: Tree 2F 123
Town End Ind. Est.
DN5: Don 6H 39
Townend La. S36: Spink 5G 175
Town End Rd. S35: Eccl 2E 93
Townend St. S10: Shef 1B 118
Town Flds. DN1: Don 1D 56
Town Flds. Av. S35: Eccl 2H 93
Town Fld. Vs. DN1: Don 1D 56
Towngate S36: Thurl 3A 176
S75: Mapp 5A 8
S75: Silk 2A 28
Towngate Gro. S35: Ough 5E 91
Towngate Rd. S35: Ough 5D 90
TOWN HEAD .1G 105
TOWNHEAD .3D 144
Townhead Rd. S17: Dore 3D 144
Townhead St. S1: Shef 3D 4 (3F 119)
Town Lands Cl. S73: Womb 6A 34
Town La. S61: Kimb P, Wing 6G 81
Town Moor Av. DN2: Don 6E 41
Town St. S9: Tins 1G 109
S60: Roth 6E 97
Town Vw. Av. DN5: Scaws 2C 38
Town Wells Ct. S25: Nth A 3G 141
Toyne St. S10: Shef 2A 118
Trafalgar Ct. S1: Shef 5C 4 (4E 119)
Trafalgar Rd. S6: Shef 6B 92
Trafalgar St. S1: Shef 4C 4 (3E 119)
Traffic Ter. S41: Has 3A 172
S43: Bar H 2G 163
Trafford Apartments S61: Kimb 4H 95
Trafford Ct. DN1: Don 1B 56
Trafford Way DN1: Don 1B 56
Tranmoor Av. DN4: Bess 5B 58
Tranmoor Ct. S74: Hoyl 1G 61
Tranmoor La. DN3: Arm 5E 43
Tranquil Wlk. DN11: New R 6A 74
Trap La. S11: Shef 2F 131
Traso Bus. Pk. S18: Dron 3A 156
Travey Rd. S2: Shef 1D 134
Travis Gdns. DN4: Hex 3G 55
Travis Pl. S10: Shef 6A 4 (4D 118)
Tredis Cl. S71: Monk B 5G 17
Treecrest Ri. S75: Barn 4D 16
Treefield Cl. S61: Wing 5B 82
Treelands S75: Barn 5A 16
Treeneuk Cl. S40: Ash 5C 166
Treeneuk Gdns. S40: Ash 5C 166

Tree Root Wlk. S10: Shef 3C 118
TREETON 2F 123
Treeton Enterprise Cen.
  S60: Tree 3G 123
Treeton Ho. DN1: Don 2B 56
                 (off Oxford Pl.)
Treeton La. S26: Augh 3B 124
  S60: Tree 1E 123
Treetown Cres. S60: Tree 1F 123
Treherne Rd. S60: Roth 5G 97
Trelawney Wlk. S70: Wors 5E 31
Trenchard Cl. S72: Grim 1B 20
Trent Cl. DN12: New E 3D 70
Trent Gdns. DN3: Kirk Sa 3C 26
Trent Gro. S18: Dron 1G 155
Trentham Cl. S60: Brins 4E 111
Trenton Cl. S13: Shef 2E 137
Trenton Ri. S13: Shef 2E 137
Trent St. S9: Shef 6B 108
Trent Ter. DN12: Con 3F 69
Trent Vs. S26: Kiv P 6A 140
Treswell Cres. S6: Shef 4B 106
Trevorrow Cres. S40: C'fld 1H 171
Trevose Cl. S40: W'ton 3D 170
Trewan Cl. S71: Monk B 5G 17
Trickett Rd. S6: Shef 5B 106
  S35: High G 6B 60
Trigon, The S1: Shef 6F 5
Trinity Cl. S41: C'fld 4G 167
Trinity Rd. S26: Kiv P 6C 140
Trinity St. S3: Shef 1D 4 (2F 119)
Trippet Cl. S10: Shef 6G 117
Trippet La. S1: Shef 3C 4 (3E 119)
Tristford Cl. S60: Cat 6E 111
Troon Cl. S40: W'ton 2D 170
Troon Wlk. S25: Din 6A 128
Tropical Butterfly House,
  Wildlife and Falconry Cen. . .2B 142
Troughbrook Hill S43: Stav 6H 163
Troughbrook Rd. S43: Hol 5G 163
Trough Dr. S65: Thry 6F 85
Troutbeck Cl. S63: Thurn 3B 36
Troutbeck Rd. S7: Shef 4D 132
Troutbeck Way DN11: New R 6F 75
TROWAY 6E 149
Trowell Way S71: Ath 6E 9
Trueman Dr. S62: Rawm 6D 64
Trueman Grn. S66: Malt 4H 101
Trueman Ter. S71: Lund 6B 18
Truman Gro. S36: Spink 3H 175
Truman St. DN5: Bntly 1H 39
Truro Av. DN2: Don 2G 41
Truro Ct. S71: Monk B 5G 17
Truswell Av. S10: Shef 2H 117
Truswell Rd. S10: Shef 3H 117
Tudor Cl. S9: Shef 6E 109
Tudor Ct. DN3: Barn D 2C 26
  S72: Grim 2B 20
Tudor Rd. DN2: Don 6F 41
  DN6: Woodl 5D 22
Tudor Sq. S1: Shef 4F 5 (3G 119)
Tudor St. DN11: New R 6C 74
  S43: Stav 4C 164
  S63: Thurn 2D 36
Tudor Way S70: Wors 5F 31
Tuffolds Cl. S2: Shef 1D 134
Tulip Tree Cl. S20: Beig 3H 137
Tullibardine Rd. S11: Shef 2A 132
Tulyar Cl. DN11: New R 6G 75
Tumbling La. S71: Monk B 2C 18
Tummon Rd. S2: Shef 4B 120
Tummon St. S61: Roth 4C 96
Tune St. S70: Barn 2F 31
  S73: Womb 2F 47
Tunstall Cl. S73: Womb 3F 47
Tunstall Grn. S40: W'ton 1E 171
Tunstall Way S40: W'ton 1E 171
Tunwell Av. S5: Shef 3G 93
Tunwell Dr. S5: Shef 3G 93
Tunwell Greave S5: Shef 3G 93
Tunwell Rd. S66: Carr 3F 115
Turham Ct. DN11: Ross 6E 75
Turie Av. S5: Shef 4F 93
Turie Cres. S5: Shef 4F 93
Turnberry Cl. S40: W'ton 2D 170
Turnberry Ct. DN5: Bntly 2H 39
Turnberry Gro. S72: Cud 6F 11
Turnberry Way S25: Din 1A 142
Turnbull Cl. S40: C'fld 1G 171

Turner Av. S73: Womb 1E 47
Turner Bus. Pk. S13: Shef 4H 121
Turner Cl. S18: Dron 3E 155
  S62: P'gte 4H 83
Turner Dr. S43: Ink 6G 163
Turner La. S60: Whis 3A 112
Turner Museum of Glass 3C 4 (3E 119)
Turner St. S74: Jum 5C 46
Turners La. S10: Shef 4B 118
Turner St. S2: Shef 5F 5 (4G 119)
  S72: Gt H 1F 35
Turnesc Gro. S63: Thurn 3C 36
Turnoaks Bus. Pk.
  S40: Birdh 3A 172
Turnoaks La. S40: Birdh 3H 171
Turnpike Cft. S35: Gren 1B 92
Turnshaw Av. S26: Augh 5B 124
Turnshaw M. S70: Barn 3F 31
Turnshaw Rd. S26: Ull 5D 124
Turquoise S41: C'fld 6A 168
                 (off Wain Av.)
Turton Rd. S65: Rav 2C 100
Tuscany Gdns. S70: Barn 2G 31
Tuscany Vs. S70: Barn 2G 31
Tutbury Gdns. DN4: Can 5D 58
Tuxford Cres. S71: Barn 6A 18
Tween Woods La. DN11: Wad 5G 71
Twelve Lands Cl. S75: Tank 1D 60
Twelve O'Clock Ct. S4: Shef 1H 119
Twentylands, The S60: Tree 3F 123
Twentywell Ct. S17: Dore 3H 145
           (off Ladies Spring Dr.)
Twentywell Dr. S17: Bradw 4A 146
Twentywell La.
  S17: Dore, Bradw 3H 145
Twentywell Ri. S17: Bradw 4A 146
Twentywell Rd. S17: Bradw 5A 146
Twentywell Vw. S17: Bradw 5A 146
Twibell St. S71: Barn 5F 17
Twickenham Cl. S20: Half 4F 151
Twickenham Ct. S20: Half 4F 151
Twickenham Cres. S20: Half 4F 151
Twickenham Glade S20: Half 5G 151
Twickenham Gro. S20: Half 4F 151
Twigg Cl. S64: Kiln 5D 66
Twigg Cres. DN3: Arm 4C 42
Twitchill Dr. S13: Shef 2C 136
TWI Technology Cen. S60: Cat 1B 122
Two Gates Way S72: Shaft 4F 11
Twyford Cl. S64: Swin 3H 65
Tyas Pl. S64: Mexb 1H 67
Tyas Rd. S5: Shef 3F 93
Tye Rd. S20: Beig 5H 137
TYERS HILL 1G 33
Tyler St. S9: Shef 2E 109
Tyler Way S9: Shef 1E 109
Tylney Rd. S2: Shef 4A 120
  S40: W'ton 2C 170
Tynedale Ct. DN3: Kirk Sa 4D 26
Tynker Av. S20: Beig 5H 137
Tyzack Rd. S8: Shef 6D 132

U

ULLEY 3D 124
Ulley Activity Cen. 3F 85
Ulley Beeches S66: Bramp M 3G 125
Ulley Country Pk. 3B 124
Ulley Country Pk. Visitor Cen. 3B 124
Ulley Cres. S13: Shef 1E 135
Ulley La. S26: Aston 5D 124
  S26: Ull 4C 124
Ulley Rd. S13: Shef 1E 135
Ulley Vw. S26: Augh 4C 124
Ullswater Av. S20: Half 4F 151
Ullswater Cl. S18: Dron W 2D 154
  S20: Half 4F 151
  S25: Nth A 1H 141
  S63: Bolt D 3B 50
Ullswater Dr. S18: Dron W 3D 154
Ullswater Gdns. DN4: Don 3G 57
Ullswater Pk. S18: Dron W 2D 154
Ullswater Pl. S18: Dron W 2D 154
Ullswater Rd. S64: Mexb 6H 51
  S71: Ard 2E 33
Ullswater Wlk. DN5: Scaws 3D 38
Ulrica Dr. S66: Thurc 6B 114

Ulverston Rd. S8: Shef 4D 132
  S41: C'fld 1E 167
Uncle Eddies Motocross Pk. 1G 23
UNDERBANK 6C 104
Underbank La. S36: Stoc 1B 174
Undercliffe Rd. S6: Shef 1G 117
Undergate Rd. S25: Din 4H 127
Underhill S70: Wors 6G 31
Underhill La. S6: Shef 5A 92
UNDER TOFTS 2E 117
Underwood Av. S70: Wors 4G 31
Underwood Rd. S8: Shef 4E 133
Union Ct. S70: Barn 2E 31
Union St. S11: Shef 2E 31
Union La. S1: Shef 5E 5 (4F 119)
Union St. DN1: Don 2B 56
  S1: Shef 5E 5 (4F 119)
  S61: Roth 4C 96
  S70: Barn 2E 31
  WF9: Hems 1F 13
Union Wlk. S40: C'fld 5H 167
Unistates Bus. Pk.
  S41: Old W 4A 162
Unity Pl. S60: Roth 4E 97
Universal Cl. S25: Nth A 6E 127
Universal Cres. S25: Nth A 6E 127
University of Derby
  Chesterfield Campus 3H 167
University off Huddersfield
  Barnsley Campus 6D 16
University of Sheffield
  Bolsover St. 3A 4 (3D 118)
  Crookesmoor Building 3B 118
  Dorset St. 4C 118
  Drama Studio 3A 4 (3D 118)
  Jessops Building 3D 118
  North Campus 3C 4 (3E 119)
  Northumberland Rd. 3C 118
  The Diamond 3E 119
  Western Bank 3C 118
University of Sheffield Stop (ST)
                 .4A 4 (3D 118)
Unsliven Rd. S36: Stoc 1A 174
UNSTONE 5B 156
Unstone Dronfield By-Pass
  S18: Dron, Uns 3E 155
UNSTONE GREEN 1F 161
Unstone Hill S18: Uns 4A 156
Unstone La. S41: Old W 1G 161
Unstone St. S2: Shef 5F 119
Unwin Cres. S36: Pen 5D 176
Unwin St. S36: Pen 5D 176
Upland Ri. S40: W'ton 1E 171
Uplands Av. S75: Kexb 6D 6
Uplands Rd. DN3: Arm 4F 43
Uplands Way S62: Rawm 2F 83
Up. Albert Rd. S8: Shef 4F 133
Up. Allen St. S3: Shef 2B 4 (2E 119)
UPPER BRADWAY 6A 146
Upper Chambers S35: Chap 6E 61
Up. Clara St. S61: Kimb 4A 96
Up. Cliffe Rd. S75: Dod 2F 29
UPPER CRABTREE 3H 107
Up. Croft Cl. S43: Brim 1D 168
UPPER CUDWORTH 6E 11
Upperfield Cl. S66: Malt 4A 102
Upperfield La.
  S75: High H, Kexb 5A 6
Upperfield Rd. S66: Malt 3H 101
Upper Folderings S75: Dod 3G 29
Up. Forest Rd. S71: Ath 6E 9
UPPER GATE 6C 104
Uppergate Rd. S6: Stan 1C 116
Up. Hanover St. S3: Shef 5A 4 (4D 118)
                 (not continuous)
UPPER HAUGH 1E 83
Up. High Royds S75: Dart 6H 7
UPPER HOYLAND 5H 45
Up. Hoyland Rd. S74: Hoyl 4G 45
Up. King St. S43: Brim 5E 163
Up. Ley Ct. S35: Chap 4F 79
Up. Ley Dell S35: Chap 3F 79
Up. Lum Cl. S41: C'fld 6C 168
Up. Lunns Cl. S71: R'ton 3B 10
Upper Mill Ga. S60: Roth 4E 97
Up. Moor St. S40: Bramp 6C 166
UPPER NEWBOLD 6B 160
Up. Newbold Cl. S41: C'fld 1C 166

Up. New St. S70: Barn 2E 31
Up. Rye Cl. S60: Whis 3C 112
Up. School La. S18: Dron 4G 155
Up. Sheffield Rd.
  S70: Barn, Wors 3F 31
UPPER SWITHEN 3C 6
UPPER TANKERSLEY 3C 60
UPPERTHORPE
  S21 . . . . .5C 152
  S6 . . . . .1A 4 (1D 118)
Upperthorpe S6: Shef 1C 118
Upperthorpe Glen S6: Shef 1C 118
Upperthorpe Rd. S6: Shef 1B 4 (1D 118)
  S21: Killa 5C 152
Upperthorpe Vs. S21: Killa 5C 152
Up. Valley Rd. S8: Shef 3F 133
UPPER WHISTON 5C 112
Up. Whiston Cl. S60: Whis 5B 112
Up. Whiston La. S60: Up W, Whis . . .5B 112
Upperwood Rd. S73: D'fld 4H 33
Up. Wortley Rd.
  S61: Kimb, Scho, Thorpe H 4B 80
Upton Cl. S66: Malt 3H 101
  S73: Womb 6E 33
  (not continuous)
Upwell Hill S4: Shef 3B 108
Upwell La. S4: Shef 3B 108
Upwell St. S4: Shef 3B 108
Upwood Cl. S40: C'fld 3B 166
Upwood Rd. S3: Shef 3A 106
Urban Rd. DN4: Hex 3H 55
Urch Cl. DN12: Con 5F 69
Usker Cl. S17: Dore 5E 177
Utah Ter. S12: Shef 5D 136
Utleys Cft. S63: Wath D 4E 49
Uttley Cl. S9: Shef 6E 109
Uttley Cft. S9: Shef 6E 109
Uttley Dr. S9: Shef 6E 109
Uttoxeter Av. S64: Mexb 6H 51

V

Vaal St. S70: Barn 2G 31
Vainor Rd. S6: Shef 2H 105
Vale Av. S65: Thry 6E 85
Vale Cl. S18: Dron 3G 155
Vale Ct. S65: Thry 6E 85
Vale Cres. S65: Thry 6E 85
Vale Gro. S6: Lox 4F 105
Valentine Cl. S5: Shef 5H 93
Valentine Cres. S5: Shef 5H 93
  (not continuous)
Valentine Rd. S5: Shef 5H 93
Vale Rd. S3: Shef 5E 107
  S65: Thry 6E 85
Valetta Ho. S62: P'gte 4G 83
  (off Allt St.)
Vale Vw. S36: Oxs 6H 177
Valiant Gdns. DN5: Sprot 1F 55
Valley Centertainment S9: Shef 4F 109
Valley Centertainment (Park & Ride)
  . . . . .5E 109
Valley Centertainment Stop (ST) 4F 109
Valley Cres. S41: C'fld 6B 168
Valley Dr. DN3: Brant 4G 59
  S21: Killa 3C 152
  S63: Wath D 6E 49
  S72: Grim 1B 20
  S74: Hoyl 1B 62
Valley Gro. S71: Lund 3C 18
Valley Park Ind. Est. S73: Womb 3B 48
Valley Rd. S8: Shef 2F 133
  S12: Shef 5D 136
  S21: Killa 3C 152
  S35: High G 2D 78
  S41: C'fld 6B 168
  S43: Mas M 2F 165
  S64: Swin 4A 66
  S73: Womb 6H 33
  S75: Mapp 5H 7
Valley Vw. DN12: Con 3H 69
  S36: Pen 4E 177
Valley Vw. Cl. S21: Ecki 2D 158
  S41: Has 3D 172
Valley Way S73: Womb 1H 47
  S74: Hoyl 6B 46
Vancouver Dr. S63: Bolt D 2A 50
Vanguard Trad. Est. S40: Birdh 3A 172

Vantage Cl. S9: Tins 6H 95
Vantage Dr. S9: Tins 1G 109
Varley Gdns. S66: Flan 4G 99
Varley Ho. S41: C'fld 2A 168
  (off Tapton Lock Hill)
Varney Rd. S63: Wath D 1F 65
Vaughan Av. DN1: Don 6C 40
Vaughan Rd. S75: Barn 5A 16
Vaughan Ter. S72: Gt H 6F 21
  (off School St.)
Vaughton Hill S36: Spink 4H 175
Vauxhall Cl. S9: Shef 6E 95
Vauxhall Rd. S9: Shef 6E 95
Velocity Twr. S1: Shef 6C 4 (5E 119)
Velvet Wood Cl. S75: Barn 5H 15
Venetian Cres. S73: D'fld 5A 34
Ventnor Cl. DN4: Balb 5G 55
Ventnor Cl. S70: Barn 3E 31
Ventnor Ct. S7: Shef 6E 119
Ventnor Pl. S7: Shef 6E 119
Venture One Bus. Pk. S20: Holb 1H 151
Venture Way S41: Whit M 5G 161
Venus Ct. S60: Brins 2D 110
Verdant Way S5: Shef 5A 94
Verdon St. S3: Shef 6G 107
Verdon Street Recreation Cen. 1G 119
Verelst Av. S26: Aston 5C 124
Vere Rd. S6: Shef 2B 106
Verger Cl. DN11: Ross 5D 74
Vernon Cl. S70: Barn 3E 31
Vernon Cres. S70: Wors 5E 31
Vernon Delph S10: Shef 3G 117
Vernon Dr. S35: Chap 3F 79
Vernon Rd. S17: Dore 4F 145
  S40: C'fld 5E 167
  S60: Roth 1A 112
  S70: Wors 5E 31
Vernon St. S70: Birdw 6E 45
  S71: Barn 6E 17
  S74: Hoyl 1H 61
Vernon St. Nth. S71: Barn 6E 17
Vernon Ter. S10: Shef 4H 117
Vernon Way S66: Malt 4H 101
  S75: Barn 5A 16
Verona Ri. S73: D'fld 5B 34
Vesey St. S62: Rawm 4G 83
Vicarage Cl. DN4: Can 5D 58
  S35: Gren 2B 92
  S64: Mexb 1H 51
  S65: Roth 2C 98
  S74: Hoyl 6B 46
Vicarage Ct. S60: Brins 5E 111
Vicarage Cres. S35: Gren 2B 92
Vicarage Dr. DN11: Wad 5E 73
Vicarage Farm Ct. S75: Silk 2B 28
Vicarage La. S17: Dore 3E 145
  S65: Roth 4E 97
  S71: R'ton 3H 9
Vicarage Rd. S9: Shef 5C 108
  S35: Gren 2B 92
Vicarage Wlk. S36: Pen 4D 176
Vicarage Way DN5: Ark 6D 24
Vicar Cres. S73: D'fld 5C 34
Vicar La. S1: Shef 3E 5 (3F 119)
  S13: Shef 1C 136
  S43: C'fld 5H 167
  S73: D'fld 5C 34
Vicar Rd. S63: Wath D 5E 49
  S73: D'fld 5C 34
Vickers Dr. S5: Shef 1A 108
Vickers Rd. S5: Shef 2A 108
  S35: High G 1C 78
Victoria Av. S43: Stav 3C 164
  S65: Roth 4G 97
  S70: Barn 6D 16
Victoria Cl. S26: Kiv P 6B 140
  S36: Stoc 3D 174
Victoria Cl. DN5: Bntly 5A 24
  S11: Shef 2C 132
  S26: Kiv P 6B 140
Victoria Cres. S70: Birdw 5D 44
  S75: Barn 6C 16
Victoria Cres. W. S75: Barn 6C 16
Victoria Gdns. S72: Brier 1E 21
Victoria Gro. S43: Brim C 3E 169
Victoria Hall S1: Shef 4C 4 (3E 119)
Victoria Ho. S3: Shef 4B 4
Victoria Jubilee Mus. 4A 14
Victoria La. DN11: New R 5B 74
Victoria M. S64: Kiln 1D 84
Victorian Cres. DN2: Don 6E 41

Victoria Pk. Rd. S43: Brim C 3E 169
Victoria Quays
  S2: Shef 2H 5 (2H 119)
Victoria Rd. DN4: Balb 4A 56
  DN5: Bntly 6A 24
  DN6: Adw S 6E 23
  DN12: New E 3C 70
  S10: Shef 6A 4 (6D 118)
  S20: Beig 4G 137
  S36: Stoc 3D 174
  S62: P'gte 4G 83
  (not continuous)
  S64: Mexb 1F 67
  S70: Barn 6D 16
  S71: R'ton 2A 10
  S73: Womb 1G 47
Victoria Rd. E. S63: Wath D 5E 49
Victoria Rd. W. S63: Wath D 5E 49
Victoria Sta. Rd.
  S4: Shef 2G 5 (2G 119)
Victoria St. S3: Shef 4B 4 (3E 119)
  S18: Dron 2E 155
  S25: Din 5B 128
  S36: Pen 4D 176
  S36: Stoc 3D 174
  S41: C'fld 4H 167
  S43: Brim 3E 163
  S60: Cat 6E 111
  S60: Roth 4C 96
  (not continuous)
  S63: Gol 5D 36
  S64: Kiln 1D 84
  S64: Mexb 1D 66
  S66: Malt 6B 102
  S70: Barn 6D 16
  S70: Stair 2A 32
  S72: Cud 1E 19
  S73: D'fld 4C 34
  S74: Hoyl 6C 46
  WF9: Hems 1F 13
Victoria St. Nth.
  S41: Old W 4G 161
Victoria St. W. S40: Bramp 6D 166
Victoria Ter. S70: Barn 2F 31
Victoria Vs. S6: Shef 1D 118
  (off Upperthorpe)
  S75: Pil .1D 60
Victoria Way S66: Malt 4G 101
Victor Rd. S17: Dore 3G 145
Victor St. S6: Shef 5C 106
Victor Ter. S70: Barn 2F 31
Viewland Cl. S72: Cud 3F 19
Viewlands S75: Silk C 5B 28
Viewlands Cl. S36: Pen 2D 176
  S66: Bram 6B 100
View Rd. S2: Shef 1F 133
  S65: Roth 2H 97
Views, The S75: Mapp 5A 8
Viewtree Cl. S62: H'ley 5A 62
Vikinglea Cl. S2: Shef 6E 121
Vikinglea Dr. S2: Shef 6E 121
  (not continuous)
Vikinglea Glade S2: Shef 5E 121
Vikinglea Rd. S2: Shef 5E 121
Viking Way S26: Kiv P 5G 140
Villa Gdns. DN5: Bntly 3H 23
Village Ct. S72: Cud 1F 19
Village St. DN5: Cus 5E 39
  DN6: Adw S 2C 22
Villa Pk. Rd. DN4: Can 4B 58
Villa Rd. DN6: Woodl 3C 22
Villiers Cl. S2: Shef 2B 134
Villiers Dr. S2: Shef 2B 134
Vincent Cres. S40: Bramp 6C 166
Vincent Ho. S1: Shef 2C 4 (2E 119)
Vincent La. S40: Bramp 6C 166
Vincent Rd. S7: Shef 6E 119
  S65: Rav 3A 100
  S71: Lund 5C 18
Vincent Ter. S63: Thurn 3E 37
Vine Cl. S60: Roth 4D 96
Vine St. S71: Monk B 4H 17
Vine Grove Ct. S20: Mosb 3E 151
Vine Grove Gdns. S20: Mosb 3E 151
Viola Bank S36: Stoc 3D 174
Violet Av. DN12: New E 5C 70
  S20: Beig 5F 137
Violet Bank Rd. S7: Shef 2D 132
Violet Farm Ct. S72: Brier 4B 12

Virgin Active
Millhouses 4D 132
Sheffield 2E 133
Vissitt La. WF9: Hems 1B 12
Vista S60: Roth 5E 97
Vivian Rd. S5: Shef 2A 108
Vizard Rd. S74: Els 6D 46
Vue Cinema
Doncaster 3F 57
Sheffield 1F 109
Vulcan Ho. S65: Roth 3H 97
Vulcan M. DN9: Auck 2C 76
Vulcan Rd. S9: Shef 2E 109
(Meadowhall Way)
S9: Shef 2F 109
(Sheffield Rd.)

W

Wadbrough Rd. S11: Shef 5C 118
Waddington Rd. S75: Barn 6A 16
Waddington Ter. S64: Mexb 2G 67
Waddington Way S65: Ald 1H 97
Wade Cl. S60: Roth 6G 97
S72: Grim 2C 20
Wade Mdw. S6: Shef 3H 105
Wade St. S4: Shef 3B 108
S75: Barn 6A 16
WADSLEY 3G 105
WADSLEY BRIDGE 1B 106
Wadsley La. S6: Shef 2H 105
Wadsley Pk. Cres. S6: Shef 3H 105
Wadsworth Av. S12: Shef 3F 135
Wadsworth Cl. S12: Shef 2G 135
Wadsworth Dr. S12: Shef 2G 135
S62: Rawm 6D 64
Wadsworth Rd. S12: Shef 3F 135
S66: Bram 6A 100
WADWORTH 5E 73
Wadworth Av. DN11: Ross 5E 75
Wadworth Cl. DN5: Barnb 1H 51
Wadworth Hall DN11: Wad 5E 73
Wadworth Hall La. DN11: Wad 1H 89
Wadworth Hill DN11: Wad 5E 73
Wadworth Riding DN12: New E 4E 71
Wadworth St. DN12: Den M 3D 68
Wager La. S72: Brier 3B 12
Wagon Rd. S61: Grea 5C 82
Wain Av. S41: C'fld 3A 168
Waingate S3: Shef 2F 5 (2G 119)
Wainwright Av. S13: Shef 6G 121
S73: Womb 1E 47
Wainwright Cres. S13: Shef 6F 121
S73: Womb 1E 47
Wainwright Pl. S73: Womb 1E 47
Wainwright Rd. DN4: Don 2D 56
S61: Kimb P 1A 96
Wakefield Rd. S71: Ath, Smi 1D 16
(not continuous)
S75: Stain 3B 8
Wakelam Dr. DN3: Arm 4C 42
Wake Rd. S7: Shef 1D 132
Walbank Rd. DN3: Arm 4F 43
Walbert Av. S63: Thurn 3B 36
Walbrook S70: Wors 6G 31
Walden Av. DN5: Scawt 1F 39
Walden Rd. S2: Shef 1G 133
Walders Av. S6: Shef 2H 105
Walders La. S36: Bolst 6E 175
WALES 6G 139
WALES BAR 5E 139
Wales Ct. S26: Wales 4G 139
Walesmoor Av. S26: Kiv P 6G 139
Wales Pl. S6: Shef 6C 106
Wales Rd. S26: Kiv P, Wales 6G 139
WALESWOOD 5C 138
Waleswood Ind. Est.
S26: Wales B 4E 139
Waleswood Rd. S26: Wales B 3B 138
(Delves La.)
S26: Wales B 4E 139
(Waleswood Ind. Est.)
Waleswood Vw. S26: Aston 2C 138
Waleswood Vs. S26: Wales B 5E 139
Waleswood Way S26: Wales B 5E 139
Walford Rd. S21: Killa 4B 152
Walgrove Av. S40: C'fld 1E 171

Walgrove Rd. S40: W'ton 1E 171
Walk, The S65: Roth 3A 98
S70: Birdw 6D 44
Walker Cl. S35: Green 2B 92
Walker La. S65: Roth 3F 97
Walker Rd. S41: Kimb P 1A 96
S75: Tank 1E 61
Walker's La. S21: Killa 4C 152
Walkers Ter. S71: Monk B 3H 17
Walker St. S3: Shef 1G 5 (1G 119)
S62: Rawm 2A 84
S70: Barn 3D 66
Walker Vw. S62: Rawm 2A 84
WALKLEY 6B 106
WALKLEY BANK 1A 118
Walkley Bank Cl. S6: Shef 5B 106
Walkley Bank Rd. S6: Shef 6H 105
Walkley Cres. Rd. S6: Shef 6A 106
Walkley La. S6: Shef 4B 106
Walkley Rd. S6: Shef 6B 106
Walkley St. S6: Shef 6B 106
Walkley Ter. S6: Shef 6H 105
Wallace Rd. DN4: Balb 6F 55
S3: Shef 5E 107
Waller Rd. S6: Shef 6H 105
Walling Cl. S9: Shef 2E 109
Wallingfield Ct.
S26: Wales B 5E 139
Walling Rd. S9: Shef 2E 109
Wallingwells La. S81: Gild 2G 143
Wallis Way S60: Cat 1C 122
Wallsend Cotts. S41: C'fld 3F 167
Wall St. S70: Barn 2D 30
Walney Fold S71: Monk B 2A 18
Walnut Av. DN9: Auck 2A 76
Walnut Cl. S70: Barn 3E 31
Walnut Dr. S21: Killa 5B 152
S25: Din 6A 128
Walnut Gro. S64: Mexb 6E 51
Walnut Pl. S35: Chap 4E 79
(not continuous)
Walnut Tree Hill DN11: Wad 5F 73
Walpole Cl. DN4: Balb 1G 71
Walpole Gro. S26: Swal 5C 124
Walseker La. S26: Wooda 2H 153
Walsham Dr. DN5: Cus 5F 39
Walshaw Gro. S35: Ough 5D 90
Walshaw Rd. S35: Ough 5E 91
Walstow Cres. DN3: Arm 4C 42
Walters Rd. S66: Malt 5C 102
Walter St. S6: Shef 5C 106
S60: Roth 3D 96
Waltham Cft. S41: Has 3B 172
Waltham Gdns. S20: Sot 6H 137
Waltham St. S70: Barn 2E 31
Waltheof Rd. S2: Shef 6D 120
WALTON 2C 170
Walton Bk. La. S42: W'ton 3A 170
Walton Cl. S18: Dron W 2B 154
S35: High G 6B 60
S40: W'ton 2C 170
Walton Ct. S8: Shef 2D 146
Walton Cres. S40: C'fld 1F 171
Walton Dr. S40: C'fld 1F 171
Walton Dr. S40: C'fld 1F 171
Walton Fields Rd. S40: C'fld 6E 167
Walton Ho. DN1: Don 2B 56
(off Grove Pl.)
Walton Rd. S11: Shef 5C 118
S40: W'ton 6E 167
Walton St. S75: Barn 5B 16
Walton St. Nth. S75: Barn 5B 16
Walton Wlk. S40: C'fld 6F 167
Walton Way S42: W'orth 6F 171
Walton Works S40: C'fld 6E 167
Wannop St. S62: P'gte 5G 83
Wansfell Rd. S4: Shef 3C 108
Wansfield Ter. S71: Barn 1F 31
Wapping, The S65: Hoot R 1A 86
Warburton Cl. S2: Shef 1H 133
Warburton Gdns. S2: Shef 1H 133
Warburton Rd. S2: Shef 1H 133
Ward Cl. S36: Pen 5D 176
Warde Aldam Cres. S66: Wick 5F 99
Warde Av. DN4: Balb 6G 55
Warden Cl. DN4: Can 4D 58
Warden St. S60: Roth 1E 111
Wardgate Way S40: C'fld 3B 166
WARD GREEN 5E 31

Wardlow Cl. S40: C'fld 2G 171
Wardlow Rd. S12: Shef 3G 135
Ward Pl. S7: Shef 6E 119
Wards Cl. S11: Shef 3E 119
(off Napier St.)
Wardsend Rd. S6: Shef 2C 106
Wardsend Rd. Nth.
S6: Shef 1B 106
Ward St. S3: Shef 1D 4 (1F 119)
S36: Pen 5D 176
Wards Yd. S18: Dron 3F 155
Wareham Ct. S20: Sot 6H 137
Wareham Gro. S75: Dod 2H 29
Warehouse La. S63: Wath D 6F 49
Warley Rd. S2: Shef 5B 120
Warminster Cl. S8: Shef 4F 133
Warminster Cres. S8: Shef 4G 133
Warminster Dr. S8: Shef 5G 133
Warminster Gdns. S8: Shef 5F 133
Warminster Pl. S8: Shef 6G 133
Warminster Rd. S8: Shef 4F 133
WARMSWORTH 1D 70
Warmsworth Ct. DN4: Warm 6E 55
Warmsworth Halt DN4: Warm 2C 70
Warmsworth Halt Ind. Est.
DN4: Warm 2D 70
Warmsworth Rd. DN4: Balb 6F 55
Warner Av. S75: Barn 6A 16
Warner Pl. S75: Barn 6B 16
Warner Rd. S6: Shef 3A 106
S75: Barn 6A 16
Warner St. S41: C'fld 1A 172
Warnington Dr. DN4: Bess 1D 74
Warning Tongue La. DN3: Can 4E 59
DN4: Bess, Can 4E 59
WARREN 6F 61
Warren, The DN11: Ross 4D 74
S26: Aston 1E 139
Warren Av. S62: Rawm 1F 83
Warren Cl. DN2: Don 6F 41
DN4: Warm 6D 54
S71: R'ton 1A 10
S81: Woods 4F 143
Warren Cres. S21: Mar L 2H 157
S70: Barn 3E 31
Warren Dr. S61: Kimb 2A 96
Warreners Dr. S65: Thry 6E 85
Warren Gdns. S35: Chap 6G 61
Warren Hill S61: Kimb P 2A 96
Warren Ho. Cl. S66: Bram 5A 100
Warren La. DN4: Bess 1C 74
DN11: Ross 2D 74
S35: Chap 5F 61
(not continuous)
S35: High G 5E 61
(not continuous)
S75: Stain 3A 8
WF4: Wool 3A 8
Warren Mt. S61: Kimb 2A 96
Warren Pl. S70: Barn 3E 31
Warren Quarry La. S70: Barn 3E 31
Warren Ri. S18: Dron 1H 155
Warren Rd. DN12: Con 5E 69
S66: Wick 5G 99
Warren St. S4: Shef 1A 120
(not continuous)
WARREN VALE 6H 65
Warren Vale S62: Rawm 1H 83
S64: Swin 1H 83
Warren Vale Rd.
S64: Swin 3H 65
Warren Vw. S70: Barn 3E 31
S74: Hoyl 2H 61
Warren Wlk. S21: Mar L 2H 157
S71: R'ton 1A 10
(Queensway)
S71: R'ton 1A 10
(Warren Cl.)
Warrington Rd. S10: Shef 2C 118
Warris Cl. S61: Kimb P 1H 95
Warris Pl. S2: Shef 3A 120
Warsop Rd. S71: Ath 5D 8
Warwick M. S63: Wath D 4E 49
Warwick Rd. DN2: Don 5G 41
S66: Malt 5F 101
S71: Monk B 5G 17
Warwick St. S10: Shef 2B 118
S40: Birdh 3A 172
S60: Roth 5F 97

Warwick St. Ind. Est. S40: Birdh 3A 172
Warwick St. Sth. S60: Roth 5F 97
Warwick Ter. S10: Shef 2B 118
Warwick Way S25: Nth A 2H 141
Wasdale Av. S20: Half 4F 151
Wasdale Cl. S20: Half 4F 151
Washfield Cres. S60: Tree 2F 123
Washfield La. S60: Tree 2F 123
Washford Rd. S9: Shef 6B 108
Wash Ho. La. S40: Bramp 6D 166
Washington Av. DN12: Con 4C 68
  S73: Womb 2E 47
Washington Cl. S25: Din 6G 127
Washington Gro. DN5: Don 3H 39
Washington Rd. DN6: Woodl 3C 22
  S11: Shef 6E 119
  S35: Eccl 1G 93
  S63: Gol 6C 36
Washington St. S64: Mexb 1G 67
Wasteneys Rd. S26: Tod 3C 143
Watch Ho. La. DN5: Don 4G 39
Watchley Gdns. S63: Gol 5B 36
Watch St. S13: Shef 6F 123
Waterdale DN1: Don 2C 56
Waterdale Cl. DN5: Sprot 4E 55
Waterdale Rd. S70: Wors 6E 31
Waterdale Shop. Cen. DN1: Don ...1C 56
Waterfield M. S20: W'fld 1F 151
Waterfield Pl. S70: Stair 2B 32
Waterfront Driving Range 4H 49
Waterfront Golf Course 4H 49
Water Hall La. S36: Pen 3D 176
  (not continuous)
Waterhall Vw. S36: Pen 3D 176
Waterhouse Cl. S65: Dalt 1D 98
Wateringbury Gro. S43: Stav 4C 164
Watering La. S71: Ard 2F 33
Watering Pl. Rd. S36: Thurl 4A 176
Water La. S17: Dore 3G 145
  S60: Roth 5E 97
  S62: Wentw 3D 62
  S65: Hoot R 2H 85
  WF9: Hems 2G 13
Waterloo Ct. S25: Laugh C 3F 127
Waterloo Rd. S3: Shef 5D 106
  S70: Barn 1C 30
Waterloo Wlk. S6: Shef 1E 119
Watermead S63: Bolt D 3C 50
Watermeade S21: Ecki 2C 158
Water Mdw. La. S41: C'fld 1C 166
Water Royd Dr. S75: Dod 3G 29
Waterside Cotts. S65: Ald 1H 97
Waterside Dr. S66: Sunn 2H 99
Waterside Ent. Pk. S25: Laugh C ..4F 127
Waterside Gdns. S35: Ough 3E 91
Waterside Pk. S73: Womb 2A 48
Waterside Vw. DN12: Con 3F 69
Water Slacks Cl. S13: Shef 2C 136
Water Slacks Dr. S13: Shef 2C 136
Water Slacks La. S13: Shef 2B 136
Water Slacks Rd. S13: Shef 2C 136
Water Slacks Wlk. S13: Shef 2C 136
Water Slacks Way S13: Shef 2C 136
Watersmeet Rd. S6: Shef 5A 106
Water St. S3: Shef 1E 5 (2F 119)
  S60: Roth 3E 97
  S65: Roth 3E 97
WATERTHORPE 6F 137
Waterthorpe Cl. S20: W'fld 2G 151
Waterthorpe Cres. S20: W'fld 2G 151
Waterthorpe Gdns. S20: W'fld 2G 151
Waterthorpe Glade S20: W'fld 2G 151
Waterthorpe Glen S20: W'fld 2G 151
Waterthorpe Greenway
  S20: Water 5E 137
Waterthorpe Ri. S20: W'fld 1G 151
Waterthorpe Stop (ST) 1G 151
Water Vole Way DN4: Balb 5B 56
Waterway La. S64: Kiln 6D 66
Watery St. S3: Shef 1B 4 (1E 119)
Wath Golf Course 4F 65
Wath Rd. S7: Shef 2D 132
  S63: Bolt D 3A 50
  S64: Mexb 6C 50
  S73: Bramp, Womb 2A 48
  S73: Hem 2E 63
  S74: Els 2E 63
WATH RDBT. 6G 49
Wath upon Deane Leisure Cen. 1G 65

WATH UPON DEARNE 6G 49
Wath West Ind. Est.
  S63: Wath D 4D 48
WATH WOOD 2G 65
Wath Wood Bottom
  S63: Wath D 3F 65
Wath Wood Dr. S64: Swin 3G 65
Wath Wood Rd. S63: Wath D 2G 65
Watkin Cl. S9: Shef 1E 121
Watkinson Gdns. S20: Water 1F 151
Watnall Rd. S71: Ath 6E 9
Watson Cl. S61: Kimb 2A 96
Watson Glen S61: Kimb 2F 95
Watson La. S42: W'orth 6D 170
Watson Rd. S10: Shef 4B 118
  S61: Kimb 2A 96
Watson St. S74: Hoyl 1G 61
Watson Wlk. S1: Shef 2F 5
Watt La. S10: Shef 4G 117
Waveney Dr. S75: High'm 5F 15
WAVERLEY 2C 122
Waverley Av. DN4: Balb 5F 55
  DN12: Con 4F 69
  S26: Kiv P 5B 140
  S66: Thurc 6C 114
Waverley Cotts. S13: Shef 3A 122
Waverley Ct. DN5: Bntly 4H 23
Waverley La. S13: Shef 3A 122
Waverley Rd. S9: Shef 2F 121
Waverley Vw. S60: Cat 1D 122
Waverley Wlk. S60: Wav 2D 122
Way, The S40: W'ton 2C 170
Waycliffe S71: Monk B 5H 17
Wayford Av. S41: Has 1A 172
  S66: Bram 4B 100
Wayland Av. S70: Wors 5E 31
Wayland Rd. S11: Shef 6C 118
Wayside S43: Brim 6C 162
Wayside Cl. S43: Brim 6C 162
Weakland Cl. S12: Shef 6A 136
Weakland Cres.
  S12: Shef 5A 136
Weakland Dr. S12: Shef 5A 136
Weakland Way S12: Shef 5A 136
Weaver Cl. S75: High'm 5F 15
Weavers Ct. S35: Gren 1B 92
Webb Av. S36: Spink 4G 175
Webb Cl. S63: Bramp B 5B 48
Webbs Av. S6: Stan 6F 105
Webster Cl. S61: Kimb 2F 95
Webster Ct. S40: C'fld 3F 167
  (off Newbold Bk. La.)
Webster Cres. S61: Kimb 2G 95
Webster Cft. S41: Old W 4A 162
Webster St. S9: Shef 3E 109
Wedgewood Cl. S62: Rawm 3G 83
Weedon St. S9: Shef 3E 109
Weetshaw Cl. S72: Shaft 5F 11
Weet Shaw La. S72: Cud 5D 10
Weetshaw La. S72: Shaft 4F 11
Weetwood Dr. S11: Shef 2H 131
Weetwood Rd. S60: Roth 2H 111
Weigh La. S2: Shef 4H 5 (3H 119)
Weir Cl. S74: Hoyl 2B 62
Weir Head S9: Shef 3E 109
Welbeck Cl. S18: Dron W 2B 154
  S43: Ink 2H 169
Welbeck Dr. S26: Aston 1E 139
  S42: W'orth 6F 171
Welbeck M. S66: Wick 1G 113
Welbeck Rd. DN4: Don 2E 57
  S6: Shef 6A 106
Welbeck St. S75: Barn 6C 16
  (not continuous)
Welbury Gdns. S20: Half 4F 151
Welby Pl. S8: Shef 3E 133
Welcome Way DN1: Don 2B 56
Welfare Av. DN12: Con 4D 68
  S40: C'fld 5E 167
Welfare Cl. S63: Thurn 2B 36
Welfare Rd. DN6: Woodl 5C 22
  S63: Thurn 2C 36
Welfare Vw. S63: Gol 6C 36
  S75: Dod 2G 29
Welham Dr. S60: Roth 6F 97
Welland Cl. S3: Shef 6E 107
Welland Ct. S75: High'm 5F 15
Welland Cres. S74: Els 6D 46
Welland Gdns. S74: Els 6D 46

Wellbeck Ct. S43: Stav 4B 164
  (off Porter St.)
Wellbourne Cl. S35: Chap 4H 79
Wellcarr Rd. S8: Shef 6F 133
Well Ct. S12: Shef 5C 136
Wellcliffe Cl. S66: Bram 4H 99
Wellcroft Cl. DN2: Don 4H 41
Wellcroft Gdns. S66: Bram 6B 100
Wellcroft Ho. S71: R'ton 3H 9
  (off Church St.)
Wellcroft M. S70: Wors 2F 45
Well Dr. S65: Thry 6F 85
Wellesley Rd. S10: Shef 3C 118
Wellfield Cl. S6: Shef 2C 118
  S12: Ridg 1H 149
Wellfield Cres. S81: Woods 4F 143
Wellfield Gdns. S71: R'ton 1A 10
Wellfield Gro. S36: Pen 2D 176
Wellfield Lodge S61: Kimb P 1H 95
Wellfield Rd. S6: Shef 1C 118
  S61: Kimb P 6H 81
  S75: Barn 5C 16
Wellgate DN12: Con 4F 69
  S60: Roth 4F 97
  S75: Mapp 5A 8
Wellgate Mt. S60: Roth 4F 97
Wellgate Ter. S60: Roth 4F 97
Well Grn. Rd. S8: Shef 1C 116
Wellhead Rd. S8: Shef 2F 133
Well Hill Gro. S71: R'ton 2H 9
Well Hill Rd. S35: Wort 1H 175
Well Ho. La. S36: Pen 1B 176
Wellhouse La. S36: Pen 2D 176
Wellhouse Way S36: Pen 2D 176
Wellingley Rd. DN4: Balb 2B 72
Wellington Av. S25: Nth A 1G 141
Wellington Cl. S71: Monk B 4G 17
Wellington Cres. S70: Wors 4H 31
Wellington Dr. DN9: Finn 4E 77
Wellington Gro. DN5: Don 3H 39
Wellington Pl. S9: Shef 2F 121
  S70: Barn 1C 30
Wellington Rd. DN12: New E 4H 67
  S6: Shef 6F 105
Wellington St. S1: Shef ...5C 4 (4E 119)
  (not continuous)
  S43: New W 2C 162
  S63: Gol 5D 36
  S64: Mexb 1F 67
  S70: Barn 1D 30
Welling Way S61: Kimb 3H 95
Well La. DN11: Wad 5F 73
  S6: Shef 5H 105
  S12: Shef 4C 136
  S26: Augh 4B 124
  S35: Eccl 2G 93
  S35: Gren 1B 92
  S60: Tree 2F 123
  S60: Up W 5C 112
  S60: Whis 3A 112
  S66: Clftn 3G 87
  S71: Monk B 3H 17
Well La. Ct. S72: Bill 4G 35
Well Meadow Dr.
  S3: Shef 2B 4 (2E 119)
Well Meadow St.
  S3: Shef 1B 4 (2E 119)
Well Rd. S8: Shef 2F 133
Wells, The S25: Nth A 3G 141
Wells Ct. S75: Mapp 6B 8
Wells Gdn. Wlk.
  S25: Nth A 3G 141
Well Spring Cl. S43: Brim 1D 168
Wellspring Cl. S42: W'orth 6A 172
Wells Rd. DN2: Don 4E 41
Well's St. S75: Dod 6F 7
Wells St. S72: Cud 2E 19
Well St. S70: Barn 1C 30
Wellsyke Ind. Est.
  DN6: Adw S 1F 23
Wellsyke Rd. DN6: Adw S 1E 23
Well Vw. Rd. S61: Kimb 2G 95
Wellway, The S66: Sunn 3G 99
Wellwyn Cl. S12: Shef 4E 135
Welney Pl. S6: Shef 6B 92
Welshpool Pl. S40: C'fld 5E 167
Welshpool Yd. S40: C'fld 6E 167
Welton Cl. DN4: Bess 6H 57

Welwyn Cl. S12: Shef 4E **135**
   S40: C'fld 5E **167**
Welwyn Rd. S12: Shef 4E **135**
Wembley Av. DN12: Con 4D **68**
Wembley Cl. DN2: Don 5H **41**
Wendel Gro. S74: Els 6E **47**
Wenlock Cl. S40: Ash 4E **167**
Wenlock Cres. S40: Ash 4D **166**
Wenlock St. S13: Shef 5A **122**
Wensley Cl. S4: Shef 3B **108**
Wensley Ct. S4: Shef 2B **108**
   S71: Smi 1D **16**
Wensley Cres. DN4: Can 5C **58**
Wensley Cft. S4: Shef 2B **108**
Wensleydale Dr. S60: Brins 5E **111**
Wensleydale Rd.
   DN5: Scaws 3E **39**
   S61: Wing 5A **82**
Wensley Dr. S4: Shef 2B **108**
Wensley Gdns. S4: Shef 2B **108**
Wensley Grn. S4: Shef 2B **108**
Wensley Rd. S60: Wav 3C **122**
   S71: Smi 1D **16**
Wensley St. S4: Shef 2B **108**
   S63: Thurn 2A **36**
Wensley Way S43: Stav 6H **163**
WENTWORTH 5D **62**
Wentworth Av. S11: Shef 6G **131**
   S26: Aston 2E **139**
   S40: W'ton 2F **171**
Wentworth Cl. DN5: Sprot 3D **54**
   S61: Thorpe H 3B **80**
   S71: Monk B 4A **18**
Wentworth Ct. S36: Pen 4D **176**
   S61: Grea 4C **82**
   S70: Barn *3E* **31**
     (off Warren Quarry La.)
Wentworth Cres. S36: Pen 4D **176**
   S75: Mapp 6C **8**
Wentworth Dr. S62: Rawm 4G **83**
   S75: Mapp 6B **8**
Wentworth Gdns. S64: Swin 5B **66**
Wentworth Gro. DN4: Bess 2C **74**
Wentworth Ho. *DN1: Don* *2B* **56**
     (off St James St.)
Wentworth Ind. Pk. S75: Tank 2C **60**
Wentworth Mdws. S36: Pen 3D **176**
Wentworth M. S36: Pen 4D **176**
   S75: Mapp 6B **8**
Wentworth Park 6F **63**
Wentworth Pl. S61: Scho 6F **81**
Wentworth Rd. DN2: Don 5D **40**
   S18: Dron W 3B **154**
   S36: Pen 3C **176**
     (not continuous)
   S61: Thorpe H 3C **80**
   S62: Rawm 5D **64**
   S64: Kiln, Swin 5H **65**
   S74: Black H 3A **46**
   S74: Els 2D **62**
   S74: Jum 5D **46**
   S75: Kexb 6E **7**
   S75: Mapp 6B **8**
Wentworth Sta. S74: Hoyl 4H **61**
Wentworth St. S70: Birdw 5D **44**
   S71: Barn 5D **16**
Wentworth Vw. S73: Womb 3G **47**
   S74: Hoyl 1B **62**
     (Millhouses St.)
   S74: Hoyl 1H **61**
     (Willow Cl.)
Wentworth Way S25: Din 1A **142**
   S75: Dod 4G **29**
   S75: Tank 2C **60**
Wentworth Woodhouse 6F **63**
Wentworth Woodhouse Gdns. 6F **63**
Wescoe Av. S72: Gt H 1F **35**
Wesley Av. S26: Aston, Swal 6C **124**
Wesley Cl. S61: Thorpe H 3C **80**
Wesley La. S10: Shef 3A **118**
Wesley Pl. S25: Sth A 4G **141**
Wesley Rd. S26: Kiv P 5A **140**
   S35: High G 1B **78**
     (not continuous)
Wesley St. S70: Barn 1E **31**
Wessenden Cl. S75: Barn 1H **29**
Wessex Cl. S43: Brim 6E **163**
Wessex Gdns. S17: Dore 5E **145**
Wessington Dr. S43: Stav 6H **163**

Westacre S36: Pen 4E **177**
West Av. DN4: Balb 5H **55**
   DN6: Woodl 3A **22**
   S62: Rawm 2G **83**
   S63: Bolt D 3A **50**
   S71: R'ton 2A **10**
   S73: Womb 1E **47**
Westbank Cl. S18: Coal A 6G **147**
Westbank Ct. S18: Coal A 6H **147**
West Bank Dr. S25: Sth A 4F **141**
W. Bank La.
   S1: Shef 3D **4** (3F **119**)
W. Bank Ri. S25: Sth A 4G **141**
West Bar S3: Shef 2E **5** (2F **119**)
Westbar Grn.
   S1: Shef 2E **5** (2F **119**)
WEST BARRIER 2A **76**
West Bars S40: C'fld 5G **167**
W. Bawtry Rd. S60: Roth 3E **111**
Westbourne Gdns. DN4: Balb 1G **71**
Westbourne Gro.
   S40: Bramp 5C **166**
   S75: Barn 5C **16**
Westbourne Rd. S10: Shef 5B **118**
Westbourne Ter. S70: Barn 1B **30**
Westbrook Bank S11: Shef 6C **118**
Westbrook Cl. S40: Bramp 6A **166**
Westbrook Dr. S40: Bramp 6A **166**
Westbrook Rd. S35: Chap 3F **79**
Westbury Av. S35: Chap 4G **79**
Westbury Cl. S75: Barn 4A **16**
Westbury St. S9: Shef 1C **120**
Westby Cl. S65: Rav 2B **100**
Westby Cres. S60: Whis 3A **112**
Westby Wlk. S66: Bram 5B **100**
W. Carr Rd. S25: Din 5G **127**
   S61: Kimb P 2H **95**
Westcott M. S26: Augh 5B **124**
West Cres. S36: Oxs 5G **177**
   S36: Stoc 3C **174**
West Cft. Cl. S43: Ink 3G **169**
Westcroft Cres. S20: W'fld 2F **151**
West Cft. Dr. S43: Ink 3G **169**
Westcroft Dr. S20: W'fld 3F **151**
Westcroft Gdns. S20: W'fld 2F **151**
Westcroft Glen S20: W'fld 3F **151**
Westcroft Gro. S20: W'fld 3F **151**
West End Dr. S6: Shef 6D **106**
West End Av. DN5: Don 3H **39**
   S71: R'ton 3F **9**
West End Ct. DN11: Ross 6E **75**
West End Cres. S71: R'ton 3F **9**
West End La. DN11: New R 5H **73**
West End Rd. S63: Wath D 5C **48**
West End Vw. S21: Ecki 2D **158**
Westerdale Rd. DN5: Scaws 3E **39**
Western Av. S25: Din 6A **128**
Western Bank S10: Shef 3A **4** (3C **118**)
Western Cl. S25: Din 6A **128**
Western Dr. WF9: Sth K 4G **13**
Western M. S70: Barn 6C **16**
Western Rd. S10: Shef 2A **118**
   S65: Roth 3H **97**
Western St. S70: Barn 6C **16**
Western Ter. S73: Womb 1F **47**
Westerton Dr. S66: Bram 6C **100**
W. Farm La. S65: Roth 2C **98**
WESTFIELD
   S20 . . . . .2F **151**
   S63 . . . . .6B **48**
Westfield Av. S12: Shef 5D **136**
   S26: Augh 5B **124**
   S36: Thurl 3A **176**
   S40: Bramp 1C **170**
Westfield Cen. S20: W'fld 2F **151**
Westfield Cl. S40: Bramp 6C **166**
Westfield Craft Pk. S62: P'gte 4F **83**
Westfield Cres. S20: Mosb 2D **150**
   S63: Thurn 2A **36**
Westfield Cft. S63: Bramp B 5B **48**
Westfield Gdns. S40: Bramp 6C **166**
Westfield Gro. S12: Shef 5C **136**
Westfield Ho. S1: Shef 4C **4**
Westfield La. DN5: Barnb 1F **51**
   S21: Midd H 4G **157**
   S36: Thurl 3A **176**
   S75: Bar G 3E **15**
Westfield Northway S20: W'fld 1F **151**
     (not continuous)

Westfield Rd. DN3: Arm 4D **42**
   DN4: Balb 4A **56**
   S18: Dron 4H **155**
   S21: Killa 5B **152**
   S62: P'gte 5F **83**
   S63: Bramp B 6B **48**
   S66: Bram 5A **100**
   S73: Bramp 6B **48**
Westfields S70: Wors 6F **31**
   S71: R'ton 2F **9**
Westfield Southway S20: W'fld 2F **151**
Westfield Sports Cen. 6G **137**
Westfield Stop (ST) 2G **151**
Westfield St. S70: Barn 1C **30**
Westfield Ter. S1: Shef 4C **4** (3E **119**)
   S25: Din 5A **128**
West Gate S64: Mexb 1H **67**
Westgate S36: Pen 5E **177**
   S60: Roth 4E **97**
   S63: Bramp B 6B **48**
   S70: Barn 1D **30**
   S71: Monk B 4G **17**
WEST GREEN 2C **18**
West Green Av. S71: Monk B 2C **18**
West Green Dr. DN3: Kirk Sa 4B **26**
West Green Way S71: Monk B 1A **18**
West Gro. DN2: Don 5F **41**
   S71: R'ton 2F **9**
West Hall Fold S62: Wentw 5D **62**
WEST HANDLEY 4G **157**
Westhaven S72: Cud 3F **19**
West Hill S61: Kimb 4F **95**
Westhill La. S3: Shef 4B **4** (3E **119**)
   S42: Gras 6D **172**
Westholme Rd. DN4: Balb 3A **56**
West House S8: Shef 4F **133**
W. Kirk La. S72: Bill, Midd 3F **35**
W. Laith Ga. DN1: Don 1B **56**
Westland Cl. S20: W'fld 1F **151**
Westland Gdns. S20: W'fld 1E **151**
Westland Gro. S20: W'fld 2F **151**
Westland Rd. S20: W'fld 2F **151**
Westlands S43: Bar H 3G **163**
West La. S6: Lox 2A **104**
   S26: Augh 5A **124**
   S66: Carr 3E **115**
West Lea S40: Bramp 6D **166**
Westleigh Cl. S40: C'fld 3F **167**
West Mall DN1: Don 1B **56**
   S20: Water 6F **137**
Westmeads S71: R'ton 3G **9**
WEST MELTON 5E **49**
Westminster Av. S10: Shef 5C **116**
Westminster Cl. S10: Shef 5C **116**
   S66: Bram 6B **100**
Westminster Cres. DN2: Don 5G **41**
   S10: Shef 5C **116**
Westminster Dr. DN7: Dunsv 4H **27**
Westminster Ho. DN2: Don 5H **41**
Westmoor Cl. S63: Gol 5B **36**
W. Moor Cres. S75: Barn 1H **29**
W. Moor La. DN3: Arm 3G **43**
     (not continuous)
   DN5: Harl 2E **51**
   S63: Bolt D 2E **51**
W. Moor Link DN3: Eden 1B **42**
W. Moor Pk. DN3: Arm 4H **43**
Westmoor Rd. S43: Brim C 4E **169**
West Mt. Av. S63: Wath D 4D **48**
Westnall Ho. *S35: Ough* *3E* **91**
     (off Glossop Row)
Westnall Rd. S5: Shef 3A **94**
Westnall Ter. S5: Shef 3A **94**
Weston Cl. S40: C'fld 3B **166**
West One Aspect S3: Shef 4B **4**
West One Central S1: Shef 4B **4**
West One City S1: Shef 4B **4**
West One Cube S1: Shef 5B **4**
West One Panorama S1: Shef 4B **4**
West One Peak S3: Shef 4B **4**
West One Plaza
   S3: Shef 4B **4** (3E **119**)
West One Reflect S3: Shef 5B **4**

West One Space—Whitehill Ter.

West One Space S3: Shef 5B 4
West One Twr. S3: Shef 4B 4
Westongales Way
DN5: Bntly 2H 39
Weston Park Mus. 3C 118
Weston Rd. DN4: Balb 6H 55
Weston St. S3: Shef 2A 4 (2D 118)
Weston Vw. S10: Shef 3B 118
Westover Rd. S10: Shef 4F 117
West Pk. Dr. S26: Swal 1A 138
West Pinfold S71: R'ton 3H 9
Westpit Hill S63: Bramp B 5B 48
West Pl. DN5: Bntly 1A 40
West Quadrant S5: Shef 1A 108
West Rd. S64: Mexb 1E 67
S75: Barn 6A 16
Westside Grange
DN4: Balb 4G 55
West St. DN1: Don 1B 56
DN12: Con 4F 69
S1: Shef 4B 4 (3E 119)
S18: Dron 2E 155
S20: Beig 5G 137
S21: Ecki 2D 158
S25: Sth A 4G 141
S40: C'fld 4G 167
S63: Gol 4D 36
S63: Wath D 6F 49
(not continuous)
S64: Mexb 2F 67
S66: Thurc 5C 114
S70: Wors 6F 31
S71: R'ton 2A 10
S72: Sth H 1H 11
S73: D'fld 5B 34
S73: Womb 1F 47
S74: Hoyl 6H 45
WF9: Sth K 5G 13
West St. La. S1: Shef 3D 4 (3F 119)
West Street Stop (ST) 4C 4 (3E 119)
WESTTHORPE 5C 152
Westthorpe Bus. Innovation Cen.
S21: Killa 6B 152
Westthorpe Flds. Rd.
S21: Killa 6B 152
Westthorpe Grn. S21: Killa 6C 152
Westthorpe Rd. S21: Killa 5C 152
West Va. Gro. S65: Thry 6E 85
West Vw. S43: Stav 5A 164
S70: Barn 3D 30
S70: Wors 6G 31
S72: Cud 3F 19
S75: Silk C 4B 28
West Vw. Cl. S17: Tot 4G 145
West Vw. Cres. S63: Gol 6B 36
West Vw. La. S17: Tot 4G 145
West Vw. Rd. S41: C'fld 2F 167
S61: Kimb 4F 95
S64: Mexb 2F 67
West Vw. Ter. *S70: Wors* *6G 31*
(off West St.)
Westville Rd. S75: Barn 5C 16
West Way S70: Barn 1D 30
Westwell Pl. S20: Mosb 4E 151
Westwick Cres. S8: Shef 3C 146
Westwick Gro. S8: Shef 3D 146
Westwick Rd. S8: Shef 4C 146
WESTWOOD 5C 60
Westwood S35: High G 5C 60
Westwood Av. S6: Shef 1G 105
S43: Stav 6H 163
Westwood Cl. S6: Shef 1G 105
S43: Ink 3H 169
Westwood Country Pk. 5C 60
Westwood Ct. S35: High G 6C 60
S70: Barn 6D 16
Westwood Dr. S43: Ink 3G 169
Westwood Dr. Gdns. S43: Ink 3G 169
Westwood La. S35: Brom 2A 60
S43: Brim C 4E 169
Westwood New Rd. S35: High G 1A 78
S75: Tank 3C 60
Westwood Rd. S11: Shef 6G 117
S35: High G 6C 60
S44: Cal 4F 169
Wetherby Cl. DN5: Scaws 5E 39
Wetherby Ct. S9: Shef 2F 121
Wetherby Dr. S26: Swal 1B 138
S64: Mexb 6G 51
Wetlands La. S43: Brim C 4D 168
Wet Moor La. S63: Wath D 5E 49
(Norton Rd.)
S63: Wath D 5G 49
(Stables Way)
Whaley Rd. S75: Barn 3G 15
Wharf Cl. S64: Swin 3D 66
Wharfedale Dr. S35: Chap 3D 78
Wharfedale Rd. S75: Barn 6A 16
Wharf La. S41: C'fld 4H 167
S43: Stav 3C 164
Wharf Rd. DN1: Don 5C 40
S9: Tins 1G 109
S64: Kiln 1D 84
Wharf St. S2: Shef 2G 5 (2H 119)
S64: Swin 3D 66
S71: Barn 5F 17
Wharncliffe S75: Dod 4H 29
Wharncliffe Av. S26: Aston 6D 124
S35: Wharn S 1A 90
S63: Wath D *6G 49*
(off Moor Rd.)
Wharncliffe Bus. Pk. S71: Ath 6G 9
Wharncliffe Cl. S62: Rawm 6E 65
S74: Hoyl 2A 62
Wharncliffe Cotts. S75: Pil 1D 60
Wharncliffe Ct. S75: Pil 1B 60
Wharncliffe Hill S65: Roth 3F 97
Wharncliffe Ind. Complex
S36: Spink 3H 175
Wharncliffe Rd. S10: Shef 6A 4 (4D 118)
S35: High G 1C 78
WHARNCLIFFE SIDE 2A 90
Wharncliffe St. DN4: Hex 2H 55
S65: Roth 3F 97
S70: Barn 1C 30
S71: Car 6A 10
Wharton Av. S26: Swal 5C 124
Wharton Dr. S41: C'fld 5A 168
Wheatacre Rd. S36: Stoc 3E 175
Wheata Dr. S5: Shef 3G 93
Wheata Pl. S5: Shef 3F 93
Wheata Rd. S5: Shef 4F 93
Wheatbridge Retail Pk. S40: C'fld 6G 167
Wheatbridge Rd. S40: C'fld 5F 167
Wheat Cft. DN12: Con 4H 69
Wheatcroft Cl. S42: W'orth 6H 171
Wheatcroft Gdns. S36: Pen 5E 177
Wheatcroft Rd. S62: Rawm 2A 84
Wheatcrofts S70: Barn 1C 30
Wheatfield Cl. DN3: Barn D 2D 26
Wheatfield Cres. S5: Shef 4A 94
Wheatfield Dr. S63: Thurn 3C 36
Wheatfield Way S42: Ash 3A 166
Wheathill Cl. S42: Ash 4A 166
S43: Brim C 4E 169
Wheathill La. S43: Brim C 4C 168
Wheathill St. S60: Roth 5E 97
Wheat Holme La.
DN5: Bntly, Holme 1B 24
Wheatlands Rd. S42: W'orth 6F 171
WHEATLEY 5D 40
Wheatley Cl. S71: Barn 4E 17
Wheatley Dr. S75: Wool G 3F 7
Wheatley Golf Course 4A 42
Wheatley Gro. S13: Shef 5H 121
Wheatley Hall Rd. DN2: Don 4D 40
Wheatley Hall Trade Pk. DN2: Don 2G 41
WHEATLEY HILLS 4H 41
Wheatley La. DN1: Don 6D 40
WHEATLEY PARK 3G 41
Wheatley Pk. Rd. DN5: Bntly 6H 23
Wheatley Pl. DN12: Den M 3C 68
Wheatley Retail Pk. DN2: Don 2G 41
Wheatley Ri. S75: Stain 4A 8
Wheatley Rd. S61: Kimb P 1H 95
S64: Kiln 1D 84
S70: Stair 3B 32
Wheatley St. DN12: Den M 3C 68
Wheats La. S1: Shef 2E 5
Wheel, The S35: Eccl 2D 92
Wheeldon Cres. S43: Brim 6C 162
Wheeldon St. S1: Shef 3B 4 (3E 119)
Wheel La. S35: Gren 2C 92
S35: Ough 3C 90
Wheldrake Rd. S5: Shef 2A 108
Whernside Av. S35: Chap 2E 79
Whinacre Cl. S8: Shef 4G 147
Whinacre Pl. S8: Shef 4F 147
Whinacre Wlk. S8: Shef 4F 147
Whinby Cft. S75: Dod 3G 29
Whinby Rd. S75: Dod, High'm 2F 29
Whin Cl. WF9: Hems 1E 13
Whin Cnr. S72: Shaft 2E 11
Whincover Vw. S71: R'ton 2B 10
Whinfell Cl. DN6: Adw S 2C 22
Whinfell Ct. S11: Shef 6F 131
Whin Gdns. S63: Thurn 1C 36
Whin Hill Rd. DN4: Bess 4A 58
Whinmoor Cl. S75: Silk 1A 28
Whinmoor Ct. S75: Silk 1A 28
Whinmoor Dr. S75: Silk 1A 28
Whinmoor Rd. S5: Shef 1C 108
S35: High G 1B 78
Whinmoor Vw. S75: Silk 1A 28
Whinmoor Way S75: Silk 2A 28
WHINNEY HILL 6D 84
Whins, The S62: Neth Hau 2D 82
Whinside Cres. S63: Thurn 1B 36
Whiphill Cl. DN4: Bess 5B 58
Whiphill La. DN3: Arm 5F 43
Whiphill Top La. DN3: Brant 3H 59
(not continuous)
WHIRLOW 6G 131
Whirlow Chapel Rd. S60: Wav 3C 122
Whirlow Ct. Rd. S11: Shef 6G 131
Whirlow Cft. S11: Shef 5G 131
Whirlowdale Cl. S11: Shef 6F 131
Whirlowdale Cres. S7: Shef 5A 132
Whirlowdale Ri. S11: Shef 6G 131
Whirlowdale Rd. S7: Shef 5B 132
S11: Shef 6F 131
Whirlow Elms Chase S11: Shef 4G 131
Whirlow Farm M. S11: Shef 5F 131
Whirlow Grange Av. S11: Shef 6F 131
Whirlow Grange Dr. S11: Shef 6F 131
Whirlow Grn. S11: Shef 6F 131
Whirlow Gro. S11: Shef 6G 131
Whirlow La. S11: Shef 5F 131
Whirlow M. S11: Shef 5G 131
Whirlow Pk. Rd. S11: Shef 6G 131
Whisperwood Dr. DN4: Balb 2A 72
WHISTON 3A 112
Whiston Brook Vw. S60: Whis 3B 112
Whiston Grange S60: Roth 3H 111
Whiston Grn. S60: Whis 4A 112
Whiston Gro. S60: Roth 6G 97
Whiston Va. S60: Whis 4A 112
Whitaker Cl. DN11: New R 6G 75
Whitaker Sq. DN11: New R 6B 74
Whitbeck Cl. DN11: Wad 5E 73
Whitbourne Cl. S71: Smi 3E 17
Whitburn Rd. DN1: Don 2D 56
Whitby Rd. DN11: New R 6B 74
S9: Shef 1F 121
Whitcomb Dr. DN11: New R 6G 75
White Apron St. WF9: Sth K 4H 13
Whitebank Cl. S41: C'fld 1A 172
Whitecedar La. S71: Lund 5B 18
Whitecotes Cl. S40: W'ton 2F 171
Whitecotes La. S40: C'fld, W'ton 2E 171
Whitecotes Pk. S40: W'ton 2G 171
White Cft. S1: Shef 2C 4 (2F 119)
Whitecroft Cres. S60: Brins 4D 110
White Cross Av. S72: Cud 3E 19
White Cross Ct. S72: Cud 3F 19
White Cross La. DN11: Wad 5H 71
S70: Swai, Wors 5A 32
White Cross Mt. S72: Cud 3F 19
Whitecross Ri. S70: Wors 5A 32
White Cross Rd. S72: Cud 3E 19
White Cross Vw. S70: Wors 5A 32
White Edge Cl. S40: C'fld 3E 167
White Ga. S25: Nth A 2A 142
Whitegate Wlk. S61: Wing 5H 81
Whitehall Rd. S61: Wing 4A 82
Whitehall Way S61: Wing 5B 82
White Hart Cnr. S21: Ecki 6F 151
Whitehead Av. S36: Spink 3F 175
Whitehead Cl. S25: Din 5H 127
Whitehead St. S43: Stav 4C 164
White Hill Av. S70: Barn 1H 29
Whitehill Av. S60: Brins 4D 110
Whitehill Dr. S60: Brins 5D 110
White Hill Gro. S70: Barn 1A 30
Whitehill La. S60: Brins 3D 110
Whitehill Rd. S60: Brins 4C 110
Whitehill Ter. S70: Barn 1H 29

Whitehill Willow S60: Brins 5D **110**
Whitehouse La. S6: Shef 6C **106**
Whitehouse Rd. S6: Shef 6C **106**
Whitehouses S41: C'fld 1A **172**
White Ho. Vw.
 DN3: Barn D 1G **27**
White La. S12: Shef 5E **135**
 S35: Chap 1G **79**
White Lane Stop (ST) 5E **135**
Whitelea Gro. S64: Mexb 2E **67**
Whitelea Grove Trad. Est.
 S64: Mexb 2E **67**
White Leas S40: Ash 4C **166**
Whitelee Rd. S64: Swin 3D **66**
Whiteley La. S10: Shef 1D **130**
Whiteleys Av. S62: Rawm 1F **83**
Whiteley Wood Cl. S11: Shef 1G **131**
WHITELEY WOOD GREEN 3D **130**
Whiteley Wood Rd. S11: Shef 2E **131**
WHITELEY WOODS 1G **131**
Whitelow La. S17: Dore 2A **144**
White Rd. S43: Stav 3D **164**
White Rose Ct. DN5: Bntly 1B **40**
White Rose Ho. S60: Roth 5E **97**
White Rose Way DN4: Don 3C **56**
White Rose Way (Park & Ride) 1D **72**
White's La. S2: Shef 3A **120**
White Thorns Cl. S8: Shef 4G **147**
White Thorns Dr. S8: Shef 5G **147**
White Thorns Vw. S8: Shef 4G **147**
White Towers Cvn. Site
 DN2: Don 4B **42**
Whiteways Cl. S4: Shef 4A **108**
Whiteways Dr. S4: Shef 4A **108**
Whiteways Gro. S4: Shef 4A **108**
Whiteways Rd. S4: Shef 4A **108**
Whitewood Cl. S71: R'ton 4G **9**
Whitfield Gdns. S81: Woods 4E **143**
Whitfield Rd. S10: Shef 1D **130**
 S62: Rawm 1E **83**
Whitham Rd. S10: Shef 4B **118**
Whiting St. S8: Shef 2F **133**
WHITLEY 6E **79**
Whitley Carr S35: Gren 6D **78**
Whitley Cft. S35: Eccl 6G **79**
Whitley La. S35: Gren, Eccl 1C **92**
Whitley Vw. S35: Eccl 6G **79**
Whitley Vw. Rd. S61: Kimb 5E **95**
Whitmoore Dr. DN9: Auck 3A **76**
Whitney Cl. DN4: Balb 1F **71**
Whittier Rd. DN4: Balb 6H **55**
Whitting M. S41: Old W 4G **161**
Whittington Hill S41: Old W 5H **161**
Whittington Ind. Est. S43: New W . . .3C **162**
Whittington La. S18: Uns 6B **156**
WHITTINGTON MOOR 6H **161**
Whittington Rd.
 S43: Bar H, New W 2D **162**
Whittington St. DN1: Don 5C **40**
Whittington Way S41: Whitt M 5H **161**
Whitting Valley Rd.
 S41: Old W 5H **161**
Whittle Way S60: Shef 2B **122**
Whitton Cl. DN4: Bess 6H **57**
Whitwell Cres. S36: Stoc 3D **174**
Whitwell La. S36: Stoc 4C **174**
Whitwell St. S9: Shef 2G **121**
Whitwell Vw. DN11: Ross 5E **75**
Whitworth Ct. DN9: Finn 3C **76**
Whitworth Cft. S10: Shef 4G **117**
Whitworth La. S9: Shef 5D **108**
 S63: Wath D 4E **49**
Whitworth Rd. S10: Shef 5F **117**
 S41: C'fld 2G **167**
Whitworth St. S63: Gol 5D **36**
Whitworth Way S63: Wath D 5F **49**
Whybourne Gro. S60: Roth 5F **97**
Whybourne Ter. S60: Roth 4F **97**
Whyn Vw. S63: Thurn 2B **36**
Wickens Pl. S43: Mas M 2E **165**
Wicker S3: Shef 1G **5** (2G **119**)
Wicker La. S3: Shef 1F **5** (2G **119**)
 (not continuous)
WICKERSLEY 6G **99**
Wickersley Ct. S66: Wick 6E **99**
Wickersley Rd. S60: Roth 6H **97**
Wickett Hern Rd. DN3: Arm 4F **43**
Wicket Way DN12: New E 3D **70**
Wickfield Cl. S12: Shef 3A **136**

Wickfield Dr. S12: Shef 3A **136**
Wickfield Gro.
 S12: Shef 4H **135**
Wickfield Rd. S12: Shef 4A **136**
Wicklow Rd. DN2: Don 5F **41**
Wickstone Dr. S72: Cud 1F **19**
Widdop Cl. S13: Shef 6G **121**
Widdop Cft. S13: Shef 6G **121**
Wigfield Dr. S70: Wors 5E **31**
Wigfield Farm 6E **31**
Wigfull Rd.
 S11: Shef 5B **118**
Wigley Rd. S43: Ink 2H **169**
Wignall Av. S66: Wick 6E **99**
Wikeley Way S43: Brim 6C **162**
Wike Rd. S71: Lund 6B **18**
Wilberforce Ct. S25: Sth A 3G **141**
Wilberforce Rd. DN2: Don 1A **42**
 S25: Sth A 3G **141**
Wilbrook Ri. S75: Barn 4H **15**
Wilby Carr Gdns. DN4: Can 3B **58**
Wilby La. S70: Barn 2F **31**
Wilcox Cl. S6: Shef 5C **92**
Wilcox Grn. S61: Wing 4B **82**
Wilcox Rd. S6: Shef 5B **92**
Wild Av. S62: Rawm 1D **82**
Wild Bank Pl. S5: Shef 3F **93**
Wilden Cft. S43: Brim 6B **162**
Wildene Dr. S64: Mexb 6F **51**
Wilder M. S61: Kimb 3A **96**
Wildflower Cl. DN11: New R 6F **75**
Wild Geese Way
 S64: Mexb 1B **68**
Wilding Cl. S61: Kimb 2H **95**
Wilding Way S61: Kimb 2H **95**
Wilford Rd. S71: Ath 5D **8**
Wilfred Cl. S9: Shef 1D **120**
Wilfred Dr. S9: Shef 1D **120**
Wilfred St. S60: Roth 4E **97**
Wilfrid Rd. S9: Shef 1D **120**
Wilkin Hill S18: Barl 5A **160**
Wilkinson Av. DN11: New R 6D **74**
Wilkinson Cl. S40: Birdh 4H **171**
Wilkinson Dr. S43: Ink 1G **169**
Wilkinson La. S10: Shef 4A **4** (3D **118**)
 (not continuous)
Wilkinson Rd. S74: Els 1D **62**
Wilkinson St. S10: Shef 4A **4** (3D **118**)
 (not continuous)
Willan Dr. S60: Cat 1D **122**
Willbury Dr. S12: Shef 2D **134**
Willersley Ct. S41: C'fld 1E **167**
 (off Newbold Rd.)
Willey St. S3: Shef 1G **5** (2G **119**)
William Brown Sq. S40: C'fld 1H **171**
William Cl. S20: Mosb 4E **151**
William Ct. WF9: Sth K 4H **13**
William Cres. S20: Mosb 3E **151**
William La. DN11: New R 4A **74**
William Nuttall Cott. Homes
 DN4: Don 2E **57**
Williamson Rd. S11: Shef 1C **132**
Williams Rd. DN5: Cus 4G **39**
Williams St. S62: P'gte 4H **83**
William St. S10: Shef 6A **4** (4D **118**)
 S21: Ecki 1E **159**
 S41: C'fld 2H **167**
 S60: Roth 4F **97**
 S63: Gol 5B **36**
 S63: Wath D 6G **49**
 S64: Swin 3D **66**
 S70: Wors 5F **31**
 S73: Womb 1F **47**
William St. Nth. S40: Old W 4G **161**
Willingham Cl. S20: Sot 1H **151**
Willingham Gdns. S20: Sot 1H **151**
Willington Rd. S5: Shef 6H **93**
Willis Rd. S6: Shef 3A **106**
Willman Rd. S71: Lund 5C **18**
Willoughby St. S4: Shef 2B **108**
Willow Av. DN4: Can 4C **58**
 S62: Rawm 3H **83**
Willow Bank S71: Barn 3C **16**
 S75: Barn 4D **16**
Willow Beck S65: Roth 2A **98**
Willow Bri. Cvn. Site DN5: Don 5A **40**
Willow Brook S75: Dart 6H **7**
Willow Chase S25: Nth A 3H **141**

Willow Cl. S25: Sth A 5G **141**
 S60: Brins 5E **111**
 S66: Flan 4H **99**
 S72: Cud 1E **19**
 S74: Hoyl 1H **61**
Willow Ct. S44: Cal 5F **169**
 S62: Rawm 2H **83**
 S63: Wath D 1F **65**
 S66: Wick 6G **99**
 S73: D'fld 5B **34**
Willow Cres. DN9: Auck 2A **76**
 S35: Chap 4F **79**
 S66: B'well 6B **88**
Willowcroft S63: Bolt D 3A **50**
Willowdale Cl. DN5: Sprot 4D **54**
Willowdale Ri. S61: Scho 6E **81**
Willow Dene Rd. S72: Grim 1B **20**
Willow Dr. DN2: New E 3D **70**
 S9: Shef 3H **121**
 S43: Mas M 2F **165**
 S64: Mexb 1E **67**
 S66: Flan 4H **99**
 WF9: Hems 1E **13**
Willow Gdns. S73: Womb 1H **47**
Willow Gth. S73: Womb 6E **33**
Willowgarth S62: Rawm 2H **83**
Willowgarth Av. S60: Brins 4D **110**
Willow Gth. Rd. S41: C'fld 6D **160**
Willow Glen DN3: Brant 4H **59**
Willow Gro. S26: Aston 6E **125**
Willow La. DN11: Ross 5D **74**
 S36: Oxs 5H **177**
 S63: Bolt D 3C **50**
Willowlees Ct. DN4: Bess 5B **58**
Willow Pl. S66: B'well 6B **88**
Willow Rd. DN3: Arm 3F **43**
 S21: Killa 5B **152**
 S36: Stoc 5D **174**
 S63: Thurn 1C **36**
 S63: Wath D 2H **65**
 S66: Malt 5G **101**
Willows, The S36: Oxs 6H **177**
 S61: Kimb P 6G **81**
 S65: Roth 5G **97**
 (off Johnson St.)
 S73: D'fld 5B **34**
Willow St. DN12: Con 4G **69**
 S70: Barn 2C **30**
Willow Tree Way S66: Wick 6G **99**
Willow Wlk. DN5: Bntly 5H **23**
 S70: Barn 3F **31**
Wilmington Dr. DN4: Don 5E **57**
Wilsden Gro. S75: Barn 5A **16**
WILSIC 4H **89**
Wilsic Ho. DN1: Don 2B **56**
 (off Grove Pl.)
Wilsic La. DN11: Tick, Wils 4H **89**
Wilsic Rd. DN11: Wils 2H **89**
Wilson Av. S36: Pen 5D **176**
 S62: Rawm 2F **83**
Wilson Ct. S73: Womb 6F **33**
Wilson Dr. S65: Dalt 1D **98**
Wilson Gro. S71: Lund 4B **18**
Wilson Pl. S8: Shef 2F **133**
Wilson Rd. S11: Shef 6B **118**
 S18: Coal A 6H **147**
 S36: Spink 4H **175**
Wilson St. S3: Shef 6F **107**
 S18: Dron 4G **155**
 S73: Womb 1E **47**
Wilson Wlk. S75: Dod 4H **29**
Wilstrop Rd. S9: Shef 1E **121**
WILTHORPE 4B **16**
Wilthorpe Av. S75: Barn 4B **16**
Wilthorpe Cres. S75: Barn 4B **16**
Wilthorpe Farm Rd. S75: Barn 4B **16**
Wilthorpe Gdns. S20: Mosb 5B **136**
Wilthorpe Grn. S75: Barn 4B **16**
Wilthorpe La. S75: Barn 4A **16**
Wilthorpe Rd. S75: Barn 4H **15**
Wilton Cl. S62: Rawm 3G **83**
Wilton Cft. S61: Kimb 3B **96**
Wilton Gdns. S61: Roth 3B **96**
Wilton La. S61: Roth 4B **96**
Wilton Pl. S10: Shef 6A **4** (4D **118**)
Wiltshire Av. DN12: Den M 3C **68**
Wiltshire Rd. DN2: Don 6H **41**
Wimborne Cres. S41: C'fld 1F **167**
Winberry Av. S25: Nth A 3H **141**

Wincanton Cl. S64: Mexb 6G 51
Winchester Av. DN2: Don 4F 41
S10: Shef 6C 116
Winchester Ct. S65: Roth 3F 97
(off Nottingham St.)
Winchester Cres. S10: Shef 6C 116
Winchester Dr. S10: Shef 6C 116
Winchester Ho. DN5: Scaws 4E 39
Winchester Rd. S10: Shef 6C 116
S41: C'fld 1F 167
Winchester Way DN5: Scaws 4F 39
S60: Brins 3B 110
S71: Ard .3D 32
WINCOBANK 1C 108
Wincobank Av. S5: Shef 1B 108
Wincobank Cl. S5: Shef 1C 108
Wincobank La. S4: Shef 3C 108
Wincobank Rd. S5: Shef 1C 108
Winco Rd. S4: Shef 3C 108
Winco Wood La. S5: Shef 1C 108
Windam Dr. DN3: Barn D 1H 27
Windermere Av. DN2: Don 5H 41
S18: Dron W 3D 154
S63: Gol .6D 36
Windermere Cl. S64: Mexb 6A 52
Windermere Ct. S25: Nth A 2H 141
Windermere Cres.
DN3: Kirk Sa 4C 26
Windermere Dr. DN4: Don 3G 57
Windermere Grange
DN12: New E 5C 70
Windermere Rd. S8: Shef 3D 132
S36: Pen .3D 176
S41: C'fld 1D 166
S71: Barn .1F 31
Winders Pl. S73: Womb 2G 47
Windgate Hill DN12: Con 3G 69
Windham Cl. S71: Barn 5E 17
WINDHILL 6H 51
Windhill Av. S64: Mexb 1H 67
S75: Stain .3H 7
Windhill Cres. S64: Mexb 6H 51
S75: Stain .3H 7
Windhill Dr. S75: Stain 3H 7
Windhill La. S75: Stain 3H 7
Windhill Mt. S75: Stain 3H 7
Windhill Ri. S75: Wool G 3F 7
Windhill Ter. S64: Mexb 6H 51
Windings, The S63: Thurn 3E 37
Winding Wheel, The 5A 168
Windle Ct. S60: Tree 2G 123
Windle Rd. DN4: Hex 3H 55
Windle Sq. DN3: Kirk Sa 4C 26
Windmill Av. DN12: Con 5G 69
S72: Grim .6A 12
Windmill Bank La.
DN6: Adw S, Woodl 4B 22
Windmill Cl. S70: Barn 3F 31
Windmill Ct. DN6: Woodl 3C 22
S61: Thorpe H 5D 80
S73: Womb 2E 47
Windmill Dr. DN11: Wad 6E 73
Windmill Est. DN12: Con 5G 69
Windmill Greenway S20: Half 5F 151
WINDMILL HILL 6E 73
Windmill Hill La. S35: Burn 4D 78
Windmill La. S5: Shef 6B 94
S18: Hun .1H 161
S36: Thurl .4A 176
Windmill Rd. S25: Nth A 2H 141
S73: Womb 2E 47
Windmill Ter. S71: R'ton 1G 9
Windmill Way S43: Brim 6B 162
Windsor Av. S36: Thurl 3A 176
S75: Kexb .6D 6
Windsor Cl. DN5: Harl 2H 51
S40: W'ton 1D 170
S66: Bram .4A 100
Windsor Ct. DN7: Dunsv 4H 27
S11: Shef .4G 131
S70: Barn .6D 16
Windsor Cres. S71: Monk B 5G 17
S72: Midd .3E 35
Windsor Dr. DN5: Barnb 1H 51
S18: Dron W 3B 154
S42: W'orth 6F 171
S64: Mexb 6H 51
S75: Dod .3G 29
Windsor Gdns. S63: Thurn 2D 36

Windsor Ri. S26: Aston 2D 138
Windsor Rd. DN2: Don 6E 41
DN12: Con 3E 69
S8: Shef .2E 133
S61: Thorpe H 4C 80
WF9: Hems 1G 13
Windsor Sq. S63: Thurn 2D 36
Windsor St. S4: Shef 6A 108
(not continuous)
S63: Thurn 2D 36
S74: Hoyl .5A 46
Windsor Vw. DN11: New R 6A 74
Windsor Wlk.
DN5: Scaws 4F 39
S25: Sth A 5F 141
S41: Has .1B 172
S72: Grim .2B 20
Windy Ho. La. S2: Shef 1C 134
Windy Ridge S26: Augh 5B 124
Winfield Rd. S63: Wath D 1G 65
WINGERWORTH 6H 171
Wingerworth Av. S8: Shef 2C 146
Wingerworth Hall Est.
S42: W'orth 6H 171
(off Longedge Ri.)
Wingerworth Way S40: Birdh 4G 171
WINGFIELD 5B 82
Wingfield Cl. S18: Dron W 4B 154
S61: Wing 5B 82
Wingfield Ct. S61: Wing 6A 82
Wingfield Cres. S12: Shef 3F 135
Wingfield Rd. S61: Wing 5H 81
S71: Ath .2F 17
Winholme DN3: Arm 4E 43
Winifred St. S60: Roth 4D 96
Winkley Ter. S5: Shef 5B 94
Winlea Av. S66: Roth 6D 98
Winmarith Ct. S71: R'ton 3G 9
Winnat Pl. S43: Ink 1H 169
Winnats Cl. S40: C'fld 3D 166
Winnats Way S10: Shef 5H 117
Winn Cl. S6: Shef 1A 106
Winn Dr. S6: Shef 1A 106
Winn Gdns. S6: Shef 1A 106
(not continuous)
Winn Gro. S6: Shef 6H 91
Winnipeg Rd. DN5: Bntly 1A 40
Winscar Rd. S64: Dron 5G 57
Winsford Rd. S6: Shef 5B 92
WINSICK 4D 172
Winster Cl. S70: Birdw 4E 45
Winster Ct. S41: C'fld 4H 167
Winster Rd. S6: Shef 3B 106
S43: Stav .6H 163
Winston Av. S36: Stoc 2B 174
Winter Av. S71: R'ton 1H 9
S75: Barn .6B 16
Winter Garden 4E 5 (3F 119)
Winter Hill La. S61: Kimb 3H 95
Winterhill Rd. S61: Kimb 4G 95
Winterhill Youth Cen. 3G 95
Winter Rd. S75: Barn 6B 16
Wintersett Dr. DN4: Don 6G 57
Winter St. S3: Shef 2D 118
Winter Ter. S75: Barn 6A 58
Winterton Cl. DN4: Bess 3F 57
Winterton Gdns. S12: Shef 5D 136
Winterwell Rd. S63: Wath D 5D 48
(not continuous)
Winton Cl. S70: Barn 3F 31
Winton Rd. DN2: Don 6G 41
Wisbech Cl. S40: W'ton 2F 171
Wisconsin Dr. DN4: Don 5F 57
Wiseley Cft. S72: Grim 6B 12
Wiseton Rd. S11: Shef 6B 118
WISEWOOD 4G 105
Wisewood Av. S6: Shef 4H 105
Wisewood La. S6: Shef 4H 105
Wisewood Pl. S6: Shef 4H 105
Wisewood Rd. S6: Shef 4H 105
Wishing Well Grn. S26: Swal 1A 138
Wiston Way S41: Has 3B 172
Witham Cl. S41: C'fld 2B 168
Witham Ct. S40: Bramp 5D 166
S75: High'm 5F 15
Witham Way S63: Bramp B 5B 48
Withens Av. S6: Shef 2A 106
Withens Ct. S75: Mapp 3F 15
Witney St. S8: Shef 6F 119

Wittsend Park Cvn. Site
DN5: Ark 5D 24
Wivelsfield Rd. DN4: Balb 5F 55
Woburn Cl. DN4: Balb 1F 71
Woburn Pl. S11: Shef 6G 131
S75: Dod .4G 29
Wolfe Cl. S40: W'ton 1E 171
Wolfe Dr. S6: Shef 5C 92
Wolfe Rd. S6: Shef 5C 92
Wollaton Av. S17: Bradw 5H 145
Wollaton Cl. S71: Ath 6D 8
Wollaton Dr. S17: Bradw 5H 145
Wollaton Rd. S17: Bradw 6G 145
Wolseley Rd. S8: Shef 1F 133
Wolsey Av. DN2: Don 1F 57
Wolverley Rd. S13: Shef 2B 136
WOMBWELL 1G 47
Wombwell Av. S63: Wath D 1F 65
Wombwell Hillies Golf Course
. . . . .3G 47
Wombwell La. S70: Stair 3B 32
S73: Womb 3B 32
S74: Black H 2A 46
Wombwell Race Circuit Go-Kart Track
. . . . .6H 33
Wombwell Rd. S74: Hoyl 5B 46
Wombwell Station (Rail) 2E 47
Wood Acres S75: Barn 4H 15
WOODALL 5H 153
Woodall La.
S26: Hart, Wooda 4H 153
Woodall Rd. S21: Killa 5E 153
S65: Roth .5B 98
Woodall Rd. Sth.
S65: Roth .5B 98
WOODALL SERVICE AREA 5G 153
Woodbank Cl. S17: Dore 3H 145
(off Ladies Spring Dr.)
Woodbank Cres. S8: Shef 3E 133
Woodbank Rd. S6: Stan 3A 116
Woodbourne Gdns. S75: Tank 1D 60
Woodbourn Gdns.
S73: Womb 5E 33
Woodbourn Hill S9: Shef 1C 120
Woodbourn Rd. S9: Shef 2C 120
Woodbourn Road Stop (ST) 1C 120
Woodbridge Ri. S40: W'ton 2C 170
Woodburn Ct. S61: Roth 3C 96
(off Alice Rd.)
Woodburn Dr. S35: Chap 3G 79
Woodbury Cl. S9: Shef 5D 94
Woodbury Rd. S9: Shef 5D 94
Wood Cliffe S10: Shef 2C 130
Wood Cl. S35: Chap 4H 79
S42: W'orth 6E 171
S62: Rawm 1F 83
S65: Rav .2H 99
Woodcock Cl.
S61: Kimb P 6A 82
Woodcock Pl. S2: Shef 3A 120
Woodcock Rd. S74: Hoyl 1B 62
Woodcock Way
DN6: Adw S 1C 22
Wood Ct. DN3: Arm 3D 42
Wood Cft. S61: Kimb P 1A 96
Woodcross Av. DN4: Can 5D 58
S72: Grim .1B 20
Wood End S35: Gren 6D 78
Wood End Av. S36: Cub 6C 176
Woodend Cl. S6: Shef 5H 105
Wood End Ct. S75: Dod 4H 29
Woodend Dr. S6: Shef 5H 105
Woodfarm Av. S6: Shef 6G 105
Woodfarm Cl. S6: Shef 6F 105
Woodfarm Dr. S6: Shef 6F 105
Woodfarm Pl. S6: Shef 6F 105
Woodfield Av. S64: Mexb 1G 67
Woodfield Cl. S73: D'fld 4B 34
Woodfield Rd. DN3: Arm 5F 43
DN4: Balb .5H 55
(not continuous)
S10: Shef .1A 118
S63: Wath D 6C 48
Wood Flds. S66: Bram 6B 100
Woodfield Vs. S60: Roth 6F 97
Woodfield Way DN4: Balb 2A 72
Wood Fold S3: Shef 5F 107
Woodfoot Rd. S60: Roth 3G 111
Woodford Rd. DN3: Barn D 1H 27

Woodford Way S43: Bar H 2G 163
Woodgrove Rd. S9: Shef 6E 95
   S65: Roth 3B 98
Woodhall Cl. S73: D'fld 4B 34
Woodhall Flats S73: D'fld 4B 34
Woodhall Ri. S64: Swin 4C 66
Woodhall Rd. S73: D'fld 4B 34
Woodhead Dr. S74: Black H 3A 46
Woodhead La. S74: Hoyl 2B 46
Woodhead M. S74: Black H 3A 46
Woodhead Rd. S2: Shef 6F 119
   S35: Gren 4A 78
Woodhead Vw. S74: Jum 4D 46
Woodhead Way S10: Shef 5H 117
WOOD HILL 4A 108
Woodholm Pl. S11: Shef 3A 132
Woodholm Rd. S11: Shef 3A 132
WOODHOUSE 2C 136
Woodhouse Av. S20: Beig 4G 137
Woodhouse Cl. S62: Rawm 6E 65
Woodhouse Ct. S20: Beig 4F 137
Woodhouse Cres. S20: Beig 4G 137
Woodhouse Gdns. S13: Shef 2D 136
Woodhouse Grn. S66: Thurc 5B 114
   (not continuous)
Wood Ho. La. DN11: Wad 1G 89
Woodhouse La. S20: Beig 3F 137
   (not continuous)
   S43: Barl 1F 165
   WF4: Wool 1H 7
WOODHOUSE MILL 6E 123
Woodhouse Rd. DN2: Don 4D 40
   S12: Shef 2E 135
   S74: Hoyl 1A 62
Woodhouse Station (Rail) 1E 137
Woodhouse Washlands Nature Reserve
   .1G 137
Woodkirk Cl. S36: Pen 5F 177
Woodknot M. DN4: Balb 2A 72
WOODLAITHES 3G 99
Woodlaithes Rd. S66: Sunn 2H 99
Woodland Av. S25: Nth A 3H 141
Woodland Cl. S60: Cat 1D 122
   S66: Wick 1H 113
Woodland Ct. S35: Chap 3C 78
Woodland Dr. S12: Shef 6E 135
   S25: Nth A 3H 141
   S70: Barn 2A 30
Woodland Gdns. S66: Malt 5C 102
Woodland Gro.
   S63: Wath D 2G 65
Woodland Pl. S17: Bradw 5G 145
Woodland Ri. S75: Silk C 5B 28
Woodland Rd. S8: Shef 5G 133
   S41: Old W 2G 161
   S63: Wath D 2G 65
WOODLANDS 3C 22
Woodlands S43: Brim 1C 168
   S60: Roth 1B 112
Woodlands, The DN3: Arm 3F 43
   S10: Shef 4H 117
Woodlands Av. S20: Beig 3G 137
Woodlands Chase S61: Kimb P 6A 82
Woodlands Cl. S26: Swal 5C 124
Woodlands Cl. S75: Wool G 3F 7
Woodlands Cres. S64: Swin 4H 65
WOODLANDS EAST 5D 22
Woodlands Farm S60: Tree 2F 123
Woodlands Gdns. DN3: Eden 1B 42
Woodlands Rd. DN6: Woodl 4C 22
   S74: Hoyl 4B 46
Woodlands Ter. DN12: New E 5C 70
Woodlands Vw. DN6: Woodl 4B 22
   S72: Gt H 6F 21
   S73: Womb 4D 46
   S74: Hoyl 5B 46
Woodlands Way DN12: Den M 3C 68
Woodland Ter. S72: Grim 3C 20
WOODLAND VIEW 6H 105
Woodland Vw. S12: Shef 6E 135
   S17: Dore 3H 145
   S64: Mexb 2H 67
   S71: Barn 1A 32
   S72: Cud 3E 19
   S75: Silk C 5B 28
Woodland Vw. Rd. S6: Shef 6H 105
Woodland Vs. S72: Grim 2C 20
   S75: Pil 1D 60
Woodland Wlk. S40: C'fld 3A 166

Woodland Way S65: Roth 5B 98
Wood La. DN11: Wad 4F 71
   DN12: Old E 1C 88
   S6: Shef 6F 105
   S12: Shef 5C 134
   S60: Cat 5B 110
   S60: Roth 1E 111
   (not continuous)
   S60: Tree 2F 123
   S66: Bram, Wick 1H 113
   S66: Bramp M 1H 125
   S66: Stain 1F 103
   S71: Car 4F 9
   (Ruscombe Rd.)
   S71: Car 5H 9
   (Woodroyd Av.)
   S71: Stain 4D 8
Wood La. Cl. S6: Shef 6F 105
Woodlea Gdns. DN4: Can 5C 58
Woodlea Gro. DN3: Arm 4E 43
Woodlea Way DN2: Don 3H 41
Woodleigh Cl. S40: C'fld 3A 166
Woodleys Av. S62: Rawm 6F 65
Woodman Dr. S64: Swin 4H 65
Woodman Dr. S41: Old W 2B 162
Woodmoor St. S71: Car 6A 10
WOODNOOK 4A 166
Wood Nook S35: Gren 1B 92
Woodnook Cl. S42: Ash 4A 166
Woodnook Gro. S21: Mar L 2H 157
Woodnook La. S42: Old B 3A 166
Woodnook Way S42: Ash 4A 166
Woodpecker Cl. S26: Aston 2D 138
Wood Rd. S6: Shef 4A 106
   S61: Kimb P 1A 96
Woodrove Av. S13: Shef 6E 121
Woodrove Cl. S13: Shef 1E 135
WOOD ROYD 4G 175
Woodroyd Av. S71: Car 5H 9
Woodroyd Cl. S71: Car 5H 9
Woodroyd Gdns.
   S73: Womb 3D 46
Wood Royd Rd. S36: Spink 3G 175
WOOD SEATS 5C 78
WOODSEATS 5E 133
Woodseats S35: Gren 5C 78
Woodseats Cl. S8: Shef 4D 132
Woodseats Ho. Rd. S8: Shef 6E 133
Woodseats M. S8: Shef 4D 132
Woodseats Rd. S8: Shef 4D 132
WOODSETTS 4F 143
Woodsetts Rd. S25: Nth A 2H 141
   S81: Gild 2G 143
Woodsett Wlk. DN12: Con 4H 69
WOODSIDE 6F 107
Woodside Av. S21: Killa 3E 153
   S63: Wath D 6G 49
Woodside Cl. S40: Ash 4C 166
   S66: Malt 5C 102
Woodside Cotts. DN6: Woodl 5B 22
Woodside Cl. DN6: Woodl 4B 22
   S66: Malt 6D 102
   (off Woodside Cl.)
   S66: Wick 1H 113
Woodside La. S3: Shef 6F 107
   (not continuous)
   S35: Gren 1B 92
Woodside Rd. DN5: Scawt 2F 39
   DN6: Woodl 4B 22
Woodside Vw. S18: Holme 4A 154
   S63: Bolt D 2C 50
Woodside Wlk. S61: Grea 5C 82
Woodspring Ct. S4: Shef 4B 108
Woodstock Dr. S41: Has 2B 172
Woodstock Gdns. S75: Barn 4C 16
Woodstock Ri. S41: Has 2B 172
Woodstock Rd. DN4: Balb 5F 55
   S6: Lox 4F 105
   S7: Shef 2D 132
   S75: Barn 4C 16
Wood St. DN1: Don 1C 56
   S6: Shef 6D 106
   S64: Mexb 1E 67
   S64: Swin 3D 66
   S65: Thry 6D 84
   S70: Barn 2D 30
   S72: Sth H 1H 11
   S73: Womb 2F 47

Wood Syke S75: Dod 3H 29
WOODTHORPE 4F 165
Woodthorpe Cres. S13: Shef 6F 121
Woodthorpe Est. S13: Shef 1F 135
Woodthorpe Rd. S13: Shef 6F 121
   (not continuous)
   S43: Woodt 4F 165
   S44: Shut 5H 165
Woodvale Cl. S40: Bramp 2B 170
   S75: High'm 4F 15
Woodvale Flats S10: Shef 4A 118
Woodvale Rd. S10: Shef 5A 118
Wood Vw. DN3: Brant 3H 59
   DN12: Con 5H 69
   DN12: New E 3D 70
   S66: Malt 5C 102
   S70: Birdw 6E 45
   S74: Els 1D 62
   (not continuous)
Woodview DN5: Sprot 3C 54
   S21: Reni 4H 159
Woodview Ho. S21: Ecki 1D 158
   (off West St.)
Wood Vw. La. S75: Barn 5H 15
Woodview Rd. S6: Shef 5B 106
Wood Vw. Ter. S11: Shef 6F 117
Woodville Hall S10: Shef 5D 118
Wood Wlk. S64: Mexb 6E 51
   S71: R'ton 1H 9
   S73: Womb 4C 46
   S74: Hoyl 4B 46
Woodway, The S66: Sunn 3G 99
WOOD WILLOWS 3F 175
Woofindin Av. S11: Shef 1F 131
Woofindin Rd. S10: Shef 1E 131
Woldale Cl. S20: Mosb 6B 136
Woldale Cft. S20: Mosb 6B 136
Woldale Dr. S20: Mosb 6B 136
Woldale Gdns. S20: Mosb 6B 136
Wooley Av. S73: Womb 2F 47
Wooley Edge La.
   S75: Wool G 3F 7
Woollen La. S6: Shef 1D 118
Woolley Colliery Rd.
   S75: Dart 5F 7
Woolley Edge La. WF4: Wool 1F 7
WOOLLEY GRANGE 3F 7
Woolley Ho. DN1: Don 2B 56
   (off Elsworth Cl.)
Woolley Rd. S36: Stoc 3C 174
Woolley Wood Rd. S5: Shef 3B 94
Woolscroft Vw. S73: Hem 5F 47
Wootton Ct. S65: Thry 6D 84
Worcester Av. DN2: Don 3E 41
Worcester Cl. S10: Shef 5C 116
Worcester Dr. S10: Shef 5C 116
Worcester Rd. S10: Shef 5B 116
Wordsworth Av. DN4: Balb 6H 55
   S5: Shef 1D 106
   S25: Din 6B 128
   S36: Pen 5C 176
Wordsworth Cl. S5: Shef 4D 92
   S36: Pen 3D 176
Wordsworth Cres. S5: Shef 6D 92
Wordsworth Dr. DN5: Don 6G 39
   S5: Shef 6D 92
   S65: Roth 4H 97
Wordsworth Pl. S18: Dron 5H 155
Wordsworth Rd. S41: C'fld 6G 161
   S63: Wath D 5D 48
   S71: Monk B 4G 17
Work Bank La.
   S36: Pen, Thurl 3A 176
WORKHOUSE GREEN 2A 130
Workhouse La.
   . . . . .1E 5 (2F 119)
Worksop Rd. S9: Shef 6D 108
   S25: Sth A 4G 141
   S26: Aston, Swal 1C 138
   S43: Mas M 3E 165
   S81: Woods 4F 143
   S81: Work 4G 141
Works Rd. S43: Hol 3G 163
Worral Av. S60: Tree 1F 123
Worral Cl. S70: Wors 4E 31
Worral Ct. DN3: Eden 6D 26
WORRALL 5E 91
Worrall Dr. S35: Ough 5E 91

Worrall Rd. S6: Ough, Shef 1F **105**
   S35: High G 2D **78**
   S35: Ough 6E **91**
Worry Goose La. S60: Whis 2B **112**
Worsborough Vw. S75: Pil 6C **44**
WORSBROUGH 6F **31**
WORSBROUGH BRIDGE 6G **31**
WORSBROUGH COMMON 3E **31**
Worsbrough Country Pk.
   Doe La. 1D **44**
   Park Rd. 1F **45**
WORSBROUGH DALE 5H **31**
Worsbrough Mill (Museum) 1E **45**
Worsbrough Rd.
   S70: Birdw, Wors 4E **45**
   S74: Black H 3A **46**
WORSBROUGH VILLAGE 2F **45**
Worsley Cl. S70: Barn 4G **31**
Worthing Cres. DN12: Con 4G **69**
Worthing Rd. S9: Shef 2B **120**
Wortley Av. DN12: Con 4D **68**
   S64: Swin 3C **66**
   S73: Womb 5E **33**
Wortley Ct. S35: High G 6C **60**
   S75: Dod 3F **29**
Wortley Dr. S35: Ough 3F **91**
Wortley M. S61: Thorpe H 4B **80**
Wortley Rd. S35: High G 6B **60**
   S36: Spink 3H **175**
   S61: Kimb 2A **96**
          (not continuous)
Wortley St. S70: Barn 1D **30**
Wortley Vw. S74: Black H 3A **46**
Wostenholm Rd. S7: Shef 1E **133**
Wragby Rd. S11: Shef 6H **117**
Wragg Rd. S2: Shef 4B **120**
Wreakes La. S18: Dron 1E **155**
Wrelton Cl. S71: R'ton 3G **9**
Wren Bank S2: Shef 4B **120**
Wren Pk. Cl. S12: Ridg 2H **149**
   S40: Birdh 3G **171**
Wrenpark Rd. S42: W'orth 6E **171**
Wrens Gdns. S63: Wath D 4F **49**
Wrens Way S70: Birdw 4E **45**
Wright Cres. S73: Womb 2G **47**
Wright's Hill S2: Shef 6E **119**
Wrightson Av. DN4: Warm 1D **70**
Wrightson Ter. DN5: Don 4A **40**
Wright St. S25: Nth A 2H **141**
Wroot Rd. DN9: Finn 3F **77**
Wroxham Cl. S66: Bram 5B **100**
Wroxham Dr. S66: Bram 5B **100**

Wroxham Way DN5: Cus 5F **39**
   S66: Bram 4B **100**
Wulfric Cl. S2: Shef 6C **120**
Wulfric Pl. S2: Shef 6C **120**
Wulfric Rd. S2: Shef 1C **134**
   S21: Ecki 1D **158**
Wyatt Av. S11: Shef 2B **132**
WYBOURN 3B **120**
Wybourn Hall Dr. S2: Shef 3B **120**
Wybourn Ho. Rd. S2: Shef 3B **120**
Wybourn Ter. S2: Shef 3B **120**
Wychwood Cl. DN4: Balb 2G **71**
Wychwood Cft. S20: Sot 6H **137**
Wychwood Glen S20: Sot 6H **137**
Wychwood Gro. S20: Sot 6H **137**
Wycombe St. S71: Lund 6B **18**
Wyedale Ct. S41: C'fld 1F **167**
Wyedale Cft. S20: Beig 4G **137**
Wyming Ho. S10: Shef 5A **116**
          (off Holyrood Av.)
Wyndthorpe Av. DN4: Bess 5B **58**
Wyn Gro. S73: Bramp 4B **48**
Wynmoor Cres. S73: Bramp 5B **48**
Wynyard Rd. S6: Shef 3A **106**
Wythburn Rd. S41: C'fld 1D **166**
Wyvern Gdns. S17: Dore 4F **145**

Yarborough Ter. DN5: Don 5A **40**
Yardley Sq. S3: Shef 2A **4** (2D **118**)
Yarmouth St. S9: Shef 3E **109**
Yarncliff Cl. S40: C'fld 3E **167**
Yarwell Dr. S66: Malt 4H **101**
Yates Cl. S66: Wick 1G **113**
Yealand Cl. DN6: Adw S 2C **22**
Yearling Chase S64: Swin 3A **66**
Yeldersley Cl. S40: C'fld 3C **166**
Yeomans Rd. S6: Shef 1D **118**
Yeomans Way S25: Sth A 4G **141**
Yewdale S70: Wors 5G **31**
Yew Greave Cres. S5: Shef 3E **93**
Yew La. S5: Shef 3D **92**
Yews, The S65: Roth 3G **97**
Yews Av. S70: Wors 5G **31**
Yews Cl. S35: Ough 6E **91**
Yews Dr. S35: Ough 6E **91**
Yews La. S70: Barn, Wors 5G **31**
Yews Pl. S70: Barn 3G **31**
Yew Tree Av. S25: Nth A 3A **142**
Yew Tree Cl. S66: Thurc 5C **114**

Yew Tree Cres. DN11: Ross 4D **74**
Yew Tree Dr. S9: Tins 3A **110**
   S21: Killa 5B **152**
   S40: Bramp 2A **170**
Yew Tree Rd. S66: Malt 4F **101**
Yewtrees La. S36: Bolst 6D **174**
Yoredale Av. S35: Chap 2E **79**
York & Lancaster Regiment Mus.
   ....4G **97**
     (within Clifton Park Mus.)
York Bldgs. DN12: New E 3C **70**
      (off Edlington La.)
York Gdns. DN4: Can 3A **58**
   S63: Wath D 5E **49**
York La. S66: Mort 5G **113**
York M. S63: Thurn 2D **36**
York Ri. S26: Swal 1B **138**
York Rd. DN5: Don, Scawt 1E **39**
   S9: Shef 1F **121**
   S36: Stoc 3D **174**
   S65: Roth 3F **97**
Yorkshire Way DN3: Arm 3G **43**
Yorkshire Wildlife Pk. 5G **59**
York Sq. S64: Mexb 2F **67**
Yorkstone Ct. S2: Shef 4B **120**
York St. DN11: New R 4B **74**
   S1: Shef 2E **5** (2F **119**)
   S41: Has 3B **172**
   S63: Thurn 1D **36**
   S64: Mexb 1E **67**
   S70: Barn 1D **30**
   S72: Cud 2D **18**
   S73: Womb 1G **47**
   S74: Hoyl 5B **46**
   WF9: Hems 1F **13**
York Way DN12: Con 3H **69**
Youlgreave Dr. S12: Shef 3G **135**
Young St. DN1: Don 1C **56**
   S1: Shef 6C **4** (4E **119**)
Yvonne Gro. S73: Womb 1E **47**

Zamor Cres. S66: Thurc 1B **126**
Zenith Pk. S75: Barn 3H **15**
Zetland Rd. DN2: Don 5E **41**
   S74: Els 1E **63**
Zion Dr. S75: Mapp 5A **8**
Zion La. S9: Shef 6C **108**
Zion Pl. S9: Shef 6C **108**
Zion Ter. S70: Stair 3B **32**